The One Year® Bible for Kids

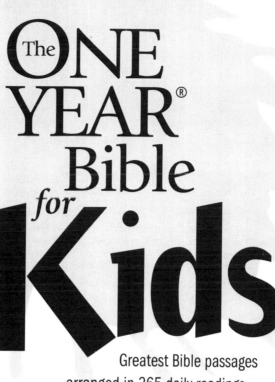

The ONE YEAR® Bible for Kids

Greatest Bible passages
arranged in 365 daily readings
from the NEW LIVING TRANSLATION

Tyndale House
Publishers, Inc.
Wheaton, Illinois

TABLE OF CONTENTS

February 2
Exodus 5:1-21
James 1:12
41

February 3
Exodus 6:1-12
Philippians 4:13
43

February 4
Exodus 7:1-13
John 14:21
44

February 5
Exodus 7:19–8:4, 8-19
Hebrews 12:10
45

February 6
Exodus 8:20–9:7
2 Thessalonians 3:3
46

February 7
Exodus 9:8-12, 22-34
Matthew 26:41
48

February 8
Exodus 10:8-27
Matthew 16:24
49

February 9
Exodus 12:1-8, 21-36
Luke 11:28
50

February 10
Exodus 14:10-31
Hebrews 13:5
52

February 11
Exodus 15:22-27
Philippians 4:19
54

February 12
Exodus 16:2-5, 13-28
Luke 12:24
55

February 13
Exodus 18:5-26
James 1:19
56

February 14
Exodus 19:3-19
John 14:6
58

February 15
Exodus 20:1-21
Mark 12:31
59

February 16
Exodus 32:1-14
James 5:16
60

February 17
Exodus 40:1-2, 33-38
Matthew 28:20
62

February 18
Numbers 12:1-15
Romans 13:1
63

February 19
Numbers 13:17-20, 25-33
1 Corinthians 16:13
64

February 20
Numbers 14:1-23
Romans 12:2
65

February 21
Numbers 21:4-9
Philippians 2:14-15
67

February 22
Numbers 22:21-38
Matthew 4:7
68

February 23
Deuteronomy 29:1-6, 9-18
John 14:15
69

February 24
Deuteronomy 30:11-20
John 14:23
70

February 25
Deuteronomy 31:1-8
Matthew 28:20
71

February 26
Deuteronomy 32:1-14
2 Corinthians 1:3-4
72

February 27
Joshua 1:1-11
2 Timothy 3:16-17
74

February 28
Joshua 2:1-16, 22-24
2 Timothy 4:18
75

March 1
Joshua 3:5-8, 14–4:7
Ephesians 6:10
77

March 2
Joshua 6:1-20
1 Corinthians 15:57
78

March 3
Joshua 7:10-22
Psalm 139:16
79

March 4
Joshua 10:7-14
2 Peter 1:3
81

March 5
Joshua 23:1-11
John 14:15
82

March 6
Joshua 24:1-18
Matthew 6:24
83

March 7
Judges 4:1-16
Luke 18:7-8
84

March 8
Judges 6:1-16
2 Corinthians 12:9
86

March 9
Judges 7:2-8
1 Corinthians 1:31
87

March 10
Judges 7:9-21
Philippians 4:6-7
88

March 11
Judges 13:1-24
James 1:5
89

March 12
Judges 15:9-19
Philippians 4:13
91

March 13
Judges 16:4-20
Romans 12:2
92

March 14
Judges 16:23-30
Hebrews 6:10
94

March 15
Ruth 1:3-19
John 15:12-13
95

March 16
Ruth 2:2-16
Matthew 5:42
96

March 17
1 Samuel 1:10-20
Matthew 7:11
97

March 18
1 Samuel 1:24–2:2, 11
2 Corinthians 9:7
98

March 19
1 Samuel 3:1-10
John 10:27
99

March 20
1 Samuel 7:3-10
Hebrews 13:5
100

March 21
1 Samuel 8:1-5
2 John 1:6
101

March 22
1 Samuel 8:6-20
James 1:22
102

March 23
1 Samuel 9:3-17
Romans 8:28
103

March 24
1 Samuel 10:1-11
2 Corinthians 5:17
104

March 25
1 Samuel 10:17-26
Philippians 4:6
105

March 26
1 Samuel 13:5-14
1 Corinthians 10:13
106

March 27
1 Samuel 14:1-15
1 Corinthians 16:13
107

March 28
1 Samuel 14:24-30, 36-45
James 5:12
108

March 29
1 Samuel 16:1-13
1 Corinthians 4:5
110

March 30
1 Samuel 17:4-11, 17-30
Mark 11:22
111

March 31
1 Samuel 17:32-51
1 Corinthians 1:28-29
113

April 1
1 Samuel 18:5-16
Hebrews 13:5
115

April 2
1 Samuel 20:1-4, 24-42
Acts 27:3
116

April 3
1 Samuel 24:2-17
Romans 12:19
117

April 4
1 Samuel 25:10-28, 32-33
Colossians 3:16
119

April 5
2 Samuel 5:17-25
Colossians 4:2
120

April 6
2 Samuel 9:1-13
Colossians 3:12
121

April 7
2 Samuel 12:1-14
1 John 1:9
122

April 8
2 Samuel 13:23-38
1 John 3:15
123

April 9
2 Samuel 15:13-36
John 14:1
125

April 10
2 Samuel 16:5-13
Luke 6:28
126

April 11
2 Samuel 18:1-14, 33
Matthew 5:44
127

April 12
2 Samuel 24:1-4, 10-25
Luke 5:20
129

April 13
1 Kings 1:16-20, 32-50
Romans 13:1
131

April 14
1 Kings 3:5-14
James 1:5
133

April 15
1 Kings 3:16-28
Colossians 3:9
134

April 16
1 Kings 10:1-13
James 3:17
135

April 17
1 Kings 12:4-19
1 Peter 5:5
136

April 18
1 Kings 17:1-16
Luke 12:29-31
137

April 19
1 Kings 18:20-39
Matthew 6:24
139

April 20
1 Kings 19:1-9
Philippians 4:13
140

April 21
1 Kings 19:9-18
1 Peter 3:13-14
141

April 22
1 Kings 21:1-19
James 4:2
142

April 23
2 Kings 2:1-15
Galatians 4:6
144

April 24
2 Kings 4:1-7
Matthew 6:26
145

April 25
2 Kings 5:1-14
John 14:21
146

April 26
2 Kings 11:1-8, 12-21
John 17:15
148

April 27
2 Chronicles 34:14-33
Hebrews 4:12
149

April 28
Ezra 3:7-13
1 Thessalonians 5:18
151

April 29
Nehemiah 4:1-21
1 Peter 3:9
152

April 30
Nehemiah 5:1-11
James 1:27
154

May 1
Nehemiah 8:2-6, 8-12
2 Timothy 3:16
155

May 2
Esther 2:5-11, 15-20
Ephesians 4:32
156

May 3
Esther 3:1-14
Romans 12:2
157

May 4
Esther 4:1–5:2
Mark 8:35
159

May 5
Esther 5:9–6:13
Galatians 6:14
160

May 6
Esther 7:1-10
Romans 13:1
162

May 7
Job 1:6-22
James 1:2-3
163

May 8
Job 2:1-10
Romans 8:35
164

May 9
Job 2:11–3:6
1 Peter 3:8
165

May 10
Job 38:1-15; 40:1-5
James 4:10
166

May 11
Job 42:1-17
2 Corinthians 7:10
167

May 12
Psalm 1:1-6
Matthew 5:6
169

May 13
Psalm 8:1-9
Ephesians 2:10
170

May 14
Psalm 23:1-6
John 10:14-15
171

May 15
Psalm 51:1-17
1 John 1:9
172

May 16
Psalm 103:1-22
1 John 4:16
173

May 17
Psalm 119:97-106
2 Timothy 3:16
174

May 18
Psalm 139:1-18
Matthew 6:8
175

May 19
Psalm 145:1-21
Matthew 5:45
177

May 20
Proverbs 4:10-27
James 1:19
178

May 21
Ecclesiastes 11:7–12:2, 9-14
1 Timothy 4:12
179

May 22
Isaiah 6:1-8
1 Peter 5:6
180

May 23
Isaiah 53:1-12
1 Peter 2:24
181

May 24
Jeremiah 1:4-12, 17-19
2 Thessalonians 3:3
182

May 25
Jeremiah 36:1-4, 21-31
Mark 1:15
183

May 26
Ezekiel 37:1-14
1 Corinthians 3:16
185

May 27
Daniel 1:3-5, 8-17
James 4:7
186

May 28
Daniel 2:1-19
Matthew 7:7
187

May 29
Daniel 3:1-18
Exodus 20:3-5
189

May 30
Daniel 3:19-28
John 14:1
190

May 31
Daniel 4:29-37
Matthew 23:12
191

June 1
Daniel 5:1-6, 13-30
1 Peter 1:3
193

July 12
Luke 8:22-39
Psalm 66:16
241

July 13
Matthew 9:27-38
Psalm 103:8
242

July 14
Mark 6:1-13
Isaiah 43:10
243

July 15
Matthew 10:16-39
Psalm 16:10
244

July 16
Mark 6:30-44
Deuteronomy 8:3
246

July 17
Mark 6:45-56
Deuteronomy 31:6
247

July 18
John 6:22-40
Psalm 14:2
248

July 19
John 6:41-71
John 14:6
249

July 20
Mark 7:1-23
Ezekiel 36:26-27
251

July 21
Matthew 16:1-12
Jeremiah 23:16
252

July 22
Luke 9:18-27
Galatians 4:4-5
253

July 23
Matthew 17:1-13
Deuteronomy 31:12
254

July 24
Matthew 18:1-10
Psalm 149:4
255

July 25
Matthew 18:12-20
Psalm 100:3
256

July 26
Matthew 18:21-35
Psalm 32:1
257

July 27
John 7:10-31
Numbers 14:11
258

July 28
John 7:32-52
Psalm 23:4-5
260

July 29
John 8:1-11
Psalm 79:9
261

July 30
John 8:12-30
Romans 6:23
262

July 31
Luke 10:1-24
Revelation 3:5
263

August 1
Luke 10:25-37
Romans 13:10
266

August 2
Luke 11:1-13
Psalm 6:9
267

August 3
Luke 11:14-28
Psalm 119:97
268

August 4
Luke 11:37-54
Psalm 24:3-4
269

August 5
Luke 12:13-21
Proverbs 28:25
270

August 6
Luke 12:22-34
Psalm 111:5
271

August 7
Luke 12:35-48
Matthew 24:36
272

August 8
Luke 13:1-17
Ezekiel 18:32
273

August 9
John 9:1-17
Psalm 119:101
275

August 10
John 9:18-41
Job 1:21
276

August 11
John 10:1-18
Psalm 23:1-2
277

August 12
Luke 14:1-14
1 Peter 5:5
278

August 13
Luke 14:15-35
2 Chronicles 16:9
280

August 14
Luke 15:1-10
Ezekiel 18:32
281

August 15
Luke 15:11-32
Psalm 103:13
282

August 16
Luke 16:1 15
Ecclesiastes 5:10
283

August 17
Luke 16:19-31
Psalm 119:15-16
285

August 18
John 11:17-36
Isaiah 57:18
286

August 19
John 11:38-52
Isaiah 53:12
287

August 20
Luke 17:1-19
Psalm 100:4-5
288

November 9
Acts 27:13-26
Psalm 69:29
390

November 10
Acts 27:27-44
Isaiah 17:7
391

November 11
Acts 28:11-31
Colossians 4:3
392

November 12
Romans 3:9-26
Ecclesiastes 7:20
394

November 13
Romans 5:1-11
Psalm 86:5
395

November 14
Romans 6:5-23
Psalm 51:1-2
396

November 15
Romans 8:1-17
Psalm 51:10-11
398

November 16
Romans 8:28-39
Psalm 94:18
399

November 17
Romans 12:1-21
1 Samuel 24:17
400

November 18
Romans 13:1-10
Colossians 2:10
402

November 19
1 Corinthians 13:1-13
Proverbs 12:25
403

November 20
1 Corinthians 15:35-58
Revelation 21:3-4
404

November 21
2 Corinthians 4:7-18
Psalm 46:1
405

November 22
2 Corinthians 9:6-15
Proverbs 14:21
406

November 23
Galatians 5:13-26
Romans 6:22
407

November 24
Ephesians 1:15-23
Ephesians 3:16
409

November 25
Ephesians 2:1-10
Matthew 6:31-33
410

November 26
Ephesians 4:17–5:2
Psalm 68:35
411

November 27
Ephesians 6:1-9
Proverbs 1:8-9
412

November 28
Ephesians 6:10-20
Romans 13:12
413

November 29
Philippians 2:1-15
2 Chronicles 7:14
414

November 30
Philippians 3:12–4:9
Psalm 100:1-2
415

December 1
Colossians 1:28–2:15
John 15:5
417

December 2
Colossians 3:1-17
Isaiah 1:18
418

December 3
1 Thessalonians 1:1-10
Galatians 5:22-23
419

December 4
1 Thessalonians 5:1-22
Mark 13:33
420

December 5
2 Thessalonians 1:1-12
Psalm 9:8
422

December 6
2 Thessalonians 3:1-18
Proverbs 14:23
423

December 7
1 Timothy 4:1-16
Joshua 1:8
424

December 8
1 Timothy 6:1-21
Matthew 6:24
425

December 9
2 Timothy 2:1-24
Psalm 119:33
427

December 10
2 Timothy 3:10–4:5
Psalm 119:9
428

December 11
Titus 2:1-15
1 Corinthians 10:13
429

December 12
Titus 3:1-11
Proverbs 12:2
431

December 13
Hebrews 4:12–5:9
Psalm 130:1-2
432

December 14
Hebrews 11:1-16
Proverbs 3:5-6
433

December 15
Hebrews 12:1-13
Psalm 18:32-33
434

December 16
Hebrews 12:14-29
Psalm 147:5
436

December 17
Hebrews 13:1-21
2 Corinthians 11:4
437

December 18
James 1:2-18
Psalm 64:10
439

INTRODUCTION TO *THE ONE YEAR BIBLE FOR KIDS*

The Bible Is a Great Book!

Did you ever wonder where the earth, animals, and people came from? Have you ever asked yourself why people suffer and die? Is there anyone or anything that can give you hope? The Bible answers all of these questions and more. In these pages, you will find out where the earth and everything in it came from. You will get to know who God is. You will read about the incredible adventures of ancient biblical heroes and the amazing things they did for God. But most important, you will get to know Jesus Christ and what he has done for you.

This Is a Great Way to Read the Bible!

If you picked up a Bible and started reading it straight through from Genesis to Revelation, it would probably take you more than a year to finish. One reason this is true is that it is hard to know how much you should read each day. *The One Year Bible for Kids* solves this problem. *The One Year Bible for Kids* helps you to read 365 passages from the Bible in a year. Every day, you get a great Bible story or an important passage on living the Christian life. After a year, you will have read a variety of passages from the Old and New Testaments.

The One Year Bible for Kids gives you:
- 365 readings from the Bible
- a short introduction to each reading to help you know what it is about
- a note to help you apply the Bible to your life
- a related verse to help you remember the message of the reading
- the easy-to-understand New Living Translation

Get Started Now!

Reading the Bible every day helps you grow in your faith. Don't wait for New Year's Day to get started. You can read the Bible daily, starting today. Check the date on a calendar. Then find that same date in *The One Year Bible for Kids.* Now you are ready to read. What are you waiting for?

A NOTE TO READERS

With 40 million copies in print, *The Living Bible* has been meeting a great need in people's hearts for more than thirty years. But even good things can be improved, so ninety evangelical scholars from various theological backgrounds and denominations were commissioned in 1989 to begin revising *The Living Bible.* The end result of this seven-year process is the *Holy Bible,* New Living Translation—a general-purpose translation that is accurate, easy to read, and excellent for study.

The goal of any Bible translation is to convey the meaning of the ancient Hebrew and Greek texts as accurately as possible to the modern reader. The New Living Translation is based on the most recent scholarship in the theory of translation. The challenge for the translators was to create a text that would make the same impact in the life of modern readers that the original text had for the original readers. In the New Living Translation, this is accomplished by translating entire thoughts (rather than just words) into natural, everyday English. The end result is a translation that is easy to read and understand and that accurately communicates the meaning of the original text.

We believe that this new translation, which combines the latest in scholarship with the best in translation style, will speak to your heart. We present the New Living Translation with the prayer that God will use it to speak his timeless truth to the church and to the world in a fresh, new way.

The Publishers
July 1996

JANUARY

Everything and everyone (except God) had a beginning.
Where did people, plants, and animals come from?

GENESIS 1:1–2:3

How It All Started

In the beginning God created* the heavens and the earth. ²The earth was empty, a formless mass cloaked in darkness. And the Spirit of God was hovering over its surface. ³Then God said, "Let there be light," and there was light. ⁴And God saw that it was good. Then he separated the light from the darkness. ⁵God called the light "day" and the darkness "night." Together these made up one day.

⁶And God said, "Let there be space between the waters, to separate water from water." ⁷And so it was. God made this space to separate the waters above from the waters below. ⁸And God called the space "sky." This happened on the second day.

⁹And God said, "Let the waters beneath the sky be gathered into one place so dry ground may appear." And so it was. ¹⁰God named the dry ground "land" and the water "seas." And God saw that it was good. ¹¹Then God said, "Let the land burst forth with every sort of grass and seed-bearing plant. And let there be trees that grow seed-bearing fruit. The seeds will then produce the kinds of plants and trees from which they came." And so it was. ¹²The land was filled with seed-bearing plants and trees, and their seeds produced plants and trees of like kind. And God saw that it was good. ¹³This all happened on the third day.

¹⁴And God said, "Let bright lights appear in the sky to separate the day from the night. They will be signs to mark off the seasons, the days, and the years. ¹⁵Let their light shine down upon the earth." And so it was. ¹⁶For God made two great lights, the sun and the moon, to shine down upon the earth. The greater one, the sun, presides during the day; the lesser one, the moon, presides through the night. He also made the stars. ¹⁷God set these lights in the heavens to light the earth,

1:1 Or *In the beginning when God created,* or *When God began to create.*

¹⁸to govern the day and the night, and to separate the light from the darkness. And God saw that it was good. ¹⁹This all happened on the fourth day.

²⁰And God said, "Let the waters swarm with fish and other life. Let the skies be filled with birds of every kind." ²¹So God created great sea creatures and every sort of fish and every kind of bird. And God saw that it was good. ²²Then God blessed them, saying, "Let the fish multiply and fill the oceans. Let the birds increase and fill the earth." ²³This all happened on the fifth day.

²⁴And God said, "Let the earth bring forth every kind of animal—livestock, small animals, and wildlife." And so it was. ²⁵God made all sorts of wild animals, livestock, and small animals, each able to reproduce more of its own kind. And God saw that it was good.

²⁶Then God said, "Let us make people* in our image, to be like ourselves. They will be masters over all life—the fish in the sea, the birds in the sky, and all the livestock, wild animals,* and small animals."

²⁷ So God created people in his own
    image;
    God patterned them after
        himself;
    male and female he created
        them.

²⁸God blessed them and told them, "Multiply and fill the earth and sub-

due it. Be masters over the fish and birds and all the animals." ²⁹And God said, "Look! I have given you the seed-bearing plants throughout the earth and all the fruit trees for your food. ³⁰And I have given all the grasses and other green plants to the animals and birds for their food." And so it was. ³¹Then God looked over all he had made, and he saw that it was excellent in every way. This all happened on the sixth day.

²:¹So the creation of the heavens and the earth and everything in them was completed. ²On the seventh day, having finished his task, God rested from all his work. ³And God blessed the seventh day and declared it holy, because it was the day when he rested from his work of creation.

Look around you. Just about everything you see was created by God. He created the sun and the moon. He created plants and animals. He even created boys and girls. After God finished creating everything, he admired it all. It was good.

**Why are you valuable
in God's sight?**
For God so loved the world that he gave his only Son, so that everyone who believes in him will not perish but have eternal life.
John 3:16

1:26a Hebrew *man;* also in 1:27. **1:26b** As in Syriac version; Hebrew reads *all the earth.*

*God created Adam and Eve and provided fruit for them to eat.
What did God command Adam and Eve not to do?*

GENESIS 3:1-19, 22-23

Adam and Eve

Now the serpent was the shrewdest of all the creatures the LORD God had made. "Really?" he asked the woman. "Did God really say you must not eat any of the fruit in the garden?"

²"Of course we may eat it," the woman told him. ³"It's only the fruit from the tree at the center of the garden that we are not allowed to eat. God says we must not eat it or even touch it, or we will die."

⁴"You won't die!" the serpent hissed. ⁵"God knows that your eyes will be opened when you eat it. You will become just like God, knowing everything, both good and evil."

⁶The woman was convinced. The fruit looked so fresh and delicious, and it would make her so wise! So she ate some of the fruit. She also gave some to her husband, who was with her. Then he ate it, too. ⁷At that moment, their eyes were opened, and they suddenly felt shame at their nakedness. So they strung fig leaves together around their hips to cover themselves.

⁸Toward evening they heard the LORD God walking about in the garden, so they hid themselves among the trees. ⁹The LORD God called to Adam,* "Where are you?"

¹⁰He replied, "I heard you, so I hid. I was afraid because I was naked."

¹¹"Who told you that you were naked?" the LORD God asked. "Have you eaten the fruit I commanded you not to eat?"

¹²"Yes," Adam admitted, "but it was the woman you gave me who brought me the fruit, and I ate it."

¹³Then the LORD God asked the woman, "How could you do such a thing?"

"The serpent tricked me," she replied. "That's why I ate it."

¹⁴So the LORD God said to the serpent, "Because you have done this, you will be punished. You are singled out from all the domestic and wild animals of the whole earth to be cursed. You will grovel in the dust as long as you live, crawling along on your belly. ¹⁵From now on, you and the woman will be enemies, and your offspring and her offspring will be enemies. He will crush your head, and you will strike his heel."

¹⁶Then he said to the woman, "You will bear children with intense pain and suffering. And though your desire will be for your husband,* he will be your master."

¹⁷And to Adam he said, "Because you listened to your wife and ate the fruit I told you not to eat, I have placed a curse

---

3:9 Hebrew *the man*, and so throughout this chapter. 3:16 Or *And though you may desire to control your husband.*

on the ground. All your life you will struggle to scratch a living from it. ¹⁸It will grow thorns and thistles for you, though you will eat of its grains. ¹⁹All your life you will sweat to produce food, until your dying day. Then you will return to the ground from which you came. For you were made from dust, and to the dust you will return."

• • •

²²Then the LORD God said, "The people have become as we are, knowing everything, both good and evil. What if they eat the fruit of the tree of life? Then they will live forever!" ²³So the LORD God banished Adam and his wife from the Garden of Eden, and he sent Adam out to cultivate the ground from which he had been made.

The serpent tempted Eve to disobey God. Then Eve offered the fruit to Adam. Sinful people want others to sin with them. That is why people who do wrong ask you to join them. But you can say no to them, for God promises to help you resist.

How can you resist temptation?
But remember that the temptations that come into your life are no different from what others experience. And God is faithful. He will keep the temptation from becoming so strong that you can't stand up against it. When you are tempted, he will show you a way out so that you will not give in to it.
1 Corinthians 10:13

J A N U A R Y

*Adam and Eve had two sons, Cain and Abel.
How did Adam and Eve's sin affect Cain and Abel?*

GENESIS 4:3-16
Cain and Abel
³At harvesttime Cain brought to the LORD a gift of his farm produce, ⁴while Abel brought several choice lambs from the best of his flock. The LORD accepted Abel and his offering, ⁵but he did not accept Cain and his offering. This made Cain very angry and dejected.

⁶"Why are you so angry?" the LORD asked him. "Why do you look so de-jected? ⁷You will be accepted if you respond in the right way. But if you refuse to respond correctly, then watch out! Sin is waiting to attack and destroy you, and you must subdue it."

⁸Later Cain suggested to his brother, Abel, "Let's go out into the fields."* And while they were together there, Cain attacked and killed his brother.

⁹Afterward the LORD asked Cain, "Where is your brother? Where is Abel?"

"I don't know!" Cain retorted. "Am

4:8 As in Samaritan Pentateuch, Greek and Syriac versions, Latin Vulgate; Masorectic Text lacks *"Let's go out into the fields."*

I supposed to keep track of him wherever he goes?"

[10]But the LORD said, "What have you done? Listen—your brother's blood cries out to me from the ground! [11]You are hereby banished from the ground you have defiled with your brother's blood. [12]No longer will it yield abundant crops for you, no matter how hard you work! From now on you will be a homeless fugitive on the earth, constantly wandering from place to place."

[13]Cain replied to the LORD, "My punishment* is too great for me to bear! [14]You have banished me from my land and from your presence; you have made me a wandering fugitive. All who see me will try to kill me!"

[15]The LORD replied, "They will not kill you, for I will give seven times your punishment to anyone who does." Then the LORD put a mark on Cain to warn anyone who might try to kill him. [16]So Cain left the LORD's presence and settled in the land of Nod,* east of Eden.

4:13 Or *My sin.* **4:16** *Nod* means "wandering." **4:20** Greek *brother.*

Cain was hurt because God rejected his sacrifice. He became jealous of Abel because God accepted his sacrifice. This bothered Cain so much that he killed Abel. Do your brothers or sisters get on your nerves? God commands you to love them because he loved you first. When your brothers and sisters annoy you, ask God to help you love them and try to say something kind to them.

When do you find it difficult to love your brother or sister?
If someone says, "I love God," but hates another Christian,* that person is a liar; for if we don't love people we can see, how can we love God, whom we have not seen?
1 John 4:20

J A N U A R Y

People had become so wicked by Noah's time that God decided to destroy them with a flood. Did God destroy everyone in the flood?

GENESIS 6:9-22
Noah Builds a Boat
[9]This is the history of Noah and his family. Noah was a righteous man, the only blameless man living on earth at the time. He consistently followed God's will and enjoyed a close relationship with him. [10]Noah had three sons: Shem, Ham, and Japheth.

[11]Now the earth had become corrupt in God's sight, and it was filled with violence. [12]God observed all this corruption in the world, and he saw violence and depravity everywhere. [13]So God said to

5

Noah, "I have decided to destroy all living creatures, for the earth is filled with violence because of them. Yes, I will wipe them all from the face of the earth!

14"Make a boat* from resinous wood and seal it with tar, inside and out. Then construct decks and stalls throughout its interior. 15Make it 450 feet long, 75 feet wide, and 45 feet high.* 16Construct an opening all the way around the boat, 18 inches* below the roof. Then put three decks inside the boat—bottom, middle, and upper—and put a door in the side.

17"Look! I am about to cover the earth with a flood that will destroy every living thing. Everything on earth will die! 18But I solemnly swear to keep you safe in the boat, with your wife and your sons and their wives. 19Bring a pair of every kind of animal—a male and a female—into the boat with you to keep them alive during the flood. 20Pairs of each kind of bird and each kind of animal, large and small alike, will come to you to be

kept alive. 21And remember, take enough food for your family and for all the animals."

22So Noah did everything exactly as God had commanded him.

A flood was coming. But God provided a way to be saved from it. He told Noah to build a boat. Noah believed God, obeyed him, and was saved. Today, God has provided a way to be saved from the coming judgment. He sent Jesus to die for our sins. If we believe that Jesus is God's Son, we will be saved.

How does God rescue us from the coming judgment?

This is a true saying, and everyone should believe it: Christ Jesus came into the world to save sinners—and I was the worst of them all.
1 Timothy 1:15

6:14 Traditionally rendered *an ark.* **6:15** Hebrew *300 cubits* [135 meters] *long, 50 cubits* [22.5 meters] *wide, and 30 cubits* [13.5 meters] *high.* **6:16** Hebrew *1 cubit* [45 centimeters].

J A N U A R Y

After Noah built the boat, God sent the flood upon the earth to punish the people for their wickedness. What did God tell Noah to do?

GENESIS 7:1-23
God Brings the Flood
Finally, the day came when the LORD said to Noah, "Go into the boat with all your family, for among all the people of the earth, I consider you

alone to be righteous. 2Take along seven pairs of each animal that I have approved for eating and for sacrifice, and take one pair of each of the others. 3Then select seven pairs of every kind of bird. There must be a male and a female in each pair to ensure that every kind of living creature will survive the flood. ⁴One week from today I will begin forty days and forty nights of rain. And I will wipe from the earth all the living things I have created."

⁵So Noah did exactly as the LORD had commanded him. ⁶He was 600 years old when the flood came, ⁷and he went aboard the boat to escape—he and his wife and his sons and their wives. ⁸With them were all the various kinds of animals—those approved for eating and sacrifice and those that were not—along with all the birds and other small animals. ⁹They came into the boat in pairs, male and female, just as God had commanded Noah. ¹⁰One week later, the flood came and covered the earth.

¹¹When Noah was 600 years old, on the seventeenth day of the second month, the underground waters burst forth on the earth, and the rain fell in mighty torrents from the sky. ¹²The rain continued to fall for forty days and forty nights. ¹³But Noah had gone into the boat that very day with his wife and his sons—Shem, Ham, and Japheth—and their wives. ¹⁴With them in the boat were pairs of every kind of breathing animal—domestic and wild, large and small—along with birds and flying insects of every kind. ¹⁵Two by two they came into the boat, ¹⁶male and female, just as God had commanded. Then the LORD shut them in.

¹⁷For forty days the floods prevailed, covering the ground and lifting the boat high above the earth. ¹⁸As the waters rose higher and higher above the ground, the boat floated safely on the surface. ¹⁹Finally, the water covered even the highest mountains on the earth, ²⁰standing more than twenty-two feet* above the highest peaks. ²¹All the living things on earth died—birds, domestic animals, wild animals, all kinds of small animals, and all the people. ²²Everything died that breathed and lived on dry land. ²³Every living thing on the earth was wiped out—people, animals both large and small, and birds. They were all destroyed, and only Noah was left alive, along with those who were with him in the boat.

God told Noah to go into the boat when it wasn't raining. Noah believed God and obeyed. Seven days later, the raging floodwaters came. Noah was safe. Today, God wants to keep us safe, too, and so he asks us to believe in his Son, Jesus.

How does God save us?
For if you confess with your mouth that Jesus is Lord and believe in your heart that God raised him from the dead, you will be saved.
Romans 10:9

7:20 Hebrew *15 cubits* [6.8 meters].

J A N U A R Y

The rain finally stopped, but the floodwater was still there.
Noah stayed in the boat. When was he able to come out?

GENESIS 8:1-16

A Long Wait

But God remembered Noah and all the animals in the boat. He sent a wind to blow across the waters, and the floods began to disappear. ²The underground water sources ceased their gushing, and the torrential rains stopped. ³So the flood gradually began to recede. After 150 days, ⁴exactly five months from the time the flood began,* the boat came to rest on the mountains of Ararat. ⁵Two and a half months later,* as the waters continued to go down, other mountain peaks began to appear.

⁶After another forty days, Noah opened the window he had made in the boat ⁷and released a raven that flew back and forth until the earth was dry. ⁸Then he sent out a dove to see if it could find dry ground. ⁹But the dove found no place to land because the water was still too high. So it returned to the boat, and Noah held out his hand and drew the dove back inside. ¹⁰Seven days later, Noah released the dove again. ¹¹This time, toward evening, the bird returned to him with a fresh olive leaf in its beak. Noah now knew that the water was almost gone. ¹²A week later, he released the dove again, and this time it did not come back.

¹³Finally, when Noah was 601 years old, ten and a half months after the flood began,* Noah lifted back the cover to look. The water was drying up. ¹⁴Two more months went by,* and at last the earth was dry! ¹⁵Then God said to Noah, ¹⁶"Leave the boat, all of you."

Noah waited for more than a year for the floodwater to dry up. Have you ever waited that long for something? There may be times in your life when God wants you to wait. It is then that you need to have patience and trust that God is doing good things in your life, even if you don't see it.

When do you find it difficult to wait patiently for God?

You, too, must be patient. And take courage, for the coming of the Lord is near.
James 5:8

8:4 Hebrew *on the seventeenth day of the seventh month;* see 7:11. **8:5** Hebrew *On the first day of the tenth month;* see 7:11 and note on 8:4. **8:13** Hebrew *on the first day of the first month;* see 7:11. **8:14** Hebrew *The twenty-seventh day of the second month arrived;* see note on 8:13.

After the Flood, God created the rainbow. Why did God create rainbows?

GENESIS 9:1-17
Rules and Rainbows

God blessed Noah and his sons and told them, "Multiply and fill the earth. [2]All the wild animals, large and small, and all the birds and fish will be afraid of you. I have placed them in your power. [3]I have given them to you for food, just as I have given you grain and vegetables. [4]But you must never eat animals that still have their lifeblood in them. [5]And murder is forbidden. Animals that kill people must die, and any person who murders must be killed. [6]Yes, you must execute anyone who murders another person, for to kill a person is to kill a living being made in God's image. [7]Now you must have many children and repopulate the earth. Yes, multiply and fill the earth!"

[8]Then God told Noah and his sons, [9]"I am making a covenant with you and your descendants, [10]and with the animals you brought with you—all these birds and livestock and wild animals. [11]I solemnly promise never to send another flood to kill all living creatures and destroy the earth." [12]And God said, "I am giving you a sign as evidence of my eternal covenant with you and all living creatures. [13]I have placed my rainbow in the clouds. It is the sign of my permanent promise to you and to all the earth. [14]When I send clouds over the earth, the rainbow will be seen in the clouds, [15]and I will remember my covenant with you and with everything that lives. Never again will there be a flood that will destroy all life. [16]When I see the rainbow in the clouds, I will remember the eternal covenant between God and every living creature on earth." [17]Then God said to Noah, "Yes, this is the sign of my covenant with all the creatures of the earth."

God promised never again to destroy the earth with a flood. He created the beautiful rainbow as a reminder of his promise. This reminder is a symbol of God's love for us.

What will you think of the next time you see a rainbow?

We know how much God loves us, and we have put our trust in him. God is love, and all who live in love live in God, and God lives in them.
1 John 4:16

All the people of the earth gathered together to build a tower.
Why was God unhappy with their plans?

GENESIS 11:1-9
The Tower of Babel

At one time the whole world spoke a single language and used the same words. ²As the people migrated eastward, they found a plain in the land of Babylonia* and settled there. ³They began to talk about construction projects. "Come," they said, "let's make great piles of burnt brick and collect natural asphalt to use as mortar. ⁴Let's build a great city with a tower that reaches to the skies—a monument to our greatness! This will bring us together and keep us from scattering all over the world."

⁵But the LORD came down to see the city and the tower the people were building. ⁶"Look!" he said. "If they can accomplish this when they have just begun to take advantage of their common language and political unity, just think of what they will do later. Nothing will be impossible for them! ⁷Come, let's go down and give them different languages. Then they won't be able to understand each other."

⁸In that way, the LORD scattered them all over the earth; and that ended the building of the city. ⁹That is why the city was called Babel,* because it was there that the LORD confused the people by giving them many languages, thus scattering them across the earth.

A tall tower would bring fame. People would admire it and say, "Look at how intelligent and strong the builders of this tower are!" Instead of thanking and admiring God, the builders were trying to gain glory for themselves. Unfortunately, we are just like them. We take pride in our intelligence and skills and forget to give thanks to God for giving us those abilities. The next time you're tempted to boast about yourself, remember to thank God for creating you. Thank him also for blessing you with your abilities.

Why is it important to be humble?
But those who exalt themselves will be humbled, and those who humble themselves will be exalted.
Matthew 23:12

11:2 Hebrew *Shinar*. **11:9** *Babel* sounds like a Hebrew term that means "confusion."

God told Abram to leave his country. Abram obeyed. What did God promise Abram?

GENESIS 12:1-9
God's Promises to Abram

Then the LORD told Abram, "Leave your country, your relatives, and your father's house, and go to the land that I will show you. ²I will cause you to become the father of a great nation. I will bless you and make you famous, and I will make you a blessing to others. ³I will bless those who bless you and curse those who curse you. All the families of the earth will be blessed through you."

⁴So Abram departed as the LORD had instructed him, and Lot went with him. Abram was seventy-five years old when he left Haran. ⁵He took his wife, Sarai, his nephew Lot, and all his wealth—his livestock and all the people who had joined his household at Haran—and finally arrived in Canaan. ⁶Traveling through Canaan, they came to a place near Shechem and set up camp beside the oak at Moreh. At that time, the area was inhabited by Canaanites.

⁷Then the LORD appeared to Abram and said, "I am going to give this land to your offspring.*" And Abram built an altar there to commemorate the LORD's visit. ⁸After that, Abram traveled southward and set up camp in the hill country between Bethel on the west and Ai on the east. There he built an altar and worshiped the LORD. ⁹Then Abram traveled south by stages toward the Negev.

God promised to make Abram's family into a great nation if he believed and obeyed God. Israel became that great nation. God has made another promise to all people, including you. He promises you eternal life if you believe in Jesus. You can trust him to come through on his promise.

What is God's promise to you?
For God so loved the world that he gave his only Son, so that everyone who believes in him will not perish but have eternal life.
John 3:16

12:7 Hebrew *seed.*

Abraham and Sarah could not have children. But God promised them a son. How would he keep his promise?

GENESIS 18:1-15

Sarah Will Have a Son

The LORD appeared again to Abraham while he was camped near the oak grove belonging to Mamre. One day about noon, as Abraham was sitting at the entrance to his tent, ²he suddenly noticed three men standing nearby. He got up and ran to meet them, welcoming them by bowing low to the ground. ³"My lord," he said, "if it pleases you, stop here for a while. ⁴Rest in the shade of this tree while my servants get some water to wash your feet. ⁵Let me prepare some food to refresh you. Please stay awhile before continuing on your journey."

"All right," they said. "Do as you have said."

⁶So Abraham ran back to the tent and said to Sarah, "Quick! Get three measures* of your best flour, and bake some bread." ⁷Then Abraham ran out to the herd and chose a fat calf and told a servant to hurry and butcher it. ⁸When the food was ready, he took some cheese curds and milk and the roasted meat, and he served it to the men. As they ate, Abraham waited on them there beneath the trees.

⁹"Where is Sarah, your wife?" they asked him.

"In the tent," Abraham replied.

¹⁰Then one of them said, "About this time next year I will return, and your wife Sarah will have a son."

Now Sarah was listening to this conversation from the tent nearby. ¹¹And since Abraham and Sarah were both very old, and Sarah was long past the age of having children, ¹²she laughed silently to herself. "How could a worn-out woman like me have a baby?" she thought. "And when my master—my husband—is also so old?"

¹³Then the LORD said to Abraham, "Why did Sarah laugh? Why did she say, 'Can an old woman like me have a baby?' ¹⁴Is anything too hard for the LORD? About a year from now, just as I told you, I will return, and Sarah will have a son." ¹⁵Sarah was afraid, so she denied that she had laughed. But he said, "That is not true. You did laugh."

Sarah could not believe it. How could she have a son? But it happened! God did the impossible! Today, he still does the impossible in our lives and the lives of others. All he asks is that we trust him.

Why is it sometimes hard for us to trust God?

But these are written so that you may believe* that Jesus is the Messiah, the Son of God, and that by believing in him you will have life.

John 20:31

18:6 Hebrew *3 seahs*, about 15 quarts or 18 liters. **20:31** Some manuscripts read *may continue to believe.*

God had decided to punish the people of Sodom and Gomorrah for their wickedness. He sent two angels to warn those who were good. Did they escape in time?

GENESIS 19:12-29

Sodom and Gomorrah

12 "Do you have any other relatives here in the city?" the angels asked. "Get them out of this place—sons-in-law, sons, daughters, or anyone else. 13 For we will destroy the city completely. The stench of the place has reached the LORD, and he has sent us to destroy it."

14 So Lot rushed out to tell his daughters' fiancés, "Quick, get out of the city! The LORD is going to destroy it." But the young men thought he was only joking.

15 At dawn the next morning the angels became insistent. "Hurry," they said to Lot. "Take your wife and your two daughters who are here. Get out of here right now, or you will be caught in the destruction of the city."

16 When Lot still hesitated, the angels seized his hand and the hands of his wife and two daughters and rushed them to safety outside the city, for the LORD was merciful. 17 "Run for your lives!" the angels warned. "Do not stop anywhere in the valley. And don't look back! Escape to the mountains, or you will die."

18 "Oh no, my lords, please," Lot begged. 19 "You have been so kind to me and saved my life, and you have granted me such mercy. But I cannot go to the mountains. Disaster would catch up to me there, and I would soon die. 20 See, there is a small village nearby. Please let me go there instead; don't you see how small it is? Then my life will be saved."

Two angels warned Lot that God's punishment was coming and that Lot and his family should leave Sodom and Gomorrah immediately. Lot hesitated. Instead, he should have acted quickly to escape. God warns people today to turn away from their sins. Don't hesitate! The best time to choose to follow and obey God is right now.

How should we respond to God's warnings in the Bible?

From then on, Jesus began to preach, "Turn from your sins and turn to God, because the Kingdom of Heaven is near.*"

Matthew 4:17

21 "All right," the angel said, "I will grant your request. I will not destroy that little village. 22 But hurry! For I can do nothing until you are there." From that time on, that village was known as Zoar.*

19:22 Zoar means "little." **4:17** Or *has come,* or *is coming soon.*

²³The sun was rising as Lot reached the village. ²⁴Then the LORD rained down fire and burning sulfur from the heavens on Sodom and Gomorrah. ²⁵He utterly destroyed them, along with the other cities and villages of the plain, eliminating all life—people, plants, and animals alike. ²⁶But Lot's wife looked back as she was following along behind him, and she became a pillar of salt.

²⁷The next morning Abraham was up early and hurried out to the place where he had stood in the LORD's presence. ²⁸He looked out across the plain to Sodom and Gomorrah and saw columns of smoke and fumes, as from a furnace, rising from the cities there. ²⁹But God had listened to Abraham's request and kept Lot safe, removing him from the disaster that engulfed the cities on the plain.

J A N U A R Y

God told Abraham to send his servant Hagar and her son, Ishmael, away from his household. In the desert, Hagar couldn't find water. What happened to Hagar and Ishmael?

GENESIS 21:8-21

Hagar and Ishmael

⁸As time went by and Isaac grew and was weaned, Abraham gave a big party to celebrate the happy occasion. ⁹But Sarah saw Ishmael—the son of Abraham and her Egyptian servant Hagar—making fun of Isaac. ¹⁰So she turned to Abraham and demanded, "Get rid of that servant and her son. He is not going to share the family inheritance with my son, Isaac. I won't have it!"

¹¹This upset Abraham very much because Ishmael was his son. ¹²But God told Abraham, "Do not be upset over the boy and your servant wife. Do just as Sarah says, for Isaac is the son through whom your descendants will be counted. ¹³But I will make a nation of the descendants of Hagar's son because he also is your son."

¹⁴So Abraham got up early the next morning, prepared food for the journey, and strapped a container of water to Hagar's shoulders. He sent her away with their son, and she walked out into the wilderness of Beersheba, wandering aimlessly. ¹⁵When the water was gone, she left the boy in the shade of a bush. ¹⁶Then she went and sat down by herself about a hundred yards* away. "I don't want to watch the boy die," she said, as she burst into tears.

¹⁷Then God heard the boy's cries, and the angel of God called to Hagar from the sky, "Hagar, what's wrong? Do not be afraid! God has heard the boy's cries from the place where you

21:16 Hebrew *a bowshot.*

14

laid him. [18]Go to him and comfort him, for I will make a great nation from his descendants."

[19]Then God opened Hagar's eyes, and she saw a well. She immediately filled her water container and gave the boy a drink. [20]And God was with the boy as he grew up in the wilderness of Paran. He became an expert archer, [21]and his mother arranged a marriage for him with a young woman from Egypt.

Hagar was worried. She had no water, and Ishmael was dying of thirst. But, just in time, God provided. Jesus tells us not to worry about our needs, such as food or clothing. God cares about you, and he will provide for your needs.

Why should you trust God to provide for your needs?

Why be like the pagans who are so deeply concerned about these things? Your heavenly Father already knows all your needs, and he will give you all you need from day to day if you live for him and make the Kingdom of God your primary concern.
Matthew 6:32-33

J A N U A R Y

God had kept his promise to Abraham and Sarah by giving them a son, Isaac. But then God tested Abraham's love for him by asking Abraham to sacrifice Isaac. Did Abraham obey God?

GENESIS 22:1-18

Abraham's Painful Decision

Later on God tested Abraham's faith and obedience. "Abraham!" God called.

"Yes," he replied. "Here I am."

[2]"Take your son, your only son— yes, Isaac, whom you love so much— and go to the land of Moriah. Sacrifice him there as a burnt offering on one of the mountains, which I will point out to you."

[3]The next morning Abraham got up early. He saddled his donkey and took two of his servants with him, along with his son Isaac. Then he chopped wood to build a fire for a burnt offering and set out for the place where God had told him to go. [4]On the third day of the journey, Abraham saw the place in the distance. [5]"Stay here with the donkey," Abraham told the young men. "The boy and I will travel a little farther. We will worship there, and then we will come right back."

[6]Abraham placed the wood for the

burnt offering on Isaac's shoulders, while he himself carried the knife and the fire. As the two of them went on together, [7]Isaac said, "Father?"

"Yes, my son," Abraham replied.

"We have the wood and the fire," said the boy, "but where is the lamb for the sacrifice?"

[8]"God will provide a lamb, my son," Abraham answered. And they both went on together.

[9]When they arrived at the place where God had told Abraham to go, he built an altar and placed the wood on it. Then he tied Isaac up and laid him on the altar over the wood. [10]And Abraham took the knife and lifted it up to kill his son as a sacrifice to the LORD. [11]At that moment the angel of the LORD shouted to him from heaven, "Abraham! Abraham!"

"Yes," he answered. "I'm listening."

[12]"Lay down the knife," the angel said. "Do not hurt the boy in any way, for now I know that you truly fear God. You have not withheld even your beloved son from me."

[13]Then Abraham looked up and saw a ram caught by its horns in a bush. So he took the ram and sacrificed it as a burnt offering on the altar in place of his son. [14]Abraham named the place "The LORD Will Provide."* This name has now become a proverb: "On the mountain of the LORD it will be provided."

[15]Then the angel of the LORD called again to Abraham from heaven, [16]"This is what the LORD says: Because you have obeyed me and have not withheld even your beloved son, I swear by my own self that [17]I will bless you richly. I will multiply your descendants into countless millions, like the stars of the sky and the sand on the seashore. They will conquer their enemies, [18]and through your descendants,* all the nations of the earth will be blessed—all because you have obeyed me."

Even though Abraham did not understand why God had asked him to sacrifice Isaac, he trusted God and took steps to obey his command. God blessed Abraham because of his obedience and provided him with a ram to sacrifice instead of his son. There may be commands from God that you don't understand, too. But God will bless you if you trust and obey him as Abraham did.

Why is it important to obey God?
He replied, "But even more blessed are all who hear the word of God and put it into practice."
Luke 11:28

22:14 Hebrew *Yahweh Yir'eh.* 22:18 Hebrew *seed.*

Abraham ordered his chief servant to find a wife for his son, Isaac. Who did the servant turn to for help?

GENESIS 24:34-48
A Wife for Isaac

[34] "I am Abraham's servant," he explained. [35] "And the LORD has blessed my master richly; he has become a great man. The LORD has given him flocks of sheep and herds of cattle, a fortune in silver and gold, and many servants and camels and donkeys. [36] When Sarah, my master's wife, was very old, she gave birth to my master's son, and my master has given him everything he owns. [37] And my master made me swear that I would not let Isaac marry one of the local Canaanite women. [38] Instead, I was to come to his relatives here in this far-off land, to his father's home. I was told to bring back a young woman from here to marry his son.

[39] "'But suppose I can't find a young woman willing to come back with me?' I asked him. [40] 'You will,' he told me, 'for the LORD, in whose presence I have walked, will send his angel with you and will make your mission successful. Yes, you must get a wife for my son from among my relatives, from my father's family. [41] But if you go to my relatives and they refuse to let her come, you will be free from your oath.'

[42] "So this afternoon when I came to the spring I prayed this prayer: 'O LORD, the God of my master, Abraham, if you are planning to make my mission a success, please guide me in a special way. [43] Here I am, standing beside this spring. I will say to some young woman who comes to draw water, "Please give me a drink of water!" [44] And she will reply, "Certainly! And I'll water your camels, too!" LORD, let her be the one you have selected to be the wife of my master's son.'

[45] "Before I had finished praying these words, I saw Rebekah coming along with her water jug on her shoulder. She went down to the spring and drew water and filled the jug. So I said to her, 'Please give me a drink.' [46] She quickly lowered the jug from her shoulder so I could drink, and she said, 'Certainly, sir, and I will water

Abraham's servant had a difficult job. How could he complete his task? He turned to God for guidance, and God answered. When something is difficult for you, remember to pray to God and trust him for an answer.

What should you do when you need God's help?

Don't worry about anything; instead, pray about everything. Tell God what you need, and thank him for all he has done.
Philippians 4:6

your camels, too!' And she did. 47When I asked her whose daughter she was, she told me, 'My father is Bethuel, the son of Nahor and his wife, Milcah.' So I gave her the ring and the bracelets.

48"Then I bowed my head and worshiped the LORD. I praised the LORD, the God of my master, Abraham, because he had led me along the right path to find a wife from the family of my master's relatives."

J A N U A R Y

Abraham's servant told Rebekah's family how God had guided him to Rebekah. Did they follow God's guidance and let Rebekah return with Abraham's servant?

GENESIS 24:50-67

Rebekah's Response

50Then Laban and Bethuel replied, "The LORD has obviously brought you here, so what can we say? 51Here is Rebekah; take her and go. Yes, let her be the wife of your master's son, as the LORD has directed."

52At this reply, Abraham's servant bowed to the ground and worshiped the LORD. 53Then he brought out silver and gold jewelry and lovely clothing for Rebekah. He also gave valuable presents to her mother and brother. 54Then they had supper, and the servant and the men with him stayed there overnight. But early the next morning, he said, "Send me back to my master."

55"But we want Rebekah to stay at least ten days," her brother and mother said. "Then she can go."

56But he said, "Don't hinder my return. The LORD has made my mission successful, and I want to report back to my master."

57"Well," they said, "we'll call Rebekah and ask her what she thinks." 58So they called Rebekah. "Are you willing to go with this man?" they asked her.

And she replied, "Yes, I will go."

59So they said good-bye to Rebekah and sent her away with Abraham's servant and his men. The woman who had been Rebekah's childhood nurse went along with her. 60They blessed her with this blessing as she parted:

"Our sister, may you become
    the mother of many millions!
May your descendants overcome
    all their enemies."

61Then Rebekah and her servants mounted the camels and left with Abraham's servant.

62Meanwhile, Isaac, whose home was in the Negev, had returned from Beer-lahairoi. 63One evening as he was taking a walk out in the fields, meditating, he looked up and saw the camels coming. 64When Rebekah looked up and saw Isaac, she quickly dismounted. ⁶⁵"Who is that man walking through the fields to meet us?" she asked the servant.

And he replied, "It is my master." So Rebekah covered her face with her veil. ⁶⁶Then the servant told Isaac the whole story.

⁶⁷And Isaac brought Rebekah into his mother's tent, and she became his wife. He loved her very much, and she was a special comfort to him after the death of his mother.

Rebekah acted on faith when she left with Abraham's servant. She had not met Isaac, her husband-to-be, and her family wanted her to stay with them a little longer. But she obeyed God and left with Abraham's servant the next day. Today, Jesus asks you to follow him. You can be like Rebekah and act in faith by obeying Jesus immediately.

Why should you obey Jesus' commands?

Jesus said to the people, "I am the light of the world. If you follow me, you won't be stumbling through the darkness, because you will have the light that leads to life."
John 8:12

J A N U A R Y

16

God blessed Isaac and Rebekah with twin boys. Esau was the older, and Jacob was the younger. How did these two boys treat each other?

GENESIS 25:21-34

Jacob versus Esau

²¹Isaac pleaded with the LORD to give Rebekah a child because she was childless. So the LORD answered Isaac's prayer, and his wife became pregnant with twins. ²²But the two children struggled with each other in her womb. So she went to ask the LORD about it. "Why is this happening to me?" she asked.

²³And the LORD told her, "The sons in your womb will become two rival nations. One nation will be stronger than the other; the descendants of your older son will serve the descendants of your younger son."

²⁴And when the time came, the twins were born. ²⁵The first was very red at birth. He was covered with so much hair that one would think he was wearing a piece of clothing. So they called him Esau.* ²⁶Then the other twin was born with his hand grasping Esau's heel. So they called him Jacob.* Isaac was sixty years old when the twins were born.

25:25 *Esau* sounds like a Hebrew term that means "hair." 25:26 *Jacob* means "he grasps the heel"; this can also figuratively mean "he deceives."

²⁷As the boys grew up, Esau became a skillful hunter, a man of the open fields, while Jacob was the kind of person who liked to stay at home. ²⁸Isaac loved Esau in particular because of the wild game he brought home, but Rebekah favored Jacob.

²⁹One day when Jacob was cooking some stew, Esau arrived home exhausted and hungry from a hunt. ³⁰Esau said to Jacob, "I'm starved! Give me some of that red stew you've made." (This was how Esau got his other name, Edom—"Red.")

³¹Jacob replied, "All right, but trade me your birthright for it."

³²"Look, I'm dying of starvation!" said Esau. "What good is my birthright to me now?"

³³So Jacob insisted, "Well then, swear to me right now that it is mine." So Esau swore an oath, thereby selling all his rights as the firstborn to his younger brother. ³⁴Then Jacob gave Esau some bread and lentil stew. Esau ate and drank and went on about his business, indifferent to the fact that he had given up his birthright.

Jacob cheated Esau out of his inheritance. Often brothers and sisters trick, tease, and pick on each other. But God commands us to love our brothers and sisters.

Why should you love your brothers and sisters?

And God himself has commanded that we must love not only him but our Christian brothers and sisters, too.
1 John 4:21

J A N U A R Y

Isaac was close to death. He told Esau, his oldest son, to prepare him a tasty meal. At this meal, he planned to bless Esau. But Jacob wanted to receive his father's blessing. What did Jacob do?

GENESIS 27:5-30
Jacob Tricks His Father

⁵But Rebekah overheard the conversation. So when Esau left to hunt for the wild game, ⁶she said to her son Jacob, "I overheard your father asking Esau ⁷to prepare him a delicious meal of wild game. He wants to bless Esau in the LORD's presence before he dies. ⁸Now, my son, do exactly as I tell you. ⁹Go out to the flocks and bring me two fine young goats. I'll prepare your father's favorite dish from them. ¹⁰Take the food to your father; then he can eat it and bless you instead of Esau before he dies."

¹¹"But Mother!" Jacob replied. "He won't be fooled that easily. Think how hairy Esau is and how smooth my skin is! ¹²What if my father touches me? He'll see that I'm trying to trick him, and then he'll curse me instead of blessing me."

¹³"Let the curse fall on me, dear son," said Rebekah. "Just do what I tell you. Go out and get the goats."

¹⁴So Jacob followed his mother's instructions, bringing her the two goats. She took them and cooked a delicious meat dish, just the way Isaac liked it. ¹⁵Then she took Esau's best clothes, which were there in the house, and dressed Jacob with them. ¹⁶She made him a pair of gloves from the hairy skin of the young goats, and she fastened a strip of the goat's skin around his neck. ¹⁷Then she gave him the meat dish, with its rich aroma, and some freshly baked bread. ¹⁸Jacob carried the platter of food to his father and said, "My father?"

"Yes, my son," he answered. "Who is it—Esau or Jacob?"

¹⁹Jacob replied, "It's Esau, your older son. I've done as you told me. Here is the wild game, cooked the way you like it. Sit up and eat it so you can give me your blessing."

²⁰Isaac asked, "How were you able to find it so quickly, my son?"

"Because the LORD your God put it in my path!" Jacob replied.

²¹Then Isaac said to Jacob, "Come over here. I want to touch you to make sure you really are Esau." ²²So Jacob went over to his father, and Isaac touched him. "The voice is Jacob's, but the hands are Esau's," Isaac said to himself. ²³But he did not recognize Jacob because Jacob's hands felt hairy just like Esau's. So Isaac pronounced his blessing on Jacob. ²⁴"Are you really my son Esau?" he asked.

"Yes, of course," Jacob replied.

²⁵Then Isaac said, "Now, my son, bring me the meat. I will eat it, and then I will give you my blessing." So Jacob took the food over to his father, and Isaac ate it. He also drank the wine that Jacob served him. Then Isaac said, ²⁶"Come here and kiss me, my son."

²⁷So Jacob went over and kissed him. And when Isaac caught the smell of his clothes, he was finally convinced, and he blessed his son. He said, "The smell of my son is the good smell of the open fields that the LORD has blessed. ²⁸May God always give you plenty of dew for healthy crops and good harvests of grain and wine. ²⁹May many nations become your servants. May you be the master of your brothers. May all your mother's sons bow low before you. All who curse you are cursed, and all who bless you are blessed."

³⁰As soon as Isaac had blessed Jacob, and almost before Jacob had left his father, Esau returned from his hunting trip.

Jacob wanted his father's blessing so much that he lied to get it. His action led to future problems with his family members. God wants us to be honest in our relationships with other people. Lying is never the right way to get what we want.

Why is it important to be honest?

Unless you are faithful in small matters, you won't be faithful in large ones. If you cheat even a little, you won't be honest with greater responsibilities.
Luke 16:10

J A N U A R Y

To get away from Esau, Jacob went to the land of his uncle Laban. Who did Jacob meet on the way?

GENESIS 28:10-22

Stairway to Heaven

¹⁰Meanwhile, Jacob left Beersheba and traveled toward Haran. ¹¹At sundown he arrived at a good place to set up camp and stopped there for the night. Jacob found a stone for a pillow and lay down to sleep. ¹²As he slept, he dreamed of a stairway that reached from earth to heaven. And he saw the angels of God going up and down on it.

¹³At the top of the stairway stood the LORD, and he said, "I am the LORD, the God of your grandfather Abraham and the God of your father, Isaac. The ground you are lying on belongs to you. I will give it to you and your descendants. ¹⁴Your descendants will be as numerous as the dust of the earth! They will cover the land from east to west and from north to south. All the families of the earth will be blessed through you and your descendants.* ¹⁵What's more, I will be with you, and I will protect you wherever you go. I will someday bring you safely back to this land. I will be with you constantly until I have finished giving you everything I have promised."

¹⁶Then Jacob woke up and said, "Surely the LORD is in this place, and I wasn't even aware of it." ¹⁷He was afraid and said, "What an awesome place this is! It is none other than the house of God—the gateway to heaven!" ¹⁸The next morning he got up very early. He took the stone he had used as a pillow and set it upright as a memorial pillar. Then he poured olive oil over it. ¹⁹He named the place Bethel—"house of God"—though the name of the nearby village was Luz.

²⁰Then Jacob made this vow: "If God will be with me and protect me on this journey and give me food and clothing, ²¹and if he will bring me back safely to my father, then I will make the LORD my God. ²²This memorial pillar will become a place for worshiping God, and I will give God a tenth of everything he gives me."

When Jacob had this dream of the stairway, he did not have a family of his own or any land or livestock. That did not matter. God was going to bless Jacob, and he let Jacob know this. Jacob believed God and gave thanks to him for his goodness.

What has God given you that you can be thankful for?
And you will always give thanks for everything to God the Father in the name of our Lord Jesus Christ.
Ephesians 5:20

28:14 Hebrew *seed.*

J A N U A R Y

Jacob returned home with his wives and children. He was afraid his brother, Esau, would hurt him. Did Esau take revenge?

GENESIS 32:3-21; 33:1-4

Jacob Returns Home

³Jacob now sent messengers to his brother, Esau, in Edom, the land of Seir. ⁴He told them, "Give this message to my master Esau: 'Humble greetings from your servant Jacob! I have been living with Uncle Laban until recently, ⁵and now I own oxen, donkeys, sheep, goats, and many servants, both men and women. I have sent these messengers to inform you of my coming, hoping that you will be friendly to us.' "

⁶The messengers returned with the news that Esau was on his way to meet Jacob—with an army of four hundred men! ⁷Jacob was terrified at the news. He divided his household, along with the flocks and herds and camels, into two camps. ⁸He thought, "If Esau attacks one group, perhaps the other can escape."

⁹Then Jacob prayed, "O God of my grandfather Abraham and my father, Isaac—O LORD, you told me to return to my land and to my relatives, and you promised to treat me kindly. ¹⁰I am not worthy of all the faithfulness and unfailing love you have shown to me, your servant. When I left home, I owned nothing except a walking stick, and now my household fills two camps! ¹¹O LORD, please rescue me from my brother, Esau. I am afraid that he is coming to kill me, along with my wives and children. ¹²But you promised to treat me kindly and to multiply my descendants until they become as numerous as the sands along the seashore—too many to count."

¹³Jacob stayed where he was for the night and prepared a present for Esau: ¹⁴two hundred female goats, twenty male goats, two hundred ewes, twenty rams, ¹⁵thirty female camels with their young, forty cows, ten bulls, twenty female donkeys, and ten male donkeys. ¹⁶He told his servants to lead them on ahead, each group of animals by itself, separated by a distance in between.

¹⁷He gave these instructions to the men leading the first group: "When you meet Esau, he will ask, 'Where are you going? Whose servants are you? Whose animals are these?' ¹⁸You should reply, 'These belong to your servant Jacob. They are a present for his master Esau! He is coming right behind us.' " ¹⁹Jacob gave the same instructions to each of the herdsmen and told them, "You are all to say the same thing to Esau when you see him. ²⁰And be sure to say, 'Your servant Jacob is right behind us.' " Jacob's plan was to appease Esau with the presents before meeting him face to face. "Perhaps," Jacob hoped, "he will

be friendly to us." ²¹So the presents were sent on ahead, and Jacob spent that night in the camp.

• • •

³³:¹Then, in the distance, Jacob saw Esau coming with his four hundred men. ²Jacob now arranged his family into a column, with his two concubines and their children at the front, Leah and her children next, and Rachel and Joseph last. ³Then Jacob went on ahead. As he approached his brother, he bowed low seven times before him. ⁴Then Esau ran to meet him and embraced him affectionately and kissed him. Both of them were in tears.

Jacob was afraid that Esau was still angry at him. He thought Esau would do him and his family harm. To deal with his fear, Jacob prayed. He asked God to protect him and his family from Esau. God answered and protected Jacob. When you are afraid of someone or something and need protection, pray to God. He will protect you.

How does God comfort us when we are afraid?

I am leaving you with a gift—peace of mind and heart. And the peace I give isn't like the peace the world gives. So don't be troubled or afraid.
John 14:27

J A N U A R Y

Joseph's brothers were jealous of him. How did they deal with their jealousy?

GENESIS 37:3-4, 12-34
Joseph and His Brothers
³Now Jacob* loved Joseph more than any of his other children because Joseph had been born to him in his old age. So one day he gave Joseph a special gift—a beautiful robe.* ⁴But his brothers hated Joseph because of their father's partiality. They couldn't say a kind word to him.

• • •

¹²Soon after this, Joseph's brothers went to pasture their father's flocks at Shechem. ¹³When they had been gone for some time, Jacob said to Joseph, "Your brothers are over at Shechem with the flocks. I'm going to send you to them."

"I'm ready to go," Joseph replied.

¹⁴"Go and see how your brothers and the flocks are getting along," Jacob said. "Then come back and bring me word." So Jacob sent him on his way, and Joseph traveled to Shechem from his home in the valley of Hebron.

¹⁵When he arrived there, a man noticed him wandering around the countryside. "What are you looking for?" he asked.

37:3a Hebrew *Israel;* also in 37:13. **37:3b** Traditionally rendered *a coat of many colors.* The exact meaning of the Hebrew is uncertain.

¹⁶"For my brothers and their flocks," Joseph replied. "Have you seen them?"

¹⁷"Yes," the man told him, "but they are no longer here. I heard your brothers say they were going to Dothan." So Joseph followed his brothers to Dothan and found them there.

¹⁸When Joseph's brothers saw him coming, they recognized him in the distance and made plans to kill him. ¹⁹"Here comes that dreamer!" they exclaimed. ²⁰"Come on, let's kill him and throw him into a deep pit. We can tell our father that a wild animal has eaten him. Then we'll see what becomes of all his dreams!"

²¹But Reuben came to Joseph's rescue. "Let's not kill him," he said. ²²"Why should we shed his blood? Let's just throw him alive into this pit here. That way he will die without our having to touch him." Reuben was secretly planning to help Joseph escape, and then he would bring him back to his father.

²³So when Joseph arrived, they pulled off his beautiful robe ²⁴and threw him into the pit. This pit was normally used to store water, but it was empty at the time. ²⁵Then, just as they were sitting down to eat, they noticed a caravan of camels in the distance coming toward them. It was a group of Ishmaelite traders taking spices, balm, and myrrh from Gilead to Egypt.

²⁶Judah said to the others, "What can we gain by killing our brother? That would just give us a guilty conscience. ²⁷Let's sell Joseph to those Ishmaelite traders. Let's not be responsible for his death; after all, he is our brother!" And his brothers agreed. ²⁸So when the traders* came by, his brothers pulled Joseph out of the pit and sold him for twenty pieces* of silver, and the Ishmaelite traders took him along to Egypt.

²⁹Some time later, Reuben returned to get Joseph out of the pit. When he discovered that Joseph was missing, he tore his clothes in anguish and frustration. ³⁰Then he went back to his brothers and lamented, "The boy is gone! What can I do now?"

³¹Then Joseph's brothers killed a goat and dipped the robe in its blood. ³²They took the beautiful robe to their father and asked him to identify it. "We found this in the field," they told him. "It's Joseph's robe, isn't it?"

³³Their father recognized it at once. "Yes," he said, "it is my son's robe. A wild animal has attacked and eaten him. Surely Joseph has been torn in pieces!" ³⁴Then Jacob tore his clothes and put on sackcloth. He mourned deeply for his son for many days.

Jacob liked his son Joseph the best. Joseph's brothers were jealous of him because of their father's favor. They let their jealousy grow into hatred and almost killed Joseph. Of whom are you jealous? Don't stay jealous. Your jealousy can lead you to hurt other people.

How can you defeat jealousy?
Yet true religion with contentment is great wealth. After all, we didn't bring anything with us when we came into the world, and we certainly cannot carry anything with us when we die. So if we have enough food and clothing, let us be content.
1 Timothy 6:6-8

37:28a Hebrew *Midianites;* also in 37:36. 37:28b Hebrew *20 shekels,* about 8 ounces or 228 grams in weight.

Joseph's master put him in charge of his entire household. But Joseph had more challenges than just the chores. How did he deal with those extra challenges?

GENESIS 39:1-23

Joseph in Trouble

Now when Joseph arrived in Egypt with the Ishmaelite traders, he was purchased by Potiphar, a member of the personal staff of Pharaoh, the king of Egypt. Potiphar was the captain of the palace guard.

²The LORD was with Joseph and blessed him greatly as he served in the home of his Egyptian master. ³Potiphar noticed this and realized that the LORD was with Joseph, giving him success in everything he did. ⁴So Joseph naturally became quite a favorite with him. Potiphar soon put Joseph in charge of his entire household and entrusted him with all his business dealings. ⁵From the day Joseph was put in charge, the LORD began to bless Potiphar for Joseph's sake. All his household affairs began to run smoothly, and his crops and livestock flourished. ⁶So Potiphar gave Joseph complete administrative responsibility over everything he owned. With Joseph there, he didn't have a worry in the world, except to decide what he wanted to eat!

Now Joseph was a very handsome and well-built young man. ⁷And about this time, Potiphar's wife began to desire him and invited him to sleep with her. ⁸But Joseph refused. "Look," he told her, "my master trusts me with everything in his entire household. ⁹No one here has more authority than I do! He has held back nothing from me except you, because you are his wife. How could I ever do such a wicked thing? It would be a great sin against God."

¹⁰She kept putting pressure on him day after day, but he refused to sleep with her, and he kept out of her way as much as possible. ¹¹One day, however, no one else was around when he was doing his work inside the house. ¹²She came and grabbed him by his shirt, demanding, "Sleep with me!" Joseph tore himself away, but as he did, his shirt came off. She was left holding it as he ran from the house.

¹³When she saw that she had his shirt and that he had fled, ¹⁴she began screaming. Soon all the men around the place came running. "My husband has brought this Hebrew slave here to insult us!" she sobbed. "He tried to rape me, but I screamed. ¹⁵When he heard my loud cries, he ran and left his shirt behind with me."

¹⁶She kept the shirt with her, and when her husband came home that night, ¹⁷she told him her story. "That Hebrew slave you've had around here tried to make a fool of me," she said.

¹⁸"I was saved only by my screams. He ran out, leaving his shirt behind!"

¹⁹After hearing his wife's story, Potiphar was furious! ²⁰He took Joseph and threw him into the prison where the king's prisoners were held. ²¹But the LORD was with Joseph there, too, and he granted Joseph favor with the chief jailer. ²²Before long, the jailer put Joseph in charge of all the other prisoners and over everything that happened in the prison. ²³The chief jailer had no more worries after that, because Joseph took care of everything. The LORD was with him, making everything run smoothly and successfully.

Potiphar's wife tempted Joseph to sin with her "day after day." But Joseph refused, choosing to respect Potiphar and to honor God. One day Potiphar's wife cornered Joseph. It would have been easy for him to give in to the temptation to sin. But Joseph obeyed God and ran away from temptation. Who or what tempts you? When the temptation to sin is more than you can handle, follow Joseph's example and run away from the temptation.

What temptation should you run from?

Run from anything that stimulates youthful lust. Follow anything that makes you want to do right. Pursue faith and love and peace, and enjoy the companionship of those who call on the Lord with pure hearts.
2 Timothy 2:22

J A N U A R Y

Although Joseph was in prison, he was not bitter and remained useful to God. How did God use Joseph there?

GENESIS 40:1-23

The Prisoners' Dreams

Some time later, Pharaoh's chief cup-bearer and chief baker offended him. ²Pharaoh became very angry with these officials, ³and he put them in the prison where Joseph was, in the palace of Potiphar, the captain of the guard. ⁴They remained in prison for quite some time, and Potiphar assigned Joseph to take care of them.

⁵One night the cup-bearer and the baker each had a dream, and each dream had its own meaning. ⁶The next morning Joseph noticed the dejected look on their faces. ⁷"Why do you look so worried today?" he asked.

⁸And they replied, "We both had dreams last night, but there is no one here to tell us what they mean."

"Interpreting dreams is God's

business," Joseph replied. "Tell me what you saw."

⁹The cup-bearer told his dream first. "In my dream," he said, "I saw a vine in front of me. ¹⁰It had three branches that began to bud and blossom, and soon there were clusters of ripe grapes. ¹¹I was holding Pharaoh's wine cup in my hand, so I took the grapes and squeezed the juice into it. Then I placed the cup in Pharaoh's hand."

¹²"I know what the dream means," Joseph said. "The three branches mean three days. ¹³Within three days Pharaoh will take you out of prison and return you to your position as his chief cup-bearer. ¹⁴And please have some pity on me when you are back in his favor. Mention me to Pharaoh, and ask him to let me out of here. ¹⁵For I was kidnapped from my homeland, the land of the Hebrews, and now I'm here in jail, but I did nothing to deserve it."

¹⁶When the chief baker saw that the first dream had such a good meaning, he told his dream to Joseph, too. "In my dream," he said, "there were three baskets of pastries on my head. ¹⁷In the top basket were all kinds of bakery goods for Pharaoh, but the birds came and ate them."

¹⁸"I'll tell you what it means," Joseph told him. "The three baskets mean three days. ¹⁹Three days from now Pharaoh will cut off your head and impale your body on a pole. Then birds will come and peck away at your flesh."

²⁰Pharaoh's birthday came three days later, and he gave a banquet for all his officials and household staff. He sent for his chief cup-bearer and chief baker, and they were brought to him from the prison. ²¹He then restored the chief cup-bearer to his former position, ²²but he sentenced the chief baker to be impaled on a pole, just as Joseph had predicted. ²³Pharaoh's cup-bearer, however, promptly forgot all about Joseph, never giving him another thought.

Joseph was in prison for doing the right thing! He had every right to complain. Instead, he worked hard and was put in charge of other prisoners. That is how Joseph was able to find out about the dreams of two prisoners—Pharaoh's chief baker and chief cup-bearer. With God's help, Joseph was able to interpret their dreams. When things are not going well in your life, you can complain. Or you can have a good attitude and do your best for God. Choose to have a good attitude. This pleases God.

When do you need to have a good attitude?

Dear brothers and sisters, whenever trouble comes your way, let it be an opportunity for joy. For when your faith is tested, your endurance has a chance to grow.
James 1:2-3

Pharaoh had a dream that no one could interpret. His chief cup-bearer remembered to tell Pharaoh about Joseph. Pharaoh called Joseph to interpret his dream. Did Joseph interpret Pharaoh's dream correctly?

GENESIS 41:15-32

A Dream in the Palace

15 "I had a dream last night," Pharaoh told him, "and none of these men can tell me what it means. But I have heard that you can interpret dreams, and that is why I have called for you."

16 "It is beyond my power to do this," Joseph replied. "But God will tell you what it means and will set you at ease."

17 So Pharaoh told him the dream. "I was standing on the bank of the Nile River," he said. 18 "Suddenly, seven fat, healthy-looking cows came up out of the river and began grazing along its bank. 19 But then seven other cows came up from the river. They were very thin and gaunt—in fact, I've never seen such ugly animals in all the land of Egypt. 20 These thin, ugly cows ate up the seven fat ones that had come out of the river first, 21 but afterward they were still as ugly and gaunt as before! Then I woke up.

22 "A little later I had another dream. This time there were seven heads of grain on one stalk, and all seven heads were plump and full. 23 Then out of the same stalk came seven withered heads, shriveled by the east wind. 24 And the withered heads swallowed up the plump ones! I told these dreams to my magicians, but not one of them could tell me what they mean."

25 "Both dreams mean the same thing," Joseph told Pharaoh. "God was telling you what he is about to do. 26 The seven fat cows and the seven plump heads of grain both represent seven years of prosperity. 27 The seven thin, ugly cows and the seven withered heads of grain represent seven years of famine. 28 This will happen just as I have described it, for God has shown you what he is about to do. 29 The next seven years will be a period of great prosperity throughout the land of Egypt. 30 But afterward there will be seven years of famine so great that all

The chief cup-bearer knew who could interpret Pharaoh's dream—Joseph. As Joseph stood before Pharaoh, he could have taken credit for his success. But he did not. Instead, he gave credit where it was due—to God. When God gives you success in anything you do, be sure to give him the credit.

Why should we give credit to God when we do well?

For everything comes from him; everything exists by his power and is intended for his glory. To him be glory evermore. Amen.
Romans 11:36

the prosperity will be forgotten and wiped out. Famine will destroy the land. [31]This famine will be so terrible that even the memory of the good years will be erased. [32]As for having the dream twice, it means that the matter has been decreed by God and that he will make these events happen soon."

J A N U A R Y

After interpreting Pharaoh's dream, Joseph gave him advice for dealing with the coming famine. How did Pharaoh respond to Joseph's advice?

GENESIS 41:33-49
Joseph in Charge

[33]"My suggestion is that you find the wisest man in Egypt and put him in charge of a nationwide program. [34]Let Pharaoh appoint officials over the land, and let them collect one-fifth of all the crops during the seven good years. [35]Have them gather all the food and grain of these good years into the royal storehouses, and store it away so there will be food in the cities. [36]That way there will be enough to eat when the seven years of famine come. Otherwise disaster will surely strike the land, and all the people will die."

[37]Joseph's suggestions were well received by Pharaoh and his advisers. [38]As they discussed who should be appointed for the job, Pharaoh said, "Who could do it better than Joseph? For he is a man who is obviously filled with the spirit of God." [39]Turning to Joseph, Pharaoh said, "Since God has revealed the meaning of the dreams to you, you are the wisest man in the land! [40]I hereby appoint you to direct this project. You will manage my household and organize all my people. Only I will have a rank higher than yours."

[41]And Pharaoh said to Joseph, "I hereby put you in charge of the entire land of Egypt." [42]Then Pharaoh placed his own signet ring on Joseph's finger as a symbol of his authority. He dressed him in beautiful clothing and placed the royal gold chain about his neck. [43]Pharaoh also gave Joseph the chariot of his second-in-command, and wherever he went the command was shouted, "Kneel down!" So Joseph was put in charge of all Egypt. [44]And Pharaoh said to Joseph, "I am the king, but no one will move a hand or a foot in the entire land of Egypt without your approval."

[45]Pharaoh renamed him Zaphenath-paneah* and gave him a wife—a young woman named Asenath, the daughter of Potiphera, priest of Heliopolis.* So Joseph took charge of the entire land of Egypt. [46]He was thirty years old when he entered the service of Pharaoh, the king of Egypt. And when Joseph left Pharaoh's pres-

41:45a *Zaphenath-paneah* probably means "God speaks and lives." **41:45b** Hebrew *of On;* also in 41:50.

ence, he made a tour of inspection throughout the land.

⁴⁷And sure enough, for the next seven years there were bumper crops everywhere. ⁴⁸During those years, Joseph took a portion of all the crops grown in Egypt and stored them for the government in nearby cities. ⁴⁹After seven years, the granaries were filled to overflowing. There was so much grain, like sand on the seashore, that the people could not keep track of the amount.

Joseph did not brag about his abilities or ask for a job after he interpreted Pharaoh's dream. Even before Joseph interpreted the dream, he told Pharaoh that it was God who would reveal its meaning (Genesis 41:16). Joseph was wise to give God the credit. God blessed Joseph and gave him wisdom to advise Pharaoh. Because Joseph was wise, Pharaoh put him in charge of all Egypt.

To whom does God give wisdom?
If you need wisdom—if you want to know what God wants you to do—ask him, and he will gladly tell you. He will not resent your asking.
James 1:5

J A N U A R Y

Driven by hunger from the famine, Joseph's brothers traveled to Egypt to buy food. What problem did they face while buying grain?

GENESIS 42:1-21

Joseph Sees His Brothers Again

When Jacob heard that there was grain available in Egypt, he said to his sons, "Why are you standing around looking at one another? ²I have heard there is grain in Egypt. Go down and buy some for us before we all starve to death." ³So Joseph's ten older brothers went down to Egypt to buy grain. ⁴Jacob wouldn't let Joseph's younger brother, Benjamin, go with them, however, for fear some harm might come to him. ⁵So Jacob's* sons arrived in Egypt along with others to buy food, for the famine had reached Canaan as well.

⁶Since Joseph was governor of all Egypt and in charge of the sale of the grain, it was to him that his brothers came. They bowed low before him, with their faces to the ground. ⁷Joseph recognized them instantly, but he pretended to be a stranger. "Where are you from?" he demanded roughly.

"From the land of Canaan," they replied. "We have come to buy grain."

42:5 Hebrew *Israel's.*

31

[8]Joseph's brothers didn't recognize him, but Joseph recognized them. [9]And he remembered the dreams he had had many years before. He said to them, "You are spies! You have come to see how vulnerable our land has become."

[10]"No, my lord!" they exclaimed. "We have come to buy food. [11]We are all brothers and honest men, sir! We are not spies!"

[12]"Yes, you are!" he insisted. "You have come to discover how vulnerable the famine has made us."

[13]"Sir," they said, "there are twelve of us brothers, and our father is in the land of Canaan. Our youngest brother is there with our father, and one of our brothers is no longer with us."

[14]But Joseph insisted, "As I said, you are spies! [15]This is how I will test your story. I swear by the life of Pharaoh that you will not leave Egypt unless your youngest brother comes here. [16]One of you go and get your brother! I'll keep the rest of you here, bound in prison. Then we'll find out whether or not your story is true. If it turns out that you don't have a younger brother, then I'll know you are spies."

[17]So he put them all in prison for three days. [18]On the third day Joseph said to them, "I am a God-fearing man. If you do as I say, you will live.

[19]We'll see how honorable you really are. Only one of you will remain in the prison. The rest of you may go on home with grain for your families. [20]But bring your youngest brother back to me. In this way, I will know whether or not you are telling me the truth. If you are, I will spare you." To this they agreed.

[21]Speaking among themselves, they said, "This has all happened because of what we did to Joseph long ago. We saw his terror and anguish and heard his pleadings, but we wouldn't listen. That's why this trouble has come upon us."

Joseph's brothers knew they had sinned. They thought God was punishing them for selling Joseph into slavery. Sometimes we might think that God is punishing us for something we have done wrong. But God wants us to confess our sins and find forgiveness.

What should you do when you know that you have sinned?

But if we confess our sins to him, he is faithful and just to forgive us and to cleanse us from every wrong.
1 John 1:9

Joseph placed his silver cup in Benjamin's sack. Then he accused Benjamin of stealing it. Did the brothers abandon Benjamin? Or did they defend him?

GENESIS 44:3-18, 32-34

Joseph Tests His Brothers

³The brothers were up at dawn and set out on their journey with their loaded donkeys. ⁴But when they were barely out of the city, Joseph said to his household manager, "Chase after them and stop them. Ask them, 'Why have you repaid an act of kindness with such evil? ⁵What do you mean by stealing my master's personal silver drinking cup, which he uses to predict the future? What a wicked thing you have done!' "

⁶So the man caught up with them and spoke to them in the way he had been instructed. ⁷"What are you talking about?" the brothers responded. "What kind of people do you think we are, that you accuse us of such a terrible thing? ⁸Didn't we bring back the money we found in our sacks? Why would we steal silver or gold from your master's house? ⁹If you find his cup with any one of us, let that one die. And all the rest of us will be your master's slaves forever."

¹⁰"Fair enough," the man replied, "except that only the one who stole it will be a slave. The rest of you may go free."

¹¹They quickly took their sacks from the backs of their donkeys and opened them. ¹²Joseph's servant began search-ing the oldest brother's sack, going on down the line to the youngest. The cup was found in Benjamin's sack! ¹³At this, they tore their clothing in despair, loaded the donkeys again, and re-turned to the city. ¹⁴Joseph was still at home when Judah and his brothers arrived, and they fell to the ground before him.

¹⁵"What were you trying to do?" Joseph demanded. "Didn't you know that a man such as I would know who stole it?"

¹⁶And Judah said, "Oh, my lord, what can we say to you? How can we plead? How can we prove our inno-cence? God is punishing us for our sins. My lord, we have all returned to be your slaves—we and our brother who had your cup in his sack."

¹⁷"No," Joseph said. "Only the man who stole the cup will be my slave. The rest of you may go home to your father."

¹⁸Then Judah stepped forward and said, "My lord, let me say just this one word to you. Be patient with me for a moment, for I know you could have me killed in an instant, as though you were Pharaoh himself.

• • •

³²My lord, I made a pledge to my father that I would take care of the

boy. I told him, 'If I don't bring him back to you, I will bear the blame forever.' ³³Please, my lord, let me stay here as a slave instead of the boy, and let the boy return with his brothers. ³⁴For how can I return to my father if the boy is not with me? I cannot bear to see what this would do to him."

Joseph tested his brothers. Could they be trusted? Judah passed the test. He stood up for his brother Benjamin. When your character is tested, follow Judah's example and stand up for what is right.

Why is it good to endure tests and trials?
God blesses the people who patiently endure testing. Afterward they will receive the crown of life that God has promised to those who love him.
James 1:12

J A N U A R Y

Joseph told his brothers who he was. Why did he forgive them?

GENESIS 45:1-15
A Brother's Forgiveness
Joseph could stand it no longer. "Out, all of you!" he cried out to his attendants. He wanted to be alone with his brothers when he told them who he was. ²Then he broke down and wept aloud. His sobs could be heard throughout the palace, and the news was quickly carried to Pharaoh's palace.

³"I am Joseph!" he said to his brothers. "Is my father still alive?" But his brothers were speechless! They were stunned to realize that Joseph was standing there in front of them. ⁴"Come over here," he said. So they came closer. And he said again, "I am Joseph, your brother whom you sold into Egypt. ⁵But don't be angry with yourselves that you did this to me, for God did it. He sent me here ahead of you to preserve your lives. ⁶These two years of famine will grow to seven, during which there will be neither plowing nor harvest. ⁷God has sent me here to keep you and your families alive so that you will become a great nation. ⁸Yes, it was God who sent me here, not you! And he has made me a counselor to Pharaoh—manager of his entire household and ruler over all Egypt.

⁹"Hurry, return to my father and tell him, 'This is what your son Joseph says: God has made me master over all the land of Egypt. Come down to me right away! ¹⁰You will live in the land of Goshen so you can be near me with all your children and grandchildren, your

flocks and herds, and all that you have. [11]I will take care of you there, for there are still five years of famine ahead of us. Otherwise you and your household will come to utter poverty.' "

[12]Then Joseph said, "You can see for yourselves, and so can my brother Benjamin, that I really am Joseph! [13]Tell my father how I am honored here in Egypt. Tell him about everything you have seen, and bring him to me quickly." [14]Weeping with joy, he embraced Benjamin, and Benjamin also began to weep. [15]Then Joseph kissed each of his brothers and wept over them, and then they began talking freely with him.

Why was Joseph sold into slavery? Why was he thrown into prison? God had a good plan for Joseph, even during these bad times. God was saving Joseph and his family from the coming famine. When you go through bad times, remember that God has good things in mind for you.

What hope do you have when you go through bad times?

And we know that God causes everything to work together* for the good of those who love God and are called according to his purpose for them.
Romans 8:28

8:28 Some manuscripts read *And we know that everything works together.*

J A N U A R Y

Joseph's brothers worried about their safety now that their father was dead. Did Joseph want to take revenge on them now?

GENESIS 50:15-21

Past Wrongs

[15]But now that their father was dead, Joseph's brothers became afraid. "Now Joseph will pay us back for all the evil we did to him," they said. [16]So they sent this message to Joseph: "Before your father died, he instructed us [17]to say to you: ' Forgive your brothers for the great evil they did to you.' So we, the servants of the God of your father, beg you to forgive us." When Joseph received the message, he broke down and wept. [18]Then his brothers

Joseph's brothers had sold him into slavery. Now Joseph had the power to get even with them. But Joseph chose to forgive them rather than get revenge. When people hurt you, don't try to get even. Forgive them instead.

Who do you need to forgive?

Then Peter came to him and asked, "Lord, how often should I forgive someone who sins against me? Seven times?" "No!" Jesus replied, "seventy times seven!"*
Matthew 18:21-22

18:22 Or *77 times.*

came and bowed low before him. "We are your slaves," they said.

¹⁹But Joseph told them, "Don't be afraid of me. Am I God, to judge and punish you? ²⁰As far as I am concerned, God turned into good what you meant for evil. He brought me to the high position I have today so I could save the lives of many people. ²¹No, don't be afraid. Indeed, I myself will take care of you and your families." And he spoke very kindly to them, reassuring them.

J A N U A R Y

Pharaoh ordered the Egyptians to throw all the Israelite baby boys into the Nile River. Sometime after this order was given, Moses, an Israelite boy, was born. How did God protect him from being killed?

EXODUS 2:1-10
Moses in the Nile

During this time, a man and woman from the tribe of Levi got married. ²The woman became pregnant and gave birth to a son. She saw what a beautiful baby he was and kept him hidden for three months. ³But when she could no longer hide him, she got a little basket made of papyrus reeds and waterproofed it with tar and pitch. She put the baby in the basket and laid it among the reeds along the edge of the Nile River. ⁴The baby's sister then stood at a distance, watching to see what would happen to him.

⁵Soon after this, one of Pharaoh's daughters came down to bathe in the river, and her servant girls walked along the riverbank. When the princess saw the little basket among the reeds, she told one of her servant girls to get it for her. ⁶As the princess opened it, she found the baby boy. His helpless cries touched her heart. "He must be one of the Hebrew children," she said.

⁷Then the baby's sister approached the princess. "Should I go and find

God caused Pharaoh's daughter to have compassion on Moses. Later, she adopted him, and he was protected from Pharaoh's evil plans. God is more powerful than any king or political leader. He can save his people from evil. When you are in danger, remember that God is watching over you. He can protect you, just as he protected Moses.

How does God protect you from evil?
But the Lord is faithful; he will make you strong and guard you from the evil one.*
2 Thessalonians 3:3

3:3 Or *from evil.*

one of the Hebrew women to nurse the baby for you?" she asked.

⁸"Yes, do!" the princess replied. So the girl rushed home and called the baby's mother.

⁹"Take this child home and nurse him for me," the princess told her. "I will pay you for your help." So the baby's mother took her baby home and nursed him.

¹⁰Later, when he was older, the child's mother brought him back to the princess, who adopted him as her son. The princess named him Moses,* for she said, "I drew him out of the water."

2:10 *Moses* sounds like a Hebrew term that means "to draw out."

J A N U A R Y

Moses made a serious mistake. How did he deal with it?

EXODUS 2:11-21

Moses on the Run

¹¹Many years later, when Moses had grown up, he went out to visit his people, the Israelites, and he saw how hard they were forced to work. During his visit, he saw an Egyptian beating one of the Hebrew slaves. ¹²After looking around to make sure no one was watching, Moses killed the Egyptian and buried him in the sand.

¹³The next day, as Moses was out visiting his people again, he saw two Hebrew men fighting. "What are you doing, hitting your neighbor like that?" Moses said to the one in the wrong.

¹⁴"Who do you think you are?" the man replied. "Who appointed you to be our prince and judge? Do you plan to kill me as you killed that Egyptian yesterday?"

Moses was badly frightened because he realized that everyone knew what he had done. ¹⁵And sure enough, when Pharaoh heard about it, he gave orders to have Moses arrested and killed. But Moses fled from Pharaoh and escaped to the land of Midian.

When Moses arrived in Midian, he sat down beside a well. ¹⁶Now it happened that the priest of Midian had seven daughters who came regularly to this well to draw water and fill the water troughs for their father's flocks. ¹⁷But other shepherds would often come and chase the girls and their flocks away. This time, however, Moses came to their aid, rescuing the girls from the shepherds. Then he helped them draw water for their flocks.

¹⁸When the girls returned to Reuel, their father, he asked, "How did you get the flocks watered so quickly today?"

¹⁹"An Egyptian rescued us from the shepherds," they told him. "And then

he drew water for us and watered our flocks."

²⁰"Well, where is he then?" their father asked. "Did you just leave him there? Go and invite him home for a meal!"

²¹Moses was happy to accept the invitation, and he settled down to live with them. In time, Reuel gave Moses one of his daughters, Zipporah, to be his wife.

Moses was angry at the Egyptian who was beating an Israelite. In a moment of rage, Moses killed the Egyptian and then tried to cover up his sin. But it did not work. People found out what he had done. If someone wrongs you, do not repay that person with evil. Only God can punish that person justly. Instead, pray to God, asking him to help you forgive that person and resist the temptation to get even.

Why shouldn't you get even with someone?
Never pay back evil for evil to anyone. Do things in such a way that everyone can see you are honorable.
Romans 12:17

JANUARY

As Moses cared for his sheep, he heard God's call. How did Moses respond?

EXODUS 3:1-15

The Burning Bush

One day Moses was tending the flock of his father-in-law, Jethro,* the priest of Midian, and he went deep into the wilderness near Sinai,* the mountain of God. ²Suddenly, the angel of the LORD appeared to him as a blazing fire in a bush. Moses was amazed because the bush was engulfed in flames, but it didn't burn up. ³"Amazing!" Moses said to himself. "Why isn't that bush burning up? I must go over to see this."

⁴When the LORD saw that he had caught Moses' attention, God called to him from the bush, "Moses! Moses!"

"Here I am!" Moses replied.

⁵"Do not come any closer," God told him. "Take off your sandals, for you are standing on holy ground." ⁶Then he said, "I am the God of your ancestors—the God of Abraham, the God of Isaac, and the God of Jacob." When Moses heard this, he hid his face in his hands because he was afraid to look at God.

⁷Then the LORD told him, "You can

3:1a Moses' father-in-law went by two names, Jethro and Reuel. **3:1b** Hebrew *Horeb*, another name for Sinai.

be sure I have seen the misery of my people in Egypt. I have heard their cries for deliverance from their harsh slave drivers. Yes, I am aware of their suffering. ⁸So I have come to rescue them from the Egyptians and lead them out of Egypt into their own good and spacious land. It is a land flowing with milk and honey—the land where the Canaanites, Hittites, Amorites, Perizzites, Hivites, and Jebusites live. ⁹The cries of the people of Israel have reached me, and I have seen how the Egyptians have oppressed them with heavy tasks. ¹⁰Now go, for I am sending you to Pharaoh. You will lead my people, the Israelites, out of Egypt."

¹¹"But who am I to appear before Pharaoh?" Moses asked God. "How can you expect me to lead the Israelites out of Egypt?"

¹²Then God told him, "I will be with you. And this will serve as proof that I have sent you: When you have brought the Israelites out of Egypt, you will return here to worship God at this very mountain."

¹³But Moses protested, "If I go to the people of Israel and tell them, 'The God of your ancestors has sent me to you,' they won't believe me. They will ask, 'Which god are you talking about? What is his name?' Then what should I tell them?"

¹⁴God replied, "I AM THE ONE WHO ALWAYS IS.* Just tell them, 'I AM has sent me to you.' " ¹⁵God also said, "Tell them, 'The LORD,* the God of your ancestors—the God of Abraham, the God of Isaac, and the God of Jacob—has sent me to you.' This will be my name forever; it has always been my name, and it will be used throughout all generations."

When Moses met God, he took off his sandals and hid his face to show respect for God. We also need to humble ourselves before God. One way we can do that is to show respect for him by kneeling when we pray.

How can you show God respect?
When you bow down before the Lord and admit your dependence on him, he will lift you up and give you honor.
James 4:10

3:14 Or *I AM WHO I AM,* or *I WILL BE WHAT I WILL BE.* **3:15** Hebrew *Yahweh;* traditionally rendered *Jehovah.*

FEBRUARY

God told Moses to go back to Egypt and lead the Israelites out of that land. Moses doubted his ability to lead. How did the Lord encourage Moses to lead the Israelites?

EXODUS 4:1-17

Moses Is Afraid

But Moses protested again, "Look, they won't believe me! They won't do what I tell them. They'll just say, 'The LORD never appeared to you.' "

²Then the LORD asked him, "What do you have there in your hand?"

"A shepherd's staff," Moses replied.

³"Throw it down on the ground," the LORD told him. So Moses threw it down, and it became a snake! Moses was terrified, so he turned and ran away.

⁴Then the LORD told him, "Take hold of its tail." So Moses reached out and grabbed it, and it became a shepherd's staff again.

⁵"Perform this sign, and they will believe you," the LORD told him. "Then they will realize that the LORD, the God of their ancestors—the God of Abraham, the God of Isaac, and the God of Jacob—really has appeared to you."

⁶Then the LORD said to Moses, "Put your hand inside your robe." Moses did so, and when he took it out again, his hand was white as snow with leprosy.*

⁷"Now put your hand back into your robe again," the LORD said. Moses did, and when he took it out this time, it was as healthy as the rest of his body.

⁸"If they do not believe the first mi-raculous sign, they will believe the second," the LORD said. ⁹"And if they do not believe you even after these two signs, then take some water from the Nile River and pour it out on the dry ground. When you do, it will turn into blood."

¹⁰But Moses pleaded with the LORD, "O Lord, I'm just not a good speaker. I never have been, and I'm not now, even after you have spoken to me. I'm clumsy with words."

¹¹"Who makes mouths?" the LORD asked him. "Who makes people so they can speak or not speak, hear or

Moses made all kinds of excuses to get out of leading the Israelites. But the Lord saw through them all. He reassured Moses that he would be with him. He even had Aaron, Moses' brother, come and help Moses lead the people. What impossible task is God calling you to do? Trust him to help you do the impossible. He is powerful and able to help you do anything.

What do we need to remember when we face impossible tasks?

He replied, "What is impossible from a human perspective is possible with God."

Luke 18:27

4:6 Or *with a contagious skin disease.* The Hebrew word used here can describe various skin diseases.

not hear, see or not see? Is it not I, the LORD? ¹²Now go, and do as I have told you. I will help you speak well, and I will tell you what to say."

¹³But Moses again pleaded, "Lord, please! Send someone else."

¹⁴Then the LORD became angry with Moses. "All right," he said. "What about your brother, Aaron the Levite? He is a good speaker. And look! He is on his way to meet you now. And when he sees you, he will be very glad. ¹⁵You will talk to him, giving him the words to say. I will help both of you to speak clearly, and I will tell you what to do. ¹⁶Aaron will be your spokesman to the people, and you will be as God to him, telling him what to say. ¹⁷And be sure to take your shepherd's staff along so you can perform the miraculous signs I have shown you."

F E B R U A R Y

Moses took God's message to Pharaoh. How did Pharaoh respond?

EXODUS 5:1-21
Pharaoh Says No

After this presentation to Israel's leaders, Moses and Aaron went to see Pharaoh. They told him, "This is what the LORD, the God of Israel, says: 'Let my people go, for they must go out into the wilderness to hold a religious festival in my honor.' "

²"Is that so?" retorted Pharaoh. "And who is the LORD that I should listen to him and let Israel go? I don't know the LORD, and I will not let Israel go."

³But Aaron and Moses persisted. "The God of the Hebrews has met with us," they declared. "Let us take a three-day trip into the wilderness so we can offer sacrifices to the LORD our God. If we don't, we will surely die by disease or the sword."

⁴"Who do you think you are," Pharaoh shouted, "distracting the people from their tasks? Get back to work! ⁵Look, there are many people here in Egypt, and you are stopping them from doing their work."

⁶That same day Pharaoh sent this order to the slave drivers and foremen he had set over the people of Israel: ⁷"Do not supply the people with any more straw for making bricks. Let them get it themselves! ⁸But don't reduce their production quotas by a single brick. They obviously don't have enough to do. If they did, they wouldn't be talking about going into the wilderness to offer sacrifices to their God. ⁹Load them down with more work. Make them sweat! That will teach them to listen to these liars!"

¹⁰So the slave drivers and foremen informed the people: "Pharaoh has ordered us not to provide straw for you. ¹¹Go and get it yourselves. Find it

wherever you can. But you must produce just as many bricks as before!" [12]So the people scattered throughout the land in search of straw.

[13]The slave drivers were brutal. "Meet your daily quota of bricks, just as you did before!" they demanded. [14]Then they whipped the Israelite foremen in charge of the work crews. "Why haven't you met your quotas either yesterday or today?" they demanded.

[15]So the Israelite foremen went to Pharaoh and pleaded with him. "Please don't treat us like this," they begged. [16]"We are given no straw, but we are still told to make as many bricks as before. We are beaten for something that isn't our fault! It is the fault of your slave drivers for making such unreasonable demands."

[17]But Pharaoh replied, "You're just lazy! You obviously don't have enough to do. If you did, you wouldn't be saying, 'Let us go, so we can offer sacrifices to the LORD.' [18]Now, get back to work! No straw will be given to you, but you must still deliver the regular quota of bricks."

[19]Since Pharaoh would not let up on his demands, the Israelite foremen could see that they were in serious trouble. [20]As they left Pharaoh's court, they met Moses and Aaron, who were waiting outside for them. [21]The foremen said to them, "May the LORD judge you for getting us into this terrible situation with Pharaoh* and his officials. You have given them an excuse to kill us!"

Moses did what God told him to. But Pharaoh made life difficult for the Israelites. Even though you may do what is right, other people might want to make your life difficult. Do not get discouraged. God will give you the strength to handle hardship from others.

How should you react when someone makes fun of you for doing right?

God blesses the people who patiently endure testing. Afterward they will receive the crown of life that God has promised to those who love him.
James 1:12

5:21 Hebrew *for making us a stench in the nostrils of Pharaoh.*

Moses and the Israelites became discouraged because of the extra work Pharaoh gave them. What did God tell Moses?

EXODUS 6:1-12
God Sends Moses Back to Pharaoh

"Now you will see what I will do to Pharaoh," the LORD told Moses. "When he feels my powerful hand upon him, he will let the people go. In fact, he will be so anxious to get rid of them that he will force them to leave his land!"

²And God continued, "I am the LORD. ³I appeared to Abraham, to Isaac, and to Jacob as God Almighty,* though I did not reveal my name, the LORD,* to them. ⁴And I entered into a solemn covenant with them. Under its terms, I swore to give them the land of Canaan, where they were living. ⁵You can be sure that I have heard the groans of the people of Israel, who are now slaves to the Egyptians. I have remembered my covenant with them.

⁶"Therefore, say to the Israelites: 'I am the LORD, and I will free you from your slavery in Egypt. I will redeem you with mighty power and great acts of judgment. ⁷I will make you my own special people, and I will be your God. And you will know that I am the LORD your God who has rescued you from your slavery in Egypt. ⁸I will bring you into the land I swore to give to Abra-

ham, Isaac, and Jacob. It will be your very own property. I am the LORD!' "

⁹So Moses told the people what the LORD had said, but they wouldn't listen anymore. They had become too discouraged by the increasing burden of their slavery.

¹⁰Then the LORD said to Moses, ¹¹"Go back to Pharaoh, and tell him to let the people of Israel leave Egypt."

¹²"But LORD!" Moses objected. "My own people won't listen to me anymore. How can I expect Pharaoh to listen? I'm no orator!"

God promised freedom from slavery. But the Israelites wanted to quit. Following God was too difficult. Following God might be hard for you, too. But God gives strength to those who trust in him.

What can we do with Christ's help?
For I can do everything with the help of Christ who gives me the strength I need.
Philippians 4:13

6:3a Hebrew *El Shaddai*.   6:3b Hebrew *Yahweh;* traditionally rendered *Jehovah*.

F E B R U A R Y

Moses and Aaron visited Pharaoh again. Did Pharaoh listen to God's message?

EXODUS 7:1-13

A Stubborn Ruler

Then the LORD said to Moses, "Pay close attention to this. I will make you seem like God to Pharaoh. Your brother, Aaron, will be your prophet; he will speak for you. [2]Tell Aaron everything I say to you and have him announce it to Pharaoh. He will demand that the people of Israel be allowed to leave Egypt. [3]But I will cause Pharaoh to be stubborn so I can multiply my miraculous signs and wonders in the land of Egypt. [4]Even then Pharaoh will refuse to listen to you. So I will crush Egypt with a series of disasters, after which I will lead the forces of Israel out with great acts of judgment. [5]When I show the Egyptians my power and force them to let the Israelites go, they will realize that I am the LORD."

[6]So Moses and Aaron did just as the LORD had commanded them. [7]Moses was eighty years old, and Aaron was eighty-three at the time they made their demands to Pharaoh.

[8]Then the LORD said to Moses and Aaron, [9]"Pharaoh will demand that you show him a miracle to prove that God has sent you. When he makes this demand, say to Aaron, 'Throw down your shepherd's staff,' and it will become a snake."

[10]So Moses and Aaron went to see Pharaoh, and they performed the miracle just as the LORD had told them. Aaron threw down his staff before Pharaoh and his court, and it became a snake. [11]Then Pharaoh called in his wise men and magicians, and they did the same thing with their secret arts. [12]Their staffs became snakes, too! But then Aaron's snake swallowed up their snakes. [13]Pharaoh's heart, however, remained hard and stubborn. He still refused to listen, just as the LORD had predicted.

Pharaoh would not listen to God, even though Moses performed miracles in front of him. But God told Moses that he would use Pharaoh's rebellion to display his power and show the Egyptians that he is God. Today, God speaks to us through the Bible. Listen to him.

How should we respond to God's commands?
Those who obey my commandments are the ones who love me. And because they love me, my Father will love them, and I will love them. And I will reveal myself to each one of them.
John 14:21

FEBRUARY

Pharaoh would not let the Israelites go. How did God respond?

EXODUS 7:19–8:4, 8-19

Blood, Frogs, and Gnats

[19]Then the LORD said to Moses: "Tell Aaron to point his staff toward the waters of Egypt—all its rivers, canals, marshes, and reservoirs. Everywhere in Egypt the water will turn into blood, even the water stored in wooden bowls and stone pots in the people's homes."

[20]So Moses and Aaron did just as the LORD had commanded them. As Pharaoh and all of his officials watched, Moses raised his staff and hit the water of the Nile. Suddenly, the whole river turned to blood! [21]The fish in the river died, and the water became so foul that the Egyptians couldn't drink it. There was blood everywhere throughout the land of Egypt. [22]But again the magicians of Egypt used their secret arts, and they, too, turned water into blood. So Pharaoh's heart remained hard and stubborn. He refused to listen to Moses and Aaron, just as the LORD had predicted. [23]Pharaoh returned to his palace and put the whole thing out of his mind. [24]Then the Egyptians dug wells along the riverbank to get drinking water, for they couldn't drink from the river. [25]An entire week passed from the time the LORD turned the water of the Nile to blood.

[8:1]Then the LORD said to Moses, "Go to Pharaoh once again and tell him, 'This is what the LORD says: Let my people go, so they can worship me. [2]If you refuse, then listen carefully to this: I will send vast hordes of frogs across your entire land from one border to the other. [3]The Nile River will swarm with them. They will come up out of the river and into your houses, even into your bedrooms and onto your beds! Every home in Egypt will be filled with them. They will fill even your ovens and your kneading bowls. [4]You and your people will be overwhelmed by frogs!' "

• • •

[8]Then Pharaoh summoned Moses and Aaron and begged, "Plead with the LORD to take the frogs away from me and my people. I will let the people go, so they can offer sacrifices to the LORD."

[9]"You set the time!" Moses replied. "Tell me when you want me to pray for you, your officials, and your people. I will pray that you and your houses will be rid of the frogs. Then only the frogs in the Nile River will remain alive."

[10]"Do it tomorrow," Pharaoh said.

"All right," Moses replied, "it will be as you have said. Then you will know that no one is as powerful as the LORD our God. [11]All the frogs will be destroyed, except those in the river."

[12]So Moses and Aaron left Pharaoh, and Moses pleaded with the LORD

45

about the frogs he had sent. 13And the LORD did as Moses had promised. The frogs in the houses, the courtyards, and the fields all died. 14They were piled into great heaps, and a terrible stench filled the land. 15But when Pharaoh saw that the frogs were gone, he hardened his heart. He refused to listen to Moses and Aaron, just as the LORD had predicted.

16So the LORD said to Moses, "Tell Aaron to strike the dust with his staff. The dust will turn into swarms of gnats throughout the land of Egypt." 17So Moses and Aaron did just as the LORD had commanded them. Suddenly, gnats infested the entire land, covering the Egyptians and their animals. All the dust in the land of Egypt turned into gnats. 18Pharaoh's magicians tried to do the same thing with their secret arts, but this time they failed. And the gnats covered all the people and animals.

19"This is the finger of God!" the magicians exclaimed to Pharaoh. But Pharaoh's heart remained hard and stubborn. He wouldn't listen to them, just as the LORD had predicted.

Pharaoh would not obey God's command. God sent frogs and gnats to get his attention. Sometimes God disciplines us to get our attention. God wants us to turn from our sin and follow him.

Why does God discipline people?
For our earthly fathers disciplined us for a few years, doing the best they knew how. But God's discipline is always right and good for us because it means we will share in his holiness.
Hebrews 12:10

F E B R U A R Y

Moses told Pharaoh to let God's people go. Pharaoh refused. How did God deal with Pharaoh's stubbornness?

EXODUS 8:20–9:7

Flies and Livestock

20Next the LORD told Moses, "Get up early in the morning and meet Pharaoh as he goes down to the river. Say to him, 'This is what the LORD says: Let my people go, so they can worship me. 21If you refuse, I will send swarms of flies throughout Egypt. Your homes will be filled with them, and the ground will be covered with them. 22But it will be very different in the land of Goshen, where the Israelites live. No flies will be found there. Then you will know that I am the LORD and that I have power even in the heart of your land. 23I will make a clear distinction between your people and my people. This miraculous sign will happen tomorrow.' "

24And the LORD did just as he had

said. There were terrible swarms of flies in Pharaoh's palace and in every home in Egypt. The whole country was thrown into chaos by the flies.

²⁵Pharaoh hastily called for Moses and Aaron. "All right! Go ahead and offer sacrifices to your God," he said. "But do it here in this land. Don't go out into the wilderness."

²⁶But Moses replied, "That won't do! The Egyptians would detest the sacrifices that we offer to the LORD our God. If we offer them here where they can see us, they will be sure to stone us. ²⁷We must take a three-day trip into the wilderness to offer sacrifices to the LORD our God, just as he has commanded us."

²⁸"All right, go ahead," Pharaoh replied. "I will let you go to offer sacrifices to the LORD your God in the wilderness. But don't go too far away. Now hurry, and pray for me."

²⁹"As soon as I go," Moses said, "I will ask the LORD to cause the swarms of flies to disappear from you and all your people. But I am warning you, don't change your mind again and refuse to let the people go to sacrifice to the LORD."

³⁰So Moses left Pharaoh and asked the LORD to remove all the flies. ³¹And the LORD did as Moses asked and caused the swarms to disappear. Not a single fly remained in the land! ³²But Pharaoh hardened his heart again and refused to let the people go.

⁹:¹"Go back to Pharaoh," the LORD commanded Moses. "Tell him, 'This is what the LORD, the God of the Hebrews, says: Let my people go, so they can worship me. ²If you continue to oppress them and refuse to let them go, ³the LORD will send a deadly plague to destroy your horses, donkeys, camels, cattle, and sheep. ⁴But the LORD will again make a distinction between the property of the Israelites and that of the Egyptians. Not a single one of Israel's livestock will die!' "

⁵The LORD announced that he would send the plague the very next day, ⁶and he did it, just as he had said. The next morning all the livestock of the Egyptians began to die, but the Israelites didn't lose a single animal from their flocks and herds. ⁷Pharaoh sent officials to see whether it was true that none of the Israelites' animals were dead. But even after he found it to be true, his heart remained stubborn. He still refused to let the people go.

Flies plagued the Egyptians, and their livestock died, too. But God protected the Israelites from harm. Today God still protects his people from harm, just as he protected the Israelites.

Who does God protect us from?

But the Lord is faithful; he will make you strong and guard you from the evil one. *
2 Thessalonians 3:3

3:3 Or *from evil.*

FEBRUARY

Despite all these plagues, Pharaoh still refused to let the Israelites go. God sent more plagues on Egypt. Did Pharaoh finally obey God?

EXODUS 9:8-12, 22-34

Boils and Hail

8Then the LORD said to Moses and Aaron, "Take soot from a furnace, and have Moses toss it into the sky while Pharaoh watches. 9It will spread like fine dust over the whole land of Egypt, causing boils to break out on people and animals alike."

10So they gathered soot from a furnace and went to see Pharaoh. As Pharaoh watched, Moses tossed the soot into the air, and terrible boils broke out on the people and animals throughout Egypt. 11Even the magicians were unable to stand before Moses, because the boils had broken out on them, too. 12But the LORD made Pharaoh even more stubborn, and he refused to listen, just as the LORD had predicted.

• • •

22Then the LORD said to Moses, "Lift your hand toward the sky, and cause the hail to fall throughout Egypt, on the people, the animals, and the crops."

23So Moses lifted his staff toward the sky, and the LORD sent thunder and hail, and lightning struck the earth. The LORD sent a tremendous hailstorm against all the land of Egypt. 24Never in all the history of Egypt had there been a storm like that, with such severe hail and continuous lightning. 25It left all of Egypt in ruins. Everything left in the fields was destroyed—people, animals, and crops alike. Even all the trees were destroyed. 26The only spot in all Egypt without hail that day was the land of Goshen, where the people of Israel lived.

27Then Pharaoh urgently sent for Moses and Aaron. "I finally admit my fault," he confessed. "The LORD is right, and my people and I are wrong. 28Please beg the LORD to end this terri-

Pharaoh kept on sinning. He knew what God wanted from him but chose to disobey God anyway. Christians choose to do the opposite of Pharaoh. They choose to obey God because Jesus has freed them from their sin. If you are a Christian, Jesus protects you from evil. When you are tempted, pray for Jesus' protection.

What should we do when we are tempted to sin?

Keep alert and pray. Otherwise temptation will overpower you. For though the spirit is willing enough, the body is weak!
Matthew 26:41

fying thunder and hail. I will let you go at once."

²⁹"All right," Moses replied. "As soon as I leave the city, I will lift my hands and pray to the LORD. Then the thunder and hail will stop. This will prove to you that the earth belongs to the LORD. ³⁰But as for you and your officials, I know that you still do not fear the LORD God as you should."

³¹All the flax and barley were destroyed because the barley was ripe and the flax was in bloom. ³²But the wheat and the spelt were not destroyed because they had not yet sprouted from the ground.

³³So Moses left Pharaoh and went out of the city. As he lifted his hands to the LORD, all at once the thunder and hail stopped, and the downpour ceased. ³⁴When Pharaoh saw this, he and his officials sinned yet again by stubbornly refusing to do as they had promised.

FEBRUARY 8

Pharaoh wanted to end his misery. Did he agree to Moses' request?

EXODUS 10:8-27

Locusts and Darkness

⁸So Moses and Aaron were brought back to Pharaoh. "All right, go and serve the LORD your God," he said. "But tell me, just whom do you want to take along?"

⁹"Young and old, all of us will go," Moses replied. "We will take our sons and daughters and our flocks and herds. We must all join together in a festival to the LORD."

¹⁰Pharaoh retorted, "The LORD will certainly need to be with you if you try to take your little ones along! I can see through your wicked intentions. ¹¹Never! Only the men may go and serve the LORD, for that is what you requested." And Pharaoh threw them out of the palace.

¹²Then the LORD said to Moses, "Raise your hand over the land of Egypt to bring on the locusts. Let them cover the land and eat all the crops still left after the hailstorm."

¹³So Moses raised his staff, and the LORD caused an east wind to blow all that day and through the night. When morning arrived, the east wind had brought the locusts. ¹⁴And the locusts swarmed over the land of Egypt from border to border. It was the worst locust plague in Egyptian history, and there has never again been one like it. ¹⁵For the locusts covered the surface of the whole country, making the ground look black. They ate all the plants and all the fruit on the trees that had survived the hailstorm. Not one green thing remained, neither tree nor plant, throughout the land of Egypt.

¹⁶Pharaoh quickly sent for Moses and Aaron. "I confess my sin against the LORD your God and against you," he

said to them. [17]"Forgive my sin only this once, and plead with the LORD your God to take away this terrible plague."

[18]So Moses left Pharaoh and pleaded with the LORD. [19]The LORD responded by sending a strong west wind that blew the locusts out into the Red Sea.* Not a single locust remained in all the land of Egypt. [20]But the LORD made Pharaoh stubborn once again, and he did not let the people go.

[21]Then the LORD said to Moses, "Lift your hand toward heaven, and a deep and terrifying darkness will descend on the land of Egypt." [22]So Moses lifted his hand toward heaven, and there was deep darkness over the entire land for three days. [23]During all that time the people scarcely moved, for they could not see. But there was light as usual where the people of Israel lived.

[24]Then Pharaoh called for Moses. "Go and worship the LORD," he said. "But let your flocks and herds stay here. You can even take your children with you."

[25]"No," Moses said, "we must take our flocks and herds for sacrifices and burnt offerings to the LORD our God. [26]All our property must go with us; not a hoof can be left behind. We will have to choose our sacrifices for the LORD our God from among these animals. And we won't know which sacrifices he will require until we get there."

[27]So the LORD hardened Pharaoh's heart once more, and he would not let them go.

Pharaoh would only agree to obey God partially. He did not want all of the Israelites to leave. Some Christians only want to obey God partially. But Jesus calls us to follow him all the way. We cannot do just what we want.

What does it mean to follow Christ?

Then Jesus said to the disciples, "If any of you wants to be my follower, you must put aside your selfish ambition, shoulder your cross, and follow me." *Matthew 16:24*

10:19 Hebrew *sea of reeds.*

F E B R U A R Y

After nine plagues, Pharaoh still wouldn't let the people go. What did it take for Pharaoh to obey?

EXODUS 12:1-8, 21-36

The Last Plague

Now the LORD gave the following instructions to Moses and Aaron while they were still in the land of Egypt: [2]"From now on, this month will be the first month of the year for you. [3]Announce to the whole community that on the tenth day of this month each family must choose a lamb or a young goat for a sacrifice. ⁴If a family is too small to eat an entire lamb, let them share the lamb with another family in the neighborhood. Whether or not they share in this way depends on the size of each family and how much they can eat. ⁵This animal must be a one-year-old male, either a sheep or a goat, with no physical defects.

⁶"Take special care of these lambs until the evening of the fourteenth day of this first month. Then each family in the community must slaughter its lamb. ⁷They are to take some of the lamb's blood and smear it on the top and sides of the doorframe of the house where the lamb will be eaten. ⁸That evening everyone must eat roast lamb with bitter herbs and bread made without yeast.

• • •

²¹Then Moses called for the leaders of Israel and said, "Tell each of your families to slaughter the lamb they have set apart for the Passover. ²²Drain each lamb's blood into a basin. Then take a cluster of hyssop branches and dip it into the lamb's blood. Strike the hyssop against the top and sides of the doorframe, staining it with the blood. And remember, no one is allowed to leave the house until morning. ²³For the LORD will pass through the land and strike down the Egyptians. But when he sees the blood on the top and sides of the doorframe, the LORD will pass over your home. He will not permit the Destroyer to enter and strike down your firstborn.

²⁴"Remember, these instructions are permanent and must be observed by you and your descendants forever. ²⁵When you arrive in the land the LORD has promised to give you, you will continue to celebrate this festival. ²⁶Then your children will ask, 'What does all this mean? What is this ceremony about?' ²⁷And you will reply, 'It is the celebration of the LORD's Passover, for he passed over the homes of the Israelites in Egypt. And though he killed the Egyptians, he spared our families and did not destroy us.' " Then all the people bowed their heads and worshiped.

²⁸So the people of Israel did just as the LORD had commanded through Moses and Aaron. ²⁹And at midnight the LORD killed all the firstborn sons in the land of Egypt, from the firstborn son of Pharaoh, who sat on the throne, to the firstborn son of the captive in the dungeon. Even the firstborn of their livestock were killed. ³⁰Pharaoh and his officials and all the people of Egypt woke up during the night, and loud wailing was heard throughout the land of Egypt. There was not a single house where someone had not died.

³¹Pharaoh sent for Moses and Aaron during the night. "Leave us!" he cried. "Go away, all of you! Go and serve the LORD as you have requested. ³²Take your flocks and herds, and be gone. Go, but give me a blessing as you leave." ³³All the Egyptians urged the people of Israel to get out of the land as quickly as possible, for they thought, "We will all die!"

³⁴The Israelites took with them their bread dough made without yeast. They wrapped their kneading bowls in their spare clothing and carried them

on their shoulders. [35]And the people of Israel did as Moses had instructed and asked the Egyptians for clothing and articles of silver and gold. [36]The LORD caused the Egyptians to look favorably on the Israelites, and they gave the Israelites whatever they asked for. So, like a victorious army, they plundered the Egyptians!

Pharaoh's rebellion against God cost him his firstborn son. The Egyptian people also paid the same price for Pharaoh's rebellion. Broken by God's judgment, Pharaoh finally let the Israelites go. Are you rebelling against God? Don't test God by disobeying him. The cost of your disobedience could be more painful than simply obeying in the first place.

What does obedience bring?
He replied, "But even more blessed are all who hear the word of God and put it into practice."
Luke 11:28

F E B R U A R Y

At the banks of the Red Sea, the Israelites faced Pharaoh's charging chariots. Did God save the Israelites?

EXODUS 14:10-31
A Narrow Escape

[10]As Pharaoh and his army approached, the people of Israel could see them in the distance, marching toward them. The people began to panic, and they cried out to the LORD for help.

[11]Then they turned against Moses and complained, "Why did you bring us out here to die in the wilderness? Weren't there enough graves for us in Egypt? Why did you make us leave? [12]Didn't we tell you to leave us alone while we were still in Egypt? Our Egyptian slavery was far better than dying out here in the wilderness!"

[13]But Moses told the people, "Don't be afraid. Just stand where you are and watch the LORD rescue you. The Egyptians that you see today will never be seen again. [14]The LORD himself will fight for you. You won't have to lift a finger in your defense!"

[15]Then the LORD said to Moses, "Why are you crying out to me? Tell the people to get moving! [16]Use your shepherd's staff—hold it out over the water, and a path will open up before you through the sea. Then all the people of Israel will walk through on dry ground. [17]Yet I will harden the hearts of the Egyptians, and they will

follow the Israelites into the sea. Then I will receive great glory at the expense of Pharaoh and his armies, chariots, and charioteers. [18]When I am finished with Pharaoh and his army, all Egypt will know that I am the LORD!"

[19]Then the angel of God, who had been leading the people of Israel, moved to a position behind them, and the pillar of cloud also moved around behind them. [20]The cloud settled between the Israelite and Egyptian camps. As night came, the pillar of cloud turned into a pillar of fire, lighting the Israelite camp. But the cloud became darkness to the Egyptians, and they couldn't find the Israelites.

[21]Then Moses raised his hand over the sea, and the LORD opened up a path through the water with a strong east wind. The wind blew all that night, turning the seabed into dry land. [22]So the people of Israel walked through the sea on dry ground, with walls of water on each side! [23]Then the Egyptians—all of Pharaoh's horses, chariots, and charioteers—followed them across the bottom of the sea. [24]But early in the morning, the LORD looked down on the Egyptian army from the pillar of fire and cloud, and he threw them into confusion. [25]Their chariot wheels began to come off, making their chariots impossible to drive. "Let's get out of here!" the Egyptians shouted. "The LORD is fighting for Israel against us!"

[26]When all the Israelites were on the other side, the LORD said to Moses, "Raise your hand over the sea again. Then the waters will rush back over the Egyptian chariots and charioteers." [27]So as the sun began to rise, Moses raised his hand over the sea. The water roared back into its usual place, and the LORD swept the terrified Egyptians into the surging currents. [28]The waters covered all the chariots and charioteers—the entire army of Pharaoh. Of all the Egyptians who had chased the Israelites into the sea, not a single one survived.

[29]The people of Israel had walked through the middle of the sea on dry land, as the water stood up like a wall on both sides. [30]This was how the LORD rescued Israel from the Egyptians that day. And the Israelites could see the bodies of the Egyptians washed up on the shore. [31]When the people of Israel saw the mighty power that the LORD had displayed against the Egyptians, they feared the LORD and put their faith in him and his servant Moses.

God fought for the Israelites. He parted the Red Sea and led the Israelites safely to the other side. As the Egyptians began crossing, God brought the walls of water crashing down on them. From whom or what do you need protection? You can let God take care of you. He protected the Israelites back then, and he can protect you today.

How do we know that God will protect us?

For God has said, "I will never fail you. I will never forsake you."*
Hebrews 13:5

13:5 Deut 31:6, 8.

FEBRUARY

In the desert, the Israelites couldn't find water. Did they die of thirst?

EXODUS 15:22-27
God Provides Water

²²Then Moses led the people of Israel away from the Red Sea, and they moved out into the Shur Desert. They traveled in this desert for three days without water. ²³When they came to Marah, they finally found water. But the people couldn't drink it because it was bitter. (That is why the place was called Marah, which means "bitter.")

²⁴Then the people turned against Moses. "What are we going to drink?" they demanded.

²⁵So Moses cried out to the LORD for help, and the LORD showed him a branch. Moses took the branch and threw it into the water. This made the water good to drink.

It was there at Marah that the LORD laid before them the following conditions to test their faithfulness to him: ²⁶"If you will listen carefully to the voice of the LORD your God and do what is right in his sight, obeying his commands and laws, then I will not make you suffer the diseases I sent on the Egyptians; for I am the LORD who heals you."

²⁷After leaving Marah, they came to Elim, where there were twelve springs and seventy palm trees. They camped there beside the springs.

God gave the Israelites water when they were thirsty. Who gives you water when you are thirsty? Although your parents might give you a drink of water, God ultimately provides everything for you. Thank God for what he gives you.

Why shouldn't we worry about our needs?
And this same God who takes care of me will supply all your needs from his glorious riches, which have been given to us in Christ Jesus.
Philippians 4:19

The Israelites were hungry and didn't have any food. How did they survive?

EXODUS 16:2-5, 13-28
Raining Bread

²There, too, the whole community of Israel spoke bitterly against Moses and Aaron.

³"Oh, that we were back in Egypt," they moaned. "It would have been better if the LORD had killed us there! At least there we had plenty to eat. But now you have brought us into this desert to starve us to death."

⁴Then the LORD said to Moses, "Look, I'm going to rain down food from heaven for you. The people can go out each day and pick up as much food as they need for that day. I will test them in this to see whether they will follow my instructions. ⁵Tell them to pick up twice as much as usual on the sixth day of each week."

• • •

¹³That evening vast numbers of quail arrived and covered the camp. The next morning the desert all around the camp was wet with dew. ¹⁴When the dew disappeared later in the morning, thin flakes, white like frost, covered the ground. ¹⁵The Israelites were puzzled when they saw it. "What is it?" they asked.

And Moses told them, "It is the food the LORD has given you. ¹⁶The LORD says that each household should gather as much as it needs. Pick up two quarts* for each person."

¹⁷So the people of Israel went out and gathered this food—some getting more, and some getting less. ¹⁸By gathering two quarts for each person, everyone had just enough. Those who gathered a lot had nothing left over, and those who gathered only a little had enough. Each family had just what it needed.

¹⁹Then Moses told them, "Do not keep any of it overnight." ²⁰But, of course, some of them didn't listen and kept some of it until morning. By then it was full of maggots and had a terrible smell. And Moses was very angry with them.

²¹The people gathered the food morning by morning, each family according to its need. And as the sun became hot, the food they had not picked up melted and disappeared. ²²On the sixth day, there was twice as much as usual on the ground—four quarts* for each person instead of two. The leaders of the people came and asked Moses why this had happened. ²³He replied, "The LORD has appointed tomorrow as a day of rest, a holy Sabbath to the LORD. On this day we will rest from our normal daily tasks. So bake or boil as much as you

16:16 Hebrew *1 omer* [2 liters]; also in 16:18, 32, 33. **16:22** Hebrew *2 omers* [4 liters].

want today, and set aside what is left for tomorrow."

²⁴The next morning the leftover food was wholesome and good, without maggots or odor. ²⁵Moses said, "This is your food for today, for today is a Sabbath to the LORD. There will be no food on the ground today. ²⁶Gather the food for six days, but the seventh day is a Sabbath. There will be no food on the ground for you on that day."

²⁷Some of the people went out anyway to gather food, even though it was the Sabbath day. But there was none to be found. ²⁸"How long will these people refuse to obey my commands and instructions?" the LORD asked Moses.

The Israelites were hungry. Again, God showed his trustworthiness by providing food for them. God cared about the Israelites, and he cares about you. You are valuable to God. You can trust him to provide food for you.

How can you be sure that God will provide for you?
Look at the ravens. They don't need to plant or harvest or put food in barns because God feeds them. And you are far more valuable to him than any birds!
Luke 12:24

F E B R U A R Y

Moses had a difficult assignment. How did he accomplish it?

EXODUS 18:5-26
Difficult Work

⁵Jethro now came to visit Moses, and he brought Moses' wife and two sons with him. They arrived while Moses and the people were camped near the mountain of God. ⁶Moses was told, "Jethro, your father-in-law, has come to visit you. Your wife and your two sons are with him."

⁷So Moses went out to meet his father-in-law. He bowed to him respectfully and greeted him warmly. They asked about each other's health and then went to Moses' tent to talk further. ⁸Moses told his father-in-law about everything the LORD had done to rescue Israel from Pharaoh and the Egyptians. He also told him about the problems they had faced along the way and how the LORD had delivered his people from all their troubles. ⁹Jethro was delighted when he heard about all that the LORD had done for Israel as he brought them out of Egypt.

¹⁰"Praise be to the LORD," Jethro said, "for he has saved you from the Egyptians and from Pharaoh. He has rescued Israel from the power of Egypt! ¹¹I know now that the LORD is greater than all other gods, because his

people have escaped from the proud and cruel Egyptians."

¹²Then Jethro presented a burnt offering and gave sacrifices to God. As Jethro was doing this, Aaron and the leaders of Israel came out to meet him. They all joined him in a sacrificial meal in God's presence.

¹³The next day, Moses sat as usual to hear the people's complaints against each other. They were lined up in front of him from morning till evening.

¹⁴When Moses' father-in-law saw all that Moses was doing for the people, he said, "Why are you trying to do all this alone? The people have been standing here all day to get your help."

¹⁵Moses replied, "Well, the people come to me to seek God's guidance. ¹⁶When an argument arises, I am the one who settles the case. I inform the people of God's decisions and teach them his laws and instructions."

¹⁷"This is not good!" his father-in-law exclaimed. ¹⁸"You're going to wear yourself out—and the people, too. This job is too heavy a burden for you to handle all by yourself. ¹⁹Now let me give you a word of advice, and may God be with you. You should continue to be the people's representative before God, bringing him their questions to be decided. ²⁰You should tell them God's decisions, teach them God's laws and instructions, and show them how to conduct their lives. ²¹But find some capable, honest men who fear God and hate bribes. Appoint them as judges over groups of one thousand, one hundred, fifty, and ten. ²²These men can

serve the people, resolving all the ordinary cases. Anything that is too important or too complicated can be brought to you. But they can take care of the smaller matters themselves. They will help you carry the load, making the task easier for you. ²³If you follow this advice, and if God directs you to do so, then you will be able to endure the pressures, and all these people will go home in peace."

²⁴Moses listened to his father-in-law's advice and followed his suggestions. ²⁵He chose capable men from all over Israel and made them judges over the people. They were put in charge of groups of one thousand, one hundred, fifty, and ten. ²⁶These men were constantly available to administer justice. They brought the hard cases to Moses, but they judged the smaller matters themselves.

Moses listened to his father-in-law's advice about appointing judges to hear the people's disputes. Then he followed it. By accepting this advice, Moses was able to focus on his more important responsibilities, such as leading the people. We all need good advice. In fact, we should ask for it. When good advice comes your way, be sure to listen.

What should we do when we receive good advice?

Dear friends,* be quick to listen, slow to speak, and slow to get angry.
James 1:19

1:19 Greek *Know this, my beloved brothers.*

*God made an appointment with the Israelites at Mount Sinai.
What did they need to do before they met with God?*

EXODUS 19:3-19

Meeting at Mount Sinai

³Then Moses climbed the mountain to appear before God. The LORD called out to him from the mountain and said, "Give these instructions to the descendants of Jacob, the people of Israel: ⁴'You have seen what I did to the Egyptians. You know how I brought you to myself and carried you on eagle's wings. ⁵Now if you will obey me and keep my covenant, you will be my own special treasure from among all the nations of the earth; for all the earth belongs to me. ⁶And you will be to me a kingdom of priests, my holy nation.' Give this message to the Israelites."

⁷Moses returned from the mountain and called together the leaders of the people and told them what the LORD had said. ⁸They all responded together, "We will certainly do everything the LORD asks of us." So Moses brought the people's answer back to the LORD.

⁹Then the LORD said to Moses, "I am going to come to you in a thick cloud so the people themselves can hear me as I speak to you. Then they will always have confidence in you."

Moses told the LORD what the people had said. ¹⁰Then the LORD told Moses, "Go down and prepare the people for my visit. Purify them today and tomorrow, and have them wash their clothing. ¹¹Be sure they are ready on the third day, for I will come down upon Mount Sinai as all the people watch. ¹²Set boundary lines that the people may not pass. Warn them, 'Be careful! Do not go up on the mountain or even touch its boundaries. Those who do will certainly die! ¹³Any people or animals that cross the boundary must be stoned to death or shot with arrows. They must not be touched by human hands.' The people must stay away from the mountain until they hear one long blast from the ram's horn. Then they must gather at the foot of the mountain."

¹⁴So Moses went down to the people. He purified them for worship and had them wash their clothing. ¹⁵He told them, "Get ready for an important event two days from now. And until then, abstain from having sexual intercourse."

¹⁶On the morning of the third day, there was a powerful thunder and lightning storm, and a dense cloud came down upon the mountain. There was a long, loud blast from a ram's horn, and all the people trembled. ¹⁷Moses led them out from the camp to meet with God, and they stood at the foot of the mountain. ¹⁸All Mount Sinai was covered with smoke

because the LORD had descended on it in the form of fire. The smoke billowed into the sky like smoke from a furnace, and the whole mountain shook with a violent earthquake. ¹⁹As the horn blast grew louder and louder, Moses spoke, and God thundered his reply for all to hear.

Moses gave God's message to the Israelites. They had to wash their clothes for their meeting with God. How can we approach God today? Jesus washes sin from our lives. He is the only way to God. Forgiven and clean, we can confidently approach the living God.

Who is the only one that can bring us to God?

Jesus told him, "I am the way, the truth, and the life. No one can come to the Father except through me."
John 14:6

F E B R U A R Y

Moses met with God to receive some special instructions for the Israelites. What did Moses bring back to the people?

EXODUS 20:1-21
The Ten Commandments

Then God instructed the people as follows:

²"I am the LORD your God, who rescued you from slavery in Egypt.
³"Do not worship any other gods besides me.
⁴"Do not make idols of any kind, whether in the shape of birds or animals or fish. ⁵You must never worship or bow down to them, for I, the LORD your God, am a jealous God who will not share your affection with any other god! I do not leave unpunished the sins of those who hate me, but I

punish the children for the sins of their parents to the third and fourth generations. ⁶But I lavish my love on those who love me and obey my commands, even for a thousand generations.
⁷"Do not misuse the name of the LORD your God. The LORD will not let you go unpunished if you misuse his name.
⁸"Remember to observe the Sabbath day by keeping it holy. ⁹Six days a week are set apart for your daily duties and regular work, ¹⁰but the seventh day is a day of rest dedicated to the LORD your God. On that day no one in your

household may do any kind of work. This includes you, your sons and daughters, your male and female servants, your livestock, and any foreigners living among you. ¹¹For in six days the LORD made the heavens, the earth, the sea, and everything in them; then he rested on the seventh day. That is why the LORD blessed the Sabbath day and set it apart as holy.

¹²"Honor your father and mother. Then you will live a long, full life in the land the LORD your God will give you.

¹³"Do not murder.

¹⁴"Do not commit adultery.

¹⁵"Do not steal.

¹⁶"Do not testify falsely against your neighbor.

¹⁷"Do not covet your neighbor's house. Do not covet your neighbor's wife, male or female servant, ox or donkey, or anything else your neighbor owns."

¹⁸When the people heard the thunder and the loud blast of the horn, and when they saw the lightning and the smoke billowing from the mountain, they stood at a distance, trembling with fear.

¹⁹And they said to Moses, "You tell us what God says, and we will listen. But don't let God speak directly to us. If he does, we will die!"

²⁰"Don't be afraid," Moses said, "for God has come in this way to show you his awesome power. From now on, let your fear of him keep you from sinning!"

²¹As the people stood in the distance, Moses entered into the deep darkness where God was.

God gave his laws to Moses. Jesus sums all of God's laws up this way: Love God and love your neighbor. Your neighbors are the people around you at school, church, and home.

How should we love our neighbors?
Love your neighbor as yourself.*
Mark 12:31

12:31 Lev 19:18.

F E B R U A R Y

While Moses was on Mount Sinai with God, the Israelites made an idol to worship. How did God respond to their disobedience?

EXODUS 32:1-14
The Golden Calf
When Moses failed to come back down the mountain right away, the people went to Aaron. "Look," they said, "make us some gods who can lead us. This man Moses, who brought us here from Egypt, has disappeared.

We don't know what has happened to him."

²So Aaron said, "Tell your wives and sons and daughters to take off their gold earrings, and then bring them to me."

³All the people obeyed Aaron and brought him their gold earrings. ⁴Then Aaron took the gold, melted it down, and molded and tooled it into the shape of a calf. The people exclaimed, "O Israel, these are the gods who brought you out of Egypt!"

⁵When Aaron saw how excited the people were about it, he built an altar in front of the calf and announced, "Tomorrow there will be a festival to the LORD!"

⁶So the people got up early the next morning to sacrifice burnt offerings and peace offerings. After this, they celebrated with feasting and drinking, and indulged themselves in pagan revelry.

⁷Then the LORD told Moses, "Quick! Go down the mountain! The people you brought from Egypt have defiled themselves. ⁸They have already turned from the way I commanded them to live. They have made an idol shaped like a calf, and they have worshiped and sacrificed to it. They are saying, 'These are your gods, O Israel, who brought you out of Egypt.' "

⁹Then the LORD said, "I have seen how stubborn and rebellious these people are. ¹⁰Now leave me alone so my anger can blaze against them and destroy them all. Then I will make you, Moses, into a great nation instead of them."

¹¹But Moses pleaded with the LORD his God not to do it. "O LORD!" he exclaimed. "Why are you so angry with your own people whom you brought from the land of Egypt with such great power and mighty acts? ¹²The Egyptians will say, 'God tricked them into coming to the mountains so he could kill them and wipe them from the face of the earth.' Turn away from your fierce anger. Change your mind about this terrible disaster you are planning against your people! ¹³Remember your covenant with your servants—Abraham, Isaac, and Jacob.* You swore by your own self, 'I will make your descendants as numerous as the stars of heaven. Yes, I will give them all of this land that I have promised to your descendants, and they will possess it forever.' "

¹⁴So the LORD withdrew his threat and didn't bring against his people the disaster he had threatened.

The Israelites knew that they were not to make and worship idols of gold or silver. Moses had told them so before returning to Mount Sinai. But their faith in God was weak. When Moses did not return right away, they disobeyed God's commands. Today, we know how God wants us to live. The Bible gives us his commands. But if we sin, we can seek God's forgiveness through Jesus.

What should we do when we sin?
Confess your sins to each other and pray for each other so that you may be healed. The earnest prayer of a righteous person has great power and wonderful results.
James 5:16

32:13 Hebrew *Israel*.

God wanted to live with his people, the Israelites. How did he do that?

EXODUS 40:1-2, 33-38
The Cloud and the Fire

The LORD now said to Moses, [2]"Set up the Tabernacle* on the first day of the new year."*

• • •

[33]Then he hung the curtains forming the courtyard around the Tabernacle and the altar. And he set up the curtain at the entrance of the courtyard. So at last Moses finished the work.

[34]Then the cloud covered the Tabernacle, and the glorious presence of the LORD filled it. [35]Moses was no longer able to enter the Tabernacle because the cloud had settled down over it, and the Tabernacle was filled with the awesome glory of the LORD.

[36]Now whenever the cloud lifted from the Tabernacle and moved, the people of Israel would set out on their journey, following it. [37]But if the cloud stayed, they would stay until it moved again. [38]The cloud of the LORD rested on the Tabernacle during the day, and at night there was fire in the cloud so all the people of Israel could see it. This continued throughout all their journeys.

God appeared to the Israelites in the form of a cloud. He did this to show the Israelites that he was with them. Does God appear as a cloud today? No, something even better happens! God sends his Spirit to live within all who believe in his Son. Besides that, his Word is always available for us to read.

What assurance do we have that God is with us?
And be sure of this: I am with you always, even to the end of the age.
Matthew 28:20

40:2a Hebrew *the Tabernacle, the Tent of Meeting;* also in 40:6, 29. **40:2b** Hebrew *the first day of the first month.* This day of the Hebrew lunar calendar occurs in March or early April.

F E B R U A R Y

Miriam and Aaron challenged Moses' authority. How did God treat them?

NUMBERS 12:1-15

Sibling Rivalry

While they were at Hazeroth, Miriam and Aaron criticized Moses because he had married a Cushite woman. [2]They said, "Has the LORD spoken only through Moses? Hasn't he spoken through us, too?" But the LORD heard them.

[3]Now Moses was more humble than any other person on earth. [4]So immediately the LORD called to Moses, Aaron, and Miriam and said, "Go out to the Tabernacle,* all three of you!" And the three of them went out. [5]Then the LORD descended in the pillar of cloud and stood at the entrance of the Tabernacle.* "Aaron and Miriam!" he called, and they stepped forward. [6]And the LORD said to them, "Now listen to me! Even with prophets, I the LORD communicate by visions and dreams. [7]But that is not how I communicate with my servant Moses. He is entrusted with my entire house. [8]I speak to him face to face, directly and not in riddles! He sees the LORD as he is. Should you not be afraid to criticize him?"

[9]The LORD was furious with them, and he departed. [10]As the cloud moved from above the Tabernacle, Miriam suddenly became white as snow with leprosy.* When Aaron saw what had happened, [11]he cried out to Moses, "Oh, my lord! Please don't punish us for this sin we have so foolishly committed. [12]Don't let her be like a stillborn baby, already decayed at birth."

[13]So Moses cried out to the LORD, "Heal her, O God, I beg you!"

[14]And the LORD said to Moses, "If her

Miriam and Aaron were jealous of Moses and questioned his authority over them. But they could not find anything wrong with Moses. So they attacked him for marrying a Cushite woman rather than an Israelite woman. Today it seems like more people than ever are challenging those in authority. Parents, teachers, pastors, and government officials are constantly under attack from those under them. Instead of going along with rebellious people, we should obey those in authority. God himself has placed these people over us. Honor God by respecting those in authority over you.

How should we behave toward those in authority?

Obey the government, for God is the one who put it there. All governments have been placed in power by God.
Romans 13:1

12:4 Hebrew *Tent of Meeting.* 12:5 Hebrew *the tent;* also in 12:10. 12:10 Or *with a contagious skin disease.* The Hebrew word used here can describe various skin diseases.

father had spit in her face, wouldn't she have been defiled for seven days? Banish her from the camp for seven days, and after that she may return."

¹⁵So Miriam was excluded from the camp for seven days, and the people waited until she was brought back before they traveled again.

F E B R U A R Y

Moses sent twelve scouts into the Promised Land. When they returned, what did they report about the land?

NUMBERS 13:17-20, 25-33

Scouting Out the Promised Land

¹⁷Moses gave the men these instructions as he sent them out to explore the land: "Go northward through the Negev into the hill country. ¹⁸See what the land is like and find out whether the people living there are strong or weak, few or many. ¹⁹What kind of land do they live in? Is it good or bad? Do their towns have walls or are they unprotected? ²⁰How is the soil? Is it fertile or poor? Are there many trees? Enter the land boldly, and bring back samples of the crops you see." (It happened to be the season for harvesting the first ripe grapes.)

• • •

²⁵After exploring the land for forty days, the men returned ²⁶to Moses, Aaron, and the people of Israel at Kadesh in the wilderness of Paran. They reported to the whole community what they had seen and showed them the fruit they had taken from the land. ²⁷This was their report to Moses: "We arrived in the land you sent us to see, and it is indeed a magnificent coun-try—a land flowing with milk and honey. Here is some of its fruit as proof. ²⁸But the people living there are powerful, and their cities and towns are fortified and very large. We also saw the descendants of Anak who are living there! ²⁹The Amalekites live in the Negev, and the Hittites, Jebusites, and Amorites live in the hill country. The Canaanites live along the coast of

The scouts said that the land was wonderful, but they also said the people living there were stronger than the Israelites. The scouts didn't think that they stood a chance against the people of the land. They failed to see that God was with them and would help them defeat their enemies. When God wants you to do something that looks impossible, trust in him to help you. He will not fail you.

What should you do when you fear failure?

Be on guard. Stand true to what you believe. Be courageous. Be strong.
1 Corinthians 16:13

the Mediterranean Sea* and along the Jordan Valley."

³⁰But Caleb tried to encourage the people as they stood before Moses. "Let's go at once to take the land," he said. "We can certainly conquer it!"

³¹But the other men who had explored the land with him answered, "We can't go up against them! They are stronger than we are!" ³²So they spread discouraging reports about the land among the Israelites: "The land we explored will swallow up any who go to live there. All the people we saw were huge. ³³We even saw giants* there, the descendants of Anak. We felt like grasshoppers next to them, and that's what we looked like to them!"

13:29 Hebrew *the sea.*   **13:33** Hebrew *nephilim.*

F E B R U A R Y

Almost all of the Israelites refused to trust in God. What did Joshua and Caleb do?

NUMBERS 14:1-23
The Wrong Crowd

Then all the people began weeping aloud, and they cried all night. ²Their voices rose in a great chorus of complaint against Moses and Aaron. "We wish we had died in Egypt, or even here in the wilderness!" they wailed. ³"Why is the LORD taking us to this country only to have us die in battle? Our wives and little ones will be carried off as slaves! Let's get out of here and return to Egypt!" ⁴Then they plotted among themselves, "Let's choose a leader and go back to Egypt!"

⁵Then Moses and Aaron fell face down on the ground before the people of Israel. ⁶Two of the men who had explored the land, Joshua son of Nun and Caleb son of Jephunneh, tore their clothing. ⁷They said to the community of Israel, "The land we explored is a wonderful land! ⁸And if the LORD is pleased with us, he will bring us safely into that land and give it to us. It is a rich land flowing with milk and honey, and he will give it to us! ⁹Do not rebel against the LORD, and don't be afraid of the people of the land. They are only helpless prey to us! They have no protection, but the LORD is with us! Don't be afraid of them!"

¹⁰But the whole community began to talk about stoning Joshua and Caleb. Then the glorious presence of the LORD appeared to all the Israelites from above the Tabernacle.* ¹¹And the LORD said to Moses, "How long will these people reject me? Will they never believe me, even after all the miraculous signs I have done among them? ¹²I will disown them and destroy them with a plague. Then I will make you into a nation far greater and mightier than they are!"

¹³"But what will the Egyptians

14:10 Hebrew *Tent of Meeting.*

65

think when they hear about it?" Moses pleaded with the LORD. "They know full well the power you displayed in rescuing these people from Egypt. [14]They will tell this to the inhabitants of this land, who are well aware that you are with this people. They know, LORD, that you have appeared in full view of your people in the pillar of cloud that hovers over them. They know that you go before them in the pillar of cloud by day and the pillar of fire by night. [15]Now if you slaughter all these people, the nations that have heard of your fame will say, [16]'The LORD was not able to bring them into the land he swore to give them, so he killed them in the wilderness.'

[17]"Please, Lord, prove that your power is as great as you have claimed it to be. For you said, [18]'The LORD is slow to anger and rich in unfailing love, forgiving every kind of sin and rebellion. Even so he does not leave sin unpunished, but he punishes the children for the sins of their parents to the third and fourth generations.' [19]Please pardon the sins of this people because of your magnificent, unfailing love, just as you have forgiven them ever since they left Egypt."

[20]Then the LORD said, "I will pardon them as you have requested. [21]But as surely as I live, and as surely as the earth is filled with the LORD's glory, [22]not one of these people will ever enter that land. They have seen my glorious presence and the miraculous signs I performed both in Egypt and in the wilderness, but again and again they tested me by refusing to listen. [23]They will never even see the land I swore to give their ancestors. None of those who have treated me with contempt will enter it."

Almost everybody refused to trust God. Yet Joshua and Caleb stood up for what was right. You can be like them. When people you know do something wrong, refuse to go along with the crowd. God will reward you for it.

What should you do when everybody else goes the wrong way?
Don't copy the behavior and customs of this world, but let God transform you into a new person by changing the way you think. Then you will know what God wants you to do, and you will know how good and pleasing and perfect his will really is.
Romans 12:2

The Israelites complained against God and Moses.
How did God respond to their complaints?

NUMBERS 21:4-9
A Bronze Snake

⁴Then the people of Israel set out from Mount Hor, taking the road to the Red Sea* to go around the land of Edom. But the people grew impatient along the way, ⁵and they began to murmur against God and Moses. "Why have you brought us out of Egypt to die here in the wilderness?" they complained. "There is nothing to eat here and nothing to drink. And we hate this wretched manna!"

⁶So the LORD sent poisonous snakes among them, and many of them were bitten and died. ⁷Then the people came to Moses and cried out, "We have sinned by speaking against the LORD and against you. Pray that the LORD will take away the snakes." So Moses prayed for the people.

⁸Then the LORD told him, "Make a replica of a poisonous snake and attach it to the top of a pole. Those who are bitten will live if they simply look at it!" ⁹So Moses made a snake out of bronze and attached it to the top of a pole. Whenever those who were bitten looked at the bronze snake, they recovered!

Instead of thanking God, the Israelites complained. So God punished them with a plague of poisonous snakes. When we complain against God today, he is not likely to send poisonous snakes after us. But that doesn't mean our complaining is less serious than that of the Israelites. The next time you are tempted to complain against God, remember the good things he has done for you in the past and thank him for his goodness to you.

How can you defeat the temptation to complain?
In everything you do, stay away from complaining and arguing, so that no one can speak a word of blame against you.
Philippians 2:14-15

21·4 Hebrew *sea of reeds.*

Balaam set out to disobey God. What surprise did God have waiting for him?

NUMBERS 22:21-38

The Talking Donkey

²¹So the next morning Balaam saddled his donkey and started off with the Moabite officials. ²²But God was furious that Balaam was going, so he sent the angel of the LORD to stand in the road to block his way. As Balaam and two servants were riding along, ²³Balaam's donkey suddenly saw the angel of the LORD standing in the road with a drawn sword in his hand. The donkey bolted off the road into a field, but Balaam beat it and turned it back onto the road. ²⁴Then the angel of the LORD stood at a place where the road narrowed between two vineyard walls. ²⁵When the donkey saw the angel of the LORD standing there, it tried to squeeze by and crushed Balaam's foot against the wall. So Balaam beat the donkey again. ²⁶Then the angel of the LORD moved farther down the road and stood in a place so narrow that the donkey could not get by at all. ²⁷This time when the donkey saw the angel, it lay down under Balaam. In a fit of rage Balaam beat it again with his staff.

²⁸Then the LORD caused the donkey to speak. "What have I done to you that deserves your beating me these three times?" it asked Balaam.

²⁹"Because you have made me look like a fool!" Balaam shouted. "If I had a sword with me, I would kill you!"

³⁰"But I am the same donkey you always ride on," the donkey answered. "Have I ever done anything like this before?"

"No," he admitted.

³¹Then the LORD opened Balaam's eyes, and he saw the angel of the LORD standing in the roadway with a drawn sword in his hand. Balaam fell face down on the ground before him.

Balaam was going with the Moabite officials to meet Balak, the Moabites' king. Balak wanted Balaam to curse the Israelites, and Balak was going to pay Balaam well for this curse. But Balaam knew that God did not want him to curse the Israelites, and he was testing God by going with the Moabites. Fortunately for Balaam, his donkey saved his life. What are you doing that you know displeases God? You don't have to be like Balaam. Instead, you can confess your sin and obey God.

What does the Bible say about testing God?

Jesus responded, "The Scriptures also say, 'Do not test the Lord your God.'* "
Matthew 4:7

4:7 Deut 6:16.

³²"Why did you beat your donkey those three times?" the angel of the LORD demanded. "I have come to block your way because you are stubbornly resisting me. ³³Three times the donkey saw me and shied away; otherwise, I would certainly have killed you by now and spared the donkey."

³⁴Then Balaam confessed to the angel of the LORD, "I have sinned. I did not realize you were standing in the road to block my way. I will go back home if you are against my going."

³⁵But the angel of the LORD told him, "Go with these men, but you may say only what I tell you to say." So Balaam went on with Balak's officials. ³⁶When King Balak heard that Balaam was on the way, he went out to meet him at a Moabite town on the Arnon River at the border of his land.

³⁷"Did I not send you an urgent invitation? Why didn't you come right away?" Balak asked Balaam. "Didn't you believe me when I said I would reward you richly?"

³⁸Balaam replied, "I have come, but I have no power to say just anything. I will speak only the messages that God gives me."

F E B R U A R Y

Moses called the Israelites for a meeting. What did he tell them?

DEUTERONOMY 29:1-6, 9-18
God's Agreement
These are the terms of the covenant the LORD commanded Moses to make with the Israelites while they were in the land of Moab, in addition to the covenant he had made with them at Mount Sinai.*

²Moses summoned all the Israelites and said to them, "You have seen with your own eyes everything the LORD did in Egypt to Pharaoh and all his servants and his whole country—³all the great tests of strength, the miraculous signs, and the amazing wonders. ⁴But to this day the LORD has not given you minds that understand, nor eyes that see, nor ears that hear! ⁵For forty years I led you through the wilderness, yet your clothes and sandals did not wear out. ⁶You had no bread or wine or other strong drink, but he gave you food so you would know that he is the LORD your God.

• • •

⁹"Therefore, obey the terms of this covenant so that you will prosper in everything you do. ¹⁰All of you—your tribal leaders, your judges, your officers, all the men of Israel—are standing today before the LORD your God. ¹¹With you are your little ones, your wives, and the foreigners living among you who chop your wood and carry

29:1 Hebrew *Horeb*, another name for Sinai.

69

your water. [12]You are standing here today to enter into a covenant with the LORD your God. The LORD is making this covenant with you today, and he has sealed it with an oath. [13]He wants to confirm you today as his people and to confirm that he is your God, just as he promised you, and as he swore to your ancestors Abraham, Isaac, and Jacob. [14]But you are not the only ones with whom the LORD is making this covenant with its obligations. [15]The LORD your God is making this covenant with you who stand in his presence today and also with all future generations of Israel.

[16]"Surely you remember how we lived in the land of Egypt and how we traveled through the lands of enemy nations as we left. [17]You have seen their detestable idols made of wood, stone, silver, and gold. [18]The LORD made this covenant with you so that no man, woman, family, or tribe among you would turn away from the LORD our God to worship these gods of other nations, and so that no root among you would bear bitter and poisonous fruit."

Moses reminded the Israelites of the covenant (or agreement) they had with God. He also reminded them of the many ways God had provided for them while they traveled through the desert. Most important, Moses told the Israelites to obey God so that they would not break their agreement with him. When Jesus came, he made a new agreement with those who would follow him. This agreement also involves obedience on the part of his followers. If you are a Christian, keep up your part of this new agreement and obey Jesus' commands.

If we love Jesus, what will we do?
If you love me, obey my commandments.
John 14:15

F E B R U A R Y

Moses challenged the Israelites to obey God in order to receive God's blessing. What would happen if they disobeyed God?

DEUTERONOMY 30:11-20
The Big Choice
[11]"This command I am giving you today is not too difficult for you to understand or perform. [12]It is not up in heaven, so distant that you must ask, 'Who will go to heaven and bring it down so we can hear and obey it?' [13]It is not beyond the sea, so far away that you must ask, 'Who will cross the sea to bring it to us so we can hear and obey it?' [14]The message is very close at hand; it is on your lips and in your heart so that you can obey it.

15"Now listen! Today I am giving you a choice between prosperity and disaster, between life and death. 16I have commanded you today to love the LORD your God and to keep his commands, laws, and regulations by walking in his ways. If you do this, you will live and become a great nation, and the LORD your God will bless you and the land you are about to enter and occupy. 17But if your heart turns away and you refuse to listen, and if you are drawn away to serve and worship other gods, 18then I warn you now that you will certainly be destroyed. You will not live a long, good life in the land you are crossing the Jordan to occupy.

19"Today I have given you the choice between life and death, between blessings and curses. I call on heaven and earth to witness the choice you make. Oh, that you would choose life, that you and your descendants might live! 20Choose to love the LORD your God and to obey him and commit yourself to him, for he is your life. Then you will live long in the land the LORD swore to give your ancestors Abraham, Isaac, and Jacob."

The Israelites had a big choice to make. They could choose to obey God, or they could choose to disobey him. If they chose to obey, God promised the Israelites that he would bless them. If they chose to disobey, Moses told them that they would lose God's blessings and their land. Today, we have a big choice to make, too. We can choose to obey Jesus' commands for living, or we can choose to do whatever we want. The second choice sounds good, but it brings a lot of troubles and sadness. Make the better choice. Obey Jesus. He wants to bless you for obeying him.

What happens when we obey God?
Jesus replied, "All those who love me will do what I say. My Father will love them, and we will come to them and live with them."
John 14:23

F E B R U A R Y

*Moses gave Joshua the scary task of conquering Canaan.
Did Joshua have the courage?*

DEUTERONOMY 31:1-8
A New Leader
When Moses had finished saying* these things to all the people of Israel, 2he said, "I am now 120 years old and am no longer able to lead you. The LORD has told me that I will not cross the Jordan River. 3But the LORD your God himself will cross over ahead of you. He will destroy the nations living

31:1 As in Dead Sea Scrolls and Greek version; Masoretic Text reads Moses went and spoke.

there, and you will take possession of their land. Joshua is your new leader, and he will go with you, just as the LORD promised. ⁴The LORD will destroy the nations living in the land, just as he destroyed Sihon and Og, the kings of the Amorites. ⁵The LORD will hand over to you the people who live there, and you will deal with them as I have commanded you. ⁶Be strong and courageous! Do not be afraid of them! The LORD your God will go ahead of you. He will neither fail you nor forsake you."

⁷Then Moses called for Joshua, and as all Israel watched he said to him, "Be strong and courageous! For you will lead these people into the land that the LORD swore to give their ancestors. You are the one who will deliver it to them as their inheritance. ⁸Do not be afraid or discouraged, for the LORD is the one who goes before you. He will be with you; he will neither fail you nor forsake you."

Joshua had a large task ahead of him. But Moses encouraged Joshua. He told Joshua that the Lord would "go before" him and "be with" him. Joshua could trust God, who is all powerful, to help him complete his task. All Christians can be encouraged by these words. Jesus promises to be with us. If we obey him, he will be with us no matter what we have to do or go through.

What should we remember when we do not have enough courage?

And be sure of this: I [Jesus] am with you always, even to the end of the age.
Matthew 28:20

FEBRUARY 26

Moses sang about God. What are some of the things for which Moses praised God?

DEUTERONOMY 32:1-14
Moses' Song

¹ "Listen, O heavens, and I will
        speak!
    Hear, O earth, the words that I
        say!
² My teaching will fall on you like
        rain;
    my speech will settle like dew.
My words will fall like rain on
        tender grass,

like gentle showers on young
        plants.
³ I will proclaim the name of the
        LORD;
    how glorious is our God!
⁴ He is the Rock; his work is perfect.
    Everything he does is just and
        fair.
He is a faithful God who does no
        wrong;
    how just and upright he is!

5 "But they have acted corruptly
toward him;
when they act like that, are they
really his children?*
They are a deceitful and twisted
generation.
6 Is this the way you repay the LORD,
you foolish and senseless people?
Isn't he your Father who created
you?
Has he not made you and
established you?
7 Remember the days of long ago;
think about the generations past.
Ask your father and he will inform
you.
Inquire of your elders, and they
will tell you.
8 When the Most High assigned
lands to the nations,
when he divided up the human
race,
he established the boundaries of
the peoples
according to the number of
angelic beings.*
9 For the people of Israel belong to
the LORD;
Jacob is his special possession.

10 "He found them in a desert land,
in an empty, howling wasteland.
He surrounded them and watched
over them;
he guarded them as his most
precious possession.*
11 Like an eagle that rouses her chicks
and hovers over her young,
so he spread his wings to take
them in
and carried them aloft on his
pinions.

12 The LORD alone guided them;
they lived without any foreign
gods.
13 He made them ride over the
highlands;
he let them feast on the crops of
the fields.
He nourished them with honey
from the cliffs,
with olive oil from the hard
rock.
14 He fed them curds from the herd
and milk from the flock,
together with the fat of lambs
and goats.
He gave them choice rams and
goats from Bashan,
together with the choicest wheat.
You drank the finest wine,
made from the juice of grapes."

*Moses praised God for his perfect and
wonderful character. He also praised
God for the way he protected Israel and
provided food for them. Like Moses, we
should praise God for who he is and
what he has done.*

What can you praise God for?
All praise to the God and Father of
our Lord Jesus Christ. He is the
source* of every mercy and the God
who comforts us. He comforts us in
all our troubles so that we can
comfort others. When others are
troubled, we will be able to give them
the same comfort God has given us.
2 Corinthians 1:3-4

32:5 The meaning of the Hebrew is uncertain. **32:8** As in Dead Sea Scrolls, which read *of the sons of God*, and Greek version, which reads *of the angels of god*; Masoretic Text reads *of the sons of Israel*. **32:10** Hebrew *as the apple of his eye*. **1:3** Greek *the Father*.

The Lord told Joshua that he would lead the Israelites into the Promised Land. What did the Lord promise Joshua?

JOSHUA 1:1-11
Joshua Leads Israel

After the death of Moses the LORD's servant, the LORD spoke to Joshua son of Nun, Moses' assistant. He said, [2]"Now that my servant Moses is dead, you must lead my people across the Jordan River into the land I am giving them. [3]I promise you what I promised Moses: 'Everywhere you go, you will be on land I have given you—[4]from the Negev Desert in the south to the Lebanon mountains in the north, from the Euphrates River on the east to the Mediterranean Sea* on the west, and all the land of the Hittites.' [5]No one will be able to stand their ground against you as long as you live. For I will be with you as I was with Moses. I will not fail you or abandon you.

[6]"Be strong and courageous, for you will lead my people to possess all the land I swore to give their ancestors. [7]Be strong and very courageous. Obey all the laws Moses gave you. Do not turn away from them, and you will be successful in everything you do. [8]Study this Book of the Law continually. Meditate on it day and night so you may be sure to obey all that is written in it. Only then will you succeed. [9]I command you—be strong and courageous! Do not be afraid or discouraged. For the LORD your God is with you wherever you go."

[10]Joshua then commanded the leaders of Israel, [11]"Go through the camp and tell the people to get their provisions ready. In three days you will cross the Jordan River and take possession of the land the LORD your God has given you."

The Lord promised to be with Joshua and to make him a successful leader. But Joshua had to do his part. In order for the Lord to fulfill his promise, Joshua had to study and obey the laws that Moses gave him. Those laws are part of what we call the Bible. Living our life by the commands of God's Word will bring us success—not the worldly kind with money and possessions, but the spiritual kind with peace, joy, and love.

Why is it good to read the Bible?
All Scripture is inspired by God and is useful to teach us what is true and to make us realize what is wrong in our lives. It straightens us out and teaches us to do what is right. It is God's way of preparing us in every way, fully equipped for every good thing God wants us to do.
2 Timothy 3:16-17

1:4 Hebrew *the Great Sea.*

Joshua sent two spies to Jericho. The king of Jericho found out about them and sent out a search party. Did the Israelite spies get out alive?

JOSHUA 2:1-16, 22-24

Trapped in Jericho

Then Joshua secretly sent out two spies from the Israelite camp at Acacia.* He instructed them, "Spy out the land on the other side of the Jordan River, especially around Jericho." So the two men set out and came to the house of a prostitute named Rahab and stayed there that night.

²But someone told the king of Jericho, "Some Israelites have come here tonight to spy out the land." ³So the king of Jericho sent orders to Rahab: "Bring out the men who have come into your house. They are spies sent here to discover the best way to attack us."

⁴Rahab, who had hidden the two men, replied, "The men were here earlier, but I didn't know where they were from. ⁵They left the city at dusk, as the city gates were about to close, and I don't know where they went. If you hurry, you can probably catch up with them." ⁶(But she had taken them up to the roof and hidden them beneath piles of flax.) ⁷So the king's men went looking for the spies along the road leading to the shallow crossing places of the Jordan River. And as soon as the king's men had left, the city gate was shut.

⁸Before the spies went to sleep that night, Rahab went up on the roof to talk with them. ⁹"I know the LORD has given you this land," she told them. "We are all afraid of you. Everyone is living in terror. ¹⁰For we have heard how the LORD made a dry path for you through the Red Sea* when you left Egypt. And we know what you did to Sihon and Og, the two Amorite kings east of the Jordan River, whose people you completely destroyed.* ¹¹No wonder our hearts have melted in fear! No one has the courage to fight after hearing such things. For the LORD your God is the supreme God of the heavens above and the earth below. ¹²Now swear to me by the LORD that you will be kind to me and my family since I have helped you. Give me some guarantee that ¹³when Jericho is conquered, you will let me live, along with my father and mother, my brothers and sisters, and all their families."

¹⁴"We offer our own lives as a guarantee for your safety," the men agreed. "If you don't betray us, we will keep our promise when the LORD gives us the land."

¹⁵Then, since Rahab's house was built into the city wall, she let them down by a rope through the window. ¹⁶"Escape to the hill country," she

---

2:1 Hebrew *Shittim.* 2:10a Hebrew *sea of reeds.* 2:10b The Hebrew term used here refers to the complete consecration of things or people to the LORD, either by destroying them or by giving them as an offering.

told them. "Hide there for three days until the men who are searching for you have returned; then go on your way."

• • •

22 The spies went up into the hill country and stayed there three days. The men who were chasing them had searched everywhere along the road, but they finally returned to the city without success. 23 Then the two spies came down from the hill country, crossed the Jordan River, and reported to Joshua all that had happened to them. 24 "The LORD will certainly give us the whole land," they said, "for all the people in the land are terrified of us."

The Israelite spies were trapped. They were inside the gates of Jericho, and the king was looking for them. But God rescued the Israelite spies from the hands of their enemies. He used Rahab, a citizen of Jericho, to hide the Israelites and help them escape from the city. There may be times when we feel trapped by evil. God is able to rescue us, too.

What can we remember when we feel trapped?
Yes, and the Lord will deliver me from every evil attack and will bring me safely to his heavenly Kingdom. To God be the glory forever and ever. Amen.
2 Timothy 4:18

M A R C H

The Israelites needed to cross the Jordan River, which was flooding. How would they cross it?

JOSHUA 3:5-8, 14–4:7
Crossing the Jordan

⁵Then Joshua told the people, "Purify yourselves, for tomorrow the LORD will do great wonders among you."

⁶In the morning Joshua said to the priests, "Lift up the Ark of the Covenant and lead the people across the river." And so they started out.

⁷The LORD told Joshua, "Today I will begin to make you great in the eyes of all the Israelites. Now they will know that I am with you, just as I was with Moses. ⁸Give these instructions to the priests who are carrying the Ark of the Covenant: 'When you reach the banks of the Jordan River, take a few steps into the river and stop.' "

• • •

¹⁴When the people set out to cross the Jordan, the priests who were carrying the Ark of the Covenant went ahead of them. ¹⁵Now it was the harvest season, and the Jordan was overflowing its banks. But as soon as the feet of the priests who were carrying the Ark touched the water at the river's edge, ¹⁶the water began piling up at a town upstream called Adam, which is near Zarethan. And the water below that point flowed on to the Dead Sea* until the riverbed was dry. Then all the people crossed over near the city of Jericho. ¹⁷Meanwhile, the priests who were carrying the Ark of the LORD's covenant stood on dry ground in the middle of the riverbed as the people passed by them. They waited there until everyone had crossed the Jordan on dry ground.

Crossing the flooding Jordan River would have been a difficult task for the Israelites. But God took care of his people by stopping up the river so that they could cross on dry ground. Are you facing a difficult or impossible situation? Trust God to guide you through it. Nothing is impossible for him.

**What should we do when we
face a difficult task?**
A final word: Be strong with
the Lord's mighty power.
Ephesians 6:10

⁴:¹When all the people were safely across the river, the LORD said to Joshua, ²"Now choose twelve men, one from each tribe. ³Tell the men to take twelve stones from where the priests are standing in the middle of the Jordan and pile them up at the place where you camp tonight."

3:16 Hebrew *the sea of the Arabah, the Salt Sea.*

⁴So Joshua called together the twelve men ⁵and told them, "Go into the middle of the Jordan, in front of the Ark of the LORD your God. Each of you must pick up one stone and carry it out on your shoulder—twelve stones in all, one for each of the twelve tribes. ⁶We will use these stones to build a memorial. In the future, your children will ask, 'What do these stones mean to you?' ⁷Then you can tell them, 'They remind us that the Jordan River stopped flowing when the Ark of the LORD's covenant went across.' These stones will stand as a permanent memorial among the people of Israel."

MARCH

Jericho had walls that were more than twenty feet thick. How did the Israelites conquer this city?

JOSHUA 6:1-20

The Battle of Jericho

Now the gates of Jericho were tightly shut because the people were afraid of the Israelites. No one was allowed to go in or out. ²But the LORD said to Joshua, "I have given you Jericho, its king, and all its mighty warriors. ³Your entire army is to march around the city once a day for six days. ⁴Seven priests will walk ahead of the Ark, each carrying a ram's horn. On the seventh day you are to march around the city seven times, with the priests blowing the horns. ⁵When you hear the priests give one long blast on the horns, have all the people give a mighty shout. Then the walls of the city will collapse, and the people can charge straight into the city."

⁶So Joshua called together the priests and said, "Take up the Ark of the Covenant, and assign seven priests to walk in front of it, each carrying a ram's horn." ⁷Then he gave orders to the people: "March around the city, and the armed men will lead the way in front of the Ark of the LORD."

⁸After Joshua spoke to the people, the seven priests with the rams' horns started marching in the presence of the LORD, blowing the horns as they marched. And the priests carrying the Ark of the LORD's covenant followed behind them. ⁹Armed guards marched both in front of the priests and behind the Ark, with the priests continually blowing the horns. ¹⁰"Do not shout; do not even talk," Joshua commanded. "Not a single word from any of you until I tell you to shout. Then shout!" ¹¹So the Ark of the LORD was carried around the city once that day, and then everyone returned to spend the night in the camp.

¹²Joshua got up early the next morning, and the priests again carried the Ark of the LORD. ¹³The seven priests with the rams' horns marched in front of the Ark of the LORD, blowing their horns. Armed guards marched both in

front of the priests with the horns and behind the Ark of the LORD. All this time the priests were sounding their horns. ¹⁴On the second day they marched around the city once and returned to the camp. They followed this pattern for six days.

¹⁵On the seventh day the Israelites got up at dawn and marched around the city as they had done before. But this time they went around the city seven times. ¹⁶The seventh time around, as the priests sounded the long blast on their horns, Joshua commanded the people, "Shout! For the LORD has given you the city! ¹⁷The city and everything in it must be completely destroyed* as an offering to the LORD. Only Rahab the prostitute and the others in her house will be spared, for she protected our spies. ¹⁸Do not take any of the things set apart for destruction, or you yourselves will be completely destroyed, and you will bring trouble on all Israel. ¹⁹Everything made from silver, gold, bronze, or iron is sacred to the LORD and must be brought into his treasury."

²⁰When the people heard the sound of the horns, they shouted as loud as they could. Suddenly, the walls of Jericho collapsed, and the Israelites charged straight into the city from every side and captured it.

God gave the Israelites some unusual instructions for conquering Jericho. Instead of using physical force to break down the walls, God had the priests blow horns and the people shout. But God worked through these unusual instructions and his people's obedience to destroy Jericho's thick walls. Today, we have Jesus' commands to obey. Some of his commands may not make sense to us, like loving our enemies. But when we obey his commands, walls of sin in our life come tumbling down.

Who gives us the victory over sin?
How we thank God, who gives us victory over sin and death through Jesus Christ our Lord!
1 Corinthians 15:57

6:17 The Hebrew term used here refers to the complete consecration of things or people to the LORD, either by destroying them or by giving them as an offering; also in 6:18, 21.

M A R C H

God was angry with Israel. What did Israel do wrong?

JOSHUA 7:10-22
Achan Sins
¹⁰But the LORD said to Joshua, "Get up! Why are you lying on your face like this? ¹¹Israel has sinned and broken my covenant! They have stolen the things that I commanded to be set apart for me. And they have not only

stolen them; they have also lied about it and hidden the things among their belongings. ¹²That is why the Israelites are running from their enemies in defeat. For now Israel has been set apart for destruction. I will not remain with you any longer unless you destroy the things among you that were set apart for destruction.

¹³"Get up! Command the people to purify themselves in preparation for tomorrow. For this is what the LORD, the God of Israel, says: Hidden among you, O Israel, are things set apart for the LORD. You will never defeat your enemies until you remove these things. ¹⁴In the morning you must present yourselves by tribes, and the LORD will point out the tribe to which the guilty man belongs. That tribe must come forward with its clans, and the LORD will point out the guilty clan. That clan will then come forward, and the LORD will point out the guilty family. Finally, each member of the guilty family must come one by one. ¹⁵The one who has stolen what was set apart for destruction will himself be burned with fire, along with everything he has, for he has broken the covenant of the LORD and has done a horrible thing in Israel."

¹⁶Early the next morning Joshua brought the tribes of Israel before the LORD, and the tribe of Judah was singled out. ¹⁷Then the clans of Judah came forward, and the clan of Zerah was singled out. Then the families of Zerah came before the LORD, and the family of Zimri was singled out. ¹⁸Every member of Zimri's family was brought forward person by person, and Achan was singled out.

¹⁹Then Joshua said to Achan, "My son, give glory to the LORD, the God of Israel, by telling the truth. Make your confession and tell me what you have done. Don't hide it from me."

²⁰Achan replied, "I have sinned against the LORD, the God of Israel. ²¹For I saw a beautiful robe imported from Babylon,* two hundred silver coins,* and a bar of gold weighing more than a pound.* I wanted them so much that I took them. They are hidden in the ground beneath my tent, with the silver buried deeper than the rest."

²²So Joshua sent some men to make a search. They ran to the tent and found the stolen goods hidden there, just as Achan had said, with the silver buried beneath the rest.

Achan disobeyed God's command to destroy everything taken from Jericho. Achan may have thought that he would get away with taking the robe, silver, and gold. God, however, knew that Achan had taken these items and buried them under his tent. Unfortunately, we act like Achan sometimes. We sin and think that we can hide our actions from God. But God sees everything, and he knows our thoughts and motives. We cannot hide anything from him.

What does God know about you?
You saw me before I was born. Every day of my life was recorded in your book. Every moment was laid out before a single day had passed.
Psalm 139:16

7:21a Hebrew *Shinar*. 7:21b Hebrew *200 shekels of silver*, about 5 pounds or 2.3 kilograms in weight. 7:21c Hebrew *50 shekels*, about 20 ounces or 570 grams in weight.

Five kings joined forces against Israel. How were the Israelites able to fight five armies at once?

JOSHUA 10:7-14
The Sun Stops

7So Joshua and the entire Israelite army left Gilgal and set out to rescue Gibeon. 8"Do not be afraid of them," the LORD said to Joshua, "for I will give you victory over them. Not a single one of them will be able to stand up to you."

9Joshua traveled all night from Gilgal and took the Amorite armies by surprise. 10The LORD threw them into a panic, and the Israelites slaughtered them in great numbers at Gibeon. Then the Israelites chased the enemy along the road to Beth-horon and attacked them at Azekah and Makkedah, killing them along the way. 11As the Amorites retreated down the road from Beth-horon, the LORD destroyed them with a terrible hailstorm that continued until they reached Azekah. The hail killed more of the enemy than the Israelites killed with the sword.

12On the day the LORD gave the Israelites victory over the Amorites, Joshua prayed to the LORD in front of all the people of Israel. He said,

"Let the sun stand still over Gibeon,
    and the moon over the valley of
    Aijalon."

10:13 Or *The Book of the Upright.*

13So the sun and moon stood still until the Israelites had defeated their enemies.

Is this event not recorded in *The Book of Jashar**? The sun stopped in the middle of the sky, and it did not set as on a normal day. 14The LORD fought for Israel that day. Never before or since has there been a day like that one, when the LORD answered such a request from a human being.

How likely would it be for one army to beat five armies? It would be nearly impossible! But God was with Israel. He helped them defeat their enemies. Like the Israelites, we may face many impossible situations in our life. But God cares for us and can help us overcome incredible odds.

What can you remember when you face an impossible situation?
As we know Jesus better, his divine power gives us everything we need for living a godly life.
2 Peter 1:3

*Joshua called the Israelites together for a meeting.
What command did he give them?*

JOSHUA 23:1-11

Wise Words

The years passed, and the LORD had given the people of Israel rest from all their enemies. Joshua, who was now very old, ²called together all the elders, leaders, judges, and officers of Israel. He said to them, "I am an old man now. ³You have seen everything the LORD your God has done for you during my lifetime. The LORD your God has fought for you against your enemies. ⁴I have allotted to you as an inheritance all the land of the nations yet unconquered, as well as the land of those we have already conquered— from the Jordan River to the Mediterranean Sea* in the west. ⁵This land will be yours, for the LORD your God will drive out all the people living there now. You will live there instead of them, just as the LORD your God promised you.

⁶"So be strong! Be very careful to follow all the instructions written in the Book of the Law of Moses. Do not deviate from them in any way. ⁷Make sure you do not associate with the other people still remaining in the land. Do not even mention the names of their gods, much less swear by them or worship them. ⁸But be faithful to the LORD your God as you have done until now.

⁹"For the LORD has driven out great and powerful nations for you, and no one has yet been able to defeat you. ¹⁰Each one of you will put to flight a thousand of the enemy, for the LORD your God fights for you, just as he has promised. ¹¹So be very careful to love the LORD your God."

Joshua commanded the Israelites to love and obey God. If they did, they would remain powerful. And no other nation would be able to defeat them. But more important, the Lord would be their God and would fight their battles for them. For Christians, it is also important to love and obey God because he sent Jesus to die for our sins.

How should we show our love for God?

If you love me, obey my commandments.
John 14:15

23:4 Hebrew *the Great Sea.*

M A R C H

Joshua told the Israelites the story of their past. He reminded them of God's faithfulness. What did he challenge them to do?

JOSHUA 24:1-18

Joshua Challenges Israel

Then Joshua summoned all the people of Israel to Shechem, along with their elders, leaders, judges, and officers. So they came and presented themselves to God.

²Joshua said to the people, "This is what the LORD, the God of Israel, says: Your ancestors, including Terah, the father of Abraham and Nahor, lived beyond the Euphrates River,* and they worshiped other gods. ³But I took your ancestor Abraham from the land beyond the Euphrates and led him into the land of Canaan. I gave him many descendants through his son Isaac. ⁴To Isaac I gave Jacob and Esau. To Esau I gave the hill country of Seir, while Jacob and his children went down into Egypt.

⁵"Then I sent Moses and Aaron, and I brought terrible plagues on Egypt; and afterward I brought you out as a free people. ⁶But when your ancestors arrived at the Red Sea,* the Egyptians chased after you with chariots and horses. ⁷When you cried out to the LORD, I put darkness between you and the Egyptians. I brought the sea crashing down on the Egyptians, drowning them. With your very own eyes you saw what I did. Then you lived in the wilderness for many years.

⁸"Finally, I brought you into the land of the Amorites on the east side of the Jordan. They fought against you, but I gave you victory over them, and you took possession of their land. ⁹Then Balak son of Zippor, king of Moab, started a war against Israel. He asked Balaam son of Beor to curse you, ¹⁰but I would not listen to him. Instead, I made Balaam bless you, and so I rescued you from Balak.

¹¹"When you crossed the Jordan River and came to Jericho, the men of Jericho fought against you. There were also many others who fought you, including the Amorites, the Perizzites, the Canaanites, the Hittites, the Girgashites, the Hivites, and the Jebusites. But I gave you victory over them. ¹²And I sent hornets ahead of you to drive out the two kings of the Amorites. It was not your swords or bows that brought you victory. ¹³I gave you land you had not worked for, and I gave you cities you did not build—the cities in which you are now living. I gave you vineyards and olive groves for food, though you did not plant them.

¹⁴"So honor the LORD and serve him wholeheartedly. Put away forever the idols your ancestors worshiped when they lived beyond the Euphrates River and in Egypt. Serve the LORD alone. ¹⁵But if you are unwilling to serve the

24:2 Hebrew *the river;* also in 24:3, 14, 15.　24:6 Hebrew *sea of reeds.*

LORD, then choose today whom you will serve. Would you prefer the gods your ancestors served beyond the Euphrates? Or will it be the gods of the Amorites in whose land you now live? But as for me and my family, we will serve the LORD."

¹⁶The people replied, "We would never forsake the LORD and worship other gods. ¹⁷For the LORD our God is the one who rescued us and our ancestors from slavery in the land of Egypt. He performed mighty miracles before our very eyes. As we traveled through the wilderness among our enemies, he preserved us. ¹⁸It was the LORD who drove out the Amorites and the other nations living here in the land. So we, too, will serve the LORD, for he alone is our God."

Joshua told the Israelites to choose whom they would serve: either the living God or other gods. They couldn't serve both. Just like the Israelites, you can't serve both the living God and other things. You can't put money or popularity before God. He has to be first in your life.

How can you better serve God with your whole heart?
No one can serve two masters. For you will hate one and love the other, or be devoted to one and despise the other. You cannot serve both God and money.
Matthew 6:24

M A R C H

The Israelites sinned against God. So he used a Canaanite king to punish them. Did God listen to the Israelites' cry for help?

JUDGES 4:1-16

Deborah Predicts Victory

After Ehud's death, the Israelites again did what was evil in the LORD's sight. ²So the LORD handed them over to King Jabin of Hazor, a Canaanite king. The commander of his army was Sisera, who lived in Harosheth-haggoyim. ³Sisera, who had nine hundred iron chariots, ruthlessly oppressed the Israelites for twenty years. Then the Israelites cried out to the LORD for help.

⁴Deborah, the wife of Lappidoth, was a prophet who had become a judge in Israel. ⁵She would hold court under the Palm of Deborah, which stood between Ramah and Bethel in the hill country of Ephraim, and the Israelites came to her to settle their disputes. ⁶One day she sent for Barak son of Abinoam, who lived in Kedesh in the land of Naphtali. She said to him, "This is what the LORD, the God of Israel, commands you: Assemble ten thousand warriors from the tribes of Naphtali and Zebulun at Mount

Tabor. [7]I will lure Sisera, commander of Jabin's army, along with his chariots and warriors, to the Kishon River. There I will give you victory over him."

[8]Barak told her, "I will go, but only if you go with me!"

[9]"Very well," she replied, "I will go with you. But since you have made this choice, you will receive no honor. For the LORD's victory over Sisera will be at the hands of a woman." So Deborah went with Barak to Kedesh. [10]At Kedesh, Barak called together the tribes of Zebulun and Naphtali, and ten thousand warriors marched up with him. Deborah also marched with them.

[11]Now Heber the Kenite, a descendant of Moses' brother-in-law* Hobab, had moved away from the other members of his tribe and pitched his tent by the Oak of Zaanannim, near Kedesh.

[12]When Sisera was told that Barak son of Abinoam had gone up to Mount Tabor, [13]he called for all nine hundred of his iron chariots and all of his warriors, and they marched from Harosheth-haggoyim to the Kishon River.

[14]Then Deborah said to Barak, "Get ready! Today the LORD will give you victory over Sisera, for the LORD is marching ahead of you." So Barak led his ten thousand warriors down the slopes of Mount Tabor into battle. [15]When Barak attacked, the LORD threw Sisera and all his charioteers and warriors into a panic. Then Sisera leaped down from his chariot and escaped on foot. [16]Barak chased the enemy and their chariots all the way to Harosheth-haggoyim, killing all of Sisera's warriors. Not a single one was left alive.

God heard his people's cry for help. He responded by rescuing them. But God's rescue required the Israelites to have faith in him and to obey his commands. When we are in trouble, we should cry out to God for help. But before he answers, we should believe that he is able to rescue us. We should also be ready and willing to obey what he commands us to do.

When do you need to ask God for help?

. . . so don't you think God will surely give justice to his chosen people who plead with him day and night? Will he keep putting them off? I tell you, he will grant justice to them quickly!
Luke 18:7-8

4:11 Or father-in-law.

MARCH

God planned on rescuing Israel from the Midianites. He had chosen Gideon to carry out his plan. But Gideon said he was weak. Gideon also did not have much faith in God. Did God use him?

JUDGES 6:1-16

The Mighty Gideon

Again the Israelites did what was evil in the LORD's sight. So the LORD handed them over to the Midianites for seven years. ²The Midianites were so cruel that the Israelites fled to the mountains, where they made hiding places for themselves in caves and dens. ³Whenever the Israelites planted their crops, marauders from Midian, Amalek, and the people of the east would attack Israel, ⁴camping in the land and destroying crops as far away as Gaza. They left the Israelites with nothing to eat, taking all the sheep, oxen, and donkeys. ⁵These enemy hordes, coming with their cattle and tents as thick as locusts, arrived on droves of camels too numerous to count. And they stayed until the land was stripped bare. ⁶So Israel was reduced to starvation by the Midianites. Then the Israelites cried out to the LORD for help.

⁷When they cried out to the LORD because of Midian, ⁸the LORD sent a prophet to the Israelites. He said, "This is what the LORD, the God of Israel, says: I brought you up out of slavery in Egypt ⁹and rescued you from the Egyptians and from all who oppressed you. I drove out your enemies and gave you their land. ¹⁰I told you, 'I am the LORD your God. You must not worship the gods of the Amorites, in whose land you now live.' But you have not listened to me."

¹¹Then the angel of the LORD came and sat beneath the oak tree at Ophrah, which belonged to Joash of the clan of Abiezer. Gideon son of Joash had been threshing wheat at the bottom of a winepress to hide the grain from the Midianites. ¹²The angel of the

Why did God choose Gideon to save Israel? Gideon was not physically strong. He also doubted God's ability to use him as a leader. But God chose Gideon because he was weak. Through Gideon, God could show the Israelites his power. And the Israelites would know that it was God, not Gideon, who delivered them from their enemies. Do you feel weak like Gideon? That is when God can use you. Be open to his leading.

Why is our weakness useful to God?

Each time he said, "My gracious favor is all you need. My power works best in your weakness." So now I am glad to boast about my weaknesses, so that the power of Christ may work through me.
2 Corinthians 12:9

LORD appeared to him and said, "Mighty hero, the LORD is with you!"

¹³"Sir," Gideon replied, "if the LORD is with us, why has all this happened to us? And where are all the miracles our ancestors told us about? Didn't they say, 'The LORD brought us up out of Egypt'? But now the LORD has abandoned us and handed us over to the Midianites."

¹⁴Then the LORD turned to him and said, "Go with the strength you have and rescue Israel from the Midianites. I am sending you!"

¹⁵"But Lord," Gideon replied, "how can I rescue Israel? My clan is the weakest in the whole tribe of Manasseh, and I am the least in my entire family!"

¹⁶The LORD said to him, "I will be with you. And you will destroy the Midianites as if you were fighting against one man."

M A R C H

Gideon had a large army ready to fight the Midianites. But God told Gideon that his army was too big. Why?

JUDGES 7:2-8

Choosing an Army

²The LORD said to Gideon, "You have too many warriors with you. If I let all of you fight the Midianites, the Israelites will boast to me that they saved themselves by their own strength. ³Therefore, tell the people, 'Whoever is timid or afraid may leave* and go home.'" Twenty-two thousand of them went home, leaving only ten thousand who were willing to fight.

⁴But the LORD told Gideon, "There are still too many! Bring them down to the spring, and I will sort out who will go with you and who will not." ⁵When Gideon took his warriors down to the water, the LORD told him, "Divide the men into two groups. In one group put all those who cup water in their hands and lap it up with their tongues like

Out of thirty-two thousand men, God chose a mere three hundred to fight. God did this because he did not want the Israelites to brag about their own strength. Instead, he wanted the Israelites to praise and thank him for defeating their enemies. God also does not want us to brag about our strength. When we brag about ourselves, we fail to see who really deserves our praise. The only one worthy of our praise is God.

What should you do when you are tempted to boast?

As the Scriptures say, "The person who wishes to boast should boast only of what the Lord has done."*

1 Corinthians 1:31

7:3 Hebrew *leave Mount Gilead*. The identity of Mount Gilead is uncertain in this context. It is perhaps used here as another name for Mount Gilboa. **1:31** Jer 9:24.

dogs. In the other group put all those who kneel down and drink with their mouths in the stream." 6Only three hundred of the men drank from their hands. All the others got down on their knees and drank with their mouths in the stream. 7The LORD told Gideon, "With these three hundred men I will rescue you and give you victory over the Midianites. Send all the others home." 8So Gideon collected the provisions and rams' horns of the other warriors and sent them home. But he kept the three hundred men with him.

Now the Midianite camp was in the valley just below Gideon.

M A R C H

Gideon faced a huge Midianite army with only three hundred soldiers. How did God calm his fears?

JUDGES 7:9-21

Gideon Is Outnumbered

9During the night, the LORD said, "Get up! Go down into the Midianite camp, for I have given you victory over them! 10But if you are afraid to attack, go down to the camp with your servant Purah. 11Listen to what the Midianites are saying, and you will be greatly encouraged. Then you will be eager to attack."

So Gideon took Purah and went down to the outposts of the enemy camp. 12The armies of Midian, Amalek, and the people of the east had settled in the valley like a swarm of locusts. Their camels were like grains of sand on the seashore—too many to count! 13Gideon crept up just as a man was telling his friend about a dream. The man said, "I had this dream, and in my dream a loaf of barley bread came tumbling down into the Midianite camp. It hit a tent, turned it over, and knocked it flat!"

14His friend said, "Your dream can mean only one thing—God has given Gideon son of Joash, the Israelite, victory over all the armies united with Midian!"

15When Gideon heard the dream and its interpretation, he thanked God. Then he returned to the Israelite camp and shouted, "Get up! For the LORD has given you victory over the Midianites!" 16He divided the three hundred men into three groups and gave each man a ram's horn and a clay jar with a torch in it. 17Then he said to them, "Keep your eyes on me. When I come to the edge of the camp, do just as I do. 18As soon as my group blows the rams' horns, those of you on the other sides of the camp blow your horns and shout, 'For the LORD and for Gideon!' "

19It was just after midnight, after the

changing of the guard, when Gideon and the one hundred men with him reached the outer edge of the Midianite camp. Suddenly, they blew the horns and broke their clay jars. ²⁰Then all three groups blew their horns and broke their jars. They held the blazing torches in their left hands and the horns in their right hands and shouted, "A sword for the LORD and for Gideon!" ²¹Each man stood at his position around the camp and watched as all the Midianites rushed around in a panic, shouting as they ran.

Gideon had a problem. He didn't trust God to do what he said he would. But God calmed Gideon's fears. Through the interpretation of a Midianite's dream, God assured Gideon that he would have victory. Gideon thanked God for this assurance. Many of us are just like Gideon. We have doubts about God's ability to help us when we are outnumbered. But God loves us. We can trust him to take care of us. If you doubt God, go to him in prayer and confess your doubts. He can strengthen your faith in him.

What should we do when we are afraid?

Don't worry about anything; instead, pray about everything. Tell God what you need, and thank him for all he has done. If you do this, you will experience God's peace, which is far more wonderful than the human mind can understand.
Philippians 4:6-7

M A R C H

Samson's father, Manoah, asked God for guidance. Did God provide it?

JUDGES 13:1-24
Samson's Birth
Again the Israelites did what was evil in the LORD's sight, so the LORD handed them over to the Philistines, who kept them in subjection for forty years.

²In those days, a man named Manoah from the tribe of Dan lived in the town of Zorah. His wife was unable to become pregnant, and they had no children. ³The angel of the LORD appeared to Manoah's wife and said, "Even though you have been unable to have children, you will soon become pregnant and give birth to a son. ⁴You must not drink wine or any other alcoholic drink or eat any forbidden

food. 5You will become pregnant and give birth to a son, and his hair must never be cut. For he will be dedicated to God as a Nazirite from birth. He will rescue Israel from the Philistines."

6The woman ran and told her husband, "A man of God appeared to me! He was like one of God's angels, terrifying to look at. I didn't ask where he was from, and he didn't tell me his name. 7But he told me, 'You will become pregnant and give birth to a son. You must not drink wine or any other alcoholic drink or eat any forbidden food. For your son will be dedicated to God as a Nazirite from the moment of his birth until the day of his death.' "

8Then Manoah prayed to the LORD. He said, "Lord, please let the man of God come back to us again and give us more instructions about this son who is to be born."

9God answered his prayer, and the angel of God appeared once again to his wife as she was sitting in the field. But her husband, Manoah, was not with her. 10So she quickly ran and told her husband, "The man who appeared to me the other day is here again!"

11Manoah ran back with his wife and asked, "Are you the man who talked to my wife the other day?"

"Yes," he replied, "I am."

12So Manoah asked him, "When your words come true, what kind of rules should govern the boy's life and work?"

13The angel of the LORD replied, "Be sure your wife follows the instructions I gave her. 14She must not eat grapes or raisins, drink wine or any other alcoholic drink, or eat any forbidden food."

15Then Manoah said to the angel of the LORD, "Please stay here until we can prepare a young goat for you to eat."

16"I will stay," the angel of the LORD replied, "but I will not eat anything. However, you may prepare a burnt offering as a sacrifice to the LORD." (Manoah didn't realize it was the angel of the LORD.)

17Then Manoah asked the angel of the LORD, "What is your name? For when all this comes true, we want to honor you."

18"Why do you ask my name?" the angel of the LORD replied. "You wouldn't understand if I told you."

19Then Manoah took a young goat and a grain offering and offered it on a rock as a sacrifice to the LORD. And as Manoah and his wife watched, the LORD did an amazing thing. 20As the flames from the altar shot up toward the sky, the angel of the LORD ascended in the fire. When Manoah and

Manoah believed everything the angel of the Lord had told his wife. He respectfully asked God for more instructions on raising his son. Manoah was seeking God's wisdom. God answered Manoah's request. When we ask God for instructions or wisdom, we must ask him respectfully. We must also believe that God is able to answer our requests.

How can you become more wise?
If you need wisdom—if you want to know what God wants you to do—ask him, and he will gladly tell you. He will not resent your asking.
James 1:5

his wife saw this, they fell with their faces to the ground.

²¹The angel did not appear again to Manoah and his wife. Manoah finally realized it was the angel of the LORD, ²²and he said to his wife, "We will die, for we have seen God!"

²³But his wife said, "If the LORD were going to kill us, he wouldn't have accepted our burnt offering and grain offering. He wouldn't have appeared to us and told us this wonderful thing and done these miracles."

²⁴When her son was born, they named him Samson. And the LORD blessed him as he grew up.

M A R C H

The Philistines wanted to capture Samson because he set fire to their fields. Did they get him?

JUDGES 15:9-19

Samson and the Jawbone

⁹The Philistines retaliated by setting up camp in Judah and raiding the town of Lehi. ¹⁰The men of Judah asked the Philistines, "Why have you attacked us?"

The Philistines replied, "We've come to capture Samson. We have come to pay him back for what he did to us."

¹¹So three thousand men of Judah went down to get Samson at the cave in the rock of Etam. They said to Samson, "Don't you realize the Philistines rule over us? What are you doing to us?"

But Samson replied, "I only paid them back for what they did to me."

¹²But the men of Judah told him, "We have come to tie you up and hand you over to the Philistines."

"All right," Samson said. "But promise that you won't kill me yourselves."

¹³"We will tie you up and hand you over to the Philistines," they replied. "We won't kill you." So they tied him up with two new ropes and led him away from the rock.

¹⁴As Samson arrived at Lehi, the Philistines came shouting in triumph. But the Spirit of the LORD powerfully took control of Samson, and he snapped the ropes on his arms as if they were burnt strands of flax, and they fell from his wrists. ¹⁵Then he picked up a donkey's jawbone that was lying on the ground and killed a thousand Philistines with it. ¹⁶And Samson said,

"With the jawbone of a donkey,
    I've made heaps on heaps!
With the jawbone of a donkey,
    I've killed a thousand men!"

¹⁷When he finished speaking, he threw away the jawbone; and the place was named Jawbone Hill.*

¹⁸Now Samson was very thirsty, and he cried out to the LORD, "You have accomplished this great victory by the strength of your servant. Must I now die of thirst and fall into the hands of these pagan people?" ¹⁹So God caused water to gush out of a hollow in the ground at Lehi, and Samson was revived as he drank. Then he named that place "The Spring of the One Who Cried Out,"* and it is still in Lehi to this day.

When the Philistines saw Samson bound, they thought that Samson was defeated. But God filled Samson with strength. Then Samson broke the ropes around his arms and killed a thousand Philistines. Samson relied upon God for the strength to defeat the Philistines. We should also rely upon God for the strength to accomplish the tasks he has given us.

In what situation do you need God's strength?

For I can do everything with the help of Christ who gives me the strength I need.
Philippians 4:13

15:17 Hebrew *Ramath-lehi.* **15:19** Hebrew *En-hakkore.*

M A R C H

Delilah nagged Samson for the secret of his strength. Did he resist telling her?

JUDGES 16:4-20
Samson and Delilah

⁴Later Samson fell in love with a woman named Delilah, who lived in the valley of Sorek. ⁵The leaders of the Philistines went to her and said, "Find out from Samson what makes him so strong and how he can be overpowered and tied up securely. Then each of us will give you eleven hundred pieces* of silver."

⁶So Delilah said to Samson, "Please tell me what makes you so strong and what it would take to tie you up securely."

⁷Samson replied, "If I am tied up with seven new bowstrings that have not yet been dried, I will be as weak as anyone else."

⁸So the Philistine leaders brought Delilah seven new bowstrings, and she tied Samson up with them. ⁹She had hidden some men in one of the rooms of her house, and she cried out, "Samson! The Philistines have come to capture you!" But Samson snapped the bowstrings as if they were string that had been burned in a

16:5 Hebrew *1,100 shekels*, about 28 pounds or 12.5 kilograms in weight.

fire. So the secret of his strength was not discovered.

[10]Afterward Delilah said to him, "You made fun of me and told me a lie! Now please tell me how you can be tied up securely."

[11]Samson replied, "If I am tied up with brand-new ropes that have never been used, I will be as weak as anyone else."

[12]So Delilah took new ropes and tied him up with them. The men were hiding in the room as before, and again Delilah cried out, "Samson! The Philistines have come to capture you!" But Samson snapped the ropes from his arms as if they were thread.

[13]Then Delilah said, "You have been making fun of me and telling me lies! Won't you please tell me how you can be tied up securely?"

Samson replied, "If you weave the seven braids of my hair into the fabric on your loom and tighten it with the loom shuttle,* I will be as weak as anyone else."

So while he slept, Delilah wove the seven braids of his hair into the fabric [14]and tightened it with the loom shuttle. Again she cried out, "Samson! The Philistines have come to capture you!" But Samson woke up, pulled back the loom shuttle, and yanked his hair away from the loom and the fabric.

[15]Then Delilah pouted, "How can you say you love me when you don't confide in me? You've made fun of me three times now, and you still haven't told me what makes you so strong!" [16]So day after day she nagged him until he couldn't stand it any longer.

[17]Finally, Samson told her his secret. "My hair has never been cut," he confessed, "for I was dedicated to God as a Nazirite from birth. If my head were shaved, my strength would leave me, and I would become as weak as anyone else."

[18]Delilah realized he had finally told her the truth, so she sent for the Philistine leaders. "Come back one more time," she said, "for he has told me everything." So the Philistine leaders returned and brought the money with them. [19]Delilah lulled Samson to sleep with his head in her lap, and she called in a man to shave off his hair, making his capture certain. And his strength left him. [20]Then she cried out, "Samson! The Philistines have come to capture you!"

When he woke up, he thought, "I will do as before and shake myself free." But he didn't realize the LORD had left him.

Samson played with trouble. After being tied up a few times, he should have realized that Delilah was out to hurt him. He should have just told Delilah no when she asked him to tell her what made him strong. Unfortunately, he told her the secret of his strength. Do friends sometimes nag you to do wrong? Be stronger than Samson. Learn to say no.

How can you avoid giving in to peer pressure?

Don't copy the behavior and customs of this world, but let God transform you into a new person by changing the way you think. Then you will know what God wants you to do, and you will know how good and pleasing and perfect his will really is.
Romans 12:2

16:13 As in Greek version; Hebrew lacks *on your loom and tighten it with the loom shuttle.*

M A R C H

The Philistines captured Samson. Would God forget about him?

JUDGES 16:23-30
Samson's Revenge

²³The Philistine leaders held a great festival, offering sacrifices and praising their god, Dagon. They said, "Our god has given us victory over our enemy Samson!"

²⁴When the people saw him, they praised their god, saying, "Our god has delivered our enemy to us! The one who killed so many of us is now in our power!"

²⁵Half drunk by now, the people demanded, "Bring out Samson so he can perform for us!" So he was brought from the prison and made to stand at the center of the temple, between the two pillars supporting the roof.

²⁶Samson said to the servant who was leading him by the hand, "Place my hands against the two pillars. I want to rest against them." ²⁷The temple was completely filled with people. All the Philistine leaders were there, and there were about three thousand on the roof who were watching Samson and making fun of him.

²⁸Then Samson prayed to the LORD, "Sovereign LORD, remember me again. O God, please strengthen me one more time so that I may pay back the Philistines for the loss of my eyes." ²⁹Then Samson put his hands on the center pillars of the temple and pushed against them with all his might. ³⁰"Let me die with the Philistines," he prayed. And the temple crashed down on the Philistine leaders and all the people. So he killed more people when he died than he had during his entire lifetime.

God did not forget Samson. He answered Samson's prayer. God promises not to forget those who serve him. God will always be with those who believe in him.

How do we know that God will remember us?
For God is not unfair. He will not forget how hard you have worked for him and how you have shown your love to him by caring for other Christians, as you still do.
Hebrews 6:10

M A R C H

Naomi had lost just about everyone in her life. Her husband died, and then her sons died. Did her daughters-in-law stay with her?

RUTH 1:3-19

Ruth and Naomi

³Elimelech died and Naomi was left with her two sons. ⁴The two sons married Moabite women. One married a woman named Orpah, and the other a woman named Ruth. But about ten years later, ⁵both Mahlon and Kilion died. This left Naomi alone, without her husband or sons.

⁶Then Naomi heard in Moab that the LORD had blessed his people in Judah by giving them good crops again. So Naomi and her daughters-in-law got ready to leave Moab to return to her homeland. ⁷With her two daughters-in-law she set out from the place where she had been living, and they took the road that would lead them back to Judah.

⁸But on the way, Naomi said to her two daughters-in-law, "Go back to your mothers' homes instead of coming with me. And may the LORD reward you for your kindness to your husbands and to me. ⁹May the LORD bless you with the security of another marriage." Then she kissed them good-bye, and they all broke down and wept.

¹⁰"No," they said. "We want to go with you to your people."

¹¹But Naomi replied, "Why should you go on with me? Can I still give birth to other sons who could grow up

to be your husbands? ¹²No, my daughters, return to your parents' homes, for I am too old to marry again. And even if it were possible, and I were to get married tonight and bear sons, then what? ¹³Would you wait for them to grow up and refuse to marry someone else? No, of course not, my daughters! Things are far more bitter for me than for you, because the LORD himself has caused me to suffer."

¹⁴And again they wept together, and

After Naomi's sons died, she told her daughters-in-law to go back to their families. Ruth chose to stay with Naomi. In fact, Ruth left friends, family, and her home to take care of Naomi back in Israel. Ruth loved Naomi that much. Ruth's actions are a good example of how to love your family members. Loving your family like Ruth loved Naomi means putting your family's needs before your own.

How should we treat our family members?

I command you to love each other in the same way that I love you. And here is how to measure it—the greatest love is shown when people lay down their lives for their friends.
John 15:12-13

Orpah kissed her mother-in-law good-bye. But Ruth insisted on staying with Naomi. ¹⁵"See," Naomi said to her, "your sister-in-law has gone back to her people and to her gods. You should do the same."

¹⁶But Ruth replied, "Don't ask me to leave you and turn back. I will go wherever you go and live wherever you live. Your people will be my people, and your God will be my God.

¹⁷I will die where you die and will be buried there. May the LORD punish me severely if I allow anything but death to separate us!" ¹⁸So when Naomi saw that Ruth had made up her mind to go with her, she stopped urging her.

¹⁹So the two of them continued on their journey. When they came to Bethlehem, the entire town was stirred by their arrival. "Is it really Naomi?" the women asked.

M A R C H

Ruth and Naomi needed food. Did God provide for their need?

RUTH 2:2-16
Ruth and Boaz

²One day Ruth said to Naomi, "Let me go out into the fields to gather leftover grain behind anyone who will let me do it."

And Naomi said, "All right, my daughter, go ahead." ³So Ruth went out to gather grain behind the harvesters. And as it happened, she found herself working in a field that belonged to Boaz, the relative of her father-in-law, Elimelech.

⁴While she was there, Boaz arrived from Bethlehem and greeted the harvesters. "The LORD be with you!" he said.

"The LORD bless you!" the harvesters replied.

⁵Then Boaz asked his foreman, "Who is that girl over there?"

⁶And the foreman replied, "She is the young woman from Moab who came back with Naomi. ⁷She asked me this morning if she could gather grain behind the harvesters. She has been hard at work ever since, except for a few minutes' rest over there in the shelter."

⁸Boaz went over and said to Ruth, "Listen, my daughter. Stay right here with us when you gather grain; don't go to any other fields. Stay right behind the women working in my field. ⁹See which part of the field they are harvesting, and then follow them. I have warned the young men not to bother you. And when you are thirsty, help yourself to the water they have drawn from the well."

¹⁰Ruth fell at his feet and thanked him warmly. "Why are you being so kind to me?" she asked. "I am only a foreigner."

¹¹"Yes, I know," Boaz replied. "But I also know about the love and kind-

ness you have shown your mother-in-law since the death of your husband. I have heard how you left your father and mother and your own land to live here among complete strangers. ¹²May the LORD, the God of Israel, under whose wings you have come to take refuge, reward you fully."

¹³"I hope I continue to please you, sir," she replied. "You have comforted me by speaking so kindly to me, even though I am not as worthy as your workers."

¹⁴At lunchtime Boaz called to her, "Come over here and help yourself to some of our food. You can dip your bread in the wine if you like." So she sat with his harvesters, and Boaz gave her food—more than she could eat.

¹⁵When Ruth went back to work again, Boaz ordered his young men, "Let her gather grain right among the sheaves without stopping her. ¹⁶And pull out some heads of barley from the bundles and drop them on purpose for her. Let her pick them up, and don't give her a hard time!"

Boaz took care of Ruth. He told his workers not to bother Ruth and to leave some grain for her to gather. He even fed her lunch. Boaz did all of this for Ruth because he knew what she had done for Naomi. Because Ruth put Naomi's needs before her own, God provided grain for Ruth through Boaz. Do you know anyone who needs food or clothing? Give that person what you can. This pleases Jesus.

How should we respond to people in need?
Give to those who ask, and don't turn away from those who want to borrow.
Matthew 5:42

M A R C H

Hannah prayed for a son. Did God answer her prayer?

1 SAMUEL 1:10-20

Answered Prayer

¹⁰Hannah was in deep anguish, crying bitterly as she prayed to the LORD. ¹¹And she made this vow: "O LORD Almighty, if you will look down upon my sorrow and answer my prayer and give me a son, then I will give him back to you. He will be yours for his entire lifetime, and as a sign that he has been dedicated to the LORD, his hair will never be cut."*

¹²As she was praying to the LORD, Eli watched her. ¹³Seeing her lips moving but hearing no sound, he thought she had been drinking. ¹⁴"Must you come here drunk?" he demanded. "Throw away your wine!"

1:11 Some manuscripts add *He will drink neither wine nor intoxicants.*

¹⁵"Oh no, sir!" she replied, "I'm not drunk! But I am very sad, and I was pouring out my heart to the LORD. ¹⁶Please don't think I am a wicked woman! For I have been praying out of great anguish and sorrow."

¹⁷"In that case," Eli said, "cheer up! May the God of Israel grant the request you have asked of him."

¹⁸"Oh, thank you, sir!" she exclaimed. Then she went back and began to eat again, and she was no longer sad.

¹⁹The entire family got up early the next morning and went to worship the LORD once more. Then they returned home to Ramah. When Elkanah slept with Hannah, the LORD remembered her request, ²⁰and in due time she gave birth to a son. She named him Samuel,* for she said, "I asked the LORD for him."

Hannah was sad and ashamed because she couldn't have children. So she asked the Lord for a son. But she didn't just think of herself when she asked. She promised the Lord that she would give her child back to him. When we ask the Lord for something, we should be like Hannah. We should be willing to dedicate whatever we ask for to him.

What kind of gifts does God give us?

If you sinful people know how to give good gifts to your children, how much more will your heavenly Father give good gifts to those who ask him.
Matthew 7:11

1:20 *Samuel* sounds like the Hebrew term for "asked of God" or "heard by God."

M A R C H

God gave Samuel to Hannah. How did Hannah respond?

1 SAMUEL 1:24–2:2, 11

Hannah and Samuel

²⁴When the child was weaned, Hannah took him to the Tabernacle in Shiloh. They brought along a three-year-old bull* for the sacrifice and half a bushel* of flour and some wine. ²⁵After sacrificing the bull, they took the child to Eli. ²⁶"Sir, do you remember me?" Hannah asked. "I am the woman who stood here several years ago praying to the LORD. ²⁷I asked the LORD to give me this child, and he has given me my request. ²⁸Now I am giving him to the LORD, and he will belong to the LORD his whole life." And they* worshiped the LORD there.

^{2:1}Then Hannah prayed:

"My heart rejoices in the LORD!
  Oh, how the LORD has blessed me!

1:24a As in Dead Sea Scrolls, Greek and Syriac versions; Masoretic Text reads *3 bulls.* **1:24b** Hebrew *and an ephah* [18 liters]. **1:28** Or *he.*

Now I have an answer for my
    enemies,
    as I delight in your deliverance.
² No one is holy like the LORD!
    There is no one besides you;
    there is no Rock like our God."

• • •

¹¹Then Elkanah and Hannah returned home to Ramah without Samuel. And the boy became the LORD's helper, for he assisted Eli the priest.

Hannah kept her promise and gave Samuel to God. Samuel served God in the Tabernacle. Today, Jesus asks all Christians to be like Samuel. We can experience God's joy by giving our entire lives to serving Jesus.

How much should we give to God?
You must each make up your own mind as to how much you should give. Don't give reluctantly or in response to pressure. For God loves the person who gives cheerfully.
2 Corinthians 9:7

M A R C H

Samuel heard someone calling him. Who was it?

1 SAMUEL 3:1-10
A Mysterious Voice

Meanwhile, the boy Samuel was serving the LORD by assisting Eli. Now in those days messages from the LORD were very rare, and visions were quite uncommon.

²One night Eli, who was almost blind by now, had just gone to bed. ³The lamp of God had not yet gone out, and Samuel was sleeping in the Tabernacle* near the Ark of God. ⁴Suddenly, the LORD called out, "Samuel! Samuel!"

"Yes?" Samuel replied. "What is it?"

⁵He jumped up and ran to Eli. "Here I am. What do you need?"

"I didn't call you," Eli replied. "Go on back to bed." So he did.

⁶Then the LORD called out again, "Samuel!"

Again Samuel jumped up and ran to Eli. "Here I am," he said. "What do you need?"

"I didn't call you, my son," Eli said. "Go on back to bed."

⁷Samuel did not yet know the LORD because he had never had a message from the LORD before. ⁸So now the LORD called a third time, and once more Samuel jumped up and ran to

3:3 Hebrew *the Temple of the LORD.*

Eli. "Here I am," he said. "What do you need?"

Then Eli realized it was the LORD who was calling the boy. ⁹So he said to Samuel, "Go and lie down again, and if someone calls again, say, 'Yes, LORD, your servant is listening.' " So Samuel went back to bed.

¹⁰And the LORD came and called as before, "Samuel! Samuel!"

And Samuel replied, "Yes, your servant is listening."

God called Samuel, but Samuel thought it was Eli. Fortunately, Eli figured out that God was calling Samuel. So Eli told Samuel what to do the next time he heard God calling. When God called, Samuel listened and obeyed. How is God calling you? Do you feel the need to change a habit or spend more time with God when you read a Bible verse or listen to your Sunday school teacher? God uses his Word and his people to speak to us. When God calls you, choose to love him by listening and obeying.

How should we respond to God's call?

My sheep recognize my voice; I know them, and they follow me.
John 10:27

M A R C H

The Philistine army advanced to destroy the Israelites. Did the Lord rescue them?

1 SAMUEL 7:3-10
The Lord Thunders

³Then Samuel said to all the people of Israel, "If you are really serious about wanting to return to the LORD, get rid of your foreign gods and your images of Ashtoreth. Determine to obey only the LORD; then he will rescue you from the Philistines." ⁴So the Israelites destroyed their images of Baal and Ashtoreth and worshiped only the LORD.

⁵Then Samuel told them, "Come to Mizpah, all of you. I will pray to the LORD for you." ⁶So they gathered there and, in a great ceremony, drew water from a well and poured it out before the LORD. They also went without food all day and confessed that they had sinned against the LORD. So it was at Mizpah that Samuel became Israel's judge.

⁷When the Philistine rulers heard that all Israel had gathered at Mizpah, they mobilized their army and advanced. The Israelites were badly frightened when they learned that the Philistines were approaching. ⁸"Plead with the LORD our God to save us from

the Philistines!" they begged Samuel. ⁹So Samuel took a young lamb and offered it to the LORD as a whole burnt offering. He pleaded with the LORD to help Israel, and the LORD answered.

¹⁰Just as Samuel was sacrificing the burnt offering, the Philistines arrived for battle. But the LORD spoke with a mighty voice of thunder from heaven, and the Philistines were thrown into such confusion that the Israelites defeated them.

The Israelites had sinned against God. Samuel advised them to turn away from their sins and follow God again. They were doing this when the Philistines came to attack them. But God didn't let the Philistines harm his people. He confused the Philistine army. And the Israelites destroyed them. God promised his people that he would never leave them. This same promise is for us, too. When danger comes your way, trust God. He will be with you.

What has God promised us?
Stay away from the love of money;
be satisfied with what you have.
For God has said,
"I will never fail you.
I will never forsake you."*
Hebrews 13:5

13:5 Deut 31:6, 8.

M A R C H
21

Samuel followed God. Did his sons do the same?

1 SAMUEL 8:1-5
Samuel's Sons
As Samuel grew old, he appointed his sons to be judges over Israel. ²Joel and Abijah, his oldest sons, held court in Beersheba. ³But they were not like their father, for they were greedy for money. They accepted bribes and perverted justice.

⁴Finally, the leaders of Israel met at Ramah to discuss the matter with Samuel. ⁵"Look," they told him, "you are now old, and your sons are not like you. Give us a king like all the other nations have."

Although Samuel followed God's ways, his sons did not follow in his footsteps. Don't be like Samuel's sons. Determine to be like those who love and obey God.

What does it mean to walk in God's ways?
Love means doing what God has commanded us, and he has commanded us to love one another, just as you heard from the beginning.
2 John 1:6

All the nations around Israel had kings. Israel also wanted a king.
Did God give them one?

1 SAMUEL 8:6-20
Israel Wants a King

⁶Samuel was very upset with their request and went to the LORD for advice. ⁷"Do as they say," the LORD replied, "for it is me they are rejecting, not you. They don't want me to be their king any longer. ⁸Ever since I brought them from Egypt they have continually forsaken me and followed other gods. And now they are giving you the same treatment. ⁹Do as they ask, but solemnly warn them about how a king will treat them."

¹⁰So Samuel passed on the LORD's warning to the people. ¹¹"This is how a king will treat you," Samuel said. "The king will draft your sons into his army and make them run before his chariots. ¹²Some will be commanders of his troops, while others will be slave laborers. Some will be forced to plow in his fields and harvest his crops, while others will make his weapons and chariot equipment. ¹³The king will take your daughters from you and force them to cook and bake and make perfumes for him. ¹⁴He will take away the best of your fields and vineyards and olive groves and give them to his own servants. ¹⁵He will take a tenth of your harvest and distribute it among his officers and attendants. ¹⁶He will want your male and female slaves and demand the finest of your cattle* and donkeys for his own use. ¹⁷He will demand a tenth of your flocks, and you will be his slaves. ¹⁸When that day comes, you will beg for relief from this king you are demanding, but the LORD will not help you."

¹⁹But the people refused to listen to Samuel's warning. "Even so, we still want a king," they said. ²⁰"We want to be like the nations around us. Our king will govern us and lead us into battle."

God told the Israelites not to ask for a king, but they refused to listen. Don't repeat the mistakes of the Israelites; instead, listen to God's warnings. Why? Because God only wants the best for you.

How should you respond to the Bible's message?
And remember, it is a message to obey, not just to listen to. If you don't obey, you are only fooling yourself.
James 1:22

8:16 As in Greek version; Hebrew reads *young men.*

Saul couldn't find his donkeys. What did he find instead?

1 SAMUEL 9:3-17
The Lost Donkeys

³One day Kish's donkeys strayed away, and he told Saul, "Take a servant with you, and go look for them." ⁴So Saul took one of his servants and traveled all through the hill country of Ephraim, the land of Shalishah, the Shaalim area, and the entire land of Benjamin, but they couldn't find the donkeys anywhere. ⁵Finally, they entered the region of Zuph, and Saul said to his servant, "Let's go home. By now my father will be more worried about us than about the donkeys!"

⁶But the servant said, "I've just thought of something! There is a man of God who lives here in this town. He is held in high honor by all the people because everything he says comes true. Let's go find him. Perhaps he can tell us which way to go."

⁷"But we don't have anything to offer him," Saul replied. "Even our food is gone, and we don't have a thing to give him."

⁸"Well," the servant said, "I have one small silver piece.* We can at least offer it to him and see what happens!"

⁹(In those days if people wanted a message from God, they would say, "Let's go and ask the seer," for prophets used to be called seers.)

¹⁰"All right," Saul agreed, "let's try it!" So they started into the town where the man of God was.

¹¹As they were climbing a hill toward the town, they met some young women coming out to draw water. So Saul and his servant asked, "Is the seer here today?"

¹²"Yes," they replied. "Stay right on this road. He is at the town gates. He has just arrived to take part in a public sacrifice up on the hill. ¹³Hurry and catch him before he goes up the hill to eat. The guests won't start until he arrives to bless the food."

¹⁴So they entered the town, and as

Saul was God's choice for king, and Samuel was the one God chose to anoint Saul. God used lost donkeys to bring Saul and Samuel together, so Saul's problem turned into a blessing. Sometimes problems are just God's way of preparing you for something better. God has a good plan for you. Trust him to bring you through your problems.

What should you remember when you feel frustrated?

And we know that God causes everything to work together* for the good of those who love God and are called according to his purpose for them.
Romans 8:28

9:8 Hebrew ¼ *shekel of silver*, about 0.1 ounces or 3 grams in weight. 8:28 Some manuscripts read *And we know that everything works together*.

they passed through the gates, Samuel was coming out toward them to climb the hill. ¹⁵Now the LORD had told Samuel the previous day, ¹⁶"About this time tomorrow I will send you a man from the land of Benjamin. Anoint him to be the leader of my people, Israel. He will rescue them from the Philistines, for I have looked down on my people in mercy and have heard their cry."

¹⁷When Samuel noticed Saul, the LORD said, "That's the man I told you about! He will rule my people."

M A R C H

Saul prophesied to a small group of prophets. What happened to Saul?

1 SAMUEL 10:1-11
A Changed Man

Then Samuel took a flask of olive oil and poured it over Saul's head. He kissed Saul on the cheek and said, "I am doing this because the LORD has appointed you to be the leader of his people Israel.* ²When you leave me today, you will see two men beside Rachel's tomb at Zelzah, on the border of Benjamin. They will tell you that the donkeys have been found and that your father is worried about you and is asking, 'Have you seen my son?'

³"When you get to the oak of Tabor, you will see three men coming toward you who are on their way to worship God at Bethel. One will be bringing three young goats, another will have three loaves of bread, and the third will be carrying a skin of wine. ⁴They will greet you and offer you two of the loaves, which you are to accept.

⁵"When you arrive at Gibeah of God,* where the garrison of the Philistines is located, you will meet a band of prophets coming down from the altar on the hill. They will be playing a harp, a tambourine, a flute, and a lyre, and they will be prophesying. ⁶At that time the Spirit of the LORD will come upon you with power, and you will prophesy with them. You will be changed into a different person. ⁷After these signs take

God changed Saul. He was a new person. When we believe in Jesus, God changes us, too. We are brand new on the inside! God places his Spirit in us. Instead of living for ourselves, we live for God.

How does God change us?
What this means is that those who become Christians become new persons. They are not the same anymore, for the old life is gone. A new life has begun!
2 Corinthians 5:17

10:1 Greek version reads *Israel. And you will rule over the LORD's people and save them from their enemies around them. This will be the sign to you that the LORD has appointed you to be leader over his inheritance.* **10:5** Hebrew *Gibeath-elohim.*

place, do whatever you think is best, for God will be with you. [8]Then go down to Gilgal ahead of me and wait for me there seven days. I will join you there to sacrifice burnt offerings and peace offerings. When I arrive, I will give you further instructions."

[9]As Saul turned and started to leave, God changed his heart, and all Samuel's signs were fulfilled that day. [10]When Saul and his servant arrived at Gibeah, they saw the prophets coming toward them. Then the Spirit of God came upon Saul, and he, too, began to prophesy. [11]When his friends heard about it, they exclaimed, "What? Is Saul a prophet? How did the son of Kish become a prophet?"

M A R C H

Samuel called a meeting for all the people of Israel. At the meeting, Saul was presented as God's choice for king. But where was Saul?

1 SAMUEL 10:17-26
Saul Becomes King

[17]Later Samuel called all the people of Israel to meet before the LORD at Mizpah. [18]And he gave them this message from the LORD, the God of Israel: "I brought you from Egypt and rescued you from the Egyptians and from all of the nations that were oppressing you. [19]But though I have done so much for you, you have rejected me and said, 'We want a king instead!' Now, therefore, present yourselves before the LORD by tribes and clans."

[20]So Samuel called the tribal leaders together before the LORD, and the tribe of Benjamin was chosen. * [21]Then he brought each family of the tribe of Benjamin before the LORD, and the family of the Matrites was chosen. And finally Saul son of Kish was chosen from among them. But when they looked for him, he had disappeared!

[22]So they asked the LORD, "Where is he?"

And the LORD replied, "He is hiding

Saul was afraid of being king. So much so that he hid when Samuel was about to present him before the people. But God had appointed Saul. If Saul had had faith in God, then he would have had nothing to fear. Many times we are just like Saul. Even though God is with us, we still worry. Don't be like Saul. Trust that God will strengthen you to do what he has called you to do.

What should we do when we worry?
Don't worry about anything; instead, pray about everything. Tell God what you need, and thank him for all he has done.
Philippians 4:6

10:20 Hebrew *chosen by lot*; also in 10:21.

among the baggage." ²³So they found him and brought him out, and he stood head and shoulders above anyone else.

²⁴Then Samuel said to all the people, "This is the man the LORD has chosen as your king. No one in all Israel is his equal!"

And all the people shouted, "Long live the king!"

²⁵Then Samuel told the people what the rights and duties of a king were. He wrote them down on a scroll and placed it before the LORD. Then Samuel sent the people home again.

²⁶When Saul returned to his home at Gibeah, a band of men whose hearts God had touched became his constant companions.

M A R C H

Saul was under pressure. The Philistines were coming, and his army was fleeing in fear. What could he do?

1 SAMUEL 13:5-14
Foolish Actions

⁵The Philistines mustered a mighty army of three thousand* chariots, six thousand horsemen, and as many warriors as the grains of sand along the seashore! They camped at Micmash east of Beth-aven. ⁶When the men of Israel saw the vast number of enemy troops, they lost their nerve entirely and tried to hide in caves, holes, rocks, tombs, and cisterns. ⁷Some of them crossed the Jordan River and escaped into the land of Gad and Gilead.

Meanwhile, Saul stayed at Gilgal, and his men were trembling with fear. ⁸Saul waited there seven days for Samuel, as Samuel had instructed him earlier, but Samuel still didn't come. Saul realized that his troops were rapidly slipping away. ⁹So he demanded, "Bring me the burnt offering and the peace offerings!" And Saul sacrificed

Under pressure, Saul disobeyed God by offering sacrifices without a priest. Saul lost his kingdom for his disobedience. Often temptation strikes when we are under pressure. Giving in to temptation is an easy way out. It may be easy to disobey, but it is never easy to live with the consequences of disobedience.

**Who will help us
to overcome temptation?**
But remember that the temptations that come into your life are no different from what others experience. And God is faithful. He will keep the temptation from becoming so strong that you can't stand up against it. When you are tempted, he will show you a way out so that you will not give in to it.
1 Corinthians 10:13

13:5 As in Greek and Syriac versions; Hebrew reads *30,000*.

the burnt offering himself. ¹⁰Just as Saul was finishing with the burnt offering, Samuel arrived. Saul went out to meet and welcome him, ¹¹but Samuel said, "What is this you have done?"

Saul replied, "I saw my men scattering from me, and you didn't arrive when you said you would, and the Philistines are at Micmash ready for battle. ¹²So I said, 'The Philistines are ready to march against us, and I haven't even asked for the LORD's help!' So I felt obliged to offer the burnt offering myself before you came."

¹³"How foolish!" Samuel exclaimed. "You have disobeyed the command of the LORD your God. Had you obeyed, the LORD would have established your kingdom over Israel forever. ¹⁴But now your dynasty must end, for the LORD has sought out a man after his own heart. The LORD has already chosen him to be king over his people, for you have not obeyed the LORD's command."

M A R C H

Jonathan and a young man fought the Philistines. Did they win?

1 SAMUEL 14:1-15

Jonathan's Courage

One day Jonathan said to the young man who carried his armor, "Come on, let's go over to where the Philistines have their outpost." But Jonathan did not tell his father what he was doing. ²Meanwhile, Saul and his six hundred men were camped on the outskirts of Gibeah, around the pomegranate tree at Migron. ³(Among Saul's men was Ahijah the priest, who was wearing the linen ephod. Ahijah was the son of Ahitub, Ichabod's brother. Ahitub was the son of Phinehas and the grandson of Eli, the priest of the LORD who had served at Shiloh.)

No one realized that Jonathan had left the Israelite camp. ⁴To reach the Philistine outpost, Jonathan had to go down between two rocky cliffs that were called Bozez and Seneh. ⁵The cliff on the north was in front of Micmash, and the one on the south was in front of Geba. ⁶"Let's go across to see those pagans," Jonathan said to his armor bearer. "Perhaps the LORD will help us, for nothing can hinder the LORD. He can win a battle whether he has many warriors or only a few!"

⁷"Do what you think is best," the youth replied. "I'm with you completely, whatever you decide."

⁸"All right then," Jonathan told him. "We will cross over and let them see us. ⁹If they say to us, 'Stay where you are or we'll kill you,' then we will stop and not go up to them. ¹⁰But if they say, 'Come on up and fight,' then we will go up. That will be the LORD's sign that he will help us defeat them."

¹¹When the Philistines saw them

coming, they shouted, "Look! The Hebrews are crawling out of their holes!" [12]Then they shouted to Jonathan, "Come on up here, and we'll teach you a lesson!"

"Come on, climb right behind me," Jonathan said to his armor bearer, "for the LORD will help us defeat them!" [13]So they climbed up using both hands and feet, and the Philistines fell back as Jonathan and his armor bearer killed them right and left. [14]They killed about twenty men in all, and their bodies were scattered over about half an acre.* [15]Suddenly, panic broke out in the Philistine army, both in the camp and in the field, including even the outposts and raiding parties. And just then an earthquake struck, and everyone was terrified.

Jonathan and another young man had courage. They took on a group of Philistines and won. The odds were against them, but they were not alone. God was with them. God gave them the strength and courage they needed to win. When the odds are against you, how can you be more courageous? Trust in God. His strength can help you to overcome the odds.

What should we do when our enemies outnumber us?
Be on guard. Stand true to what you believe. Be courageous. Be strong.
1 Corinthians 16:13

14:14 Hebrew *half a yoke;* a "yoke" was the amount of land plowed by a pair of yoked oxen in one day.

M A R C H

Saul said that anyone who ate before he got revenge on his enemies would be cursed. What was the outcome of his vow?

1 SAMUEL 14:24-30, 36-45

Jonathan Has a Snack

[24]Now the men of Israel were worn out that day, because Saul had made them take an oath, saying, "Let a curse fall on anyone who eats before evening— before I have full revenge on my enemies." So no one ate a thing all day, [25]even though they found honeycomb on the ground in the forest. [26]They didn't even touch the honey because they all feared the oath they had taken.

[27]But Jonathan had not heard his father's command, and he dipped a stick into a piece of honeycomb and ate the honey. After he had eaten it, he felt much better. [28]But one of the men saw him and said, "Your father made the army take a strict oath that anyone who eats food today will be cursed. That is why everyone is weary and faint."

[29]"My father has made trouble for us all!" Jonathan exclaimed. "A com-

mand like that only hurts us. See how much better I feel now that I have eaten this little bit of honey. ³⁰If the men had been allowed to eat freely from the food they found among our enemies, think how many more we could have killed!"

• • •

³⁶Then Saul said, "Let's chase the Philistines all night and destroy every last one of them."

His men replied, "We'll do whatever you think is best."

But the priest said, "Let's ask God first."

³⁷So Saul asked God, "Should we go after the Philistines? Will you help us defeat them?" But God made no reply that day.

³⁸Then Saul said to the leaders, "Something's wrong! I want all my army commanders to come here. We must find out what sin was committed today. ³⁹I vow by the name of the LORD who rescued Israel that the sinner will surely die, even if it is my own son Jonathan!" But no one would tell him what the trouble was. ⁴⁰Then Saul said, "Jonathan and I will stand over here, and all of you stand over there." And the people agreed.

⁴¹Then Saul prayed, "O LORD, God of Israel, please show us who is guilty and who is innocent. Are Jonathan and I guilty, or is the sin among the others?"* And Jonathan and Saul were chosen* as the guilty ones, and the people were declared innocent.

⁴²Then Saul said, "Now choose* between me and Jonathan." And Jonathan was shown to be the guilty one.

⁴³"Tell me what you have done," Saul demanded of Jonathan.

"I tasted a little honey," Jonathan admitted. "It was only a little bit on the end of a stick. Does that deserve death?"

⁴⁴"Yes, Jonathan," Saul said, "you must die! May God strike me dead if you are not executed for this."

⁴⁵But the people broke in and said to Saul, "Should Jonathan, who saved Israel today, die? Far from it! As surely as the LORD lives, not one hair on his head will be touched, for he has been used of God to do a mighty miracle today." So the people rescued Jonathan, and he was not put to death.

Saul's reckless vow got him into trouble. His own son Jonathan ate before all of the Philistines were killed. Reckless words are dangerous. They can injure others. Eventually, your words can come back to haunt you. Be careful what you say to others and to God.

How should we talk?
But most of all, dear brothers and sisters, never take an oath, by heaven or earth or anything else. Just say a simple yes or no, so that you will not sin and be condemned for it.
James 5:12

14:41a Greek version adds *If the fault is with me or my son Jonathan, respond with Urim; but if the men of Israel are at fault, respond with Thummim.* **14:41b** Hebrew *chosen by lot.* **14:42** Hebrew *draw lots.*

The Lord rejected Saul as Israel's king. He then told Samuel to anoint another king. Whom did the Lord choose for Samuel to anoint?

1 SAMUEL 16:1-13
Samuel and David

Finally, the LORD said to Samuel, "You have mourned long enough for Saul. I have rejected him as king of Israel. Now fill your horn with olive oil and go to Bethlehem. Find a man named Jesse who lives there, for I have selected one of his sons to be my new king."

²But Samuel asked, "How can I do that? If Saul hears about it, he will kill me."

"Take a heifer with you," the LORD replied, "and say that you have come to make a sacrifice to the LORD. ³Invite Jesse to the sacrifice, and I will show you which of his sons to anoint for me."

⁴So Samuel did as the LORD instructed him. When he arrived at Bethlehem, the leaders of the town became afraid. "What's wrong?" they asked. "Do you come in peace?"

⁵"Yes," Samuel replied. "I have come to sacrifice to the LORD. Purify yourselves and come with me to the sacrifice." Then Samuel performed the purification rite for Jesse and his sons and invited them, too.

⁶When they arrived, Samuel took one look at Eliab and thought, "Surely this is the LORD's anointed!" ⁷But the LORD said to Samuel, "Don't judge by his appearance or height, for I have rejected him. The LORD doesn't make decisions the way you do! People judge by outward appearance, but the LORD looks at a person's thoughts and intentions."

⁸Then Jesse told his son Abinadab to step forward and walk in front of Samuel. But Samuel said, "This is not

Eliab was tall and handsome. Samuel thought that Eliab was to be the next king. But the Lord ignored Eliab's appearance. Instead, he chose David because he knew that David's heart was good. As 1 Samuel 16:7 says, the Lord does not judge people by their appearance. He judges people by their thoughts and intentions. Do not judge a person's ability to do anything by his or her appearance. Instead, watch his or her attitude and actions. These will tell you more about who that person really is than his or her appearance ever will.

Why is it wrong to judge a person by his or her appearance?
So be careful not to jump to conclusions before the Lord returns as to whether or not someone is faithful. When the Lord comes, he will bring our deepest secrets to light and will reveal our private motives. And then God will give to everyone whatever praise is due.
1 Corinthians 4:5

the one the LORD has chosen." ⁹Next Jesse summoned Shammah, but Samuel said, "Neither is this the one the LORD has chosen." ¹⁰In the same way all seven of Jesse's sons were presented to Samuel. But Samuel said to Jesse, "The LORD has not chosen any of these." ¹¹Then Samuel asked, "Are these all the sons you have?"

"There is still the youngest," Jesse replied. "But he's out in the fields watching the sheep."

"Send for him at once," Samuel said. "We will not sit down to eat until he arrives."

¹²So Jesse sent for him. He was ruddy and handsome, with pleasant eyes. And the LORD said, "This is the one; anoint him."

¹³So as David stood there among his brothers, Samuel took the olive oil he had brought and poured it on David's head. And the Spirit of the LORD came mightily upon him from that day on. Then Samuel returned to Ramah.

M A R C H

The Philistines had a mighty warrior named Goliath. Goliath challenged the Israelite army to send out someone to fight him. Did anyone take up that challenge?

1 SAMUEL 17:4-11, 17-30
Goliath's Challenge

⁴Then Goliath, a Philistine champion from Gath, came out of the Philistine ranks to face the forces of Israel. He was a giant of a man, measuring over nine feet* tall! ⁵He wore a bronze helmet and a coat of mail that weighed 125 pounds.* ⁶He also wore bronze leggings, and he slung a bronze javelin over his back. ⁷The shaft of his spear was as heavy and thick as a weaver's beam, tipped with an iron spearhead that weighed fifteen pounds.* An armor bearer walked ahead of him carrying a huge shield.

⁸Goliath stood and shouted across to the Israelites, "Do you need a whole army to settle this? Choose someone to fight for you, and I will represent the Philistines. We will settle this dispute in single combat! ⁹If your man is able to kill me, then we will be your slaves. But if I kill him, you will be our slaves! ¹⁰I defy the armies of Israel! Send me a man who will fight with me!" ¹¹When Saul and the Israelites heard this, they were terrified and deeply shaken.

• • •

¹⁷One day Jesse said to David, "Take this half-bushel* of roasted grain and these ten loaves of bread to your brothers. ¹⁸And give these ten cuts of

17:4 Hebrew *6 cubits and 1 span* [which totals about 9.75 feet or 3 meters]; Greek version and Dead Sea Scrolls read *4 cubits and 1 span* [which totals about 6.75 feet or 2 meters]. **17:5** Hebrew *5,000 shekels* [57 kilograms]. **17:7** Hebrew *600 shekels* [6.8 kilograms]. **17:17** Hebrew *ephah* [18 liters].

cheese to their captain. See how your brothers are getting along, and bring me back a letter from them.*"

¹⁹David's brothers were with Saul and the Israelite army at the valley of Elah, fighting against the Philistines. ²⁰So David left the sheep with another shepherd and set out early the next morning with the gifts. He arrived at the outskirts of the camp just as the Israelite army was leaving for the battlefield with shouts and battle cries. ²¹Soon the Israelite and Philistine forces stood facing each other, army against army. ²²David left his things with the keeper of supplies and hurried out to the ranks to greet his brothers. ²³As he was talking with them, he saw Goliath, the champion from Gath, come out from the Philistine ranks, shouting his challenge to the army of Israel.

²⁴As soon as the Israelite army saw him, they began to run away in fright. ²⁵"Have you seen the giant?" the men were asking. "He comes out each day to challenge Israel. And have you heard about the huge reward the king has offered to anyone who kills him? The king will give him one of his daughters for a wife, and his whole family will be exempted from paying taxes!"

²⁶David talked to some others standing there to verify the report. "What will a man get for killing this Philistine and putting an end to his abuse of Israel?" he asked them. "Who is this pagan Philistine anyway, that he is allowed to defy the armies of the living God?" ²⁷And David received the same reply as before: "What you have been hearing is true. That is the reward for killing the giant."

²⁸But when David's oldest brother, Eliab, heard David talking to the men, he was angry. "What are you doing around here anyway?" he demanded. "What about those few sheep you're supposed to be taking care of? I know about your pride and dishonesty. You just want to see the battle!"

²⁹"What have I done now?" David replied. "I was only asking a question!" ³⁰He walked over to some others and asked them the same thing and received the same answer.

Not one Israelite soldier took up Goliath's challenge. All of them were too afraid to fight him. When David found out about Goliath's challenge, he was amazed that Goliath was "allowed to defy the armies of the living God." David was not a soldier, and he was physically small. But he had great faith. He believed that God could and would defeat Goliath. You don't need to be an adult or a strong person to have faith. You only need to do two things. First, believe that God is who he says he is. And second, trust that God will do what he says he will do.

What should we do when we face Goliath-size problems?

Then Jesus said to the disciples, "Have faith in God."
Mark 11:22

17:18 Hebrew and take their pledge.

David responded to Goliath's challenge. Did David win?

1 SAMUEL 17:32-51

David and Goliath

³²"Don't worry about a thing," David told Saul. "I'll go fight this Philistine!"

³³"Don't be ridiculous!" Saul replied. "There is no way you can go against this Philistine. You are only a boy, and he has been in the army since he was a boy!"

³⁴But David persisted. "I have been taking care of my father's sheep," he said. "When a lion or a bear comes to steal a lamb from the flock, ³⁵I go after it with a club and take the lamb from its mouth. If the animal turns on me, I catch it by the jaw and club it to death. ³⁶I have done this to both lions and bears, and I'll do it to this pagan Philistine, too, for he has defied the armies of the living God! ³⁷The LORD who saved me from the claws of the lion and the bear will save me from this Philistine!"

Saul finally consented. "All right, go ahead," he said. "And may the LORD be with you!"

³⁸Then Saul gave David his own armor—a bronze helmet and a coat of mail. ³⁹David put it on, strapped the sword over it, and took a step or two to see what it was like, for he had never worn such things before. "I can't go in these," he protested. "I'm not used to them." So he took them off again. ⁴⁰He picked up five smooth stones from a stream and put them in his shepherd's bag. Then, armed only with his shepherd's staff and sling, he started across to fight Goliath.

⁴¹Goliath walked out toward David with his shield bearer ahead of him, ⁴²sneering in contempt at this ruddy-faced boy. ⁴³"Am I a dog," he roared at David, "that you come at me with a stick?" And he cursed David by the names of his gods. ⁴⁴"Come over here, and I'll give your flesh to the birds and wild animals!" Goliath yelled.

⁴⁵David shouted in reply, "You come to me with sword, spear, and javelin, but I come to you in the name

David was not an experienced soldier. Why did God use him? God wanted to show his power. David could not triumph over Goliath by himself. But with God's help, David killed Goliath with one small stone. Like David, we cannot triumph over huge odds on our own. But with God, we can conquer anything.

Why does God use unlikely people to do his will?

God chose things despised by the world, things counted as nothing at all, and used them to bring to nothing what the world considers important, so that no one can ever boast in the presence of God.
1 Corinthians 1:28-29

of the LORD Almighty—the God of the armies of Israel, whom you have defied. [46]Today the LORD will conquer you, and I will kill you and cut off your head. And then I will give the dead bodies of your men to the birds and wild animals, and the whole world will know that there is a God in Israel! [47]And everyone will know that the LORD does not need weapons to rescue his people. It is his battle, not ours. The LORD will give you to us!"

[48]As Goliath moved closer to attack, David quickly ran out to meet him. [49]Reaching into his shepherd's bag and taking out a stone, he hurled it from his sling and hit the Philistine in the forehead. The stone sank in, and Goliath stumbled and fell face downward to the ground. [50]So David triumphed over the Philistine giant with only a stone and sling. And since he had no sword, [51]he ran over and pulled Goliath's sword from its sheath. David used it to kill the giant and cut off his head.

A P R I L

God gave David success in whatever he did.
How did Saul respond to David's success?

1 SAMUEL 18:5-16
Trouble between Saul and David

⁵Whatever Saul asked David to do, David did it successfully. So Saul made him a commander in his army, an appointment that was applauded by the fighting men and officers alike. ⁶But something happened when the victorious Israelite army was returning home after David had killed Goliath. Women came out from all the towns along the way to celebrate and to cheer for King Saul, and they sang and danced for joy with tambourines and cymbals.* ⁷This was their song:

"Saul has killed his thousands,
    and David his ten thousands!"

⁸This made Saul very angry. "What's this?" he said. "They credit David with ten thousands and me with only thousands. Next they'll be making him their king!" ⁹So from that time on Saul kept a jealous eye on David.

¹⁰The very next day, in fact, a tormenting spirit from God overwhelmed Saul, and he began to rave like a madman. David began to play the harp, as he did whenever this happened. But Saul, who had a spear in his hand, ¹¹suddenly hurled it at David, intending to pin him to the wall. But David jumped aside and escaped. This happened another time, too, ¹²for Saul was afraid of him, and he was jealous because the LORD had left him and was now with David. ¹³Finally, Saul banned him from his presence and appointed him commander over only a thousand men, but David faithfully led his troops into battle.

¹⁴David continued to succeed in everything he did, for the LORD was with him. ¹⁵When Saul recognized this, he became even more afraid of him. ¹⁶But all Israel and Judah loved David because he was so successful at leading his troops into battle.

Saul was jealous of David's success. His jealousy got so out of control that he attempted to kill David. Jealousy is a dangerous attitude or feeling that we all experience at some time in our life. Although we experience jealousy, we don't have to give in to it. We can choose instead to celebrate with our friends and family members who are successful.

How can we avoid becoming jealous?
Stay away from the love of money; be satisfied with what you have. For God has said, "I will never fail you. I will never forsake you."*
Hebrews 13:5

18:6 The type of instrument represented by the final word is uncertain.   13:5 Deut 31:6, 8.

Saul wanted to kill David. Who helped David escape from Saul?

1 SAMUEL 20:1-4, 24-42

David and Jonathan

David now fled from Naioth in Ramah and found Jonathan. "What have I done?" he exclaimed. "What is my crime? How have I offended your father that he is so determined to kill me?"

²"That's not true!" Jonathan protested. "I'm sure he's not planning any such thing, for he always tells me everything he's going to do, even the little things. I know he wouldn't hide something like this from me. It just isn't so!"

³Then David took an oath before Jonathan and said, "Your father knows perfectly well about our friendship, so he has said to himself, 'I won't tell Jonathan—why should I hurt him?' But I swear to you that I am only a step away from death! I swear it by the LORD and by your own soul!"

⁴"Tell me what I can do!" Jonathan exclaimed.

• • •

²⁴So David hid himself in the field, and when the new moon festival began, the king sat down to eat. ²⁵He sat at his usual place against the wall, with Jonathan sitting opposite him* and Abner beside him. But David's place was empty. ²⁶Saul didn't say anything about it that day, for he said to himself, "Something must have made David ceremonially unclean. Yes, that must be why he's not here." ²⁷But when David's place was empty again the next day, Saul asked Jonathan, "Why hasn't the son of Jesse been here for dinner either yesterday or today?"

²⁸Jonathan replied, "David earnestly asked me if he could go to Bethlehem. ²⁹He wanted to take part in a family sacrifice. His brother demanded that he be there, so I told him he could go. That's why he isn't here."

³⁰Saul boiled with rage at Jonathan. "You stupid son of a whore!"* he swore at him. "Do you think I don't know that you want David to be king in your place, shaming yourself and your mother? ³¹As long as that son of Jesse is alive, you'll never be king. Now go and get him so I can kill him!"

³²"But what has he done?" Jonathan demanded. "Why should he be put to death?" ³³Then Saul hurled his spear at Jonathan, intending to kill him. So at last Jonathan realized that his father was really determined to kill David. ³⁴Jonathan left the table in fierce anger and refused to eat all that day, for he was crushed by his father's shameful behavior toward David.

³⁵The next morning, as agreed, Jonathan went out into the field and took a young boy with him to gather his

20:25 As in Greek version; Hebrew reads *with Jonathan standing.* **20:30** Hebrew *You son of a perverse and rebellious woman.*

arrows. ³⁶"Start running," he told the boy, "so you can find the arrows as I shoot them." So the boy ran, and Jonathan shot an arrow beyond him. ³⁷When the boy had almost reached the arrow, Jonathan shouted, "The arrow is still ahead of you. ³⁸Hurry, hurry, don't wait." So the boy quickly gathered up the arrows and ran back to his master. ³⁹He, of course, didn't understand what Jonathan meant; only Jonathan and David knew. ⁴⁰Then Jonathan gave his bow and arrows to the boy and told him to take them back to the city.

⁴¹As soon as the boy was gone, David came out from where he had been hiding near the stone pile.* Then David bowed to Jonathan with his face to the ground. Both of them were in tears as they embraced each other and said good-bye, especially David. ⁴²At last Jonathan said to David, "Go in peace, for we have made a pact in the LORD's name. We have entrusted each other and each other's children into the LORD's hands forever." Then David left, and Jonathan returned to the city.

Jonathan found out firsthand that his father, Saul, was trying to kill David. Even though Jonathan loved his father, he helped David stay alive. Jonathan was a good friend to David. Would you like to have a good friend like Jonathan? If you would, then choose to be someone your friends can count on in hard times. You will be amazed at how close your friendships will grow.

What do friends do for one another?
The next day when we docked at Sidon, Julius was very kind to Paul and let him go ashore to visit with friends so they could provide for his needs.
Acts 27:3

20:41 As in Greek version; Hebrew reads *near the south edge.*

A P R I L

Saul was an arm's length away from David. Did David take revenge?

1 SAMUEL 24:2-17
Too Close for Comfort
²So Saul chose three thousand special troops from throughout Israel and went to search for David and his men near the rocks of the wild goats. ³At the place where the road passes some sheepfolds, Saul went into a cave to relieve himself. But as it happened, David and his men were hiding in that very cave!

⁴"Now's your opportunity!" David's men whispered to him. "Today is the day the LORD was talking about when he said, 'I will certainly put Saul into your power, to do with as you wish.' "

Then David crept forward and cut off a piece of Saul's robe.

⁵But then David's conscience began bothering him because he had cut Saul's robe. ⁶"The LORD knows I shouldn't have done it," he said to his men. "It is a serious thing to attack the LORD's anointed one, for the LORD himself has chosen him." ⁷So David sharply rebuked his men and did not let them kill Saul.

After Saul had left the cave and gone on his way, ⁸David came out and shouted after him, "My lord the king!" And when Saul looked around, David bowed low before him.

⁹Then he shouted to Saul, "Why do you listen to the people who say I am trying to harm you? ¹⁰This very day you can see with your own eyes it isn't true. For the LORD placed you at my mercy back there in the cave, and some of my men told me to kill you, but I spared you. For I said, 'I will never harm him—he is the LORD's anointed one.' ¹¹Look, my father, at what I have in my hand. It is a piece of your robe! I cut it off, but I didn't kill you. This proves that I am not trying to harm you and that I have not sinned against you, even though you have been hunting for me to kill me. ¹²The LORD will decide between us. Perhaps the LORD will punish you for what you

are trying to do to me, but I will never harm you. ¹³As that old proverb says, 'From evil people come evil deeds.' So you can be sure I will never harm you. ¹⁴Who is the king of Israel trying to catch anyway? Should he spend his time chasing one who is as worthless as a dead dog or a flea? ¹⁵May the LORD judge which of us is right and punish the guilty one. He is my advocate, and he will rescue me from your power!"

¹⁶Saul called back, "Is that really you, my son David?" Then he began to cry. ¹⁷And he said to David, "You are a better man than I am, for you have repaid me good for evil."

Saul had driven David into hiding. Yet David did not take revenge on Saul when he had the chance. When a person wrongs you, do not plan your revenge. Instead, plan how you can show Jesus' love to that person.

Why shouldn't we take revenge?
Dear friends, never avenge yourselves. Leave that to God. For it is written, "I will take vengeance; I will repay those who deserve it,"* says the Lord.
Romans 12:19

12:19 Deut 32:35.

*David was angry because Nabal had insulted him.
Did Abigail smooth over Nabal's wrongs?*

1 SAMUEL 25:10-28, 32-33

David and Abigail

¹⁰"Who is this fellow David?" Nabal sneered. "Who does this son of Jesse think he is? There are lots of servants these days who run away from their masters. ¹¹Should I take my bread and water and the meat I've slaughtered for my shearers and give it to a band of outlaws who come from who knows where?" ¹²So David's messengers returned and told him what Nabal had said.

¹³"Get your swords!" was David's reply as he strapped on his own. Four hundred men started off with David, and two hundred remained behind to guard their equipment.

¹⁴Meanwhile, one of Nabal's servants went to Abigail and told her, "David sent men from the wilderness to talk to our master, and he insulted them. ¹⁵But David's men were very good to us, and we never suffered any harm from them. Nothing was stolen from us the whole time they were with us. ¹⁶In fact, day and night they were like a wall of protection to us and the sheep. ¹⁷You'd better think fast, for there is going to be trouble for our master and his whole family. He's so ill-tempered that no one can even talk to him!"

¹⁸Abigail lost no time. She quickly gathered two hundred loaves of bread, two skins of wine, five dressed sheep, nearly a bushel* of roasted grain, one hundred raisin cakes, and two hundred fig cakes. She packed them on donkeys and said to her servants, ¹⁹"Go on ahead. I will follow you shortly." But she didn't tell her husband what she was doing.

²⁰As she was riding her donkey into a mountain ravine, she saw David and his men coming toward her. ²¹David had just been saying, "A lot of good it did to help this fellow. We protected his flocks in the wilderness, and nothing he owned was lost or stolen. But he has repaid me evil for good. ²²May God deal with me severely if even one man of his household is still alive tomorrow morning!"

²³When Abigail saw David, she quickly got off her donkey and bowed low before him. ²⁴She fell at his feet and said, "I accept all blame in this matter, my lord. Please listen to what I have to say. ²⁵I know Nabal is a wicked and ill-tempered man; please don't pay any attention to him. He is a fool, just as his name suggests.* But I never even saw the messengers you sent.

²⁶"Now, my lord, as surely as the LORD lives and you yourself live, since the LORD has kept you from murdering and taking vengeance into your

25:18 Hebrew *5 seahs* [30 liters].   **25:25** The name *Nabal* means "fool."

119

own hands, let all your enemies be as cursed as Nabal is. [27]And here is a present I have brought to you and your young men. [28]Please forgive me if I have offended in any way. The LORD will surely reward you with a lasting dynasty, for you are fighting the LORD's battles. And you have not done wrong throughout your entire life."

• • •

[32]David replied to Abigail, "Praise the LORD, the God of Israel, who has sent you to meet me today! [33]Thank God for your good sense! Bless you for keeping me from murdering the man and carrying out vengeance with my own hands."

David had done Nabal a big favor. But Nabal treated David with disrespect. In contrast, Nabal's wife, Abigail, showed David respect. She also gave David what he had asked Nabal for—food and drink. When someone does us a favor, we should not repay that person with insults. Instead, we should show that person gratitude for the kindness he or she has shown us.

Who do you need to show gratitude to this week?

Let the words of Christ, in all their richness, live in your hearts and make you wise. Use his words to teach and counsel each other. Sing psalms and hymns and spiritual songs to God with thankful hearts.
Colossians 3:16

A P R I L

The Philistine army advanced to fight David. What did David do?

2 SAMUEL 5:17-25
David and the Philistines

[17]When the Philistines heard that David had been anointed king of Israel, they mobilized all their forces to capture him. But David was told they were coming and went into the stronghold. [18]The Philistines arrived and spread out across the valley of Rephaim. [19]So David asked the LORD, "Should I go out to fight the Philistines? Will you hand them over to me?"

The LORD replied, "Yes, go ahead. I will certainly give you the victory."

[20]So David went to Baal-perazim and defeated the Philistines there. "The LORD has done it!" David exclaimed. "He burst through my enemies like a raging flood!" So David named that place Baal-perazim (which means "the Lord who bursts through"). [21]The Philistines had abandoned their idols there, so David and his troops confiscated them.

²²But after a while the Philistines returned and again spread out across the valley of Rephaim. ²³And once again David asked the LORD what to do. "Do not attack them straight on," the LORD replied. "Instead, circle around behind them and attack them near the balsam trees. ²⁴When you hear a sound like marching feet in the tops of the balsam trees, attack! That will be the signal that the LORD is moving ahead of you to strike down the Philistines." ²⁵So David did what the LORD commanded, and he struck down the Philistines all the way from Gibeon* to Gezer.

When the Philistines came to capture David, he fled to a stronghold, or fortress. There he asked God for direction. God answered his prayer and gave him victory over his enemies. David's example is one that we can follow anytime. Whenever we are faced with problems or decisions, we can go to God in prayer. We can seek his direction for our life. If we truly want his guidance, he will answer our prayers.

What can you do when you aren't sure what to do?
Devote yourselves to prayer with an alert mind and a thankful heart.
Colossians 4:2

5:25 As in Greek version (see also 1 Chr 14:16); Hebrew reads *Geba*.

A P R I L

After David became king, he set out to keep his promise to Jonathan. What was that promise?

2 SAMUEL 9:1-13
The King's Kindness

One day David began wondering if anyone in Saul's family was still alive, for he had promised Jonathan that he would show kindness to them. ²He summoned a man named Ziba, who had been one of Saul's servants. "Are you Ziba?" the king asked.

"Yes sir, I am," Ziba replied.

³The king then asked him, "Is anyone still alive from Saul's family? If so, I want to show God's kindness to them in any way I can."

Ziba replied, "Yes, one of Jonathan's sons is still alive, but he is crippled."

⁴"Where is he?" the king asked.

"In Lo-debar," Ziba told him, "at the home of Makir son of Ammiel." ⁵So David sent for him and brought him from Makir's home. ⁶His name was Mephibosheth*; he was Jonathan's son and Saul's grandson. When he

9:6 Also known as *Meribbaal*.

came to David, he bowed low in great fear and said, "I am your servant."

⁷But David said, "Don't be afraid! I've asked you to come so that I can be kind to you because of my vow to your father, Jonathan. I will give you all the land that once belonged to your grandfather Saul, and you may live here with me at the palace!"

⁸Mephibosheth fell to the ground before the king. "Should the king show such kindness to a dead dog like me?" he exclaimed.

⁹Then the king summoned Saul's servant Ziba and said, "I have given your master's grandson everything that belonged to Saul and his family. ¹⁰You and your sons and servants are to farm the land for him to produce food for his family. But Mephibosheth will live here at the palace with me."

Ziba, who had fifteen sons and twenty servants, replied, ¹¹"Yes, my lord; I will do all that you have commanded." And from that time on, Mephibosheth ate regularly with David, as though he were one of his own sons. ¹²Mephibosheth had a young son named Mica. And from then on, all the members of Ziba's household were Mephibosheth's servants. ¹³And Mephibosheth, who was crippled in both feet, moved to Jerusalem to live at the palace.

David had promised to show kindness to Jonathan's family. This was unusual back then. A new king usually killed off the old king and his entire family. And Jonathan and his family were part of King Saul's family. Rather than follow the custom of the day, David chose to show kindness. We may never be as powerful as King David. But we can show kindness to those who are weaker than we are.

Why should we be kind to others?
Since God chose you to be the holy people whom he loves, you must clothe yourselves with tenderhearted mercy, kindness, humility, gentleness, and patience.
Colossians 3:12

APRIL

David had sinned. God sent Nathan to confront David. How did David respond?

2 SAMUEL 12:1-14
The Poor Man's Lamb
So the LORD sent Nathan the prophet to tell David this story: "There were two men in a certain town. One was rich, and one was poor. ²The rich man owned many sheep and cattle. ³The poor man owned nothing but a little lamb he had worked hard to buy. He raised that little lamb, and it grew up with his children. It ate from the man's own plate and drank from his cup. He

cuddled it in his arms like a baby daughter. ⁴One day a guest arrived at the home of the rich man. But instead of killing a lamb from his own flocks for food, he took the poor man's lamb and killed it and served it to his guest."

⁵David was furious. "As surely as the LORD lives," he vowed, "any man who would do such a thing deserves to die! ⁶He must repay four lambs to the poor man for the one he stole and for having no pity."

⁷Then Nathan said to David, "You are that man! The LORD, the God of Israel, says, 'I anointed you king of Israel and saved you from the power of Saul. ⁸I gave you his house and his wives and the kingdoms of Israel and Judah. And if that had not been enough, I would have given you much, much more. ⁹Why, then, have you despised the word of the LORD and done this horrible deed? For you have murdered Uriah and stolen his wife. ¹⁰From this time on, the sword will be a constant threat to your family, because you have despised me by taking Uriah's wife to be your own. ¹¹"'Because of what you have done, I, the LORD, will cause your own house-hold to rebel against you. I will give your wives to another man, and he will go to bed with them in public view. ¹²You did it secretly, but I will do this to you openly in the sight of all Israel.'"

¹³Then David confessed to Nathan, "I have sinned against the LORD."

Nathan replied, "Yes, but the LORD has forgiven you, and you won't die for this sin. ¹⁴But you have given the enemies of the LORD great opportunity to despise and blaspheme him, so your child will die."

David confessed his sin to Nathan. God forgave David and took away his sin. Through Jesus, we also can be forgiven. When we confess our sins, Jesus takes them away from us. Our sins are no longer with us. We are clean!

What should we do when we sin?
But if we confess our sins to him, he is faithful and just to forgive us and to cleanse us from every wrong.
1 John 1:9

A P R I L

8

Absalom hated his half brother Amnon. Where did his hate lead him?

2 SAMUEL 13:23-38
Absalom and Amnon
²³Two years later, when Absalom's sheep were being sheared at Baal-hazor near Ephraim, Absalom invited all the king's sons to come to a feast. ²⁴He went to the king and said, "My sheep-shearers are now at work. Would the king

and his servants please come to celebrate the occasion with me?"

²⁵The king replied, "No, my son. If we all came, we would be too much of a burden on you." Absalom pressed him, but the king wouldn't come, though he sent his thanks.

²⁶"Well, then," Absalom said, "if you can't come, how about sending my brother Amnon instead?"

"Why Amnon?" the king asked. ²⁷But Absalom kept on pressing the king until he finally agreed to let all his sons attend, including Amnon.

²⁸Absalom told his men, "Wait until Amnon gets drunk; then at my signal, kill him! Don't be afraid. I'm the one who has given the command. Take courage and do it!" ²⁹So at Absalom's signal they murdered Amnon. Then the other sons of the king jumped on their mules and fled.

³⁰As they were on the way back to Jerusalem, this report reached David: "Absalom has killed all your sons; not one is left alive!" ³¹The king jumped up, tore his robe, and fell prostrate on the ground. His advisers also tore their clothes in horror and sorrow.

³²But just then Jonadab, the son of David's brother Shimea, arrived and said, "No, not all your sons have been killed! It was only Amnon! Absalom has been plotting this ever since Amnon raped his sister Tamar. ³³No, your sons aren't all dead! It was only Amnon." ³⁴Meanwhile Absalom escaped.

Then the watchman on the Jerusalem wall saw a great crowd coming toward the city from the west. He ran to tell the king, "I see a crowd of people coming from the Horonaim road* along the side of the hill."

³⁵"Look!" Jonadab told the king. "There they are now! Your sons are coming, just as I said." ³⁶They soon arrived, weeping and sobbing, and the king and his officials wept bitterly with them. ³⁷And David mourned many days for his son Amnon.

Absalom fled to his grandfather, Talmai son of Ammihud, the king of Geshur. ³⁸He stayed there in Geshur for three years.

Amnon had done a terrible thing to his half sister Tamar. She was Absalom's sister, and Absalom had not forgiven Amnon for this act. Absalom's hatred of Amnon led him to plot the murder of his half brother. Not everyone who hates someone will commit murder. But that doesn't mean hatred isn't serious. Jesus said that even to be angry with someone would put us in danger of judgment (Matthew 5:21-22). Hatred is far more serious than anger.

What can hatred make you?
Anyone who hates another Christian is really a murderer at heart. And you know that murderers don't have eternal life within them.
1 John 3:15

13:34 As in Greek version; Hebrew reads *from the road behind him.*

Absalom was coming with an army. David had to flee. How did David react?

2 SAMUEL 15:13-36
David in Distress

¹³A messenger soon arrived in Jerusalem to tell King David, "All Israel has joined Absalom in a conspiracy against you!"

¹⁴"Then we must flee at once, or it will be too late!" David urged his men. "Hurry! If we get out of the city before he arrives, both we and the city of Jerusalem will be spared from disaster."

¹⁵"We are with you," his advisers replied. "Do what you think is best." ¹⁶So the king and his household set out at once. He left no one behind except ten of his concubines to keep the palace in order. ¹⁷The king and his people set out on foot, and they paused at the edge of the city ¹⁸to let David's troops move past to lead the way. There were six hundred Gittites who had come with David from Gath, along with the king's bodyguard.*

¹⁹Then the king turned to Ittai, the captain of the Gittites, and asked, "Why are you coming with us? Go on back with your men to King Absalom, for you are a guest in Israel, a foreigner in exile. ²⁰You arrived only yesterday, and now should I force you to wander with us? I don't even know where we will go. Go on back and take your troops with you, and may the LORD show you his unfailing love and faithfulness.*"

²¹But Ittai said to the king, "I vow by the LORD and by your own life that I will go wherever you go, no matter what happens—whether it means life or death."

²²David replied, "All right, come with us." So Ittai and his six hundred men and their families went along.

²³There was deep sadness throughout the land as the king and his followers passed by. They crossed the Kidron Valley and then went out toward the wilderness.

²⁴Abiathar and Zadok and the Levites took the Ark of the Covenant of God and set it down beside the road. Then they offered sacrifices there until everyone had passed by. ²⁵David instructed Zadok to take the Ark of God back into the city. "If the LORD sees fit," David said, "he will bring me back to see the Ark and the Tabernacle again. ²⁶But if he is through with me, then let him do what seems best to him."

²⁷Then the king told Zadok the priest, "Look,* here is my plan. You and Abiathar* should return quietly to the city with your son Ahimaaz and Abiathar's son Jonathan. ²⁸I will stop at the shallows of the Jordan River* and wait there for a message from you.

15:18 Hebrew *the Kerethites and Pelethites.* **15:20** As in Greek version; Hebrew reads *and may unfailing love and faithfulness go with you.*
15:27a As in Greek version; Hebrew reads *Are you a seer?* or *Do you see?* **15:27b** Hebrew lacks *and Abiathar;* compare 15:29.
15:28 Hebrew *at the crossing points of the wilderness.*

Let me know what happens in Jerusalem before I disappear into the wilderness." ²⁹So Zadok and Abiathar took the Ark of God back to the city and stayed there.

³⁰David walked up the road that led to the Mount of Olives, weeping as he went. His head was covered and his feet were bare as a sign of mourning. And the people who were with him covered their heads and wept as they climbed the mountain. ³¹When someone told David that his adviser Ahithophel was now backing Absalom, David prayed, "O LORD, let Ahithophel give Absalom foolish advice!"

³²As they reached the spot at the top of the Mount of Olives where people worshiped God, David found Hushai the Arkite waiting for him. Hushai had torn his clothing and put dirt on his head as a sign of mourning. ³³But David told him, "If you go with me, you will only be a burden. ³⁴Return to Jerusalem and tell Absalom, 'I will now be your adviser, just as I was your father's adviser in the past.' Then you can frustrate and counter Ahithophel's advice. ³⁵Zadok and Abiathar, the priests, are there. Tell them the plans that are being made to capture me, ³⁶and they will send their sons Ahimaaz and Jonathan to find me and tell me what is going on."

David could have fought Absalom, but he chose to flee instead. He made this choice not only to save himself but to save Jerusalem as well. A battle between David and Absalom would have destroyed Jerusalem. In addition, David was content to trust in God's plan for his future. David knew that if God wanted him to be king, God would bring him back to Jerusalem. When we face problems, we can do what David did. We can trust that God will take care of us and help us through our problems. Give your problems to God.

Who can we trust with our problems?

[Jesus said,] "Don't be troubled. You trust God, now trust in me."
John 14:1

A P R I L
10

As David fled from Absalom, Shimei cursed David and threw stones at him. How did David respond?

2 SAMUEL 16:5-13

Don't Throw Stones

⁵As David and his party passed Bahurim, a man came out of the village cursing them. It was Shimei son of Gera, a member of Saul's family. ⁶He threw stones at the king and the king's officers and all the mighty warriors

who surrounded them. [7]"Get out of here, you murderer, you scoundrel!" he shouted at David. [8]"The LORD is paying you back for murdering Saul and his family. You stole his throne, and now the LORD has given it to your son Absalom. At last you will taste some of your own medicine, you murderer!"

[9]"Why should this dead dog curse my lord the king?" Abishai son of Zeruiah demanded. "Let me go over and cut off his head!"

[10]"No!" the king said. "What am I going to do with you sons of Zeruiah! If the LORD has told him to curse me, who am I to stop him?" [11]Then David said to Abishai and the other officers, "My own son is trying to kill me. Shouldn't this relative of Saul* have even more reason to do so? Leave him alone and let him curse, for the LORD has told him to do it. [12]And perhaps the LORD will see that I am being wronged and will bless me because of these curses." [13]So David and his men continued on, and Shimei kept pace with them on a nearby hillside, cursing as he went and throwing stones at David and tossing dust into the air.

David ignored Shimei's hateful insults. Instead of fighting back, David prayed that God would see his suffering. Today there are many people like Shimei who wrongly insult and curse others. If you are insulted, remember that you can act like David. You don't have to pay back someone who insults you. God sees your suffering and will take care of you.

How should we respond to those who curse us?
Pray for the happiness of those who curse you. Pray for those who hurt you.
Luke 6:28

16:11 Hebrew *this Benjaminite.*

A P R I L

David's army killed Absalom. How did David respond?

2 SAMUEL 18:1-14, 33
Absalom's Death
David now appointed generals and captains to lead his troops. [2]One-third were placed under Joab, one-third under Joab's brother Abishai son of Zeruiah, and one-third under Ittai the Gittite. The king told his troops, "I am going out with you."

[3]But his men objected strongly. "You must not go," they urged. "If we have to turn and run—and even if half of us die—it will make no difference to Absalom's troops; they will be looking only for you. You are worth ten thousand of us, and it is better that you stay here in the city and send us help if we need it."

⁴"If you think that's the best plan, I'll do it," the king finally agreed. So he stood at the gate of the city as all the divisions of troops passed by. ⁵And the king gave this command to Joab, Abishai, and Ittai: "For my sake, deal gently with young Absalom." And all the troops heard the king give this order to his commanders.

⁶So the battle began in the forest of Ephraim, ⁷and the Israelite troops were beaten back by David's men. There was a great slaughter, and twenty thousand men laid down their lives that day. ⁸The battle raged all across the countryside, and more men died because of the forest than were killed by the sword.

⁹During the battle, Absalom came unexpectedly upon some of David's men. He tried to escape on his mule, but as he rode beneath the thick branches of a great oak, his head got caught. His mule kept going and left him dangling in the air. ¹⁰One of David's men saw what had happened and told Joab, "I saw Absalom dangling in a tree."

¹¹"What?" Joab demanded. "You saw him there and didn't kill him? I would have rewarded you with ten pieces of silver* and a hero's belt!"

¹²"I wouldn't do it for a thousand pieces of silver,*" the man replied. "We all heard the king say to you and Abishai and Ittai, 'For my sake, please don't harm young Absalom.' ¹³And if I had betrayed the king by killing his son—and the king would certainly find out who did it—you yourself would be the first to abandon me."

¹⁴"Enough of this nonsense," Joab said. Then he took three daggers and plunged them into Absalom's heart as he dangled from the oak still alive.

• • •

³³The king was overcome with emotion. He went up to his room over the gateway and burst into tears. And as he went, he cried, "O my son Absalom! My son, my son Absalom! If only I could have died instead of you! O Absalom, my son, my son."

Even though Absalom had wronged him, David loved his son and was saddened by his death. David had told his army not to hurt Absalom. But one commander disobeyed David's order. He killed Absalom because it made sense to kill David's enemies. Getting back at our enemies may seem to make perfect sense, but this choice does not please Jesus. He loved us when we were his enemies. We need to love those who are against us.

How should we treat those who wrong us?
But I say, love your enemies!* Pray for those who persecute you!
Matthew 5:44

18:11 Hebrew *10 shekels of silver,* about 4 ounces or 114 grams in weight. 18:12 Hebrew *1,000 shekels,* about 25 pounds or 11.4 kilograms in weight. 5:44 Some manuscripts add *Bless those who curse you, do good to those who hate you.*

APRIL

David sinned and God punished Israel for it. David realized that he had sinned and cried out to God for forgiveness. Did God have mercy on David?

2 SAMUEL 24:1-4, 10-25

David Counts His Soldiers

Once again the anger of the LORD burned against Israel, and he caused David to harm them by taking a census. "Go and count the people of Israel and Judah," the LORD told him.

²So the king said to Joab, the commander of his army, "Take a census of all the people in the land—from Dan in the north to Beersheba in the south—so that I may know how many people there are."

³But Joab replied to the king, "May the LORD your God let you live until there are a hundred times as many people in your kingdom as there are now! But why do you want to do this?"

⁴But the king insisted that they take the census, so Joab and his officers went out to count the people of Israel.

• • •

¹⁰But after he had taken the census, David's conscience began to bother him. And he said to the LORD, "I have sinned greatly and shouldn't have taken the census. Please forgive me, LORD, for doing this foolish thing."

¹¹The next morning the word of the LORD came to the prophet Gad, who was David's seer. This was the message: ¹²"Go and say to David, 'This is what the LORD says: I will give you three choices. Choose one of these punishments, and I will do it.' "

¹³So Gad came to David and asked him, "Will you choose three* years of famine throughout the land, three months of fleeing from your enemies, or three days of severe plague throughout your land? Think this over and let me know what answer to give the LORD."

¹⁴"This is a desperate situation!" David replied to Gad. "But let us fall into the hands of the LORD, for his mercy is great. Do not let me fall into human hands."

¹⁵So the LORD sent a plague upon Israel that morning, and it lasted for three days. Seventy thousand people died throughout the nation. ¹⁶But as the death angel was preparing to destroy Jerusalem, the LORD relented and said to the angel, "Stop! That is enough!" At that moment the angel of the LORD was by the threshing floor of Araunah the Jebusite.

¹⁷When David saw the angel, he said to the LORD, "I am the one who has sinned and done wrong! But these people are innocent—what have they done? Let your anger fall against me and my family."

¹⁸That day Gad came to David and

24:13 As in Greek version (see also 1 Chr 21:12); Hebrew reads *seven*.

said to him, "Go and build an altar to the LORD on the threshing floor of Araunah the Jebusite."

¹⁹So David went to do what the LORD had commanded him. ²⁰When Araunah saw the king and his men coming toward him, he came forward and bowed before the king with his face to the ground. ²¹"Why have you come, my lord?" Araunah asked.

And David replied, "I have come to buy your threshing floor and to build an altar to the LORD there, so that the LORD will stop the plague."

²²"Take it, my lord, and use it as you wish," Araunah said to David. "Here are oxen for the burnt offering, and you can use the threshing tools and ox yokes for wood to build a fire on the altar. ²³I will give it all to you, and may the LORD your God accept your sacrifice."

²⁴But the king replied to Araunah, "No, I insist on buying it, for I cannot present burnt offerings to the LORD my God that have cost me nothing." So David paid him fifty pieces of silver* for the threshing floor and the oxen. ²⁵David built an altar there to the LORD and offered burnt offerings and peace offerings. And the LORD answered his prayer, and the plague was stopped.

David sinned by trusting in his army rather than trusting in God. But David confessed his sin, and God sent a prophet to him. Through the prophet, God let David choose the punishment for his sin. David did not specifically choose one of the three options. But he did choose to have God punish him rather than men. His choice showed that he had renewed his trust and faith in God. As a result, God decided to show mercy to David by sparing Jerusalem from the plague. What sins do you need to confess to God? Make the wise choice of following David's example. Choose to confess your sins and trust God to discipline you out of love. His punishment is merciful.

What will Jesus do if we confess our sins?

Seeing their faith, Jesus said to the man, "Son, your sins are forgiven."
Luke 5:20

24:24 Hebrew *50 shekels of silver,* about 20 ounces or 570 grams in weight.

A P R I L

Adonijah made himself king. But he wasn't God's choice or David's choice. What did David do about this?

1 KINGS 1:16-20, 32-50
Solomon Is King

¹⁶Bathsheba bowed low before him.

"What can I do for you?" he asked her.

¹⁷She replied, "My lord, you vowed to me by the LORD your God that my son Solomon would be the next king and would sit on your throne. ¹⁸But instead, Adonijah has become the new king, and you do not even know about it. ¹⁹He has sacrificed many oxen, fattened calves, and sheep, and he has invited all your sons and Abiathar the priest and Joab, the commander of the army. But he did not invite your servant Solomon. ²⁰And now, my lord the king, all Israel is waiting for your decision as to who will become king after you."

• • •

³²Then King David ordered, "Call Zadok the priest, Nathan the prophet, and Benaiah son of Jehoiada." When they came into the king's presence, ³³the king said to them, "Take Solomon and my officers down to Gihon Spring. Solomon is to ride on my personal mule. ³⁴There Zadok the priest and Nathan the prophet are to anoint him king over Israel. Then blow the trumpets and shout, 'Long live King Solomon!' ³⁵When you bring him back here, he will sit on my throne. He will succeed me as king, for I have appointed him to be ruler over Israel and Judah."

³⁶"Amen!" Benaiah son of Jehoiada replied. "May the LORD, the God of my lord the king, decree it to be so. ³⁷And may the LORD be with Solomon as he has been with you, and may he make Solomon's reign even greater than yours!"

³⁸So Zadok the priest, Nathan the prophet, Benaiah son of Jehoiada, and the king's bodyguard* took Solomon down to Gihon Spring, and Solomon rode on King David's personal mule. ³⁹There Zadok the priest took a flask of olive oil from the sacred tent and poured it on Solomon's head. Then the trumpets were blown, and all the people shouted, "Long live King Solomon!" ⁴⁰And all the people returned with Solomon to Jerusalem, playing flutes and shouting for joy. The celebration was so joyous and noisy that the earth shook with the sound.

⁴¹Adonijah and his guests heard the celebrating and shouting just as they were finishing their banquet. When Joab heard the sound of trumpets, he asked, "What's going on? Why is the city in such an uproar?"

⁴²And while he was still speaking,

1:38 Hebrew *the Kerethites and Pelethites;* also in 1:44.

Jonathan son of Abiathar the priest arrived. "Come in," Adonijah said to him, "for you are a good man. You must have good news."

[43] "Not at all!" Jonathan replied. "Our lord King David has just declared Solomon king! [44] The king sent him down to Gihon Spring with Zadok the priest, Nathan the prophet, and Benaiah son of Jehoiada, protected by the king's bodyguard. They had him ride on the king's own mule, [45] and Zadok and Nathan have anointed him as the new king. They have just returned, and the whole city is celebrating and rejoicing. That's what all the noise is about. [46] Moreover, Solomon is now sitting on the royal throne as king. [47] All the royal officials went to King David and congratulated him, saying, 'May your God make Solomon's fame even greater than your own, and may Solomon's kingdom be even greater than yours!' Then the king bowed his head in worship as he lay in his bed, [48] and he spoke these words: 'Blessed be the LORD, the God of Israel, who today has chosen someone to sit on my throne while I am still alive to see it.' "

[49] Then all of Adonijah's guests jumped up in panic from the banquet table and quickly went their separate ways. [50] Adonijah himself was afraid of Solomon, so he rushed to the sacred tent and caught hold of the horns of the altar.

Adonijah was wrong to make himself king. He did not have the authority to do that. Only David had the authority on earth to appoint the next king. When David found out what Adonijah had done, he had Zadok anoint Solomon as Israel's next king. Just like Adonijah, many people today want power and authority. But it is wrong to take what is not ours. If you want authority, then work to earn it. Also, ask God if he wants you to be a leader of some kind. But in the meantime, choose to respect those in authority over you.

How are we to respond to those in authority over us?

Obey the government, for God is the one who put it there. All governments have been placed in power by God.
Romans 13:1

A P R I L

Solomon had a wonderful dream. In it God asked Solomon what he wanted. Why did Solomon ask for wisdom?

1 KINGS 3:5-14
Solomon Asks for Wisdom

⁵That night the LORD appeared to Solomon in a dream, and God said, "What do you want? Ask, and I will give it to you!"

⁶Solomon replied, "You were wonderfully kind to my father, David, because he was honest and true and faithful to you. And you have continued this great kindness to him today by giving him a son to succeed him. ⁷O LORD my God, now you have made me king instead of my father, David, but I am like a little child who doesn't know his way around. ⁸And here I am among your own chosen people, a nation so great they are too numerous to count! ⁹Give me an understanding mind so that I can govern your people well and know the difference between right and wrong. For who by himself is able to govern this great nation of yours?"

¹⁰The Lord was pleased with Solomon's reply and was glad that he had asked for wisdom. ¹¹So God replied, "Because you have asked for wisdom in governing my people and have not asked for a long life or riches for yourself or the death of your enemies—¹²I will give you what you asked for! I will give you a wise and understanding mind such as no one else has ever had or ever will have! ¹³And I will also give you what you did not ask for—riches and honor! No other king in all the world will be compared to you for the rest of your life! ¹⁴And if you follow me and obey my commands as your father, David, did, I will give you a long life."

Solomon could have had anything he wanted. God told him to ask and he would get it. He could have chosen riches, long life, or the death of his enemies. But he asked God for wisdom instead. God does not come to us today and ask us what we want. But we, like Solomon, can ask God for wisdom. He loves to grant this request.

How can you be wise?
If you need wisdom—if you want to know what God wants you to do—ask him, and he will gladly tell you. He will not resent your asking.
James 1:5

APRIL

Solomon had to settle a difficult case between two women. How did he do it?

1 KINGS 3:16-28
Two Women and a Baby

[16]Some time later, two prostitutes came to the king to have an argument settled. [17]"Please, my lord," one of them began, "this woman and I live in the same house. I gave birth to a baby while she was with me in the house. [18]Three days later, she also had a baby. We were alone; there were only two of us in the house. [19]But her baby died during the night when she rolled over on it. [20]Then she got up in the night and took my son from beside me while I was asleep. She laid her dead child in my arms and took mine to sleep beside her. [21]And in the morning when I tried to nurse my son, he was dead! But when I looked more closely in the morning light, I saw that it wasn't my son at all."

[22]Then the other woman interrupted, "It certainly was your son, and the living child is mine."

"No," the first woman said, "the dead one is yours, and the living one is mine." And so they argued back and forth before the king.

[23]Then the king said, "Let's get the facts straight. Both of you claim the living child is yours, and each says that the dead child belongs to the other. [24]All right, bring me a sword." So a sword was brought to the king. [25]Then he said, "Cut the living child in two and give half to each of these women!"

[26]Then the woman who really was the mother of the living child, and who loved him very much, cried out, "Oh no, my lord! Give her the child— please do not kill him!"

But the other woman said, "All right, he will be neither yours nor mine; divide him between us!"

[27]Then the king said, "Do not kill him, but give the baby to the woman who wants him to live, for she is his mother!"

[28]Word of the king's decision spread quickly throughout all Israel, and the people were awed as they realized the great wisdom God had given him to render decisions with justice.

One of the women was lying. But Solomon didn't have any evidence to prove either woman's claim to the baby. So he asked for a sword to divide the baby. By doing so, Solomon was able to find out who the real mother was. No one can hide a lie for long. Eventually lies are uncovered, and liars are embarrassed. You don't have to experience the uncomfortable feelings that come with lying. If you always tell the truth, you will never experience embarrassment from being caught in a lie.

If you are a Christian, why shouldn't you lie?
Don't lie to each other, for you have stripped off your old evil nature and all its wicked deeds.
Colossians 3:9

A P R I L

The queen of Sheba heard of Solomon's wisdom and went to test him.
What did she find?

1 KINGS 10:1-13

A Queen's Visit

When the queen of Sheba heard of Solomon's reputation, which brought honor to the name of the LORD, she came to test him with hard questions. ²She arrived in Jerusalem with a large group of attendants and a great caravan of camels loaded with spices, huge quantities of gold, and precious jewels. When she met with Solomon, they talked about everything she had on her mind. ³Solomon answered all her questions; nothing was too hard for the king to explain to her. ⁴When the queen of Sheba realized how wise Solomon was, and when she saw the palace he had built, ⁵she was breathless. She was also amazed at the food on his tables, the organization of his officials and their splendid clothing, the cup-bearers and their robes, and the burnt offerings Solomon made at the Temple of the LORD.

⁶She exclaimed to the king, "Everything I heard in my country about your achievements and wisdom is true! ⁷I didn't believe it until I arrived here and saw it with my own eyes. Truly I had not heard the half of it! Your wisdom and prosperity are far greater than what I was told. ⁸How happy these people must be! What a privilege for your officials to stand here day after day, listening to your wisdom! ⁹The LORD your God is great indeed! He delights in you and has placed you on the throne of Israel. Because the LORD loves Israel with an eternal love, he has made you king so you can rule with justice and righteousness."

¹⁰Then she gave the king a gift of nine thousand pounds* of gold, and

The queen of Sheba was amazed at Solomon's wisdom. She concluded that God had blessed Solomon, and she praised God for his greatness. The wisdom that God gives is greater than any wisdom we can get from people or books. His wisdom amazes people and helps people live godly lives. What is wisdom? Wisdom is the ability to make good decisions in all situations. If you need wisdom, ask God. He gives his wisdom freely to those who love and serve him.

What is God's wisdom like?

But the wisdom that comes from heaven is first of all pure. It is also peace loving, gentle at all times, and willing to yield to others. It is full of mercy and good deeds. It shows no partiality and is always sincere.
James 3:17

10:10 Hebrew *120 talents* [4 metric tons].

great quantities of spices and precious jewels. Never again were so many spices brought in as those the queen of Sheba gave to Solomon.

¹¹(When Hiram's ships brought gold from Ophir, they also brought rich cargoes of almug wood and precious jewels. ¹²The king used the almug wood to make railings for the Temple of the LORD and the royal palace, and to construct harps and lyres for the musicians. Never before or since has there been such a supply of beautiful almug wood.)

¹³King Solomon gave the queen of Sheba whatever she asked for, besides all the other customary gifts he had so generously given. Then she and all her attendants left and returned to their own land.

A P R I L

Rehoboam was a young king with a hard choice to make. Whose advice did he follow?

1 KINGS 12:4-19

Good and Bad Advice

⁴"Your father was a hard master," they said. "Lighten the harsh labor demands and heavy taxes that your father imposed on us. Then we will be your loyal subjects."

⁵Rehoboam replied, "Give me three days to think this over. Then come back for my answer." So the people went away.

⁶Then King Rehoboam went to discuss the matter with the older men who had counseled his father, Solomon. "What is your advice?" he asked. "How should I answer these people?"

⁷The older counselors replied, "If you are willing to serve the people today and give them a favorable answer, they will always be your loyal subjects."

⁸But Rehoboam rejected the advice of the elders and instead asked the opinion of the young men who had grown up with him and who were now his advisers. ⁹"What is your advice?" he asked them. "How should I answer these people who want me to lighten the burdens imposed by my father?"

¹⁰The young men replied, "This is what you should tell those complainers: 'My little finger is thicker than my father's waist—if you think he was hard on you, just wait and see what I'll be like! ¹¹Yes, my father was harsh on you, but I'll be even harsher! My father used whips on you, but I'll use scorpions!' "

¹²Three days later, Jeroboam and all the people returned to hear Rehoboam's decision, just as the king had requested. ¹³But Rehoboam spoke harshly to them, for he rejected the advice of the older counselors ¹⁴and followed the counsel of his younger advisers. He told the people, "My

father was harsh on you, but I'll be even harsher! My father used whips on you, but I'll use scorpions!" ¹⁵So the king paid no attention to the people's demands. This turn of events was the will of the LORD, for it fulfilled the LORD's message to Jeroboam son of Nebat through the prophet Ahijah from Shiloh.

¹⁶When all Israel realized that the king had rejected their request, they shouted, "Down with David and his dynasty! We have no share in Jesse's son! Let's go home, Israel! Look out for your own house, O David!" So the people of Israel returned home. ¹⁷But Rehoboam continued to rule over the Israelites who lived in the towns of Judah.

¹⁸King Rehoboam sent Adoniram,* who was in charge of the labor force, to restore order, but all Israel stoned him to death. When this news reached King Rehoboam, he quickly jumped into his chariot and fled to Jerusalem.

¹⁹The northern tribes of Israel have refused to be ruled by a descendant of David to this day.

Rehoboam had to decide how he would treat his subjects. He asked for advice from his father's counselors. But he did not take it. Instead, he listened to his friends, who gave him bad advice. In the end, he lost most of his kingdom. If we act like Rehoboam and do not listen to older people's advice, we only hurt ourselves. Older people have more experience than we do. They can help us make good decisions.

How should we treat older people?
You younger men, accept the authority of the elders. And all of you, serve each other in humility, for "God sets himself against the proud, but he shows favor to the humble."*
1 Peter 5:5

12:18 As in some Greek manuscripts and Syriac version (see also 4:6; 5:14); Hebrew reads *Adoram*. **5:5** Prov 3:34.

A P R I L

It didn't rain in Israel for a few years, and Israel was running out of food. How did God provide food for Elijah?

1 KINGS 17:1-16
Ravens Feed Elijah
Now Elijah, who was from Tishbe in Gilead, told King Ahab, "As surely as the LORD, the God of Israel, lives— the God whom I worship and serve— there will be no dew or rain during the next few years unless I give the word!"

²Then the LORD said to Elijah, ³"Go to the east and hide by Kerith Brook at a place east of where it enters the Jordan River. ⁴Drink from the brook and eat what the ravens bring you, for I

have commanded them to bring you food."

⁵So Elijah did as the LORD had told him and camped beside Kerith Brook. ⁶The ravens brought him bread and meat each morning and evening, and he drank from the brook. ⁷But after a while the brook dried up, for there was no rainfall anywhere in the land.

⁸Then the LORD said to Elijah, ⁹"Go and live in the village of Zarephath, near the city of Sidon. There is a widow there who will feed you. I have given her my instructions."

¹⁰So he went to Zarephath. As he arrived at the gates of the village, he saw a widow gathering sticks, and he asked her, "Would you please bring me a cup of water?" ¹¹As she was going to get it, he called to her, "Bring me a bite of bread, too."

¹²But she said, "I swear by the LORD your God that I don't have a single piece of bread in the house. And I have only a handful of flour left in the jar and a little cooking oil in the bottom of the jug. I was just gathering a few sticks to cook this last meal, and then my son and I will die."

¹³But Elijah said to her, "Don't be afraid! Go ahead and cook that 'last meal,' but bake me a little loaf of bread first. Afterward there will still be enough food for you and your son. ¹⁴For this is what the LORD, the God of Israel, says: There will always be plenty of flour and oil left in your containers until the time when the LORD sends rain and the crops grow again!"

¹⁵So she did as Elijah said, and she and Elijah and her son continued to eat from her supply of flour and oil for many days. ¹⁶For no matter how much they used, there was always enough left in the containers, just as the LORD had promised through Elijah.

God provided food for Elijah through ravens and a widow. While Elijah lived by a brook, ravens brought bread and meat to him twice a day. When the brook dried up, God told Elijah to go to a certain village. There a widow gave him food. God did not let Elijah starve. He provided for Elijah's needs daily. Today, God continues to show his love to his followers by caring for them. If you love God, trust him to provide for your needs. He will take care of you.

Why shouldn't we worry about what we will eat?

And don't worry about food—what to eat and drink. Don't worry whether God will provide it for you. . . . He will give you all you need from day to day if you make the Kingdom of God your primary concern.
Luke 12:29, 31

A P R I L

Elijah challenged the Israelites to follow God. How did God prove himself to them?

1 KINGS 18:20-39
The Fire of God

²⁰So Ahab summoned all the people and the prophets to Mount Carmel. ²¹Then Elijah stood in front of them and said, "How long are you going to waver between two opinions? If the LORD is God, follow him! But if Baal is God, then follow him!" But the people were completely silent.

²²Then Elijah said to them, "I am the only prophet of the LORD who is left, but Baal has 450 prophets. ²³Now bring two bulls. The prophets of Baal may choose whichever one they wish and cut it into pieces and lay it on the wood of their altar, but without setting fire to it. I will prepare the other bull and lay it on the wood on the altar, but not set fire to it. ²⁴Then call on the name of your god, and I will call on the name of the LORD. The god who answers by setting fire to the wood is the true God!" And all the people agreed.

²⁵Then Elijah said to the prophets of Baal, "You go first, for there are many of you. Choose one of the bulls and prepare it and call on the name of your god. But do not set fire to the wood."

²⁶So they prepared one of the bulls and placed it on the altar. Then they called on the name of Baal all morning, shouting, "O Baal, answer us!" But there was no reply of any kind.

Then they danced wildly around the altar they had made.

²⁷About noontime Elijah began mocking them. "You'll have to shout louder," he scoffed, "for surely he is a god! Perhaps he is deep in thought, or he is relieving himself. Or maybe he is away on a trip, or he is asleep and needs to be wakened!"

²⁸So they shouted louder, and following their normal custom, they cut themselves with knives and swords until the blood gushed out. ²⁹They raved all afternoon until the time of the evening sacrifice, but still there was no reply, no voice, no answer.

³⁰Then Elijah called to the people, "Come over here!" They all crowded around him as he repaired the altar of the LORD that had been torn down. ³¹He took twelve stones, one to represent each of the tribes of Israel,* ³²and he used the stones to rebuild the LORD's altar. Then he dug a trench around the altar large enough to hold about three gallons.* ³³He piled wood on the altar, cut the bull into pieces, and laid the pieces on the wood. Then he said, "Fill four large jars with water, and pour the water over the offering and the wood." After they had done this, ³⁴he said, "Do the same thing again!" And when they were finished, he said, "Now do it a third time!" So they did as he said,

18:31 Hebrew *each of the tribes of the sons of Jacob to whom the LORD had said, "Your name will be Israel."* 18:32 Hebrew *2 seahs* [12 liters] *of seed.*

³⁵and the water ran around the altar and even overflowed the trench.

³⁶At the customary time for offering the evening sacrifice, Elijah the prophet walked up to the altar and prayed, "O LORD, God of Abraham, Isaac, and Jacob,* prove today that you are God in Israel and that I am your servant. Prove that I have done all this at your command. ³⁷O LORD, answer me! Answer me so these people will know that you, O LORD, are God and that you have brought them back to yourself."

³⁸Immediately the fire of the LORD flashed down from heaven and burned up the young bull, the wood, the stones, and the dust. It even licked up all the water in the ditch! ³⁹And when the people saw it, they fell on their faces and cried out, "The LORD is God! The LORD is God!"

18:36 Hebrew *and Israel.*

God sent fire from heaven that burned up the altar and the bull. The altar of the false god Baal remained untouched. God proved to the Israelites that he is the only living God. Elijah's challenge to follow the living God is still valid for us today. What keeps you from completely following God? God does not want halfhearted followers. Choose to serve God completely.

Why is it hard to serve God and something else at the same time?
No one can serve two masters. For you will hate one and love the other, or be devoted to one and despise the other. You cannot serve both God and money.
Matthew 6:24

APRIL

Jezebel wanted to kill Elijah. He found out about it and fled for his life. What did Elijah pray to God?

1 KINGS 19:1-9

An Angel Feeds Elijah

When Ahab got home, he told Jezebel what Elijah had done and that he had slaughtered the prophets of Baal. ²So Jezebel sent this message to Elijah: "May the gods also kill me if by this time tomorrow I have failed to take your life like those whom you killed."

³Elijah was afraid and fled for his life. He went to Beersheba, a town in Judah, and he left his servant there. ⁴Then he went on alone into the desert, traveling all day. He sat down under a solitary broom tree and prayed that he might die. "I have had enough, LORD," he said. "Take my life, for I am no better than my ancestors."

⁵Then he lay down and slept under the broom tree. But as he was sleeping, an angel touched him and told him, "Get up and eat!" ⁶He looked around

and saw some bread baked on hot stones and a jar of water! So he ate and drank and lay down again.

⁷Then the angel of the LORD came again and touched him and said, "Get up and eat some more, for there is a long journey ahead of you."

⁸So he got up and ate and drank, and the food gave him enough strength to travel forty days and forty nights to Mount Sinai,* the mountain of God. ⁹There he came to a cave, where he spent the night.

Elijah felt like quitting, and he prayed that he might die. But God helped Elijah. He sent an angel to feed him. He also allowed Elijah to rest before continuing his long journey. When do you feel like quitting? Giving up is easy to do when we are tired and face difficulties. But God can encourage us in these times. He has promised to be with us and to never leave us. The next time you feel like quitting, look to God for strength and encouragement. He will be there for you.

Who helps us when we feel like giving up?

For I can do everything with the help of Christ who gives me the strength I need.
Philippians 4:13

19:8 Hebrew *Horeb*, another name for Sinai.

A P R I L

Elijah met with the Lord at Mount Sinai. What did the Lord tell him?

1 KINGS 19:9-18
In a Whisper
⁹But the LORD said to him, "What are you doing here, Elijah?"

¹⁰Elijah replied, "I have zealously served the LORD God Almighty. But the people of Israel have broken their covenant with you, torn down your altars, and killed every one of your prophets. I alone am left, and now they are trying to kill me, too."

¹¹"Go out and stand before me on the mountain," the LORD told him. And as Elijah stood there, the LORD passed by, and a mighty windstorm hit the mountain. It was such a terrible blast that the rocks were torn loose, but the LORD was not in the wind. After the wind there was an earthquake, but the LORD was not in the earthquake. ¹²And after the earthquake there was a fire, but the LORD was not

in the fire. And after the fire there was the sound of a gentle whisper. [13]When Elijah heard it, he wrapped his face in his cloak and went out and stood at the entrance of the cave.

And a voice said, "What are you doing here, Elijah?"

[14]He replied again, "I have zealously served the LORD God Almighty. But the people of Israel have broken their covenant with you, torn down your altars, and killed every one of your prophets. I alone am left, and now they are trying to kill me, too."

[15]Then the LORD told him, "Go back the way you came, and travel to the wilderness of Damascus. When you arrive there, anoint Hazael to be king of Aram. [16]Then anoint Jehu son of Nimshi to be king of Israel, and anoint Elisha son of Shaphat from Abel-me-holah to replace you as my prophet. [17]Anyone who escapes from Hazael will be killed by Jehu, and those who escape Jehu will be killed by Elisha! [18]Yet I will preserve seven thousand others in Israel who have never bowed to Baal or kissed him!"

Elijah was asleep in a cave when the Lord spoke to him. The Lord told Elijah to go out and stand before him. Outside the cave, Elijah witnessed the Lord's power in a windstorm, earthquake, and fire. But the Lord did not speak to Elijah in any of these. Instead, he spoke to Elijah in a whisper. Perhaps God displayed his power to show Elijah that he did not need to fear Jezebel, the queen who was going to kill him. For in a gentle whisper the Lord told Elijah to go back. There may be times when we are scared of those who threaten us. But if we trust God, we don't need to be afraid. With God's help, we can face our fears and defeat them.

Why don't we need to worry when others threaten us?

Now, who will want to harm you if you are eager to do good? But even if you suffer for doing what is right, God will reward you for it. So don't be afraid and don't worry.
1 Peter 3:13-14

A P R I L

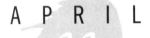

King Ahab wanted Naboth's vineyard. But Naboth would not give it to him. Did Ahab get the vineyard?

1 KINGS 21:1-19
Naboth's Vineyard
King Ahab had a palace in Jezreel, and near the palace was a vineyard owned by a man named Naboth. [2]One day Ahab said to Naboth, "Since your vineyard is so convenient to the palace, I would like to buy it to use as a vegetable garden. I will give you a better vineyard in exchange, or if you prefer, I will pay you for it."

[3]But Naboth replied, "The LORD

forbid that I should give you the inheritance that was passed down by my ancestors." ⁴So Ahab went home angry and sullen because of Naboth's answer. The king went to bed with his face to the wall and refused to eat!

⁵"What in the world is the matter?" his wife, Jezebel, asked him. "What has made you so upset that you are not eating?"

⁶"I asked Naboth to sell me his vineyard or to trade it, and he refused!" Ahab told her.

⁷"Are you the king of Israel or not?" Jezebel asked. "Get up and eat and don't worry about it. I'll get you Naboth's vineyard!"

⁸So she wrote letters in Ahab's name, sealed them with his seal, and sent them to the elders and other leaders of the city where Naboth lived. ⁹In her letters she commanded: "Call the citizens together for fasting and prayer and give Naboth a place of honor. ¹⁰Find two scoundrels* who will accuse him of cursing God and the king. Then take him out and stone him to death."

¹¹So the elders and other leaders followed the instructions Jezebel had written in the letters. ¹²They called for a fast and put Naboth at a prominent place before the people. ¹³Then two scoundrels accused him before all the people of cursing God and the king. So he was dragged outside the city and stoned to death. ¹⁴The city officials then sent word to Jezebel, "Naboth has been stoned to death."

¹⁵When Jezebel heard the news, she said to Ahab, "You know the vineyard Naboth wouldn't sell you? Well, you can have it now! He's dead!" ¹⁶So

Ahab immediately went down to the vineyard to claim it.

¹⁷But the LORD said to Elijah, who was from Tishbe, ¹⁸"Go down to meet King Ahab, who rules in Samaria. He will be at Naboth's vineyard in Jezreel, taking possession of it. ¹⁹Give him this message: 'This is what the LORD says: Isn't killing Naboth bad enough? Must you rob him, too? Because you have done this, dogs will lick your blood outside the city just as they licked the blood of Naboth!' "

Ahab got the vineyard, but Naboth didn't give it to him. Jezebel, Ahab's wife, had Naboth killed so Ahab could take the vineyard. Although Jezebel did the dirty work, Ahab shouldn't have pouted when he didn't get what he wanted. Instead, he should have accepted Naboth's response and moved on. How do you respond when you don't get something you want? We all desire something. But we can't let our desires control us. To be free of their control, we can commit our desires to God. He will keep us free from sin.

What are the wrong way and the right way to get something you want?

You want what you don't have, so you scheme and kill to get it. You are jealous for what others have, and you can't possess it, so you fight and quarrel to take it away from them. And yet the reason you don't have what you want is that you don't ask God for it.
James 4:2

21:10 Hebrew *two sons of Belial*; also in 21:13.

A P R I L

Before Elijah went to heaven, Elisha asked him for one big favor.
What did Elisha ask for?

2 KINGS 2:1-15

Fiery Chariots

When the LORD was about to take Elijah up to heaven in a whirlwind, Elijah and Elisha were traveling from Gilgal. ²And Elijah said to Elisha, "Stay here, for the LORD has told me to go to Bethel."

But Elisha replied, "As surely as the LORD lives and you yourself live, I will never leave you!" So they went on together to Bethel.

³The group of prophets from Bethel came to Elisha and asked him, "Did you know that the LORD is going to take your master away from you today?"

"Quiet!" Elisha answered. "Of course I know it."

⁴Then Elijah said to Elisha, "Stay here, for the LORD has told me to go to Jericho."

But Elisha replied again, "As surely as the LORD lives and you yourself live, I will never leave you." So they went on together to Jericho.

⁵Then the group of prophets from Jericho came to Elisha and asked him, "Did you know that the LORD is going to take your master away from you today?"

"Quiet!" he answered again. "Of course I know it."

⁶Then Elijah said to Elisha, "Stay here, for the LORD has told me to go to the Jordan River."

But again Elisha replied, "As surely as the LORD lives and you yourself live, I will never leave you." So they went on together.

⁷Fifty men from the group of prophets also went and watched from a distance as Elijah and Elisha stopped beside the Jordan River. ⁸Then Elijah folded his cloak together and struck the water with it. The river divided, and the two of them went across on dry ground!

⁹When they came to the other side, Elijah said to Elisha, "What can I do for you before I am taken away?"

And Elisha replied, "Please let me become your rightful successor."*

¹⁰"You have asked a difficult thing," Elijah replied. "If you see me when I am taken from you, then you will get your request. But if not, then you won't."

¹¹As they were walking along and talking, suddenly a chariot of fire appeared, drawn by horses of fire. It drove between them, separating them, and Elijah was carried by a whirlwind into heaven. ¹²Elisha saw it and cried out, "My father! My father! The chariots and charioteers of Israel!" And as they disappeared from sight, Elisha tore his robe in two.

2:9 Hebrew *Let me inherit a double share of your spirit.*

144

¹³Then Elisha picked up Elijah's cloak and returned to the bank of the Jordan River. ¹⁴He struck the water with the cloak and cried out, "Where is the LORD, the God of Elijah?" Then the river divided, and Elisha went across.

¹⁵When the group of prophets from Jericho saw what happened, they exclaimed, "Elisha has become Elijah's successor!"* And they went to meet him and bowed down before him.

Elisha asked to become Elijah's successor. This meant that he wanted to be the next prophet of Israel. He wanted to be filled with God's Spirit. Elisha's request was a difficult one to grant. But he did what Elijah told him, and Elisha was filled with God's Spirit. Today, God freely gives his Spirit to those who believe in Jesus. If you're a Christian, ask God to fill you with his Spirit.

To whom does God give his Spirit?
And because you Gentiles
have become his children,
God has sent the Spirit of his Son
into your hearts, and now you can
call God your dear Father.*
Galatians 4:6

2:15 Hebrew *The spirit of Elijah rests upon Elisha.* **4:6** Greek *into your hearts, crying, "Abba, Father." Abba* is an Aramaic term for "father."

A P R I L

A widow couldn't pay her bills. How did God provide for her?

2 KINGS 4:1-7
The Widow's Oil

One day the widow of one of Elisha's fellow prophets came to Elisha and cried out to him, "My husband who served you is dead, and you know how he feared the LORD. But now a creditor has come, threatening to take my two sons as slaves."

²"What can I do to help you?" Elisha asked. "Tell me, what do you have in the house?"

"Nothing at all, except a flask of olive oil," she replied.

³And Elisha said, "Borrow as many empty jars as you can from your friends and neighbors. ⁴Then go into your house with your sons and shut the door behind you. Pour olive oil from your flask into the jars, setting the jars aside as they are filled."

⁵So she did as she was told. Her sons brought many jars to her, and she

filled one after another. ⁶Soon every container was full to the brim!

"Bring me another jar," she said to one of her sons.

"There aren't any more!" he told her. And then the olive oil stopped flowing.

⁷When she told the man of God what had happened, he said to her, "Now sell the olive oil and pay your debts, and there will be enough money left over to support you and your sons."

God multiplied the widow's flask of olive oil. She was able to fill many jars with oil and sell it to pay her bills. God knew the needs of that widow, and he knows your needs, too. He is loving and generous and will provide everything you need.

Why does God provide for our needs?

Look at the birds. They don't need to plant or harvest or put food in barns because your heavenly Father feeds them. And you are far more valuable to him than they are.

Matthew 6:26

A P R I L

Naaman had leprosy. He went to Elisha to be healed. What did Elisha tell Naaman to do?

2 KINGS 5:1-14

The Healing of Naaman

The king of Aram had high admiration for Naaman, the commander of his army, because through him the LORD had given Aram great victories. But though Naaman was a mighty warrior, he suffered from leprosy.*

²Now groups of Aramean raiders had invaded the land of Israel, and among their captives was a young girl who had been given to Naaman's wife as a maid. ³One day the girl said to her mistress, "I wish my master would go to see the prophet in Samaria. He would heal him of his leprosy."

⁴So Naaman told the king what the young girl from Israel had said. ⁵"Go and visit the prophet," the king told him. "I will send a letter of introduction for you to carry to the king of Israel." So Naaman started out, taking as gifts 750 pounds of silver, 150 pounds of gold,* and ten sets of clothing. ⁶The letter to the king of Israel said: "With this letter I present my servant Naaman. I want you to heal him of his leprosy."

5:1 Or *from a contagious skin disease.* The Hebrew word used here and throughout this passage can describe various skin diseases.
5:5 Hebrew *10 talents* [340 kilograms] *of silver, 6,000 shekels* [68 kilograms] *of gold.*

[7]When the king of Israel read it, he tore his clothes in dismay and said, "This man sends me a leper to heal! Am I God, that I can kill and give life? He is only trying to find an excuse to invade us again."

[8]But when Elisha, the man of God, heard about the king's reaction, he sent this message to him: "Why are you so upset? Send Naaman to me, and he will learn that there is a true prophet here in Israel."

[9]So Naaman went with his horses and chariots and waited at the door of Elisha's house. [10]But Elisha sent a messenger out to him with this message: "Go and wash yourself seven times in the Jordan River. Then your skin will be restored, and you will be healed of leprosy."

[11]But Naaman became angry and stalked away. "I thought he would surely come out to meet me!" he said. "I expected him to wave his hand over the leprosy and call on the name of the LORD his God and heal me! [12]Aren't the Abana River and Pharpar River of Damascus better than all the rivers of Israel put together? Why shouldn't I wash in them and be healed?" So Naaman turned and went away in a rage.

[13]But his officers tried to reason with him and said, "Sir, if the prophet had told you to do some great thing, wouldn't you have done it? So you should certainly obey him when he says simply to go and wash and be cured!" [14]So Naaman went down to the Jordan River and dipped himself seven times, as the man of God had instructed him. And his flesh became as healthy as a young child's, and he was healed!

Elisha told Naaman to wash himself seven times in the Jordan River. At first Naaman didn't want to do this. He was full of pride and thought that washing himself in the Jordan was beneath him. But his officers convinced him to do what Elisha had said. When Naaman obeyed, he was healed. Obedience isn't always fun. But obeying, even when we don't want to, can bring blessing.

What does Jesus promise to do for those who obey him?

Those who obey my commandments are the ones who love me. And because they love me, my Father will love them, and I will love them. And I will reveal myself to each one of them.

John 14:21

Athaliah tried to kill all her grandchildren. What happened to her grandson Joash?

2 KINGS 11:1-8, 12-21

A Seven-Year-Old King

When Athaliah, the mother of King Ahaziah of Judah, learned that her son was dead, she set out to destroy the rest of the royal family. ²But Ahaziah's sister Jehosheba, the daughter of King Jehoram,* took Ahaziah's infant son, Joash, and stole him away from among the rest of the king's children, who were about to be killed. Jehosheba put Joash and his nurse in a bedroom to hide him from Athaliah, so the child was not murdered. ³Joash and his nurse remained hidden in the Temple of the LORD for six years while Athaliah ruled over the land.

⁴In the seventh year of Athaliah's reign, Jehoiada the priest summoned the commanders, the Carite mercenaries, and the guards to come to the Temple of the LORD. He made a pact with them and made them swear an oath of loyalty there in the LORD's Temple; then he showed them the king's son.

⁵Jehoiada told them, "This is what you must do. A third of you who are on duty on the Sabbath are to guard the royal palace itself. ⁶Another third of you are to stand guard at the Sur Gate. And the final third must stand guard behind the palace guard. These three groups will all guard the palace.

⁷The other two units who are off duty on the Sabbath must stand guard for the king at the LORD's Temple. ⁸Form a bodyguard for the king and keep your weapons in hand. Any unauthorized person who approaches you must be killed. Stay right beside the king at all times."

• • •

¹²Then Jehoiada brought out Joash, the king's son, and placed the crown on his head. He presented Joash with a copy of God's covenant and proclaimed him king. They anointed him, and all the people clapped their hands and shouted, "Long live the king!"

¹³When Athaliah heard all the noise made by the guards and the people, she hurried to the LORD's Temple to see what was happening. ¹⁴And she saw the newly crowned king standing in his place of authority by the pillar, as was the custom at times of coronation. The officers and trumpeters were surrounding him, and people from all over the land were rejoicing and blowing trumpets. When Athaliah saw all this, she tore her clothes in despair and shouted, "Treason! Treason!"

¹⁵Then Jehoiada the priest ordered the commanders who were in charge of the troops, "Take her out of the Temple, and kill anyone who tries to

11:2 Hebrew *Joram*, a variant name for Jehoram.

rescue her. Do not kill her here in the Temple of the LORD." ¹⁶So they seized her and led her out to the gate where horses enter the palace grounds, and she was killed there.

¹⁷Then Jehoiada made a covenant between the LORD and the king and the people that they would be the LORD's people. He also made a covenant between the king and the people. ¹⁸And all the people of the land went over to the temple of Baal and tore it down. They demolished the altars and smashed the idols to pieces, and they killed Mattan the priest of Baal in front of the altars.

Jehoiada the priest stationed guards at the Temple of the LORD. ¹⁹Then the commanders, the Carite mercenaries, the guards, and all the people of the land escorted the king from the Temple of the LORD. They went through the gate of the guards and into the palace, and the king took his seat on the royal throne. ²⁰So all the people of the land rejoiced, and the city was peaceful because Athaliah had been killed at the king's palace.

²¹Joash* was seven years old when he became king.

11:21 Hebrew *Jehoash*, a variant name for Joash.

Athaliah wanted to rule Judah. When her son, the king, died, she tried to kill all the rightful successors to the throne. But God used a few people to protect Joash, one of the king's sons. Years later Athaliah was removed from the throne, and Joash was made king. Unlike Joash, we may never have to hide from a killer. But there may be many times when we are in some kind of danger. In those times we can trust God to protect us.

Who does God protect us from?
I'm not asking you to take them out of the world, but to keep them safe from the evil one.
John 17:15

A P R I L

27

God's Word was lost. But Hilkiah, the high priest, found it.
How did King Josiah react?

2 CHRONICLES 34:14-33
Lost and Found

¹⁴As Hilkiah the high priest was recording the money collected at the LORD's Temple, he found the Book of the Law of the LORD as it had been given through Moses. ¹⁵Hilkiah said to Shaphan the court secretary, "I have found the Book of the Law in the LORD's Temple!" Then Hilkiah gave the scroll to Shaphan.

¹⁶Shaphan took the scroll to the king and reported, "Your officials are doing everything they were assigned

to do. [17]The money that was collected at the Temple of the LORD has been given to the supervisors and workmen." [18]Shaphan also said to the king, "Hilkiah the priest has given me a scroll." So Shaphan read it to the king.

[19]When the king heard what was written in the law, he tore his clothes in despair. [20]Then he gave these orders to Hilkiah, Ahikam son of Shaphan, Acbor son of Micaiah,* Shaphan the court secretary, and Asaiah the king's personal adviser: [21]"Go to the Temple and speak to the LORD for me and for all the remnant of Israel and Judah. Ask him about the words written in this scroll that has been found. The LORD's anger has been poured out against us because our ancestors have not obeyed the word of the LORD. We have not been doing what this scroll says we must do."

[22]So Hilkiah and the other men went to the newer Mishneh section* of Jerusalem to consult with the prophet Huldah. She was the wife of Shallum son of Tikvah and grandson of Harhas,* the keeper of the Temple wardrobe. [23]She said to them, "The LORD, the God of Israel, has spoken! Go and tell the man who sent you, [24]'This is what the LORD says: I will certainly destroy this city and its people. All the curses written in the scroll you have read will come true. [25]For the people of Judah have abandoned me and worshiped pagan gods, and I am very angry with them for everything they have done. My anger will be poured out against this place, and nothing will be able to stop it.'

[26]"But go to the king of Judah who sent you to seek the LORD and tell him: 'This is what the LORD, the God of Israel, says concerning the message you have just heard: [27]You were sorry and humbled yourself before God when you heard what I said against this city and its people. You humbled yourself and tore your clothing in despair and wept before me in repentance. So I have indeed heard you, says the LORD. [28]I will not send the promised disaster against this city and its people until after you have died and been buried in peace. You will not see the disaster I am going to bring on this place.' " So they took her message back to the king.

[29]Then the king summoned all the leaders of Judah and Jerusalem. [30]And

King Josiah was sorry for his sins and for the sins of his people as well. He then did what many kings of Israel before him had not done: He read God's Word to the people, and he promised to obey it. One reason the Israelites disobeyed God was because they didn't have his Word. We cannot use this excuse for our disobedience. There are plenty of copies of God's Word available to us today. We can know what God desires from us by reading the Bible.

Why is it important to read the Bible?

For the word of God is full of living power. It is sharper than the sharpest knife, cutting deep into our innermost thoughts and desires. It exposes us for what we really are.
Hebrews 4:12

34:20 As in parallel text at 2 Kgs 22:12; Hebrew reads *Abdon son of Micah.* **34:22a** Or *the Second Quarter,* a newer section of Jerusalem. **34:22b** As in parallel text at 2 Kgs 22:14; Hebrew reads *son of Tokhath, son of Hasrah.*

the king went up to the Temple of the LORD with all the people of Judah and Jerusalem and the priests and the Levites—all the people from the greatest to the least. There the king read to them the entire Book of the Covenant that had been found in the LORD's Temple. ³¹The king took his place of authority beside the pillar and renewed the covenant in the LORD's presence. He pledged to obey the LORD by keeping all his commands, regulations, and laws with all his heart and soul. He promised to obey all the terms of the covenant that were written in the scroll. ³²And he required everyone in Jerusalem and the people of Benjamin to make a similar pledge. As the people of Jerusalem did this, they renewed their covenant with God, the God of their ancestors.

³³So Josiah removed all detestable idols from the entire land of Israel and required everyone to worship the LORD their God. And throughout the rest of his lifetime, they did not turn away from the LORD, the God of their ancestors.

APRIL

28

God had Israel rebuild the Temple. What did the priests do when the Temple foundation was laid?

EZRA 3:7-13

Rebuilding the Temple

⁷Then they hired masons and carpenters and bought cedar logs from the people of Tyre and Sidon, paying them with food, wine, and olive oil. The logs were brought down from the Lebanon mountains and floated along the coast of the Mediterranean Sea to Joppa, for King Cyrus had given permission for this.

⁸The construction of the Temple of God began in midspring,* during the second year after they arrived in Jerusalem. The work force was made up of everyone who had returned from exile, including Zerubbabel son of Shealtiel,

Jeshua son of Jehozadak and his fellow priests, and all the Levites. The Levites who were twenty years old or older were put in charge of rebuilding the LORD's Temple. ⁹The workers at the Temple of God were supervised by Jeshua with his sons and relatives, and Kadmiel and his sons, all descendants of Hodaviah.* They were helped in this task by the Levites of the family of Henadad.

¹⁰When the builders completed the foundation of the LORD's Temple, the priests put on their robes and took their places to blow their trumpets. And the Levites, descendants of Asaph, clashed their cymbals to praise the LORD, just as King David had prescribed. ¹¹With

3:8 Hebrew *in the second month*. This month of the Hebrew lunar calendar occurred in April and May 536 B.C.   3:9 Hebrew *sons of Judah* (i.e., *bene Yehudah*). *Bene* might also be read here as the proper name Binnui; *Yehudah* is probably another name for Hodaviah. Compare 2:40; Neh 7:43; 1 Esdras 5:58.

praise and thanks, they sang this song to the LORD:

> "He is so good!
> His faithful love for Israel
> endures forever!"

Then all the people gave a great shout, praising the LORD because the foundation of the LORD's Temple had been laid. [12]Many of the older priests, Levites, and other leaders remembered the first Temple, and they wept aloud when they saw the new Temple's foundation. The others, however, were shouting for joy. [13]The joyful shouting and weeping mingled together in a loud commotion that could be heard far in the distance.

When the Temple's foundation was completed, the Israelites celebrated. They praised God and thanked him for his goodness to them. Can you list five things you can thank God for right now? God enjoys giving you gifts. But he also likes to hear a thank-you.

When should you thank God?
No matter what happens, always be thankful, for this is God's will for you who belong to Christ Jesus.
1 Thessalonians 5:18

APRIL

*As the Israelites rebuilt Jerusalem's walls, their enemies mocked them.
Their enemies also plotted to attack them.
Did the insults and threats stop the Israelites?*

NEHEMIAH 4:1-21
Rebuilding Jerusalem
Sanballat was very angry when he learned that we were rebuilding the wall. He flew into a rage and mocked the Jews, [2]saying in front of his friends and the Samarian army officers, "What does this bunch of poor, feeble Jews think they are doing? Do they think they can build the wall in a day if they offer enough sacrifices? Look at those charred stones they are pulling out of the rubbish and using again!" [3]Tobiah the Ammonite, who was

standing beside him, remarked, "That stone wall would collapse if even a fox walked along the top of it!"

[4]Then I prayed, "Hear us, O our God, for we are being mocked. May their scoffing fall back on their own heads, and may they themselves become captives in a foreign land! [5]Do not ignore their guilt. Do not blot out their sins, for they have provoked you to anger here in the presence of* the builders."

[6]At last the wall was completed to half its original height around the en-

4:5 Or *for they have thrown insults in the face of.*

tire city, for the people had worked very hard. ⁷But when Sanballat and Tobiah and the Arabs, Ammonites, and Ashdodites heard that the work was going ahead and that the gaps in the wall were being repaired, they became furious. ⁸They all made plans to come and fight against Jerusalem and to bring about confusion there. ⁹But we prayed to our God and guarded the city day and night to protect ourselves.

¹⁰Then the people of Judah began to complain that the workers were becoming tired. There was so much rubble to be moved that we could never get it done by ourselves. ¹¹Meanwhile, our enemies were saying, "Before they know what's happening, we will swoop down on them and kill them and end their work."

¹²The Jews who lived near the enemy came and told us again and again, "They will come from all directions and attack us!"* ¹³So I placed armed guards behind the lowest parts of the wall in the exposed areas. I stationed the people to stand guard by families, armed with swords, spears, and bows.

¹⁴Then as I looked over the situation, I called together the leaders and the people and said to them, "Don't be afraid of the enemy! Remember the Lord, who is great and glorious, and fight for your friends, your families, and your homes!"

¹⁵When our enemies heard that we knew of their plans and that God had frustrated them, we all returned to our work on the wall. ¹⁶But from then on, only half my men worked while the other half stood guard with spears, shields, bows, and coats of mail. The officers stationed themselves behind the people of Judah ¹⁷who were building the wall. The common laborers carried on their work with one hand supporting their load and one hand holding a weapon. ¹⁸All the builders had a sword belted to their side. The trumpeter stayed with me to sound the alarm.

¹⁹Then I explained to the nobles and officials and all the people, "The work is very spread out, and we are widely separated from each other along the wall. ²⁰When you hear the blast of the trumpet, rush to wherever it is sounding. Then our God will fight for us!"

²¹We worked early and late, from sunrise to sunset. And half the men were always on guard.

The insults and threats meant to discourage Nehemiah and the Israelites backfired. Nehemiah didn't get distracted by his enemies' actions. Instead, he prayed to God and concentrated on leading the Israelites to complete the walls. Like the Israelites, you may have enemies that will try to discourage you. Don't be distracted by their insults. Continue to do good and pray for them.

What should you do when people insult you?

Don't repay evil for evil. Don't retaliate when people say unkind things about you. Instead, pay them back with a blessing. That is what God wants you to do, and he will bless you for it.
1 Peter 3:9

4:12 The meaning of the Hebrew is uncertain.

A P R I L

The poor were treated unfairly. They cried out to Nehemiah. How did he respond?

NEHEMIAH 5:1-11

Nehemiah Defends the Poor

About this time some of the men and their wives raised a cry of protest against their fellow Jews. ²They were saying, "We have such large families. We need more money just so we can buy the food we need to survive." ³Others said, "We have mortgaged our fields, vineyards, and homes to get food during the famine." ⁴And others said, "We have already borrowed to the limit on our fields and vineyards to pay our taxes. ⁵We belong to the same family, and our children are just like theirs. Yet we must sell our children into slavery just to get enough money to live. We have already sold some of our daughters, and we are helpless to do anything about it, for our fields and vineyards are already mortgaged to others."

⁶When I heard their complaints, I was very angry. ⁷After thinking about the situation, I spoke out against these nobles and officials. I told them, "You are oppressing your own relatives by charging them interest when they borrow money!" Then I called a public meeting to deal with the problem.

⁸At the meeting I said to them, "The rest of us are doing all we can to redeem our Jewish relatives who have had to sell themselves to pagan foreigners, but you are selling them back into slavery again. How often must we redeem them?" And they had nothing to say in their defense.

⁹Then I pressed further, "What you are doing is not right! Should you not walk in the fear of our God in order to avoid being mocked by enemy nations? ¹⁰I myself, as well as my brothers and my workers, have been lending the people money and grain, but now let us stop this business of loans. ¹¹You must restore their fields, vineyards, olive groves, and homes to them this very day. Repay the interest you charged on their money, grain, wine, and olive oil."

The Jewish nobles charged interest on the loans they made to the poor. As a result, the poor couldn't pay their bills and had to sell their children into slavery. The nobles sinned because God had instructed his people not to charge each other interest on loans. Nehemiah listened to the poor and defended them. Do you know anyone who is treated unfairly? Do what you can to help that person.

Who are some people we can help?

Pure and lasting religion in the sight of God our Father means that we must care for orphans and widows in their troubles, and refuse to let the world corrupt us.
James 1:27

M A Y

Ezra read God's Word to the Israelites. How did they react?

NEHEMIAH 8:2-6, 8-12

Reading and Weeping

²So on October 8* Ezra the priest brought the scroll of the law before the assembly, which included the men and women and all the children old enough to understand. ³He faced the square just inside the Water Gate from early morning until noon and read aloud to everyone who could understand. All the people paid close attention to the Book of the Law. ⁴Ezra the scribe stood on a high wooden platform that had been made for the occasion. To his right stood Mattithiah, Shema, Anaiah, Uriah, Hilkiah, and Maaseiah. To his left stood Pedaiah, Mishael, Malkijah, Hashum, Hashbaddanah, Zechariah, and Meshullam. ⁵Ezra stood on the platform in full view of all the people. When they saw him open the book, they all rose to their feet.

⁶Then Ezra praised the LORD, the great God, and all the people chanted, "Amen! Amen!" as they lifted their hands toward heaven. Then they bowed down and worshiped the LORD with their faces to the ground.

• • •

⁸They read from the Book of the Law of God and clearly explained the meaning of what was being read, helping the people understand each passage. ⁹Then Nehemiah the governor, Ezra the priest and scribe, and the Levites who were interpreting for the people said to them, "Don't weep on such a day as this! For today is a sacred day before the LORD your God." All the people had been weeping as they listened to the words of the law.

¹⁰And Nehemiah* continued, "Go and celebrate with a feast of choice

As Ezra read God's Word, a group of Levites explained to the people what it meant. The Israelites listened and understood. Their understanding caused them to weep because they realized that they had offended God. And they were sorry for their sin. God's Word is just as powerful today as it was for the Israelites thousands of years ago. When we understand God's Word, its power changes our lives.

Why should we read the Bible?

All Scripture is inspired by God and is useful to teach us what is true and to make us realize what is wrong in our lives. It straightens us out and teaches us to do what is right.

2 Timothy 3:16

8:2 Hebrew *on the first day of the seventh month,* of the Hebrew calendar. This event occurred on October 8, 445 B.C.; also see note on 1:1.
8:10 Hebrew *he.*

foods and sweet drinks, and share gifts of food with people who have nothing prepared. This is a sacred day before our Lord. Don't be dejected and sad, for the joy of the LORD is your strength!"

¹¹And the Levites, too, quieted the people, telling them, "Hush! Don't weep! For this is a sacred day." ¹²So the people went away to eat and drink at a festive meal, to share gifts of food, and to celebrate with great joy because they had heard God's words and understood them.

M A Y

The king of Persia was looking for a new queen. Whom did he choose?

ESTHER 2:5-11, 15-20

Esther before the King

⁵Now at the fortress of Susa there was a certain Jew named Mordecai son of Jair. He was from the tribe of Benjamin and was a descendant of Kish and Shimei. ⁶His family* had been exiled from Jerusalem to Babylon by King Nebuchadnezzar, along with King Jehoiachin* of Judah and many others. ⁷This man had a beautiful and lovely young cousin, Hadassah, who was also called Esther. When her father and mother had died, Mordecai adopted her into his family and raised her as his own daughter. ⁸As a result of the king's decree, Esther, along with many other young women, was brought to the king's harem at the fortress of Susa and placed in Hegai's care. ⁹Hegai was very impressed with Esther and treated her kindly. He quickly ordered a special menu for her and provided her with beauty treatments. He also assigned her seven maids specially chosen from the king's palace, and he moved her and her maids into the best place in the harem.

¹⁰Esther had not told anyone of her nationality and family background, for Mordecai had told her not to. ¹¹Every day Mordecai would take a walk near the courtyard of the harem to ask about Esther and to find out what was happening to her.

• • •

¹⁵When it was Esther's turn* to go to the king, she accepted the advice of Hegai, the eunuch in charge of the harem. She asked for nothing except what he suggested, and she was admired by everyone who saw her. ¹⁶When Esther was taken to King Xerxes at the royal palace in early winter* of the seventh year of his reign, ¹⁷the king loved her more than any of the

2:6a Hebrew *He.* 2:6b Hebrew *Jeconiah,* a variant name for Jehoiachin. 2:15 Hebrew *the turn of Esther, the daughter of Abihail, who was Mordecai's uncle, who had adopted her.* 2:16 Hebrew *in the tenth month, the month of Tebeth.* A number of dates in the book of Esther can be cross-checked with dates in surviving Persian records and related accurately to our modern calendar. This month of the Hebrew lunar calendar occurred in December 479 B.C. and January 478 B.C.

other young women. He was so delighted with her that he set the royal crown on her head and declared her queen instead of Vashti. [18]To celebrate the occasion, he gave a banquet in Esther's honor for all his princes and servants, giving generous gifts to everyone and declaring a public festival for the provinces.

[19]Even after all the young women had been transferred to the second harem* and Mordecai had become a palace official, [20]Esther continued to keep her nationality and family background a secret. She was still following Mordecai's orders, just as she did when she was living in his home.

The king chose Esther. Esther was beautiful, but she was also a nice person to be around. People enjoyed being in her presence because she was humble and a good listener. Do people enjoy being around you? You don't have to be physically beautiful for people to enjoy your company. With a kind smile and a listening ear, you can make many friends who will love to spend time with you.

How can you make your company enjoyable for others?
Instead, be kind to each other, tenderhearted, forgiving one another, just as God through Christ has forgiven you.
Ephesians 4:32

2:19 The meaning of the Hebrew is uncertain.

M A Y

The king ordered his officials to bow to Haman. What did Mordecai do?

ESTHER 3:1-14
Haman and Mordecai
Some time later, King Xerxes promoted Haman son of Hammedatha the Agagite to prime minister, making him the most powerful official in the empire next to the king himself. [2]All the king's officials would bow down before Haman to show him respect whenever he passed by, for so the king had commanded. But Mordecai refused to bow down or show him respect.

[3]Then the palace officials at the king's gate asked Mordecai, "Why are you disobeying the king's command?" [4]They spoke to him day after day, but still he refused to comply with the order. So they spoke to Haman about this to see if he would tolerate Mordecai's conduct, since Mordecai had told them he was a Jew.

[5]When Haman saw that Mordecai would not bow down or show him respect, he was filled with rage. [6]So he

decided it was not enough to lay hands on Mordecai alone. Since he had learned that Mordecai was a Jew, he decided to destroy all the Jews throughout the entire empire of Xerxes.

[7]So in the month of April,* during the twelfth year of King Xerxes' reign, lots were cast (the lots were called *purim*) to determine the best day and month to take action. And the day selected was March 7, nearly a year later.*

[8]Then Haman approached King Xerxes and said, "There is a certain race of people scattered through all the provinces of your empire. Their laws are different from those of any other nation, and they refuse to obey even the laws of the king. So it is not in the king's interest to let them live. [9]If it please Your Majesty, issue a decree that they be destroyed, and I will give 375 tons* of silver to the government administrators so they can put it into the royal treasury."

[10]The king agreed, confirming his decision by removing his signet ring from his finger and giving it to Haman son of Hammedatha the Agagite—the enemy of the Jews. [11]"Keep the money," the king told Haman, "but go ahead and do as you like with these people."

[12]On April 17* Haman called in the king's secretaries and dictated letters to the princes, the governors of the respective provinces, and the local officials of each province in their own scripts and languages. These letters were signed in the name of King Xerxes, sealed with his ring, [13]and sent by messengers into all the provinces of the empire. The letters decreed that all Jews—young and old, including women and children—must be killed, slaughtered, and annihilated on a single day. This was scheduled to happen nearly a year later on March 7.* The property of the Jews would be given to those who killed them. [14]A copy of this decree was to be issued in every province and made known to all the people, so that they would be ready to do their duty on the appointed day.

All of the king's officials were bowing before Haman. But Mordecai wouldn't kneel. He knew that it was wrong to bow before anyone but God. So he refused to do what everybody else was doing. When have your friends pressured you to do wrong? You don't have to join them. With God's help, you can resist bad peer pressure.

How can we resist bad peer pressure?

Don't copy the behavior and customs of this world, but let God transform you into a new person by changing the way you think. Then you will know what God wants you to do, and you will know how good and pleasing and perfect his will really is.
Romans 12:2

3:7a Hebrew *in the first month, the month of Nisan.* This month of the Hebrew lunar calendar occurred in April and May 474 B.C.; also see note on 2:16.   3:7b As in Greek version, which reads *the thirteenth day of the twelfth month, the month of Adar* (see also 3:13). Hebrew reads *in the twelfth month,* of the Hebrew calendar. The date selected was March 7, 473 B.C.; also see note on 2:16.   3:9 Hebrew *10,000 talents* [340 metric tons].   3:12 Hebrew *On the thirteenth day of the first month,* of the Hebrew calendar. This event occurred on April 17, 474 B.C.; also see note on 2:16.   3:13 Hebrew *on the thirteenth day of the twelfth month, the month of Adar,* of the Hebrew calendar. The date selected was March 7, 473 B.C.; also see note on 2:16.

M A Y

Mordecai was mourning over the king's order to kill the Jews.
When Esther found out about Mordecai's grief, what did she do?

ESTHER 4:1–5:2

Esther Risks Her Life

When Mordecai learned what had been done, he tore his clothes, put on sackcloth and ashes, and went out into the city, crying with a loud and bitter wail. ²He stood outside the gate of the palace, for no one was allowed to enter while wearing clothes of mourning. ³And as news of the king's decree reached all the provinces, there was great mourning among the Jews. They fasted, wept, and wailed, and many people lay in sackcloth and ashes.

⁴When Queen Esther's maids and eunuchs came and told her about Mordecai, she was deeply distressed. She sent clothing to him to replace the sackcloth, but he refused it. ⁵Then Esther sent for Hathach, one of the king's eunuchs who had been appointed as her attendant. She ordered him to go to Mordecai and find out what was troubling him and why he was in mourning. ⁶So Hathach went out to Mordecai in the square in front of the palace gate.

⁷Mordecai told him the whole story and told him how much money Haman had promised to pay into the royal treasury for the destruction of the Jews. ⁸Mordecai gave Hathach a copy of the decree issued in Susa that called for the death of all Jews, and he asked Hathach to show it to Esther. He

also asked Hathach to explain it to her and to urge her to go to the king to beg for mercy and plead for her people. ⁹So Hathach returned to Esther with Mordecai's message.

¹⁰Then Esther told Hathach to go back and relay this message to Mordecai: ¹¹"The whole world knows that anyone who appears before the king in his inner court without being invited is doomed to die unless the king holds out his gold scepter. And the king has not called for me to come to him in more than a month." ¹²So Hathach gave Esther's message to Mordecai.

¹³Mordecai sent back this reply to Esther: "Don't think for a moment that you will escape there in the palace when all other Jews are killed. ¹⁴If you keep quiet at a time like this, deliverance for the Jews will arise from some other place, but you and your relatives will die. What's more, who can say but that you have been elevated to the palace for just such a time as this?"

¹⁵Then Esther sent this reply to Mordecai: ¹⁶"Go and gather together all the Jews of Susa and fast for me. Do not eat or drink for three days, night or day. My maids and I will do the same. And then, though it is against the law, I will go in to see the king. If I must die, I am willing to die." ¹⁷So Mordecai went away and did as Esther told him.

5:1 Three days later, Esther put on her royal robes and entered the inner court of the palace, just across from the king's hall. The king was sitting on his royal throne, facing the entrance. **2** When he saw Queen Esther standing there in the inner court, he welcomed her, holding out the gold scepter to her. So Esther approached and touched its tip.

Esther was afraid to approach the king to plead for the Jews. She knew that she could lose her life. But Mordecai convinced her to act, and she risked her life in order to save the Jews. Sometimes we have to risk losing something in order to do what is right. But whatever we lose on earth for Jesus, we will gain in heaven.

What do we need to give to Jesus?
If you try to keep your life for yourself, you will lose it. But if you give up your life for my sake and for the sake of the Good News, you will find true life.
Mark 8:35

M A Y

Haman boasted to his friends and his wife about how important he was. What happened to him?

ESTHER 5:9–6:13

Haman Humiliated

9 What a happy man Haman was as he left the banquet! But when he saw Mordecai sitting at the gate, not standing up or trembling nervously before him, he was furious. **10** However, he restrained himself and went on home. Then he gathered together his friends and Zeresh, his wife, **11** and boasted to them about his great wealth and his many children. He bragged about the honors the king had given him and how he had been promoted over all the other officials and leaders.

12 Then Haman added, "And that's not all! Queen Esther invited only me and the king himself to the banquet she prepared for us. And she has invited me to dine with her and the king again tomorrow!" **13** Then he added, "But all this is meaningless as long as I see Mordecai the Jew just sitting there at the palace gate."

14 So Haman's wife, Zeresh, and all his friends suggested, "Set up a gallows* that stands seventy-five feet* tall, and in the morning ask the king to hang Mordecai on it. When this is done, you can go on your merry way

5:14a Or *a pole*. 5:14b Hebrew *50 cubits* [22.5 meters].

160

to the banquet with the king." This pleased Haman immensely, and he ordered the gallows set up.

⁶:¹That night the king had trouble sleeping, so he ordered an attendant to bring the historical records of his kingdom so they could be read to him. ²In those records he discovered an account of how Mordecai had exposed the plot of Bigthana and Teresh, two of the eunuchs who guarded the door to the king's private quarters. They had plotted to assassinate the king. ³"What reward or recognition did we ever give Mordecai for this?" the king asked.

His attendants replied, "Nothing has been done."

⁴"Who is that in the outer court?" the king inquired. Now, as it happened, Haman had just arrived in the outer court of the palace to ask the king to hang Mordecai from the gallows* he had prepared.

⁵So the attendants replied to the king, "Haman is out there."

"Bring him in," the king ordered. ⁶So Haman came in, and the king said, "What should I do to honor a man who truly pleases me?"

Haman thought to himself, "Whom would the king wish to honor more than me?" ⁷So he replied, "If the king wishes to honor someone, ⁸he should bring out one of the king's own royal robes, as well as the king's own horse with a royal emblem on its head. ⁹Instruct one of the king's most noble princes to dress the man in the king's robe and to lead him through the city square on the king's own horse. Have the prince shout as they go, 'This is what happens to those the king wishes to honor!' "

¹⁰"Excellent!" the king said to Haman. "Hurry and get the robe and my horse, and do just as you have said for Mordecai the Jew, who sits at the gate of the palace. Do not fail to carry out everything you have suggested."

¹¹So Haman took the robe and put it on Mordecai, placed him on the king's own horse, and led him through the city square, shouting, "This is what happens to those the king wishes to honor!" ¹²Afterward

After Haman boasted, he went to the palace to ask the king for permission to hang Mordecai. Before Haman could make his request, the king asked him a question. Thinking that the king wanted to honor him, Haman gave his answer. But Haman was humbled and humiliated when the king honored Mordecai. Haman's experience shows that boasting about yourself is dangerous. Be careful that you do not boast about yourself. Instead, boast about God. Tell others what he has done for you, and thank him for his gifts.

What can we boast about?
As for me, God forbid that I should boast about anything except the cross of our Lord Jesus Christ. Because of that cross,* my interest in this world died long ago, and the world's interest in me is also long dead.
Galatians 6:14

6:4 Or from the pole. **6:14** Or Because of him.

Mordecai returned to the palace gate, but Haman hurried home dejected and completely humiliated.

¹³When Haman told his wife, Zeresh, and all his friends what had happened, they said, "Since Mordecai—this man who has humiliated you—is a Jew, you will never succeed in your plans against him. It will be fatal to continue to oppose him."

M A Y

Esther asked the king to save her and her people. How did the king respond?

ESTHER 7:1-10
Haman Hanged

So the king and Haman went to Queen Esther's banquet. ²And while they were drinking wine that day, the king again asked her, "Tell me what you want, Queen Esther. What is your request? I will give it to you, even if it is half the kingdom!"

³And so Queen Esther replied, "If Your Majesty is pleased with me and wants to grant my request, my petition is that my life and the lives of my people will be spared. ⁴For my people and I have been sold to those who would kill, slaughter, and annihilate us. If we had only been sold as slaves, I could remain quiet, for that would have been a matter too trivial to warrant disturbing the king."

⁵"Who would do such a thing?" King Xerxes demanded. "Who would dare touch you?"

⁶Esther replied, "This wicked Haman is our enemy." Haman grew pale with fright before the king and queen. ⁷Then the king jumped to his feet in a rage and went out into the palace garden.

But Haman stayed behind to plead for his life with Queen Esther, for he knew that he was doomed. ⁸In despair he fell on the couch where Queen Esther was reclining, just as the king returned from the palace garden. "Will he even assault the queen right here in the palace, before my very eyes?" the king roared. And as soon as the king

The king loved Esther. When he found out that Esther's life was in danger, he was outraged and asked who would hurt her. She told the king that it was Haman, and the king had Haman executed. Through Esther, God protected the Jews. God has power over kings and presidents. We can trust God to raise up people who will influence those in authority for good.

Who gives authorities their power?

Obey the government, for God is the one who put it there. All governments have been placed in power by God.
Romans 13:1

spoke, his attendants covered Haman's face, signaling his doom.

⁹Then Harbona, one of the king's eunuchs, said, "Haman has set up a gallows* that stands seventy-five feet* tall in his own courtyard. He intended to use it to hang Mordecai, the man who saved the king from assassination."

"Then hang Haman on it!" the king ordered. ¹⁰So they hanged Haman on the gallows he had set up for Mordecai, and the king's anger was pacified.

7:9a Or *a pole*; also in 7:10.   7:9b Hebrew *50 cubits* [22.5 meters].

M A Y

Job was a good man who lost all his children and possessions in one day. What was his response?

JOB 1:6-22

Job's Problems

⁶One day the angels* came to present themselves before the LORD, and Satan the Accuser came with them. ⁷"Where have you come from?" the LORD asked Satan.

And Satan answered the LORD, "I have been going back and forth across the earth, watching everything that's going on."

⁸Then the LORD asked Satan, "Have you noticed my servant Job? He is the finest man in all the earth—a man of complete integrity. He fears God and will have nothing to do with evil."

⁹Satan replied to the LORD, "Yes, Job fears God, but not without good reason! ¹⁰You have always protected him and his home and his property from harm. You have made him prosperous in everything he does. Look how rich he is! ¹¹But take away everything he has, and he will surely curse you to your face!"

¹²"All right, you may test him," the LORD said to Satan. "Do whatever you want with everything he possesses, but don't harm him physically." So Satan left the LORD's presence.

¹³One day when Job's sons and daughters were dining at the oldest brother's house, ¹⁴a messenger arrived at Job's home with this news: "Your oxen were plowing, with the donkeys feeding beside them, ¹⁵when the Sabeans raided us. They stole all the animals and killed all the farmhands. I am the only one who escaped to tell you."

¹⁶While he was still speaking, another messenger arrived with this news: "The fire of God has fallen from heaven and burned up your sheep and all the shepherds. I am the only one who escaped to tell you."

¹⁷While he was still speaking, a third messenger arrived with this news: "Three bands of Chaldean raiders have stolen your camels and killed

1:6 Hebrew *the sons of God.*

your servants. I am the only one who escaped to tell you."

[18]While he was still speaking, another messenger arrived with this news: "Your sons and daughters were feasting in their oldest brother's home. [19]Suddenly, a powerful wind swept in from the desert and hit the house on all sides. The house collapsed, and all your children are dead. I am the only one who escaped to tell you."

[20]Job stood up and tore his robe in grief. Then he shaved his head and fell to the ground before God. [21]He said,

"I came naked from my mother's
    womb,
  and I will be stripped of
    everything when I die.
The LORD gave me everything I had,
  and the LORD has taken it away.
Praise the name of the LORD!"

[22]In all of this, Job did not sin by blaming God.

Satan wanted to test Job because he thought Job's faith was based on God's blessings. But when Job lost just about everything, he didn't curse God. Instead, he expressed sorrow over his losses and then praised God for his goodness. How could Job react this way? Job had the right perspective. He knew that God is good. When troubles came, Job's faith in God did not evaporate. We may never lose everything and everyone like Job did. But the same God Job praised is still here today for us to trust. He loves us and gives us the strength we need to get through hard times.

What can result from troubles?
Dear brothers and sisters, whenever trouble comes your way, let it be an opportunity for joy. For when your faith is tested, your endurance has a chance to grow.
James 1:2-3

M A Y

8

Satan took away Job's health. What did Job do?

JOB 2:1-10
Job in Ashes
One day the angels* came again to present themselves before the LORD, and Satan the Accuser came with them. [2]"Where have you come from?" the LORD asked Satan.

And Satan answered the LORD, "I have been going back and forth across the earth, watching everything that's going on."

[3]Then the LORD asked Satan, "Have you noticed my servant Job? He is the finest man in all the earth—a man of complete integrity. He fears God and will have nothing to do with evil. And

2:1 Hebrew *the sons of God.*

he has maintained his integrity, even though you persuaded me to harm him without cause."

⁴Satan replied to the LORD, "Skin for skin—he blesses you only because you bless him. A man will give up everything he has to save his life. ⁵But take away his health, and he will surely curse you to your face!"

⁶"All right, do with him as you please," the LORD said to Satan. "But spare his life." ⁷So Satan left the LORD's presence, and he struck Job with a terrible case of boils from head to foot.

⁸Then Job scraped his skin with a piece of broken pottery as he sat among the ashes. ⁹His wife said to him, "Are you still trying to maintain your integrity? Curse God and die."

¹⁰But Job replied, "You talk like a godless woman. Should we accept only good things from the hand of God and never anything bad?" So in all this, Job said nothing wrong.

Job had remained faithful to God even after he lost his possessions and children. But Satan still thought that Job would curse God if he suffered the right hardship. So Satan asked God for permission to make Job sick. God let Satan inflict Job with boils, a painful skin disease. Job did not curse God though. Instead, he accepted his illness and scolded his wife for suggesting that he curse God. Job's example gives us encouragement to obey God when we have problems. Cling to God through the good and the bad times. God will not leave you.

Can troubles separate us from God?
Can anything ever separate us from Christ's love? Does it mean he no longer loves us if we have trouble or calamity, or are persecuted, or are hungry or cold or in danger or threatened with death?
Romans 8:35

M A Y

Three of Job's friends visited him. How did they act?

JOB 2:11–3:6
Job's Friends

¹¹Three of Job's friends were Eliphaz the Temanite, Bildad the Shuhite, and Zophar the Naamathite. When they heard of the tragedy he had suffered, they got together and traveled from their homes to comfort and console him. ¹²When they saw Job from a distance, they scarcely recognized him.

Wailing loudly, they tore their robes and threw dust into the air over their heads to demonstrate their grief. ¹³Then they sat on the ground with him for seven days and nights. And no one said a word, for they saw that his suffering was too great for words.

³:¹At last Job spoke, and he cursed the day of his birth. ²He said:

165

³"Cursed be the day of my birth, and cursed be the night when I was conceived. ⁴Let that day be turned to darkness. Let it be lost even to God on high, and let it be shrouded in darkness. ⁵Yes, let the darkness and utter gloom claim it for its own. Let a black cloud overshadow it, and let the darkness terrify it. ⁶Let that night be blotted off the calendar, never again to be counted among the days of the year, never again to appear among the months."

Job's friends showed him compassion. They wept with him, sat in silence with him, and listened to him. Their response shows us how we can comfort our friends when they are suffering. Even if we have nothing comforting to say, we can at least sit with them and listen as they talk about their sorrow and pain.

How should we treat a friend who is hurting?
Finally, all of you should be of one mind, full of sympathy toward each other, loving one another with tender hearts and humble minds.
1 Peter 3:8

M A Y

Job questioned why he was suffering. God responded to Job's questions. How did Job react?

JOB 38:1-15; 40:1-5
God Speaks

Then the LORD answered Job from the whirlwind:

²"Who is this that questions my wisdom with such ignorant words? ³Brace yourself, because I have some questions for you, and you must answer them.

⁴"Where were you when I laid the foundations of the earth? Tell me, if you know so much. ⁵Do you know how its dimensions were determined and who did the surveying? ⁶What supports its foundations, and who laid its cornerstone ⁷as the morning stars sang together and all the angels* shouted for joy?

⁸"Who defined the boundaries of the sea as it burst from the womb, ⁹and as I clothed it with clouds and thick darkness? ¹⁰For I locked it behind barred gates, limiting its shores. ¹¹I said, 'Thus far and no farther will you come. Here your proud waves must stop!'

¹²"Have you ever commanded the morning to appear and caused the

38:7 Hebrew *sons of God*.

166

dawn to rise in the east? [13]Have you ever told the daylight to spread to the ends of the earth, to bring an end to the night's wickedness? [14]For the features of the earth take shape as the light approaches, and the dawn is robed in red. [15]The light disturbs the haunts of the wicked, and it stops the arm that is raised in violence."

• • •

[40:1]Then the LORD said to Job, [2]"Do you still want to argue with the Almighty? You are God's critic, but do you have the answers?"

[3]Then Job replied to the LORD, [4]"I am nothing—how could I ever find the answers? I will put my hand over my mouth in silence. [5]I have said too much already. I have nothing more to say."

In questioning God's ways or reasons, Job came close to accusing God of being unfair. So God questioned Job. He did this to show Job that his power is unlimited and that Job was no one to be questioning him. Job responded by humbly admitting that he had said too much. Like Job, we may have questions for God about why we, or others, suffer. When we do, we should be careful how we ask them. Asking with the wrong attitude insults God. But asking with a humble attitude honors him.

How should we come to God?
When you bow down before the Lord and admit your dependence on him, he will lift you up and give you honor.
James 4:10

M A Y

God continued questioning Job. What did Job do? How did God respond?

JOB 42:1-17
Job's Reply to God
Then Job replied to the LORD:

[2]"I know that you can do anything, and no one can stop you. [3]You ask, 'Who is this that questions my wisdom with such ignorance?' It is I. And I was talking about things I did not understand, things far too wonderful for me.

[4]"You said, 'Listen and I will speak! I have some questions for you, and you must answer them.'

[5]"I had heard about you before, but now I have seen you with my own eyes. [6]I take back everything I said, and I sit in dust and ashes to show my repentance."

[7]After the LORD had finished speaking to Job, he said to Eliphaz the Temanite: "I am angry with you and with your two friends, for you have not been right in what you said about me, as my servant Job was. [8]Now take seven young bulls and seven rams and go to my servant Job and offer a burnt offering for yourselves. My servant Job will pray for you, and I will accept his

prayer on your behalf. I will not treat you as you deserve, for you have not been right in what you said about me, as my servant Job was."

⁹So Eliphaz the Temanite, Bildad the Shuhite, and Zophar the Naamathite did as the LORD commanded them, and the LORD accepted Job's prayer.

¹⁰When Job prayed for his friends, the LORD restored his fortunes. In fact, the LORD gave him twice as much as before! ¹¹Then all his brothers, sisters, and former friends came and feasted with him in his home. And they consoled him and comforted him because of all the trials the LORD had brought against him. And each of them brought him a gift of money* and a gold ring.

¹²So the LORD blessed Job in the second half of his life even more than in the beginning. For now he had fourteen thousand sheep, six thousand camels, one thousand teams of oxen, and one thousand female donkeys. ¹³He also gave Job seven more sons and three more daughters. ¹⁴He named his first daughter Jemimah, the second Keziah, and the third Keren-happuch. ¹⁵In all the land there were no other women as lovely as the daughters of Job. And their father put them into his will along with their brothers.

¹⁶Job lived 140 years after that, living to see four generations of his children and grandchildren. ¹⁷Then he died, an old man who had lived a long, good life.

Job admitted that he was wrong to question God. He also praised God for his power. God forgave Job and blessed him with other children and more possessions. Like Job, we have all sinned against God. But we can also have God's forgiveness. Christ died so our sins can be forgiven. If we confess our sins to Jesus, he will forgive us.

Why should we be sorry for our sins?

For God can use sorrow in our lives to help us turn away from sin and seek salvation. We will never regret that kind of sorrow. But sorrow without repentance is the kind that results in death.
2 Corinthians 7:10

42:11 Hebrew *a kesitah;* the value or weight of the kesitah is no longer known.

M A Y

This psalm says that there are two paths one can choose in life. One is good and the other is bad. What are the rewards for taking the good path?

PSALM 1:1-6

The Right and the Wrong Way

¹ Oh, the joys of those
     who do not follow the advice of
     the wicked,
     or stand around with sinners,
     or join in with scoffers.
² But they delight in doing
     everything the LORD wants;
     day and night they think about
     his law.
³ They are like trees planted along
     the riverbank,
     bearing fruit each season
     without fail.
   Their leaves never wither,
     and in all they do, they prosper.

⁴ But this is not true of the wicked.
     They are like worthless chaff,
     scattered by the wind.
⁵ They will be condemned at the
     time of judgment.

Sinners will have no place
     among the godly.

⁶ For the LORD watches over the path
     of the godly,
     but the path of the wicked leads
     to destruction.

Those who choose the good path in life will be successful. God will watch over them and protect them from evil. Those who choose the bad path will face God's judgment. Their lives will end in destruction. You don't have to choose the bad path. You can choose the good path by giving your life to Jesus.

Whom does God bless?
God blesses those who are hungry
and thirsty for justice, for they
will receive it in full.
Matthew 5:6

MAY

*David wrote this psalm to praise God for creating people.
What inspired David to write this psalm?*

PSALM 8:1-9
The Work of God's Fingers

*For the choir director: A psalm of David, to
be accompanied by a stringed instrument.**

¹ O LORD, our Lord, the majesty of
  your name fills the earth!
  Your glory is higher than the
  heavens.

² You have taught children and
  nursing infants
  to give you praise.*
  They silence your enemies
  who were seeking revenge.

³ When I look at the night sky and
  see the work of your fingers—
  the moon and the stars you
  have set in place—
⁴ what are mortals that you should
  think of us,
  mere humans that you should
  care for us?*
⁵ For you made us only a little lower
  than God,*
  and you crowned us with glory
  and honor.
⁶ You put us in charge of everything
  you made,
  giving us authority over all
  things—

⁷ the sheep and the cattle
  and all the wild animals,
⁸ the birds in the sky, the fish in the
  sea,
  and everything that swims the
  ocean currents.

⁹ O LORD, our Lord, the majesty of
  your name fills the earth!

*God made the sun, moon, stars, plants,
animals, and people. Even though he
made all of these things, he was most
concerned with people. This fact
amazed David. How could the same
God that made the universe be concerned with little things like human
beings? Yet God showed his love for
people by placing them in authority
over everything he made. He also
showed his love for us when he sent his
Son, Jesus, to die for our sins. Our lives
are valuable because God loves us. This
fact alone is worth praising God for.*

What did God create you to do?
For we are God's masterpiece. He
has created us anew in Christ Jesus,
so that we can do the good things he
planned for us long ago.
Ephesians 2:10

8:TITLE Hebrew *according to the gittith.*   **8:2** As in Greek version; Hebrew reads *to show strength.*   **8:4** Hebrew *what is man that you should
think of him, the son of man that you should care for him?*   **8:5** Or *a little lower than the angels;* Hebrew reads *Elohim.*

M A Y

In this psalm, David called the Lord his shepherd. How is God like a shepherd?

PSALM 23:1-6
The Good Shepherd
A psalm of David.

¹ The LORD is my shepherd;
    I have everything I need.
² He lets me rest in green meadows;
    he leads me beside peaceful
        streams.
³   He renews my strength.
  He guides me along right paths,
    bringing honor to his name.

⁴ Even when I walk
    through the dark valley of
        death,*
  I will not be afraid,
    for you are close beside me.
  Your rod and your staff
    protect and comfort me.

⁵ You prepare a feast for me
    in the presence of my enemies.
  You welcome me as a guest,
    anointing my head with oil.
    My cup overflows with blessings.

⁶ Surely your goodness and
    unfailing love will pursue me
  all the days of my life,
  and I will live in the house of the
    LORD
    forever.

David saw at least three ways God was like a shepherd. He guided David throughout his life, he provided for David's needs, and he protected David from his enemies. Like David, we have a good shepherd. His name is Jesus. He not only takes care of us, but he died to save us. Follow Jesus. He will show you the way to heaven.

What does Jesus do for us?
I am the good shepherd; I know
my own sheep, and they know me,
just as my Father knows me and
I know the Father. And I lay down
my life for the sheep.
John 10:14-15

23:4 Or *the darkest valley.*

M A Y

David sinned against God. What did he ask God to do?

PSALM 51:1-17

A Psalm of Forgiveness

*For the choir director: A psalm of David,
regarding the time Nathan the prophet came
to him after David had committed adultery
with Bathsheba.*

¹ Have mercy on me, O God,
   because of your unfailing love.
Because of your great compassion,
   blot out the stain of my sins.
² Wash me clean from my guilt.
   Purify me from my sin.

³ For I recognize my shameful
      deeds—
   they haunt me day and night.
⁴ Against you, and you alone, have I
      sinned;
   I have done what is evil in your
      sight.
You will be proved right in what
      you say,
   and your judgment against me
      is just.

⁵ For I was born a sinner—
   yes, from the moment my
      mother conceived me.
⁶ But you desire honesty from the
      heart,
   so you can teach me to be wise
      in my inmost being.

⁷ Purify me from my sins,* and I
   will be clean;

wash me, and I will be whiter
   than snow.
⁸ Oh, give me back my joy again;
   you have broken me—
   now let me rejoice.
⁹ Don't keep looking at my sins.
   Remove the stain of my guilt.
¹⁰ Create in me a clean heart, O God.
   Renew a right spirit within me.
¹¹ Do not banish me from your
      presence,
   and don't take your Holy Spirit
      from me.
¹² Restore to me again the joy of your
      salvation,

*David had taken another man's wife as
his own. When a prophet confronted
David about this sin, David confessed it
to God. He also asked God to forgive
him, and God did. In this psalm, David
expresses his sorrow for his sin. If sin is
keeping you from God, follow David's
example and ask for forgiveness. Confess
your sin and trust in God to forgive you.*

What will God do when
you confess your sins?
But if we confess our sins to him, he
is faithful and just to forgive us and
to cleanse us from every wrong.
1 John 1:9

51:7 Hebrew *Purify me with the hyssop branch.*

172

and make me willing to obey you.
¹³ Then I will teach your ways to
sinners,
and they will return to you.
¹⁴ Forgive me for shedding blood,
O God who saves;
then I will joyfully sing of your
forgiveness.
¹⁵ Unseal my lips, O Lord,
that I may praise you.

¹⁶ You would not be pleased with
sacrifices,
or I would bring them.
If I brought you a burnt offering,
you would not accept it.
¹⁷ The sacrifice you want is a broken
spirit.
A broken and repentant heart,
O God,
you will not despise.

M A Y

David thought of many things to praise God for. He wrote a lot of them down in this psalm. What does this psalm say about God?

PSALM 103:1-22
Praise the LORD!
A psalm of David.

¹ Praise the LORD, I tell myself;
with my whole heart, I will
praise his holy name.
² Praise the LORD, I tell myself,
and never forget the good things
he does for me.
³ He forgives all my sins
and heals all my diseases.
⁴ He ransoms me from death
and surrounds me with love and
tender mercies.
⁵ He fills my life with good things.
My youth is renewed like the
eagle's!
⁶ The LORD gives righteousness
and justice to all who are treated
unfairly.
⁷ He revealed his character to Moses
and his deeds to the people of
Israel.

⁸ The LORD is merciful and gracious;
he is slow to get angry and full
of unfailing love.
⁹ He will not constantly accuse us,
nor remain angry forever.
¹⁰ He has not punished us for all our
sins,
nor does he deal with us as we
deserve.
¹¹ For his unfailing love toward those
who fear him
is as great as the height of the
heavens above the earth.
¹² He has removed our rebellious acts
as far away from us as the east is
from the west.
¹³ The LORD is like a father to his
children,
tender and compassionate to
those who fear him.
¹⁴ For he understands how weak we
are;
he knows we are only dust.

¹⁵ Our days on earth are like grass;
   like wildflowers, we bloom and
   die.
¹⁶ The wind blows, and we are gone—
   as though we had never been
   here.
¹⁷ But the love of the LORD remains
   forever
   with those who fear him.
   His salvation extends to the
   children's children
¹⁸   of those who are faithful to his
   covenant,
   of those who obey his
   commandments!

¹⁹ The LORD has made the heavens
   his throne;
   from there he rules over
   everything.
²⁰ Praise the LORD, you angels of his,
   you mighty creatures who carry
   out his plans,
   listening for each of his
   commands.
²¹ Yes, praise the LORD, you armies of
   angels
   who serve him and do his will!

²² Praise the LORD, everything he has
   created,
   everywhere in his kingdom.
   As for me—I, too, will praise the
   LORD.

God is forgiving. He forgives our sins and places them out of his sight forever. God is also generous. He gives us good things like parents, food, and clothing. God is gracious. He doesn't punish us for our sins as much as we deserve to be punished. God is compassionate and understanding. He knows our weaknesses but loves us anyway. Think about how God has shown his forgiveness, generosity, and compassion to you. Then praise and thank him for his love and kindness.

What do we know about God?
We know how much God loves us, and we have put our trust in him. God is love, and all who live in love live in God, and God lives in them.
1 John 4:16

M A Y

This psalm lists the rewards of reading Scripture. What are these rewards?

PSALM 119:97-106
A Lamp to My Feet
⁹⁷ Oh, how I love your law!
   I think about it all day long.
⁹⁸ Your commands make me wiser
   than my enemies,
for your commands are my
   constant guide.
⁹⁹ Yes, I have more insight than my
   teachers,
   for I am always thinking of your
   decrees.

¹⁰⁰ I am even wiser than my elders,
    for I have kept your
    commandments.
¹⁰¹ I have refused to walk on any path
    of evil,
    that I may remain obedient to
    your word.
¹⁰² I haven't turned away from your
    laws,
    for you have taught me well.
¹⁰³ How sweet are your words to my
    taste;
    they are sweeter than honey.
¹⁰⁴ Your commandments give me
    understanding;
    no wonder I hate every false way
    of life.
¹⁰⁵ Your word is a lamp for my feet
    and a light for my path.
¹⁰⁶ I've promised it once, and I'll
    promise again:
    I will obey your wonderful laws.

The writer of this psalm loved reading God's Word. He was able to grow close to God by spending time reading Scripture. He also gained wisdom and knowledge. Today we can follow this writer's example. We can spend some time each day reading the Bible. It tells us the right way to go. It also gives us wisdom and knowledge for living a life that pleases God.

Why should you read the Bible?
All Scripture is inspired by God and is useful to teach us what is true and to make us realize what is wrong in our lives. It straightens us out and teaches us to do what is right.
2 Timothy 3:16

M A Y 18

David wrote this psalm to praise God for his knowledge. What does God know?

PSALM 139:1-18
God Knows Everything
For the choir director: A psalm of David.

¹ O LORD, you have examined my
    heart
    and know everything about me.
² You know when I sit down or
    stand up.
    You know my every thought
    when far away.

³ You chart the path ahead of me
    and tell me where to stop and
    rest.
    Every moment you know where
    I am.
⁴ You know what I am going to say
    even before I say it, LORD.
⁵ You both precede and follow me
    You place your hand of blessing
    on my head.

⁶ Such knowledge is too wonderful
     for me,
       too great for me to know!

⁷ I can never escape from your spirit!
     I can never get away from your
       presence!
⁸ If I go up to heaven, you are there;
     if I go down to the place of the
       dead,* you are there.
⁹ If I ride the wings of the morning,
     if I dwell by the farthest oceans,
¹⁰ even there your hand will guide
     me,
       and your strength will support
       me.
¹¹ I could ask the darkness to hide me
     and the light around me to
       become night—
¹²   but even in darkness I cannot
       hide from you.
   To you the night shines as bright as
     day.
       Darkness and light are both
       alike to you.

¹³ You made all the delicate, inner
     parts of my body
       and knit me together in my
       mother's womb.
¹⁴ Thank you for making me so
     wonderfully complex!
       Your workmanship is
       marvelous—and how well I
       know it.
¹⁵ You watched me as I was being
     formed in utter seclusion,
as I was woven together in the
     dark of the womb.
¹⁶ You saw me before I was born.
     Every day of my life was
       recorded in your book.
   Every moment was laid out
       before a single day had passed.

¹⁷ How precious are your thoughts
     about me,* O God!
       They are innumerable!
¹⁸ I can't even count them;
     they outnumber the grains of
       sand!
   And when I wake up in the
     morning,
       you are still with me!

*God knows everything. He knows our
thoughts and words. He knows our
past and our future. He even saw us
and put us together while we were in
our mothers' wombs. He also knows all
of our needs. Only a great and powerful God could know all of this. Like
David, let us praise God for his knowledge of us and concern for us.*

What does God know about you?
Your Father knows exactly what you
need even before you ask him!
Matthew 6:8

139:8 Hebrew *to Sheol.* **139:17** Or *How precious to me are your thoughts.*

God is good and deserves to be praised. How does he show his goodness?

PSALM 145:1-21
A God for All People

A psalm of praise of David.

¹ I will praise you, my God and King,
and bless your name forever and
ever.
² I will bless you every day,
and I will praise you forever.
³ Great is the LORD! He is most
worthy of praise!
His greatness is beyond
discovery!

⁴ Let each generation tell its children
of your mighty acts.
⁵ I will meditate* on your majestic,
glorious splendor
and your wonderful miracles.
⁶ Your awe-inspiring deeds will be
on every tongue;
I will proclaim your greatness.
⁷ Everyone will share the story of
your wonderful goodness;
they will sing with joy of your
righteousness.

⁸ The LORD is kind and merciful,
slow to get angry, full of
unfailing love.
⁹ The LORD is good to everyone.
He showers compassion on all
his creation.
¹⁰ All of your works will thank you,
LORD,

and your faithful followers will
bless you.
¹¹ They will talk together about the
glory of your kingdom;
they will celebrate examples of
your power.
¹² They will tell about your mighty
deeds
and about the majesty and glory
of your reign.
¹³ For your kingdom is an everlasting
kingdom.
You rule generation after
generation.

The LORD is faithful in all he says;
he is gracious in all he does.*
¹⁴ The LORD helps the fallen
and lifts up those bent beneath
their loads.
¹⁵ All eyes look to you for help;
you give them their food as they
need it.
¹⁶ When you open your hand,
you satisfy the hunger and thirst
of every living thing.

¹⁷ The LORD is righteous in
everything he does;
he is filled with kindness.
¹⁸ The LORD is close to all who call
on him,
yes, to all who call on him
sincerely.

145:5 Some manuscripts read *They will speak.* 145:13 The last two lines of 145:13 are not found in many of the ancient manuscripts.

¹⁹ He fulfills the desires of those who
fear him;
he hears their cries for help and
rescues them.
²⁰ The LORD protects all those who
love him,
but he destroys the wicked.

²¹ I will praise the LORD,
and everyone on earth will bless
his holy name
forever and forever.

*One way God shows his goodness is by
treating all people fairly. He never
shows favoritism to one person over
another. That is because God loves all
people. He created everyone, and he
cares for all people. Thank God for
being perfectly just and fair.*

**Does God treat evil
people unfairly?**

For he gives his sunlight to both the
evil and the good, and he sends rain
on the just and on the unjust, too.
Matthew 5:45

M A Y

20

*King Solomon wrote these wise sayings called proverbs.
What did he say about living a good life?*

PROVERBS 4:10-27

Wise Words

¹⁰ My child,* listen to me and do as I
say, and you will have a long, good
life. ¹¹ I will teach you wisdom's ways
and lead you in straight paths. ¹² If
you live a life guided by wisdom, you
won't limp or stumble as you run.
¹³ Carry out my instructions; don't
forsake them. Guard them, for they
will lead you to a fulfilled life.

¹⁴ Do not do as the wicked do or
follow the path of evildoers. ¹⁵ Avoid
their haunts. Turn away and go some-
where else, ¹⁶ for evil people cannot
sleep until they have done their evil
deed for the day. They cannot rest unless they have caused someone to
stumble. ¹⁷ They eat wickedness and
drink violence!

¹⁸ The way of the righteous is like the
first gleam of dawn, which shines ever
brighter until the full light of day. ¹⁹ But
the way of the wicked is like complete
darkness. Those who follow it have no
idea what they are stumbling over.

²⁰ Pay attention, my child, to what I
say. Listen carefully. ²¹ Don't lose sight
of my words. Let them penetrate deep
within your heart, ²² for they bring life
and radiant health to anyone who dis-
covers their meaning.

4:10 Hebrew *My son;* also in 4:20.

²³Above all else, guard your heart, for it affects everything you do.*

²⁴Avoid all perverse talk; stay far from corrupt speech.

²⁵Look straight ahead, and fix your eyes on what lies before you. ²⁶Mark out a straight path for your feet; then stick to the path and stay safe. ²⁷Don't get sidetracked; keep your feet from following evil.

Solomon said that living a good life involves two things. The first thing is wisdom. Wisdom helps us make good decisions in life. The second thing is to avoid following evil people. Imitating their actions only brings sorrow and pain. How are you living? Are you following Solomon's advice? Living by his advice is one of the wisest things you can do.

How can we act wisely?
Dear friends,* be quick to listen, slow to speak, and slow to get angry.
James 1:19

4:23 Hebrew *for from it flow the springs of life.* **1:19** Greek *Know this, my beloved brothers.*

M A Y

Solomon wrote down a lot of advice during his life. What did he advise young people to do?

ECCLESIASTES 11:7–12:2, 9-14
Be Happy, Don't Sin

⁷Light is sweet; it's wonderful to see the sun! ⁸When people live to be very old, let them rejoice in every day of life. But let them also remember that the dark days will be many. Everything still to come is meaningless.

⁹Young man, it's wonderful to be young! Enjoy every minute of it. Do everything you want to do; take it all in. But remember that you must give an account to God for everything you do. ¹⁰So banish grief and pain, but remember that youth, with a whole life before it, still faces the threat of meaninglessness.

¹²:¹Don't let the excitement of youth cause you to forget your Creator. Honor him in your youth before you grow old and no longer enjoy living. ²It will be too late then to remember him, when the light of the sun and moon and stars is dim to your old eyes, and there is no silver lining left among the clouds.

• • •

⁹Because the Teacher was wise, he taught the people everything he knew.

179

He collected proverbs and classified them. [10]Indeed, the Teacher taught the plain truth, and he did so in an interesting way.

[11]A wise teacher's words spur students to action and emphasize important truths. The collected sayings of the wise are like guidance from a shepherd.

[12]But, my child,* be warned: There is no end of opinions ready to be expressed. Studying them can go on forever and become very exhausting!

[13]Here is my final conclusion: Fear God and obey his commands, for this is the duty of every person. [14]God will judge us for everything we do, including every secret thing, whether good or bad.

12:12 Hebrew *my son.*

Solomon advised young people to enjoy being young. But he also advised young people to fear God and obey his commands. By obeying God, we can have a clear conscience before him. We will also have a life that is filled with meaning and purpose. Obeying God is a wise thing to do.

How can you show that you have God's wisdom?

Don't let anyone think less of you because you are young. Be an example to all believers in what you teach, in the way you live, in your love, your faith, and your purity.
1 Timothy 4:12

M A Y

Isaiah had a scary experience. He saw the Lord sitting on a throne in the Temple. What did Isaiah do before the Lord?

ISAIAH 6:1-8
God's Throne

In the year King Uzziah died, I saw the Lord. He was sitting on a lofty throne, and the train of his robe filled the Temple. [2]Hovering around him were mighty seraphim, each with six wings. With two wings they covered their faces, with two they covered their feet, and with the remaining two they flew. [3]In a great chorus they sang, "Holy, holy, holy is the LORD Almighty! The whole earth is filled with his glory!" [4]The glorious singing shook the Temple to its foundations, and the entire sanctuary was filled with smoke.

[5]Then I said, "My destruction is sealed, for I am a sinful man and a member of a sinful race. Yet I have seen the King, the LORD Almighty!"

[6]Then one of the seraphim flew over to the altar, and he picked up a burning coal with a pair of tongs. [7]He

touched my lips with it and said, "See, this coal has touched your lips. Now your guilt is removed, and your sins are forgiven."

⁸Then I heard the Lord asking, "Whom should I send as a messenger to my people? Who will go for us?"

And I said, "Lord, I'll go! Send me."

In God's presence, Isaiah cried out. Isaiah did this because he knew that he was a sinner. He also knew that a sinner could not be in the presence of a holy God and live. But because Isaiah was sorry for his sin, God spared his life and cleansed him of his sin. Coming into God's presence is just as serious today as it was in Isaiah's day. Each time we pray, we come before God. Let us honor God by coming with a humble and repentant heart.

How should we approach God?
So humble yourselves under the mighty power of God, and in his good time he will honor you.
1 Peter 5:6

M A Y

Isaiah predicted Jesus' suffering. He referred to Jesus as the man of sorrows. Why was Jesus sorrowful?

ISAIAH 53:1-12
The Man of Sorrows
Who has believed our message? To whom will the LORD reveal his saving power? ²My servant grew up in the LORD's presence like a tender green shoot, sprouting from a root in dry and sterile ground. There was nothing beautiful or majestic about his appearance, nothing to attract us to him. ³He was despised and rejected—a man of sorrows, acquainted with bitterest grief.

We turned our backs on him and looked the other way when he went by. He was despised, and we did not care.

⁴Yet it was our weaknesses he carried; it was our sorrows* that weighed him down. And we thought his troubles were a punishment from God for his own sins! ⁵But he was wounded and crushed for our sins. He was beaten that we might have peace. He was whipped, and we were healed! ⁶All of us have strayed away like sheep.

53:4 Or *Yet it was our sicknesses he carried; it was our diseases.*

We have left God's paths to follow our own. Yet the LORD laid on him the guilt and sins of us all.

⁷He was oppressed and treated harshly, yet he never said a word. He was led as a lamb to the slaughter. And as a sheep is silent before the shearers, he did not open his mouth. ⁸From prison and trial they led him away to his death. But who among the people realized that he was dying for their sins—that he was suffering their punishment? ⁹He had done no wrong, and he never deceived anyone. But he was buried like a criminal; he was put in a rich man's grave.

¹⁰But it was the LORD's good plan to crush him and fill him with grief. Yet when his life is made an offering for sin, he will have a multitude of children, many heirs. He will enjoy a long life, and the LORD's plan will prosper in his hands. ¹¹When he sees all that is accomplished by his anguish, he will be satisfied. And because of what he has experienced, my righteous servant will make it possible for many to be counted righteous, for he will bear all their sins. ¹²I will give him the honors of one who is mighty and great, because he exposed himself to death. He was counted among those who were sinners. He bore the sins of many and interceded for sinners.

Jesus was sorrowful because he took the punishment that every person deserves on himself. The punishment was death on a cross. But Jesus didn't deserve to die. He was the Son of God, and he never sinned. Even though he willingly died for everyone, he was hated by many. How do you feel about Jesus? Are you thankful that he died for you?

What did Jesus do for us?
He personally carried away our sins in his own body on the cross so we can be dead to sin and live for what is right. You have been healed by his wounds!
1 Peter 2:24

M A Y

God called Jeremiah to be his prophet. What did God promise him?

JEREMIAH 1:4-12, 17-19

The Rescuer

⁴The LORD gave me a message. He said, ⁵"I knew you before I formed you in your mother's womb. Before you were born I set you apart and appointed you as my spokesman to the world."

⁶"O Sovereign LORD," I said, "I can't speak for you! I'm too young!"

⁷"Don't say that," the LORD replied, "for you must go wherever I send you and say whatever I tell you. ⁸And don't be afraid of the people, for I will be with you and take care of you. I, the LORD, have spoken!"

⁹Then the LORD touched my mouth and said, "See, I have put my words in your mouth! ¹⁰Today I appoint you to stand up against nations and kingdoms. You are to uproot some and tear them down, to destroy and overthrow them. You are to build others up and plant them."

¹¹Then the LORD said to me, "Look, Jeremiah! What do you see?"

And I replied, "I see a branch from an almond tree."

¹²And the LORD said, "That's right, and it means that I am watching,* and I will surely carry out my threats of punishment."

• • •

¹⁷"Get up and get dressed. Go out, and tell them whatever I tell you to say. Do not be afraid of them, or I will make you look foolish in front of them. ¹⁸For see, today I have made you immune to their attacks. You are strong like a fortified city that cannot be captured, like an iron pillar or a bronze wall. None of the kings, officials, priests, or people of Judah will be able to stand against you. ¹⁹They will try, but they will fail. For I am with you, and I will take care of you. I, the LORD, have spoken!"

God promised to rescue Jeremiah from any troubles he would face. God may have made this promise because Jeremiah was afraid of being a prophet. This promise reassured Jeremiah that God would be with him. Before Jesus went to heaven, he made a similar promise to all of his followers. He promised that he would be with us. No matter what we go through, we can trust Jesus to be by our side.

Who protects you?
But the Lord is faithful; he will make you strong and guard you from the evil one.*
2 Thessalonians 3:3

1:12 The Hebrew word for "watching" sounds like the word for "almond tree."   **3:3** Or *from evil.*

M A Y

God gave Jeremiah some bad news about Judah's future. The king heard the news. How did he respond?

JEREMIAH 36:1-4, 21-31
A Book Burning
During the fourth year that Jehoiakim son of Josiah was king in Judah,* the LORD gave this message to Jeremiah: ²"Get a scroll, and write down all my messages against Israel, Judah, and the other nations. Begin with the

36:1 The fourth year of Jehoiakim's reign was 605 B.C.

first message back in the days of Josiah, and write down every message you have given, right up to the present time. ³Perhaps the people of Judah will repent if they see in writing all the terrible things I have planned for them. Then I will be able to forgive their sins and wrongdoings."

⁴So Jeremiah sent for Baruch son of Neriah, and as Jeremiah dictated, Baruch wrote down all the prophecies that the LORD had given him.

• • •

²¹The king sent Jehudi to get the scroll. Jehudi brought it from Elishama's room and read it to the king as all his officials stood by. ²²It was late autumn, and the king was in a winterized part of the palace, sitting in front of a fire to keep warm. ²³Whenever Jehudi finished reading three or four columns, the king took his knife and cut off that section of the scroll. He then threw it into the fire, section by section, until the whole scroll was burned up. ²⁴Neither the king nor his officials showed any signs of fear or repentance at what they heard. ²⁵Even when Elnathan, Delaiah, and Gemariah begged the king not to burn the scroll, he wouldn't listen.

²⁶Then the king commanded his son Jerahmeel, Seraiah son of Azriel, and Shelemiah son of Abdeel to arrest Baruch and Jeremiah. But the LORD had hidden them.

²⁷After the king had burned Jeremiah's scroll, the LORD gave Jeremiah another message. He said, ²⁸"Get another scroll, and write everything again just as you did on the scroll King Jehoiakim burned. ²⁹Then say to the king, 'This is what the LORD says: You burned the scroll because it said the king of Babylon would destroy this land and everything in it. ³⁰Now this is what the LORD says about King Jehoiakim of Judah: He will have no heirs to sit on the throne of David. His dead body will be thrown out to lie unburied—exposed to hot days and frosty nights. ³¹I will punish him and his family and his officials because of their sins. I will pour out on them and on all the people of Judah and Jerusalem all the disasters I have promised, for they would not listen to my warnings.' "

The king didn't like what God had to say. So he cut up God's message and threw it into the fire. But the king could not destroy God's Word. God had Jeremiah write everything again just as he had done on the scroll the king had burned. God's Word lasts forever. Like this king, we can not ignore God's Word or get rid of it. Instead, we should read it and believe it.

How should we respond to what the Bible says?
The Kingdom of God is near! Turn from your sins and believe this Good News!
Mark 1:15

God gave Ezekiel a message of hope. What did God tell Ezekiel?

EZEKIEL 37:1-14

Dry Bones Live

The LORD took hold of me, and I was carried away by the Spirit of the LORD to a valley filled with bones. [2] He led me around among the old, dry bones that covered the valley floor. They were scattered everywhere across the ground. [3] Then he asked me, "Son of man, can these bones become living people again?"

"O Sovereign LORD," I replied, "you alone know the answer to that."

[4] Then he said to me, "Speak to these bones and say, 'Dry bones, listen to the word of the LORD! [5] This is what the Sovereign LORD says: Look! I am going to breathe into you and make you live again! [6] I will put flesh and muscles on you and cover you with skin. I will put breath into you, and you will come to life. Then you will know that I am the LORD.'"

[7] So I spoke these words, just as he told me. Suddenly as I spoke, there was a rattling noise all across the valley. The bones of each body came together and attached themselves as they had been before. [8] Then as I watched, muscles and flesh formed over the bones. Then skin formed to cover their bodies, but they still had no breath in them.

[9] Then he said to me, "Speak to the winds and say: 'This is what the Sovereign LORD says: Come, O breath, from the four winds! Breathe into these dead bodies so that they may live again.'"

[10] So I spoke as he commanded me, and the wind entered the bodies, and they began to breathe. They all came to life and stood up on their feet—a great army of them.

[11] Then he said to me, "Son of man,

The Israelites were captives in a foreign land. They had little hope that they would ever see their home again. But God had a message for them that he gave to Ezekiel. He told Ezekiel that he would restore the Israelites' hope and bring them back home. He gave this message using a valley of dry bones. Through a miracle or a vision, God caused dry bones to be clothed with flesh. He then brought these bodies back to life. This is what he would do for Israel. This is also what it is like when we receive Jesus as our Savior and he fills us with his Spirit. We are reborn and filled with hope.

How does God make us alive spiritually?

Don't you realize that all of you together are the temple of God and that the Spirit of God lives in* you?
1 Corinthians 3:16

3:16 Or *among.*

these bones represent the people of Israel. They are saying, 'We have become old, dry bones—all hope is gone.' ¹²Now give them this message from the Sovereign LORD: O my people, I will open your graves of exile and cause you to rise again. Then I will bring you back to the land of Israel.

¹³When this happens, O my people, you will know that I am the LORD. ¹⁴I will put my Spirit in you, and you will live and return home to your own land. Then you will know that I am the LORD. You will see that I have done everything just as I promised. I, the LORD, have spoken!"

M A Y 27

The king ordered Daniel and his friends to eat food God had told the Israelites not to eat. What did Daniel do?

DANIEL 1:3-5, 8-17

Vegetables and Water

• • •

³Then the king ordered Ashpenaz, who was in charge of the palace officials, to bring to the palace some of the young men of Judah's royal family and other noble families, who had been brought to Babylon as captives. ⁴"Select only strong, healthy, and good-looking young men," he said. "Make sure they are well versed in every branch of learning, are gifted with knowledge and good sense, and have the poise needed to serve in the royal palace. Teach these young men the language and literature of the Babylonians.*" ⁵The king assigned them a daily ration of the best food and wine from his own kitchens. They were to be trained for a three-year period, and then some of them would be made his advisers in the royal court.

⁸But Daniel made up his mind not to defile himself by eating the food and wine given to them by the king. He asked the chief official for permission to eat other things instead. ⁹Now God had given the chief official great respect for Daniel. ¹⁰But he was alarmed by Daniel's suggestion. "My lord the king has ordered that you eat this food and wine," he said. "If you become pale and thin compared to the other youths your age, I am afraid the king will have me beheaded for neglecting my duties."

¹¹Daniel talked it over with the attendant who had been appointed by the chief official to look after Daniel, Hananiah, Mishael, and Azariah. ¹²"Test us for ten days on a diet of vegetables and water," Daniel said. ¹³"At the end of the ten days, see how we look compared to the other young

1:4 *Or of the Chaldeans.*

men who are eating the king's rich food. Then you can decide whether or not to let us continue eating our diet." ¹⁴So the attendant agreed to Daniel's suggestion and tested them for ten days.

¹⁵At the end of the ten days, Daniel and his three friends looked healthier and better nourished than the young men who had been eating the food assigned by the king. ¹⁶So after that, the attendant fed them only vegetables instead of the rich foods and wines. ¹⁷God gave these four young men an unusual aptitude for learning the literature and science of the time. And God gave Daniel special ability in understanding the meanings of visions and dreams.

Daniel decided not to sin. Then he came up with a good idea. He asked an official to allow him and his friends to eat only vegetables for ten days. If he and his friends looked sickly after that time, they would eat the king's food. But if they looked healthy, the official would allow them to continue this diet. The plan worked, and Daniel and his friends didn't have to disobey God. Daniel's commitment to obey God is a good commitment for us to make, too. God gave Daniel the power to obey. He also will give us the power we need to follow him each day.

How can we avoid sinning?
So humble yourselves before God.
Resist the Devil, and he
will flee from you.
James 4:7

M A Y
28

The king ordered his astrologers to describe to him a dream he had had. He also told them to interpret the dream or they would die. What did Daniel do in this crisis?

DANIEL 2:1-19

Guessing the King's Dream

One night during the second year of his reign,* Nebuchadnezzar had a dream that disturbed him so much that he couldn't sleep. ²He called in his magicians, enchanters, sorcerers, and astrologers,* and he demanded that they tell him what he had dreamed. As they stood before the king, ³he said, "I have had a dream that troubles me. Tell me what I dreamed, for I must know what it means."

⁴Then the astrologers answered the

2:1 The second year of Nebuchadnezzar's reign was 603 B.C. 2:2 Or *Chaldeans*; also in 2:4, 5, 10. 2:4 The original text from this point through chapter 7 is in Aramaic.

king in Aramaic,* "Long live the king! Tell us the dream, and we will tell you what it means."

⁵But the king said to the astrologers, "I am serious about this. If you don't tell me what my dream was and what it means, you will be torn limb from limb, and your houses will be demolished into heaps of rubble! ⁶But if you tell me what I dreamed and what the dream means, I will give you many wonderful gifts and honors. Just tell me the dream and what it means!"

⁷They said again, "Please, Your Majesty. Tell us the dream, and we will tell you what it means."

⁸The king replied, "I can see through your trick! You are trying to stall for time because you know I am serious about what I said. ⁹If you don't tell me the dream, you will be condemned. You have conspired to tell me lies in hopes that something will change. But tell me the dream, and then I will know that you can tell me what it means."

¹⁰The astrologers replied to the king, "There isn't a man alive who can tell Your Majesty his dream! And no king, however great and powerful, has ever asked such a thing of any magician, enchanter, or astrologer! ¹¹This is an impossible thing the king requires. No one except the gods can tell you your dream, and they do not live among people."

¹²The king was furious when he heard this, and he sent out orders to execute all the wise men of Babylon. ¹³And because of the king's decree, men were sent to find and kill Daniel and his friends. ¹⁴When Arioch, the commander of the king's guard, came to kill them, Daniel handled the situation with wisdom and discretion. ¹⁵He asked Arioch, "Why has the king issued such a harsh decree?" So Arioch told him all that had happened. ¹⁶Daniel went at once to see the king and requested more time so he could tell the king what the dream meant.

¹⁷Then Daniel went home and told his friends Hananiah, Mishael, and Azariah what had happened. ¹⁸He urged them to ask the God of heaven to show them his mercy by telling them the secret, so they would not be executed along with the other wise men of Babylon. ¹⁹That night the secret was revealed to Daniel in a vision. . . .

Daniel prayed. He also asked others to pray for him. Have you ever faced a crisis? Do what Daniel did. Pray and ask for prayer. Then trust God to give you the answer you need.

How did Jesus tell us to pray?
Keep on asking, and you will be given what you ask for. Keep on looking, and you will find. Keep on knocking, and the door will be opened.
Matthew 7:7

The king ordered everyone to worship his statue or die.
What did Shadrach, Meshach, and Abednego do?

DANIEL 3:1-18

The Gold Statue

King Nebuchadnezzar made a gold statue ninety feet tall and nine feet wide* and set it up on the plain of Dura in the province of Babylon. 2Then he sent messages to the princes, prefects, governors, advisers, counselors, judges, magistrates, and all the provincial officials to come to the dedication of the statue he had set up. 3When all these officials* had arrived and were standing before the image King Nebuchadnezzar had set up, 4a herald shouted out, "People of all races and nations and languages, listen to the king's command! 5When you hear the sound of the horn, flute, zither, lyre, harp, pipes, and other instruments,* bow to the ground to worship King Nebuchadnezzar's gold statue. 6Anyone who refuses to obey will immediately be thrown into a blazing furnace."

7So at the sound of the musical instruments,* all the people, whatever their race or nation or language, bowed to the ground and worshiped the statue that King Nebuchadnezzar had set up.

8But some of the astrologers* went to the king and informed on the Jews. 9They said to King Nebuchadnezzar, "Long live the king! 10You issued a decree requiring all the people to bow down and worship the gold statue when they hear the sound of the musical instruments.* 11That decree also states that those who refuse to obey must be thrown into a blazing furnace. 12But there are some Jews—Shadrach, Meshach, and Abednego—whom you have put in charge of the province of Babylon. They have defied Your Majesty by refusing to serve your gods or to worship the gold statue you have set up."

13Then Nebuchadnezzar flew into a rage and ordered Shadrach, Meshach, and Abednego to be brought before him. When they were brought in, 14Nebuchadnezzar said to them, "Is it true, Shadrach, Meshach, and Abednego, that you refuse to serve my gods or to worship the gold statue I have set up? 15I will give you one more chance. If you bow down and worship the statue I have made when you hear the sound of the musical instruments, all will be well. But if you refuse, you will be thrown immediately into the blazing furnace. What

---

3:1 Aramaic *60 cubits* [27 meters] *tall and 6 cubits* [2.7 meters] *wide.* 3:3 Aramaic *the princes, prefects, governors, advisers, counselors, judges, magistrates, and all the provincial officials.* 3:5 The identification of some of these musical instruments is uncertain. 3:7 Aramaic *the horn, flute, zither, lyre, harp, and other instruments of the musical ensemble.* 3:8 Aramaic *Chaldeans.* 3:10 Aramaic *the horn, flute, zither, lyre, harp, pipes, and other instruments of the musical ensemble;* also in 3:15.

god will be able to rescue you from my power then?"

[16]Shadrach, Meshach, and Abednego replied, "O Nebuchadnezzar, we do not need to defend ourselves before you. [17]If we are thrown into the blazing furnace, the God whom we serve is able to save us. He will rescue us from your power, Your Majesty. [18]But even if he doesn't, Your Majesty can be sure that we will never serve your gods or worship the gold statue you have set up."

Shadrach, Meshach, and Abednego would only worship the true God. They refused to worship the statue, even though they could be killed. Today there aren't many authorities who force us to worship people or things other than God. But there are many things or people that we may worship without realizing it. We may idolize sports stars, movie stars, or rock stars. Putting anything or anyone before God in our life is wrong. Instead, we should follow the example of Shadrach, Meshach, and Abednego and worship only God. He is the only one worthy of our worship.

What has God told us about worshiping him?

Do not worship any other gods besides me. Do not make idols of any kind, whether in the shape of birds or animals or fish. You must never worship or bow down to them, for I, the LORD your God, am a jealous God who will not share your affection with any other god!
Exodus 20:3-5

M A Y

The king threw Shadrach, Meshach, and Abednego into a blazing furnace. What happened to them?

DANIEL 3:19-28

The Blazing Furnace

[19]Nebuchadnezzar was so furious with Shadrach, Meshach, and Abednego that his face became distorted with rage. He commanded that the furnace be heated seven times hotter than usual. [20]Then he ordered some of the strongest men of his army to bind Shadrach, Meshach, and Abednego

and throw them into the blazing furnace. ²¹So they tied them up and threw them into the furnace, fully clothed. ²²And because the king, in his anger, had demanded such a hot fire in the furnace, the flames leaped out and killed the soldiers as they threw the three men in! ²³So Shadrach, Meshach, and Abednego, securely tied, fell down into the roaring flames.

²⁴But suddenly, as he was watching, Nebuchadnezzar jumped up in amazement and exclaimed to his advisers, "Didn't we tie up three men and throw them into the furnace?"

"Yes," they said, "we did indeed, Your Majesty."

²⁵"Look!" Nebuchadnezzar shouted. "I see four men, unbound, walking around in the fire. They aren't even hurt by the flames! And the fourth looks like a divine being*!"

²⁶Then Nebuchadnezzar came as close as he could to the door of the flaming furnace and shouted: "Shadrach, Meshach, and Abednego, servants of the Most High God, come out! Come here!" So Shadrach, Meshach, and Abednego stepped out of the fire.

3:25 Aramaic *like a son of the gods.*

²⁷Then the princes, prefects, governors, and advisers crowded around them and saw that the fire had not touched them. Not a hair on their heads was singed, and their clothing was not scorched. They didn't even smell of smoke!

²⁸Then Nebuchadnezzar said, "Praise to the God of Shadrach, Meshach, and Abednego! He sent his angel to rescue his servants who trusted in him. They defied the king's command and were willing to die rather than serve or worship any god except their own God."

Shadrach, Meshach, and Abednego trusted God with their lives. God rewarded their trust. Even in a raging fire, God protected them. How do you need to trust God? You may never get thrown into a blazing furnace, but God is still there for you. He cares about you, and he will not abandon you.

Who did Jesus say we could trust?
Don't be troubled. You trust God,
now trust in me.
John 14:1

M A Y

The king boasted about what he had done. What did God do to him?

DANIEL 4:29-37
A King Eats Grass
²⁹"Twelve months later, he was taking a walk on the flat roof of the royal palace in Babylon. ³⁰As he looked out across the city, he said, 'Just look at this great city of Babylon! I, by my own mighty

power, have built this beautiful city as my royal residence and as an expression of my royal splendor.'

31 "While he was still speaking these words, a voice called down from heaven, 'O King Nebuchadnezzar, this message is for you! You are no longer ruler of this kingdom. 32 You will be driven from human society. You will live in the fields with the wild animals, and you will eat grass like a cow. Seven periods of time will pass while you live this way, until you learn that the Most High rules over the kingdoms of the world and gives them to anyone he chooses.'

33 "That very same hour the prophecy was fulfilled, and Nebuchadnezzar was driven from human society. He ate grass like a cow, and he was drenched with the dew of heaven. He lived this way until his hair was as long as eagles' feathers and his nails were like birds' claws.

34 "After this time had passed, I, Nebuchadnezzar, looked up to heaven. My sanity returned, and I praised and worshiped the Most High and honored the one who lives forever.

His rule is everlasting,
    and his kingdom is eternal.
35 All the people of the earth
    are nothing compared to him.

He has the power to do as he pleases
    among the angels of heaven
    and with those who live on earth.
No one can stop him or
    challenge him,
    saying, 'What do you mean
        by doing these things?'

36 "When my sanity returned to me, so did my honor and glory and kingdom. My advisers and officers sought me out, and I was reestablished as head of my kingdom, with even greater honor than before.

37 "Now I, Nebuchadnezzar, praise and glorify and honor the King of heaven. All his acts are just and true, and he is able to humble those who are proud."

God humbled this king so much by making the king crazy enough to act like an animal and eat grass. This shows how much God hates boasting. Boasting steals the credit that God deserves. Be careful not to boast about yourself. Give God the credit instead.

Who does God exalt or honor?
But those who exalt themselves will be humbled, and those who humble themselves will be exalted.
Matthew 23:12

JUNE

*Strange writing appeared on a wall. What did the words mean?
What did the king do wrong?*

DANIEL 5:1-6, 13-30

Writing on the Wall

A number of years later, King Belshazzar gave a great feast for a thousand of his nobles and drank wine with them. ²While Belshazzar was drinking, he gave orders to bring in the gold and silver cups that his predecessor,* Nebuchadnezzar, had taken from the Temple in Jerusalem, so that he and his nobles, his wives, and his concubines might drink from them. ³So they brought these gold cups taken from the Temple of God in Jerusalem, and the king and his nobles, his wives, and his concubines drank from them. ⁴They drank toasts from them to honor their idols made of gold, silver, bronze, iron, wood, and stone.

⁵At that very moment they saw the fingers of a human hand writing on the plaster wall of the king's palace, near the lampstand. The king himself saw the hand as it wrote, ⁶and his face turned pale with fear. Such terror gripped him that his knees knocked together and his legs gave way beneath him.

• • •

¹³So Daniel was brought in before the king. The king asked him, "Are you Daniel, who was exiled from Judah by my predecessor, King Nebuchadnezzar? ¹⁴I have heard that you have the spirit of the gods within you and that you are filled with insight, understanding, and wisdom. ¹⁵My wise men and enchanters have tried to read this writing on the wall, but they cannot. ¹⁶I am told that you can give interpretations and solve difficult problems. If you can read these words and tell me their meaning, you will be clothed in purple robes of royal honor, and you will wear a gold chain around your neck. You will become the third highest ruler in the kingdom."

¹⁷Daniel answered the king, "Keep your gifts or give them to someone else, but I will tell you what the writing means. ¹⁸Your Majesty, the Most High God gave sovereignty, majesty, glory, and honor to your predecessor, Nebuchadnezzar. ¹⁹He made him so great that people of all races and nations and languages trembled before him in fear. He killed those he wanted to kill and spared those he wanted to spare. He honored those he wanted to honor and disgraced those he wanted to disgrace. ²⁰But when his heart and mind were hardened with pride, he was brought down from his royal throne and stripped of his glory. ²¹He was driven from human society. He was given the mind of an animal, and he

5:2 Aramaic *father;* also in 5:11, 13, 18.

lived among the wild donkeys. He ate grass like a cow, and he was drenched with the dew of heaven, until he learned that the Most High God rules the kingdoms of the world and appoints anyone he desires to rule over them.

22"You are his successor,* O Belshazzar, and you knew all this, yet you have not humbled yourself. 23For you have defied the Lord of heaven and have had these cups from his Temple brought before you. You and your nobles and your wives and concubines have been drinking wine from them while praising gods of silver, gold, bronze, iron, wood, and stone—gods that neither see nor hear nor know anything at all. But you have not honored the God who gives you the breath of life and controls your destiny! 24So God has sent this hand to write a message.

25"This is the message that was written: MENE, MENE, TEKEL, PARSIN. 26This is what these words mean:

Mene means 'numbered'—God has numbered the days of your reign and has brought it to an end.
27 Tekel means 'weighed'—you have been weighed on the balances and have failed the test.

28 Parsin* means 'divided'—your kingdom has been divided and given to the Medes and Persians."

29Then at Belshazzar's command, Daniel was dressed in purple robes, a gold chain was hung around his neck, and he was proclaimed the third highest ruler in the kingdom.

30That very night Belshazzar, the Babylonian* king, was killed.*

The king refused to honor God. In fact, he insulted God by using the gold cups from God's Temple for a wild party. The king and his nobles even drank toasts to their idols from these cups. So God decided to take away his kingdom, which was the message he wrote on the wall. God opposes those who oppose him. But God supports those who honor him. We can honor God by worshiping him and by obeying his commands.

Who deserves our praise and honor?
All honor to the God and Father of our Lord Jesus Christ, for it is by his boundless mercy that God has given us the privilege of being born again.
1 Peter 1:3

5:22 Aramaic *son*. **5:28** Aramaic *Peres*, the singular of *Parsin*. **5:30a** Or *Chaldean*. **5:30b** The Persians and Medes conquered Babylon in October 539 B.C.

J U N E

Daniel was an excellent administrator. His enemies were jealous and tried to find some fault in him. What did they find?

DANIEL 6:1-10
Faultfinders

Darius the Mede decided to divide the kingdom into 120 provinces, and he appointed a prince to rule over each province. ²The king also chose Daniel and two others as administrators to supervise the princes and to watch out for the king's interests. ³Daniel soon proved himself more capable than all the other administrators and princes. Because of his great ability, the king made plans to place him over the entire empire. ⁴Then the other administrators and princes began searching for some fault in the way Daniel was handling his affairs, but they couldn't find anything to criticize. He was faithful and honest and always responsible. ⁵So they concluded, "Our only chance of finding grounds for accusing Daniel will be in connection with the requirements of his religion."

⁶So the administrators and princes went to the king and said, "Long live King Darius! ⁷We administrators, prefects, princes, advisers, and other officials have unanimously agreed that Your Majesty should make a law that will be strictly enforced. Give orders that for the next thirty days anyone who prays to anyone, divine or human—except to Your Majesty—will be thrown to the lions. ⁸And let Your Majesty issue and sign this law so it cannot be changed, a law of the Medes and Persians, which cannot be revoked." ⁹So King Darius signed the law.

¹⁰But when Daniel learned that the law had been signed, he went home and knelt down as usual in his upstairs room, with its windows open toward Jerusalem. He prayed three times a day, just as he had always done, giving thanks to his God.

Daniel's enemies could not find a single fault in him. He worked hard and did what was right. So they decided to attack Daniel's faith in God. They had the king pass a law that made it illegal to pray to anyone other than the king. Like Daniel, we should live faultless lives, obeying God at all costs. The only way we can do this is to depend on God to help us live obedient lives.

How can we live a faultless life?
In everything you do, stay away from complaining and arguing, so that no one can speak a word of blame against you. You are to live clean, innocent lives as children of God in a dark world full of crooked and perverse people. Let your lives shine brightly before them.
Philippians 2:14-15

JUNE

Daniel was arrested and thrown into the lions' den for praying to God. Did he survive the night?

DANIEL 6:11-27
Hungry Lions

¹¹The officials went together to Daniel's house and found him praying and asking for God's help. ¹²So they went back to the king and reminded him about his law. "Did you not sign a law that for the next thirty days anyone who prays to anyone, divine or human—except to Your Majesty—will be thrown to the lions?"

"Yes," the king replied, "that decision stands; it is a law of the Medes and Persians, which cannot be revoked."

¹³Then they told the king, "That man Daniel, one of the captives from Judah, is paying no attention to you or your law. He still prays to his God three times a day."

¹⁴Hearing this, the king was very angry with himself for signing the law, and he tried to find a way to save Daniel. He spent the rest of the day looking for a way to get Daniel out of this predicament. ¹⁵In the evening the men went together to the king and said, "Your Majesty knows that according to the law of the Medes and the Persians, no law that the king signs can be changed."

¹⁶So at last the king gave orders for Daniel to be arrested and thrown into the den of lions. The king said to him, "May your God, whom you worship continually, rescue you." ¹⁷A stone was brought and placed over the mouth of the den. The king sealed the stone with his own royal seal and the seals of his nobles, so that no one could rescue Daniel from the lions. ¹⁸Then the king returned to his palace and spent the night fasting. He refused his usual entertainment and couldn't sleep at all that night.

¹⁹Very early the next morning, the king hurried out to the lions' den. ²⁰When he got there, he called out in anguish, "Daniel, servant of the living God! Was your God, whom you worship continually, able to rescue you from the lions?"

²¹Daniel answered, "Long live the king! ²²My God sent his angel to shut the lions' mouths so that they would not hurt me, for I have been found innocent in his sight. And I have not wronged you, Your Majesty."

²³The king was overjoyed and ordered that Daniel be lifted from the den. Not a scratch was found on him because he had trusted in his God. ²⁴Then the king gave orders to arrest the men who had maliciously accused Daniel. He had them thrown into the lions' den, along with their wives and children. The lions leaped on them and tore them apart before they even hit the floor of the den.

²⁵Then King Darius sent this mes-

sage to the people of every race and nation and language throughout the world:

"Peace and prosperity to you!

26 "I decree that everyone throughout my kingdom should tremble with fear before the God of Daniel.

For he is the living God,
  and he will endure forever.
His kingdom will never be
    destroyed,
  and his rule will never end.
27 He rescues and saves his people;
  he performs miraculous signs
    and wonders
  in the heavens and on earth.
He has rescued Daniel
  from the power of the lions."

Hungry lions waited to make Daniel their supper. But God came to the rescue. He shut the lions' mouths and kept Daniel safe. God has rescued his followers in some amazing ways. The most amazing way, though, was when he sent his Son, Jesus, to die for our sins. Jesus has rescued us from a death worse than being eaten by lions. He has rescued us from spending eternity in hell. Praise God for rescuing you from eternal death.

What has Jesus rescued us from?
May grace and peace be yours from God our Father and from the Lord Jesus Christ. He died for our sins, just as God our Father planned, in order to rescue us from this evil world in which we live.
Galatians 1:3-4

J U N E

God wanted Jonah to go to Nineveh. What did Jonah do?

JONAH 1:1-15
On the Run
The LORD gave this message to Jonah son of Amittai: 2 "Get up and go to the great city of Nineveh! Announce my judgment against it because I have seen how wicked its people are."

3 But Jonah got up and went in the opposite direction in order to get away from the LORD. He went down to the seacoast, to the port of Joppa, where he found a ship leaving for Tarshish.

He bought a ticket and went on board, hoping that by going away to the west he could escape from the LORD.

4 But as the ship was sailing along, suddenly the LORD flung a powerful wind over the sea, causing a violent storm that threatened to send them to the bottom. 5 Fearing for their lives, the desperate sailors shouted to their gods for help and threw the cargo overboard to lighten the ship. And all this time Jonah was sound asleep down in

the hold. ⁶So the captain went down after him. "How can you sleep at a time like this?" he shouted. "Get up and pray to your god! Maybe he will have mercy on us and spare our lives."

⁷Then the crew cast lots to see which of them had offended the gods and caused the terrible storm. When they did this, Jonah lost the toss. ⁸"What have you done to bring this awful storm down on us?" they demanded. "Who are you? What is your line of work? What country are you from? What is your nationality?"

⁹And Jonah answered, "I am a Hebrew, and I worship the LORD, the God of heaven, who made the sea and the land." ¹⁰Then he told them that he was running away from the LORD.

The sailors were terrified when they heard this. "Oh, why did you do it?" they groaned. ¹¹And since the storm was getting worse all the time, they asked him, "What should we do to you to stop this storm?"

¹²"Throw me into the sea," Jonah said, "and it will become calm again. For I know that this terrible storm is all my fault."

¹³Instead, the sailors tried even harder to row the boat ashore. But the stormy sea was too violent for them, and they couldn't make it. ¹⁴Then they cried out to the LORD, Jonah's God. "O LORD," they pleaded, "don't make us die for this man's sin. And don't hold us responsible for his death, because it isn't our fault. O LORD, you have sent this storm upon him for your own good reasons."

¹⁵Then the sailors picked Jonah up and threw him into the raging sea, and the storm stopped at once!

Jonah tried to run from God. But he did not get far. God caused a storm that almost sank the ship he was on. The sailors had to throw Jonah overboard to save themselves. Jonah learned that running from God only got him into more trouble. We can also learn from Jonah's mistake. Do not try to run from God. You will just run into trouble.

What do we need to be careful of?
Be careful then, dear friends.* Make sure that your own hearts are not evil and unbelieving, turning you away from the living God.
Hebrews 3:12

3:12 Greek *brothers.*

J U N E

*A great fish swallowed Jonah. With seaweed wrapped around his head,
Jonah prayed to God. What happened?*

JONAH 1:17–2:10

A Fish Full

¹⁷Now the LORD had arranged for a great fish to swallow Jonah. And Jonah was inside the fish for three days and three nights.

^{2:1}Then Jonah prayed to the LORD his God from inside the fish. ²He said, "I cried out to the LORD in my great trouble, and he answered me. I called to you from the world of the dead,* and LORD, you heard me! ³You threw me into the ocean depths, and I sank down to the heart of the sea. I was buried beneath your wild and stormy waves. ⁴Then I said, 'O LORD, you have driven me from your presence. How will I ever again see your holy Temple?'

⁵"I sank beneath the waves, and death was very near. The waters closed in around me, and seaweed wrapped itself around my head. ⁶I sank down to the very roots of the mountains. I was locked out of life and imprisoned in the land of the dead. But you, O LORD my God, have snatched me from the yawning jaws of death!

⁷"When I had lost all hope, I turned my thoughts once more to the LORD.

And my earnest prayer went out to you in your holy Temple. ⁸Those who worship false gods turn their backs on all God's mercies. ⁹But I will offer sacrifices to you with songs of praise, and I will fulfill all my vows. For my salvation comes from the LORD alone."

¹⁰Then the LORD ordered the fish to spit up Jonah on the beach, and it did.

Jonah was not too comfortable. He was inside a fish! He thought he was as good as dead. But then he prayed. God heard Jonah's prayer and had the fish spit him up on the beach. Prayer is important in our relationship with God. We should not let anything stop us from talking to him, not even our problems. Keep praying in rough situations.

What can you do when bad things happen?

Pray at all times and on every occasion in the power of the Holy Spirit. Stay alert and be persistent in your prayers for all Christians everywhere.

Ephesians 6:18

2:2 Hebrew *from Sheol.*

J U N E

*Jonah went to Nineveh and gave the people God's message.
How did the people of Nineveh respond?*

JONAH 3:1-10
News for Nineveh

Then the LORD spoke to Jonah a second time: [2] "Get up and go to the great city of Nineveh, and deliver the message of judgment I have given you."

[3] This time Jonah obeyed the LORD's command and went to Nineveh, a city so large that it took three days to see it all. [4] On the day Jonah entered the city, he shouted to the crowds: "Forty days from now Nineveh will be destroyed!" [5] The people of Nineveh believed God's message, and from the greatest to the least, they decided to go without food and wear sackcloth to show their sorrow.

[6] When the king of Nineveh heard what Jonah was saying, he stepped down from his throne and took off his royal robes. He dressed himself in sackcloth and sat on a heap of ashes. [7] Then the king and his nobles sent this decree throughout the city: "No one, not even the animals, may eat or drink anything at all. [8] Everyone is required to wear sackcloth and pray earnestly to God. Everyone must turn from their evil ways and stop all their violence. [9] Who can tell? Perhaps even yet God will have pity on us and hold back his fierce anger from destroying us."

[10] When God saw that they had put a stop to their evil ways, he had mercy on them and didn't carry out the destruction he had threatened.

The people of Nineveh listened to Jonah and stopped sinning. They also prayed and fasted so that God would forgive them. God saw their humilty and sorrow. He had mercy on them and didn't destroy them. God also calls us to turn away from our sin. He calls us to be obedient to his Word, the Bible. We should not ignore his call. We need to turn away from our sins so that we can be forgiven.

Why doesn't God destroy bad people?

The Lord isn't really being slow about his promise to return, as some people think. No, he is being patient for your sake. He does not want anyone to perish, so he is giving more time for everyone to repent.
2 Peter 3:9

JUNE

*Jonah was mad that God had spared the people of Nineveh.
What did God teach him?*

JONAH 4:1-11
A Hungry Worm

This change of plans upset Jonah, and he became very angry. ²So he complained to the LORD about it: "Didn't I say before I left home that you would do this, LORD? That is why I ran away to Tarshish! I knew that you were a gracious and compassionate God, slow to get angry and filled with unfailing love. I knew how easily you could cancel your plans for destroying these people. ³Just kill me now, LORD! I'd rather be dead than alive because nothing I predicted is going to happen."

⁴The LORD replied, "Is it right for you to be angry about this?"

⁵Then Jonah went out to the east side of the city and made a shelter to sit under as he waited to see if anything would happen to the city. ⁶And the LORD God arranged for a leafy plant to grow there, and soon it spread its broad leaves over Jonah's head, shading him from the sun. This eased some of his discomfort, and Jonah was very grateful for the plant.

⁷But God also prepared a worm! The next morning at dawn the worm ate through the stem of the plant, so that it soon died and withered away. ⁸And as the sun grew hot, God sent a scorching east wind to blow on Jonah. The sun beat down on his head until he grew faint and wished to die. "Death is certainly better than this!" he exclaimed.

⁹Then God said to Jonah, "Is it right for you to be angry because the plant died?"

"Yes," Jonah retorted, "even angry enough to die!"

¹⁰Then the LORD said, "You feel sorry about the plant, though you did nothing to put it there. And a plant is only, at best, short lived. ¹¹But Nineveh has more than 120,000 people living in spiritual darkness,* not to mention all the animals. Shouldn't I feel sorry for such a great city?"

Jonah was outraged that God forgave the Ninevites. But God taught Jonah that he is a loving and forgiving God. Through a vine, God showed Jonah that people are valuable to him. He wants everyone to run to him for mercy and forgiveness.

How does God treat people who turn from their sin?

What can we say? Was God being unfair? Of course not! For God said to Moses, "I will show mercy to anyone I choose, and I will show compassion to anyone I choose."*
Romans 9:14-15

4:11 Hebrew *people who don't know their right hands from their left.* **9:15** Exod 33:19.

In the Temple, an angel appeared to Zechariah and gave him a message from God. How did Zechariah respond to the message?

LUKE 1:11-25
The Angel and Zechariah

[11]Zechariah was in the sanctuary when an angel of the Lord appeared, standing to the right of the incense altar. [12]Zechariah was overwhelmed with fear. [13]But the angel said, "Don't be afraid, Zechariah! For God has heard your prayer, and your wife, Elizabeth, will bear you a son! And you are to name him John. [14]You will have great joy and gladness, and many will rejoice with you at his birth, [15]for he will be great in the eyes of the Lord. He must never touch wine or hard liquor, and he will be filled with the Holy Spirit, even before his birth.* [16]And he will persuade many Israelites to turn to the Lord their God. [17]He will be a man with the spirit and power of Elijah, the prophet of old. He will precede the coming of the Lord, preparing the people for his arrival. He will turn the hearts of the fathers to their children, and he will change disobedient minds to accept godly wisdom."*

[18]Zechariah said to the angel, "How can I know this will happen? I'm an old man now, and my wife is also well along in years."

[19]Then the angel said, "I am Gabriel! I stand in the very presence of God. It was he who sent me to bring you this good news! [20]And now, since you didn't believe what I said, you won't be able to speak until the child is born. For my words will certainly come true at the proper time."

[21]Meanwhile, the people were waiting for Zechariah to come out, wondering why he was taking so long. [22]When he finally did come out, he couldn't speak to them. Then they realized from his gestures that he must have seen a vision in the Temple sanctuary.

[23]He stayed at the Temple until his term of service was over, and then he

---

Zechariah was amazed. He couldn't believe that God would bless him and his wife with a child in their old age. But nothing is too difficult for God! Zechariah learned this lesson the hard way. Because of his unbelief, he couldn't speak until his child was born. We can learn from Zechariah's example. When God says he will do something, we can believe that he will.

How do we know that God is able to help us?

I am the LORD, the God of all the peoples of the world. Is anything too hard for me?
Jeremiah 32:27

1:15 Or *even from birth.*   1:17 See Mal 4:5-6.

returned home. [24]Soon afterward his wife, Elizabeth, became pregnant and went into seclusion for five months. [25]"How kind the Lord is!" she exclaimed. "He has taken away my disgrace of having no children!"

JUNE

The angel Gabriel appeared to Mary. What did he tell her?

LUKE 1:26-38

An Angel and Mary

[26]In the sixth month of Elizabeth's pregnancy, God sent the angel Gabriel to Nazareth, a village in Galilee, [27]to a virgin named Mary. She was engaged to be married to a man named Joseph, a descendant of King David. [28]Gabriel appeared to her and said, "Greetings, favored woman! The Lord is with you!*"

[29]Confused and disturbed, Mary tried to think what the angel could mean. [30]"Don't be frightened, Mary," the angel told her, "for God has decided to bless you! [31]You will become pregnant and have a son, and you are to name him Jesus. [32]He will be very great and will be called the Son of the Most High. And the Lord God will give him the throne of his ancestor David. [33]And he will reign over Israel* forever; his Kingdom will never end!"

[34]Mary asked the angel, "But how can I have a baby? I am a virgin."

[35]The angel replied, "The Holy Spirit will come upon you, and the power of the Most High will overshadow you. So the baby born to you will be holy, and he will be called the Son of God.

[36]What's more, your relative Elizabeth has become pregnant in her old age! People used to say she was barren, but she's already in her sixth month. [37]For nothing is impossible with God."

[38]Mary responded, "I am the Lord's servant, and I am willing to accept whatever he wants. May everything you have said come true." And then the angel left.

Gabriel told Mary that she would give birth to God's Son, Jesus. Mary humbly accepted Gabriel's message. She made herself available for God to use. God wants to be able to use all of his followers for his service. But he dosen't force his followers to serve him. Instead, he lets them choose whether they want to serve him or not. Mary chose to serve God and was greatly blessed for it. You can serve God, too. He wants to bless you.

How can we serve God?

Serve only the LORD your God and fear him alone. Obey his commands, listen to his voice, and cling to him.
Deuteronomy 13:4

1:28 Some manuscripts add *Blessed are you among women.* **1:33** Greek *over the house of Jacob.*

J U N E
10

God gave Elizabeth and Zechariah a son. How did Zechariah respond to God's gift?

LUKE 1:57-80

John's Birth

57Now it was time for Elizabeth's baby to be born, and it was a boy. 58The word spread quickly to her neighbors and relatives that the Lord had been very kind to her, and everyone rejoiced with her.

59When the baby was eight days old, all the relatives and friends came for the circumcision ceremony. They wanted to name him Zechariah, after his father. 60But Elizabeth said, "No! His name is John!"

61"What?" they exclaimed. "There is no one in all your family by that name." 62So they asked the baby's father, communicating to him by making gestures. 63He motioned for a writing tablet, and to everyone's surprise he wrote, "His name is John!" 64Instantly Zechariah could speak again, and he began praising God.

65Wonder fell upon the whole neighborhood, and the news of what had happened spread throughout the Judean hills. 66Everyone who heard about it reflected on these events and asked, "I wonder what this child will turn out to be? For the hand of the Lord is surely upon him in a special way."

67Then his father, Zechariah, was filled with the Holy Spirit and gave this prophecy:

68 "Praise the Lord, the God of Israel,
   because he has visited his
      people and redeemed them.

69 He has sent us a mighty Savior
   from the royal line of his servant
      David,
70 just as he promised
   through his holy prophets long ago.
71 Now we will be saved from our
      enemies
   and from all who hate us.
72 He has been merciful to our
      ancestors
   by remembering his sacred
      covenant with them,
73 the covenant he gave to our
      ancestor Abraham.
74 We have been rescued from our
      enemies,
   so we can serve God without fear,

Zechariah thanked God for giving him a son. In fact, the first words Zechariah spoke after his son was born were praises to God. What has God given you? You can thank him for everything, from the food on your plate to the clothes in your closet. Like Zechariah, express your thankfulness to God.

Why should we thank God?
Give thanks to the LORD, for he is good! His faithful love endures forever.
Psalm 118:29

75 in holiness and righteousness
forever.

76 "And you, my little son,
will be called the prophet of the
Most High,
because you will prepare the
way for the Lord.
77 You will tell his people how to find
salvation
through forgiveness of their sins.
78 Because of God's tender mercy,
the light from heaven is about
to break upon us,
79 to give light to those who sit in
darkness and in the shadow
of death,
and to guide us to the path of
peace."

80 John grew up and became strong
in spirit. Then he lived out in the wilderness until he began his public ministry to Israel.

J U N E

An angel came to Joseph in a dream. What did the angel tell him?

MATTHEW 1:18-25
An Angel and Joseph

18 Now this is how Jesus the Messiah was born. His mother, Mary, was engaged to be married to Joseph. But while she was still a virgin, she became pregnant by the Holy Spirit. 19 Joseph, her fiancé, being a just man, decided to break the engagement quietly, so as not to disgrace her publicly.

20 As he considered this, he fell asleep, and an angel of the Lord appeared to him in a dream. "Joseph, son of David," the angel said, "do not be afraid to go ahead with your marriage to Mary. For the child within her has been conceived by the Holy Spirit. 21 And she will have a son, and you are to name him Jesus,* for he will save his people from their sins." 22 All of this happened to fulfill the Lord's message through his prophet:

Joseph knew that Mary was pregnant. He thought she had been unfaithful to him, so he was planning to break off their engagement to be married. But an angel appeared to Joseph in a dream and told him to marry her. The angel told Joseph that Mary's child was God's Son, Jesus. Jesus would save his people from their sins. When Joseph woke up, he did what the angel had told him. Angels don't often appear to us in our dreams. But God does have other ways in which he speaks to us. His Word, the Bible, is the main way he tells us his truth. He can also use others, as well as his Spirit, to give us direction in life and answers to our prayers.

What can we do when we feel that God is speaking to us?
I listen carefully to what God the LORD is saying, for he speaks peace to his people, his faithful ones.
Psalm 85:8

1:21 *Jesus* means "The LORD saves."

23 "Look! The virgin will conceive a child!
She will give birth to a son,
and he will be called Immanuel*
(meaning, God is with us)."

24When Joseph woke up, he did what the angel of the Lord commanded. He brought Mary home to be his wife, 25but she remained a virgin until her son was born. And Joseph named him Jesus.

1:23 Isa 7:14; 8:8, 10.

J U N E

Jesus was born in Bethlehem. Angels announced his birth to some shepherds. What did the shepherds do?

LUKE 2:4-20

Jesus Is Born

4And because Joseph was a descendant of King David, he had to go to Bethlehem in Judea, David's ancient home. He traveled there from the village of Nazareth in Galilee. 5He took with him Mary, his fiancée, who was obviously pregnant by this time.

6And while they were there, the time came for her baby to be born. 7She gave birth to her first child, a son. She wrapped him snugly in strips of cloth and laid him in a manger, because there was no room for them in the village inn.

8That night some shepherds were in the fields outside the village, guarding their flocks of sheep. 9Suddenly, an angel of the Lord appeared among them, and the radiance of the Lord's glory surrounded them. They were terribly frightened, 10but the angel reassured them. "Don't be afraid!" he said. "I bring you good news of great joy for everyone! 11The Savior—yes, the Messiah, the Lord—has been born tonight in Bethlehem, the city of David! 12And this is how you will recognize him: You will find a baby lying in a manger, wrapped snugly in strips of cloth!"

13Suddenly, the angel was joined by a vast host of others—the armies of heaven—praising God:

The shepherds went to find Jesus. When they found him, they told everyone there that angels had appeared to them and told them about Jesus. Then the shepherds went back to their fields, praising God. How have you responded to Jesus' birth? Have you praised God for Jesus? If not, think about all the good things Jesus has done for you. Then you can praise God for sending Jesus to earth to die for our sins.

How can we celebrate Jesus' birth?

Praise the Lord; praise God our savior!
For each day he carries us in his arms.
Psalm 68:19

¹⁴ "Glory to God in the highest heaven,
    and peace on earth to all whom
        God favors.*"

¹⁵When the angels had returned to heaven, the shepherds said to each other, "Come on, let's go to Bethlehem! Let's see this wonderful thing that has happened, which the Lord has told us about."

¹⁶They ran to the village and found Mary and Joseph. And there was the baby, lying in the manger. ¹⁷Then the shepherds told everyone what had happened and what the angel had said to them about this child. ¹⁸All who heard the shepherds' story were astonished, ¹⁹but Mary quietly treasured these things in her heart and thought about them often. ²⁰The shepherds went back to their fields and flocks, glorifying and praising God for what the angels had told them, and because they had seen the child, just as the angel had said.

2:14 Or and peace on earth for all those pleasing God; some manuscripts read and peace on earth, goodwill among people.

J U N E

Simeon had been waiting a long time to see Jesus.
What did Simeon say when he finally saw him?

LUKE 2:21-35

A Long Wait

²¹Eight days later, when the baby was circumcised, he was named Jesus, the name given him by the angel even before he was conceived.

²²Then it was time for the purification offering, as required by the law of Moses after the birth of a child; so his parents took him to Jerusalem to present him to the Lord. ²³The law of the Lord says, "If a woman's first child is a boy, he must be dedicated to the Lord."* ²⁴So they offered a sacrifice according to what was required in the law of the Lord—"either a pair of turtledoves or two young pigeons."*

²⁵Now there was a man named Simeon who lived in Jerusalem. He was a righteous man and very devout. He was filled with the Holy Spirit, and he eagerly expected the Messiah to come and rescue Israel. ²⁶The Holy Spirit had revealed to him that he would not die until he had seen the Lord's Messiah. ²⁷That day the Spirit led him to the Temple. So when Mary and Joseph came to present the baby Jesus to the Lord as the law required, ²⁸Simeon was there. He took the child in his arms and praised God, saying,

²⁹ "Lord, now I can die in peace!
    As you promised me,
³⁰ I have seen the Savior
³¹   you have given to all people.

2:23 Exod 13:2. **2:24** Lev 12:8.

³² He is a light to reveal God to the nations,
   and he is the glory of your people Israel!"

³³ Joseph and Mary were amazed at what was being said about Jesus. ³⁴ Then Simeon blessed them, and he said to Mary, "This child will be rejected by many in Israel, and it will be their undoing. But he will be the greatest joy to many others. ³⁵ Thus, the deepest thoughts of many hearts will be revealed. And a sword will pierce your very soul."

Simeon said that he had seen God's salvation. What did he mean? He had seen Jesus as an infant. More than thirty years later, Jesus would die on the cross for everyone's sin. God sent Jesus to save all those who choose to believe in him. You can be one of those people that Jesus came to save. Believe that he died for your sins and came back to life so you could live with him in heaven. Trust your life to him. He came to save you.

What has Jesus done for us?
I thank you for answering my prayer and saving me!
Psalm 118:21

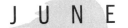

JUNE 14

Wise men from the east searched for Jesus. What did they do when they found him?

MATTHEW 2:1-12
The Wise Men

Jesus was born in the town of Bethlehem in Judea, during the reign of King Herod. About that time some wise men* from eastern lands arrived in Jerusalem, asking, ² "Where is the newborn king of the Jews? We have seen his star as it arose,* and we have come to worship him."

³ Herod was deeply disturbed by their question, as was all of Jerusalem. ⁴ He called a meeting of the leading priests and teachers of religious law.

"Where did the prophets say the Messiah would be born?" he asked them. ⁵ "In Bethlehem," they said, "for this is what the prophet wrote:

⁶ 'O Bethlehem of Judah,
   you are not just a lowly village in Judah,
for a ruler will come from you
   who will be the shepherd for my people Israel.'* "

⁷ Then Herod sent a private message to the wise men, asking them to come see him. At this meeting he learned the exact

2:1 Or *royal astrologers;* Greek reads *magi;* also in 2:7, 16. 2:2 Or *in the east.* 2:6 Mic 5:2; 2 Sam 5:2.

time when they first saw the star. [8]Then he told them, "Go to Bethlehem and search carefully for the child. And when you find him, come back and tell me so that I can go and worship him, too!"

[9]After this interview the wise men went their way. Once again the star appeared to them, guiding them to Bethlehem. It went ahead of them and stopped over the place where the child was. [10]When they saw the star, they were filled with joy! [11]They entered the house where the child and his mother, Mary, were, and they fell down before him and worshiped him. Then they opened their treasure chests and gave him gifts of gold, frankincense, and myrrh. [12]But when it was time to leave, they went home another way, because God had warned them in a dream not to return to Herod.

The wise men knelt before Jesus, worshiped him, and offered him gifts. Even though they respected Jesus, they did not know him as God's Son. Today we know that Jesus is God's Son. Because we know this, we should be more willing than the wise men to kneel before Jesus and worship him.

How can we show Jesus our love and respect for him?
Come, let us worship and bow down.
Let us kneel before the
Lord our maker.
Psalm 95:6

J U N E

15

Herod wanted to kill Jesus. Did Jesus escape?

MATTHEW 2:13-23

The Escape

[13]After the wise men were gone, an angel of the Lord appeared to Joseph in a dream. "Get up and flee to Egypt with the child and his mother," the angel said. "Stay there until I tell you to return, because Herod is going to try to kill the child." [14]That night Joseph left for Egypt with the child and Mary, his mother, [15]and they stayed there until Herod's death. This fulfilled what the Lord had spoken through the prophet: "I called my Son out of Egypt."*

[16]Herod was furious when he learned that the wise men had outwitted him. He sent soldiers to kill all the boys in and around Bethlehem who were two years old and under, because the wise men had told him the star first appeared to them about two years earlier.* [17]Herod's brutal action fulfilled the prophecy of Jeremiah:

2:15 Hos 11:1. **2:16** Or *according to the time he calculated from the wise men.*

¹⁸ "A cry of anguish is heard in
  Ramah—
  weeping and mourning
  unrestrained.
Rachel weeps for her children,
  refusing to be comforted—for
  they are dead."*

¹⁹When Herod died, an angel of the Lord appeared in a dream to Joseph in Egypt and told him, ²⁰"Get up and take the child and his mother back to the land of Israel, because those who were trying to kill the child are dead." ²¹So Joseph returned immediately to Israel with Jesus and his mother. ²²But when he learned that the new ruler was Herod's son Archelaus, he was afraid. Then, in another dream, he was warned to go to Galilee. ²³So they went and lived in a town called Nazareth.

2:18 Jer 31:15.

This fulfilled what was spoken by the prophets concerning the Messiah: "He will be called a Nazarene."

God sent an angel to warn Joseph of Herod's plan. Joseph took Mary and Jesus and fled to Egypt. God rescued Jesus and his family from danger. The world is filled with danger. But God can rescue his people. Rely on him. He will watch over you.

**How do we know that God
will rescue us from danger?**
The LORD says, "I will rescue those
who love me. I will protect those
who trust in my name."
Psalm 91:14

JUNE

Jesus and his family were in Jerusalem for the Passover festival. His parents were going home, but Jesus wasn't with them. Where did Jesus go?

LUKE 2:41-52

Jesus at the Temple

⁴¹Every year Jesus' parents went to Jerusalem for the Passover festival. ⁴²When Jesus was twelve years old, they attended the festival as usual. ⁴³After the celebration was over, they started home to Nazareth, but Jesus stayed behind in Jerusalem. His parents didn't miss him at first, ⁴⁴because they assumed he was with friends among the other travelers. But when he didn't show up that evening, they started to look for him among their relatives and friends. ⁴⁵When they couldn't find him, they went back to Jerusalem to search for him there. ⁴⁶Three days later they finally discovered him. He was in the Temple, sitting among the religious teachers, discussing deep questions with them. ⁴⁷And all who heard him were amazed at his understanding and his answers.

⁴⁸His parents didn't know what to

think. "Son!" his mother said to him. "Why have you done this to us? Your father and I have been frantic, searching for you everywhere."

⁴⁹"But why did you need to search?" he asked. "You should have known that I would be in my Father's house."* ⁵⁰But they didn't understand what he meant.

⁵¹Then he returned to Nazareth with them and was obedient to them; and his mother stored all these things in her heart. ⁵²So Jesus grew both in height and in wisdom, and he was loved by God and by all who knew him.

When Mary and Joseph realized that Jesus wasn't with them, they went back to Jerusalem to search for him. They found him at the Temple, talking with the religious leaders. The answers Jesus gave to the leaders were so wise that they marveled at his wisdom and understanding. How can we be wise? Above all, we need to fear God. To fear God means to realize who he is, to love him, and to obey him.

How can you become wise?
Fear of the LORD is the beginning of wisdom. Knowledge of the Holy One results in understanding.
Proverbs 9:10

2:49 Or "Didn't you realize that I should be involved with my Father's affairs?"

J U N E

John the Baptist lived in the desert. He ate locusts and honey. What did he say to the people?

MATTHEW 3:1-17
A Desert Hermit's Message
In those days John the Baptist began preaching in the Judean wilderness. His message was, ²"Turn from your sins and turn to God, because the Kingdom of Heaven is near.*" ³Isaiah had spoken of John when he said,

"He is a voice shouting in the wilderness:

'Prepare a pathway for the Lord's coming!
Make a straight road for him!' "*

⁴John's clothes were woven from camel hair, and he wore a leather belt; his food was locusts and wild honey. ⁵People from Jerusalem and from every section of Judea and from all over the Jordan Valley went out to the wilderness to hear him preach. ⁶And

3:2 Or has come, or is coming soon. **3:3** Isa 40:3.

when they confessed their sins, he baptized them in the Jordan River.

⁷But when he saw many Pharisees and Sadducees coming to be baptized, he denounced them. "You brood of snakes!" he exclaimed. "Who warned you to flee God's coming judgment? ⁸Prove by the way you live that you have really turned from your sins and turned to God. ⁹Don't just say, 'We're safe—we're the descendants of Abraham.' That proves nothing. God can change these stones here into children of Abraham. ¹⁰Even now the ax of God's judgment is poised, ready to sever your roots. Yes, every tree that does not produce good fruit will be chopped down and thrown into the fire.

¹¹"I baptize with* water those who turn from their sins and turn to God. But someone is coming soon who is far greater than I am—so much greater that I am not even worthy to be his slave.* He will baptize you with the Holy Spirit and with fire.* ¹²He is ready to separate the chaff from the grain with his winnowing fork. Then he will clean up the threshing area, storing the grain in his barn but burning the chaff with never-ending fire."

¹³Then Jesus went from Galilee to the Jordan River to be baptized by John. ¹⁴But John didn't want to baptize him. "I am the one who needs to be baptized by you," he said, "so why are you coming to me?"

¹⁵But Jesus said, "It must be done, because we must do everything that is right.*" So then John baptized him.

¹⁶After his baptism, as Jesus came up out of the water, the heavens were opened and he saw the Spirit of God descending like a dove and settling on him. ¹⁷And a voice from heaven said, "This is my beloved Son, and I am fully pleased with him."

John the Baptist was sent by God to prepare people for Jesus' coming. He told the people to repent, which means to turn away from sin. Today we can prepare ourselves for Jesus' second coming. This means believing that he died for our sins and living in obedience to his Word.

How should we prepare ourselves for Jesus' return?
Turn from your sins! Don't let them destroy you!
Ezekiel 18:30

3:11a Or in.   **3:11b** Greek to carry his sandals.   **3:11c** Or in the Holy Spirit and in fire.   **3:15** Or we must fulfill all righteousness.

J U N E

The Devil tempted Jesus when Jesus was hungry and tired.
How did Jesus respond to temptation?

MATTHEW 4:1-11
Jesus and the Devil

Then Jesus was led out into the wilderness by the Holy Spirit to be tempted there by the Devil. ²For forty days and forty nights he ate nothing and became very hungry. ³Then the Devil* came and said to him, "If you are the Son of God, change these stones into loaves of bread."

⁴But Jesus told him, "No! The Scriptures say,

'People need more than bread for
their life;
they must feed on every word of
God.'* "

⁵Then the Devil took him to Jerusalem, to the highest point of the Temple, ⁶and said, "If you are the Son of God, jump off! For the Scriptures say,

'He orders his angels to protect
you.
And they will hold you with their
hands
to keep you from striking your
foot on a stone.'* "

⁷Jesus responded, "The Scriptures also say, 'Do not test the Lord your God.'* "
⁸Next the Devil took him to the peak of a very high mountain and showed him the nations of the world and all their glory. ⁹"I will give it all to you," he said, "if you will only kneel down and worship me."

¹⁰"Get out of here, Satan," Jesus told him. "For the Scriptures say,

'You must worship the Lord your
God;
serve only him.'* "

¹¹Then the Devil went away, and angels came and cared for Jesus.

Though Jesus was tempted, he never gave in. Instead, he used God's Word to defend himself against Satan's attacks. When you are tempted, you can do the same thing as Jesus. You can also turn to God's Word for help. Jesus knows what you are going through. He will help you resist temptation and escape from it.

What will God do when we are tempted?
But remember that the temptations that come into your life are no different from what others experience. And God is faithful. He will keep the temptation from becoming so strong that you can't stand up against it. When you are tempted, he will show you a way out so that you will not give in to it.
1 Corinthians 10:13

4:3 Greek *the tempter.* **4:4** Deut 8:3. **4:6** Ps 91:11-12. **4:7** Deut 6:16. **4:10** Deut 6:13.

J U N E

Jesus called Peter, Philip, and Nathanael to follow him. How did they respond?

JOHN 1:35-51
Follow Me

[35]The following day, John was again standing with two of his disciples. [36]As Jesus walked by, John looked at him and then declared, "Look! There is the Lamb of God!" [37]Then John's two disciples turned and followed Jesus.

[38]Jesus looked around and saw them following. "What do you want?" he asked them.

They replied, "Rabbi" (which means Teacher), "where are you staying?"

[39]"Come and see," he said. It was about four o'clock in the afternoon when they went with him to the place, and they stayed there the rest of the day.

[40]Andrew, Simon Peter's brother, was one of these men who had heard what John said and then followed Jesus. [41]The first thing Andrew did was to find his brother, Simon, and tell him, "We have found the Messiah" (which means the Christ).

[42]Then Andrew brought Simon to meet Jesus. Looking intently at Simon, Jesus said, "You are Simon, the son of John—but you will be called Cephas" (which means Peter*).

[43]The next day Jesus decided to go to Galilee. He found Philip and said to him, "Come, be my disciple." [44]Philip was from Bethsaida, Andrew and Peter's hometown.

[45]Philip went off to look for Nathanael and told him, "We have found the very person Moses and the prophets wrote about! His name is Jesus, the son of Joseph from Nazareth."

[46]"Nazareth!" exclaimed Nathanael. "Can anything good come from there?"

"Just come and see for yourself," Philip said.

[47]As they approached, Jesus said, "Here comes an honest man—a true son of Israel."

[48]"How do you know about me?" Nathanael asked.

When Jesus called these disciples, they followed. They left everything behind to know Jesus. Nothing in the world is worth more than knowing Jesus as your Savior, Lord, and friend. He wants you to follow him. Don't let anything stop you from following Jesus.

What has Jesus promised to those who follow him?
Jesus replied, ". . . I assure you, everyone who has given up house or wife or brothers or parents or children, for the sake of the Kingdom of God, will be repaid many times over in this life, as well as receiving eternal life in the world to come."
Luke 18:29-30

1:42 The names *Cephas* and *Peter* both mean "rock."

And Jesus replied, "I could see you under the fig tree before Philip found you."

[49]Nathanael replied, "Teacher, you are the Son of God—the King of Israel!"

[50]Jesus asked him, "Do you believe all this just because I told you I had seen you under the fig tree? You will see greater things than this." [51]Then he said, "The truth is, you will all see heaven open and the angels of God going up and down upon the Son of Man."*

JUNE

Jesus went to the Temple to worship God. What did he find there?

JOHN 2:12-23
Jesus Clears the Temple

[12]After the wedding he went to Capernaum for a few days with his mother, his brothers, and his disciples.

[13]It was time for the annual Passover celebration, and Jesus went to Jerusalem. [14]In the Temple area he saw merchants selling cattle, sheep, and doves for sacrifices; and he saw money changers behind their counters. [15]Jesus made a whip from some ropes and chased them all out of the Temple. He drove out the sheep and oxen, scattered the money changers' coins over the floor, and turned over their tables. [16]Then, going over to the people who sold doves, he told them, "Get these things out of here. Don't turn my Father's house into a marketplace!"

[17]Then his disciples remembered this prophecy from the Scriptures: "Passion for God's house burns within me."*

[18]"What right do you have to do these things?" the Jewish leaders demanded. "If you have this authority from God, show us a miraculous sign to prove it."

[19]"All right," Jesus replied. "Destroy this temple, and in three days I will raise it up."

[20]"What!" they exclaimed. "It took forty-six years to build this Temple, and you can do it in three days?" [21]But by "this temple," Jesus meant his

Jesus expected to find people worshiping God in the Temple. Instead, he found merchants selling cattle, sheep, and doves. They were distracting the people from worshiping God. Jesus became angry and drove the merchants out of God's house. As Jesus' actions show us, worshiping God is important. We shouldn't let anything or anyone distract us from it.

What should you do in church?
O God, we meditate on your unfailing love as we worship in your Temple.
Psalm 48:9

1:51 See Gen 28:10-17, the account of Jacob's ladder. **2:17** Or "Concern for God's house will be my undoing." Ps 69:9

body. ²²After he was raised from the dead, the disciples remembered that he had said this. And they believed both Jesus and the Scriptures.

²³Because of the miraculous signs he did in Jerusalem at the Passover celebration, many people were convinced that he was indeed the Messiah.

JUNE

Under the cover of night, Nicodemus, a Jewish religious leader, sought advice from Jesus. What did Jesus tell him?

JOHN 3:1-21

Jesus and Nicodemus

After dark one evening, a Jewish religious leader named Nicodemus, a Pharisee, ²came to speak with Jesus. "Teacher," he said, "we all know that God has sent you to teach us. Your miraculous signs are proof enough that God is with you."

³Jesus replied, "I assure you, unless you are born again,* you can never see the Kingdom of God."

⁴"What do you mean?" exclaimed Nicodemus. "How can an old man go back into his mother's womb and be born again?"

⁵Jesus replied, "The truth is, no one can enter the Kingdom of God without being born of water and the Spirit.* ⁶Humans can reproduce only human life, but the Holy Spirit gives new life from heaven. ⁷So don't be surprised at my statement that you* must be born again. ⁸Just as you can hear the wind but can't tell where it comes from or where it is going, so you can't explain how people are born of the Spirit."

⁹"What do you mean?" Nicodemus asked.

¹⁰Jesus replied, "You are a respected Jewish teacher, and yet you don't understand these things? ¹¹I assure you, I am telling you what we know and have seen, and yet you won't believe us. ¹²But if you don't even believe me when I tell you about things that happen here on earth, how can you possibly believe if I tell you what is going on in heaven? ¹³For only I, the Son of Man,* have come to earth and will return to heaven again. ¹⁴And as Moses lifted up the bronze snake on a pole in the wilderness, so I, the Son of Man, must be lifted up on a pole,* ¹⁵so that everyone who believes in me will have eternal life.

¹⁶"For God so loved the world that he gave his only Son, so that everyone who believes in him will not perish but have eternal life. ¹⁷God did not send his Son into the world to condemn it, but to save it.

¹⁸"There is no judgment awaiting those who trust him. But those who do not trust him have already been

3:3 Or *born from above;* also in 3:7. **3:5** Or *spirit.* The Greek word for *Spirit* can also be translated *wind;* see 3:8. **3:7** The Greek word for *you* is plural; also in 3:12. **3:13** Some manuscripts add *who lives in heaven.* **3:14** Greek *must be lifted up.*

judged for not believing in the only Son of God. [19]Their judgment is based on this fact: The light from heaven came into the world, but they loved the darkness more than the light, for their actions were evil. [20]They hate the light because they want to sin in the darkness. They stay away from the light for fear their sins will be exposed and they will be punished. [21]But those who do what is right come to the light gladly, so everyone can see that they are doing what God wants."

Jesus told Nicodemus that he must be born again. What does that mean? It means that the Holy Spirit changes our heart so we can follow Jesus. We all need a changed heart to spend eternity with Jesus in heaven. Have you been born again? If not, right now you can ask Jesus to forgive your sins, to come into your life, and to make you a new person.

What can you do to be saved?
They replied, "Believe on the Lord Jesus and you will be saved, along with your entire household."
Acts 16:31

J U N E

Jesus was baptizing many people. John the Baptist's followers became jealous. What did John say?

JOHN 3:22-36
Jesus' Ministry Grows
[22]Afterward Jesus and his disciples left Jerusalem, but they stayed in Judea for a while and baptized there.

[23]At this time John the Baptist was baptizing at Aenon, near Salim, because there was plenty of water there and people kept coming to him for baptism. [24]This was before John was put into prison. [25]At that time a certain Jew began an argument with John's disciples over ceremonial cleansing. [26]John's disciples came to him and said, "Teacher, the man you met on the other side of the Jordan River, the one you said was the Messiah, is also baptizing people. And everybody is going over there instead of coming here to us."

[27]John replied, "God in heaven appoints each person's work. [28]You yourselves know how plainly I told you that I am not the Messiah. I am here to prepare the way for him—that is all. [29]The bride will go where the bridegroom is. A bridegroom's friend rejoices with him. I am the bridegroom's friend, and I am filled with joy at his success. [30]He must become greater and greater, and I must become less and less.

31 "He has come from above and is greater than anyone else. I am of the earth, and my understanding is limited to the things of earth, but he has come from heaven.* 32 He tells what he has seen and heard, but how few believe what he tells them! 33 Those who believe him discover that God is true. 34 For he is sent by God. He speaks God's words, for God's Spirit is upon him without measure or limit. 35 The Father loves his Son, and he has given him authority over everything. 36 And all who believe in God's Son have eternal life. Those who don't obey the Son will never experience eternal life, but the wrath of God remains upon them."

John knew that Jesus is God's Son. Because John knew this, he was happy that Jesus' ministry was growing. In fact, John was even willing for his ministry to fade out so that Jesus' would continue to expand. That was God's plan, and John was fitting into it. When it comes to helping out in church ministries, we can follow John's example. We should not fight for popularity in our church. Bringing attention to ourselves will only give us a bad name among fellow believers and even unbelievers.

How can we be an example of Christ's love to the world?

Now, dear brothers and sisters, I appeal to you by the authority of the Lord Jesus Christ to stop arguing among yourselves. Let there be real harmony so there won't be divisions in the church. I plead with you to be of one mind, united in thought and purpose.
1 Corinthians 1:10

3:31 Some manuscripts omit *but he has come from heaven.*

JUNE

23

The disciples had gone to get food for Jesus. What did they find when they returned?

JOHN 4:27-42
The Harvest
27 Just then his disciples arrived. They were astonished to find him talking to a woman, but none of them asked him why he was doing it or what they had been discussing. 28 The woman left her water jar beside the well and went back to the village and told everyone, 29 "Come and meet a man who told me everything I ever did! Can this be the Messiah?" 30 So the people came streaming from the village to see him.

31 Meanwhile, the disciples were urg-

ing Jesus to eat. ³²"No," he said, "I have food you don't know about."

³³"Who brought it to him?" the disciples asked each other.

³⁴Then Jesus explained: "My nourishment comes from doing the will of God, who sent me, and from finishing his work. ³⁵Do you think the work of harvesting will not begin until the summer ends four months from now? Look around you! Vast fields are ripening all around us and are ready now for the harvest. ³⁶The harvesters are paid good wages, and the fruit they harvest is people brought to eternal life. What joy awaits both the planter and the harvester alike! ³⁷You know the saying, 'One person plants and someone else harvests.' And it's true. ³⁸I sent you to harvest where you didn't plant; others had already done the work, and you will gather the harvest."

³⁹Many Samaritans from the village believed in Jesus because the woman had said, "He told me everything I ever did!" ⁴⁰When they came out to see him, they begged him to stay at their village. So he stayed for two days, ⁴¹long enough for many of them to hear his message and believe. ⁴²Then they said to the woman, "Now we believe because we have heard him ourselves, not just because of what you told us. He is indeed the Savior of the world."

When the disciples returned, they found Jesus speaking to a woman with a bad reputation. The disciples urged Jesus to eat. But he said that he had food they didn't know about. This confused the disciples. Jesus wasn't talking about physical food, though. He was talking about spiritual food, which for him was doing God's will. As human beings, we need physical food to feed our body. But as Christians, we also need to feed our soul. We can do this by obeying God. Don't neglect to feed your soul.

Besides eating food, what else do we need to consume?
People need more than bread for their life; real life comes by feeding on every word of the LORD.
Deuteronomy 8:3

J U N E

A man's son was sick and about to die. How did this man help his son?

JOHN 4:46-54
A Sick Son
⁴⁶In the course of his journey through Galilee, he arrived at the town of Cana, where he had turned the water into wine. There was a government official in the city of Capernaum whose son was very sick. ⁴⁷When he heard that Jesus had come from Judea and was traveling in Galilee, he went over to

Cana. He found Jesus and begged him to come to Capernaum with him to heal his son, who was about to die.

⁴⁸Jesus asked, "Must I do miraculous signs and wonders before you people will believe in me?"

⁴⁹The official pleaded, "Lord, please come now before my little boy dies."

⁵⁰Then Jesus told him, "Go back home. Your son will live!" And the man believed Jesus' word and started home.

⁵¹While he was on his way, some of his servants met him with the news that his son was alive and well. ⁵²He asked them when the boy had begun to feel better, and they replied, "Yesterday afternoon at one o'clock his fever suddenly disappeared!" ⁵³Then the father realized it was the same time that Jesus had told him, "Your son will live." And the officer and his entire household believed in Jesus. ⁵⁴This was Jesus' second miraculous sign in Galilee after coming from Judea.

4:7 Deut 6:16.

The man heard that Jesus was in a nearby town. So he went to plead with Jesus to heal his son. Jesus didn't go with the man, but he did heal the boy. When the man found out that his son was healed, he and his entire household believed in Jesus. Unfortunately, he didn't believe until Jesus acted. Be careful that you do not ask God to prove himself to you. Instead, look at what he has already done and put your trust in him.

What is wrong with testing God?
Jesus responded, "The Scriptures also say, 'Do not test the Lord your God.'*"
Matthew 4:7

J U N E

Jesus went back home to Nazareth. How did the people treat him?

LUKE 4:16-30

Jesus in Nazareth

¹⁶When he came to the village of Nazareth, his boyhood home, he went as usual to the synagogue on the Sabbath and stood up to read the Scriptures. ¹⁷The scroll containing the messages of Isaiah the prophet was handed to him, and he unrolled the scroll to the place where it says:

¹⁸ "The Spirit of the Lord is upon me,
for he has appointed me to
preach Good News to the poor.
He has sent me to proclaim
that captives will be released,
that the blind will see,
that the downtrodden will be
freed from their oppressors,
¹⁹ and that the time of the Lord's
favor has come.*"

4:18-19 Or *and to proclaim the acceptable year of the Lord.* Isa 61:1-2.

²⁰He rolled up the scroll, handed it back to the attendant, and sat down. Everyone in the synagogue stared at him intently. ²¹Then he said, "This Scripture has come true today before your very eyes!"

²²All who were there spoke well of him and were amazed by the gracious words that fell from his lips. "How can this be?" they asked. "Isn't this Joseph's son?"

²³Then he said, "Probably you will quote me that proverb, 'Physician, heal yourself'—meaning, 'Why don't you do miracles here in your hometown like those you did in Capernaum?' ²⁴But the truth is, no prophet is accepted in his own hometown.

²⁵"Certainly there were many widows in Israel who needed help in Elijah's time, when there was no rain for three and a half years and hunger stalked the land. ²⁶Yet Elijah was not sent to any of them. He was sent instead to a widow of Zarephath—a foreigner in the land of Sidon. ²⁷Or think of the prophet Elisha, who healed Naaman, a Syrian, rather than the many lepers in Israel who needed help."

²⁸When they heard this, the people in the synagogue were furious. ²⁹Jumping up, they mobbed him and took him to the edge of the hill on which the city was built. They intended to push him over the cliff, ³⁰but he slipped away through the crowd and left them.

Jesus was rejected in his hometown. The people of Nazareth thought that Jesus was Joseph's son. They didn't believe that he was God's Son. Many people today do not believe that Jesus is the Son of God. But God wants everyone to believe in Jesus. Putting your faith in Jesus is the only way to get to heaven. Don't follow the bad example of those from Jesus' hometown. Don't reject Jesus.

What will happen if we reject Jesus?

For the LORD sees every heart and understands and knows every plan and thought. If you seek him, you will find him. But if you forsake him, he will reject you forever.

1 Chronicles 28:9

J U N E
26

Some fishermen could not catch any fish. What did Jesus do?

LUKE 5:1-11

Fishermen's Catch

One day as Jesus was preaching on the shore of the Sea of Galilee,* great crowds pressed in on him to listen to the word of God. ²He noticed two empty boats at the water's edge, for the fishermen had left them and were

5:1 Greek *Lake Gennesaret*, another name for the Sea of Galilee.

washing their nets. ³Stepping into one of the boats, Jesus asked Simon,* its owner, to push it out into the water. So he sat in the boat and taught the crowds from there.

⁴When he had finished speaking, he said to Simon, "Now go out where it is deeper and let down your nets, and you will catch many fish."

⁵"Master," Simon replied, "we worked hard all last night and didn't catch a thing. But if you say so, we'll try again." ⁶And this time their nets were so full they began to tear! ⁷A shout for help brought their partners in the other boat, and soon both boats were filled with fish and on the verge of sinking.

⁸When Simon Peter realized what had happened, he fell to his knees before Jesus and said, "Oh, Lord, please leave me—I'm too much of a sinner to be around you." ⁹For he was awestruck by the size of their catch, as were the others with him. ¹⁰His partners, James and John, the sons of Zebedee, were also amazed.

Jesus replied to Simon, "Don't be afraid! From now on you'll be fishing for people!" ¹¹And as soon as they landed, they left everything and followed Jesus.

5:3 *Simon* is called *Peter* in 6:14 and thereafter.

Jesus told Simon Peter, James, and John to go out to the deep part of the lake and let down their nets. They did this and caught so many fish that their nets began to tear. When they came back on shore, they left everything to follow Jesus. We also may have to leave something we love to follow Jesus. Even so, we should follow him with our whole heart. Jesus will give us something more valuable in return—eternal life.

Why isn't it so bad to give things up to follow Jesus?
And Jesus replied, "I assure you that everyone who has given up house or brothers or sisters or mother or father or children or property, for my sake and for the Good News, will receive now in return, a hundred times over, houses, brothers, sisters, mothers, children, and property—with persecutions. And in the world to come they will have eternal life."
Mark 10:29-30

J U N E

27

Jesus noticed a man who could not walk. What did Jesus do?

JOHN 5:1-18
Jesus Heals a Lame Man

Afterward Jesus returned to Jerusalem for one of the Jewish holy days. ²Inside the city, near the Sheep Gate, was the pool of Bethesda,* with five covered porches. ³Crowds of sick people—blind, lame, or paralyzed—lay on the porches.* ⁵One of the men lying there had been sick for thirty-eight years. ⁶When Jesus saw him and knew how long he had been ill, he asked him, "Would you like to get well?"

⁷"I can't, sir," the sick man said, "for I have no one to help me into the pool when the water is stirred up. While I am trying to get there, someone else always gets in ahead of me."

⁸Jesus told him, "Stand up, pick up your sleeping mat, and walk!"

⁹Instantly, the man was healed! He rolled up the mat and began walking! But this miracle happened on the Sabbath day. ¹⁰So the Jewish leaders objected. They said to the man who was cured, "You can't work on the Sabbath! It's illegal to carry that sleeping mat!"

¹¹He replied, "The man who healed me said to me, 'Pick up your sleeping mat and walk.' "

¹²"Who said such a thing as that?" they demanded.

Jesus asked the man if he would like to be healed. The man told Jesus that he couldn't be healed because he couldn't get into the pool when it was stirred up. He had put his hope in water. But Jesus had compassion on him and healed him. How many times do we put our hope in people or things? Only Jesus has what we really need. What we need is forgiveness for our sins. Put your hope in Jesus. You will not be disappointed.

What can we hope for in the future?

All honor to the God and Father of our Lord Jesus Christ, for it is by his boundless mercy that God has given us the privilege of being born again. Now we live with a wonderful expectation because Jesus Christ rose again from the dead. For God has reserved a priceless inheritance for his children. It is kept in heaven for you, pure and undefiled, beyond the reach of change and decay.
1 Peter 1:3-4

¹³The man didn't know, for Jesus had disappeared into the crowd. ¹⁴But afterward Jesus found him in the Temple and told him, "Now you are well; so stop sinning, or something even worse may happen to you."

5:2 Some manuscripts read *Beth-zatha;* other manuscripts read *Bethsaida.* **5:3** Some manuscripts add *waiting for a certain movement of the water,* ⁴*for an angel of the Lord came from time to time and stirred up the water. And the first person to step down into it afterward was healed.*

¹⁵Then the man went to find the Jewish leaders and told them it was Jesus who had healed him.

¹⁶So the Jewish leaders began harassing Jesus for breaking the Sabbath rules. ¹⁷But Jesus replied, "My Father never stops working, so why should I?" ¹⁸So the Jewish leaders tried all the more to kill him. In addition to disobeying the Sabbath rules, he had spoken of God as his Father, thereby making himself equal with God.

J U N E

28

As Jesus was preaching in a house, part of the roof was removed. Then a paralyzed man was lowered to him. What did Jesus do?

MARK 2:1-12

A Hole in the Roof

Several days later Jesus returned to Capernaum, and the news of his arrival spread quickly through the town. ²Soon the house where he was staying was so packed with visitors that there wasn't room for one more person, not even outside the door. And he preached the word to them. ³Four men arrived carrying a paralyzed man on a mat. ⁴They couldn't get to Jesus through the crowd, so they dug through the clay roof above his head. Then they lowered the sick man on his mat, right down in front of Jesus. ⁵Seeing their faith, Jesus said to the paralyzed man, "My son, your sins are forgiven."

⁶But some of the teachers of religious law who were sitting there said to themselves, ⁷"What? This is blasphemy! Who but God can forgive sins!"

⁸Jesus knew what they were discussing among themselves, so he said to them, "Why do you think this is blasphemy? ⁹Is it easier to say to the paralyzed man, 'Your sins are forgiven' or 'Get up, pick up your mat, and walk'? ¹⁰I will prove that I, the Son of Man, have the authority on earth to forgive sins." Then Jesus turned to the paralyzed man and said, ¹¹"Stand up, take

Jesus saw that this man had faith in him. So he forgave the paralyzed man of his sins. But Jesus' words stirred up trouble. Some of the religious teachers accused Jesus of blasphemy, which is insulting God. But Jesus showed the teachers that he is God by healing the man. What doubts do you have about Jesus? Let his actions recorded in the Bible show you that he is God.

What must we believe about Jesus?
All who proclaim that Jesus is the Son of God have God living in them, and they live in God.
1 John 4:15

your mat, and go on home, because you are healed!"

¹²The man jumped up, took the mat, and pushed his way through the stunned onlookers. Then they all praised God. "We've never seen anything like this before!" they exclaimed.

JUNE

On a mountainside Jesus taught his followers about the people God blesses. Who does God bless?

MATTHEW 5:1-12

The Beatitudes

One day as the crowds were gathering, Jesus went up the mountainside with his disciples and sat down to teach them.

²This is what he taught them:

³ "God blesses those who realize
their need for him,*
for the Kingdom of Heaven is
given to them.
⁴God blesses those who mourn,
for they will be comforted.
⁵God blesses those who are gentle
and lowly,
for the whole earth will belong
to them.
⁶God blesses those who are hungry
and thirsty for justice,
for they will receive it in full.
⁷God blesses those who are
merciful,
for they will be shown mercy.
⁸God blesses those whose hearts are
pure,
for they will see God.
⁹God blesses those who work for
peace,

Jesus said that God blesses those people who are gentle, merciful, and peacemakers. Those people who long for justice, who are sorry for their sins, and who are persecuted for their faith also receive God's blessings. These people are blessed by God because they value what he values. Do you live by God's values? Have you been blessed by him? When you live by God's values, he will bless you. True happiness comes from living God's way.

What can people who live God's way do?

But let the godly rejoice. Let them be glad in God's presence. Let them be filled with joy.
Psalm 68:3

for they will be called the
children of God.
¹⁰ God blesses those who are
persecuted because they live
for God,
for the Kingdom of Heaven is
theirs.

5:3 Greek *the poor in spirit.*

225

¹¹"God blesses you when you are mocked and persecuted and lied about because you are my followers. ¹²Be happy about it! Be very glad! For a great reward awaits you in heaven. And remember, the ancient prophets were persecuted, too."

JUNE 30

Jesus taught about many things in his Sermon on the Mount. One big thing he taught about was anger. What did he say about it?

MATTHEW 5:17-26

About Anger

¹⁷"Don't misunderstand why I have come. I did not come to abolish the law of Moses or the writings of the prophets. No, I came to fulfill them. ¹⁸I assure you, until heaven and earth disappear, even the smallest detail of God's law will remain until its purpose is achieved. ¹⁹So if you break the smallest commandment and teach others to do the same, you will be the least in the Kingdom of Heaven. But anyone who obeys God's laws and teaches them will be great in the Kingdom of Heaven.

²⁰"But I warn you—unless you obey God better than the teachers of religious law and the Pharisees do, you can't enter the Kingdom of Heaven at all!

²¹"You have heard that the law of Moses says, 'Do not murder. If you commit murder, you are subject to judgment.'* ²²But I say, if you are angry with someone,* you are subject to judgment! If you call someone an idiot,* you are in danger of being brought before the high council. And if you curse someone,* you are in danger of the fires of hell.

²³"So if you are standing before the altar in the Temple, offering a sacrifice to God, and you suddenly remember that someone has something against you, ²⁴leave your sacrifice there beside the altar. Go and be reconciled to that person. Then come and offer your sac-

Jesus told his disciples not to be angry with others. He said that being angry with someone could get you into trouble with God. Instead, Jesus said people should forgive and love others. Are you angry with anyone? If so, forgive that person and ask him or her to forgive you for being angry.

What does God say we should do about holding a grudge?
Never seek revenge or bear a grudge against anyone, but love your neighbor as yourself. I am the LORD.
Leviticus 19:18

5:21 Exod 20:13; Deut 5:17. **5:22a** Some manuscripts add *without cause.* **5:22b** Greek uses an Aramaic term of contempt: *If you say to your brother, 'Raca.'* **5:22c** Greek *if you say, 'You fool.'*

226

rifice to God. [25]Come to terms quickly with your enemy before it is too late and you are dragged into court, handed over to an officer, and thrown in jail. [26]I assure you that you won't be free again until you have paid the last penny."

J U L Y

*Jesus taught his disciples how to treat their enemies.
What was unusual about his teaching?*

MATTHEW 5:38-48
Loving Enemies

³⁸ "You have heard that the law of Moses says, 'If an eye is injured, injure the eye of the person who did it. If a tooth gets knocked out, knock out the tooth of the person who did it.'* ³⁹ But I say, don't resist an evil person! If you are slapped on the right cheek, turn the other, too. ⁴⁰ If you are ordered to court and your shirt is taken from you, give your coat, too. ⁴¹ If a soldier demands that you carry his gear for a mile,* carry it two miles. ⁴² Give to those who ask, and don't turn away from those who want to borrow.

⁴³ "You have heard that the law of Moses says, 'Love your neighbor'* and hate your enemy. ⁴⁴ But I say, love your enemies!* Pray for those who persecute you! ⁴⁵ In that way, you will be acting as true children of your Father in heaven. For he gives his sunlight to both the evil and the good, and he sends rain on the just and on the un-just, too. ⁴⁶ If you love only those who love you, what good is that? Even corrupt tax collectors do that much. ⁴⁷ If you are kind only to your friends,* how are you different from anyone else? Even pagans do that. ⁴⁸ But you are to be perfect, even as your Father in heaven is perfect."

In Jesus' day, some people may have thought that hating one's enemies was OK. But Jesus taught his followers to love their enemies. If you follow Jesus, he wants you to love your enemies, too. This may be hard to do, but Jesus will help you love those you love to hate.

When your enemies attack you, how should you respond?
Never seek revenge or bear a grudge against anyone, but love your neighbor as yourself. I am the LORD.
Leviticus 19:18

5:38 Greek *'An eye for an eye and a tooth for a tooth.'* Exod 21:24; Lev 24:20; Deut 19:21. **5:41** Greek *milion* [4,854 feet or 1,478 meters]. **5:43** Lev 19:18. **5:44** Some manuscripts add *Bless those who curse you, do good to those who hate you.* **5:47** Greek *your brothers.*

J U L Y

Jesus taught his followers about prayer. He gave them an example to follow. How did he begin the prayer?

MATTHEW 6:5-18
The Model Prayer

⁵"And now about prayer. When you pray, don't be like the hypocrites who love to pray publicly on street corners and in the synagogues where everyone can see them. I assure you, that is all the reward they will ever get. ⁶But when you pray, go away by yourself, shut the door behind you, and pray to your Father secretly. Then your Father, who knows all secrets, will reward you.

⁷"When you pray, don't babble on and on as people of other religions do. They think their prayers are answered only by repeating their words again and again. ⁸Don't be like them, because your Father knows exactly what you need even before you ask him! ⁹Pray like this:

Our Father in heaven,
　　may your name be honored.
¹⁰ May your Kingdom come soon.
　　May your will be done here on earth,
　　　　just as it is in heaven.
¹¹ Give us our food for today,*
¹² and forgive us our sins,
　　　just as we have forgiven those
　　　　who have sinned against us.
¹³ And don't let us yield to temptation,
　　　but deliver us from the evil one.*

¹⁴"If you forgive those who sin against you, your heavenly Father will forgive you. ¹⁵But if you refuse to forgive others, your Father will not forgive your sins.

¹⁶"And when you fast, don't make it obvious, as the hypocrites do, who try to look pale and disheveled so people will admire them for their fasting. I assure you, that is the only reward they will ever get. ¹⁷But when you fast, comb your hair and wash your face. ¹⁸Then no one will suspect you are fasting, except your Father, who knows what you do in secret. And your Father, who knows all secrets, will reward you."

Jesus started this famous prayer by praising God. He did this to show the importance of honoring God through prayer. Praying like Jesus not only honors God, but it also helps us to have the right view of our relationship with him. When you pray, remember to praise God for his goodness and love. Thank him for his kindness to you.

What is a good way to begin your prayers?

Praise the LORD, all you who fear him! Honor him, all you descendants of Jacob! Show him reverence, all you descendants of Israel!
Psalm 22:23

6:11 Or *for tomorrow.* **6:13** Or *from evil.* Some manuscripts add *For yours is the kingdom and the power and the glory forever. Amen*

J U L Y

Jesus spent a lot of time teaching about needs.
What did Jesus tell the people not to do about food and clothing?

MATTHEW 6:19-34

Birds and Lilies

¹⁹"Don't store up treasures here on earth, where they can be eaten by moths and get rusty, and where thieves break in and steal. ²⁰Store your treasures in heaven, where they will never become moth-eaten or rusty and where they will be safe from thieves. ²¹Wherever your treasure is, there your heart and thoughts will also be.

²²"Your eye is a lamp for your body. A pure eye lets sunshine into your soul. ²³But an evil eye shuts out the light and plunges you into darkness. If the light you think you have is really darkness, how deep that darkness will be!

²⁴"No one can serve two masters. For you will hate one and love the other, or be devoted to one and despise the other. You cannot serve both God and money.

²⁵"So I tell you, don't worry about everyday life—whether you have enough food, drink, and clothes. Doesn't life consist of more than food and clothing? ²⁶Look at the birds. They don't need to plant or harvest or put food in barns because your heavenly Father feeds them. And you are far more valuable to him than they are. ²⁷Can all your worries add a single moment to your life? Of course not. ²⁸"And why worry about your clothes? Look at the lilies and how they grow. They don't work or make their clothing, ²⁹yet Solomon in all his glory was not dressed as beautifully as they are. ³⁰And if God cares so wonderfully for flowers that are here today and gone tomorrow, won't he more surely care for you? You have so little faith!

Jesus told the people not to worry about what they would eat or wear. He said that God would provide for their needs. As an example of God's care, Jesus pointed to the birds. They don't work to get their food, but they always have enough to eat, because God looks out for them. Concerning clothing, Jesus said that the lilies don't make clothes, but God has clothed them more beautifully than the richest king of Israel. He made these points to show how much God cares for and loves people. If God feeds the birds and clothes the flowers, he will provide food and clothing for you, too. Trust in God for what you need. He will provide.

Why shouldn't we worry about meeting our needs?

And this same God who takes care of me will supply all your needs from his glorious riches, which have been given to us in Christ Jesus.
Philippians 4:19

230

³¹"So don't worry about having enough food or drink or clothing. ³²Why be like the pagans who are so deeply concerned about these things? Your heavenly Father already knows all your needs, ³³and he will give you all you need from day to day if you live for him and make the Kingdom of God your primary concern.

³⁴"So don't worry about tomorrow, for tomorrow will bring its own worries. Today's trouble is enough for today."

JULY

Jesus taught people how to treat each other. What one rule did he tell them to follow?

MATTHEW 7:1-12

The Golden Rule

"Stop judging others, and you will not be judged. ²For others will treat you as you treat them.* Whatever measure you use in judging others, it will be used to measure how you are judged. ³And why worry about a speck in your friend's eye* when you have a log in your own? ⁴How can you think of saying, 'Let me help you get rid of that speck in your eye,' when you can't see past the log in your own eye? ⁵Hypocrite! First get rid of the log from your own eye; then perhaps you will see well enough to deal with the speck in your friend's eye.

⁶"Don't give what is holy to unholy people.* Don't give pearls to swine! They will trample the pearls, then turn and attack you.

⁷"Keep on asking, and you will be given what you ask for. Keep on looking, and you will find. Keep on knocking, and the door will be opened. ⁸For everyone who asks, receives. Everyone who seeks, finds. And the door is opened to everyone who knocks. ⁹You parents—if your children ask for a loaf of bread, do you give them a stone instead? ¹⁰Or if they ask for a fish, do you give them a snake? Of course not! ¹¹If you sinful people know how to give good gifts to your children, how

Jesus told people to treat others as they like to be treated. No one wants to be mistreated, picked on, or abused. Instead, people like to be loved, accepted, and treated with kindness. When you treat people as you like to be treated, you fulfill Jesus' command to love your neighbor as yourself. How do you treat others?

Why should we be kind to others?
Your own soul is nourished when you are kind, but you destroy yourself when you are cruel.
Proverbs 11:17

7:2 Or *For God will treat you as you treat others;* Greek reads *For with the judgment you judge you will be judged.* **7:3** Greek *your brother's eye;* also in 7:5. **7:6** Greek *Don't give the sacred to dogs.*

much more will your heavenly Father give good gifts to those who ask him.

¹²"Do for others what you would like them to do for you. This is a summary of all that is taught in the law and the prophets."

JULY

In part of his Sermon on the Mount, Jesus talked about living in obedience to his teachings. What did he compare an obedient person's life to?

MATTHEW 7:13-27

Rock Solid

¹³"You can enter God's Kingdom only through the narrow gate. The highway to hell* is broad, and its gate is wide for the many who choose the easy way. ¹⁴But the gateway to life is small, and the road is narrow, and only a few ever find it.

¹⁵"Beware of false prophets who come disguised as harmless sheep, but are really wolves that will tear you apart. ¹⁶You can detect them by the way they act, just as you can identify a tree by its fruit. You don't pick grapes from thornbushes, or figs from thistles. ¹⁷A healthy tree produces good fruit, and an unhealthy tree produces bad fruit. ¹⁸A good tree can't produce bad fruit, and a bad tree can't produce good fruit. ¹⁹So every tree that does not produce good fruit is chopped down and thrown into the fire. ²⁰Yes, the way to identify a tree or a person is by the kind of fruit that is produced.

²¹"Not all people who sound religious are really godly. They may refer to me as 'Lord,' but they still won't enter the Kingdom of Heaven. The decisive issue is whether they obey my Father in heaven. ²²On judgment day many will tell me, 'Lord, Lord, we prophesied in your name and cast out demons in your name and performed many miracles in your name.' ²³But I will reply, 'I never knew you. Go away; the things you did were unauthorized.*'

²⁴"Anyone who listens to my teach-

Jesus compared an obedient person's life to a house that was built on a rock. When the storms came, the house survived because its foundation was solid. There is nothing more solid on which we can build our lives than Jesus' teachings. Living life his way helps us survive the problems we face daily. What are you building your life on? You can choose Jesus. He is a firm foundation.

Why should we obey Jesus' teachings?

This is my happy way of life: obeying your commandments. LORD, you are mine! I promise to obey your words!
Psalm 119:56-57

7:13 Greek *The way that leads to destruction.* **7:23** Or *unlawful.*

ing and obeys me is wise, like a person who builds a house on solid rock. ²⁵Though the rain comes in torrents and the floodwaters rise and the winds beat against that house, it won't collapse, because it is built on rock. ²⁶But anyone who hears my teaching and ignores it is foolish, like a person who builds a house on sand. ²⁷When the rains and floods come and the winds beat against that house, it will fall with a mighty crash."

J U L Y

A Roman officer's servant was about to die. What did the officer do?

LUKE 7:1-17

An Officer's Faith

When Jesus had finished saying all this, he went back to Capernaum. ²Now the highly valued slave of a Roman officer was sick and near death. ³When the officer heard about Jesus, he sent some respected Jewish leaders to ask him to come and heal his slave. ⁴So they earnestly begged Jesus to come with them and help the man. "If anyone deserves your help, it is he," they said, ⁵"for he loves the Jews and even built a synagogue for us."

⁶So Jesus went with them. But just before they arrived at the house, the officer sent some friends to say, "Lord, don't trouble yourself by coming to my home, for I am not worthy of such an honor. ⁷I am not even worthy to come and meet you. Just say the word from where you are, and my servant will be healed. ⁸I know because I am under the authority of my superior officers, and I have authority over my soldiers. I only need to say, 'Go,' and they go, or 'Come,' and they come.

And if I say to my slaves, 'Do this or that,' they do it."

⁹When Jesus heard this, he was amazed. Turning to the crowd, he said, "I tell you, I haven't seen faith like this

The officer sent messengers to ask Jesus to heal his servant. But before Jesus could get to his house, the officer sent Jesus another message. He asked Jesus not to trouble himself by coming to his home. Instead, he asked Jesus to just say a word and the servant would be healed. The officer believed that Jesus could heal his servant even though Jesus was not there. The officer showed humility and faith, and his servant was healed. Today, we can follow the officer's example. We can believe in Jesus and trust him to answer our prayers.

**How can we show
our faith in Jesus?**
Then at last his people believed his promises. Then they finally sang his praise.
Psalm 106:12

in all the land of Israel!" ¹⁰And when the officer's friends returned to his house, they found the slave completely healed.

¹¹Soon afterward Jesus went with his disciples to the village of Nain, with a great crowd following him. ¹²A funeral procession was coming out as he approached the village gate. The boy who had died was the only son of a widow, and many mourners from the village were with her. ¹³When the Lord saw her, his heart overflowed with compassion. "Don't cry!" he said. ¹⁴Then he walked over to the coffin and touched it, and the bearers stopped. "Young man," he said, "get up." ¹⁵Then the dead boy sat up and began to talk to those around him! And Jesus gave him back to his mother.

¹⁶Great fear swept the crowd, and they praised God, saying, "A mighty prophet has risen among us," and "We have seen the hand of God at work today." ¹⁷The report of what Jesus had done that day spread all over Judea and even out across its borders.

JULY

John the Baptist sent his disciples to ask Jesus if he was God's Son. How did Jesus answer John?

MATTHEW 11:1-19

John's Question

When Jesus had finished giving these instructions to his twelve disciples, he went off teaching and preaching in towns throughout the country.

²John the Baptist, who was now in prison, heard about all the things the Messiah was doing. So he sent his disciples to ask Jesus, ³"Are you really the Messiah we've been waiting for, or should we keep looking for someone else?"

⁴Jesus told them, "Go back to John and tell him about what you have heard and seen—⁵the blind see, the lame walk, the lepers are cured, the deaf hear, the dead are raised to life, and the Good News is being preached to the poor. ⁶And tell him: 'God blesses those who are not offended by me.*' "

⁷When John's disciples had gone, Jesus began talking about him to the crowds. "Who is this man in the wilderness that you went out to see? Did you find him weak as a reed, moved by every breath of wind? ⁸Or were you expecting to see a man dressed in expensive clothes? Those who dress like that live in palaces, not out in the wilderness. ⁹Were you looking for a prophet? Yes, and he is more than a prophet. ¹⁰John is the man to whom the Scriptures refer when they say,

'Look, I am sending my messenger
  before you,
  and he will prepare your way
    before you.'*

11:6 Or *who don't fall away because of me.* **11:10** Mal 3:1.

[11]"I assure you, of all who have ever lived, none is greater than John the Baptist. Yet even the most insignificant person in the Kingdom of Heaven is greater than he is! [12]And from the time John the Baptist began preaching and baptizing until now, the Kingdom of Heaven has been forcefully advancing, and violent people attack it.* [13]For before John came, all the teachings of the Scriptures looked forward to this present time. [14]And if you are willing to accept what I say, he is Elijah, the one the prophets said would come.* [15]Anyone who is willing to hear should listen and understand!

[16] "How shall I describe this generation? These people are like a group of children playing a game in the public square. They complain to their friends, [17]'We played wedding songs, and you weren't happy, so we played funeral songs, but you weren't sad.' [18]For John the Baptist didn't drink wine and he often fasted, and you say, 'He's demon possessed.' [19] And I, the Son of Man, feast and drink, and you say, 'He's a glutton and a drunkard, and a friend of the worst sort of sinners!' But wisdom is shown to be right by what results from it."

Jesus told John's disciples that amazing things were happening in his ministry. The blind could see. The lame could walk. Lepers were cured, the dead were raised, and the poor heard the good news of Jesus Christ. Old Testament prophets predicted that the Messiah would do all of these things. Jesus fulfilled all their prophecies. He is the promised Savior.

What are some of the things the Messiah would do when he came?
Say to those who are afraid, "Be strong, and do not fear, for your God is coming to destroy your enemies. He is coming to save you." And when he comes, he will open the eyes of the blind and unstop the ears of the deaf. *Isaiah 35:4-5*

11:12 Or *until now, eager multitudes have been pressing into the Kingdom of Heaven.* **11:14** See Mal 4:5.

J U L Y

A Pharisee and a sinful woman treated Jesus differently. Who did Jesus forgive?

LUKE 7:36-50
Perfume for Jesus
[36]One of the Pharisees asked Jesus to come to his home for a meal, so Jesus accepted the invitation and sat down to eat. [37]A certain immoral woman heard he was there and brought a beautiful jar* filled with expensive perfume. [38]Then she knelt behind him at his feet, weeping. Her tears fell on

7:37 Greek *an alabaster jar.*

his feet, and she wiped them off with her hair. Then she kept kissing his feet and putting perfume on them.

[39]When the Pharisee who was the host saw what was happening and who the woman was, he said to himself, "This proves that Jesus is no prophet. If God had really sent him, he would know what kind of woman is touching him. She's a sinner!"

[40]Then Jesus spoke up and answered his thoughts. "Simon," he said to the Pharisee, "I have something to say to you."

"All right, Teacher," Simon replied, "go ahead."

[41]Then Jesus told him this story: "A man loaned money to two people—five hundred pieces of silver* to one and fifty pieces to the other. [42]But neither of them could repay him, so he kindly forgave them both, canceling their debts. Who do you suppose loved him more after that?"

[43]Simon answered, "I suppose the one for whom he canceled the larger debt."

"That's right," Jesus said. [44]Then he turned to the woman and said to Simon, "Look at this woman kneeling here. When I entered your home, you didn't offer me water to wash the dust from my feet, but she has washed them with her tears and wiped them with her hair. [45]You didn't give me a kiss of greeting, but she has kissed my feet again and again from the time I first came in. [46]You neglected the courtesy of olive oil to anoint my head, but she has anointed my feet with rare perfume. [47]I tell you, her sins—and they are many—have been forgiven, so she has shown me much love. But a person who is forgiven little shows only little love." [48]Then Jesus said to the woman, "Your sins are forgiven."

[49]The men at the table said among themselves, "Who does this man think he is, going around forgiving sins?"

[50]And Jesus said to the woman, "Your faith has saved you; go in peace."

Jesus forgave the sinful woman because she was sorry for her sins. Although Simon, a Pharisee, was also a sinner, he wasn't sorry for his sins. There are many people like Simon in the world. But you don't have to be one of them. You can be like the woman, instead. You can humble yourself before Jesus and cry over your sins. And you can worship him, thanking him for the forgiveness he offers you.

How much should we love Jesus?
And you must love the LORD your God with all your heart, all your soul, and all your strength.
Deuteronomy 6:5

7:41 Greek *500 denarii*. A denarius was the equivalent of a full day's wage.

236

JULY

*The Pharisees accused Jesus of getting his power from Satan.
How did Jesus respond to them?*

MATTHEW 12:22-37
The Pharisees' Charge

²²Then a demon-possessed man, who was both blind and unable to talk, was brought to Jesus. He healed the man so that he could both speak and see. ²³The crowd was amazed. "Could it be that Jesus is the Son of David, the Messiah?" they wondered out loud.

²⁴But when the Pharisees heard about the miracle, they said, "No wonder he can cast out demons. He gets his power from Satan,* the prince of demons."

²⁵Jesus knew their thoughts and replied, "Any kingdom at war with itself is doomed. A city or home divided against itself is doomed. ²⁶And if Satan is casting out Satan, he is fighting against himself. His own kingdom will not survive. ²⁷And if I am empowered by the prince of demons,* what about your own followers? They cast out demons, too, so they will judge you for what you have said. ²⁸But if I am casting out demons by the Spirit of God, then the Kingdom of God has arrived among you. ²⁹Let me illustrate this. You can't enter a strong man's house and rob him without first tying him up. Only then can his house be robbed!* ³⁰Anyone who isn't helping me opposes me, and anyone who isn't working with me is actually working against me.

³¹"Every sin or blasphemy can be forgiven—except blasphemy against the Holy Spirit, which can never be forgiven. ³²Anyone who blasphemes against me, the Son of Man, can be forgiven, but blasphemy against the Holy Spirit will never be forgiven, either in this world or in the world to come.

Jesus responded to the Pharisees' charge that he got his power from Satan with questions. His questions showed the Pharisees how foolish their charge was. If Jesus got his power from Satan, why would he destroy Satan's kingdom by casting out demons? The Pharisees may have made this charge against Jesus out of jealousy. But no matter what the reason, no one should say bad things about Jesus. He died for everyone's sins and loves everyone very much. Let us love him in return.

Why shouldn't people say bad things about Jesus?
Do not blaspheme God* or curse anyone who rules over you.
Exodus 22:28

12:24 Greek *Beelzeboul.* 12:27 Greek *by Beelzeboul.* 12:29 Or *One cannot rob Satan's kingdom without first tying him up. Only then can his demons be cast out.* 22:28 Or *Do not revile your judges.*

³³"A tree is identified by its fruit. Make a tree good, and its fruit will be good. Make a tree bad, and its fruit will be bad. ³⁴You brood of snakes! How could evil men like you speak what is good and right? For whatever is in your heart determines what you say. ³⁵A good person produces good words from a good heart, and an evil person produces evil words from an evil heart. ³⁶And I tell you this, that you must give an account on judgment day of every idle word you speak. ³⁷The words you say now reflect your fate then; either you will be justified by them or you will be condemned."

J U L Y

Jesus explained a parable to his disciples. What does the seed sown in the good soil represent?

MARK 4:1-20

Soil and Toil

Once again Jesus began teaching by the lakeshore. There was such a large crowd along the shore that he got into a boat and sat down and spoke from there. ²He began to teach the people by telling many stories such as this one:

³"Listen! A farmer went out to plant some seed. ⁴As he scattered it across his field, some seed fell on a footpath, and the birds came and ate it. ⁵Other seed fell on shallow soil with underlying rock. The plant sprang up quickly, ⁶but it soon wilted beneath the hot sun and died because the roots had no nourishment in the shallow soil. ⁷Other seed fell among thorns that shot up and choked out the tender blades so that it produced no grain. ⁸Still other seed fell on fertile soil and produced a crop that was thirty, sixty, and even a hundred times as much as had been planted." Then he said,

⁹"Anyone who is willing to hear should listen and understand!"

¹⁰Later, when Jesus was alone with the twelve disciples and with the others who were gathered around, they asked him, "What do your stories mean?"

¹¹He replied, "You are permitted to understand the secret about the Kingdom of God. But I am using these stories to conceal everything about it from outsiders, ¹²so that the Scriptures might be fulfilled:

'They see what I do,
　　but they don't perceive its
　　　　meaning.
They hear my words,
　　but they don't understand.
So they will not turn from their sins
　　and be forgiven.'*

¹³"But if you can't understand this story, how will you understand all the others I am going to tell? ¹⁴The farmer I talked about is the one who brings God's

4:12 Isa 6:9-10.

238

message to others. [15]The seed that fell on the hard path represents those who hear the message, but then Satan comes at once and takes it away from them. [16]The rocky soil represents those who hear the message and receive it with joy. [17]But like young plants in such soil, their roots don't go very deep. At first they get along fine, but they wilt as soon as they have problems or are persecuted because they believe the word. [18]The thorny ground represents those who hear and accept the Good News, [19]but all too quickly the message is crowded out by the cares of this life, the lure of wealth, and the desire for nice things, so no crop is produced. [20]But the good soil represents those who hear and accept God's message and produce a huge harvest—thirty, sixty, or even a hundred times as much as had been planted."

The seed sown in the good soil represents those people who hear God's Word and put it into practice. Their lives are filled with good works that please God. They don't let worries distract them from their desire to serve Jesus. Is your life like the seed in the good soil? If not, let God change you through his Word. And don't let troubles, worries, or the attraction of wealth steal God's truth from you.

How should you respond to the Bible's teachings?
So obey the LORD your God by keeping all these commands and laws that I am giving you today.
Deuteronomy 27:10

J U L Y

Jesus described God's kingdom as a wheat field. What happened to the weeds? What happened to the wheat?

MATTHEW 13:24-43
Wheat and Weeds
[24]Here is another story Jesus told: "The Kingdom of Heaven is like a farmer who planted good seed in his field. [25]But that night as everyone slept, his enemy came and planted weeds among the wheat. [26]When the crop began to grow and produce grain, the weeds also grew. [27]The farmer's servants came and told him, 'Sir, the field where you planted that good seed is full of weeds!'

[28]" 'An enemy has done it!' the farmer exclaimed.

"'Shall we pull out the weeds?' they asked.

[29]"He replied, 'No, you'll hurt the wheat if you do. [30]Let both grow together until the harvest. Then I will tell the harvesters to sort out the weeds

and burn them and to put the wheat in the barn.' "

³¹Here is another illustration Jesus used: "The Kingdom of Heaven is like a mustard seed planted in a field. ³²It is the smallest of all seeds, but it becomes the largest of garden plants and grows into a tree where birds can come and find shelter in its branches."

³³Jesus also used this illustration: "The Kingdom of Heaven is like yeast used by a woman making bread. Even though she used a large amount* of flour, the yeast permeated every part of the dough."

³⁴Jesus always used stories and illustrations like these when speaking to the crowds. In fact, he never spoke to them without using such parables. ³⁵This fulfilled the prophecy that said,

"I will speak to you in parables.
    I will explain mysteries hidden
        since the creation of the
        world."*

³⁶Then, leaving the crowds outside, Jesus went into the house. His disciples said, "Please explain the story of the weeds in the field."

³⁷"All right," he said. "I, the Son of Man, am the farmer who plants the good seed. ³⁸The field is the world, and the good seed represents the people of the Kingdom. The weeds are the people who belong to the evil one. ³⁹The enemy who planted the weeds among the wheat is the Devil. The harvest is the end of the world, and the harvesters are the angels.

⁴⁰"Just as the weeds are separated out and burned, so it will be at the end of the world. ⁴¹I, the Son of Man, will send my angels, and they will remove from my Kingdom everything that causes sin and all who do evil, ⁴²and they will throw them into the furnace and burn them. There will be weeping and gnashing of teeth. ⁴³Then the godly will shine like the sun in their Father's Kingdom. Anyone who is willing to hear should listen and understand!"

The wheat planted in this field represents God's people. The weeds represent those who do not believe in Jesus. When Jesus returns, he will separate those who believe in him from those who don't. The believers will go to heaven, and the nonbelievers will be thrown into hell. What side will you be on? Choose to be part of the wheat. Accept Jesus as your Savior before it's too late.

What has God done for those who believe in his Son, Jesus?

See, God has come to save me. I will trust in him and not be afraid. The LORD GOD is my strength and my song; he has become my salvation.
Isaiah 12:2

13:33 Greek *3 measures*. **13:35** Ps 78:2.

Jesus cast some demons out of a man. What did Jesus tell the man to do?

LUKE 8:22-39

A Demon-Possessed Man

²²One day Jesus said to his disciples, "Let's cross over to the other side of the lake." So they got into a boat and started out. ²³On the way across, Jesus lay down for a nap, and while he was sleeping the wind began to rise. A fierce storm developed that threatened to swamp them, and they were in real danger.

²⁴The disciples woke him up, shouting, "Master, Master, we're going to drown!"

So Jesus rebuked the wind and the raging waves. The storm stopped and all was calm! ²⁵Then he asked them, "Where is your faith?"

And they were filled with awe and amazement. They said to one another, "Who is this man, that even the winds and waves obey him?"

²⁶So they arrived in the land of the Gerasenes,* across the lake from Galilee. ²⁷As Jesus was climbing out of the boat, a man who was possessed by demons came out to meet him. Homeless and naked, he had lived in a cemetery for a long time. ²⁸As soon as he saw Jesus, he shrieked and fell to the ground before him, screaming, "Why are you bothering me, Jesus, Son of the Most High God? Please, I beg you, don't torture me!" ²⁹For Jesus had already commanded the evil spirit to come out of him. This spirit had often taken control of the man. Even when he was shackled with chains, he simply broke them and rushed out into the wilderness, completely under the demon's power.

³⁰"What is your name?" Jesus asked.

"Legion," he replied—for the man was filled with many demons. ³¹The demons kept begging Jesus not to send them into the Bottomless Pit. ³²A large herd of pigs was feeding on the hillside nearby, and the demons pleaded with him to let them enter into the pigs. Jesus gave them permission. ³³So the demons came out of the man and entered the pigs, and the whole herd plunged down the steep hillside into the lake, where they drowned.

³⁴When the herdsmen saw it, they fled to the nearby city and the surrounding countryside, spreading the news as they ran. ³⁵A crowd soon gathered around Jesus, for they wanted to see for themselves what had happened. And they saw the man who had been possessed by demons sitting quietly at Jesus' feet, clothed and sane. And the whole crowd was afraid. ³⁶Then those who had seen what happened told the others how the demon-possessed man had been healed.

8:26 Some manuscripts read *Gadarenes;* other manuscripts read *Gergesenes.* See Matt 8:28; Mark 5:1.

37And all the people in that region begged Jesus to go away and leave them alone, for a great wave of fear swept over them.

So Jesus returned to the boat and left, crossing back to the other side of the lake. 38The man who had been demon possessed begged to go, too, but Jesus said, 39"No, go back to your family and tell them all the wonderful things God has done for you." So he went all through the city telling about the great thing Jesus had done for him.

Jesus had changed this man's life. The man wanted to go with Jesus. But Jesus told him to go back and tell his family all that God had done for him. When we accept Jesus as our Savior, he changes our life, too. Like the man in this story, God wants us to tell others about how he has changed us. Who have you told about Jesus lately?

How can we show our appreciation to God for what he has done for us?
Come and listen, all you who fear God, and I will tell you what he did for me.
Psalm 66:16

J U L Y 13

Jesus drew crowds wherever he went. How did Jesus react to the crowds?

MATTHEW 9:27-38
Sheep without a Shepherd
27After Jesus left the girl's home, two blind men followed along behind him, shouting, "Son of David, have mercy on us!"

28They went right into the house where he was staying, and Jesus asked them, "Do you believe I can make you see?"

"Yes, Lord," they told him, "we do."

29Then he touched their eyes and said, "Because of your faith, it will happen." 30And suddenly they could see! Jesus sternly warned them, "Don't tell anyone about this." 31But instead, they spread his fame all over the region.

32When they left, some people brought to him a man who couldn't speak because he was possessed by a demon. 33So Jesus cast out the demon, and instantly the man could talk. The crowds marveled. "Nothing like this has ever happened in Israel!" they exclaimed.

34But the Pharisees said, "He can cast out demons because he is empowered by the prince of demons."

35Jesus traveled through all the cities

and villages of that area, teaching in the synagogues and announcing the Good News about the Kingdom. And wherever he went, he healed people of every sort of disease and illness. ³⁶He felt great pity for the crowds that came, because their problems were so great and they didn't know where to go for help. They were like sheep without a shepherd. ³⁷He said to his disciples, "The harvest is so great, but the workers are so few. ³⁸So pray to the Lord who is in charge of the harvest; ask him to send out more workers for his fields."

Jesus took pity on the crowds. He wanted to protect them and guide them to the truth. Jesus wants to do the same for us. He wants to be our shepherd. Will you let him be your shepherd?

How does Jesus treat us?
The LORD is merciful and gracious;
he is slow to get angry and
full of unfailing love.
Psalm 103:8

JULY

Jesus visited his hometown of Nazareth. How did the people treat him?

MARK 6:1-13
Preach It
Jesus left that part of the country and returned with his disciples to Nazareth, his hometown. ²The next Sabbath he began teaching in the synagogue, and many who heard him were astonished. They asked, "Where did he get all his wisdom and the power to perform such miracles? ³He's just the carpenter, the son of Mary and brother of James, Joseph,* Judas, and Simon. And his sisters live right here among us." They were deeply offended and refused to believe in him.

⁴Then Jesus told them, "A prophet is honored everywhere except in his own hometown and among his rela- tives and his own family." ⁵And be- cause of their unbelief, he couldn't do any mighty miracles among them ex- cept to place his hands on a few sick people and heal them. ⁶And he was amazed at their unbelief.

Then Jesus went out from village to village, teaching. ⁷And he called his twelve disciples together and sent them out two by two, with authority to cast out evil spirits. ⁸He told them to take nothing with them except a walk- ing stick—no food, no traveler's bag, no money. ⁹He told them to wear san- dals but not to take even an extra coat. ¹⁰"When you enter each village, be a guest in only one home," he said. ¹¹"And if a village won't welcome you

6:3 Greek *Joses;* see Matt 13:55.

243

or listen to you, shake off its dust from your feet as you leave. It is a sign that you have abandoned that village to its fate."

¹²So the disciples went out, telling all they met to turn from their sins. ¹³And they cast out many demons and healed many sick people, anointing them with olive oil.

The people from Jesus' hometown did not believe in him. Because of their unbelief, Jesus could not do many miracles among them. Are you limiting Jesus' work in your life because you do not believe? Jesus is powerful. He wants to free us from sin. Believe in him because he has the power to change you.

How should you respond to Jesus?
"But you are my witnesses, O Israel!" says the LORD. "And you are my servant. You have been chosen to know me, believe in me, and understand that I alone am God. There is no other God; there never has been and never will be."
Isaiah 43:10

J U L Y

Jesus warned the disciples that it would be difficult to follow him. What comfort did he give them?

MATTHEW 10:16-39
Sheep among Wolves

¹⁶"Look, I am sending you out as sheep among wolves. Be as wary as snakes and harmless as doves. ¹⁷But beware! For you will be handed over to the courts and beaten in the synagogues. ¹⁸And you must stand trial before governors and kings because you are my followers. This will be your opportunity to tell them about me— yes, to witness to the world. ¹⁹When

you are arrested, don't worry about what to say in your defense, because you will be given the right words at the right time. ²⁰For it won't be you doing the talking—it will be the Spirit of your Father speaking through you.

²¹"Brother will betray brother to death, fathers will betray their own children, and children will rise against their parents and cause them to be killed. ²²And everyone will hate you because of your allegiance to me. But

those who endure to the end will be saved. [23] When you are persecuted in one town, flee to the next. I assure you that I, the Son of Man, will return before you have reached all the towns of Israel.

[24] "A student is not greater than the teacher. A servant is not greater than the master. [25] The student shares the teacher's fate. The servant shares the master's fate. And since I, the master of the household, have been called the prince of demons,* how much more will it happen to you, the members of the household! [26] But don't be afraid of those who threaten you. For the time is coming when everything will be revealed; all that is secret will be made public. [27] What I tell you now in the darkness, shout abroad when daybreak comes. What I whisper in your ears, shout from the housetops for all to hear!

[28] "Don't be afraid of those who want to kill you. They can only kill your body; they cannot touch your soul. Fear only God, who can destroy both soul and body in hell. [29] Not even a sparrow, worth only half a penny, can fall to the ground without your Father knowing it. [30] And the very hairs on your head are all numbered. [31] So don't be afraid; you are more valuable to him than a whole flock of sparrows.

[32] "If anyone acknowledges me publicly here on earth, I will openly acknowledge that person before my Father in heaven. [33] But if anyone denies me here on earth, I will deny that person before my Father in heaven.

[34] "Don't imagine that I came to bring peace to the earth! No, I came to bring a sword. [35] I have come to set a man against his father, and a daughter against her mother, and a daughter-in-law against her mother-in-law. [36] Your enemies will be right in your own household! [37] If you love your father or mother more than you love me, you are not worthy of being mine; or if you love your son or daughter more than me, you are not worthy of being mine. [38] If you refuse to take up your cross and follow me, you are not worthy of being mine. [39] If you cling to your life, you will lose it; but if you give it up for me, you will find it."

Jesus told his followers that they would be beaten, betrayed, and forced to stand trial because of their belief in him. But he also told them that God's Spirit would be with them, comforting them and speaking through them. As Jesus' followers today, we also may have trouble with people because of our faith in him. When we do, we can trust God to comfort us and strengthen us to endure our troubles.

When we endure suffering, what can we trust God to do?

For you will not leave my soul among the dead* or allow your godly one* to rot in the grave.
Psalm 16:10

10:25 Greek *Beelzeboul.* **16:10a** Hebrew *in Sheol.* **16:10b** Or *your Holy One.*

J U L Y

*One afternoon, Jesus taught more than five thousand people.
By the time he finished teaching, it was close to dinnertime
and the crowd was hungry. What did Jesus give them?*

MARK 6:30-44

Feeding Five Thousand

[30] The apostles returned to Jesus from their ministry tour and told him all they had done and what they had taught. [31] Then Jesus said, "Let's get away from the crowds for a while and rest." There were so many people coming and going that Jesus and his apostles didn't even have time to eat. [32] They left by boat for a quieter spot. [33] But many people saw them leaving, and people from many towns ran ahead along the shore and met them as they landed. [34] A vast crowd was there as he stepped from the boat, and he had compassion on them because they were like sheep without a shepherd. So he taught them many things.

[35] Late in the afternoon his disciples came to him and said, "This is a desolate place, and it is getting late. [36] Send the crowds away so they can go to the nearby farms and villages and buy themselves some food."

[37] But Jesus said, "You feed them."

"With what?" they asked. "It would take a small fortune* to buy food for all this crowd!"

[38] "How much food do you have?" he asked. "Go and find out."

They came back and reported, "We have five loaves of bread and two fish."

[39] Then Jesus told the crowd to sit down in groups on the green grass. [40] So they sat in groups of fifty or a hundred.

[41] Jesus took the five loaves and two fish, looked up toward heaven, and asked God's blessing on the food. Breaking the loaves into pieces, he kept giving the bread and fish to the disciples to give to the people. [42] They all ate as much as they wanted, [43] and they picked up twelve baskets of leftover bread and fish. [44] Five thousand men had eaten from those five loaves!

With just five loaves of bread and two fish, Jesus fed more than five thousand people. Everyone had enough to eat, and there were even twelve basketfuls of food left over. This miracle showed that Jesus was able to provide for his followers' needs. He can provide for your needs, too. Trust Jesus to take care of you. He loves you and will not leave you.

Why is God's Word better than food?

Real life comes by feeding on every word of the LORD.
Deuteronomy 8:3

6:37 Greek *200 denarii.* A denarius was the equivalent of a full day's wage.

JULY

*In the dark and stormy sea, the disciples thought they had seen a ghost.
What did they see?*

MARK 6:45-56

Jesus Walks on Water

⁴⁵Immediately after this, Jesus made his disciples get back into the boat and head out across the lake to Bethsaida, while he sent the people home. ⁴⁶Afterward he went up into the hills by himself to pray.

⁴⁷During the night, the disciples were in their boat out in the middle of the lake, and Jesus was alone on land. ⁴⁸He saw that they were in serious trouble, rowing hard and struggling against the wind and waves. About three o'clock in the morning* he came to them, walking on the water. He started to go past them, ⁴⁹but when they saw him walking on the water, they screamed in terror, thinking he was a ghost. ⁵⁰They were all terrified when they saw him. But Jesus spoke to them at once. "It's all right," he said. "I am here! Don't be afraid." ⁵¹Then he climbed into the boat, and the wind stopped. They were astonished at what they saw. ⁵²They still didn't understand the significance of the miracle of the multiplied loaves, for their hearts were hard and they did not believe.

⁵³When they arrived at Gennesaret on the other side of the lake, they anchored the boat ⁵⁴and climbed out.

6:48 Greek *About the fourth watch of the night.*

The people standing there recognized him at once, ⁵⁵and they ran throughout the whole area and began carrying sick people to him on mats. ⁵⁶Wherever he went—in villages and cities and out on the farms—they laid the sick in the market plazas and streets. The sick begged him to let them at least touch the fringe of his robe, and all who touched it were healed.

The disciples saw Jesus walking on the water. At first they were afraid because they thought Jesus was a ghost. But then Jesus calmed his disciples' fears by talking to them and getting into their boat. Today, the Spirit of God is with all Christians. When we are afraid, we can trust the Holy Spirit to comfort us. The next time you are afraid of something, take courage. God cares for you and will protect you.

What should you do when you are afraid?

Be strong and courageous! Do not be afraid of them! The LORD your God will go ahead of you. He will neither fail you nor forsake you.
Deuteronomy 31:6

247

Many people followed Jesus in order to be fed. But what did Jesus tell them to do?

JOHN 6:22-40
The Bread of Life

²²The next morning, back across the lake, crowds began gathering on the shore, waiting to see Jesus. For they knew that he and his disciples had come over together and that the disciples had gone off in their boat, leaving him behind. ²³Several boats from Tiberias landed near the place where the Lord had blessed the bread and the people had eaten. ²⁴When the crowd saw that Jesus wasn't there, nor his disciples, they got into the boats and went across to Capernaum to look for him. ²⁵When they arrived and found him, they asked, "Teacher, how did you get here?"

²⁶Jesus replied, "The truth is, you want to be with me because I fed you, not because you saw the miraculous sign. ²⁷But you shouldn't be so concerned about perishable things like food. Spend your energy seeking the eternal life that I, the Son of Man, can give you. For God the Father has sent me for that very purpose."

²⁸They replied, "What does God want us to do?"

²⁹Jesus told them, "This is what God wants you to do: Believe in the one he has sent."

³⁰They replied, "You must show us a miraculous sign if you want us to be-

lieve in you. What will you do for us? ³¹After all, our ancestors ate manna while they journeyed through the wilderness! As the Scriptures say, 'Moses gave them bread from heaven to eat.'* "

³²Jesus said, "I assure you, Moses didn't give them bread from heaven. My Father did. And now he offers you

---

The crowd was looking for Jesus for the wrong reason. They wanted him to feed them again. Jesus wanted them to look for something more lasting, instead. He wanted them to look for eternal life. But most of them weren't interested. They wanted what they could get then and there. Today, Jesus wants us to look for eternal life through a personal relationship with him. Like the crowd that searched for Jesus, we can be distracted by what we want from him. But we need to understand that a relationship with Jesus is more important than anything we could want from a store. Don't trade a relationship with Jesus for something that won't last forever.

What does God look for in us?
The LORD looks down from heaven on the entire human race; he looks to see if there is even one with real understanding, one who seeks for God.
Psalm 14:2

6:31 Exod 16:4; Ps 78:24.

the true bread from heaven. ³³The true bread of God is the one who comes down from heaven and gives life to the world."

³⁴"Sir," they said, "give us that bread every day of our lives."

³⁵Jesus replied, "I am the bread of life. No one who comes to me will ever be hungry again. Those who believe in me will never thirst. ³⁶But you haven't believed in me even though you have seen me. ³⁷However, those the Father has given me will come to me, and I will never reject them. ³⁸For I have come down from heaven to do the will of God who sent me, not to do what I want. ³⁹And this is the will of God, that I should not lose even one of all those he has given me, but that I should raise them to eternal life at the last day. ⁴⁰For it is my Father's will that all who see his Son and believe in him should have eternal life—that I should raise them at the last day."

J U L Y

Many people stopped following Jesus. Why did Simon Peter stay with him?

JOHN 6:41-71

Jesus Is Rejected

⁴¹Then the people* began to murmur in disagreement because he had said, "I am the bread from heaven." ⁴²They said, "This is Jesus, the son of Joseph. We know his father and mother. How can he say, 'I came down from heaven'?"

⁴³But Jesus replied, "Don't complain about what I said. ⁴⁴For people can't come to me unless the Father who sent me draws them to me, and at the last day I will raise them from the dead. ⁴⁵As it is written in the Scriptures, 'They will all be taught by God.'* Everyone who hears and learns from the Father comes to me. ⁴⁶(Not that anyone has ever seen the Father; only I, who was sent from God, have seen him.)

⁴⁷"I assure you, anyone who believes in me already has eternal life. ⁴⁸Yes, I am the bread of life! ⁴⁹Your ancestors ate manna in the wilderness, but they all died. ⁵⁰However, the bread from heaven gives eternal life to everyone who eats it. ⁵¹I am the living bread that came down out of heaven. Anyone who eats this bread will live forever; this bread is my flesh, offered so the world may live."

⁵²Then the people began arguing with each other about what he meant. "How can this man give us his flesh to eat?" they asked.

⁵³So Jesus said again, "I assure you, unless you eat the flesh of the Son of Man and drink his blood, you cannot have eternal life within you. ⁵⁴But those who eat my flesh and drink my blood have eternal life, and I will raise

6:41 Greek *Jewish people*; also in 6:52. 6:45 Isa 54:13.

249

them at the last day. ⁵⁵For my flesh is the true food, and my blood is the true drink. ⁵⁶All who eat my flesh and drink my blood remain in me, and I in them. ⁵⁷I live by the power of the living Father who sent me; in the same way, those who partake of me will live because of me. ⁵⁸I am the true bread from heaven. Anyone who eats this bread will live forever and not die as your ancestors did, even though they ate the manna."

⁵⁹He said these things while he was teaching in the synagogue in Capernaum.

⁶⁰Even his disciples said, "This is very hard to understand. How can anyone accept it?"

⁶¹Jesus knew within himself that his disciples were complaining, so he said to them, "Does this offend you? ⁶²Then what will you think if you see me, the Son of Man, return to heaven again? ⁶³It is the Spirit who gives eternal life. Human effort accomplishes nothing. And the very words I have spoken to you are spirit and life. ⁶⁴But some of you don't believe me." (For Jesus knew from the beginning who didn't believe, and he knew who would betray him.) ⁶⁵Then he said, "That is what I meant when I said that people can't come to me unless the Father brings them to me."

⁶⁶At this point many of his disciples turned away and deserted him. ⁶⁷Then Jesus turned to the Twelve and asked, "Are you going to leave, too?"

⁶⁸Simon Peter replied, "Lord, to whom would we go? You alone have the words that give eternal life. ⁶⁹We believe them, and we know you are the Holy One of God."

⁷⁰Then Jesus said, "I chose the twelve of you, but one is a devil." ⁷¹He was speaking of Judas, son of Simon Iscariot, one of the Twelve, who would betray him.

Many people didn't believe what Jesus said about himself. They stopped following him from then on. When Jesus asked his twelve disciples if they wanted to leave too, Peter asked who else they would follow. Peter knew that Jesus is the true Son of God. He knew that there was no one else he could go to for eternal life. Like Peter, we should follow Jesus. He is our only hope.

Who is the only way to God?

Jesus told him, "I am the way, the truth, and the life. No one can come to the Father except through me."
John 14:6

J U L Y

The Pharisees questioned the disciples' washing habits.
How did Jesus answer them?

MARK 7:1-23

A Clean Heart

One day some Pharisees and teachers of religious law arrived from Jerusalem to confront Jesus. ²They noticed that some of Jesus' disciples failed to follow the usual Jewish ritual of hand washing before eating. ³(The Jews, especially the Pharisees, do not eat until they have poured water over their cupped hands,* as required by their ancient traditions. ⁴Similarly, they eat nothing bought from the market unless they have immersed their hands in water. This is but one of many traditions they have clung to—such as their ceremony of washing cups, pitchers, and kettles.*) ⁵So the Pharisees and teachers of religious law asked him, "Why don't your disciples follow our age-old customs? For they eat without first performing the hand-washing ceremony."

⁶Jesus replied, "You hypocrites! Isaiah was prophesying about you when he said,

⁷'These people honor me with their
   lips,
   but their hearts are far away.
 Their worship is a farce,
   for they replace God's
      commands with their own
      man-made teachings.'*

⁸For you ignore God's specific laws and substitute your own traditions."

⁹Then he said, "You reject God's laws in order to hold on to your own traditions. ¹⁰For instance, Moses gave you this law from God: 'Honor your father and mother.' and 'Anyone who speaks evil of father or mother must be put to death.'* ¹¹But you say it is all right for people to say to their parents, 'Sorry, I can't help you. For I have vowed to give to God what I could have given to you.'* ¹²You let them disregard their needy parents. ¹³As such, you break the law of God in order to protect your own tradition. And this is only one example. There are many, many others."

¹⁴Then Jesus called to the crowd to come and hear. "All of you listen," he said, "and try to understand. ¹⁵You are not defiled by what you eat; you are defiled by what you say and do!*"

¹⁷Then Jesus went into a house to get away from the crowds, and his disciples asked him what he meant by the statement he had made. ¹⁸"Don't you understand either?" he asked. "Can't you see that what you eat won't defile you? ¹⁹Food doesn't come in contact with your heart, but only passes through the stomach and

---

7:3 Greek *washed with the fist.* **7:4** Some Greek manuscripts add *and dining couches.* **7:7** Isa 29:13. **7:10** Exod 20:12; 21:17; Lev 20:9; Deut 5:16. **7:11** Greek *'What I could have given to you is Corban' (that is, a gift).* **7:15** Some manuscripts add verse 16, *Anyone who is willing to hear should listen and understand.*

then comes out again." (By saying this, he showed that every kind of food is acceptable.)

²⁰And then he added, "It is the thought-life that defiles you. ²¹For from within, out of a person's heart, come evil thoughts, sexual immorality, theft, murder, ²²adultery, greed, wickedness, deceit, eagerness for lustful pleasure, envy, slander, pride, and foolishness. ²³All these vile things come from within; they are what defile you and make you unacceptable to God."

The Pharisees were more concerned with following empty, man-made rituals than with following God's commands. Jesus knew this. So when the Pharisees came to him about his disciples, Jesus told the Pharisees that God is more concerned about people than rituals. Instead, God wants people to have clean hearts. A clean heart is free from hatred and pride. A clean heart is full of love for others and hope in God. Give your heart to God. He will make it clean.

What does it mean to have a clean heart?

And I will give you a new heart with new and right desires, and I will put a new spirit in you. I will take out your stony heart of sin and give you a new, obedient heart.* And I will put my Spirit in you so you will obey my laws and do whatever I command.
Ezekiel 36:26-27

36:26 Hebrew *a heart of flesh.*

J U L Y

The Pharisees and Sadducees asked Jesus to prove that he was God's Son. After they left, what did Jesus warn his disciples about?

MATTHEW 16:1-12
Jesus and the Pharisees
One day the Pharisees and Sadducees came to test Jesus' claims by asking him to show them a miraculous sign from heaven.

²He replied, "You know the saying, 'Red sky at night means fair weather tomorrow, ³red sky in the morning means foul weather all day.' You are good at reading the weather signs in the sky, but you can't read the obvious signs of the times!* ⁴Only an evil, faithless generation would ask for a

16:2-3 Several manuscripts do not include any of the words in 16:2-3 after *He replied.*

miraculous sign, but the only sign I will give them is the sign of the prophet Jonah." Then Jesus left them and went away.

⁵Later, after they crossed to the other side of the lake, the disciples discovered they had forgotten to bring any food. ⁶"Watch out!" Jesus warned them. "Beware of the yeast of the Pharisees and Sadducees."

⁷They decided he was saying this because they hadn't brought any bread. ⁸Jesus knew what they were thinking, so he said, "You have so little faith! Why are you worried about having no food? ⁹Won't you ever understand? Don't you remember the five thousand I fed with five loaves, and the baskets of food that were left over? ¹⁰Don't you remember the four thousand I fed with seven loaves, with baskets of food left over? ¹¹How could you even think I was talking about food? So again I say, 'Beware of the yeast of the Pharisees and Sadducees.' "

¹²Then at last they understood that he wasn't speaking about yeast or bread but about the false teaching of the Pharisees and Sadducees.

The Pharisees and Sadducees were leading people away from God with their teachings. Jesus warned his disciples to beware of these false teachers. Today some people want to lead people away from Jesus. These people teach things that are against God's commands. We should not listen to them. Instead, we should listen only to those who teach what the Bible says.

Whom should we ignore?

"This is my warning to my people," says the LORD Almighty. "Do not listen to these prophets when they prophesy to you, filling you with futile hopes. They are making up everything they say. They do not speak for the LORD!"
Jeremiah 23:16

J U L Y

Jesus asked his disciples who they thought he was. What did Peter say?

LUKE 9:18-27
Peter's Reply
¹⁸One day as Jesus was alone, praying, he came over to his disciples and asked them, "Who do people say I am?"

¹⁹"Well," they replied, "some say John the Baptist, some say Elijah, and others say you are one of the other ancient prophets risen from the dead."

²⁰Then he asked them, "Who do you say I am?"

Peter replied, "You are the Messiah sent from God!"

²¹Jesus warned them not to tell anyone about this. ²²"For I, the Son of

Man, must suffer many terrible things," he said. "I will be rejected by the leaders, the leading priests, and the teachers of religious law. I will be killed, but three days later I will be raised from the dead."

[23]Then he said to the crowd, "If any of you wants to be my follower, you must put aside your selfish ambition, shoulder your cross daily, and follow me. [24]If you try to keep your life for yourself, you will lose it. But if you give up your life for me, you will find true life. [25]And how do you benefit if you gain the whole world but lose or forfeit your own soul in the process? [26]If a person is ashamed of me and my message, I, the Son of Man, will be ashamed of that person when I return in my glory and in the glory of the Father and the holy angels. [27]And I assure you that some of you standing here right now will not die before you see the Kingdom of God."

Peter said that Jesus is the Son of God. To say this, Peter had to trust that Jesus was telling the truth. Who do you say Jesus is? Do you trust that he is God's only Son? If not, ask God to open your heart and mind so that you will know that Jesus is his Son.

Whom did God send to save us from our sins?

But when the right time came, God sent his Son, born of a woman, subject to the law. God sent him to buy freedom for us who were slaves to the law, so that he could adopt us as his very own children.
Galatians 4:4-5

JULY 23

Jesus took three disciples up the side of a mountain. There God spoke to them. What did he say about Jesus?

MATTHEW 17:1-13

A Voice from a Cloud

Six days later Jesus took Peter and the two brothers, James and John, and led them up a high mountain. [2]As the men watched, Jesus' appearance changed so that his face shone like the sun, and his clothing became dazzling white. [3]Suddenly, Moses and Elijah appeared and began talking with Jesus. [4]Peter blurted out, "Lord, this is wonderful! If you want me to, I'll make three shrines,* one for you, one for Moses, and one for Elijah."

[5]But even as he said it, a bright cloud came over them, and a voice from the cloud said, "This is my beloved Son, and I am fully pleased with him. Listen to him." [6]The disciples were terrified and fell face down on the ground.

17:4 Or *shelters;* Greek reads *tabernacles.*

⁷Jesus came over and touched them. "Get up," he said, "don't be afraid." ⁸And when they looked, they saw only Jesus with them. ⁹As they descended the mountain, Jesus commanded them, "Don't tell anyone what you have seen until I, the Son of Man, have been raised from the dead."

¹⁰His disciples asked, "Why do the teachers of religious law insist that Elijah must return before the Messiah comes*?"

¹¹Jesus replied, "Elijah is indeed coming first to set everything in order. ¹²But I tell you, he has already come, but he wasn't recognized, and he was badly mistreated. And soon the Son of Man will also suffer at their hands." ¹³Then the disciples realized he had been speaking of John the Baptist.

17:10 Greek *that Elijah must come first.*

As Jesus and three disciples were on the mountaintop, a bright cloud appeared over them. God spoke from the cloud. He told the disciples that Jesus was his Son and that he was pleased with him. He also ordered the disciples to listen to Jesus. God's command is also for us. We must listen to Jesus because he speaks for God and tells us how to live the right way.

How should we respond to Jesus' words?

Call them all together—men, women, children, and the foreigners living in your towns—so they may listen and learn to fear the LORD your God and carefully obey all the terms of this law.
Deuteronomy 31:12

JULY 24

The disciples asked Jesus which one of them would be the greatest in heaven. What did Jesus tell them about greatness?

MATTHEW 18:1-10

The Greatest

About that time the disciples came to Jesus and asked, "Which of us is greatest in the Kingdom of Heaven?"

²Jesus called a small child over to him and put the child among them. ³Then he said, "I assure you, unless you turn from your sins and become as little children, you will never get into the Kingdom of Heaven. ⁴Therefore, anyone who becomes as humble as this little child is the greatest in the Kingdom of Heaven. ⁵And anyone who welcomes a little child like this on my behalf is welcoming me. ⁶But if anyone causes one of these little ones who trusts in me to lose faith, it would be better for that person to be thrown into the sea with a large millstone tied around the neck.

⁷"How terrible it will be for anyone who causes others to sin. Temptation to do wrong is inevitable, but how

terrible it will be for the person who does the tempting. ⁸So if your hand or foot causes you to sin, cut it off and throw it away. It is better to enter heaven* crippled or lame than to be thrown into the unquenchable fire with both of your hands and feet. ⁹And if your eye causes you to sin, gouge it out and throw it away. It is better to enter heaven half blind than to have two eyes and be thrown into hell.

¹⁰"Beware that you don't despise a single one of these little ones. For I tell you that in heaven their angels are always in the presence of my heavenly Father.*"

Jesus told his disciples that those who turn away from their sins and humble themselves will be the greatest in heaven. His instructions for greatness sound easy. But they're not. Our sinful nature and pride get in the way of obeying Jesus' commands. That's why Jesus says we must be humble like a little child. We need to understand that we depend on Jesus to forgive us of our sins. There is nothing in ourselves that will save us.

Whom does the Lord honor?
For the LORD delights in his people;
he crowns the humble with salvation.
Psalm 149:4

18:8 Greek *enter life*; also in 18:9.　**18:10** Some manuscripts add verse 11, *And I, the Son of Man, have come to save the lost.*

J U L Y

Jesus told his followers the story of the lost sheep.
What did he teach about God through this story?

MATTHEW 18:12-20
Lost Sheep
¹²"If a shepherd has one hundred sheep, and one wanders away and is lost, what will he do? Won't he leave the ninety-nine others and go out into the hills to search for the lost one? ¹³And if he finds it, he will surely rejoice over it more than over the ninety-nine that didn't wander away! ¹⁴In the same way, it is not my heavenly Father's will that even one of these little ones should perish.

¹⁵"If another believer* sins against you, go privately and point out the fault. If the other person listens and confesses it, you have won that person back. ¹⁶But if you are unsuccessful, take one or two others with you and go back again, so that everything you say may be confirmed by two or three witnesses. ¹⁷If that person still refuses to listen, take your case to the church. If the church decides you are right, but the other person won't accept it, treat

18:15 Greek *your brother.*

that person as a pagan or a corrupt tax collector. ¹⁸I tell you this: Whatever you prohibit on earth is prohibited in heaven, and whatever you allow on earth is allowed in heaven.

¹⁹"I also tell you this: If two of you agree down here on earth concerning anything you ask, my Father in heaven will do it for you. ²⁰For where two or three gather together because they are mine,* I am there among them."

Jesus taught that God does not want anyone to be lost. Being lost means that a person has strayed away from God and is heading for eternal destruction. God loves lost people so much that he sent his only Son, Jesus, to save them. When a lost person is found, or saved from eternal destruction, God is happy and rejoices.

What do saved people become?
Acknowledge that the LORD is God! He made us, and we are his. We are his people, the sheep of his pasture.
Psalm 100:3

18:20 Greek *gather together in my name.*

J U L Y

Peter asked Jesus how many times he should forgive someone who sins against him. What did Jesus tell him?

MATTHEW 18:21-35
Forgive and Forget
²¹Then Peter came to him and asked, "Lord, how often should I forgive someone* who sins against me? Seven times?"

²²"No!" Jesus replied, "seventy times seven!*

²³"For this reason, the Kingdom of Heaven can be compared to a king who decided to bring his accounts up to date with servants who had borrowed money from him. ²⁴In the process, one of his debtors was brought in who owed him millions of dollars.* ²⁵He couldn't pay, so the king ordered that he, his wife, his children, and everything he had be sold to pay the debt. ²⁶But the man fell down before the king and begged him, 'Oh, sir, be patient with me, and I will pay it all.' ²⁷Then the king was filled with pity for him, and he released him and forgave his debt.

²⁸"But when the man left the king, he went to a fellow servant who owed him a few thousand dollars.* He grabbed him by the throat and demanded instant payment. ²⁹His fellow servant fell down before him and

18:21 Greek *my brother.* **18:22** Or *77 times.* **18:24** Greek *10,000 talents.* **18:28** Greek *100 denarii.* A denarius was the equivalent of a full day's wage.

257

begged for a little more time. 'Be patient and I will pay it,' he pleaded. ³⁰But his creditor wouldn't wait. He had the man arrested and jailed until the debt could be paid in full.

³¹"When some of the other servants saw this, they were very upset. They went to the king and told him what had happened. ³²Then the king called in the man he had forgiven and said, 'You evil servant! I forgave you that tremendous debt because you pleaded with me. ³³Shouldn't you have mercy on your fellow servant, just as I had mercy on you?' ³⁴Then the angry king sent the man to prison until he had paid every penny.

³⁵"That's what my heavenly Father will do to you if you refuse to forgive your brothers and sisters in your heart."

Jesus told Peter to forgive others "seventy times seven" times. In saying this, Jesus was not telling Peter he could stop forgiving someone after 490 offenses. Instead, he was saying that people should forgive one another like God forgives them—continually. The next time someone sins against you, remember Jesus' words. Show God's love by forgiving that person over and over.

What feeling or attitude might a forgiven person have?
Oh, what joy for those whose rebellion is forgiven, whose sin is put out of sight!
Psalm 32:1

J U L Y

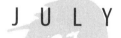

Jesus went to Jerusalem and taught in the Temple. Some of the religious leaders criticized him publicly. What did Jesus say to his critics?

JOHN 7:10-31
Jesus Teaches at the Temple
¹⁰But after his brothers had left for the festival, Jesus also went, though secretly, staying out of public view. ¹¹The Jewish leaders tried to find him at the festival and kept asking if anyone had seen him. ¹²There was a lot of discussion about him among the crowds. Some said, "He's a wonderful man," while others said, "He's nothing but a fraud, deceiving the people." ¹³But no one had the courage to speak favor-

ably about him in public, for they were afraid of getting in trouble with the Jewish leaders.

¹⁴Then, midway through the festival, Jesus went up to the Temple and began to teach. ¹⁵The Jewish leaders were surprised when they heard him. "How does he know so much when he hasn't studied everything we've studied?" they asked.

¹⁶So Jesus told them, "I'm not teaching my own ideas, but those of God who sent me. ¹⁷Anyone who wants to

do the will of God will know whether my teaching is from God or is merely my own. [18]Those who present their own ideas are looking for praise for themselves, but those who seek to honor the one who sent them are good and genuine. [19]None of you obeys the law of Moses! In fact, you are trying to kill me."

[20]The crowd replied, "You're demon possessed! Who's trying to kill you?"

[21]Jesus replied, "I worked on the Sabbath by healing a man, and you were offended. [22]But you work on the Sabbath, too, when you obey Moses' law of circumcision. (Actually, this tradition of circumcision is older than the law of Moses; it goes back to Abraham.) [23]For if the correct time for circumcising your son falls on the Sabbath, you go ahead and do it, so as not to break the law of Moses. So why should I be condemned for making a man completely well on the Sabbath? [24]Think this through and you will see that I am right."

[25]Some of the people who lived there in Jerusalem said among themselves, "Isn't this the man they are trying to kill? [26]But here he is, speaking in public, and they say nothing to him. Can it be that our leaders know that he really is the Messiah? [27]But how could he be? For we know where this man comes from. When the Messiah comes, he will simply appear; no one will know where he comes from."

[28]While Jesus was teaching in the Temple, he called out, "Yes, you know me, and you know where I come from. But I represent one you don't know, and he is true. [29]I know him because I have come from him, and he sent me to you." [30]Then the leaders tried to arrest him; but no one laid a hand on him, because his time had not yet come.

[31]Many among the crowds at the Temple believed in him. "After all," they said, "would you expect the Messiah to do more miraculous signs than this man has done?"

When the religious leaders criticized Jesus' teachings, he told them that they weren't his teachings but God's. He also told them that those who really want to do God's will would know if Jesus' teachings were from God or not. If his critics were serious about serving God, then they would know that Jesus was his Son.

Why is rejecting Jesus wrong?
And the LORD said to Moses, "How long will these people reject me? Will they never believe me, even after all the miraculous signs I have done among them?"
Numbers 14:11

The Pharisees wanted to arrest Jesus. Why did the guards refuse to arrest him?

JOHN 7:32-52

An Attempted Arrest

[32]When the Pharisees heard that the crowds were murmuring such things, they and the leading priests sent Temple guards to arrest Jesus. [33]But Jesus told them, "I will be here a little longer. Then I will return to the one who sent me. [34]You will search for me but not find me. And you won't be able to come where I am."

[35]The Jewish leaders were puzzled by this statement. "Where is he planning to go?" they asked. "Maybe he is thinking of leaving the country and going to the Jews in other lands, or maybe even to the Gentiles! [36]What does he mean when he says, 'You will search for me but not find me,' and 'You won't be able to come where I am'?"

[37]On the last day, the climax of the festival, Jesus stood and shouted to the crowds, "If you are thirsty, come to me! [38]If you believe in me, come and drink! For the Scriptures declare that rivers of living water will flow out from within."* [39](When he said "living water," he was speaking of the Spirit, who would be given to everyone believing in him. But the Spirit had not yet been given, because Jesus had not yet entered into his glory.)

[40]When the crowds heard him say this, some of them declared, "This man surely is the Prophet."* [41]Others said, "He is the Messiah." Still others said, "But he can't be! Will the Messiah come from Galilee? [42]For the Scriptures clearly state that the Messiah will be born of the royal line of David, in Bethlehem, the village where King David was born."* [43]So the crowd was divided in their opinion about him. [44]And some wanted him arrested, but no one touched him.

[45]The Temple guards who had been sent to arrest him returned to the leading priests and Pharisees. "Why didn't you bring him in?" they demanded.

The guards didn't arrest Jesus because they were amazed by what he said. The chief priests criticized the guards for listening to Jesus. Like the guards, we might be criticized for listening to Jesus. But stand firm. Jesus rewards those who are not ashamed of him.

What does God do for his followers?

Your rod and your staff protect and comfort me. You prepare a feast for me in the presence of my enemies.
Psalm 23:4-5

7:37-38 Or *"Let anyone who is thirsty come to me and drink.* [38]*For the Scriptures declare that rivers of living water will flow from the heart of those who believe in me."* **7:40** See Deut 18:15, 18. **7:42** See Mic 5:2.

46"We have never heard anyone talk like this!" the guards responded.

47"Have you been led astray, too?" the Pharisees mocked. 48"Is there a single one of us rulers or Pharisees who believes in him? 49These ignorant crowds do, but what do they know about it? A curse on them anyway!"

50Nicodemus, the leader who had met with Jesus earlier, then spoke up. 51"Is it legal to convict a man before he is given a hearing?" he asked.

52They replied, "Are you from Galilee, too? Search the Scriptures and see for yourself—no prophet ever comes from Galilee!"

J U L Y

The Pharisees brought to Jesus a woman they accused of sin.
How did Jesus respond to the situation?

JOHN 8:1-11

A Forgiven Woman

Jesus returned to the Mount of Olives, 2but early the next morning he was back again at the Temple. A crowd soon gathered, and he sat down and taught them. 3As he was speaking, the teachers of religious law and Pharisees brought a woman they had caught in the act of adultery. They put her in front of the crowd.

4"Teacher," they said to Jesus, "this woman was caught in the very act of adultery. 5The law of Moses says to stone her. What do you say?"

6They were trying to trap him into saying something they could use against him, but Jesus stooped down and wrote in the dust with his finger. 7They kept demanding an answer, so he stood up again and said, "All right, stone her. But let those who have never sinned throw the first stones!" 8Then he stooped down again and wrote in the dust.

9When the accusers heard this, they slipped away one by one, beginning with the oldest, until only Jesus was left

The Pharisees brought this woman to Jesus to trap him. They hoped he would say something they could arrest him for. They didn't expect Jesus to forgive her. Like the Pharisees, we may not expect Jesus to forgive some bad people we know. We may not even expect him to forgive us when we really blow it. But Jesus wants everyone to turn away from sin and experience his forgiveness. Only Jesus can free us from the trap of sin. Turn to Jesus and be free.

What can we pray when we sin?
Help us, O God of our salvation!
Help us for the honor of your name.
Oh, save us and forgive our sins
for the sake of your name.
Psalm 79:9

in the middle of the crowd with the woman. [10]Then Jesus stood up again and said to her, "Where are your accusers? Didn't even one of them condemn you?"

[11]"No, Lord," she said.

And Jesus said, "Neither do I. Go and sin no more."

JULY

Jesus talked about going away. Where was he going?

JOHN 8:12-30

The Light of the World

[12]Jesus said to the people, "I am the light of the world. If you follow me, you won't be stumbling through the darkness, because you will have the light that leads to life."

[13]The Pharisees replied, "You are making false claims about yourself!"

[14]Jesus told them, "These claims are valid even though I make them about myself. For I know where I came from and where I am going, but you don't know this about me. [15]You judge me with all your human limitations,* but I am not judging anyone. [16]And if I did, my judgment would be correct in every respect because I am not alone— I have with me the Father who sent me. [17]Your own law says that if two people agree about something, their witness is accepted as fact.* [18]I am one witness, and my Father who sent me is the other."

[19]"Where is your father?" they asked.

Jesus answered, "Since you don't know who I am, you don't know who my Father is. If you knew me, then you would know my Father, too." [20]Jesus made these statements while he was teaching in the section of the Temple known as the Treasury. But he was not arrested, because his time had not yet come.

[21]Later Jesus said to them again, "I am going away. You will search for me and die in your sin. You cannot come where I am going."

[22]The Jewish leaders asked, "Is he planning to commit suicide? What does he mean, 'You cannot come where I am going'?"

[23]Then he said to them, "You are from below; I am from above. You are of this world; I am not. [24]That is why I said that you will die in your sins; for unless you believe that I am who I say I am, you will die in your sins."

[25]"Tell us who you are," they demanded.

Jesus replied, "I am the one I have always claimed to be.* [26]I have much to say about you and much to condemn, but I won't. For I say only what I have heard from the one who sent me, and he is true." [27]But they still

---

8:15 Or *judge me by human standards.*   **8:17** See Deut 19:15.   **8:25** Or *"Why do I speak to you at all?"*

didn't understand that he was talking to them about his Father.

28 So Jesus said, "When you have lifted up the Son of Man on the cross, then you will realize that I am he and that I do nothing on my own, but I speak what the Father taught me. 29 And the one who sent me is with me—he has not deserted me. For I always do those things that are pleasing to him." 30 Then many who heard him say these things believed in him.

Jesus was going back to heaven. The people he talked to didn't understand this. Some thought he was going to kill himself. But that wasn't what Jesus was talking about at all. He told the people about his return to warn them that they wouldn't go to heaven if they didn't believe him. The same warning is still true today. If we don't believe Jesus, then we will not go to be with him in heaven. But if we believe that he is God's Son and seek his forgiveness for our sins, then we will spend eternity with him in heaven.

What free gift does Jesus give to those who believe in him?

For the wages of sin is death, but the free gift of God is eternal life through Christ Jesus our Lord.
Romans 6:23

J U L Y

Jesus sent out seventy-two disciples to tell people that God's kingdom was near. What would happen to those who rejected Jesus' disciples?

LUKE 10:1-24

Two by Two

The Lord now chose seventy-two* other disciples and sent them on ahead in pairs to all the towns and villages he planned to visit. 2 These were his instructions to them: "The harvest is so great, but the workers are so few. Pray to the Lord who is in charge of the harvest, and ask him to send out more workers for his fields. 3 Go now, and remember that I am sending you out as lambs among wolves. 4 Don't take along any money, or a traveler's bag, or even an extra pair of sandals. And don't stop to greet anyone on the road.

5 "Whenever you enter a home, give it your blessing. 6 If those who live

10:1 Some manuscripts read *70;* also in 10:17.

there are worthy, the blessing will stand; if they are not, the blessing will return to you. [7]When you enter a town, don't move around from home to home. Stay in one place, eating and drinking what they provide you. Don't hesitate to accept hospitality, because those who work deserve their pay.

[8]"If a town welcomes you, eat whatever is set before you [9]and heal the sick. As you heal them, say, 'The Kingdom of God is near you now.' [10]But if a town refuses to welcome you, go out into its streets and say, [11]'We wipe the dust of your town from our feet as a public announcement of your doom. And don't forget the Kingdom of God is near!' [12]The truth is, even wicked Sodom will be better off than such a town on the judgment day.

[13]"What horrors await you, Korazin and Bethsaida! For if the miracles I did in you had been done in wicked Tyre and Sidon, their people would have sat in deep repentance long ago, clothed in sackcloth and throwing ashes on their heads to show their remorse. [14]Yes, Tyre and Sidon will be better off on the judgment day than you. [15]And you people of Capernaum, will you be exalted to heaven? No, you will be brought down to the place of the dead.*"

[16]Then he said to the disciples, "Anyone who accepts your message is also accepting me. And anyone who rejects you is rejecting me. And anyone who rejects me is rejecting God who sent me."

[17]When the seventy-two disciples returned, they joyfully reported to him, "Lord, even the demons obey us when we use your name!"

[18]"Yes," he told them, "I saw Satan falling from heaven as a flash of lightning! [19]And I have given you authority over all the power of the enemy, and you can walk among snakes and scorpions and crush them. Nothing will injure you. [20]But don't rejoice just because evil spirits obey you; rejoice because your names are registered as citizens of heaven."

[21]Then Jesus was filled with the joy of the Holy Spirit and said, "O Father, Lord of heaven and earth, thank you for hiding the truth from those who think themselves so wise and clever, and for revealing it to the childlike. Yes, Father, it pleased you to do it this way.

[22]"My Father has given me authority

Those who rejected the disciples' message were rejecting Jesus. Because they rejected Jesus, they also rejected God. God would eventually judge them for rejecting him. Rejecting God is a serious sin with terrible consequences. Don't be like those who rejected Jesus' disciples. Accept Jesus and God, who sent him. This is the best decision you can ever make.

What promise has Jesus made to his followers?

All who are victorious will be clothed in white. I will never erase their names from the Book of Life, but I will announce before my Father and his angels that they are mine.
Revelation 3:5

10:15 Greek *to Hades.*

over everything. No one really knows the Son except the Father, and no one really knows the Father except the Son and those to whom the Son chooses to reveal him."

²³Then when they were alone, he turned to the disciples and said, "How privileged you are to see what you have seen. ²⁴I tell you, many prophets and kings have longed to see and hear what you have seen and heard, but they could not."

A man asked Jesus who his neighbor was. What did Jesus tell this man?

LUKE 10:25-37

The Good Neighbor

²⁵One day an expert in religious law stood up to test Jesus by asking him this question: "Teacher, what must I do to receive eternal life?"

²⁶Jesus replied, "What does the law of Moses say? How do you read it?"

²⁷The man answered, "'You must love the Lord your God with all your heart, all your soul, all your strength, and all your mind.' And, 'Love your neighbor as yourself.' "*

²⁸"Right!" Jesus told him. "Do this and you will live!"

²⁹The man wanted to justify his actions, so he asked Jesus, "And who is my neighbor?"

³⁰Jesus replied with an illustration: "A Jewish man was traveling on a trip from Jerusalem to Jericho, and he was attacked by bandits. They stripped him of his clothes and money, beat him up, and left him half dead beside the road.

³¹"By chance a Jewish priest came along; but when he saw the man lying there, he crossed to the other side of the road and passed him by. ³²A Temple assistant* walked over and looked at him lying there, but he also passed by on the other side.

³³"Then a despised Samaritan came along, and when he saw the man, he felt deep pity. ³⁴Kneeling beside him, the Samaritan soothed his wounds with medicine and bandaged them. Then he put the man on his own donkey and took him to an inn, where he took care of him. ³⁵The next day he handed the innkeeper two pieces of silver* and told him to take care of the man. 'If his bill runs higher than that,' he said, 'I'll pay the difference the next time I am here.'

Jesus answered this man's question with the story of the Good Samaritan. In Jesus' day, Jews and Samaritans were enemies. Through the story, Jesus taught the man that his neighbors include his enemies. That meant that to obey God's command to love his neighbor, the man had to love his enemies. Do you have neighbors that are difficult to love? Keep in mind the Good Samaritan's example. Love those with whom you don't get along. Then you will be keeping God's command to love your neighbor as yourself.

Why is loving your neighbor a good thing to do?
Love does no wrong to anyone, so love satisfies all of God's requirements.
Romans 13:10

10:27 Deut 6:5; Lev 19:18. **10:32** Greek *A Levite*. **10:35** Greek *2 denarii*. A denarius was the equivalent of a full day's wage.

³⁶"Now which of these three would you say was a neighbor to the man who was attacked by bandits?" Jesus asked.

³⁷The man replied, "The one who showed him mercy."

Then Jesus said, "Yes, now go and do the same."

A U G U S T

Jesus taught his disciples how to pray.
What did he teach them about asking God for something?

LUKE 11:1-13

Keep Asking

Once when Jesus had been out praying, one of his disciples came to him as he finished and said, "Lord, teach us to pray, just as John taught his disciples."

²He said, "This is how you should pray:

"Father, may your name be
     honored.
   May your Kingdom come soon.
³ Give us our food day by day.
⁴ And forgive us our sins—
     just as we forgive those who
       have sinned against us.
   And don't let us yield to
     temptation.*"

⁵Then, teaching them more about prayer, he used this illustration: "Suppose you went to a friend's house at midnight, wanting to borrow three loaves of bread. You would say to him, ⁶'A friend of mine has just arrived for a visit, and I have nothing for him to eat.' ⁷He would call out from his bedroom, 'Don't bother me. The door is locked for the night, and we are all in bed. I can't help you this time.' ⁸But I tell you this—though he won't do it as a friend, if you keep knocking long enough, he will get up and give you what you want so his reputation won't be damaged.*

⁹"And so I tell you, keep on asking, and you will be given what you ask for. Keep on looking, and you will find. Keep on knocking, and the door will be opened. ¹⁰For everyone who asks,

Jesus told his disciples that God gives to those who ask. He encouraged them to keep asking God for good things. Don't be afraid to ask God for something. He likes to give his children good gifts. Sometimes he will say no, and sometimes he will make you wait. But he always wants to give you what is best.

**Why should we keep asking
God for good things?**

The LORD has heard my plea;
the LORD will answer my prayer.

Psalm 6:9

11:2-4 Some manuscripts add additional portions of the Lord's Prayer as it reads in Matt 6:9-13. **11:8** Greek *in order to avoid shame*, or *because of [your] persistence.*

receives. Everyone who seeks, finds. And the door is opened to everyone who knocks.

[11] "You fathers—if your children ask* for a fish, do you give them a snake instead? [12] Or if they ask for an egg, do you give them a scorpion? Of course not! [13] If you sinful people know how to give good gifts to your children, how much more will your heavenly Father give the Holy Spirit to those who ask him."

11:11 Some manuscripts add *for bread, do you give them a stone? Or if they ask.*

AUGUST 3

A woman blessed Jesus' mother. How did Jesus respond?

LUKE 11:14-28

True Joy

[14] One day Jesus cast a demon out of a man who couldn't speak, and the man's voice returned to him. The crowd was amazed, [15] but some said, "No wonder he can cast out demons. He gets his power from Satan,* the prince of demons!" [16] Trying to test Jesus, others asked for a miraculous sign from heaven to see if he was from God.

[17] He knew their thoughts, so he said, "Any kingdom at war with itself is doomed. A divided home is also doomed. [18] You say I am empowered by the prince of demons.* But if Satan is fighting against himself by empowering me to cast out his demons, how can his kingdom survive? [19] And if I am empowered by the prince of demons, what about your own followers? They cast out demons, too, so they will judge you for what you have said. [20] But if I am casting out demons by the power of God, then the Kingdom of God has arrived among you. [21] For when Satan,* who is completely armed, guards his palace, it is safe— [22] until someone who is stronger attacks and overpowers him, strips him of his weapons, and carries off his belongings.

[23] "Anyone who isn't helping me opposes me, and anyone who isn't work-

Jesus said that the person who reads the Bible and does what it says is more blessed than his mother. Mary was truly blessed or joyful. God had chosen her to have his Son, Jesus. To be more joyful than Mary is real happiness. Continue reading the Bible. God blesses those who listen to him and obey his Word.

What attitude helps us to keep reading the Bible?
Oh, how I love your law!
I think about it all day long.
Psalm 119:97

11:15 Greek *Beelzeboul.* 11:18 Greek *by Beelzeboul;* also in 11:19. 11:21 Greek *the strong one.*

ing with me is actually working against me.

24 "When an evil spirit leaves a person, it goes into the desert, searching for rest. But when it finds none, it says, 'I will return to the person I came from.' 25 So it returns and finds that its former home is all swept and clean. 26 Then the spirit finds seven other spirits more evil than itself, and they all enter the person and live there. And so that person is worse off than before."

27 As he was speaking, a woman in the crowd called out, "God bless your mother—the womb from which you came, and the breasts that nursed you!"

28 He replied, "But even more blessed are all who hear the word of God and put it into practice."

AUGUST

A Pharisee invited Jesus to his house for a meal. What happened while Jesus was there?

LUKE 11:37-54
Foolish Pharisees

37 As Jesus was speaking, one of the Pharisees invited him home for a meal. So he went in and took his place at the table. 38 His host was amazed to see that he sat down to eat without first performing the ceremonial washing required by Jewish custom. 39 Then the Lord said to him, "You Pharisees are so careful to clean the outside of the cup and the dish, but inside you are still filthy—full of greed and wickedness! 40 Fools! Didn't God make the inside as well as the outside? 41 So give to the needy what you greedily possess, and you will be clean all over.

42 "But how terrible it will be for you Pharisees! For you are careful to tithe even the tiniest part of your income,* but you completely forget about justice and the love of God. You should tithe, yes, but you should not leave undone the more important things.

43 "How terrible it will be for you Pharisees! For how you love the seats of honor in the synagogues and the respectful greetings from everyone as you walk through the markets! 44 Yes, how terrible it will be for you. For you are like hidden graves in a field. People walk over them without knowing the corruption they are stepping on."

45 "Teacher," said an expert in religious law, "you have insulted us, too, in what you just said."

46 "Yes," said Jesus, "how terrible it will be for you experts in religious law! For you crush people beneath impossible religious demands, and you never lift a finger to help ease the burden. 47 How terrible it will be for you! For you build tombs for the very prophets your ancestors killed long ago. 48 Murderers!

11:42 Greek *to tithe the mint and the rue and every herb.*

You agree with your ancestors that what they did was right. You would have done the same yourselves. ⁴⁹This is what God in his wisdom said about you:* 'I will send prophets and apostles to them, and they will kill some and persecute the others.'

⁵⁰"And you of this generation will be held responsible for the murder of all God's prophets from the creation of the world—⁵¹from the murder of Abel to the murder of Zechariah, who was killed between the altar and the sanctuary. Yes, it will surely be charged against you.

⁵²"How terrible it will be for you experts in religious law! For you hide the key to knowledge from the people. You don't enter the Kingdom yourselves, and you prevent others from entering."

⁵³As Jesus finished speaking, the Pharisees and teachers of religious law were furious. From that time on they grilled him with many hostile questions, ⁵⁴trying to trap him into saying something they could use against him.

11:49 Greek *Therefore, the wisdom of God said.*

At the Pharisee's house, Jesus didn't follow the Jewish custom of washing before eating. The Pharisees were amazed at him and critical of him. Jesus used their reaction to scold them for being hypocrites. Although they washed their arms and hands, their hearts were full of greed and wickedness. From God's view it was more important that people have clean hearts than clean hands. How clean is your heart? Take Jesus' warnings to the Pharisees seriously. You don't want to end up like them.

Why is it important to have a clean heart?

Who may climb the mountain of the LORD? Who may stand in his holy place? Only those whose hands and hearts are pure, who do not worship idols and never tell lies.
Psalm 24:3-4

A U G U S T

Jesus told a story about a rich man and his wealth. What happened to that man?

LUKE 12:13-21

A Rich Fool

¹³Then someone called from the crowd, "Teacher, please tell my brother to divide our father's estate with me."

¹⁴Jesus replied, "Friend, who made me a judge over you to decide such things as that?" ¹⁵Then he said, "Beware! Don't be greedy for what you don't have. Real life is not measured by how much we own."

¹⁶And he gave an illustration: "A rich man had a fertile farm that produced fine crops. ¹⁷In fact, his barns were full to overflowing. ¹⁸So he said,

'I know! I'll tear down my barns and build bigger ones. Then I'll have room enough to store everything. ¹⁹And I'll sit back and say to myself, My friend, you have enough stored away for years to come. Now take it easy! Eat, drink, and be merry!'

²⁰"But God said to him, 'You fool! You will die this very night. Then who will get it all?'

²¹"Yes, a person is a fool to store up earthly wealth but not have a rich relationship with God."

In this story, God took the life of the rich man. He did this because the rich man trusted in his wealth rather than in God. The rich man also kept all of his wealth for himself. He didn't share with anyone. So God took everything from him in an instant. We should not trust in money or hold on to all of our stuff like the rich man. New clothes, new shoes, or the latest computer game cannot make us truly happy. They will all pass away.

Why is it dangerous to trust in money?
Greed causes fighting; trusting the LORD leads to prosperity.
Proverbs 28:25

A U G U S T

Jesus encouraged his disciples not to worry about food and clothing. Why did he say this?

LUKE 12:22-34
Don't Worry

²²Then turning to his disciples, Jesus said, "So I tell you, don't worry about everyday life—whether you have enough food to eat or clothes to wear. ²³For life consists of far more than food and clothing. ²⁴Look at the ravens. They don't need to plant or harvest or put food in barns because God feeds them. And you are far more valuable to him than any birds! ²⁵Can all your worries add a single moment to your life? Of course not! ²⁶And if worry can't do little things like that, what's the use of worrying over bigger things?

²⁷"Look at the lilies and how they grow. They don't work or make their clothing, yet Solomon in all his glory was not dressed as beautifully as they are. ²⁸And if God cares so wonderfully for flowers that are here today and gone tomorrow, won't he more surely care for you? You have so little faith! ²⁹And don't worry about food—what to eat and drink. Don't worry whether God will provide it for you. ³⁰These things dominate the thoughts of most people, but your Father already knows

your needs. [31]He will give you all you need from day to day if you make the Kingdom of God your primary concern.

[32]"So don't be afraid, little flock. For it gives your Father great happiness to give you the Kingdom.

[33]"Sell what you have and give to those in need. This will store up treasure for you in heaven! And the purses of heaven have no holes in them. Your treasure will be safe—no thief can steal it and no moth can destroy it. [34]Wherever your treasure is, there your heart and thoughts will also be."

Jesus wanted his disciples to trust in God for their needs. If they worried about food or clothing, then the concerns of the world would distract them from building God's kingdom. Like the disciples, we have more important things to do than worry. If we don't worry about our needs, we can spend our time and energy telling others about Jesus. Spend your time wisely. Trust God to take care of you, and work to expand his kingdom here on earth.

Why should you not worry about food and clothes?
He gives food to those who trust him; he always remembers his covenant.
Psalm 111:5

A U G U S T

Jesus told his disciples to be ready. What were they to be ready for?

LUKE 12:35-48

A Faithful Servant

[35]"Be dressed for service and well prepared, [36]as though you were waiting for your master to return from the wedding feast. Then you will be ready to open the door and let him in the moment he arrives and knocks. [37]There will be special favor for those who are ready and waiting for his return. I tell you, he himself will seat them, put on an apron, and serve them as they sit and eat! [38]He may come in the middle of the night or just before dawn.* But whenever he comes, there will be special favor for his servants who are ready!

[39]"Know this: A homeowner who knew exactly when a burglar was coming would not permit the house to be broken into. [40]You must be ready all the time, for the Son of Man will come when least expected."

[41]Peter asked, "Lord, is this illustration just for us or for everyone?"

[42]And the Lord replied, "I'm talking to any faithful, sensible servant to

12:38 Greek *in the second or third watch.*

272

whom the master gives the responsibility of managing his household and feeding his family. ⁴³If the master returns and finds that the servant has done a good job, there will be a reward. ⁴⁴I assure you, the master will put that servant in charge of all he owns. ⁴⁵But if the servant thinks, 'My master won't be back for a while,' and begins oppressing the other servants, partying, and getting drunk—⁴⁶well, the master will return unannounced and unexpected. He will tear the servant apart and banish him with the unfaithful. ⁴⁷The servant will be severely punished, for though he knew his duty, he refused to do it.

⁴⁸"But people who are not aware that they are doing wrong will be punished only lightly. Much is required from those to whom much is given, and much more is required from those to whom much more is given."

24:36 Some manuscripts omit the phrase *or the Son himself.*

Jesus' disciples were to be ready for his return. He told them that he would be coming again soon. But no one knew when. So they would have to be ready at all times. Being ready means obeying Jesus' commands and serving him daily. If you believe in Jesus, then this command applies to you also. Continue to obey and serve him. When Jesus comes, he will reward you for serving him.

Why don't we know when Jesus will return?
However, no one knows the day or the hour when these things will happen, not even the angels in heaven or the Son himself.* Only the Father knows.
Matthew 24:36

A U G U S T

Jesus talked about some bad things that happened to people in his day. What did he have to say?

LUKE 13:1-17
A Call to Repent
About this time Jesus was informed that Pilate had murdered some people from Galilee as they were sacrificing at the Temple in Jerusalem. ²"Do you think those Galileans were worse sinners than other people from Galilee?" he asked. "Is that why they suffered? ³Not at all! And you will also perish unless you turn from your evil ways and turn to God. ⁴And what about the eighteen men who died when the Tower of Siloam fell on them? Were they the worst sinners in Jerusalem? ⁵No, and I tell you again that unless you repent, you will also perish."

⁶Then Jesus used this illustration: "A

man planted a fig tree in his garden and came again and again to see if there was any fruit on it, but he was always disappointed. ⁷Finally, he said to his gardener, 'I've waited three years, and there hasn't been a single fig! Cut it down. It's taking up space we can use for something else.'

⁸"The gardener answered, 'Give it one more chance. Leave it another year, and I'll give it special attention and plenty of fertilizer. ⁹If we get figs next year, fine. If not, you can cut it down.' "

¹⁰One Sabbath day as Jesus was teaching in a synagogue, ¹¹he saw a woman who had been crippled by an evil spirit. She had been bent double for eighteen years and was unable to stand up straight. ¹²When Jesus saw her, he called her over and said, "Woman, you are healed of your sickness!" ¹³Then he touched her, and instantly she could stand straight. How she praised and thanked God!

¹⁴But the leader in charge of the synagogue was indignant that Jesus had healed her on the Sabbath day. "There are six days of the week for working," he said to the crowd. "Come on those days to be healed, not on the Sabbath."

¹⁵But the Lord replied, "You hypocrite! You work on the Sabbath day!

13:16 Greek *this woman, a daughter of Abraham.*

Don't you untie your ox or your donkey from their stalls on the Sabbath and lead them out for water? ¹⁶Wasn't it necessary for me, even on the Sabbath day, to free this dear woman* from the bondage in which Satan has held her for eighteen years?" ¹⁷This shamed his enemies. And all the people rejoiced at the wonderful things he did.

A belief commonly held by people in Jesus' day was that those who suffered a painful death were bad people. Jesus said that belief wasn't true. The fact that these people died tragically and suddenly showed how important Jesus' message to us was. We should all turn away from our sins and accept Jesus as our Savior before it is too late. Why do you think people suffer today? Don't assume that they're bad people. Instead, see their situation as a reminder to turn away from your sins and follow Jesus.

Why is it important to turn away from sin?

I don't want you to die, says the Sovereign LORD. Turn back and live!
Ezekiel 18:32

A U G U S T

Jesus told a blind man to wash his eyes in a pool. What did the blind man do?

JOHN 9:1-17
The Blind Man Sees

As Jesus was walking along, he saw a man who had been blind from birth. [2]"Teacher," his disciples asked him, "why was this man born blind? Was it a result of his own sins or those of his parents?"

[3]"It was not because of his sins or his parents' sins," Jesus answered. "He was born blind so the power of God could be seen in him. [4]All of us must quickly carry out the tasks assigned us by the one who sent me, because there is little time left before the night falls and all work comes to an end. [5]But while I am still here in the world, I am the light of the world."

[6]Then he spit on the ground, made mud with the saliva, and smoothed the mud over the blind man's eyes. [7]He told him, "Go and wash in the pool of Siloam" (Siloam means Sent). So the man went and washed, and came back seeing!

[8]His neighbors and others who knew him as a blind beggar asked each other, "Is this the same man—that beggar?" [9]Some said he was, and others said, "No, but he surely looks like him!"

And the beggar kept saying, "I am the same man!"

[10]They asked, "Who healed you? What happened?"

[11]He told them, "The man they call Jesus made mud and smoothed it over my eyes and told me, 'Go to the pool of Siloam and wash off the mud.' I went and washed, and now I can see!"

[12]"Where is he now?" they asked.

"I don't know," he replied.

[13]Then they took the man to the Pharisees. [14]Now as it happened, Jesus had healed the man on a Sabbath. [15]The Pharisees asked the man all about it. So he told them, "He smoothed the mud over my eyes, and when it was washed away, I could see!"

[16]Some of the Pharisees said, "This man Jesus is not from God, for he is working on the Sabbath." Others said, "But how could an ordinary sinner do

The blind man followed Jesus' instructions. He washed his eyes in a pool and was healed. Like the blind man, we need to follow Jesus' instructions. If we listen to and obey Jesus, we will be changed.

How should we respond to Jesus' commands?

I have refused to walk on any path of evil, that I may remain obedient to your word.
Psalm 119:101

such miraculous signs?" So there was a deep division of opinion among them.

¹⁷Then the Pharisees once again questioned the man who had been blind and demanded, "This man who opened your eyes—who do you say he is?"

The man replied, "I think he must be a prophet."

A U G U S T

The Pharisees asked the man who healed him. What did he say?

JOHN 9:18-41

One Man's Faith

¹⁸The Jewish leaders wouldn't believe he had been blind, so they called in his parents. ¹⁹They asked them, "Is this your son? Was he born blind? If so, how can he see?"

²⁰His parents replied, "We know this is our son and that he was born blind, ²¹but we don't know how he can see or who healed him. He is old enough to speak for himself. Ask him." ²²They said this because they were afraid of the Jewish leaders, who had announced that anyone saying Jesus was the Messiah would be expelled from the synagogue. ²³That's why they said, "He is old enough to speak for himself. Ask him."

²⁴So for the second time they called in the man who had been blind and told him, "Give glory to God by telling the truth,* because we know Jesus is a sinner."

²⁵"I don't know whether he is a sinner," the man replied. "But I know this: I was blind, and now I can see!"

²⁶"But what did he do?" they asked. "How did he heal you?"

²⁷"Look!" the man exclaimed. "I told you once. Didn't you listen? Why do you want to hear it again? Do you want to become his disciples, too?"

²⁸Then they cursed him and said, "You are his disciple, but we are disciples of Moses. ²⁹We know God spoke to Moses, but as for this man, we don't know anything about him."

³⁰"Why, that's very strange!" the man replied. "He healed my eyes, and yet you don't know anything about him! ³¹Well, God doesn't listen to sinners, but he is ready to hear those who worship him and do his will. ³²Never since the world began has anyone been able to open the eyes of someone born blind. ³³If this man were not from God, he couldn't do it."

³⁴"You were born in sin!" they answered. "Are you trying to teach us?" And they threw him out of the synagogue.

³⁵When Jesus heard what had happened, he found the man and said, "Do you believe in the Son of Man*?"

9:24 Or *Give glory to God, not to Jesus*; Greek reads *Give glory to God*. 9:35 Some manuscripts read *the Son of God*.

³⁶The man answered, "Who is he, sir, because I would like to."

³⁷"You have seen him," Jesus said, "and he is speaking to you!"

³⁸"Yes, Lord," the man said, "I believe!" And he worshiped Jesus.

³⁹Then Jesus told him, "I have come to judge the world. I have come to give sight to the blind and to show those who think they see that they are blind."

⁴⁰The Pharisees who were standing there heard him and asked, "Are you saying we are blind?"

⁴¹"If you were blind, you wouldn't be guilty," Jesus replied. "But you remain guilty because you claim you can see."

The man said that Jesus had healed him. The Pharisees didn't want to believe this. They thought Jesus was a sinner and tried to stop his ministry. But the man defended Jesus against their attacks and was kicked out of the synagogue (the Jewish "church") for it. Today, if we stand up for our faith in Jesus, we may have to endure personal attacks from unbelievers, too. But this shouldn't discourage us. Instead, we should keep standing up for Jesus. Eternal life with him will be worth any trouble we endure here because of him.

How should we respond when we suffer for our faith?

[Job] said, "I came naked from my mother's womb, and I will be stripped of everything when I die. The LORD gave me everything I had, and the LORD has taken it away. Praise the name of the LORD!"
Job 1:21

A U G U S T

11

Jesus called himself the good shepherd. What did he mean by this?

JOHN 10:1-18
The Good Shepherd

"I assure you, anyone who sneaks over the wall of a sheepfold, rather than going through the gate, must surely be a thief and a robber! ²For a shepherd enters through the gate. ³The gatekeeper opens the gate for him, and the sheep hear his voice and come to him. He calls his own sheep by name and leads them out. ⁴After he has gathered his own flock, he walks ahead of them, and they follow him because they recognize his voice. ⁵They won't follow a stranger; they will run from him because they don't recognize his voice."

⁶Those who heard Jesus use this illustration didn't understand what he

meant, [7]so he explained it to them. "I assure you, I am the gate for the sheep," he said. [8]"All others who came before me were thieves and robbers. But the true sheep did not listen to them. [9]Yes, I am the gate. Those who come in through me will be saved. Wherever they go, they will find green pastures. [10]The thief's purpose is to steal and kill and destroy. My purpose is to give life in all its fullness.

[11]"I am the good shepherd. The good shepherd lays down his life for the sheep. [12]A hired hand will run when he sees a wolf coming. He will leave the sheep because they aren't his and he isn't their shepherd. And so the wolf attacks them and scatters the flock. [13]The hired hand runs away because he is merely hired and has no real concern for the sheep.

[14]"I am the good shepherd; I know my own sheep, and they know me, [15]just as my Father knows me and I know the Father. And I lay down my life for the sheep. [16]I have other sheep, too, that are not in this sheepfold. I must bring them also, and they will listen to my voice; and there will be one flock with one shepherd.

[17]"The Father loves me because I lay down my life that I may have it back again. [18]No one can take my life from me. I lay down my life voluntarily. For I have the right to lay it down when I want to and also the power to take it again. For my Father has given me this command."

Those who believe in and follow Jesus are his sheep. Jesus is their leader or shepherd. He is a good shepherd because he cares for his sheep. He willingly died to save them from their sins, and he leads them to heaven. Follow Jesus. He will not lead you the wrong way.

Where does the Lord lead his followers?
The LORD is my shepherd; I have everything I need. He lets me rest in green meadows; he leads me beside peaceful streams.
Psalm 23:1-2

A U G U S T

Jesus was at someone's home for dinner. He noticed that the guests were trying to sit at the best seats near the head of the table. What did he say?

LUKE 14:1-14
Watch Where You Sit
One Sabbath day Jesus was in the home of a leader of the Pharisees. The people were watching him closely, [2]because there was a man there whose arms and legs were swollen.* [3]Jesus asked the Pharisees and experts in reli-

14:2 Traditionally translated *who had dropsy.*

gious law, "Well, is it permitted in the law to heal people on the Sabbath day, or not?" [4]When they refused to answer, Jesus touched the sick man and healed him and sent him away. [5]Then he turned to them and asked, "Which of you doesn't work on the Sabbath? If your son* or your cow falls into a pit, don't you proceed at once to get him out?" [6]Again they had no answer.

[7]When Jesus noticed that all who had come to the dinner were trying to sit near the head of the table, he gave them this advice: [8]"If you are invited to a wedding feast, don't always head for the best seat. What if someone more respected than you has also been invited? [9]The host will say, 'Let this person sit here instead.' Then you will be embarrassed and will have to take whatever seat is left at the foot of the table!

[10]"Do this instead—sit at the foot of the table. Then when your host sees you, he will come and say, 'Friend, we have a better place than this for you!' Then you will be honored in front of all the other guests. [11]For the proud will be humbled, but the humble will be honored."

[12]Then he turned to his host. "When you put on a luncheon or a dinner," he said, "don't invite your friends, brothers, relatives, and rich neighbors. For they will repay you by inviting you back. [13]Instead, invite the poor, the crippled, the lame, and the blind. [14]Then at the resurrection of the godly, God will reward you for inviting those who could not repay you."

Jesus used the guests' pride to teach them about humility. He told the guests not to take the best seats at a wedding feast. If they did and someone more important came along, they would be embarrassed because they would have to give up their seat. But if they took a seat at the end of the table, the master of the feast might come along and move them up to a better seat. Then they would be honored. The point Jesus made to the guests still applies to us today. We should not think too highly of ourselves. Instead, if we humble ourselves, God may honor us.

To whom does God show favor?
And all of you, serve each other in humility, for "God sets himself against the proud, but he shows favor to the humble."*
1 Peter 5:5

14:5 Some manuscripts read *donkey.* **5:5** Prov 3:34.

Jesus said that people must be willing to give up everything to follow him. Why did he say that?

LUKE 14:15-35
Following Jesus

¹⁵Hearing this, a man sitting at the table with Jesus exclaimed, "What a privilege it would be to have a share in the Kingdom of God!"

¹⁶Jesus replied with this illustration: "A man prepared a great feast and sent out many invitations. ¹⁷When all was ready, he sent his servant around to notify the guests that it was time for them to come. ¹⁸But they all began making excuses. One said he had just bought a field and wanted to inspect it, so he asked to be excused. ¹⁹Another said he had just bought five pair of oxen and wanted to try them out. ²⁰Another had just been married, so he said he couldn't come.

²¹"The servant returned and told his master what they had said. His master was angry and said, 'Go quickly into the streets and alleys of the city and invite the poor, the crippled, the lame, and the blind.' ²²After the servant had done this, he reported, 'There is still room for more.' ²³So his master said, 'Go out into the country lanes and behind the hedges and urge anyone you find to come, so that the house will be full. ²⁴For none of those I invited first will get even the smallest taste of what I had prepared for them.' "

²⁵Great crowds were following Jesus. He turned around and said to them, ²⁶"If you want to be my follower you must love me more than* your own father and mother, wife and children, brothers and sisters—yes, more than your own life. Otherwise, you cannot be my disciple. ²⁷And you cannot be my disciple if you do not carry your own cross and follow me.

²⁸"But don't begin until you count the cost. For who would begin construction of a building without first getting estimates and then checking to see if there is enough money to pay the

Jesus wanted committed followers. He did not want people to follow him and then decide that doing so was too hard. Even though following Jesus is hard, it is worth the cost. Jesus has promised that if you give up anything to follow him, you will be rewarded with much better treasures such as love, peace, and joy. Decide to follow Jesus no matter what the cost.

Whom does the Lord strengthen?
The eyes of the LORD search the whole earth in order to strengthen those whose hearts are fully committed to him.
2 Chronicles 16:9

14:26 Greek *you must hate.*

bills? ²⁹Otherwise, you might complete only the foundation before running out of funds. And then how everyone would laugh at you! ³⁰They would say, 'There's the person who started that building and ran out of money before it was finished!'

³¹"Or what king would ever dream of going to war without first sitting down with his counselors and discussing whether his army of ten thousand is strong enough to defeat the twenty thousand soldiers who are marching against him? ³²If he is not able, then while the enemy is still far away, he will send a delegation to discuss terms of peace. ³³So no one can become my disciple without giving up everything for me.

³⁴"Salt is good for seasoning. But if it loses its flavor, how do you make it salty again? ³⁵Flavorless salt is good neither for the soil nor for fertilizer. It is thrown away. Anyone who is willing to hear should listen and understand!"

A U G U S T

The Pharisees complained about the kind of people Jesus taught.
How did Jesus respond to their complaints?

LUKE 15:1-10
Lost and Found

Tax collectors and other notorious sinners often came to listen to Jesus teach. ²This made the Pharisees and teachers of religious law complain that he was associating with such despicable people—even eating with them!

³So Jesus used this illustration: ⁴"If you had one hundred sheep, and one of them strayed away and was lost in the wilderness, wouldn't you leave the ninety-nine others to go and search for the lost one until you found it? ⁵And then you would joyfully carry it home on your shoulders. ⁶When you arrived, you would call together your friends and neighbors to rejoice with you because your lost sheep was found. ⁷In the same way, heaven will be happier over

The tax collectors and other sinners who listened to Jesus were lost. The Pharisees didn't care about them and thought Jesus shouldn't be around these people. Jesus knew about the Pharisees' hateful attitude. So he told some stories to show the Pharisees how much God loves sinners. How do you treat people who are known for their sins? Remember that God loves them, too. Instead of ignoring them or being mean to them, make an effort to show them how much God cares for them.

Why does God love the lost sinner?
I don't want you to die, says the Sovereign LORD. Turn back and live!
Ezekiel 18:32

one lost sinner who returns to God than over ninety-nine others who are righteous and haven't strayed away!

⁸"Or suppose a woman has ten valuable silver coins* and loses one. Won't she light a lamp and look in every corner of the house and sweep every nook and cranny until she finds it? ⁹And when she finds it, she will call in her friends and neighbors to rejoice with her because she has found her lost coin. ¹⁰In the same way, there is joy in the presence of God's angels when even one sinner repents."

15:8 Greek *10 drachmas*. A drachma was the equivalent of a full day's wage.

A U G U S T

Jesus told the Pharisees another story about God's love.
How was God's love shown in this story?

LUKE 15:11-32

A Runaway Son

¹¹To illustrate the point further, Jesus told them this story: "A man had two sons. ¹²The younger son told his father, 'I want my share of your estate now, instead of waiting until you die.' So his father agreed to divide his wealth between his sons.

¹³"A few days later this younger son packed all his belongings and took a trip to a distant land, and there he wasted all his money on wild living. ¹⁴About the time his money ran out, a great famine swept over the land, and he began to starve. ¹⁵He persuaded a local farmer to hire him to feed his pigs. ¹⁶The boy became so hungry that even the pods he was feeding the pigs looked good to him. But no one gave him anything.

¹⁷"When he finally came to his senses, he said to himself, 'At home even the hired men have food enough to spare, and here I am, dying of hunger! ¹⁸I will go home to my father and say, "Father, I have sinned against both heaven and you, ¹⁹and I am no longer worthy of being called your son. Please take me on as a hired man." '

²⁰"So he returned home to his father. And while he was still a long distance away, his father saw him coming. Filled with love and compassion, he ran to his son, embraced him, and kissed him. ²¹His son said to him, 'Father, I have sinned against both heaven and you, and I am no longer worthy of being called your son.*'

²²"But his father said to the servants, 'Quick! Bring the finest robe in the house and put it on him. Get a ring for his finger, and sandals for his feet. ²³And kill the calf we have been fattening in the pen. We must celebrate with a feast, ²⁴for this son of mine was dead and has now returned to life. He was

15:21 Some manuscripts add *Please take me on as a hired man.*

lost, but now he is found.' So the party began.

²⁵"Meanwhile, the older son was in the fields working. When he returned home, he heard music and dancing in the house, ²⁶and he asked one of the servants what was going on. ²⁷'Your brother is back,' he was told, 'and your father has killed the calf we were fattening and has prepared a great feast. We are celebrating because of his safe return.'

²⁸"The older brother was angry and wouldn't go in. His father came out and begged him, ²⁹but he replied, 'All these years I've worked hard for you and never once refused to do a single thing you told me to. And in all that time you never gave me even one young goat for a feast with my friends. ³⁰Yet when this son of yours comes back after squandering your money on prostitutes, you celebrate by killing the finest calf we have.'

³¹"His father said to him, 'Look, dear son, you and I are very close, and everything I have is yours. ³²We had to celebrate this happy day. For your brother was dead and has come back to life! He was lost, but now he is found!' "

God's love was shown in the father's forgiveness and acceptance of his runaway son. Even though his son had left and taken part of his fortune, the father was willing to forgive him. In fact, he was overjoyed to see him return. Like this father, God longs for us to turn away from our sin and turn to him. He loves us and wants us to come home.

How does the Lord treat his followers?
The LORD is like a father to his children, tender and compassionate to those who fear him.
Psalm 103:13

A U G U S T

Jesus taught many lessons about money. What did he teach about giving money away?

LUKE 16:1-15
The Shrewd Manager
Jesus told this story to his disciples: "A rich man hired a manager to handle his affairs, but soon a rumor went around that the manager was thoroughly dishonest. ²So his employer called him in and said, 'What's this I hear about your stealing from me? Get your report in order, because you are going to be dismissed.'

³"The manager thought to himself, 'Now what? I'm through here, and I don't have the strength to go out and dig ditches, and I'm too proud to beg. ⁴I know just the thing! And then I'll

have plenty of friends to take care of me when I leave!'

⁵"So he invited each person who owed money to his employer to come and discuss the situation. He asked the first one, 'How much do you owe him?' ⁶The man replied, 'I owe him eight hundred gallons of olive oil.' So the manager told him, 'Tear up that bill and write another one for four hundred gallons.*'

⁷" 'And how much do you owe my employer?' he asked the next man. 'A thousand bushels of wheat,' was the reply. 'Here,' the manager said, 'take your bill and replace it with one for only eight hundred bushels.*'

⁸"The rich man had to admire the dishonest rascal for being so shrewd. And it is true that the citizens of this world are more shrewd than the godly are. ⁹I tell you, use your worldly resources to benefit others and make friends. In this way, your generosity stores up a reward for you in heaven.*

¹⁰"Unless you are faithful in small matters, you won't be faithful in large ones. If you cheat even a little, you won't be honest with greater responsibilities. ¹¹And if you are untrustworthy about worldly wealth, who will trust you with the true riches of heaven? ¹²And if you are not faithful with other people's money, why should you be trusted with money of your own?

¹³"No one can serve two masters. For you will hate one and love the other, or be devoted to one and despise the other. You cannot serve both God and money."

¹⁴The Pharisees, who dearly loved their money, naturally scoffed at all this. ¹⁵Then he said to them, "You like to look good in public, but God knows your evil hearts. What this world honors is an abomination in the sight of God."

Jesus taught his disciples to use their money to help others. Doing this would not only help people who needed it here on earth, but it would also store up rewards in heaven for the giver. Rather than always buying new things for yourself, look for ways to give to others. You will benefit more from giving some of your money away than you will from keeping it all to yourself.

Why shouldn't we store up money for ourselves?

Those who love money will never have enough. How absurd to think that wealth brings true happiness!
Ecclesiastes 5:10

16:6 Greek *100 baths . . . 50 [baths]*. **16:7** Greek *100 korous . . . 80 [korous]*. **16:9** Or *Then when you run out at the end of this life, your friends will welcome you into eternal homes.*

A U G U S T

Jesus told a story about a rich man and a beggar. What was the point of his story?

LUKE 16:19-31

A Rich Man Begs

[19]Jesus said, "There was a certain rich man who was splendidly clothed and who lived each day in luxury. [20]At his door lay a diseased beggar named Lazarus. [21]As Lazarus lay there longing for scraps from the rich man's table, the dogs would come and lick his open sores. [22]Finally, the beggar died and was carried by the angels to be with Abraham.* The rich man also died and was buried, [23]and his soul went to the place of the dead.* There, in torment, he saw Lazarus in the far distance with Abraham.

[24]"The rich man shouted, 'Father Abraham, have some pity! Send Lazarus over here to dip the tip of his finger in water and cool my tongue, because I am in anguish in these flames.'

[25]"But Abraham said to him, 'Son, remember that during your lifetime you had everything you wanted, and Lazarus had nothing. So now he is here being comforted, and you are in anguish. [26]And besides, there is a great chasm separating us. Anyone who wanted to cross over to you from here is stopped at its edge, and no one there can cross over to us.'

[27]"Then the rich man said, 'Please, Father Abraham, send him to my father's home. [28]For I have five broth-ers, and I want him to warn them about this place of torment so they won't have to come here when they die.'

[29]"But Abraham said, 'Moses and the prophets have warned them. Your brothers can read their writings anytime they want to.'

[30]"The rich man replied, 'No, Father Abraham! But if someone is sent to

Through this story, Jesus pointed out that God has warned everyone about the suffering in hell. He has also told everyone that they need to turn away from their sins. This message was also given by God's prophets before Jesus came to earth. Jesus said that those people who didn't believe the prophets wouldn't believe someone who came back from the dead. Don't be foolish like the rich man and his brothers. Listen to what God has said to us all. Read his Word, the Bible, and obey his commands found there.

Why is it important to read the Bible?
I will study your commandments
and reflect on your ways.
I will delight in your principles
and not forget your word.
Psalm 119:15-16

16:22 Greek *into Abraham's bosom.* **16:23** Greek *to Hades.*

them from the dead, then they will turn from their sins.'

[31] "But Abraham said, 'If they won't listen to Moses and the prophets, they won't listen even if someone rises from the dead.' "

A U G U S T

Jesus went to visit Lazarus's sisters, Mary and Martha, after Lazarus had died. What did he do when he got there?

JOHN 11:17-36

Lazarus Dies

[17] When Jesus arrived at Bethany, he was told that Lazarus had already been in his grave for four days. [18] Bethany was only a few miles* down the road from Jerusalem, [19] and many of the people* had come to pay their respects and console Martha and Mary on their loss. [20] When Martha got word that Jesus was coming, she went to meet him. But Mary stayed at home. [21] Martha said to Jesus, "Lord, if you had been here, my brother would not have died. [22] But even now I know that God will give you whatever you ask."

[23] Jesus told her, "Your brother will rise again."

[24] "Yes," Martha said, "when everyone else rises, on resurrection day."

[25] Jesus told her, "I am the resurrection and the life.* Those who believe in me, even though they die like everyone else, will live again. [26] They are given eternal life for believing in me and will never perish. Do you believe this, Martha?"

[27] "Yes, Lord," she told him. "I have always believed you are the Messiah, the Son of God, the one who has come into the world from God." [28] Then she left him and returned to Mary. She called Mary aside from the mourners and told her, "The Teacher is here and wants to see you." [29] So Mary immediately went to him.

[30] Now Jesus had stayed outside the village, at the place where Martha met him. [31] When the people who were at the house trying to console Mary saw her leave so hastily, they assumed she

Jesus cared about his friends Lazarus, Mary, and Martha. When he met Martha, he comforted her with God's truth. He then cried with Mary. If troubles surround you, pray to Jesus for help. He knows your problems and wants to comfort you.

How does God help you when you go through difficult situations?
I have seen what they do, but I will heal them anyway! I will lead them and comfort those who mourn.
Isaiah 57:18

11:18 Greek *was about 15 stadia* [about 2.8 kilometers]. **11:19** Greek *Jewish people;* also 11:31, 33, 36, 45, 54. **11:25** Some manuscripts do not include *and the life.*

286

was going to Lazarus's grave to weep. So they followed her there. ³²When Mary arrived and saw Jesus, she fell down at his feet and said, "Lord, if you had been here, my brother would not have died."

³³When Jesus saw her weeping and saw the other people wailing with her, he was moved with indignation and was deeply troubled. ³⁴"Where have you put him?" he asked them.

They told him, "Lord, come and see." ³⁵Then Jesus wept. ³⁶The people who were standing nearby said, "See how much he loved him."

A U G U S T

Jesus raised Lazarus from the dead. How did the Pharisees react?

JOHN 11:38-52

Lazarus Lives

³⁸And again Jesus was deeply troubled. Then they came to the grave. It was a cave with a stone rolled across its entrance. ³⁹"Roll the stone aside," Jesus told them.

But Martha, the dead man's sister, said, "Lord, by now the smell will be terrible because he has been dead for four days."

⁴⁰Jesus responded, "Didn't I tell you that you will see God's glory if you believe?" ⁴¹So they rolled the stone aside. Then Jesus looked up to heaven and said, "Father, thank you for hearing me. ⁴²You always hear me, but I said it out loud for the sake of all these people standing here, so they will believe you sent me." ⁴³Then Jesus shouted, "Lazarus, come out!" ⁴⁴And Lazarus came out, bound in graveclothes, his face wrapped in a headcloth. Jesus told them, "Unwrap him and let him go!"

⁴⁵Many of the people who were with Mary believed in Jesus when they saw this happen. ⁴⁶But some went to the

Jesus had just performed an incredible miracle. The Pharisees were not happy with him, though. They feared that everyone would follow Jesus, which would give the Roman army a reason to destroy Israel. So the Pharisees began to plot Jesus' death. What the Pharisees didn't know was that by plotting his death they were fulfilling God's plan. God had sent Jesus to die for everyone's sins, not to liberate Israel from Roman rule. Even though the Pharisees were doing evil against Jesus, God used their evil plan to save the world. Because of Jesus' death, we can receive forgiveness for our sins and become children of God.

What did Jesus do for us on the cross?

I will give him the honors of one who is mighty and great, because he exposed himself to death. He was counted among those who were sinners. He bore the sins of many and interceded for sinners.

Isaiah 53:12

287

Pharisees and told them what Jesus had done. ⁴⁷Then the leading priests and Pharisees called the high council* together to discuss the situation. "What are we going to do?" they asked each other. "This man certainly performs many miraculous signs. ⁴⁸If we leave him alone, the whole nation will follow him, and then the Roman army will come and destroy both our Temple and our nation."

⁴⁹And one of them, Caiaphas, who was high priest that year, said, "How can you be so stupid? ⁵⁰Why should the whole nation be destroyed? Let this one man die for the people."

⁵¹This prophecy that Jesus should die for the entire nation came from Caiaphas in his position as high priest. He didn't think of it himself; he was inspired to say it. ⁵²It was a prediction that Jesus' death would be not for Israel only, but for the gathering together of all the children of God scattered around the world.

11:47 Greek the Sanhedrin.

A U G U S T

Jesus healed ten lepers. Why did one leper return to Jesus?

LUKE 17:1-19

Ten Lepers

One day Jesus said to his disciples, "There will always be temptations to sin, but how terrible it will be for the person who does the tempting. ²It would be better to be thrown into the sea with a large millstone tied around the neck than to face the punishment in store for harming one of these little ones. ³I am warning you! If another believer* sins, rebuke him; then if he repents, forgive him. ⁴Even if he wrongs you seven times a day and each time turns again and asks forgiveness, forgive him."

⁵One day the apostles said to the Lord, "We need more faith; tell us how to get it."

⁶"Even if you had faith as small as a mustard seed," the Lord answered, "you could say to this mulberry tree, 'May God uproot you and throw you into the sea,' and it would obey you!

⁷"When a servant comes in from plowing or taking care of sheep, he doesn't just sit down and eat. ⁸He must first prepare his master's meal and serve him his supper before eating his own. ⁹And the servant is not even thanked, because he is merely doing what he is supposed to do. ¹⁰In the same way, when you obey me you should say, 'We are not worthy of praise. We are servants who have simply done our duty.' "

¹¹As Jesus continued on toward Jerusalem, he reached the border between Galilee and Samaria. ¹²As he entered a village there, ten lepers stood at a dis-

17:3 Greek your brother.

tance, ¹³crying out, "Jesus, Master, have mercy on us!"

¹⁴He looked at them and said, "Go show yourselves to the priests." And as they went, their leprosy disappeared.

¹⁵One of them, when he saw that he was healed, came back to Jesus, shouting, "Praise God, I'm healed!" ¹⁶He fell face down on the ground at Jesus' feet, thanking him for what he had done. This man was a Samaritan.

¹⁷Jesus asked, "Didn't I heal ten men? Where are the other nine? ¹⁸Does only this foreigner return to give glory to God?" ¹⁹And Jesus said to the man, "Stand up and go. Your faith has made you well."

One leper returned to thank Jesus. Where were the other nine lepers? They forgot or didn't think to thank Jesus for healing them. When Jesus does something for you, are you more like the one leper or the other nine? There are many things you can thank Jesus for daily, like his forgiveness and kindness. Remember to thank Jesus for what he has done for you.

How can we praise God for his goodness to us?

Enter his gates with thanksgiving; go into his courts with praise. Give thanks to him and bless his name. For the LORD is good. His unfailing love continues forever, and his faithfulness continues to each generation.
Psalm 100:4-5

A U G U S T

Jesus described two types of prayer. Which prayer pleased God?

LUKE 18:1-14
A Tax Collector Prays

One day Jesus told his disciples a story to illustrate their need for constant prayer and to show them that they must never give up. ²"There was a judge in a certain city," he said, "who was a godless man with great contempt for everyone. ³A widow of that city came to him repeatedly, appealing for justice against someone who had harmed her. ⁴The judge ignored her for a while, but eventually she wore him out. 'I fear neither God nor man,' he said to himself, ⁵'but this woman is driving me crazy. I'm going to see that she gets justice, because she is wearing me out with her constant requests!' "

⁶Then the Lord said, "Learn a lesson from this evil judge. ⁷Even he rendered a just decision in the end, so don't you think God will surely give justice to his chosen people who plead with him day and night? Will he keep putting

them off? [8]I tell you, he will grant justice to them quickly! But when I, the Son of Man, return, how many will I find who have faith?"

[9]Then Jesus told this story to some who had great self-confidence and scorned everyone else: [10]"Two men went to the Temple to pray. One was a Pharisee, and the other was a dishonest tax collector. [11]The proud Pharisee stood by himself and prayed this prayer: 'I thank you, God, that I am not a sinner like everyone else, especially like that tax collector over there! For I never cheat, I don't sin, I don't commit adultery, [12]I fast twice a week, and I give you a tenth of my income.'

[13]"But the tax collector stood at a distance and dared not even lift his eyes to heaven as he prayed. Instead, he beat his chest in sorrow, saying, 'O God, be merciful to me, for I am a sinner.' [14]I tell you, this sinner, not the Pharisee, returned home justified before God. For the proud will be humbled, but the humble will be honored."

The tax collector's prayer pleased God. The tax collector came to God humbly. He confessed his sin and was truly sorry for it. The Pharisee, on the other hand, boasted that he wasn't a sinner. He also bragged about his fasting and giving. The Pharisee's attitude insulted God, and God did not accept his prayer. When you pray, follow the tax collector's example. Humble yourself before God. Ask him to forgive you. God listens to the humble person.

How should you pray to God?
Have mercy on me, O God, have mercy! I look to you for protection. I will hide beneath the shadow of your wings until this violent storm is past.
Psalm 57:1

A U G U S T

A rich man asked Jesus how he could be saved. What was Jesus' response?

MARK 10:17-31

A Rich Man's Question

[17]As he was starting out on a trip, a man came running up to Jesus, knelt down, and asked, "Good Teacher, what should I do to get eternal life?"

[18]"Why do you call me good?" Jesus asked. "Only God is truly good. [19]But as for your question, you know the commandments: 'Do not murder. Do not commit adultery. Do not steal. Do not testify falsely. Do not cheat. Honor your father and mother.'* "

[20]"Teacher," the man replied, "I've obeyed all these commandments since I was a child."

10:19 Exod 20:12-16; Deut 5:16-20.

²¹Jesus felt genuine love for this man as he looked at him. "You lack only one thing," he told him. "Go and sell all you have and give the money to the poor, and you will have treasure in heaven. Then come, follow me." ²²At this, the man's face fell, and he went sadly away because he had many possessions.

²³Jesus looked around and said to his disciples, "How hard it is for rich people to get into the Kingdom of God!" ²⁴This amazed them. But Jesus said again, "Dear children, it is very hard* to get into the Kingdom of God. ²⁵It is easier for a camel to go through the eye of a needle than for a rich person to enter the Kingdom of God!"

²⁶The disciples were astounded. "Then who in the world can be saved?" they asked.

²⁷Jesus looked at them intently and said, "Humanly speaking, it is impossible. But not with God. Everything is possible with God."

²⁸Then Peter began to mention all that he and the other disciples had left behind. "We've given up everything to follow you," he said.

²⁹And Jesus replied, "I assure you that everyone who has given up house or brothers or sisters or mother or father or children or property, for my sake and for the Good News, ³⁰will receive now in return, a hundred times over, houses, brothers, sisters, mothers, children, and property—with persecutions. And in the world to come they will have eternal life. ³¹But many who seem to be important now will be the least important then, and those who are considered least here will be the greatest then.*"

The rich man wanted to know what he could do to get eternal life. Jesus told him to sell his riches, give the money to the poor, and follow him. The man went away sad. He wouldn't give up his riches to follow Jesus. Following Jesus is not easy, especially when we have to give up something. But anything we give up to follow him will be well worth it. Don't let anything keep you from Jesus. Knowing him is worth more than anything you could have here on earth.

Why should we trust in God rather than money?

Trust in your money and down you go! But the godly flourish like leaves in spring.
Proverbs 11:28

10:24 Some manuscripts add *for those who trust in riches.* **10:31** Greek *But many who are first will be last; and the last, first.*

AUGUST

23

Jesus told a story about vineyard workers receiving equal pay for unequal work. What was Jesus talking about?

MATTHEW 20:1-19

Equal Pay

"For the Kingdom of Heaven is like the owner of an estate who went out early one morning to hire workers for his vineyard. ²He agreed to pay the normal daily wage* and sent them out to work.

³"At nine o'clock in the morning he was passing through the marketplace and saw some people standing around doing nothing. ⁴So he hired them, telling them he would pay them whatever was right at the end of the day. ⁵At noon and again around three o'clock he did the same thing. ⁶At five o'clock that evening he was in town again and saw some more people standing around. He asked them, 'Why haven't you been working today?'

⁷"They replied, 'Because no one hired us.'

"The owner of the estate told them, 'Then go on out and join the others in my vineyard.'

⁸"That evening he told the foreman to call the workers in and pay them, beginning with the last workers first. ⁹When those hired at five o'clock were paid, each received a full day's wage. ¹⁰When those hired earlier came to get their pay, they assumed they would receive more. But they, too, were paid a day's wage. ¹¹When they received their pay, they protested, ¹²'Those people worked only one hour, and yet you've paid them just as much as you paid us who worked all day in the scorching heat.'

¹³"He answered one of them, 'Friend, I haven't been unfair! Didn't you agree to work all day for the usual wage? ¹⁴Take it and go. I wanted to pay this last worker the same as you. ¹⁵Is it

Jesus was talking about eternal life. The workers in the vineyard were those who accepted Jesus' forgiveness for their sins and followed him as their God. The wage, or pay, was eternal life. All who worked in the field, whether they started in the morning or in the evening, received the same wage. Some of the workers who had been in the vineyard since morning expected a greater reward than those who started in the evening. But God does not work that way. Everyone who believes in Jesus will receive eternal life, no matter when they believe.

What does God want us to do?
Jesus told them, "This is what God wants you to do: Believe in the one he has sent."
John 6:29

20:2 Greek *a denarius*, the payment for a full day's labor; also in 20:9, 10, 13.

against the law for me to do what I want with my money? Should you be angry because I am kind?'

¹⁶"And so it is, that many who are first now will be last then; and those who are last now will be first then."

¹⁷As Jesus was on the way to Jerusalem, he took the twelve disciples aside privately and told them what was go-ing to happen to him. ¹⁸"When we get to Jerusalem," he said, "the Son of Man will be betrayed to the leading priests and the teachers of religious law. They will sentence him to die. ¹⁹Then they will hand him over to the Romans to be mocked, whipped, and crucified. But on the third day he will be raised from the dead."

A U G U S T

Two brothers wanted to sit next to Jesus in heaven. What did Jesus tell them?

MARK 10:35-45

A Great Question

³⁵Then James and John, the sons of Zebedee, came over and spoke to him. "Teacher," they said, "we want you to do us a favor."

³⁶"What is it?" he asked.

³⁷"In your glorious Kingdom, we want to sit in places of honor next to you," they said, "one at your right and the other at your left."

³⁸But Jesus answered, "You don't know what you are asking! Are you able to drink from the bitter cup of sorrow I am about to drink? Are you able to be baptized with the baptism of suffering I must be baptized with?"

³⁹"Oh yes," they said, "we are able!"

And Jesus said, "You will indeed drink from my cup and be baptized with my baptism, ⁴⁰but I have no right to say who will sit on the thrones next to mine. God has prepared those places for the ones he has chosen."

⁴¹When the ten other disciples discovered what James and John had asked, they were indignant. ⁴²So Jesus called them together and said, "You know that in this world kings are

James and John were seeking positions of honor and greatness in heaven. Jesus told them that he couldn't give them what they asked for because it wasn't his to give. But he did tell them that to be great they needed to be servants. Do you want to be great in God's kingdom? If you do, you need to serve others. Remember, when you serve others you are really serving God.

How did Jesus humble himself?

He made himself nothing;* he took the humble position of a slave and appeared in human form.*

Philippians 2:7

2:7a Or *He laid aside his mighty power and glory.* **2:7b** Greek *and was born in the likeness of men and was found in appearance as a man.*

tyrants, and officials lord it over the people beneath them. ⁴³But among you it should be quite different. Whoever wants to be a leader among you must be your servant, ⁴⁴and whoever wants to be first must be the slave of all. ⁴⁵For even I, the Son of Man, came here not to be served but to serve others, and to give my life as a ransom for many."

A U G U S T

Zacchaeus climbed a tree to see Jesus. What happened to Zacchaeus that day?

LUKE 19:1-10
A Tax Collector in a Tree
Jesus entered Jericho and made his way through the town. ²There was a man there named Zacchaeus. He was one of the most influential Jews in the Roman tax-collecting business, and he had become very rich. ³He tried to get a look at Jesus, but he was too short to see over the crowds. ⁴So he ran ahead and climbed a sycamore tree beside the road, so he could watch from there.

⁵When Jesus came by, he looked up at Zacchaeus and called him by name. "Zacchaeus!" he said. "Quick, come down! For I must be a guest in your home today."

⁶Zacchaeus quickly climbed down and took Jesus to his house in great excitement and joy. ⁷But the crowds were displeased. "He has gone to be the guest of a notorious sinner," they grumbled.

⁸Meanwhile, Zacchaeus stood there and said to the Lord, "I will give half my wealth to the poor, Lord, and if I have overcharged people on their taxes, I will give them back four times as much!"

⁹Jesus responded, "Salvation has come to this home today, for this man has shown himself to be a son of Abraham. ¹⁰And I, the Son of Man, have come to seek and save those like him who are lost."

Zacchaeus met Jesus, and Jesus changed his life. Zacchaeus pledged to give half of his wealth to the poor. He also promised to give back four times the amount of money he had overcharged people in taxes. Zacchaeus repented of his sins and received salvation from Jesus. Jesus came to call all of us to repent. Listen to his call, and turn away from your sins.

Why is it important to turn away from sin?
Then if my people who are called by my name will humble themselves and pray and seek my face and turn from their wicked ways, I will hear from heaven and will forgive their sins and heal their land.
2 Chronicles 7:14

Judas criticized Mary for pouring perfume on Jesus' feet. How did Jesus respond?

JOHN 12:1-11
Mary's Perfume

Six days before the Passover ceremonies began, Jesus arrived in Bethany, the home of Lazarus—the man he had raised from the dead. ²A dinner was prepared in Jesus' honor. Martha served, and Lazarus sat at the table with him. ³Then Mary took a twelve-ounce jar* of expensive perfume made from essence of nard, and she anointed Jesus' feet with it and wiped his feet with her hair. And the house was filled with fragrance.

⁴But Judas Iscariot, one of his disciples—the one who would betray him—said, ⁵"That perfume was worth a small fortune.* It should have been sold and the money given to the poor." ⁶Not that he cared for the poor—he was a thief who was in charge of the disciples' funds, and he often took some for his own use.

⁷Jesus replied, "Leave her alone. She did it in preparation for my burial. ⁸You will always have the poor among you, but I will not be here with you much longer."

⁹When all the people* heard of Jesus' arrival, they flocked to see him and also to see Lazarus, the man Jesus had raised from the dead. ¹⁰Then the leading priests decided to kill Lazarus, too, ¹¹for it was because of him that many of the people had deserted them and believed in Jesus.

Jesus told Judas to leave Mary alone. Mary had shown her love for Jesus by anointing his feet with expensive perfume. Judas called her act of worship a waste. He was wrong. Worshiping Jesus is never a waste of time or resources, as long as it is done with the right motives. Don't let others stop you from giving Jesus the praise and worship he deserves. Follow Mary's example and worship Jesus no matter what others think or say.

What are two good attitudes to have when we worship Jesus?
Worship the LORD with gladness.
Come before him, singing with joy.
Psalm 100:2

12:3 Greek took 1 litra [327 grams]. 12:5 Greek 300 denarii. A denarius was equivalent to a full day's wage 12:9 Greek Jewish people; also in 12:11.

A U G U S T

Jesus entered Jerusalem on a donkey. How did the crowd welcome him?

MATTHEW 21:1-17
A King on a Donkey

As Jesus and the disciples approached Jerusalem, they came to the town of Bethphage on the Mount of Olives. Jesus sent two of them on ahead. ²"Go into the village over there," he said, "and you will see a donkey tied there, with its colt beside it. Untie them and bring them here. ³If anyone asks what you are doing, just say, 'The Lord needs them,' and he will immediately send them." ⁴This was done to fulfill the prophecy,

⁵ "Tell the people of Israel,*
    'Look, your King is coming to
        you.
    He is humble, riding on a donkey—
        even on a donkey's colt.' "*

⁶The two disciples did as Jesus said. ⁷They brought the animals to him and threw their garments over the colt, and he sat on it.* ⁸Most of the crowd spread their coats on the road ahead of Jesus, and others cut branches from the trees and spread them on the road. ⁹He was in the center of the procession, and the crowds all around him were shouting,

"Praise God* for the Son of David!
Bless the one who comes in the
    name of the Lord!
Praise God in highest heaven!"*

¹⁰The entire city of Jerusalem was stirred as he entered. "Who is this?" they asked.

¹¹And the crowds replied, "It's Jesus, the prophet from Nazareth in Galilee."

¹²Jesus entered the Temple and began to drive out the merchants and their customers. He knocked over the tables of the money changers and the stalls of those selling doves. ¹³He said, "The Scriptures declare, 'My Temple will be called a place of prayer,' but

The crowd shouted praises to Jesus. They even placed their coats or branches from trees in Jesus' path. Their actions showed that they welcomed Jesus as a king. Like the crowd, we should honor Jesus as our king. How can we do this? We can obey his commands. We can treat him with respect when we pray to him, and we can serve him with our lives.

Why should we praise Jesus?

O LORD, our Lord, the majesty of your name fills the earth! Your glory is higher than the heavens. You have taught children and nursing infants to give you praise.* They silence your enemies who were seeking revenge.

Psalm 8:1-2

21:5a Greek *Tell the daughter of Zion.* Isa 62:11. 21:5b Zech 9:9. 21:7 Greek *over them, and he sat on them.* 21:9a Greek *Hosanna,* an exclamation of praise that literally means "save now"; also in 21:9b, 15. 21:9b Pss 118:25-26; 148:1. 8:2 As in Greek version; Hebrew reads *to show strength.*

you have turned it into a den of thieves!"*

¹⁴The blind and the lame came to him, and he healed them there in the Temple. ¹⁵The leading priests and the teachers of religious law saw these wonderful miracles and heard even the little children in the Temple shouting, "Praise God for the Son of David."

But they were indignant ¹⁶and asked Jesus, "Do you hear what these children are saying?"

"Yes," Jesus replied. "Haven't you ever read the Scriptures? For they say, 'You have taught children and infants to give you praise.'* " ¹⁷Then he returned to Bethany, where he stayed overnight.

21:13 Isa 56:7; Jer 7:11. **21:16** Ps 8:2.

A U G U S T

Jesus told a crowd that he would die soon. What did they think of his comment?

JOHN 12:20-36

Jesus Predicts His Death

²⁰Some Greeks who had come to Jerusalem to attend the Passover ²¹paid a visit to Philip, who was from Bethsaida in Galilee. They said, "Sir, we want to meet Jesus." ²²Philip told Andrew about it, and they went together to ask Jesus.

²³Jesus replied, "The time has come for the Son of Man to enter into his glory. ²⁴The truth is, a kernel of wheat must be planted in the soil. Unless it dies it will be alone—a single seed. But its death will produce many new kernels—a plentiful harvest of new lives. ²⁵Those who love their life in this world will lose it. Those who despise their life in this world will keep it for eternal life. ²⁶All those who want to be my disciples must come and follow me, because my servants must be where I am. And if they fol-

low me, the Father will honor them. ²⁷Now my soul is deeply troubled. Should I pray, 'Father, save me from what lies ahead'? But that is the very reason why I came! ²⁸Father, bring glory to your name."

Then a voice spoke from heaven, saying, "I have already brought it glory, and I will do it again." ²⁹When the crowd heard the voice, some thought it was thunder, while others declared an angel had spoken to him.

³⁰Then Jesus told them, "The voice was for your benefit, not mine. ³¹The time of judgment for the world has come, when the prince of this world* will be cast out. ³²And when I am lifted up on the cross,* I will draw everyone to myself." ³³He said this to indicate how he was going to die.

³⁴"Die?" asked the crowd. "We understood from Scripture that the Messiah would live forever. Why are you

12:31 *The prince of this world* is a name for Satan. **12:32** Greek *lifted up from the earth.*

297

saying the Son of Man will die? Who is this Son of Man you are talking about?"

³⁵Jesus replied, "My light will shine out for you just a little while longer. Walk in it while you can, so you will not stumble when the darkness falls. If you walk in the darkness, you cannot see where you are going. ³⁶Believe in the light while there is still time; then you will become children of the light." After saying these things, Jesus went away and was hidden from them.

The crowd was confused. They thought that Jesus was the Messiah, Israel's future king, and that he would live forever. They were right to think that Jesus was the Messiah. But they were wrong to think that he would never die. Jesus had to die to pay for our sins. He didn't stay dead forever, though. He came back to life after three days so that those who believe in him can live with him in heaven forever.

How do we know that Jesus rose from the dead?

And we apostles are witnesses of all he did throughout Israel and in Jerusalem. They put him to death by crucifying him, but God raised him to life three days later. . . . We were those who ate and drank with him after he rose from the dead.
Acts 10:39-41

A U G U S T

Jesus performed many miracles. But most of the people didn't believe he was God's Son. What did Jesus say to them?

JOHN 12:37-50
Jesus' Message

³⁷But despite all the miraculous signs he had done, most of the people did not believe in him. ³⁸This is exactly what Isaiah the prophet had predicted:

"Lord, who has believed our message?
To whom will the Lord reveal his saving power?"*

³⁹But the people couldn't believe, for as Isaiah also said,

12:38 Isa 53:1.

40 "The Lord has blinded their eyes
    and hardened their hearts—
so their eyes cannot see,
    and their hearts cannot
        understand,
and they cannot turn to me
    and let me heal them."*

41 Isaiah was referring to Jesus when he made this prediction, because he was given a vision of the Messiah's glory. 42 Many people, including some of the Jewish leaders, believed in him. But they wouldn't admit it to anyone because of their fear that the Pharisees would expel them from the synagogue. 43 For they loved human praise more than the praise of God.

44 Jesus shouted to the crowds, "If you trust me, you are really trusting God who sent me. 45 For when you see me, you are seeing the one who sent me. 46 I have come as a light to shine in this dark world, so that all who put their trust in me will no longer remain in the darkness. 47 If anyone hears me and doesn't obey me, I am not his judge— for I have come to save the world and not to judge it. 48 But all who reject me and my message will be judged at the day of judgment by the truth I have spoken. 49 I don't speak on my own authority. The Father who sent me gave me his own instructions as to what I should say. 50 And I know his instructions lead to eternal life; so I say whatever the Father tells me to say!"

Jesus said that those who reject him will be judged by the truth of his words on judgment day. Their judgment will be eternity in hell. But those people who believe in Jesus will not face this judgment. They will spend eternity in heaven. Choose to spend eternity with Jesus. Take him at his word.

**Whom did God show
to the disciples?**

This one who is life from God was shown to us, and we have seen him. And now we testify and announce to you that he is the one who is eternal life. He was with the Father, and then he was shown to us.
1 John 1:2

12:40 Isa 6:10.

AUGUST

Jesus told a story about vineyard workers. Whom was Jesus talking about?

MATTHEW 21:33-46
A Hostile Takeover
33 "Now listen to this story. A certain landowner planted a vineyard, built a wall around it, dug a pit for pressing out the grape juice, and built a lookout tower. Then he leased the vineyard to tenant farmers and moved to another

country. ³⁴At the time of the grape harvest he sent his servants to collect his share of the crop. ³⁵But the farmers grabbed his servants, beat one, killed one, and stoned another. ³⁶So the landowner sent a larger group of his servants to collect for him, but the results were the same.

³⁷"Finally, the owner sent his son, thinking, 'Surely they will respect my son.'

³⁸"But when the farmers saw his son coming, they said to one another, 'Here comes the heir to this estate. Come on, let's kill him and get the estate for ourselves!' ³⁹So they grabbed him, took him out of the vineyard, and murdered him.

⁴⁰"When the owner of the vineyard returns," Jesus asked, "what do you think he will do to those farmers?"

⁴¹The religious leaders replied, "He will put the wicked men to a horrible death and lease the vineyard to others who will give him his share of the crop after each harvest."

⁴²Then Jesus asked them, "Didn't you ever read this in the Scriptures?

'The stone rejected by the builders
has now become the
cornerstone.
This is the Lord's doing,
and it is marvelous to see.'*

⁴³What I mean is that the Kingdom of God will be taken away from you and given to a nation that will produce the proper fruit. ⁴⁴Anyone who stumbles over that stone will be broken to pieces, and it will crush anyone on whom it falls.*"

⁴⁵When the leading priests and Pharisees heard Jesus, they realized he was pointing at them—that they were the farmers in his story. ⁴⁶They wanted to arrest him, but they were afraid to try because the crowds considered Jesus to be a prophet.

The vineyard workers in this story were the Pharisees. The owner represented God, and the owner's only son represented Jesus. Just like the bad workers, the Pharisees rejected Jesus and had him killed. They would face a horrible eternity for killing Jesus. But the Pharisees aren't the only ones who face this eternity. All those who reject Jesus will suffer forever. Listen carefully to the warning in Jesus' story. Accept him as your Lord and Savior and live.

Why is it dangerous to reject Jesus?
And anyone whose name was not found recorded in the Book of Life was thrown into the lake of fire.
Revelation 20:15

21:42 Ps 118:22-23. 21:44 This verse is omitted in some early manuscripts.

Jesus told another story to wake up the religious leaders.
Why were sinners entering God's kingdom ahead of them?

MATTHEW 21:23-32
Two Sons

[23]When Jesus returned to the Temple and began teaching, the leading priests and other leaders came up to him. They demanded, "By whose authority did you drive out the merchants from the Temple?* Who gave you such authority?"

[24]"I'll tell you who gave me the authority to do these things if you answer one question," Jesus replied. [25]"Did John's baptism come from heaven or was it merely human?"

They talked it over among themselves. "If we say it was from heaven, he will ask why we didn't believe him. [26]But if we say it was merely human, we'll be mobbed, because the people think he was a prophet." [27]So they finally replied, "We don't know."

And Jesus responded, "Then I won't answer your question either.

[28]"But what do you think about this? A man with two sons told the older boy, 'Son, go out and work in the vineyard today.' [29]The son answered, 'No, I won't go,' but later he changed his mind and went anyway. [30]Then the father told the other son, 'You go,' and he said, 'Yes, sir, I will.' But he didn't go. [31]Which of the two was obeying his father?"

They replied, "The first, of course."

Then Jesus explained his meaning:

"I assure you, corrupt tax collectors and prostitutes will get into the Kingdom of God before you do. [32]For John the Baptist came and showed you the way to life, and you didn't believe him, while tax collectors and prostitutes did. And even when you saw this happening, you refused to turn from your sins and believe him."

Jesus said that sinners would enter God's Kingdom before the religious leaders. That's because the sinners were obeying God by turning away from their sins. The religious leaders acted like they were obeying God, but their obedience was just a show. They were like the second son who said he would obey his father but didn't. God is interested in obedience. He doesn't want lip service from those who say they follow him. If you say you will obey God, then do it. Don't act like the second son in Jesus' story.

Why is what you do just as important as what you say?

Dear brothers and sisters, what's the use of saying you have faith if you don't prove it by your actions? That kind of faith can't save anyone.
James 2:14

21:23 Or *By whose authority do you do these things?*

Jesus told a story about a wedding feast. Who was invited to the feast?

MATTHEW 22:1-14

The Wedding Feast

Jesus told them several other stories to illustrate the Kingdom. He said, ²"The Kingdom of Heaven can be illustrated by the story of a king who prepared a great wedding feast for his son. ³Many guests were invited, and when the banquet was ready, he sent his servants to notify everyone that it was time to come. But they all refused! ⁴So he sent other servants to tell them, 'The feast has been prepared, and choice meats have been cooked. Everything is ready. Hurry!' ⁵But the guests he had invited ignored them and went about their business, one to his farm, another to his store. ⁶Others seized his messengers and treated them shamefully, even killing some of them.

⁷"Then the king became furious. He sent out his army to destroy the murderers and burn their city. ⁸And he said to his servants, 'The wedding feast is ready, and the guests I invited aren't worthy of the honor. ⁹Now go out to the street corners and invite everyone you see.'

¹⁰"So the servants brought in everyone they could find, good and bad alike, and the banquet hall was filled with guests. ¹¹But when the king came in to meet the guests, he noticed a man who wasn't wearing the proper clothes for a wedding. ¹²'Friend,' he asked, 'how is it that you are here without wedding clothes?' And the man had no reply. ¹³Then the king said to his aides, 'Bind him hand and foot and throw him out into the outer darkness, where there is weeping and gnashing of teeth.' ¹⁴For many are called, but few are chosen."

Many people were invited to the feast. But many of them refused to come. The wedding feast was eternal life with Christ. Those who received the invitations knew about Jesus but refused to believe in him. You have also received an invitation to the wedding feast. Will you go? Don't miss out on the greatest celebration to come. Accept Jesus as your Savior today.

How should you respond to God for inviting you to heaven?

Enter his gates with thanksgiving; go into his courts with praise. Give thanks to him and bless his name. *Psalm 100:4*

302

S E P T E M B E R

The Pharisees tried to trap Jesus. What did Jesus say to escape?

LUKE 20:20-40

Trick Questions

20Watching for their opportunity, the leaders sent secret agents pretending to be honest men. They tried to get Jesus to say something that could be reported to the Roman governor so he would arrest Jesus. 21They said, "Teacher, we know that you speak and teach what is right and are not influenced by what others think. You sincerely teach the ways of God. 22Now tell us—is it right to pay taxes to the Roman government or not?"

23He saw through their trickery and said, 24"Show me a Roman coin.* Whose picture and title are stamped on it?"

"Caesar's," they replied.

25"Well then," he said, "give to Caesar what belongs to him. But everything that belongs to God must be given to God." 26So they failed to trap him in the presence of the people. Instead, they were amazed by his answer, and they were silenced.

27Then some Sadducees stepped forward—a group of Jews who say there is no resurrection after death. 28They posed this question: "Teacher, Moses gave us a law that if a man dies, leaving a wife but no children, his brother should marry the widow and have a child who will be the brother's heir.*

29Well, there were seven brothers. The oldest married and then died without children. 30His brother married the widow, but he also died. Still no children. 31And so it went, one after the other, until each of the seven had married her and died, leaving no children. 32Finally, the woman died, too. 33So tell us, whose wife will she be in the resurrection? For all seven were married to her!"

34Jesus replied, "Marriage is for people here on earth. 35But that is not

The Pharisees thought they had Jesus this time. If Jesus said it was wrong to pay taxes to Caesar, he would be in trouble with the Romans. But if Jesus said it was right, he would turn the Jewish people against him. So Jesus answered their question in a way that avoided their trap. Today some people may try to trap us as the Pharisees tried to trap Jesus. But we can trust Jesus to help us escape their traps. He is wise and has been there. He can make a way for us to escape our enemies.

How can we avoid being trapped by sin?

When you are tempted, [God] will show you a way out so that you will not give into it.
1 Corinthians 10:13

20:24 Greek *a denarius.*   **20:28** Deut 25:5-6.

the way it will be in the age to come. For those worthy of being raised from the dead won't be married then. ³⁶And they will never die again. In these respects they are like angels. They are children of God raised up to new life. ³⁷But now, as to whether the dead will be raised—even Moses proved this when he wrote about the burning bush. Long after Abraham, Isaac, and Jacob had died, he referred to the Lord* as 'the God of Abraham, the God of Isaac, and the God of Jacob.'* ³⁸So he is the God of the living, not the dead. They are all alive to him."

³⁹"Well said, Teacher!" remarked some of the teachers of religious law who were standing there. ⁴⁰And that ended their questions; no one dared to ask any more.

20:37a Greek *when he wrote about the bush. He referred to the Lord.* 20:37b Exod 3:6.

S E P T E M B E R

A religious leader asked Jesus which was the most important command. What did Jesus tell him?

MARK 12:28-37

The Greatest Command

²⁸One of the teachers of religious law was standing there listening to the discussion. He realized that Jesus had answered well, so he asked, "Of all the commandments, which is the most important?"

²⁹Jesus replied, "The most important commandment is this: 'Hear, O Israel! The Lord our God is the one and only Lord. ³⁰And you must love the Lord your God with all your heart, all your soul, all your mind, and all your strength.'* ³¹The second is equally important: 'Love your neighbor as yourself.'* No other commandment is greater than these."

³²The teacher of religious law replied, "Well said, Teacher. You have spoken the truth by saying that there is only one God and no other. ³³And I know it is important to love him with all my heart and all my understanding and all my strength, and to love my neighbors as myself. This is more important than to offer all of the burnt offerings and sacrifices required in the law."

³⁴Realizing this man's understanding, Jesus said to him, "You are not far from the Kingdom of God." And after that, no one dared to ask him any more questions.

³⁵Later, as Jesus was teaching the people in the Temple, he asked, "Why do the teachers of religious law claim that the Messiah will be the son of

12:29-30 Deut 6:4-5. 12:31 Lev 19:18.

David? [36]For David himself, speaking under the inspiration of the Holy Spirit, said,

'The LORD said to my Lord,
Sit in honor at my right hand
    until I humble your enemies
        beneath your feet.'*

[37]Since David himself called him Lord, how can he be his son at the same time?" And the crowd listened to him with great interest.

Jesus told the religious leader that the most important commandment is to love God with all your heart, soul, mind, and strength. There is no commandment more important than this. How can we live by this command? We can start by obeying God's commands found in his Word, the Bible. We can spend time getting to know God in prayer. And we can put our wants, dreams, and goals after God's plan for our life.

What has God commmanded us to do?
And you must love the LORD your God with all your heart, all your soul, and all your strength.
Deuteronomy 6:5

12:36 Ps 110:1.

S E P T E M B E R

Jesus rebuked the Pharisees for their actions. What didn't they do?

MATTHEW 23:1-26
Dirty on the Inside
Then Jesus said to the crowds and to his disciples, [2]"The teachers of religious law and the Pharisees are the official interpreters of the Scriptures. [3]So practice and obey whatever they say to you, but don't follow their example. For they don't practice what they teach. [4]They crush you with impossible religious demands and never lift a finger to help ease the burden.

[5]"Everything they do is for show. On their arms they wear extra wide prayer boxes with Scripture verses inside,* and they wear extra long tassels on their robes. [6]And how they love to sit at the head table at banquets and in the most prominent seats in the synagogue! [7]They enjoy the attention they get on the streets, and they enjoy being called 'Rabbi.'* [8]Don't ever let anyone call you 'Rabbi,' for you have only one teacher, and all of you are on the same level as brothers and sisters. [9]And don't address anyone here on earth as

23:5 Greek *They enlarge their phylacteries.* **23:7** *Rabbi,* from Aramaic, means "master" or "teacher."

'Father,' for only God in heaven is your spiritual Father. [10]And don't let anyone call you 'Master,' for there is only one master, the Messiah. [11]The greatest among you must be a servant. [12]But those who exalt themselves will be humbled, and those who humble themselves will be exalted.

[13]"How terrible it will be for you teachers of religious law and you Pharisees. Hypocrites! For you won't let others enter the Kingdom of Heaven, and you won't go in yourselves.* [15]Yes, how terrible it will be for you teachers of religious law and you Pharisees. For you cross land and sea to make one convert, and then you turn him into twice the son of hell as you yourselves are.

[16]"Blind guides! How terrible it will be for you! For you say that it means nothing to swear 'by God's Temple'— you can break that oath. But then you say that it is binding to swear 'by the gold in the Temple.' [17]Blind fools! Which is greater, the gold, or the Temple that makes the gold sacred? [18]And you say that to take an oath 'by the altar' can be broken, but to swear 'by the gifts on the altar' is binding! [19]How blind! For which is greater, the gift on the altar, or the altar that makes the gift sacred? [20]When you swear 'by the altar,' you are swearing by it and by everything on it. [21]And when you swear 'by the Temple,' you are swearing by it and by God, who lives in it. [22]And when you swear 'by heaven,' you are swearing by the throne of God and by God, who sits on the throne.

[23]"How terrible it will be for you teachers of religious law and you Pharisees. Hypocrites! For you are careful to tithe even the tiniest part of your income,* but you ignore the important things of the law—justice, mercy, and faith. You should tithe, yes, but you should not leave undone the more important things. [24]Blind guides! You strain your water so you won't accidentally swallow a gnat; then you swallow a camel!

[25]"How terrible it will be for you teachers of religious law and you Pharisees. Hypocrites! You are so careful to clean the outside of the cup and the dish, but inside you are filthy—full of greed and self-indulgence! [26]Blind Pharisees! First wash the inside of the cup, and then the outside will become clean, too."

The Pharisees didn't obey God's commands. Instead, they made up their own rules to live by and insisted that others live by them, too. As a result, their lives were full of sin. Living by man-made rules didn't work for the Pharisees, and it won't work for us. To live a life that pleases God, we must trust in Jesus to take away our sin. He will fill us with his Holy Spirit to help us live in a way that pleases him.

Who lives in us to help us please God?

With the help of the Holy Spirit who lives within us, carefully guard what has been entrusted to you.
2 Timothy 1:14

23:13 Some manuscripts add verse 14, *How terrible it will be for you teachers of religious law and you Pharisees. Hypocrites! You shamelessly cheat widows out of their property, and then, to cover up the kind of people you really are, you make long prayers in public. Because of this, your punishment will be the greater.* **23:23** Greek *to tithe the mint, the dill, and the cumin.*

*Jesus told his disciples some bad news about the future.
What did he say to comfort them?*

LUKE 21:5-19

The Future

[5]Some of his disciples began talking about the beautiful stonework of the Temple and the memorial decorations on the walls. But Jesus said, [6]"The time is coming when all these things will be so completely demolished that not one stone will be left on top of another."

[7]"Teacher," they asked, "when will all this take place? And will there be any sign ahead of time?"

[8]He replied, "Don't let anyone mislead you. For many will come in my name, claiming to be the Messiah* and saying, 'The time has come!' But don't believe them. [9]And when you hear of wars and insurrections, don't panic. Yes, these things must come, but the end won't follow immediately." [10]Then he added, "Nations and kingdoms will proclaim war against each other. [11]There will be great earthquakes, and there will be famines and epidemics in many lands, and there will be terrifying things and great miraculous signs in the heavens.

[12]"But before all this occurs, there will be a time of great persecution. You will be dragged into synagogues and prisons, and you will be accused before kings and governors of being my followers. [13]This will be your opportunity to tell them about me. [14]So don't worry about how to answer the charges against you, [15]for I will give you the right words and such wisdom that none of your opponents will be able to reply! [16]Even those closest to you—your parents, brothers, relatives, and friends—will betray you. And some of you will be killed. [17]And everyone will hate you because of your allegiance to me. [18]But not a hair of your head will perish! [19]By standing firm, you will win your souls."

Jesus told his disciples that hard times were ahead of them. But he also told them that he would give them wisdom and the words to say when they were brought before the authorities for their faith. This promise holds true for us, too. We can stand firm because God is with us. He will give us strength and wisdom in difficult times.

What should we remember in times of trouble?

So you see, the Lord knows how to rescue godly people from their trials, even while punishing the wicked right up until the day of judgment.

2 Peter 2:9

21:8 Greek *name, saying, 'I am.'*

S E P T E M B E R

Jesus taught his disciples about the end of the world.
What did he tell his disciples to do to prepare for the end?

LUKE 21:25-36
Watch and Pray

25 "And there will be strange events in the skies—signs in the sun, moon, and stars. And down here on earth the nations will be in turmoil, perplexed by the roaring seas and strange tides. 26 The courage of many people will falter because of the fearful fate they see coming upon the earth, because the stability of the very heavens will be broken up. 27 Then everyone will see the Son of Man arrive on the clouds with power and great glory.* 28 So when all these things begin to happen, stand straight and look up, for your salvation is near!"

29 Then he gave them this illustration: "Notice the fig tree, or any other tree. 30 When the leaves come out, you know without being told that summer is near. 31 Just so, when you see the events I've described taking place, you can be sure that the Kingdom of God is near. 32 I assure you, this generation* will not pass from the scene until all these events have taken place. 33 Heaven and earth will disappear, but my words will remain forever.

34 "Watch out! Don't let me find you living in careless ease and drunkenness, and filled with the worries of this life. Don't let that day catch you unaware, 35 as in a trap. For that day will come upon everyone living on the earth. 36 Keep a constant watch. And pray that, if possible, you may escape these horrors and stand before the Son of Man."

Jesus told his disciples to be ready for his return. He warned them to watch for the signs of his return, to pray, and to not live carelessly. As followers of Jesus, we need to pay attention to this warning as well. Jesus will return from heaven one day to take us with him. We must be ready for his return.

What can we do to be ready for Jesus' return?
Devote yourselves to prayer with an alert mind and a thankful heart.
Colossians 4:2

21:27 See Dan 7:13. **21:32** Or *this age*, or *this nation*.

S E P T E M B E R

Jesus told a story about ten bridesmaids. Why did he tell this story?

MATTHEW 25:1-13

Ready and Waiting

"The Kingdom of Heaven can be illustrated by the story of ten bridesmaids* who took their lamps and went to meet the bridegroom. ²Five of them were foolish, and five were wise. ³The five who were foolish took no oil for their lamps, ⁴but the other five were wise enough to take along extra oil. ⁵When the bridegroom was delayed, they all lay down and slept. ⁶At midnight they were roused by the shout, 'Look, the bridegroom is coming! Come out and welcome him!'

⁷"All the bridesmaids got up and prepared their lamps. ⁸Then the five foolish ones asked the others, 'Please give us some of your oil because our lamps are going out.' ⁹But the others replied, 'We don't have enough for all of us. Go to a shop and buy some for yourselves.'

¹⁰"But while they were gone to buy oil, the bridegroom came, and those who were ready went in with him to the marriage feast, and the door was locked. ¹¹Later, when the other five bridesmaids returned, they stood outside, calling, 'Sir, open the door for us!' ¹²But he called back, 'I don't know you!'

¹³"So stay awake and be prepared, because you do not know the day or hour of my return."

Jesus told this story to prepare the disciples for his return. In the story, five bridesmaids were not ready when the bridegroom came. They lost out and did not get into the marriage feast. Just like the bridegroom in this story, Jesus will return. Be prepared for his return. Live each day as if he might come at any moment.

Who will help us get ready for Jesus' return?

As for me, I look to the LORD for his help. I wait confidently for God to save me, and my God will certainly hear me.
Micah 7:7

25:1 Or *virgins*; also in 25:7, 11.

Jesus told the story of a master who left three of his servants in charge of some money. What was Jesus teaching about in this story?

MATTHEW 25:14-30

The Three Servants

¹⁴"Again, the Kingdom of Heaven can be illustrated by the story of a man going on a trip. He called together his servants and gave them money to invest for him while he was gone. ¹⁵He gave five bags of gold* to one, two bags of gold to another, and one bag of gold to the last—dividing it in proportion to their abilities—and then left on his trip. ¹⁶The servant who received the five bags of gold began immediately to invest the money and soon doubled it. ¹⁷The servant with two bags of gold also went right to work and doubled the money. ¹⁸But the servant who received the one bag of gold dug a hole in the ground and hid the master's money for safe-keeping.

¹⁹"After a long time their master returned from his trip and called them to give an account of how they had used his money. ²⁰The servant to whom he had entrusted the five bags of gold said, 'Sir, you gave me five bags of gold to invest, and I have doubled the amount.' ²¹The master was full of praise. 'Well done, my good and faithful servant. You have been faithful in handling this small amount, so now I will give you many more responsibilities. Let's celebrate together!'

²²"Next came the servant who had received the two bags of gold, with the report, 'Sir, you gave me two bags of gold to invest, and I have doubled the amount.' ²³The master said, 'Well done, my good and faithful servant. You have been faithful in handling this small

Jesus used this story to teach his disciples about stewardship. Stewardship is the responsible use of all that God gives us. In Jesus' story, the first servant was a good steward. This servant managed what the master had given him so well that he doubled the master's wealth. The last servant, on the other hand, was a bad steward. He hid what his master had given him and didn't increase his master's wealth. Jesus wants all of his followers to be good stewards of what he gives them. Use what Jesus has given you to serve him well.

How should we use the gifts that God has given us?

God has given each of us the ability to do certain things well. So if God has given you the ability to prophesy, speak out when you have faith that God is speaking through you.
Romans 12:6

25:15 Greek *talents*; also throughout the story. A talent is equal to 75 pounds or 34 kilograms.

amount, so now I will give you many more responsibilities. Let's celebrate together!'

²⁴"Then the servant with the one bag of gold came and said, 'Sir, I know you are a hard man, harvesting crops you didn't plant and gathering crops you didn't cultivate. ²⁵I was afraid I would lose your money, so I hid it in the earth and here it is.'

²⁶"But the master replied, 'You wicked and lazy servant! You think I'm a hard man, do you, harvesting crops I didn't plant and gathering crops I didn't cultivate? ²⁷Well, you should at least have put my money into the bank so I could have some interest. ²⁸Take the money from this servant and give it to the one with the ten bags of gold. ²⁹To those who use well what they are given, even more will be given, and they will have an abundance. But from those who are unfaithful,* even what little they have will be taken away. ³⁰Now throw this useless servant into outer darkness, where there will be weeping and gnashing of teeth.'"

25:29 Or who have nothing.

S E P T E M B E R

Jesus described how he would judge people at the end of the world. Who will enter God's kingdom?

MATTHEW 25:31-46
The Sheep and the Goats
³¹"But when the Son of Man comes in his glory, and all the angels with him, then he will sit upon his glorious throne. ³²All the nations will be gathered in his presence, and he will separate them as a shepherd separates the sheep from the goats. ³³He will place the sheep at his right hand and the goats at his left. ³⁴Then the King will say to those on the right, 'Come, you who are blessed by my Father, inherit the Kingdom prepared for you from the foundation of the world. ³⁵For I was hungry, and you fed me. I was thirsty, and you gave me a drink. I was a stranger, and you invited me into your home. ³⁶I was naked, and you gave me clothing. I was sick, and you cared for me. I was in prison, and you visited me.'

³⁷"Then these righteous ones will reply, 'Lord, when did we ever see you hungry and feed you? Or thirsty and give you something to drink? ³⁸Or a stranger and show you hospitality? Or naked and give you clothing? ³⁹When did we ever see you sick or in prison, and visit you?' ⁴⁰And the King will tell them, 'I assure you, when you did it to one of the least of these my brothers and sisters, you were doing it to me!'

⁴¹"Then the King will turn to those on the left and say, 'Away with you, you cursed ones, into the eternal fire

prepared for the Devil and his demons! [42]For I was hungry, and you didn't feed me. I was thirsty, and you didn't give me anything to drink. [43]I was a stranger, and you didn't invite me into your home. I was naked, and you gave me no clothing. I was sick and in prison, and you didn't visit me.'

[44]"Then they will reply, 'Lord, when did we ever see you hungry or thirsty or a stranger or naked or sick or in prison, and not help you?' [45]And he will answer, 'I assure you, when you refused to help the least of these my brothers and sisters, you were refusing to help me.' [46]And they will go away into eternal punishment, but the righteous will go into eternal life."

Some people in this story fed and clothed the poor. They helped the sick and those in need. These are the people who were called sheep. They followed the example of their shepherd, Jesus, by loving people and taking care of their needs. The sheep were rewarded by God for their faith and obedience. They entered into God's kingdom. If you want to spend eternity with Jesus, put your trust in him. Then follow his lead and show his love to all those who need it.

Whom should we help?
There will always be some among you who are poor. That is why I am commanding you to share your resources freely with the poor and with other Israelites in need.
Deuteronomy 15:11

SEPTEMBER

*The time of Jesus' death was near.
How did he spend his last evening with his disciples?*

LUKE 22:1-20

The Last Supper

The Festival of Unleavened Bread, which begins with the Passover celebration, was drawing near. [2]The leading priests and teachers of religious law were actively plotting Jesus' murder. But they wanted to kill him without starting a riot, a possibility they greatly feared.

[3]Then Satan entered into Judas Iscariot, who was one of the twelve disciples, [4]and he went over to the leading priests and captains of the Temple guard to discuss the best way to betray Jesus to them. [5]They were delighted that he was ready to help them, and they promised him a reward. [6]So he began looking for an opportunity to betray Jesus so they could arrest him quietly when the crowds weren't around.

[7]Now the Festival of Unleavened Bread arrived, when the Passover

lambs were sacrificed. [8]Jesus sent Peter and John ahead and said, "Go and prepare the Passover meal, so we can eat it together."

[9]"Where do you want us to go?" they asked him.

[10]He replied, "As soon as you enter Jerusalem, a man carrying a pitcher of water will meet you. Follow him. At the house he enters, [11]say to the owner, 'The Teacher asks, Where is the guest room where I can eat the Passover meal with my disciples?' [12]He will take you upstairs to a large room that is already set up. That is the place. Go ahead and prepare our supper there." [13]They went off to the city and found everything just as Jesus had said, and they prepared the Passover supper there.

[14]Then at the proper time Jesus and the twelve apostles sat down together at the table. [15]Jesus said, "I have looked forward to this hour with deep longing, anxious to eat this Passover meal with you before my suffering begins. [16]For I tell you now that I won't eat it again until it comes to fulfillment in the Kingdom of God."

[17]Then he took a cup of wine, and when he had given thanks for it, he said, "Take this and share it among yourselves. [18]For I will not drink wine again until the Kingdom of God has come."

[19]Then he took a loaf of bread; and when he had thanked God for it, he broke it in pieces and gave it to the disciples, saying, "This is my body, given for you. Do this in remembrance of me." [20]After supper he took another cup of wine and said, "This wine is the token of God's new covenant to save you—an agreement sealed with the blood I will pour out for you.*"

Jesus celebrated the Passover meal with his disciples. At their meal, he began the tradition called Communion. Communion is a remembrance of Jesus' death for sinners. It is also a celebration of the new agreement God made with people through Jesus' death. Only Jesus' followers can take part in Communion. If you follow Jesus, be sure to participate in this time of remembering what he has done for you.

Why should we be careful of how we take Communion?

So if anyone eats this bread or drinks this cup of the Lord unworthily, that person is guilty of sinning against the body and the blood of the Lord.
1 Corinthians 11:27

22:19-20 Some manuscripts omit 22:19b-20, *given for you . . . I will pour out for you.*

Jesus washed his disciples' feet. What did he tell the disciples to do?

JOHN 13:1-17

Washing Feet

Before the Passover celebration, Jesus knew that his hour had come to leave this world and return to his Father. He now showed the disciples the full extent of his love.* ²It was time for supper, and the Devil had already enticed Judas, son of Simon Iscariot, to carry out his plan to betray Jesus. ³Jesus knew that the Father had given him authority over everything and that he had come from God and would return to God. ⁴So he got up from the table, took off his robe, wrapped a towel around his waist, ⁵and poured water into a basin. Then he began to wash the disciples' feet and to wipe them with the towel he had around him.

⁶When he came to Simon Peter, Peter said to him, "Lord, why are you going to wash my feet?"

⁷Jesus replied, "You don't understand now why I am doing it; someday you will."

⁸"No," Peter protested, "you will never wash my feet!"

Jesus replied, "But if I don't wash you, you won't belong to me."

⁹Simon Peter exclaimed, "Then wash my hands and head as well, Lord, not just my feet!"

¹⁰Jesus replied, "A person who has bathed all over does not need to wash, except for the feet,* to be entirely clean. And you are clean, but that isn't true of everyone here." ¹¹For Jesus knew who would betray him. That is what he meant when he said, "Not all of you are clean."

¹²After washing their feet, he put on his robe again and sat down and asked, "Do you understand what I was doing? ¹³You call me 'Teacher' and 'Lord,' and you are right, because it is true. ¹⁴And since I, the Lord and Teacher, have washed your feet, you

Jesus told his disciples to follow his example. As the king of heaven and earth, no one was above him in power or authority. Yet he lowered himself to the point of washing his disciples' dirty feet. He served the very people that should have been serving him. Jesus wants all his followers to be like him. If you follow Jesus, humble yourself and be willing to serve others.

Why should we serve others humbly?

And all of you, serve each other in humility, for "God sets himself against the proud, but he shows favor to the humble."*
1 Peter 5:5

13:1 Or *He loved his disciples to the very end.* **13:10** Some manuscripts do not include *except for the feet.* **5:5** Prov 3:34.

ought to wash each other's feet. [15]I have given you an example to follow. Do as I have done to you. [16]How true it is that a servant is not greater than the master. Nor are messengers more important than the one who sends them. [17]You know these things—now do them! That is the path of blessing."

S E P T E M B E R

Jesus gave a new command. What was this command?

JOHN 13:18-38

A New Command

[18]"I am not saying these things to all of you; I know so well each one of you I chose. The Scriptures declare, 'The one who shares my food has turned against me,'* and this will soon come true. [19]I tell you this now, so that when it happens you will believe I am the Messiah. [20]Truly, anyone who welcomes my messenger is welcoming me, and anyone who welcomes me is welcoming the Father who sent me."

[21]Now Jesus was in great anguish of spirit, and he exclaimed, "The truth is, one of you will betray me!"

[22]The disciples looked at each other, wondering whom he could mean. [23]One of Jesus' disciples, the one Jesus loved, was sitting next to Jesus at the table.* [24]Simon Peter motioned to him to ask who would do this terrible thing. [25]Leaning toward Jesus, he asked, "Lord, who is it?"

[26]Jesus said, "It is the one to whom I give the bread dipped in the sauce." And when he had dipped it, he gave it to Judas, son of Simon Iscariot. [27]As soon as Judas had eaten the bread, Satan entered into him. Then Jesus told him, "Hurry. Do it now." [28]None of the others at the table knew what Jesus meant. [29]Since Judas was their treasurer, some thought Jesus was telling him to go and pay for the food or to give some money to the poor. [30]So Judas left at once, going out into the night.

[31]As soon as Judas left the room, Jesus said, "The time has come for me, the Son of Man, to enter into my glory, and God will receive glory because of all that happens to me. [32]And God will bring* me into my glory very soon. [33]Dear children, how brief are these moments before I must go away and leave you! Then, though you search for me, you cannot come to me—just as I told the Jewish leaders. [34]So now I am giving you a new commandment: Love each other. Just as I have loved you, you should love each other. [35]Your love for one another will prove to the world that you are my disciples."

13:18 Ps 41:9. **13:23** Greek *was reclining on Jesus' bosom.* The "disciple whom Jesus loved" was probably John. **13:32** Some manuscripts read *And if God is glorified in him (the Son of Man), God will bring.*

³⁶Simon Peter said, "Lord, where are you going?"

And Jesus replied, "You can't go with me now, but you will follow me later."

³⁷"But why can't I come now, Lord?" he asked. "I am ready to die for you."

³⁸Jesus answered, "Die for me? No, before the rooster crows tomorrow morning, you will deny three times that you even know me."

The new command that Jesus gave his disciples was to love each other as he loved them. Jesus said that when they did this, the world would know that they were his disciples. That is because loving someone the way Jesus does is hard. It requires putting that person's needs before your own. In a selfish world, this kind of love stands out like a spotlight in the night sky. Love others just as Jesus does. Then the world will know to whom you belong.

**How should we love
our neighbors?**

Never seek revenge or bear a grudge against anyone, but love your neighbor as yourself. I am the LORD.
Leviticus 19:18

S E P T E M B E R

Jesus declared that he is the only way to God. How could he make this claim?

JOHN 14:1-14
The Only Way

"Don't be troubled. You trust God, now trust in me. ²There are many rooms in my Father's home, and I am going to prepare a place for you. If this were not so, I would tell you plainly. ³When everything is ready, I will come and get you, so that you will always be with me where I am. ⁴And you know where I am going and how to get there."

⁵"No, we don't know, Lord," Thomas said. "We haven't any idea where you are going, so how can we know the way?"

⁶Jesus told him, "I am the way, the truth, and the life. No one can come to the Father except through me. ⁷If you had known who I am, then you would have known who my Father is.* From now on you know him and have seen him!"

⁸Philip said, "Lord, show us the Father and we will be satisfied."

⁹Jesus replied, "Philip, don't you even yet know who I am, even after all

14:7 Some manuscripts read *If you really have known me, you will know who my Father is.*

the time I have been with you? Anyone who has seen me has seen the Father! So why are you asking to see him? [10]Don't you believe that I am in the Father and the Father is in me? The words I say are not my own, but my Father who lives in me does his work through me. [11]Just believe that I am in the Father and the Father is in me. Or at least believe because of what you have seen me do.

[12]"The truth is, anyone who believes in me will do the same works I have done, and even greater works, because I am going to be with the Father. [13]You can ask for anything in my name, and I will do it, because the work of the Son brings glory to the Father. [14]Yes, ask anything in my name, and I will do it!"

Jesus could make this claim because he was God's only Son. As his Son, Jesus not only knew God's plan for saving people from their sins, but he was the way in which God would save people. There is no other way for a person to be saved. That is why Jesus can say he is "the way, the truth, and the life." And that is why we should believe in him.

Can salvation be found in anyone but Jesus?
There is salvation in no one else! There is no other name in all of heaven for people to call on to save them.
Acts 4:12

S E P T E M B E R

Jesus was leaving his disciples to return to God. Whom did he promise to send to help them?

JOHN 14:15-31
The Spirit of Truth
[15]"If you love me, obey my commandments. [16]And I will ask the Father, and he will give you another Counselor,* who will never leave you. [17]He is the Holy Spirit, who leads into all truth. The world at large cannot receive him, because it isn't looking for him and doesn't recognize him. But you do, because he lives with you now and later will be in you. [18]No, I will not abandon you as orphans—I will come to you. [19]In just a little while the world will not see me again, but you will. For I will live again, and you will, too. [20]When I am raised to life again, you will know that I am in my Father, and you are in me, and I am in you. [21]Those who obey my commandments are the ones who love me. And because they love me, my Father will love them, and I will love them. And I will reveal myself to each one of them."

[22]Judas (not Judas Iscariot, but the other disciple with that name) said to

14:16 Or *Comforter*, or *Encourager*, or *Advocate*. Greek *Paraclete*; also in 14:26.

him, "Lord, why are you going to reveal yourself only to us and not to the world at large?"

²³Jesus replied, "All those who love me will do what I say. My Father will love them, and we will come to them and live with them. ²⁴Anyone who doesn't love me will not do what I say. And remember, my words are not my own. This message is from the Father who sent me. ²⁵I am telling you these things now while I am still with you. ²⁶But when the Father sends the Counselor as my representative—and by the Counselor I mean the Holy Spirit—he will teach you everything and will remind you of everything I myself have told you.

²⁷"I am leaving you with a gift—peace of mind and heart. And the peace I give isn't like the peace the world gives. So don't be troubled or afraid. ²⁸Remember what I told you: I am going away, but I will come back to you again. If you really love me, you will be very happy for me, because now I can go to the Father, who is greater than I am. ²⁹I have told you these things be-

fore they happen so that you will believe when they do happen.

³⁰"I don't have much more time to talk to you, because the prince of this world approaches. He has no power over me, ³¹but I will do what the Father requires of me, so that the world will know that I love the Father. Come, let's be going."

Jesus promised to send the Holy Spirit, also called the Counselor. The Holy Spirit lives in all Christians. He teaches us God's truths and helps us live by God's commands.

How does God change us so that we can obey him?

And I will give them singleness of heart and put a new spirit within them. I will take away their hearts of stone and give them tender hearts* instead, so they will obey my laws and regulations. Then they will truly be my people, and I will be their God.
Ezekiel 11:19-20

11:19 Hebrew *hearts of flesh.*

S E P T E M B E R

Jesus said that he was the vine. Who did he say were the branches?

JOHN 15:1-17
The Vine and the Branches
"I am the true vine, and my Father is the gardener. ²He cuts off every branch that doesn't produce fruit, and he

prunes the branches that do bear fruit so they will produce even more. ³You have already been pruned for greater fruitfulness by the message I have given you. ⁴Remain in me, and I will remain in you. For a branch cannot produce fruit if it is severed from the vine, and you cannot be fruitful apart from me.

5 "Yes, I am the vine; you are the branches. Those who remain in me, and I in them, will produce much fruit. For apart from me you can do nothing. 6 Anyone who parts from me is thrown away like a useless branch and withers. Such branches are gathered into a pile to be burned. 7 But if you stay joined to me and my words remain in you, you may ask any request you like, and it will be granted! 8 My true disciples produce much fruit. This brings great glory to my Father.

9 "I have loved you even as the Father has loved me. Remain in my love. 10 When you obey me, you remain in my love, just as I obey my Father and remain in his love. 11 I have told you this so that you will be filled with my joy. Yes, your joy will overflow! 12 I command you to love each other in the same way that I love you. 13 And here is how to measure it—the greatest love is shown when people lay down their lives for their friends. 14 You are my friends if you obey me. 15 I no longer call you servants, because a master doesn't confide in his servants. Now you are my friends, since I have told you everything the Father told me. 16 You didn't choose me. I chose you. I appointed you to go and produce fruit that will last, so that the Father will give you whatever you ask for, using my name. 17 I command you to love each other."

The branches were Jesus' followers. He used this illustration to show his followers how much they needed to stay connected to him. When a branch falls off a vine, it turns brown and dies. When a Christian abandons Christ, that person's spirit withers and dies. That is why it is important to stay connected to Jesus. He is your life and strength. If you cut yourself off from him, you will not grow spiritually and become like Jesus.

What is another reason we should stay connected to Jesus?
Now the Holy Spirit tells us clearly that in the last times some will turn away from what we believe; they will follow lying spirits and teachings that come from demons.
1 Timothy 4:1

Jesus was going away for a while. The disciples were sad.
What did Jesus say to comfort them?

JOHN 16:16-33

Sadness to Joy

[16] "In just a little while I will be gone, and you won't see me anymore. Then, just a little while after that, you will see me again."

[17] The disciples asked each other, "What does he mean when he says, 'You won't see me, and then you will see me'? And what does he mean when he says, 'I am going to the Father'? [18] And what does he mean by 'a little while'? We don't understand."

[19] Jesus realized they wanted to ask him, so he said, "Are you asking yourselves what I meant? I said in just a little while I will be gone, and you won't see me anymore. Then, just a little while after that, you will see me again. [20] Truly, you will weep and mourn over what is going to happen to me, but the world will rejoice. You will grieve, but your grief will suddenly turn to wonderful joy when you see me again. [21] It will be like a woman experiencing the pains of labor. When her child is born, her anguish gives place to joy because she has brought a new person into the world. [22] You have sorrow now, but I will see you again; then you will rejoice, and no one can rob you of that joy. [23] At that time you won't need to ask me for anything. The truth is, you can go directly to the Father and ask him, and he will grant your request because you use my name. [24] You haven't done this before. Ask, using my name, and you will receive, and you will have abundant joy.

[25] "I have spoken of these matters in parables, but the time will come when this will not be necessary, and I will tell you plainly all about the Father.

Jesus told his disciples that they would see him again soon. When he spoke these words, it was almost time for him to die on the cross. His death would bring sadness to the disciples. But his resurrection would fill his disciples with a joy that could never be taken from them. Jesus' resurrection can bring us comfort and joy, too. Knowing that we are saved from our sins and that Jesus is alive and will come back for us gives us all the hope we need to live through hard times.

How can we thank God for giving us his Son?

All honor to the God and Father of our Lord Jesus Christ, for it is by his boundless mercy that God has given us the privilege of being born again. Now we live with a wonderful expectation because Jesus Christ rose again from the dead.
1 Peter 1:3

²⁶Then you will ask in my name. I'm not saying I will ask the Father on your behalf, ²⁷for the Father himself loves you dearly because you love me and believe that I came from God. ²⁸Yes, I came from the Father into the world, and I will leave the world and return to the Father."

²⁹Then his disciples said, "At last you are speaking plainly and not in parables. ³⁰Now we understand that you know everything and don't need anyone to tell you anything.* From this we believe that you came from God."

³¹Jesus asked, "Do you finally believe? ³²But the time is coming—in fact, it is already here—when you will be scattered, each one going his own way, leaving me alone. Yet I am not alone because the Father is with me. ³³I have told you all this so that you may have peace in me. Here on earth you will have many trials and sorrows. But take heart, because I have overcome the world."

16:30 Or *don't need that anyone should ask you anything.*

S E P T E M B E R

Jesus knew he would die soon. He prayed for his disciples and for those who would believe in him in the future. What did Jesus want for us?

JOHN 17:1-26

Jesus Prays for Us

When Jesus had finished saying all these things, he looked up to heaven and said, "Father, the time has come. Glorify your Son so he can give glory back to you. ²For you have given him authority over everyone in all the earth. He gives eternal life to each one you have given him. ³And this is the way to have eternal life—to know you, the only true God, and Jesus Christ, the one you sent to earth. ⁴I brought glory to you here on earth by doing everything you told me to do. ⁵And now, Father, bring me into the glory we shared before the world began.

⁶"I have told these men about you. They were in the world, but then you gave them to me. Actually, they were always yours, and you gave them to me; and they have kept your word. ⁷Now they know that everything I have is a gift from you, ⁸for I have passed on to them the words you gave me; and they accepted them and know that I came from you, and they believe you sent me.

⁹"My prayer is not for the world, but for those you have given me, because they belong to you. ¹⁰And all of them, since they are mine, belong to you; and you have given them back to me, so they are my glory! ¹¹Now I am departing the world; I am leaving them behind and coming to you. Holy Father, keep them and care for them—all those you have given me—so that

they will be united just as we are. [12]During my time here, I have kept them safe.* I guarded them so that not one was lost, except the one headed for destruction, as the Scriptures foretold.

[13]"And now I am coming to you. I have told them many things while I was with them so they would be filled with my joy. [14]I have given them your word. And the world hates them because they do not belong to the world, just as I do not. [15]I'm not asking you to take them out of the world, but to keep them safe from the evil one. [16]They are not part of this world any more than I am. [17]Make them pure and holy by teaching them your words of truth. [18]As you sent me into the world, I am sending them into the world. [19]And I give myself entirely to you so they also might be entirely yours.

[20]"I am praying not only for these disciples but also for all who will ever believe in me because of their testimony. [21]My prayer for all of them is that they will be one, just as you and I are one, Father—that just as you are in me and I am in you, so they will be in us, and the world will believe you sent me.

[22]"I have given them the glory you gave me, so that they may be one, as we are—[23]I in them and you in me, all being perfected into one. Then the world will know that you sent me and will understand that you love them as much as you love me. [24]Father, I want these whom you've given me to be with me, so they can see my glory. You gave me the glory because you loved me even before the world began!

[25]"O righteous Father, the world doesn't know you, but I do; and these disciples know you sent me. [26]And I have revealed you to them and will keep on revealing you. I will do this so that your love for me may be in them and I in them."

While Jesus was with his disciples, he kept them safe. But Jesus wasn't going to be on the earth forever. So he prayed that God would keep and care for his disciples after he left. His prayer wasn't just for the twelve disciples though. It was also for us. God has protected you and will continue to do so. Give him the thanks that he deserves for protecting you.

Whom can you pray to when you are in a dangerous situation?
I am suffering and in pain. Rescue me, O God, by your saving power.
Psalm 69:29

17:12 Greek *I have kept in your name those whom you have given me.*

Just before his arrest, Jesus prayed to God. What did he pray?

MARK 14:32-42

A Painful Prayer

³²And they came to an olive grove called Gethsemane, and Jesus said, "Sit here while I go and pray." ³³He took Peter, James, and John with him, and he began to be filled with horror and deep distress. ³⁴He told them, "My soul is crushed with grief to the point of death. Stay here and watch with me."

³⁵He went on a little farther and fell face down on the ground. He prayed that, if it were possible, the awful hour awaiting him might pass him by. ³⁶"Abba,* Father," he said, "everything is possible for you. Please take this cup of suffering away from me. Yet I want your will, not mine."

³⁷Then he returned and found the disciples asleep. "Simon!" he said to Peter. "Are you asleep? Couldn't you stay awake and watch with me even one hour? ³⁸Keep alert and pray. Otherwise temptation will overpower you. For though the spirit is willing enough, the body is weak."

³⁹Then Jesus left them again and prayed, repeating his pleadings. ⁴⁰Again he returned to them and found them sleeping, for they just couldn't keep their eyes open. And they didn't know what to say.

⁴¹When he returned to them the third time, he said, "Still sleeping? Still resting?* Enough! The time has come. I, the Son of Man, am betrayed into the hands of sinners. ⁴²Up, let's be going. See, my betrayer is here!"

Jesus did not want to face the hardships of torture and death that lay ahead of him. What did he do? He prayed. He asked God to help him. At the same time, he was willing to obey God's plan. His example is an excellent one for us to follow. When we face life's problems, we can pray to God, asking him for help. We can also be obedient to him and trust him to bring us through the hard times.

What attitude can we have to help us obey God when we don't want to do it?

I take joy in doing your will, my God, for your law is written on my heart.

Psalm 40:8

14:36 *Abba* is an Aramaic term for "father."   **14:41** Or *Sleep on, take your rest.*

Judas led a group of soldiers to arrest Jesus.
What did the soldiers do when Jesus identified himself?

JOHN 18:1-24

Betrayed!

After saying these things, Jesus crossed the Kidron Valley with his disciples and entered a grove of olive trees. ²Judas, the betrayer, knew this place, because Jesus had gone there many times with his disciples. ³The leading priests and Pharisees had given Judas a battalion of Roman soldiers and Temple guards to accompany him. Now with blazing torches, lanterns, and weapons, they arrived at the olive grove.

⁴Jesus fully realized all that was going to happen to him. Stepping forward to meet them, he asked, "Whom are you looking for?"

⁵"Jesus of Nazareth," they replied.

"I am he,"* Jesus said. Judas was standing there with them when Jesus identified himself. ⁶And as he said, "I am he," they all fell backward to the ground! ⁷Once more he asked them, "Whom are you searching for?"

And again they replied, "Jesus of Nazareth."

⁸"I told you that I am he," Jesus said. "And since I am the one you want, let these others go." ⁹He did this to fulfill his own statement: "I have not lost a single one of those you gave me."*

¹⁰Then Simon Peter drew a sword and slashed off the right ear of Malchus, the high priest's servant. ¹¹But Jesus said to Peter, "Put your sword back into its sheath. Shall I not drink from the cup the Father has given me?"

¹²So the soldiers, their commanding officer, and the Temple guards arrested Jesus and tied him up. ¹³First they took him to Annas, the father-in-law of Caiaphas, the high priest that year. ¹⁴Caiaphas was the one who had told the other Jewish leaders, "Better that one should die for all."

¹⁵Simon Peter followed along behind, as did another of the disciples. That other disciple was acquainted with the high priest, so he was allowed to enter the courtyard with Jesus. ¹⁶Peter stood outside the gate. Then the other disciple spoke to the woman watching at the gate, and she let Peter in. ¹⁷The woman asked Peter, "Aren't you one of Jesus' disciples?"

"No," he said, "I am not."

¹⁸The guards and the household servants were standing around a charcoal fire they had made because it was cold. And Peter stood there with them, warming himself.

¹⁹Inside, the high priest began asking Jesus about his followers and what he had been teaching them. ²⁰Jesus replied, "What I teach is widely known, because I have preached regularly in the synagogues and the

18:5 Greek *I am*; also in 18:6, 8. 18:9 See John 6:39 and 17:12.

Temple. I have been heard by people* everywhere, and I teach nothing in private that I have not said in public. ²¹Why are you asking me this question? Ask those who heard me. They know what I said."

²²One of the Temple guards standing there struck Jesus on the face. "Is that the way to answer the high priest?" he demanded.

²³Jesus replied, "If I said anything wrong, you must give evidence for it. Should you hit a man for telling the truth?"

²⁴Then Annas bound Jesus and sent him to Caiaphas, the high priest.

The soldiers fell to the ground when Jesus identified himself. They were frightened of him and powerless to arrest him. In order for the soldiers to arrest Jesus, he had to willingly give himself up. This fact should encourage everyone who follows Jesus. No one is more powerful than he is. He can easily defeat those who do evil. Trust Jesus to handle the bad people in this world.

Who can rescue us from our trials?
So you see, the Lord knows how to rescue godly people from their trials, even while punishing the wicked right up until the day of judgment.
2 Peter 2:9

18:20 Greek *Jewish people;* also in 18:38.

S E P T E M B E R

The high priest questioned Jesus. What did Jesus say to make him angry?

MATTHEW 26:57-68
Jesus on Trial

⁵⁷Then the people who had arrested Jesus led him to the home of Caiaphas, the high priest, where the teachers of religious law and other leaders had gathered. ⁵⁸Meanwhile, Peter was following far behind and eventually came to the courtyard of the high priest's house. He went in, sat with the guards, and waited to see what was going to happen to Jesus.

⁵⁹Inside, the leading priests and the entire high council* were trying to find witnesses who would lie about Jesus, so they could put him to death. ⁶⁰But even though they found many who agreed to give false witness, there was no testimony they could use. Finally, two men were found ⁶¹who declared, "This man said, 'I am able to destroy the Temple of God and rebuild it in three days.' "

⁶²Then the high priest stood up and said to Jesus, "Well, aren't you going to answer these charges? What do you

26:59 Greek *the Sanhedrin.*

have to say for yourself?" [63]But Jesus remained silent. Then the high priest said to him, "I demand in the name of the living God that you tell us whether you are the Messiah, the Son of God."

[64]Jesus replied, "Yes, it is as you say. And in the future you will see me, the Son of Man, sitting at God's right hand in the place of power and coming back on the clouds of heaven."*

[65]Then the high priest tore his clothing to show his horror, shouting, "Blasphemy! Why do we need other witnesses? You have all heard his blasphemy. [66]What is your verdict?"

"Guilty!" they shouted. "He must die!"

[67]Then they spit in Jesus' face and hit him with their fists. And some slapped him, [68]saying, "Prophesy to us, you Messiah! Who hit you that time?"

Jesus said that he was God's Son. This angered the high priest because Jesus' statement implied that he was God. That was considered blasphemy, or an insult to God, in Jewish law. But Jesus' answer wasn't blasphemy. He is God's Son. For those people who didn't believe him then and for those who don't believe him now, there will be a rude awakening on judgment day.

What did God say about his Son, Jesus?
Then a voice from the cloud said, "This is my Son, my Chosen One.* Listen to him."
Luke 9:35

26:64 See Ps 110:1; Dan 7:13. **9:35** Some manuscripts read *This is my beloved Son.*

S E P T E M B E R

Peter denied ever knowing Jesus. What did he do after the rooster crowed?

MATTHEW 26:69-75
Peter's Denial
[69]Meanwhile, as Peter was sitting outside in the courtyard, a servant girl came over and said to him, "You were one of those with Jesus the Galilean."

[70]But Peter denied it in front of everyone. "I don't know what you are talking about," he said.

[71]Later, out by the gate, another servant girl noticed him and said to those standing around, "This man was with Jesus of Nazareth."

[72]Again Peter denied it, this time with an oath. "I don't even know the man," he said.

[73]A little later some other bystanders came over to him and said, "You must

be one of them; we can tell by your Galilean accent."

⁷⁴Peter said, "I swear by God, I don't know the man." And immediately the rooster crowed. ⁷⁵Suddenly, Jesus' words flashed through Peter's mind: "Before the rooster crows, you will deny me three times." And he went away, crying bitterly.

When the rooster crowed, Peter remembered Jesus' words and began to weep. He was ashamed that he had denied knowing Jesus. There may be times in our own life when we deny knowing Jesus by our actions or words. When we realize what we have done, we are often ashamed and sorry. We can be thankful that Jesus forgives us for denying him.

How have many people treated Jesus?
He was despised and rejected. . . . We turned our backs on him and looked the other way when he went by. He was despised, and we did not care.
Isaiah 53:3

S E P T E M B E R

Jesus was brought before Herod. How did Jesus respond to Herod's questions?

LUKE 23:1-12
Herod Questions Jesus
Then the entire council took Jesus over to Pilate, the Roman governor. ²They began at once to state their case: "This man has been leading our people to ruin by telling them not to pay their taxes to the Roman government and by claiming he is the Messiah, a king."

³So Pilate asked him, "Are you the King of the Jews?"

Jesus replied, "Yes, it is as you say."

⁴Pilate turned to the leading priests and to the crowd and said, "I find nothing wrong with this man!"

⁵Then they became desperate. "But he is causing riots everywhere he goes, all over Judea, from Galilee to Jerusalem!"

⁶"Oh, is he a Galilean?" Pilate asked. ⁷When they answered that he was, Pilate sent him to Herod Antipas, because Galilee was under Herod's jurisdiction, and Herod happened to be in Jerusalem at the time.

⁸Herod was delighted at the opportunity to see Jesus, because he had heard about him and had been hoping for a long time to see him perform a miracle. ⁹He asked Jesus question

after question, but Jesus refused to answer. [10]Meanwhile, the leading priests and the teachers of religious law stood there shouting their accusations. [11]Now Herod and his soldiers began mocking and ridiculing Jesus. Then they put a royal robe on him and sent him back to Pilate. [12]Herod and Pilate, who had been enemies before, became friends that day.

Jesus was silent. He did not answer Herod's questions because Herod only wanted to make fun of the truth. Herod's example proves that some people do not want the truth. When they are given it, they will only mock it. Like Jesus, we need to know when people are interested in the truth and when they only want to make fun of it. When you come across people who don't care about truth, it is usually better not to answer their questions at all.

Whose life is full of joy?
Oh, the joys of those who do not
follow the advice of the wicked,
or stand around with sinners,
or join in with scoffers.
Psalm 1:1

S E P T E M B E R

Pilate gave in to the demands of the crowd. What did he do for them?

MARK 15:6-24

Sentenced to Death

[6]Now it was the governor's custom to release one prisoner each year at Passover time—anyone the people requested. [7]One of the prisoners at that time was Barabbas, convicted along with others for murder during an insurrection. [8]The mob began to crowd in toward Pilate, asking him to release a prisoner as usual. [9]"Should I give you the King of the Jews?" Pilate asked. [10](For he realized by now that the lead-ing priests had arrested Jesus out of envy.) [11]But at this point the leading priests stirred up the mob to demand the release of Barabbas instead of Jesus. [12]"But if I release Barabbas," Pilate asked them, "what should I do with this man you call the King of the Jews?"

[13]They shouted back, "Crucify him!"

[14]"Why?" Pilate demanded. "What crime has he committed?"

But the crowd only roared the louder, "Crucify him!"

¹⁵So Pilate, anxious to please the crowd, released Barabbas to them. He ordered Jesus flogged with a lead-tipped whip, then turned him over to the Roman soldiers to crucify him.

¹⁶The soldiers took him into their headquarters* and called out the entire battalion. ¹⁷They dressed him in a purple robe and made a crown of long, sharp thorns and put it on his head. ¹⁸Then they saluted, yelling, "Hail! King of the Jews!" ¹⁹And they beat him on the head with a stick, spit on him, and dropped to their knees in mock worship. ²⁰When they were finally tired of mocking him, they took off the purple robe and put his own clothes on him again. Then they led him away to be crucified.

²¹A man named Simon, who was from Cyrene,* was coming in from the country just then, and they forced him to carry Jesus' cross. (Simon is the father of Alexander and Rufus.) ²²And they brought Jesus to a place called Golgotha (which means Skull Hill). ²³They offered him wine drugged with myrrh, but he refused it. ²⁴Then they nailed him to the cross. They gambled for his clothes, throwing dice* to decide who would get them.

Pilate knew that Jesus was innocent. Yet he gave in to the crowd's demands. Do not give in to those who urge you to do wrong. Instead, look for friends who will encourage you to do good.

What should you do when others urge you to do something wrong?
Do not join a crowd that intends to do evil. When you are on the witness stand, do not be swayed in your testimony by the opinion of the majority.
Exodus 23:2

15:16 Greek *the courtyard, which is the praetorium.* **15:21** *Cyrene* was a city in northern Africa. **15:24** Greek *casting lots.* See Ps 22:18.

S E P T E M B E R

Jesus hung on a cross between two criminals.
What did the criminals say to Jesus as he was dying?

LUKE 23:32-49
Jesus Crucified
³²Two others, both criminals, were led out to be executed with him. ³³Finally, they came to a place called The Skull.* All three were crucified there—Jesus on the center cross, and the two criminals on either side.

³⁴Jesus said, "Father, forgive these people, because they don't know what they are doing."* And the soldiers gambled for his clothes by throwing dice.*

23:33 Sometimes rendered *Calvary,* which comes from the Latin word for "skull." **23:34a** This sentence is not included in many ancient manuscripts. **23:34b** Greek *by casting lots.* See Ps 22:18.

35The crowd watched, and the leaders laughed and scoffed. "He saved others," they said, "let him save himself if he is really God's Chosen One, the Messiah." 36The soldiers mocked him, too, by offering him a drink of sour wine. 37They called out to him, "If you are the King of the Jews, save yourself!" 38A signboard was nailed to the cross above him with these words: "This is the King of the Jews."

39One of the criminals hanging beside him scoffed, "So you're the Messiah, are you? Prove it by saving yourself—and us, too, while you're at it!"

40But the other criminal protested, "Don't you fear God even when you are dying? 41We deserve to die for our evil deeds, but this man hasn't done anything wrong." 42Then he said, "Jesus, remember me when you come into your Kingdom."

43And Jesus replied, "I assure you, today you will be with me in paradise."

44By this time it was noon, and darkness fell across the whole land until three o'clock. 45The light from the sun was gone. And suddenly, the thick veil hanging in the Temple was torn apart. 46Then Jesus shouted, "Father, I entrust my spirit into your hands!"* And with those words he breathed his last.

47When the captain of the Roman soldiers handling the executions saw what had happened, he praised God and said, "Surely this man was innocent.*" 48And when the crowd that came to see the crucifixion saw all that had happened, they went home in deep sorrow.* 49But Jesus' friends, including the women who had followed him from Galilee, stood at a distance watching.

One criminal mocked Jesus, telling Jesus to save himself and them. But the other criminal repented of his sins and asked Jesus to remember him in heaven. Jesus told the second criminal that he would be in heaven that same day. As this second criminal's actions show, it is almost never too late to believe in Jesus. The only time it is too late is after you die. While you are living, trust in Jesus as your Savior. He wants to forgive you and is waiting for you to call on him.

How do we know that if we believe in Jesus, we will have eternal life?

For God so loved the world that he gave his only Son, so that everyone who believes in him will not perish but have eternal life.
John 3:16

23:46 Ps 31:5. 23:47 Or righteous. 23:48 Greek beating their breasts.

According to Jewish law, Jesus had to be buried before the sun set on Friday, which was the start of the Sabbath. Who buried Jesus?

MATTHEW 27:57-66

In the Tomb

[57] As evening approached, Joseph, a rich man from Arimathea who was one of Jesus' followers, [58] went to Pilate and asked for Jesus' body. And Pilate issued an order to release it to him. [59] Joseph took the body and wrapped it in a long linen cloth. [60] He placed it in his own new tomb, which had been carved out of the rock. Then he rolled a great stone across the entrance as he left. [61] Both Mary Magdalene and the other Mary were sitting nearby watching.

[62] The next day—on the first day of the Passover ceremonies*—the leading priests and Pharisees went to see Pilate. [63] They told him, "Sir, we remember what that deceiver once said while he was still alive: 'After three days I will be raised from the dead.' [64] So we request that you seal the tomb until the third day. This will prevent his disciples from coming and stealing his body and then telling everyone he came back to life! If that happens, we'll be worse off than we were at first."

[65] Pilate replied, "Take guards and secure it the best you can." [66] So they sealed the tomb and posted guards to protect it.

Joseph of Arimathea took a big risk when he placed Jesus in his own grave. The religious leaders could have punished him for his loyalty to Jesus. But Joseph was willing to take that risk. He was not ashamed of his belief in Jesus. Like Joseph, we should not be ashamed to identify ourselves as followers of Jesus. He is our king and God. Let people know that you serve him.

What should we be willing to risk for Jesus?

Then Nebuchadnezzar said, "Praise to the God of Shadrach, Meshach, and Abednego! He sent his angel to rescue his servants who trusted in him. They defied the king's command and were willing to die rather than serve or worship any god except their own God."
Daniel 3:28

27:62 Or *On the next day, which is after the Preparation.*

The stone to Jesus' tomb had been rolled away. What happened to Jesus?

JOHN 20:1-18

Jesus Is Alive!

Early Sunday morning,* while it was still dark, Mary Magdalene came to the tomb and found that the stone had been rolled away from the entrance. ²She ran and found Simon Peter and the other disciple, the one whom Jesus loved. She said, "They have taken the Lord's body out of the tomb, and I don't know where they have put him!"

³ Peter and the other disciple ran to the tomb to see. ⁴The other disciple outran Peter and got there first. ⁵He stooped and looked in and saw the linen cloth lying there, but he didn't go in. ⁶Then Simon Peter arrived and went inside. He also noticed the linen wrappings lying there, ⁷while the cloth that had covered Jesus' head was folded up and lying to the side. ⁸Then the other disciple also went in, and he saw and believed—⁹for until then they hadn't realized that the Scriptures said he would rise from the dead. ¹⁰Then they went home.

¹¹Mary was standing outside the tomb crying, and as she wept, she stooped and looked in. ¹² She saw two white-robed angels sitting at the head and foot of the place where the body of Jesus had been lying. ¹³"Why are you crying?" the angels asked her.

"Because they have taken away my Lord," she replied, "and I don't know where they have put him."

¹⁴She glanced over her shoulder and saw someone standing behind her. It was Jesus, but she didn't recognize him. ¹⁵"Why are you crying?" Jesus asked her. "Who are you looking for?"

She thought he was the gardener. "Sir," she said, "if you have taken him away, tell me where you have put him, and I will go and get him."

¹⁶"Mary!" Jesus said.

She turned toward him and exclaimed, "Teacher!"*

¹⁷"Don't cling to me," Jesus said, "for I haven't yet ascended to the

Jesus came back to life! Death could not hold him down. He kept his promise that he would rise from the grave. Believe in the living Jesus. He alone is worthy of your belief and trust.

What did God do for his Son, Jesus?

For you will not leave my soul among the dead* or allow your godly one* to rot in the grave.
Psalm 16:10

20:1 Greek *On the first day of the week.* **20:16** Greek *and said in Hebrew, "Rabboni," which means "Teacher."* **16:10a** Hebrew *in Sheol.* **16:10b** Or *your Holy One.*

Father. But go find my brothers and tell them that I am ascending to my Father and your Father, my God and your God."

[18]Mary Magdalene found the disciples and told them, "I have seen the Lord!" Then she gave them his message.

S E P T E M B E R

Jesus was alive, and the religious leaders were not happy about it. What did they do?

MATTHEW 28:1-15

The Guards' Lie

Early on Sunday morning,[*] as the new day was dawning, Mary Magdalene and the other Mary went out to see the tomb. [2]Suddenly there was a great earthquake, because an angel of the Lord came down from heaven and rolled aside the stone and sat on it. [3]His face shone like lightning, and his clothing was as white as snow. [4]The guards shook with fear when they saw him, and they fell into a dead faint.

[5]Then the angel spoke to the women. "Don't be afraid!" he said. "I know you are looking for Jesus, who was crucified. [6]He isn't here! He has been raised from the dead, just as he said would happen. Come, see where his body was lying. [7]And now, go quickly and tell his disciples he has been raised from the dead, and he is going ahead of you to Galilee. You will see him there. Remember, I have told you."

[8]The women ran quickly from the tomb. They were very frightened but also filled with great joy, and they rushed to find the disciples to give

The religious leaders came up with a lie and paid the guards to spread it. The religious leaders couldn't accept the truth about Jesus, even though the guards were eyewitnesses to the greatest miracle ever. Even today, there are people who refuse to believe that Jesus is God's Son. Some of those people even spread false information about Jesus' life and death. But those people are wrong. Jesus is God's Son, and he rose from the dead. He is alive today in heaven, and he wants you to believe and trust in him.

As Christians, what do we need to be aware of?

But there were also false prophets in Israel, just as there will be false teachers among you. They will cleverly teach their destructive heresies about God and even turn against their Master who bought them. Theirs will be a swift and terrible end.

2 Peter 2:1

28:1 Greek *After the Sabbath, on the first day of the week.*

333

them the angel's message. [9]And as they went, Jesus met them. "Greetings!" he said. And they ran to him, held his feet, and worshiped him. [10]Then Jesus said to them, "Don't be afraid! Go tell my brothers to leave for Galilee, and they will see me there."

[11]As the women were on their way into the city, some of the men who had been guarding the tomb went to the leading priests and told them what had happened. [12]A meeting of all the religious leaders was called, and they decided to bribe the soldiers. [13]They told the soldiers, "You must say, 'Jesus' disciples came during the night while we were sleeping, and they stole his body.' [14]If the governor hears about it, we'll stand up for you and everything will be all right." [15]So the guards accepted the bribe and said what they were told to say. Their story spread widely among the Jews, and they still tell it today.

S E P T E M B E R

28

*Jesus appeared to two of his followers on a road.
What were his followers slow to do?*

LUKE 24:13-35
The Walk to Emmaus
[13]That same day two of Jesus' followers were walking to the village of Emmaus, seven miles* out of Jerusalem. [14]As they walked along they were talking about everything that had happened. [15]Suddenly, Jesus himself came along and joined them and began walking beside them. [16]But they didn't know who he was, because God kept them from recognizing him.

[17]"You seem to be in a deep discussion about something," he said. "What are you so concerned about?"

They stopped short, sadness written across their faces. [18]Then one of them, Cleopas, replied, "You must be the only person in Jerusalem who hasn't heard about all the things that have happened there the last few days."

[19]"What things?" Jesus asked.

"The things that happened to Jesus, the man from Nazareth," they said. "He was a prophet who did wonderful miracles. He was a mighty teacher, highly regarded by both God and all the people. [20]But our leading priests and other religious leaders arrested him and handed him over to be condemned to death, and they crucified him. [21]We had thought he was the Messiah who had come to rescue Israel. That all happened three days ago. [22]Then some women from our group of his followers were at his tomb early this morning, and they came back with an amazing report. [23]They said his body was missing, and they had

24:13 Greek *60 stadia* [11.1 kilometers].

334

seen angels who told them Jesus is alive! 24Some of our men ran out to see, and sure enough, Jesus' body was gone, just as the women had said."

25Then Jesus said to them, "You are such foolish people! You find it so hard to believe all that the prophets wrote in the Scriptures. 26Wasn't it clearly predicted by the prophets that the Messiah would have to suffer all these things before entering his time of glory?" 27Then Jesus quoted passages from the writings of Moses and all the prophets, explaining what all the Scriptures said about himself.

28By this time they were nearing Emmaus and the end of their journey. Jesus would have gone on, 29but they begged him to stay the night with them, since it was getting late. So he went home with them. 30As they sat down to eat, he took a small loaf of bread, asked God's blessing on it, broke it, then gave it to them. 31Suddenly, their eyes were opened, and they recognized him. And at that moment he disappeared!

32They said to each other, "Didn't our hearts feel strangely warm as he talked with us on the road and explained the Scriptures to us?" 33And within the hour they were on their way back to Jerusalem, where the eleven disciples and the other followers of Jesus were gathered. When they arrived, they were greeted with the report, 34"The Lord has really risen! He appeared to Peter*!"

35Then the two from Emmaus told their story of how Jesus had appeared to them as they were walking along the road and how they had recognized him as he was breaking the bread.

Jesus' followers were slow to understand the reason why he came. The two on the road even began to doubt that Jesus was God's Son because he died on the cross. So Jesus used the Scriptures to teach his followers who he was. Today we have the same Scriptures that Jesus used to teach his followers. These Scriptures are in the Bible. We can study the Bible to learn more about Jesus. Make an effort to get to know him personally. Read your Bible every day.

What can we learn from God's Word?
I believe in your commands; now teach me good judgment and knowledge.
Psalm 119:66

24:34 Greek *Simon.*

Thomas didn't believe that Jesus was alive. What changed his mind?

JOHN 20:19-31

Thomas's Unbelief

[19]That evening, on the first day of the week, the disciples were meeting behind locked doors because they were afraid of the Jewish leaders. Suddenly, Jesus was standing there among them! "Peace be with you," he said. [20]As he spoke, he held out his hands for them to see, and he showed them his side. They were filled with joy when they saw their Lord! [21]He spoke to them again and said, "Peace be with you. As the Father has sent me, so I send you." [22]Then he breathed on them and said to them, "Receive the Holy Spirit. [23]If you forgive anyone's sins, they are forgiven. If you refuse to forgive them, they are unforgiven."

[24]One of the disciples, Thomas (nicknamed the Twin*), was not with the others when Jesus came. [25]They told him, "We have seen the Lord!" But he replied, "I won't believe it unless I see the nail wounds in his hands, put my fingers into them, and place my hand into the wound in his side."

[26]Eight days later the disciples were together again, and this time Thomas was with them. The doors were locked; but suddenly, as before, Jesus was standing among them. He said, "Peace be with you." [27]Then he said to Thomas, "Put your finger here and see

my hands. Put your hand into the wound in my side. Don't be faithless any longer. Believe!"

[28]"My Lord and my God!" Thomas exclaimed.

[29]Then Jesus told him, "You believe

Jesus appeared to Thomas personally. He even fulfilled Thomas's words by having him touch the wounds in his hands and side. This was important because Jesus had not been physically present when Thomas had spoken those words. After this experience, Thomas believed that Jesus was God. Many people today are like Thomas. They want to see Jesus personally before they believe in him. But Jesus said that he is pleased with those people who believe in him even though they haven't seen him. Do you believe in Jesus? If so, your faith pleases Jesus. Keep believing in him. You will not be disappointed when he comes back.

Why is doubting God or Jesus an insult to him?

And the LORD said to Moses, "How long will these people reject me? Will they never believe me, even after all the miraculous signs I have done among them?"
Numbers 14:11

20:24 Greek *the one who was called Didymus.*

because you have seen me. Blessed are those who haven't seen me and believe anyway."

[30]Jesus' disciples saw him do many other miraculous signs besides the ones recorded in this book. [31]But these are written so that you may believe* that Jesus is the Messiah, the Son of God, and that by believing in him you will have life.

20:31 Some manuscripts read *may continue to believe.*

S E P T E M B E R

Jesus asked Peter some painful questions. How did Peter respond?

JOHN 21:15-25

Do You Love Me?

[15]After breakfast Jesus said to Simon Peter, "Simon son of John, do you love me more than these?"

"Yes, Lord," Peter replied, "you know I love you."

"Then feed my lambs," Jesus told him.

[16]Jesus repeated the question: "Simon son of John, do you love me?"

"Yes, Lord," Peter said, "you know I love you."

"Then take care of my sheep," Jesus said.

[17]Once more he asked him, "Simon son of John, do you love me?"

Peter was grieved that Jesus asked the question a third time. He said, "Lord, you know everything. You know I love you."

Jesus said, "Then feed my sheep. [18]The truth is, when you were young, you were able to do as you liked and go wherever you wanted to. But when you are old, you will stretch out your hands, and others will direct you and take you where you don't want to go."

Jesus asked Peter one tough question three times: Do you love me more than anything else? Peter told Jesus that he loved him, but Peter was hurt because Jesus asked him three times. Jesus didn't mean to hurt Peter's feelings. But his questions show us how important it is to love Jesus more than anything or anyone else. Loving Jesus means putting him ahead of everything and everyone else in your life.

What does God require of us?

And now, Israel, what does the LORD your God require of you? He requires you to fear him, to live according to his will, to love and worship him with all your heart and soul.
Deuteronomy 10:12

[19]Jesus said this to let him know what kind of death he would die to glorify God. Then Jesus told him, "Follow me."

[20]Peter turned around and saw the disciple Jesus loved following them—

337

the one who had leaned over to Jesus during supper and asked, "Lord, who among us will betray you?" ²¹Peter asked Jesus, "What about him, Lord?"

²²Jesus replied, "If I want him to remain alive until I return, what is that to you? You follow me." ²³So the rumor spread among the community of believers* that that disciple wouldn't die. But that isn't what Jesus said at all. He only said, "If I want him to remain alive until I return, what is that to you?"

²⁴This is that disciple who saw these events and recorded them here. And we all know that his account of these things is accurate.

²⁵And I suppose that if all the other things Jesus did were written down, the whole world could not contain the books.

21:23 Greek *the brothers.*

Jesus gave his disciples a mission to accomplish. What did he tell them to do?

MATTHEW 28:8-10, 16-20

The Mission

[8]The women ran quickly from the tomb. They were very frightened but also filled with great joy, and they rushed to find the disciples to give them the angel's message. [9]And as they went, Jesus met them. "Greetings!" he said. And they ran to him, held his feet, and worshiped him. [10]Then Jesus said to them, "Don't be afraid! Go tell my brothers to leave for Galilee, and they will see me there."

• • •

[16]Then the eleven disciples left for Galilee, going to the mountain where Jesus had told them to go. [17]When they saw him, they worshiped him—but some of them still doubted! [18]Jesus came and told his disciples, "I have been given complete authority in heaven and on earth. [19]Therefore, go and make disciples of all the nations, baptizing them in the name of the Father and the Son and the Holy Spirit. [20]Teach these new disciples to obey all the commands I have given you. And be sure of this: I am with you always, even to the end of the age."

Jesus told his disciples to go and tell others about him. In addition, they were to baptize those who trusted in Jesus as their Savior and teach them to obey all of Jesus' commands. This mission was not just given to his disciples back then. It also applies to all of those who trust Jesus as their Savior today. If Jesus is your Savior, obey his command and tell your friends about Jesus' love for them.

Why is it important to tell people about Jesus?

Tell all the people, "This is what the LORD says: Take your choice of life or death!"
Jeremiah 21:8

Jesus was returning to heaven. What did he promise his followers before he disappeared from their sight?

ACTS 1:1-11

Jesus Returns Home

Dear Theophilus:

In my first book* I told you about everything Jesus began to do and teach ²until the day he ascended to heaven after giving his chosen apostles further instructions from the Holy Spirit. ³During the forty days after his crucifixion, he appeared to the apostles from time to time and proved to them in many ways that he was actually alive. On these occasions he talked to them about the Kingdom of God.

⁴In one of these meetings as he was eating a meal with them, he told them, "Do not leave Jerusalem until the Father sends you what he promised. Remember, I have told you about this before. ⁵John baptized with* water, but in just a few days you will be baptized with the Holy Spirit."

⁶When the apostles were with Jesus, they kept asking him, "Lord, are you going to free Israel now and restore our kingdom?"

⁷"The Father sets those dates," he replied, "and they are not for you to know. ⁸But when the Holy Spirit has come upon you, you will receive power and will tell people about me everywhere—in Jerusalem, throughout Judea, in Samaria, and to the ends of the earth."

⁹It was not long after he said this that he was taken up into the sky while they were watching, and he disappeared into a cloud. ¹⁰As they were straining their eyes to see him, two white-robed men suddenly stood there among them. ¹¹They said, "Men of Galilee, why are you standing here staring at the sky? Jesus has been taken away from you into heaven. And someday, just as you saw him go, he will return!"

Jesus promised to send the Holy Spirit to help his followers. The Holy Spirit would give power to Jesus' followers so that they would tell others about Jesus. If you are one of Jesus' followers, the Holy Spirit will help you, too. He can give you the courage you need to tell others about Jesus. Ask Jesus to fill you with his Spirit. You will be amazed at how God can work through you.

How do we receive the Holy Spirit?

And God has actually given us his Spirit (not the world's spirit) so we can know the wonderful things God has freely given us.
1 Corinthians 2:12

1:1 The reference is to the book of Luke. **1:5** Or *in*; also in 1:5b.

O C T O B E R

*Jesus' followers were meeting together one day.
What happened to them during the meeting?*

ACTS 2:1-13

Tongues of Fire

On the day of Pentecost, seven weeks after Jesus' resurrection,* the believers were meeting together in one place. ²Suddenly, there was a sound from heaven like the roaring of a mighty windstorm in the skies above them, and it filled the house where they were meeting. ³Then, what looked like flames or tongues of fire appeared and settled on each of them. ⁴And everyone present was filled with the Holy Spirit and began speaking in other languages,* as the Holy Spirit gave them this ability.

⁵Godly Jews from many nations were living in Jerusalem at that time. ⁶When they heard this sound, they came running to see what it was all about, and they were bewildered to hear their own languages being spoken by the believers.

⁷They were beside themselves with wonder. "How can this be?" they exclaimed. "These people are all from Galilee, ⁸and yet we hear them speaking the languages of the lands where we were born! ⁹Here we are—Parthians, Medes, Elamites, people from Mesopotamia, Judea, Cappadocia, Pontus, the province of Asia, ¹⁰Phrygia, Pamphylia, Egypt, and the areas of Libya toward Cyrene, visitors from Rome (both Jews and converts to Judaism), ¹¹Cretans, and Arabians. And we all hear these people speaking in our own languages about the wonderful things God has done!" ¹²They stood there amazed and perplexed. "What can this mean?" they asked each other. ¹³But others in the crowd were mocking. "They're drunk, that's all!" they said.

Jesus' followers were filled with the Holy Spirit. The Spirit enabled them to speak about Jesus in languages they didn't know. God's Spirit worked in an amazing way that day so more people would hear the good news about Jesus. Today, God's Spirit can still work in some amazing ways. But to see his mighty work, we need to be willing to obey him, to put his will before our own, and to believe he is able to do things we cannot.

What did God promise to do after Jesus returned to heaven?

In those days, I will pour out my Spirit even on servants, men and women alike.
Joel 2:29

2:1 Greek *When the day of Pentecost arrived.* This annual celebration came 50 days after the Passover ceremonies. See Lev 23:16. **2:4** Or *in other tongues.*

OCTOBER

Some people said that Jesus' followers were drunk.
How did Peter respond to this charge?

ACTS 2:14-40
Peter Preaches

14Then Peter stepped forward with the eleven other apostles and shouted to the crowd, "Listen carefully, all of you, fellow Jews and residents of Jerusalem! Make no mistake about this. 15Some of you are saying these people are drunk. It isn't true! It's much too early for that. People don't get drunk by nine o'clock in the morning. 16No, what you see this morning was predicted centuries ago by the prophet Joel:

17 'In the last days, God said,
  I will pour out my Spirit upon
    all people.
Your sons and daughters will
    prophesy,
  your young men will see visions,
  and your old men will dream
    dreams.
18 In those days I will pour out my
    Spirit
  upon all my servants, men and
    women alike,
  and they will prophesy.
19 And I will cause wonders in the
    heavens above
  and signs on the earth below—
  blood and fire and clouds of
    smoke.

20 The sun will be turned into
    darkness,
  and the moon will turn
    bloodred,
  before that great and glorious
    day of the Lord arrives.
21 And anyone who calls on the
    name of the Lord
  will be saved.'*

22 "People of Israel, listen! God publicly endorsed Jesus of Nazareth by doing wonderful miracles, wonders, and signs through him, as you well know. 23But you followed God's prearranged plan. With the help of lawless Gentiles, you nailed him to the cross and murdered him. 24However, God released him from the horrors of death and raised him back to life again, for death could not keep him in its grip. 25King David said this about him:

'I know the Lord is always with me.
  I will not be shaken, for he is
    right beside me.
26 No wonder my heart is filled with
    joy,
  and my mouth shouts his
    praises!
  My body rests in hope.
27 For you will not leave my soul
    among the dead*

2:17-21 Joel 2:28-32. 2:27 Greek *in Hades;* also in 2:31.

342

or allow your Holy One to rot
in the grave.
²⁸ You have shown me the way of life,
and you will give me wonderful
joy in your presence.'*

²⁹"Dear brothers, think about this! David wasn't referring to himself when he spoke these words I have quoted, for he died and was buried, and his tomb is still here among us. ³⁰But he was a prophet, and he knew God had promised with an oath that one of David's own descendants would sit on David's throne as the Messiah. ³¹David was looking into the future and predicting the Messiah's resurrection. He was saying that the Messiah would not be left among the dead and that his body would not rot in the grave.

³²"This prophecy was speaking of Jesus, whom God raised from the dead, and we all are witnesses of this. ³³Now he sits on the throne of highest honor in heaven, at God's right hand. And the Father, as he had promised, gave him the Holy Spirit to pour out upon us, just as you see and hear today. ³⁴For David himself never ascended into heaven, yet he said,

'The LORD said to my Lord,
Sit in honor at my right hand
³⁵   until I humble your enemies,
making them a footstool under
your feet.'*

³⁶So let it be clearly known by everyone in Israel that God has made this Jesus whom you crucified to be both Lord and Messiah!"

³⁷Peter's words convicted them deeply, and they said to him and to the other apostles, "Brothers, what should we do?"

³⁸Peter replied, "Each of you must turn from your sins and turn to God, and be baptized in the name of Jesus Christ for the forgiveness of your sins. Then you will receive the gift of the Holy Spirit. ³⁹This promise is to you and to your children, and even to the Gentiles*—all who have been called by the Lord our God." ⁴⁰Then Peter continued preaching for a long time, strongly urging all his listeners, "Save yourselves from this generation that has gone astray!"

Peter told the crowd that Jesus' followers were not drunk but were filled with God's Spirit. Then he told the crowd about Jesus. You may or may not have the opportunity to stand before a crowd and tell them about Jesus. But you will probably have the chance to tell your friends, neighbors, and family members about Jesus. When you do, follow Peter's example and boldly tell them why Jesus came and died.

What has Jesus done for us?
Then I will sprinkle clean water on you, and you will be clean. Your filth will be washed away, and you will no longer worship idols. And I will give you a new heart with new and right desires, and I will put a new spirit in you. I will take out your stony heart of sin and give you a new, obedient heart.*
Ezekiel 36:25-26

2:25-28 Ps 16:8-11. 2:34-35 Ps 110:1. 2:39 Greek to those far away. 36:26 Hebrew a heart of flesh.

O C T O B E R

A beggar asked Peter and John for money. What did Peter give him instead?

ACTS 2:41–3:11
A Beggar Is Healed

⁴¹Those who believed what Peter said were baptized and added to the church—about three thousand in all. ⁴²They joined with the other believers and devoted themselves to the apostles' teaching and fellowship, sharing in the Lord's Supper and in prayer.

⁴³A deep sense of awe came over them all, and the apostles performed many miraculous signs and wonders. ⁴⁴And all the believers met together constantly and shared everything they had. ⁴⁵They sold their possessions and shared the proceeds with those in need. ⁴⁶They worshiped together at the Temple each day, met in homes for the Lord's Supper, and shared their meals with great joy and generosity—⁴⁷all the while praising God and enjoying the goodwill of all the people. And each day the Lord added to their group those who were being saved.

³:¹Peter and John went to the Temple one afternoon to take part in the three o'clock prayer service. ²As they approached the Temple, a man lame from birth was being carried in. Each day he was put beside the Temple gate, the one called the Beautiful Gate, so he could beg from the people going into the Temple. ³When he saw Peter and John about to enter, he asked them for some money.

⁴Peter and John looked at him intently, and Peter said, "Look at us!" ⁵The lame man looked at them eagerly, expecting a gift. ⁶But Peter said, "I don't have any money for you. But I'll give you what I have. In the name of Jesus Christ of Nazareth, get up and walk!"

⁷Then Peter took the lame man by the right hand and helped him up. And as he did, the man's feet and anklebones were healed and strengthened. ⁸He jumped up, stood on his feet, and began to walk! Then, walking, leaping,

By the power of God's Spirit, Peter gave the man the ability to walk again. When the man realized that he was healed, he praised God for the miracle. Today, we sometimes hear about healings and other miracles done in Jesus' name. We can thank God and praise him for these wonderful displays of his love and power. But whether or not we experience these miracles, praising God is something we should always do. For Jesus has given us enough to praise him for by dying on the cross and rising from the dead.

What can you praise God for?
Sing to the LORD; bless his name.
Each day proclaim the good
news that he saves.
Psalm 96:2

and praising God, he went into the Temple with them.

⁹All the people saw him walking and heard him praising God. ¹⁰When they realized he was the lame beggar they had seen so often at the Beautiful Gate, they were absolutely astounded! ¹¹They all rushed out to Solomon's Colonnade, where he was holding tightly to Peter and John. Everyone stood there in awe of the wonderful thing that had happened.

O C T O B E R

A crowd had seen Peter heal the beggar, and they were amazed.
How did Peter react to the crowd?

ACTS 3:12-26

Peter Preaches at the Temple

¹²Peter saw his opportunity and addressed the crowd. "People of Israel," he said, "what is so astounding about this? And why look at us as though we had made this man walk by our own power and godliness? ¹³For it is the God of Abraham, the God of Isaac, the God of Jacob, the God of all our ancestors who has brought glory to his servant Jesus by doing this. This is the same Jesus whom you handed over and rejected before Pilate, despite Pilate's decision to release him. ¹⁴You rejected this holy, righteous one and instead demanded the release of a murderer. ¹⁵You killed the author of life, but God raised him to life. And we are witnesses of this fact!

¹⁶"The name of Jesus has healed this man—and you know how lame he was before. Faith in Jesus' name has caused this healing before your very eyes.

¹⁷"Friends,* I realize that what you did to Jesus was done in ignorance; and the same can be said of your leaders. ¹⁸But God was fulfilling what all the prophets had declared about the Messiah beforehand—that he must suffer all these things. ¹⁹Now turn from your sins and turn to God, so you can be cleansed of your sins. ²⁰Then wonderful times of refreshment will come from the presence of the Lord, and he will send Jesus your Messiah to you again. ²¹For he must remain in heaven until the time for the final restoration of all things, as God promised long ago through his prophets. ²²Moses said, 'The Lord your God will raise up a Prophet like me from among your own people. Listen carefully to everything he tells you.'* ²³Then Moses said, 'Anyone who will not listen to that Prophet will be cut off from God's people and utterly destroyed.'*

²⁴"Starting with Samuel, every prophet spoke about what is happening today. ²⁵You are the children of

3:17 Greek *Brothers*. **3:22** Deut 18:15. **3:23** Deut 18:19; Lev 23:29.

those prophets, and you are included in the covenant God promised to your ancestors. For God said to Abraham, 'Through your descendants all the families on earth will be blessed.'* 26When God raised up his servant, he sent him first to you people of Israel, to bless you by turning each of you back from your sinful ways."

Peter saw the crowd's reaction. He knew that they thought he was a prophet. It would have been easy for him to take credit for this miracle. But Peter was humble and gave the credit to Jesus, who filled Peter with the power to perform the miracle. Taking the credit for something good that we didn't do is tempting. But it's not right. When people praise you for something you shouldn't take credit for, follow Peter's example and give credit to the person who deserves it.

Who does God honor?
For the LORD delights in his people;
he crowns the humble with salvation.
Psalm 149:4

3:25 Gen 22:18.

O C T O B E R

The Jewish council ordered Peter and John to stop speaking about Jesus. What did Peter and John tell the council?

ACTS 4:5-22
Peter and John

5The next day the council of all the rulers and elders and teachers of religious law met in Jerusalem. 6Annas the high priest was there, along with Caiaphas, John, Alexander, and other relatives of the high priest. 7They brought in the two disciples and demanded, "By what power, or in whose name, have you done this?"

8Then Peter, filled with the Holy Spirit, said to them, "Leaders and elders of our nation, 9are we being questioned because we've done a good deed for a crippled man? Do you want to know how he was healed? 10Let me clearly state to you and to all the people of Israel that he was healed in the name and power of Jesus Christ from Nazareth, the man you crucified, but whom God raised from the dead. 11For Jesus is the one referred to in the Scriptures, where it says,

'The stone that you builders
rejected
has now become the
cornerstone.'*

[12]There is salvation in no one else! There is no other name in all of heaven for people to call on to save them."

[13]The members of the council were amazed when they saw the boldness of Peter and John, for they could see that they were ordinary men who had had no special training. They also recognized them as men who had been with Jesus. [14]But since the man who had been healed was standing right there among them, the council had nothing to say. [15]So they sent Peter and John out of the council chamber* and conferred among themselves.

[16]"What should we do with these men?" they asked each other. "We can't deny they have done a miraculous sign, and everybody in Jerusalem knows about it. [17]But perhaps we can stop them from spreading their propaganda. We'll warn them not to speak to anyone in Jesus' name again." [18]So they called the apostles back in and told them never again to speak or teach about Jesus.

[19]But Peter and John replied, "Do you think God wants us to obey you rather than him? [20]We cannot stop telling about the wonderful things we have seen and heard."

[21]The council then threatened them further, but they finally let them go because they didn't know how to punish them without starting a riot. For everyone was praising God [22]for this miraculous sign—the healing of a man who had been lame for more than forty years.

Peter and John asked the council a simple question: "Do you think God wants us to obey you rather than him?" (Acts 4:19). They then told the council that they couldn't stop telling others about what they had seen. There may be times in your life when someone in authority over you orders you to do something wrong. It is then that you can follow Peter and John's example and obey God first. Obeying God is always the right thing to do.

Who is the only one we should fear?
Serve only the LORD your God and fear him alone. Obey his commands, listen to his voice, and cling to him.
Deuteronomy 13:4

4:11 Ps 118:22. 4:15 Greek *the Sanhedrin*.

The believers prayed that they would speak boldly for Jesus. What happened?

ACTS 4:23-31

Bold Prayer

[23]As soon as they were freed, Peter and John found the other believers and told them what the leading priests and elders had said. [24]Then all the believers were united as they lifted their voices in prayer: "O Sovereign Lord, Creator of heaven and earth, the sea, and everything in them—[25]you spoke long ago by the Holy Spirit through our ancestor King David, your servant, saying,

'Why did the nations rage?
    Why did the people waste their
        time with futile plans?
[26] The kings of the earth prepared for
        battle;
    the rulers gathered together
against the Lord
    and against his Messiah.'*

[27]"That is what has happened here in this city! For Herod Antipas, Pontius Pilate the governor, the Gentiles, and the people of Israel were all united against Jesus, your holy servant, whom you anointed. [28]In fact, everything they did occurred according to your eternal will and plan. [29]And now, O Lord, hear their threats, and give your servants great boldness in their preaching. [30]Send your healing power; may miraculous signs and wonders be done through the name of your holy servant Jesus."

[31]After this prayer, the building where they were meeting shook, and they were all filled with the Holy Spirit. And they preached God's message with boldness.

Soon after the believers prayed, God shook the building they met in and filled them with the Holy Spirit. The believers then preached God's message with boldness. God wants us, like those first believers, to speak boldly about his Son, Jesus. We should not let threats or peer pressure stop us from speaking out for him. When we are threatened, we can pray for boldness and strength to speak out no matter what happens to us.

What should you do when you are afraid to tell others about Jesus?

I have not kept this good news hidden in my heart; I have talked about your faithfulness and saving power. I have told everyone in the great assembly of your unfailing love and faithfulness.
Psalm 40:10

4:25-26 Ps 2:1-2.

OCTOBER

Many believers were giving generously to the church. What did Ananias and Sapphira give?

ACTS 4:34-35; 5:1-11

Dishonest Dealings

[34]There was no poverty among them, because people who owned land or houses sold them [35]and brought the money to the apostles to give to others in need.

• • •

[5:1]There was also a man named Ananias who, with his wife, Sapphira, sold some property. [2]He brought part of the money to the apostles, but he claimed it was the full amount. His wife had agreed to this deception.

[3]Then Peter said, "Ananias, why has Satan filled your heart? You lied to the Holy Spirit, and you kept some of the money for yourself. [4]The property was yours to sell or not sell, as you wished. And after selling it, the money was yours to give away. How could you do a thing like this? You weren't lying to us but to God."

[5]As soon as Ananias heard these words, he fell to the floor and died. Everyone who heard about it was terrified. [6]Then some young men wrapped him in a sheet and took him out and buried him.

[7]About three hours later his wife came in, not knowing what had happened. [8]Peter asked her, "Was this the

Ananias and Sapphira sold some land and gave part of the money to the church. Giving just a part of the money wasn't wrong—saying that they gave the full price for the land was. They thought they could get away with a lie and look good in the eyes of the people. But they couldn't fool the Holy Spirit, and both of them died for lying. Not everyone who lies will be killed like Ananias and Sapphira. But that doesn't mean it's OK to lie. God has commanded us to tell the truth. We should take his commands seriously and obey them.

What has God commanded us concerning lying?
Do not steal. Do not cheat one another. Do not lie.
Leviticus 19:11

price you and your husband received for your land?"

"Yes," she replied, "that was the price."

[9]And Peter said, "How could the two of you even think of doing a thing like this—conspiring together to test the Spirit of the Lord? Just outside that door are the young men who buried your husband, and they will carry you out, too."

¹⁰Instantly, she fell to the floor and died. When the young men came in and saw that she was dead, they carried her out and buried her beside her husband. ¹¹Great fear gripped the entire church and all others who heard what had happened.

O C T O B E R

The high priest and the Jewish council were jealous of the apostles, so they had them arrested. What did Gamaliel say about the apostles' actions?

ACTS 5:12-39

An Arresting Thought

¹²Meanwhile, the apostles were performing many miraculous signs and wonders among the people. And the believers were meeting regularly at the Temple in the area known as Solomon's Colonnade. ¹³No one else dared to join them, though everyone had high regard for them. ¹⁴And more and more people believed and were brought to the Lord—crowds of both men and women. ¹⁵As a result of the apostles' work, sick people were brought out into the streets on beds and mats so that Peter's shadow might fall across some of them as he went by. ¹⁶Crowds came in from the villages around Jerusalem, bringing their sick and those possessed by evil spirits, and they were all healed.

¹⁷The high priest and his friends, who were Sadducees, reacted with violent jealousy. ¹⁸They arrested the apostles and put them in the jail. ¹⁹But an angel of the Lord came at night, opened the gates of the jail, and brought them out. Then he told them,

²⁰"Go to the Temple and give the people this message of life!" ²¹So the apostles entered the Temple about daybreak and immediately began teaching.

When the high priest and his officials arrived, they convened the high council,* along with all the elders of Israel. Then they sent for the apostles to be brought for trial. ²²But when the Temple guards went to the jail, the men were gone. So they returned to the council and reported, ²³"The jail was locked, with the guards standing outside, but when we opened the gates, no one was there!"

²⁴When the captain of the Temple guard and the leading priests heard this, they were perplexed, wondering where it would all end. ²⁵Then someone arrived with the news that the men they had jailed were out in the Temple, teaching the people.

²⁶The captain went with his Temple guards and arrested them, but without violence, for they were afraid the people would kill them if they treated the apostles roughly. ²⁷Then they

5:21 Greek *Sanhedrin;* also in 5:27, 41.

350

brought the apostles in before the council. [28]"Didn't we tell you never again to teach in this man's name?" the high priest demanded. "Instead, you have filled all Jerusalem with your teaching about Jesus, and you intend to blame us for his death!"

[29]But Peter and the apostles replied, "We must obey God rather than human authority. [30]The God of our ancestors raised Jesus from the dead after you killed him by crucifying him. [31]Then God put him in the place of honor at his right hand as Prince and Savior. He did this to give the people of Israel an opportunity to turn from their sins and turn to God so their sins would be forgiven. [32]We are witnesses of these things and so is the Holy Spirit, who is given by God to those who obey him."

[33]At this, the high council was furious and decided to kill them. [34]But one member had a different perspective. He was a Pharisee named Gamaliel, who was an expert on religious law and was very popular with the people. He stood up and ordered that the apostles be sent outside the council chamber for a while. [35]Then he addressed his colleagues as follows: "Men of Israel, take care what you are planning to do to these men! [36]Some time ago there was that fellow Theudas, who pretended to be someone great. About four hundred others joined him, but he was killed, and his followers went their various ways. The whole movement came to nothing.

[37]After him, at the time of the census, there was Judas of Galilee. He got some people to follow him, but he was killed, too, and all his followers were scattered.

[38]"So my advice is, leave these men alone. If they are teaching and doing these things merely on their own, it will soon be overthrown. [39]But if it is of God, you will not be able to stop them. You may even find yourselves fighting against God."

Gamaliel said that if the apostles were acting on their own, then their works would soon come to an end. But if the apostles were acting on God's commands, then the high priest and the Jewish council's attempts to stop them would be useless. That is because the high priest and the Jewish council would be fighting against God. We may not fight against God by opposing those who speak out for Jesus, but we may fight against God in other ways. For example, every time we disobey his Word, we fight against him. In what ways are you fighting against God? Confess your sins to him, and ask for his help to fight with him, not against him.

Why shouldn't we fight against God?

The LORD is a jealous God, filled with vengeance and wrath. He takes revenge on all who oppose him and furiously destroys his enemies!
Nahum 1:2

*Some men debated with Stephen about spiritual matters.
They couldn't win the debate. What did they do to Stephen?*

ACTS 6:8-15

Stephen Is Seized

⁸Stephen, a man full of God's grace and power, performed amazing miracles and signs among the people. ⁹But one day some men from the Synagogue of Freed Slaves, as it was called, started to debate with him. They were Jews from Cyrene, Alexandria, Cilicia, and the province of Asia. ¹⁰None of them was able to stand against the wisdom and Spirit by which Stephen spoke.

¹¹So they persuaded some men to lie about Stephen, saying, "We heard him blaspheme Moses, and even God." ¹²Naturally, this roused the crowds, the elders, and the teachers of religious law. So they arrested Stephen and brought him before the high council.* ¹³The lying witnesses said, "This man is always speaking against the Temple and against the law of Moses. ¹⁴We have heard him say that this Jesus of Nazareth will destroy the Temple and change the customs Moses handed down to us." ¹⁵At this point everyone in the council stared at Stephen because his face became as bright as an angel's.

6:12 Greek *Sanhedrin;* also in 6:15.

These men were angry or jealous that they couldn't beat Stephen in the debate. So they had some people spread lies about him. Their lies got Stephen in trouble with the crowd and the religious leaders. In spreading the lies, these men sinned. They broke God's commandment that says, "Do not testify falsely against your neighbor" (Exodus 20:16). Have you ever spread rumors about someone to whom you lost an argument or a game? Don't be like the men in this story. If you lose to someone, don't let anger or jealousy make you a sore loser.

How should you treat those to whom you lose?

Do for others what you would like them to do for you. This is a summary of all that is taught in the law and the prophets.
Matthew 7:12

OCTOBER

The high priest asked Stephen if what people were saying about him was true.
What did Stephen say in his defense?

ACTS 7:37-53
Stephen Speaks Out

37 "Moses himself told the people of Israel, 'God will raise up a Prophet like me from among your own people.'* 38 Moses was with the assembly of God's people in the wilderness. He was the mediator between the people of Israel and the angel who gave him life-giving words on Mount Sinai to pass on to us.

39 "But our ancestors rejected Moses and wanted to return to Egypt. 40 They told Aaron, 'Make us some gods who can lead us, for we don't know what has become of this Moses, who brought us out of Egypt.' 41 So they made an idol shaped like a calf, and they sacrificed to it and rejoiced in this thing they had made. 42 Then God turned away from them and gave them up to serve the sun, moon, and stars as their gods! In the book of the prophets it is written,

'Was it to me you were bringing
    sacrifices
  during those forty years in the
    wilderness, Israel?
43 No, your real interest was in your
    pagan gods—
  the shrine of Molech,
  the star god Rephan,

and the images you made to
    worship them.
So I will send you into captivity
  far away in Babylon.'*

44 "Our ancestors carried the Tabernacle* with them through the wilderness. It was constructed in exact accordance with the plan shown to Moses by God. 45 Years later, when Joshua led the battles against the Gentile nations that God drove out of this land, the Tabernacle was taken with them into their new territory. And it was used there until the time of King David.

46 "David found favor with God and asked for the privilege of building a permanent Temple for the God of Jacob.* 47 But it was Solomon who actually built it. 48 However, the Most High doesn't live in temples made by human hands. As the prophet says,

49 'Heaven is my throne,
    and the earth is my footstool.
  Could you ever build me a temple
    as good as that?'
  asks the Lord.
  'Could you build a dwelling place
    for me?
50   Didn't I make everything in
    heaven and earth?'*

7:37 Deut 18:15. **7:42-43** Amos 5:25-27. **7:44** Greek *the tent of witness.* **7:46** Some manuscripts read *the house of Jacob.*
7:49-50 Isa 66:1-2.

[51] "You stubborn people! You are heathen at heart and deaf to the truth. Must you forever resist the Holy Spirit? But your ancestors did, and so do you! [52] Name one prophet your ancestors didn't persecute! They even killed the ones who predicted the coming of the Righteous One—the Messiah whom you betrayed and murdered. [53] You deliberately disobeyed God's law, though you received it from the hands of angels.*"

Stephen began reciting Israel's history. As he did this, he brought up many examples of how the Israelites had disobeyed God. Sadly, we Christians are no different. We, like the Israelites, often choose to go our own way rather than obey God. This makes God sad. But we don't have to spend our whole life displeasing God. We can please him by obeying the commands found in his Word, the Bible. When we do that, we will not only make God happy but we will also be happy ourselves because we will have a closer relationship with God.

Why should you obey God?
Your decrees are wonderful.
No wonder I obey them!
Psalm 119:129

7:53 Greek *received the Law as it was ordained by angels.*

O C T O B E R

Stephen said some things that upset the Jewish leaders. What did they do to him?

ACTS 7:54-60
Jewish Leaders Stone Stephen
[54] The Jewish leaders were infuriated by Stephen's accusation, and they shook their fists in rage.* [55] But Stephen, full of the Holy Spirit, gazed steadily upward into heaven and saw the glory of God, and he saw Jesus standing in the place of honor at God's right hand. [56] And he told them, "Look, I see the heavens opened and the Son of Man standing in the place of honor at God's right hand!"

[57] Then they put their hands over their ears, and drowning out his voice with their shouts, they rushed at him.

7:54 Greek *they were grinding their teeth against him.*

⁵⁸They dragged him out of the city and began to stone him. The official witnesses took off their coats and laid them at the feet of a young man named Saul.*

⁵⁹And as they stoned him, Stephen prayed, "Lord Jesus, receive my spirit." ⁶⁰And he fell to his knees, shouting, "Lord, don't charge them with this sin!" And with that, he died.

The Jewish leaders stoned Stephen. As they did this, Stephen prayed that God would forgive them. To ask God to forgive these murderers, Stephen had to have forgiven them already. Could you forgive someone who was trying to kill you? It's not easy to do. But this type of forgiveness doesn't depend on your ability to give it. This forgiveness can only come from having a personal relationship with Jesus. It is Jesus who gives you the strength to forgive your enemies. Trust in him to help you love those who hate you.

Who set the example for forgiving one's enemies?
But God showed his great love for us by sending Christ to die for us while we were still sinners.
Romans 5:8

7:58 *Saul* is later called Paul; see 13:9.

O C T O B E R

Simon tried to buy the Holy Spirit. What happened to him?

ACTS 8:1-25
Money Can't Buy It
Saul was one of the official witnesses at the killing of Stephen.

A great wave of persecution began that day, sweeping over the church in Jerusalem, and all the believers except the apostles fled into Judea and Samaria. ²(Some godly people came and buried Stephen with loud weeping.) ³Saul was going everywhere to devas-tate the church. He went from house to house, dragging out both men and women to throw them into jail.

⁴But the believers who had fled Jerusalem went everywhere preaching the Good News about Jesus. ⁵Philip, for example, went to the city of Samaria and told the people there about the Messiah. ⁶Crowds listened intently to what he had to say because of the miracles he did. ⁷Many evil spirits

were cast out, screaming as they left their victims. And many who had been paralyzed or lame were healed. [8]So there was great joy in that city.

[9]A man named Simon had been a sorcerer there for many years, claiming to be someone great. [10]The Samaritan people, from the least to the greatest, often spoke of him as "the Great One—the Power of God." [11]He was very influential because of the magic he performed. [12]But now the people believed Philip's message of Good News concerning the Kingdom of God and the name of Jesus Christ. As a result, many men and women were baptized. [13]Then Simon himself believed and was baptized. He began following Philip wherever he went, and he was amazed by the great miracles and signs Philip performed.

[14]When the apostles back in Jerusalem heard that the people of Samaria had accepted God's message, they sent Peter and John there. [15]As soon as they arrived, they prayed for these new Christians to receive the Holy Spirit. [16]The Holy Spirit had not yet come upon any of them, for they had only been baptized in the name of the Lord Jesus. [17]Then Peter and John laid their hands upon these believers, and they received the Holy Spirit.

[18]When Simon saw that the Holy Spirit was given when the apostles placed their hands upon people's heads, he offered money to buy this power. [19]"Let me have this power, too," he exclaimed, "so that when I lay my hands on people, they will receive the Holy Spirit!"

[20]But Peter replied, "May your money perish with you for thinking God's gift can be bought! [21]You can have no part in this, for your heart is not right before God. [22]Turn from your wickedness and pray to the Lord. Perhaps he will forgive your evil thoughts, [23]for I can see that you are full of bitterness and held captive by sin."

[24]"Pray to the Lord for me," Simon exclaimed, "that these terrible things won't happen to me!"

[25]After testifying and preaching the word of the Lord in Samaria, Peter and John returned to Jerusalem. And they stopped in many Samaritan villages along the way to preach the Good News to them, too.

Simon saw people receiving the Holy Spirit when the apostles laid their hands on them. He wanted this power and was willing to pay the apostles for it. When he asked the apostles if he could buy this power, Peter scolded him for having evil motives. The Holy Spirit cannot be bought. Only true followers of Jesus Christ can receive the Holy Spirit in their lives. To think that God's power through the Holy Spirit can be bought is an insult to God. Be careful of the attitudes you have toward the Holy Spirit.

How can we honor the Holy Spirit?
And do not bring sorrow to God's Holy Spirit by the way you live. Remember, he is the one who has identified you as his own, guaranteeing that you will be saved on the day of redemption.
Ephesians 4:30

An angle guided Philip to an Ethiopian who needed to hear about Jesus.
How did the Ethiopian respond to the Good News?

ACTS 8:26-40

Unexpected Appointment

²⁶As for Philip, an angel of the Lord said to him, "Go south* down the desert road that runs from Jerusalem to Gaza." ²⁷So he did, and he met the treasurer of Ethiopia, a eunuch of great authority under the queen of Ethiopia.* The eunuch had gone to Jerusalem to worship, ²⁸and he was now returning. Seated in his carriage, he was reading aloud from the book of the prophet Isaiah.

²⁹The Holy Spirit said to Philip, "Go over and walk along beside the carriage."

³⁰Philip ran over and heard the man reading from the prophet Isaiah; so he asked, "Do you understand what you are reading?"

³¹The man replied, "How can I, when there is no one to instruct me?" And he begged Philip to come up into the carriage and sit with him. ³²The passage of Scripture he had been reading was this:

"He was led as a sheep to the
    slaughter.
And as a lamb is silent before
    the shearers,
he did not open his mouth.
³³ He was humiliated and received
    no justice.

Who can speak of his
    descendants?
For his life was taken from the
    earth."*

³⁴The eunuch asked Philip, "Was Isaiah talking about himself or someone else?" ³⁵So Philip began with this same Scripture and then used many

The Ethiopian welcomed the Good News and believed in Jesus. Philip had the chance to lead the Ethiopian to Christ because Philip listened to and obeyed the Holy Spirit's leading. Like Philip, we can be open to the Holy Spirit's leading and take advantage of the chances he gives us to tell others about Jesus. If you haven't had any chances, you can ask God to bring some your way. In the meantime, think of what you might say to someone who doesn't know Jesus. This will help you be ready when the time to speak out for Jesus comes.

What attitude will help us be open to the Holy Spirit's leading?
Teach me your ways, O LORD, that
I may live according to your truth!
Grant me purity of heart,
that I may honor you.
Psalm 86:11

8:26 Or *Go at noon.* **8:27** Greek *under the Candace, the queen of Ethiopia.* **8:32-33** Isa 53:7-8.

others to tell him the Good News about Jesus.

³⁶As they rode along, they came to some water, and the eunuch said, "Look! There's some water! Why can't I be baptized?"* ³⁸He ordered the carriage to stop, and they went down into the water, and Philip baptized him.

³⁹When they came up out of the water, the Spirit of the Lord caught Philip away. The eunuch never saw him again but went on his way rejoicing. ⁴⁰Meanwhile, Philip found himself farther north at the city of Azotus! He preached the Good News there and in every city along the way until he came to Caesarea.

8:36 Some manuscripts add verse 37, "You can," Philip answered, "if you believe with all your heart." And the eunuch replied, "I believe that Jesus Christ is the Son of God."

O C T O B E R

Saul wanted to put Christians in prison. But Jesus had other plans for Saul. How did he change Saul's mind?

ACTS 9:1-19

Blindsided

Meanwhile, Saul was uttering threats with every breath. He was eager to destroy the Lord's followers,* so he went to the high priest. ²He requested letters addressed to the synagogues in Damascus, asking their cooperation in the arrest of any followers of the Way he found there. He wanted to bring them—both men and women—back to Jerusalem in chains.

³As he was nearing Damascus on this mission, a brilliant light from heaven suddenly beamed down upon him! ⁴He fell to the ground and heard a voice saying to him, "Saul! Saul! Why are you persecuting me?"

⁵"Who are you, sir?" Saul asked.

And the voice replied, "I am Jesus, the one you are persecuting! ⁶Now get up and go into the city, and you will be told what you are to do."

⁷The men with Saul stood speechless with surprise, for they heard the sound of someone's voice, but they saw no one! ⁸As Saul picked himself up off the ground, he found that he was blind. ⁹So his companions led him by the hand to Damascus. He remained there blind for three days. And all that time he went without food and water.

¹⁰Now there was a believer* in Damascus named Ananias. The Lord spoke to him in a vision, calling, "Ananias!"

"Yes, Lord!" he replied.

¹¹The Lord said, "Go over to Straight Street, to the house of Judas. When you arrive, ask for Saul of Tarsus. He is praying to me right now. ¹²I have shown him a vision of a man named Ananias coming in and laying his hands on him so that he can see again."

9:1 Greek *disciples.* **9:10** Greek *disciple;* also in 9:36.

¹³"But Lord," exclaimed Ananias, "I've heard about the terrible things this man has done to the believers in Jerusalem! ¹⁴And we hear that he is authorized by the leading priests to arrest every believer in Damascus."

¹⁵But the Lord said, "Go and do what I say. For Saul is my chosen instrument to take my message to the Gentiles and to kings, as well as to the people of Israel. ¹⁶And I will show him how much he must suffer for me."

¹⁷So Ananias went and found Saul. He laid his hands on him and said, "Brother Saul, the Lord Jesus, who appeared to you on the road, has sent me so that you may get your sight back and be filled with the Holy Spirit." ¹⁸Instantly something like scales fell from Saul's eyes, and he regained his sight. Then he got up and was baptized. ¹⁹Afterward he ate some food and was strengthened.

Saul stayed with the believers* in Damascus for a few days.

9:19 Greek *disciples;* also in 9:26.

Saul was traveling to Damascus to arrest Christians. On the way, Jesus stopped Saul with a blinding light from heaven. Jesus then asked Saul why he was persecuting him. This encounter with Jesus changed Saul's mission in life. He would no longer persecute Christians. Instead, he would take the good news of Jesus Christ to the Gentiles. How has Jesus changed your life? You may never have an experience like Saul's, but Jesus can work in many amazing ways in your life. Listen for his voice, and let him change your life.

What does following Jesus do for people?

What this means is that those who become Christians become new persons. They are not the same anymore, for the old life is gone. A new life has begun!
2 Corinthians 5:17

OCTOBER

Saul preached about Jesus in Damascus. Some of the Jewish leaders there weren't happy with Saul and planned to kill him. How did God protect Saul?

ACTS 9:20-31
Escape from Damascus

²⁰And immediately he began preaching about Jesus in the synagogues, saying, "He is indeed the Son of God!"

²¹All who heard him were amazed. "Isn't this the same man who perse-cuted Jesus' followers with such devastation in Jerusalem?" they asked. "And we understand that he came here to arrest them and take them in chains to the leading priests."

²²Saul's preaching became more and more powerful, and the Jews in

Damascus couldn't refute his proofs that Jesus was indeed the Messiah. ²³After a while the Jewish leaders decided to kill him. ²⁴But Saul was told about their plot, and that they were watching for him day and night at the city gate so they could murder him. ²⁵So during the night, some of the other believers* let him down in a large basket through an opening in the city wall.

²⁶When Saul arrived in Jerusalem, he tried to meet with the believers, but they were all afraid of him. They thought he was only pretending to be a believer! ²⁷Then Barnabas brought him to the apostles and told them how Saul had seen the Lord on the way to Damascus. Barnabas also told them what the Lord had said to Saul and how he boldly preached in the name of Jesus in Damascus. ²⁸Then the apostles accepted Saul, and after that he was constantly with them in Jerusalem, preaching boldly in the name of the Lord. ²⁹He debated with some Greek-speaking Jews, but they plotted to murder him. ³⁰When the believers* heard about it, however, they took him to Caesarea and sent him on to his hometown of Tarsus.

³¹The church then had peace throughout Judea, Galilee, and Samaria, and it grew in strength and numbers. The believers were walking in the fear of the Lord and in the comfort of the Holy Spirit.

9:25 Greek *his disciples.* 9:30 Greek *brothers.*

Saul was trapped. He couldn't leave the city, because people were waiting at the gate to kill him. God saw Saul's situation and provided him with a way of escape. With the help of some fellow Christians, Saul was able to get out of Damascus during the night. He avoided those who plotted his murder. You may never have to run for your life. But if you do, you have a God who cares for you and can rescue you from your enemies.

Who can you turn to when someone is out to hurt you?
Save me from my enemies, LORD; I run to you to hide me.
Psalm 143:9

O C T O B E R

God used Peter to heal others. How did the people who saw these miracles react?

ACTS 9:32-43
It's a Miracle!
³²Peter traveled from place to place to visit the believers, and in his travels he came to the Lord's people in the town of Lydda. ³³There he met a man named Aeneas, who had been paralyzed and bedridden for eight years. ³⁴Peter said

to him, "Aeneas, Jesus Christ heals you! Get up and make your bed!" And he was healed instantly. [35]Then the whole population of Lydda and Sharon turned to the Lord when they saw Aeneas walking around.

[36]There was a believer in Joppa named Tabitha (which in Greek is Dorcas*). She was always doing kind things for others and helping the poor. [37]About this time she became ill and died. Her friends prepared her for burial and laid her in an upstairs room. [38]But they had heard that Peter was nearby at Lydda, so they sent two men to beg him, "Please come as soon as possible!"

[39]So Peter returned with them; and as soon as he arrived, they took him to the upstairs room. The room was filled with widows who were weeping and showing him the coats and other garments Dorcas had made for them. [40]But Peter asked them all to leave the room; then he knelt and prayed. Turning to the body he said, "Get up, Tabitha." And she opened her eyes! When she saw Peter, she sat up! [41]He gave her his hand and helped her up. Then he called in the widows and all the believers, and he showed them that she was alive.

[42]The news raced through the whole town, and many believed in the Lord. [43]And Peter stayed a long time in Joppa, living with Simon, a leatherworker.

Peter healed a man, and the people believed in Jesus. In another town, Peter raised a woman from the dead, and the people there believed in Jesus. God wants everyone to believe in his Son. But you do not have to wait for a miracle to believe. God wants you to believe in his Son today. So don't delay!

Why should you believe in Jesus?
There is salvation in no one else!
There is no other name in all
of heaven for people to call
on to save them.
Acts 4:12

9:36 The names *Tabitha* in Aramaic and *Dorcas* in Greek both mean "gazelle."

O C T O B E R

A Roman officer named Cornelius had a vision. What did he see?

ACTS 10:1-23
An Angel's Message
In Caesarea there lived a Roman army officer named Cornelius, who was a captain of the Italian Regiment. [2]He was a devout man who feared the God of Israel, as did his entire household. He gave generously to charity and was a man who regularly prayed to God. [3]One afternoon about three o'clock, he had a vision in which he saw an angel of God coming toward him. "Cornelius!" the angel said.

⁴Cornelius stared at him in terror. "What is it, sir?" he asked the angel.

And the angel replied, "Your prayers and gifts to the poor have not gone unnoticed by God! ⁵Now send some men down to Joppa to find a man named Simon Peter. ⁶He is staying with Simon, a leatherworker who lives near the shore. Ask him to come and visit you."

⁷As soon as the angel was gone, Cornelius called two of his household servants and a devout soldier, one of his personal attendants. ⁸He told them what had happened and sent them off to Joppa.

⁹The next day as Cornelius's messengers were nearing the city, Peter went up to the flat roof to pray. It was about noon, ¹⁰and he was hungry. But while lunch was being prepared, he fell into a trance. ¹¹He saw the sky open, and something like a large sheet was let down by its four corners. ¹²In the sheet were all sorts of animals, reptiles, and birds. ¹³Then a voice said to him, "Get up, Peter; kill and eat them."

¹⁴"Never, Lord," Peter declared. "I have never in all my life eaten anything forbidden by our Jewish laws.*"

¹⁵The voice spoke again, "If God says something is acceptable, don't say it isn't."* ¹⁶The same vision was repeated three times. Then the sheet was pulled up again to heaven.

¹⁷Peter was very perplexed. What could the vision mean? Just then the men sent by Cornelius found the house and stood outside at the gate. ¹⁸They asked if this was the place where Simon Peter was staying.

¹⁹Meanwhile, as Peter was puzzling over the vision, the Holy Spirit said to him, "Three men have come looking for you. ²⁰Go down and go with them without hesitation. All is well, for I have sent them."

²¹So Peter went down and said, "I'm the man you are looking for. Why have you come?"

²²They said, "We were sent by Cornelius, a Roman officer. He is a devout man who fears the God of Israel and is well respected by all the Jews. A holy angel instructed him to send for you so you can go to his house and give him a message." ²³So Peter invited the men to be his guests for the night. The next day he went with them, accompanied by some other believers* from Joppa.

Cornelius feared God and prayed regularly. This pleased God, so he sent an angel to Cornelius in a vision. The angel told Cornelius to send for Peter, who would tell him the good news of Jesus Christ. God knows who is seeking him, and he makes himself known to those people. Are you seeking God? If not, decide today to get to know him. It's the best thing you can do.

What does God do for those who follow him?

The eyes of the LORD search the whole earth in order to strengthen those whose hearts are fully committed to him.
2 Chronicles 16:9

10:14 Greek *anything common and unclean.* **10:15** Greek *"What God calls clean you must not call unclean."* **10:23** Greek *brothers.*

Peter went to Cornelius's house.
What did Peter learn about God while he was there?

ACTS 10:24-48

Peter Visits Cornelius

[24]They arrived in Caesarea the following day. Cornelius was waiting for him and had called together his relatives and close friends to meet Peter. [25]As Peter entered his home, Cornelius fell to the floor before him in worship. [26]But Peter pulled him up and said, "Stand up! I'm a human being like you!" [27]So Cornelius got up, and they talked together and went inside where the others were assembled.

[28]Peter told them, "You know it is against the Jewish laws for me to come into a Gentile home like this. But God has shown me that I should never think of anyone as impure. [29]So I came as soon as I was sent for. Now tell me why you sent for me."

[30]Cornelius replied, "Four days ago I was praying in my house at three o'clock in the afternoon. Suddenly, a man in dazzling clothes was standing in front of me. [31]He told me, 'Cornelius, your prayers have been heard, and your gifts to the poor have been noticed by God! [32]Now send some men to Joppa and summon Simon Peter. He is staying in the home of Simon, a leatherworker who lives near the shore.' [33]So I sent for you at once, and it was good of you to come. Now here we are, waiting before God to hear the message the Lord has given you."

[34]Then Peter replied, "I see very clearly that God doesn't show partiality. [35]In every nation he accepts those who fear him and do what is right. [36]I'm sure you have heard about the Good News for the people of Israel—that there is peace with God through Jesus Christ, who is Lord of all. [37]You know what happened all through Judea, beginning in Galilee after John the Baptist began preaching. [38]And no doubt you know that God anointed Jesus of Nazareth with the Holy Spirit and with power. Then Jesus went around doing good and healing all who were oppressed by the Devil, for God was with him.

[39]"And we apostles are witnesses of all he did throughout Israel and in Jerusalem. They put him to death by crucifying him, [40]but God raised him to life three days later. Then God allowed him to appear, [41]not to the general public,* but to us whom God had chosen beforehand to be his witnesses. We were those who ate and drank with him after he rose from the dead. [42]And he ordered us to preach everywhere and to testify that Jesus is ordained of God to be the judge of all—the living and the dead. [43]He is the one all the prophets testified about, saying that everyone

10:41 Greek *the people.*

who believes in him will have their sins forgiven through his name."

⁴⁴Even as Peter was saying these things, the Holy Spirit fell upon all who had heard the message. ⁴⁵The Jewish believers who came with Peter were amazed that the gift of the Holy Spirit had been poured out upon the Gentiles, too. ⁴⁶And there could be no doubt about it, for they heard them speaking in tongues and praising God.

Then Peter asked, ⁴⁷"Can anyone object to their being baptized, now that they have received the Holy Spirit just as we did?" ⁴⁸So he gave orders for them to be baptized in the name of Jesus Christ. Afterward Cornelius asked him to stay with them for several days.

Peter learned that God does not play favorites. He loves everyone and wants all to come to him. Follow God's example. Don't show favoritism to people because of their age, color, gender, or religion. Instead, show love to everyone.

Why shouldn't we play favorites?
The LORD is good to everyone.
He showers compassion
on all his creation.
Psalm 145:9

O C T O B E R

A famine was coming. What did the church in Antioch do to prepare for it?

ACTS 11:19-30
The Church in Antioch

¹⁹Meanwhile, the believers who had fled from Jerusalem during the persecution after Stephen's death traveled as far as Phoenicia, Cyprus, and Antioch of Syria. They preached the Good News, but only to Jews. ²⁰However, some of the believers who went to Antioch from Cyprus and Cyrene began preaching to Gentiles* about the Lord Jesus. ²¹The power of the Lord was upon them, and large numbers of these Gentiles believed and turned to the Lord.

²²When the church at Jerusalem heard what had happened, they sent Barnabas to Antioch. ²³When he arrived and saw this proof of God's favor, he was filled with joy, and he encouraged the believers to stay true to the Lord. ²⁴Barnabas was a good man, full of the Holy Spirit and strong in faith. And large numbers of people were brought to the Lord.

²⁵Then Barnabas went on to Tarsus to find Saul. ²⁶When he found him, he brought him back to Antioch. Both of them stayed there with the church for a full year, teaching great

11:20 Greek *the Greeks;* other manuscripts read *the Hellenists.*

numbers of people. (It was there at Antioch that the believers* were first called Christians.)

²⁷During this time, some prophets traveled from Jerusalem to Antioch. ²⁸One of them named Agabus stood up in one of the meetings to predict by the Spirit that a great famine was coming upon the entire Roman world. (This was fulfilled during the reign of Claudius.) ²⁹So the believers in Antioch decided to send relief to the brothers and sisters in Judea, everyone giving as much as they could. ³⁰This they did, entrusting their gifts to Barnabas and Saul to take to the elders of the church in Jerusalem.

11:26 Greek *disciples;* also in 11:29a.

The church in Antioch decided to send relief to the believers in Judea. They gave as much as they could and trusted Saul and Barnabas to deliver their gift to the church in Jerusalem. Like these believers, we should help those around us who are in need. When you see people in need, do what you can to help them.

How do we serve God by helping the poor?
Those who oppress the poor insult their Maker, but those who help the poor honor him.
Proverbs 14:31

O C T O B E R

Herod had Peter arrested and placed in jail. He was going to put Peter on trial and possibly kill him. What did the believers do while Peter was in prison?

ACTS 12:1-19
Jailbreak

About that time King Herod Agrippa* began to persecute some believers in the church. ²He had the apostle James (John's brother) killed with a sword. ³When Herod saw how much this pleased the Jewish leaders, he arrested Peter during the Passover celebration* ⁴and imprisoned him, placing him under the guard of four squads of four soldiers each. Herod's intention was to bring Peter out for public trial after the Passover. ⁵But while Peter was in prison, the church prayed very earnestly for him.

⁶The night before Peter was to be placed on trial, he was asleep, chained between two soldiers, with others standing guard at the prison gate. ⁷Suddenly, there was a bright light in the cell, and an angel of the Lord stood before Peter. The angel tapped him on the side to awaken him and said, "Quick! Get up!" And the chains fell off his wrists. ⁸Then the angel told

12:1 Greek *Herod the king.* He was the nephew of Herod Antipas and a grandson of Herod the Great. **12:3** Greek *the days of unleavened bread.*

him, "Get dressed and put on your sandals." And he did. "Now put on your coat and follow me," the angel ordered.

⁹So Peter left the cell, following the angel. But all the time he thought it was a vision. He didn't realize it was really happening. ¹⁰They passed the first and second guard posts and came to the iron gate to the street, and this opened to them all by itself. So they passed through and started walking down the street, and then the angel suddenly left him.

¹¹Peter finally realized what had happened. "It's really true!" he said to himself. "The Lord has sent his angel and saved me from Herod and from what the Jews were hoping to do to me!"

¹²After a little thought, he went to the home of Mary, the mother of John Mark, where many were gathered for prayer. ¹³He knocked at the door in the gate, and a servant girl named Rhoda came to open it. ¹⁴When she recognized Peter's voice, she was so overjoyed that, instead of opening the door, she ran back inside and told everyone, "Peter is standing at the door!"

¹⁵"You're out of your mind," they said. When she insisted, they decided, "It must be his angel."

¹⁶Meanwhile, Peter continued knocking. When they finally went out and opened the door, they were amazed. ¹⁷He motioned for them to quiet down and told them what had happened and how the Lord had led him out of jail. "Tell James and the other brothers what happened," he said. And then he went to another place.

¹⁸At dawn, there was a great commotion among the soldiers about what had happened to Peter. ¹⁹Herod Agrippa ordered a thorough search for him. When he couldn't be found, Herod interrogated the guards and sentenced them to death. Afterward Herod left Judea to stay in Caesarea for a while.

The believers prayed for Peter. God heard their prayer and sent an angel to free Peter. When people you know are surrounded by problems, you can pray for them, just as the believers prayed for Peter. You can also ask others to pray for you. Remember that God is powerful. He can rescue you or give you the strength to endure. Ask him for help.

What should you remember when you have problems?
God is our refuge and strength, always ready to help in times of trouble.
Psalm 46:1

Elymas tried to stop the spread of the Good News. What happened to him?

ACTS 13:1-12

Unstoppable

Among the prophets and teachers of the church at Antioch of Syria were Barnabas, Simeon (called "the black man"*), Lucius (from Cyrene), Manaen (the childhood companion of King Herod Antipas*), and Saul. ⁷One day as these men were worshiping the Lord and fasting, the Holy Spirit said, "Dedicate Barnabas and Saul for the special work I have for them." ³So after more fasting and prayer, the men laid their hands on them and sent them on their way.

⁴Sent out by the Holy Spirit, Saul and Barnabas went down to the seaport of Seleucia and then sailed for the island of Cyprus. ⁵There, in the town of Salamis, they went to the Jewish synagogues and preached the word of God. (John Mark went with them as their assistant.)

⁶Afterward they preached from town to town across the entire island until finally they reached Paphos, where they met a Jewish sorcerer, a false prophet named Bar-Jesus. ⁷He had attached himself to the governor, Sergius Paulus, a man of considerable insight and understanding. The governor invited Barnabas and Saul to visit him, for he wanted to hear the word of God. ⁸But Elymas, the sorcerer (as his name means in Greek), interfered and urged the governor to pay no attention to what Saul and Barnabas said. He was trying to turn the governor away from the Christian faith.

⁹Then Saul, also known as Paul, filled with the Holy Spirit, looked the sorcerer in the eye and said, ¹⁰"You son

---

Elymas thought he could stop Paul and Barnabas from sharing the Good News with the governor of Cyprus. He was wrong, and God blinded Elymas for his actions. Today there are many people who try to stop Christians from sharing the good news of Jesus with others. In fact, someone may have tried to stop you from sharing your faith. At times these people seem to be winning, but they will not succeed. God is more powerful than they are, and he will get his message out, no matter what these people try. Like Paul and Barnabas, we can keep sharing the Good News, no matter who opposes us.

Why shouldn't we worry when people try to stop us from talking about Jesus?
If God is for us, who can ever be against us?
Romans 8:31

13:1a Greek *who was called Niger.* **13:1b** Greek *Herod the tetrarch.*

of the Devil, full of every sort of trickery and villainy, enemy of all that is good, will you never stop perverting the true ways of the Lord? ¹¹And now the Lord has laid his hand of punishment upon you, and you will be stricken awhile with blindness." Instantly mist and darkness fell upon him, and he began wandering around begging for someone to take his hand and lead him. ¹²When the governor saw what had happened, he believed and was astonished at what he learned about the Lord.

O C T O B E R

The crowd thought Paul and Barnabas were gods. How did Paul and Barnabas react?

ACTS 14:8-20

Mistaken Identity

⁸While they were at Lystra, Paul and Barnabas came upon a man with crippled feet. He had been that way from birth, so he had never walked. ⁹He was listening as Paul preached, and Paul noticed him and realized he had faith to be healed. ¹⁰So Paul called to him in a loud voice, "Stand up!" And the man jumped to his feet and started walking.

¹¹When the listening crowd saw what Paul had done, they shouted in their local dialect, "These men are gods in human bodies!" ¹²They decided that Barnabas was the Greek god Zeus and that Paul, because he was the chief speaker, was Hermes. ¹³The temple of Zeus was located on the outskirts of the city. The priest of the temple and the crowd brought oxen and wreaths of flowers, and they prepared to sacrifice to the apostles at the city gates.

¹⁴But when Barnabas and Paul heard what was happening, they tore their clothing in dismay and ran out among the people, shouting, ¹⁵"Friends,* why are you doing this? We are merely human beings like yourselves! We have come to bring you the Good News that

Paul and Barnabas were saddened by the people's response. They wanted the people to know and worship the one true God, Jesus Christ. They didn't want the people to worship them. Their desire for the people to know and worship Jesus showed their true humility and servanthood. How would you respond if people worshiped you?

Why shouldn't we worship anyone but God?

You must worship no other gods, but only the LORD, for he is a God who is passionate about his relationship with you.
Exodus 34:14

14:15 Greek *Men.*

368

you should turn from these worthless things to the living God, who made heaven and earth, the sea, and everything in them. [16]In earlier days he permitted all the nations to go their own ways, [17]but he never left himself without a witness. There were always his reminders, such as sending you rain and good crops and giving you food and joyful hearts." [18]But even so, Paul and Barnabas could scarcely restrain the people from sacrificing to them.

[19]Now some Jews arrived from Antioch and Iconium and turned the crowds into a murderous mob. They stoned Paul and dragged him out of the city, apparently dead. [20]But as the believers* stood around him, he got up and went back into the city. The next day he left with Barnabas for Derbe.

14:20 Greek *disciples;* also in 14:22, 28.

O C T O B E R

Some Jewish Christians thought that the Gentile Christians should follow Jewish laws. The apostles met to discuss this matter. What did they decide?

ACTS 15:1-21

An Important Meeting

While Paul and Barnabas were at Antioch of Syria, some men from Judea arrived and began to teach the Christians*: "Unless you keep the ancient Jewish custom of circumcision taught by Moses, you cannot be saved." [2]Paul and Barnabas, disagreeing with them, argued forcefully and at length. Finally, Paul and Barnabas were sent to Jerusalem, accompanied by some local believers, to talk to the apostles and elders about this question. [3]The church sent the delegates to Jerusalem, and they stopped along the way in Phoenicia and Samaria to visit the believers.* They told them—much to everyone's joy—that the Gentiles, too, were being converted.

[4]When they arrived in Jerusalem, Paul and Barnabas were welcomed by the whole church, including the apostles and elders. They reported on what God had been doing through their ministry. [5]But then some of the men who had been Pharisees before their conversion stood up and declared that all Gentile converts must be circumcised and be required to follow the law of Moses.

[6]So the apostles and church elders got together to decide this question. [7]At the meeting, after a long discussion, Peter stood and addressed them as follows: "Brothers, you all know that God chose me from among you some time ago to preach to the Gentiles so that they could hear the Good News and believe. [8]God, who knows people's hearts, confirmed that he accepts Gentiles by giving them the Holy

15:1 Greek *brothers;* also in 15:32, 33. **15:3** Greek *brothers;* also in 15:23, 36, 40.

369

Spirit, just as he gave him to us. [9]He made no distinction between us and them, for he also cleansed their hearts through faith. [10]Why are you now questioning God's way by burdening the Gentile believers* with a yoke that neither we nor our ancestors were able to bear? [11]We believe that we are all saved the same way, by the special favor of the Lord Jesus."

[12]There was no further discussion, and everyone listened as Barnabas and Paul told about the miraculous signs and wonders God had done through them among the Gentiles.

[13]When they had finished, James stood and said, "Brothers, listen to me. [14]Peter* has told you about the time God first visited the Gentiles to take from them a people for himself. [15]And this conversion of Gentiles agrees with what the prophets predicted. For instance, it is written:

[16]'Afterward I will return,
  and I will restore the fallen
    kingdom of David.
From the ruins I will rebuild it,
  and I will restore it,
[17] so that the rest of humanity might
    find the Lord,
  including the Gentiles—
all those I have called to be
    mine.
This is what the Lord says,
[18] he who made these things
    known long ago.'*

[19]And so my judgment is that we should stop troubling the Gentiles who turn to God, [20]except that we should write to them and tell them to abstain from eating meat sacrificed to idols, from sexual immorality, and from consuming blood or eating the meat of strangled animals. [21]For these laws of Moses have been preached in Jewish synagogues in every city on every Sabbath for many generations."

The apostles decided that the Gentile Christians didn't have to live by their Jewish laws. During the meeting, Peter pointed out that the Jewish people couldn't even live by their own laws, so why should they make other people try to live by them? When you become a Christian, some believers may want you to live by a list of do's and don'ts. But the Christian life is not a bunch of rules. Rather, it is a relationship with Jesus, which changes your attitudes and behaviors. If you are a Christian, be sure to work on your relationship with Jesus instead of strictly following a list of rules.

What does God want his people to do?
No, O people, the LORD has already told you what is good, and this is what he requires: to do what is right, to love mercy, and to walk humbly with your God.
Micah 6:8

15:10 Greek *disciples*. **15:14** Greek *Simon*. **15:16-18** Amos 9:11-12; Isa 45:21.

Paul and Barnabas had a disagreement. What was the outcome?

ACTS 15:22-41
Parting Company

[22]Then the apostles and elders and the whole church in Jerusalem chose delegates, and they sent them to Antioch of Syria with Paul and Barnabas to report on this decision. The men chosen were two of the church leaders*—Judas (also called Barsabbas) and Silas. [23]This is the letter they took along with them:

"This letter is from the apostles and elders, your brothers in Jerusalem. It is written to the Gentile believers in Antioch, Syria, and Cilicia. Greetings! [24]"We understand that some men from here have troubled you and upset you with their teaching, but they had no such instructions from us. [25]So it seemed good to us, having unanimously agreed on our decision, to send you these official representatives, along with our beloved Barnabas and Paul, [26]who have risked their lives for the sake of our Lord Jesus Christ. [27]So we are sending Judas and Silas to tell you what we have decided concerning your question. [28]"For it seemed good to the Holy Spirit and to us to lay no greater burden on you than these requirements: [29]You must abstain from eating food offered to idols, from consuming blood or eating the meat of strangled animals, and

from sexual immorality. If you do this, you will do well. Farewell."

[30]The four messengers went at once to Antioch, where they called a general meeting of the Christians and delivered the letter. [31]And there was great joy throughout the church that day as they read this encouraging message.

[32]Then Judas and Silas, both being prophets, spoke extensively to the Christians, encouraging and strengthening their faith. [33]They stayed for a while, and then Judas and Silas were sent back to Jerusalem, with the bless-

Paul and Barnabas decided to go their separate ways. They split up because they couldn't agree on taking John Mark on their mission trip. Disagreement between Christians is OK as long as it is handled well and doesn't lead to broken relationships. Have you ever had a disagreement with another Christian that led to hurt feelings? With the help of the Holy Spirit, you can forgive that person and mend your relationship.

What kinds of disagreements should you avoid?
Again I say, don't get involved in foolish, ignorant arguments that only start fights.
2 Timothy 2:23

15:22 Greek *were leaders among the brothers.*

ings of the Christians, to those who had sent them.* [35]Paul and Barnabas stayed in Antioch to assist many others who were teaching and preaching the word of the Lord there.

[36]After some time Paul said to Barnabas, "Let's return to each city where we previously preached the word of the Lord, to see how the new believers are getting along." [37]Barnabas agreed and wanted to take along John Mark.

[38]But Paul disagreed strongly, since John Mark had deserted them in Pamphylia and had not shared in their work. [39]Their disagreement over this was so sharp that they separated. Barnabas took John Mark with him and sailed for Cyprus. [40]Paul chose Silas, and the believers sent them off, entrusting them to the Lord's grace. [41]So they traveled throughout Syria and Cilicia to strengthen the churches there.

15:33 Some manuscripts add verse 34, *But Silas decided to stay there.*

O C T O B E R

Paul tried to enter a part of Asia Minor. But the Holy Spirit stopped him from going there. Where did God want Paul to go?

ACTS 16:1-15

A New Direction

Paul and Silas went first to Derbe and then on to Lystra. There they met Timothy, a young disciple whose mother was a Jewish believer, but whose father was a Greek. [2]Timothy was well thought of by the believers* in Lystra and Iconium, [3]so Paul wanted him to join them on their journey. In deference to the Jews of the area, he arranged for Timothy to be circumcised before they left, for everyone knew that his father was a Greek. [4]Then they went from town to town, explaining the decision regarding the commandments that were to be obeyed, as decided by the apostles and elders in Jerusalem. [5]So the churches were strengthened in their faith and grew daily in numbers.

[6]Next Paul and Silas traveled through the area of Phrygia and Galatia, because the Holy Spirit had told them not to go into the province of Asia at that time. [7]Then coming to the borders of Mysia, they headed for the province of Bithynia,* but again the Spirit of Jesus did not let them go. [8]So instead, they went on through Mysia to the city of Troas.

[9]That night Paul had a vision. He saw a man from Macedonia in northern Greece, pleading with him, "Come over here and help us." [10]So we* decided to leave for Macedonia at once, for we could only conclude that God was calling us to preach the Good News there.

[11]We boarded a boat at Troas and

16:2 Greek *brothers;* also in 16:40. **16:6-7** *Phrygia, Galatia, Asia, Mysia,* and *Bithynia* were all districts in the land now called Turkey. **16:10** Luke, the writer of this book, here joined Paul and accompanied him on his journey.

sailed straight across to the island of Samothrace, and the next day we landed at Neapolis. ¹²From there we reached Philippi, a major city of the district of Macedonia and a Roman colony; we stayed there several days.

¹³On the Sabbath we went a little way outside the city to a riverbank, where we supposed that some people met for prayer, and we sat down to speak with some women who had come together. ¹⁴One of them was Lydia from Thyatira, a merchant of expensive purple cloth. She was a worshiper of God. As she listened to us, the Lord opened her heart, and she accepted what Paul was saying. ¹⁵She was baptized along with other members of her household, and she asked us to be her guests. "If you agree that I am faithful to the Lord," she said, "come and stay at my home." And she urged us until we did.

Through a vision, God instructed Paul to go to Macedonia. There he met some people with whom he shared the good news of Jesus Christ. Because Paul was obedient to the Holy Spirit's direction, more people were saved, and the message of Jesus Christ spread. Following the Holy Spirit's direction is important. When we follow his guidance, we will be used by him in ways we can't even imagine.

What does the Holy Spirit do in the life of a Christian?

When the Spirit of truth comes, he will guide you into all truth. He will not be presenting his own ideas; he will be telling you what he has heard. He will tell you about the future.
John 16:13

OCTOBER 28

Paul and Silas were arrested, beaten, and thrown into jail. How did God use them, despite the bad day they had?

ACTS 16:16-34
Prayer and Praise

¹⁶One day as we were going down to the place of prayer, we met a demon possessed slave girl. She was a fortune-teller who earned a lot of money for her masters. ¹⁷She followed along behind us shouting, "These men are servants of the Most High God, and they have come to tell you how to be saved."

¹⁸This went on day after day until Paul got so exasperated that he turned and spoke to the demon within her. "I command you in the name of Jesus Christ to come out of her," he said. And instantly it left her.

¹⁹Her masters' hopes of wealth were now shattered, so they grabbed Paul and Silas and dragged them before the authorities at the marketplace. ²⁰"The whole city is in an uproar because of

these Jews!" they shouted. [21]"They are teaching the people to do things that are against Roman customs."

[22]A mob quickly formed against Paul and Silas, and the city officials ordered them stripped and beaten with wooden rods. [23]They were severely beaten, and then they were thrown into prison. The jailer was ordered to make sure they didn't escape. [24]So he took no chances but put them into the inner dungeon and clamped their feet in the stocks.

[25]Around midnight, Paul and Silas were praying and singing hymns to God, and the other prisoners were listening. [26]Suddenly, there was a great earthquake, and the prison was shaken to its foundations. All the doors flew open, and the chains of every prisoner fell off! [27]The jailer woke up to see the prison doors wide open. He assumed the prisoners had escaped, so he drew his sword to kill himself. [28]But Paul shouted to him, "Don't do it! We are all here!"

[29]Trembling with fear, the jailer called for lights and ran to the dungeon and fell down before Paul and Silas. [30]He brought them out and asked, "Sirs, what must I do to be saved?"

[31]They replied, "Believe on the Lord Jesus and you will be saved, along with your entire household." [32]Then they shared the word of the Lord with him and all who lived in his household. [33]That same hour the jailer washed their wounds, and he and everyone in his household were immediately baptized. [34]Then he brought them into his house and set a meal before them. He and his entire household rejoiced because they all believed in God.

God used Paul and Silas to save the jailer's life twice. First, they stopped the jailer from killing himself. Second, they told him about Jesus. That night, the jailer and his entire family accepted Jesus as their Savior. God took Paul and Silas's bad situation and used it for good. Bad circumstances are not always bad experiences. God can, and sometimes does, work miracles through hard times. The next time life doesn't treat you fairly, pray that God will use your bad circumstances for good.

Does anything good come out of our troubles?

Dear brothers and sisters, whenever trouble comes your way, let it be an opportunity for joy. For when your faith is tested, your endurance has a chance to grow.
James 1:2-3

OCTOBER

*Paul noticed that the people of Athens had the altar To an Unknown God.
What did Paul have to say about the unknown God?*

ACTS 17:16-34

Paul in Athens

[16]While Paul was waiting for them in Athens, he was deeply troubled by all the idols he saw everywhere in the city. [17]He went to the synagogue to debate with the Jews and the God-fearing Gentiles, and he spoke daily in the public square to all who happened to be there.

[18]He also had a debate with some of the Epicurean and Stoic philosophers. When he told them about Jesus and his resurrection, they said, "This babbler has picked up some strange ideas." Others said, "He's pushing some foreign religion."

[19]Then they took him to the Council of Philosophers.* "Come and tell us more about this new religion," they said. [20]"You are saying some rather startling things, and we want to know what it's all about." [21](It should be explained that all the Athenians as well as the foreigners in Athens seemed to spend all their time discussing the latest ideas.)

[22]So Paul, standing before the Council,* addressed them as follows: "Men of Athens, I notice that you are very religious, [23]for as I was walking along I saw your many altars. And one of them had this inscription on it—'To an Unknown God.' You have been worshiping him without knowing who he is, and now I wish to tell you about him.

[24]"He is the God who made the world and everything in it. Since he is Lord of heaven and earth, he doesn't live in man-made temples, [25]and human hands can't serve his needs—for he has no needs. He himself gives life and breath to everything, and he satisfies every need there is. [26]From one man he created all the nations throughout the whole earth. He decided beforehand which should rise and fall, and he determined their boundaries.

[27]"His purpose in all of this was that the nations should seek after God and perhaps feel their way toward him and find him—though he is not far from any one of us. [28]For in him we live and move and exist. As one of your own poets says, 'We are his offspring.' [29]And since this is true, we shouldn't think of God as an idol designed by craftsmen from gold or silver or stone. [30]God overlooked people's former ignorance about these things, but now he commands everyone everywhere to turn away from idols and turn to him.* [31]For he has set a day for judging the world with justice by the man he

17:19 Greek *the Areopagus.* **17:22** Or *in the middle of Mars Hill;* Greek reads *in the middle of the Areopagus.* **17:30** Greek *everywhere to repent.*

375

has appointed, and he proved to everyone who this is by raising him from the dead."

32When they heard Paul speak of the resurrection of a person who had been dead, some laughed, but others said, "We want to hear more about this later." 33That ended Paul's discussion with them, 34but some joined him and became believers. Among them were Dionysius, a member of the Council,* a woman named Damaris, and others.

Paul said that the "unknown God" was the one true God. Then he told the people of Athens about Jesus, God's Son. Today we, like Paul, are surrounded by people who don't really know God or his Son, Jesus. Will you tell them about Jesus?

Why should we tell others about Jesus?

Therefore, go and make disciples of all the nations, baptizing them in the name of the Father and the Son and the Holy Spirit.
Matthew 28:19

17:34 Greek *an Areopagite.*

OCTOBER 30

The Jews opposed Paul's preaching. What did God tell him to do?

ACTS 18:1-11
Paul in Corinth

Then Paul left Athens and went to Corinth.* 2There he became acquainted with a Jew named Aquila, born in Pontus, who had recently arrived from Italy with his wife, Priscilla. They had been expelled from Italy as a result of Claudius Caesar's order to deport all Jews from Rome. 3Paul lived and worked with them, for they were tentmakers* just as he was.

4Each Sabbath found Paul at the synagogue, trying to convince the Jews and Greeks alike. 5And after Silas and Timothy came down from Macedonia, Paul spent his full time preaching and testifying to the Jews, telling them, "The Messiah you are looking for is Jesus." 6But when the Jews opposed him and insulted him, Paul shook the dust from his robe and said, "Your blood be upon your own heads—I am innocent. From now on I will go to the Gentiles."

7After that he stayed with Titius Justus, a Gentile who worshiped God and lived next door to the synagogue.

18:1 *Athens* and *Corinth* were major cities in Achaia, the region on the southern end of the Greek peninsula. 18:3 Or *leatherworkers.*

⁸Crispus, the leader of the synagogue, and all his household believed in the Lord. Many others in Corinth also became believers and were baptized.

⁹One night the Lord spoke to Paul in a vision and told him, "Don't be afraid! Speak out! Don't be silent! ¹⁰For I am with you, and no one will harm you because many people here in this city belong to me." ¹¹So Paul stayed there for the next year and a half, teaching the word of God.

God told Paul to keep speaking out for him. He also told Paul that there was nothing to fear, because he was with Paul. There may be times in our life when we are afraid to speak out for God. But God tells us that we have nothing to fear. He is our protector, and he watches over us. Remember this the next time you are afraid to speak up for Jesus.

What should we remember when we are afraid?

But when I am afraid,
I put my trust in you.
Psalm 56:3

O C T O B E R

Paul performed miracles in Ephesus. The people confessed their sins. What did they do to show that they had turned away from their sins?

ACTS 19:1-20
Paul in Ephesus
While Apollos was in Corinth, Paul traveled through the interior provinces. Finally, he came to Ephesus, where he found several believers.* ²"Did you receive the Holy Spirit when you believed?" he asked them.

"No," they replied, "we don't know what you mean. We haven't even heard that there is a Holy Spirit."

³"Then what baptism did you experience?" he asked.

And they replied, "The baptism of John."

⁴Paul said, "John's baptism was to demonstrate a desire to turn from sin and turn to God. John himself told the people to believe in Jesus, the one John said would come later."

⁵As soon as they heard this, they were baptized in the name of the Lord Jesus. ⁶Then when Paul laid his hands on them, the Holy Spirit came on them, and they spoke in other tongues and prophesied. ⁷There were about twelve men in all.

19:1 Greek *disciples;* also in 19:9, 30.

8Then Paul went to the synagogue and preached boldly for the next three months, arguing persuasively about the Kingdom of God. 9But some rejected his message and publicly spoke against the Way, so Paul left the synagogue and took the believers with him. Then he began preaching daily at the lecture hall of Tyrannus. 10This went on for the next two years, so that people throughout the province of Asia—both Jews and Greeks—heard the Lord's message.

11God gave Paul the power to do unusual miracles, 12so that even when handkerchiefs or cloths that had touched his skin were placed on sick people, they were healed of their diseases, and any evil spirits within them came out.

13A team of Jews who were traveling from town to town casting out evil spirits tried to use the name of the Lord Jesus. The incantation they used was this: "I command you by Jesus, whom Paul preaches, to come out!" 14Seven sons of Sceva, a leading priest, were doing this. 15But when they tried it on a man possessed by an evil spirit, the spirit replied, "I know Jesus, and I know Paul. But who are you?" 16And he leaped on them and attacked them with such violence that they fled from the house, naked and badly injured.

17The story of what happened spread quickly all through Ephesus, to Jews and Greeks alike. A solemn fear descended on the city, and the name of the Lord Jesus was greatly honored. 18Many who became believers confessed their sinful practices. 19A number of them who had been practicing magic brought their incantation books and burned them at a public bonfire. The value of the books was several million dollars.* 20So the message about the Lord spread widely and had a powerful effect.

The people burned the books that had led them away from God. If something causes us to sin, we should get rid of it. Turning away from our sins shows that we really love God.

What should we do when we sin?
But I confess my sins; I am deeply sorry for what I have done.
Psalm 38:18

19:19 Greek *50,000 pieces of silver,* each of which was the equivalent of a day's wage.

Some Ephesian silversmiths were worried that their idol-making business would slow down. Whom did they blame?

ACTS 19:21-41

A Riot

²¹Afterward Paul felt impelled by the Holy Spirit* to go over to Macedonia and Achaia before returning to Jerusalem. "And after that," he said, "I must go on to Rome!" ²²He sent his two assistants, Timothy and Erastus, on ahead to Macedonia while he stayed awhile longer in the province of Asia.

²³But about that time, serious trouble developed in Ephesus concerning the Way. ²⁴It began with Demetrius, a silversmith who had a large business manufacturing silver shrines of the Greek goddess Artemis.* He kept many craftsmen busy. ²⁵He called the craftsmen together, along with others employed in related trades, and addressed them as follows:

"Gentlemen, you know that our wealth comes from this business. ²⁶As you have seen and heard, this man Paul has persuaded many people that handmade gods aren't gods at all. And this is happening not only here in Ephesus but throughout the entire province! ²⁷Of course, I'm not just talking about the loss of public respect for our business. I'm also concerned that the temple of the great goddess Artemis will lose its influence and that Artemis this magnificent goddess worshiped throughout the province of Asia and all around the world—will be robbed of her prestige!"

²⁸At this their anger boiled, and they began shouting, "Great is Artemis of the Ephesians!" ²⁹A crowd began to gather, and soon the city was filled with confusion. Everyone rushed to the amphitheater, dragging along Gaius and Aristarchus, who were Paul's traveling companions from Macedonia. ³⁰Paul wanted to go in, but the believers wouldn't let him. ³¹Some of the officials of the province, friends of Paul, also sent a message to him, begging him not to risk his life by entering the amphitheater.

³²Inside, the people were all shouting, some one thing and some another. Everything was in confusion. In fact, most of them didn't even know why they were there. ³³Alexander was thrust forward by some of the Jews, who encouraged him to explain the situation. He motioned for silence and tried to speak in defense. ³⁴But when the crowd realized he was a Jew, they started shouting again and kept it up for two hours: "Great is Artemis of the Ephesians! Great is Artemis of the Ephesians!"

³⁵At last the mayor was able to quiet them down enough to speak. "Citizens of Ephesus," he said. "Everyone knows that Ephesus is the official

19:21 Or *purposed in his spirit.* 19:24 *Artemis* is otherwise known as Diana.

guardian of the temple of the great Artemis, whose image fell down to us from heaven. ³⁶Since this is an indisputable fact, you shouldn't be disturbed, no matter what is said. Don't do anything rash. ³⁷You have brought these men here, but they have stolen nothing from the temple and have not spoken against our goddess. ³⁸If Demetrius and the craftsmen have a case against them, the courts are in session and the judges can take the case at once. Let them go through legal channels. ³⁹And if there are complaints about other matters, they can be settled in a legal assembly. ⁴⁰I am afraid we are in danger of being charged with rioting by the Roman government, since there is no cause for all this commotion. And if Rome demands an explanation, we won't know what to say." ⁴¹Then he dismissed them, and they dispersed.

The silversmiths blamed Paul. They believed he threatened their business because he taught the Ephesians that handmade idols were not gods; therefore, people should not worship idols. Those who believed Paul no longer had a need for idols and most likely didn't buy any more from the silversmiths. Although Christians today don't bow down to idols, many of them put things before their relationship with Christ. When this happens, they are setting up idols in their hearts. Is there anything or anyone you value more than Jesus? If so, you need to make some changes. Begin by putting Jesus first in your life. That is the position he deserves.

Why should we put Jesus first in our life?

But God showed his great love for us by sending Christ to die for us while we were still sinners.
Romans 5:8

N O V E M B E R

Paul knew he would face trouble in the future. What did he determine to do?

ACTS 20:13-38
Paul Says Good-Bye
¹³Paul went by land to Assos, where he had arranged for us to join him, and we went on ahead by ship. ¹⁴He joined us there and we sailed together to Mitylene. ¹⁵The next day we passed the island of Kios. The following day, we crossed to the island of Samos. And a day later we arrived at Miletus.

¹⁶Paul had decided against stopping at Ephesus this time because he didn't want to spend further time in the province of Asia. He was hurrying to get to Jerusalem, if possible, for the Festival of Pentecost. ¹⁷But when we landed at Miletus, he sent a message to the elders of the church at Ephesus, asking them to come down to meet him.

¹⁸When they arrived he declared,

"You know that from the day I set foot in the province of Asia until now [19]I have done the Lord's work humbly—yes, and with tears. I have endured the trials that came to me from the plots of the Jews. [20]Yet I never shrank from telling you the truth, either publicly or in your homes. [21]I have had one message for Jews and Gentiles alike—the necessity of turning from sin and turning to God, and of faith in our Lord Jesus.

[22]"And now I am going to Jerusalem, drawn there irresistibly by the Holy Spirit,* not knowing what awaits me, [23]except that the Holy Spirit has told me in city after city that jail and suffering lie ahead. [24]But my life is worth nothing unless I use it for doing the work assigned me by the Lord Jesus—the work of telling others the Good News about God's wonderful kindness and love.

[25]"And now I know that none of you to whom I have preached the Kingdom will ever see me again. [26]Let me say plainly that I have been faithful. No one's damnation can be blamed on me,* [27]for I didn't shrink from declaring all that God wants for you.

[28]"And now beware! Be sure that you feed and shepherd God's flock—his church, purchased with his blood—over whom the Holy Spirit has appointed you as elders.* [29]I know full well that false teachers, like vicious wolves, will come in among you after I leave, not sparing the flock. [30]Even some of you will distort the truth in order to draw a following. [31]Watch out! Remember the three years I was with you—my constant watch and care over you night and day, and my many tears for you.

[32]"And now I entrust you to God and the word of his grace—his message that is able to build you up and give you an inheritance with all those he has set apart for himself.

[33]"I have never coveted anyone's money or fine clothing. [34]You know that these hands of mine have worked to pay my own way, and I have even supplied the needs of those who were with me. [35]And I have been a constant example of how you can help the poor by working hard. You should remember the words of the Lord Jesus: 'It is more blessed to give than to receive.' "

[36]When he had finished speaking, he knelt and prayed with them. [37]They wept aloud as they embraced him in farewell, [38]sad most of all because he had said that they would never see him again. Then they accompanied him down to the ship.

Even during times of trouble, Paul was determined to serve God. He was willing to give up everything—even his life—for the Lord Jesus Christ. Today, Jesus demands no less from you. To be a true disciple, you have to dedicate everything you have to God's service. Will you do that?

How can you give everything you have to Jesus?

And you must love the LORD your God with all your heart, all your soul, and all your strength.
Deuteronomy 6:5

20:22 Or by my spirit, or by an inner compulsion; Greek reads by the spirit. 20:26 Greek I am innocent of the blood of all. 20:28 Greek overseers.

As Paul traveled to Jerusalem, many people begged him not to go, because he would be arrested. How did Paul respond to them?

ACTS 21:1-17
A Difficult Journey

After saying farewell to the Ephesian elders, we sailed straight to the island of Cos. The next day we reached Rhodes and then went to Patara. ²There we boarded a ship sailing for the Syrian province of Phoenicia. ³We sighted the island of Cyprus, passed it on our left, and landed at the harbor of Tyre, in Syria, where the ship was to unload. ⁴We went ashore, found the local believers,* and stayed with them a week. These disciples prophesied through the Holy Spirit that Paul should not go on to Jerusalem. ⁵When we returned to the ship at the end of the week, the entire congregation, including wives and children, came down to the shore with us. There we knelt, prayed, ⁶and said our farewells. Then we went aboard, and they returned home.

⁷The next stop after leaving Tyre was Ptolemais, where we greeted the brothers and sisters but stayed only one day. ⁸Then we went on to Caesarea and stayed at the home of Philip the Evangelist, one of the seven men who had been chosen to distribute food. ⁹He had four unmarried daughters who had the gift of prophecy.

¹⁰During our stay of several days, a man named Agabus, who also had the gift of prophecy, arrived from Judea.

¹¹When he visited us, he took Paul's belt and bound his own feet and hands with it. Then he said, "The Holy Spirit declares, 'So shall the owner of this belt be bound by the Jewish leaders in Jerusalem and turned over to the Romans.' " ¹²When we heard this, we who were traveling with him, as well as the local believers, begged Paul not to go on to Jerusalem.

¹³But he said, "Why all this weeping? You are breaking my heart! For I am ready not only to be jailed at Jerusalem but also to die for the sake of the Lord Jesus." ¹⁴When it was clear that we couldn't persuade him, we gave up

Paul was touched by the believers' concern for him. But he told them that he would continue to Jerusalem anyway. He was ready to die for Jesus, if necessary. His response showed the depth of his commitment to Jesus. How committed to Jesus are you?

What should you do when you face difficult times?

Hear my prayer, O LORD; listen to my plea! Answer me because you are faithful and righteous.

Psalm 143:1

21:4 Greek *disciples;* also in 21:16.

and said, "The will of the Lord be done."

¹⁵Shortly afterward we packed our things and left for Jerusalem. ¹⁶Some believers from Caesarea accompanied us, and they took us to the home of Mnason, a man originally from Cyprus and one of the early disciples. ¹⁷All the brothers and sisters in Jerusalem welcomed us cordially.

N O V E M B E R

Paul was in the Temple when some Jewish men grabbed him and began beating him. Who came to Paul's rescue?

ACTS 21:26-40

Paul Is Arrested

²⁶So Paul agreed to their request, and the next day he went through the purification ritual with the men and went to the Temple. Then he publicly announced the date when their vows would end and sacrifices would be offered for each of them.

²⁷The seven days were almost ended when some Jews from the province of Asia saw Paul in the Temple and roused a mob against him. They grabbed him, ²⁸yelling, "Men of Israel! Help! This is the man who teaches against our people and tells everybody to disobey the Jewish laws. He speaks against the Temple—and he even defiles it by bringing Gentiles in!" ²⁹(For earlier that day they had seen him in the city with Trophimus, a Gentile from Ephesus, * and they assumed Paul had taken him into the Temple.)

³⁰The whole population of the city was rocked by these accusations, and a great riot followed. Paul was dragged out of the Temple, and immediately the gates were closed behind him. ³¹As they were trying to kill him, word reached the commander of the Roman regiment that all Jerusalem was in an uproar. ³²He immediately called out his soldiers and officers and ran down among the crowd. When the mob saw the commander and the troops coming, they stopped beating Paul. ³³The commander arrested him and ordered him bound with two chains. Then he asked the crowd who he was and what he had done. ³⁴Some shouted one thing and some another. He couldn't find out the truth in all the uproar and confusion, so he ordered Paul to be taken to the fortress. ³⁵As they reached the stairs, the mob grew so violent the soldiers had to lift Paul to their shoulders to protect him. ³⁶And the crowd followed behind shouting, "Kill him, kill him!"

³⁷As Paul was about to be taken inside, he said to the commander, "May I have a word with you?"

"Do you know Greek?" the commander asked, surprised. ³⁸"Aren't

21:29 Greek *Trophimus, the Ephesian.*

383

you the Egyptian who led a rebellion some time ago and took four thousand members of the Assassins out into the desert?"

[39]"No," Paul replied, "I am a Jew from Tarsus in Cilicia, which is an important city. Please, let me talk to these people." [40]The commander agreed, so Paul stood on the stairs and motioned to the people to be quiet. Soon a deep silence enveloped the crowd, and he addressed them in their own language, Aramaic.*

A commander of the Roman army heard about the uproar near the Temple. He broke up the riot and arrested Paul. Even though Paul hadn't done anything wrong and didn't deserve to be arrested, the commander's actions saved Paul's life. Sometimes God works in strange ways for our own good. We may not see the good in our circumstances, but we can trust God to care for us and guide us.

What truth about God can help us through bad times?
And we know that God causes everything to work together* for the good of those who love God and are called according to his purpose for them.
Romans 8:28

21:40 Or *Hebrew.* **8:28** Some manuscripts read *And we know that everything works together.*

N O V E M B E R

Paul told the crowd how he had met Jesus. He also told them about his new mission in life. How did the crowd respond?

ACTS 22:1-23
Paul's Story

"Brothers and esteemed fathers," Paul said, "listen to me as I offer my defense." [2]When they heard him speaking in their own language,* the silence was even greater. [3]"I am a Jew, born in Tarsus, a city in Cilicia, and I was brought up and educated here in Jeru-salem under Gamaliel. At his feet I learned to follow our Jewish laws and customs very carefully. I became very zealous to honor God in everything I did, just as all of you are today. [4]And I persecuted the followers of the Way, hounding some to death, binding and delivering both men and women to prison. [5]The high priest and the whole

22:2 Greek *in Aramaic.*

council of leaders can testify that this is so. For I received letters from them to our Jewish brothers in Damascus, authorizing me to bring the Christians from there to Jerusalem, in chains, to be punished.

⁶"As I was on the road, nearing Damascus, about noon a very bright light from heaven suddenly shone around me. ⁷I fell to the ground and heard a voice saying to me, 'Saul, Saul, why are you persecuting me?'

⁸"'Who are you, sir?' I asked. And he replied, 'I am Jesus of Nazareth, the one you are persecuting.' ⁹The people with me saw the light but didn't hear the voice.

¹⁰"I said, 'What shall I do, Lord?' And the Lord told me, 'Get up and go into Damascus, and there you will be told all that you are to do.'

¹¹"I was blinded by the intense light and had to be led into Damascus by my companions. ¹²A man named Ananias lived there. He was a godly man in his devotion to the law, and he was well thought of by all the Jews of Damascus. ¹³He came to me and stood beside me and said, 'Brother Saul, receive your sight.' And that very hour I could see him!

¹⁴"Then he told me, 'The God of our ancestors has chosen you to know his will and to see the Righteous One and hear him speak. ¹⁵You are to take his message everywhere, telling the whole world what you have seen and heard. ¹⁶And now, why delay? Get up and be baptized, and have your sins washed away, calling on the name of the Lord.'

¹⁷"One day after I returned to Jerusalem, I was praying in the Temple, and I fell into a trance. ¹⁸I saw a vision of Jesus saying to me, 'Hurry! Leave Jerusalem, for the people here won't believe you when you give them your testimony about me.'

¹⁹"'But Lord,' I argued, 'they certainly know that I imprisoned and beat those in every synagogue who believed on you. ²⁰And when your witness Stephen was killed, I was standing there agreeing. I kept the coats they laid aside as they stoned him.'

²¹"But the Lord said to me, 'Leave Jerusalem, for I will send you far away to the Gentiles!'"

²²The crowd listened until Paul came to that word; then with one voice they shouted, "Away with such a fellow! Kill him! He isn't fit to live!" ²³They yelled, threw off their coats, and tossed handfuls of dust into the air.

At first the crowd listened to what Paul had to say. But as soon as Paul said the word Gentile, the crowd went crazy. That's because the crowd was made up of devout Jews who believed Gentiles weren't worthy of entering God's kingdom. Their reaction showed their judgmental attitude. As Christians, we should not have judgmental attitudes toward others. We are sinners saved by God's grace. Therefore, we should show God's grace to others. We can do this by having a humble attitude and not judging others.

What did Jesus say about those who didn't know him?

And I, the Son of Man, have come to seek and save those like him who are lost.

Luke 19:10

Some men plotted to kill Paul. Did Paul escape from these evil men?

ACTS 23:6-24

A Murder Plot

⁶Paul realized that some members of the high council were Sadducees and some were Pharisees, so he shouted, "Brothers, I am a Pharisee, as were all my ancestors! And I am on trial because my hope is in the resurrection of the dead!"

⁷This divided the council—the Pharisees against the Sadducees—⁸for the Sadducees say there is no resurrection or angels or spirits, but the Pharisees believe in all of these. ⁹So a great clamor arose. Some of the teachers of religious law who were Pharisees jumped up to argue that Paul was all right. "We see nothing wrong with him," they shouted. "Perhaps a spirit or an angel spoke to him." ¹⁰The shouting grew louder and louder, and the men were tugging at Paul from both sides, pulling him this way and that. Finally, the commander, fearing they would tear him apart, ordered his soldiers to take him away from them and bring him back to the fortress.

¹¹That night the Lord appeared to Paul and said, "Be encouraged, Paul. Just as you have told the people about me here in Jerusalem, you must preach the Good News in Rome."

¹²The next morning a group of Jews got together and bound themselves with an oath to neither eat nor drink until they had killed Paul. ¹³There

were more than forty of them. ¹⁴They went to the leading priests and other leaders and told them what they had done. "We have bound ourselves under oath to neither eat nor drink until we have killed Paul. ¹⁵You and the high council should tell the commander to bring Paul back to the council again," they requested. "Pretend you want to examine his case more fully. We will kill him on the way."

¹⁶But Paul's nephew heard of their plan and went to the fortress and told Paul. ¹⁷Paul called one of the officers and said, "Take this young man to the commander. He has something important to tell him."

¹⁸So the officer did, explaining, "Paul, the prisoner, called me over and asked me to bring this young man to you because he has something to tell you."

¹⁹The commander took him by the arm, led him aside, and asked, "What is it you want to tell me?"

²⁰Paul's nephew told him, "Some Jews are going to ask you to bring Paul before the Jewish high council tomorrow, pretending they want to get some more information. ²¹But don't do it! There are more than forty men hiding along the way ready to jump him and kill him. They have vowed not to eat or drink until they kill him. They are

ready, expecting you to agree to their request."

²²"Don't let a soul know you told me this," the commander warned the young man as he sent him away.

²³Then the commander called two of his officers and ordered, "Get two hundred soldiers ready to leave for Caesarea at nine o'clock tonight. Also take two hundred spearmen and seventy horsemen. ²⁴Provide horses for Paul to ride, and get him safely to Governor Felix."

God frustrated the plans of the men who plotted to kill Paul. First, Paul's nephew overheard the men's plans. Second, he reported their plans to the Roman commander. Third, the commander had 470 Roman soldiers move Paul to a city far away from Jerusalem. Paul escaped and was safe from these men. God is more powerful than any person or group of people. He can prevent evil people from carrying out their plans. Trust him to watch over and protect you.

What should you remember when people are planning to hurt you?

The LORD . . . frustrates the plans of the wicked.
Psalm 146:9

N O V E M B E R

Paul defended himself against the Jews' charges before the governor, Felix. How did Felix respond to Paul's message?

ACTS 24:10-25

Paul Speaks to Felix

¹⁰Now it was Paul's turn. The governor motioned for him to rise and speak. Paul said, "I know, sir, that you have been a judge of Jewish affairs for many years, and this gives me confidence as I make my defense. ¹¹You can quickly discover that it was no more than twelve days ago that I arrived in Jerusalem to worship at the Temple. ¹²I didn't argue with anyone in the Temple, nor did I incite a riot in any synagogue or on the streets of the city. ¹³These men certainly cannot prove the things they accuse me of doing.

¹⁴"But I admit that I follow the Way, which they call a sect. I worship the God of our ancestors, and I firmly believe the Jewish law and everything written in the books of prophecy. ¹⁵I have hope in God, just as these men do, that he will raise both the righteous and the ungodly. ¹⁶Because of this, I always

try to maintain a clear conscience before God and everyone else.

[17]"After several years away, I returned to Jerusalem with money to aid my people and to offer sacrifices to God. [18]My accusers saw me in the Temple as I was completing a purification ritual. There was no crowd around me and no rioting. [19]But some Jews from the province of Asia were there—and they ought to be here to bring charges if they have anything against me! [20]Ask these men here what wrongdoing the Jewish high council* found in me, [21]except for one thing I said when I shouted out, 'I am on trial before you today because I believe in the resurrection of the dead!' "

[22]Felix, who was quite familiar with the Way, adjourned the hearing and said, "Wait until Lysias, the garrison commander, arrives. Then I will decide the case." [23]He ordered an officer to keep Paul in custody but to give him some freedom and allow his friends to visit him and take care of his needs.

[24]A few days later Felix came with his wife, Drusilla, who was Jewish. Sending for Paul, they listened as he told them about faith in Christ Jesus. [25]As he reasoned with them about righteousness and self-control and the judgment to come, Felix was terrified. "Go away for now," he replied. "When it is more convenient, I'll call for you again."

When Paul spoke of the Good News, Felix became afraid. Felix had not accepted God's free gift of salvation and could only expect punishment for his sins. But Christians do not have to be afraid of the coming judgment. All who believe in Jesus have nothing to fear.

What can Christians look forward to when Jesus returns?
It will happen in a moment, in the blinking of an eye, when the last trumpet is blown. For when the trumpet sounds, the Christians who have died* will be raised with transformed bodies. And then we who are living will be transformed so that we will never die.
1 Corinthians 15:52

24:20 Greek *Sanhedrin*. **15:52** Greek *the dead*.

N O V E M B E R

Paul spoke before King Agrippa about what Jesus had done for him. Why was Paul so open about his faith?

ACTS 26:1-3, 9-29
Paul Speaks to Agrippa
Then Agrippa said to Paul, "You may speak in your defense."

So Paul, with a gesture of his hand, started his defense: [2]"I am fortunate, King Agrippa, that you are the one hearing my defense against all these accusations made by the Jewish leaders, ³for I know you are an expert on Jewish customs and controversies. Now please listen to me patiently!"

• • •

⁹"I used to believe that I ought to do everything I could to oppose the followers of Jesus of Nazareth.* ¹⁰Authorized by the leading priests, I caused many of the believers in Jerusalem to be sent to prison. And I cast my vote against them when they were condemned to death. ¹¹Many times I had them whipped in the synagogues to try to get them to curse Christ. I was so violently opposed to them that I even hounded them in distant cities of foreign lands.

¹²"One day I was on such a mission to Damascus, armed with the authority and commission of the leading priests. ¹³About noon, Your Majesty, a light from heaven brighter than the sun shone down on me and my companions. ¹⁴We all fell down, and I heard a voice saying to me in Aramaic,* 'Saul, Saul, why are you persecuting me? It is hard for you to fight against my will.*'

¹⁵"'Who are you, sir?' I asked.

"And the Lord replied, 'I am Jesus, the one you are persecuting. ¹⁶Now stand up! For I have appeared to you to appoint you as my servant and my witness. You are to tell the world about this experience and about other times I will appear to you. ¹⁷And I will protect you from both your own people and the Gentiles. Yes, I am going to send you to the Gentiles, ¹⁸to open their eyes so they may turn from darkness to light, and from the power of

Paul wanted his audience to be saved. Unfortunately, Agrippa and the rest of Paul's audience were not interested in knowing Jesus as their Savior. If you tell others about Jesus, you may get the same reaction that Paul did. Not every person you meet will be interested in Jesus. But don't give up.

What do we need to have when we tell others about Jesus?
Patience can persuade a prince, and soft speech can crush strong opposition.
Proverbs 25:15

Satan to God. Then they will receive forgiveness for their sins and be given a place among God's people, who are set apart by faith in me.'

¹⁹"And so, O King Agrippa, I was not disobedient to that vision from heaven. ²⁰I preached first to those in Damascus, then in Jerusalem and throughout all Judea, and also to the Gentiles, that all must turn from their sins and turn to God—and prove they have changed by the good things they do. ²¹Some Jews arrested me in the Temple for preaching this, and they tried to kill me. ²²But God protected me so that I am still alive today to tell these facts to everyone, from the least to the greatest. I teach nothing except what the prophets and Moses said would happen—²³that the Messiah would suffer and be the first to rise from the dead as a light to Jews and Gentiles alike."

²⁴Suddenly, Festus shouted, "Paul, you are insane. Too much study has made you crazy!"

26:9 Greek *oppose the name of Jesus the Nazarene.* 26:14a Or *Hebrew.* 26:14b Greek *It is hard for you to kick against the oxgoads.*

²⁵But Paul replied, "I am not insane, Most Excellent Festus. I am speaking the sober truth. ²⁶And King Agrippa knows about these things. I speak frankly, for I am sure these events are all familiar to him, for they were not done in a corner! ²⁷King Agrippa, do you believe the prophets? I know you do—"

²⁸Agrippa interrupted him. "Do you think you can make me a Christian so quickly?"*

²⁹Paul replied, "Whether quickly or not, I pray to God that both you and everyone here in this audience might become the same as I am, except for these chains."

26:28 Or "A little more, and your arguments would make me a Christian."

N O V E M B E R

Paul was on a ship headed for Rome. The ship got caught in a storm. What did Paul say to encourage the ship's crew?

ACTS 27:13-26

Caught in a Storm

¹³When a light wind began blowing from the south, the sailors thought they could make it. So they pulled up anchor and sailed along close to shore. ¹⁴But the weather changed abruptly, and a wind of typhoon strength (a "northeaster," they called it) caught the ship and blew it out to sea. ¹⁵They couldn't turn the ship into the wind, so they gave up and let it run before the gale.

¹⁶We sailed behind a small island named Cauda,* where with great difficulty we hoisted aboard the lifeboat that was being towed behind us. ¹⁷Then we banded the ship with ropes to strengthen the hull. The sailors were afraid of being driven across to the sandbars of Syrtis off the African coast, so they lowered the sea anchor and were thus driven before the wind.

¹⁸The next day, as gale-force winds continued to batter the ship, the crew began throwing the cargo overboard. ¹⁹The following day they even threw out the ship's equipment and anything else they could lay their hands on. ²⁰The terrible storm raged unabated for many days, blotting out the sun and the stars, until at last all hope was gone.

²¹No one had eaten for a long time. Finally, Paul called the crew together and said, "Men, you should have listened to me in the first place and not left Fair Havens. You would have avoided all this injury and loss. ²²But take courage! None of you will lose your lives, even though the ship will go down. ²³For last night an angel of the God to whom I belong and whom I serve stood beside me, ²⁴and

27:16 Some manuscripts read *Clauda.*

he said, 'Don't be afraid, Paul, for you will surely stand trial before Caesar! What's more, God in his goodness has granted safety to everyone sailing with you.' ²⁵So take courage! For I believe God. It will be just as he said. ²⁶But we will be shipwrecked on an island."

Paul told the ship's crew that the ship would be lost but that no one on board would die. An angel of God had told Paul this. Therefore, Paul was confident that God would protect him and everyone else on the ship. Like Paul, we can trust God to protect us in times of danger. Commit your safety to him. He will take care of you.

What can you pray when you are in danger?
Rescue me, O God, by your saving power.
Psalm 69:29

N O V E M B E R

A storm raged around Paul. Yet he remained calm and thanked God. How was he able to do this?

ACTS 27:27-44
Shipwrecked

²⁷About midnight on the fourteenth night of the storm, as we were being driven across the Sea of Adria,* the sailors sensed land was near. ²⁸They took soundings and found the water was only 120 feet deep. A little later they sounded again and found only 90 feet.* ²⁹At this rate they were afraid we would soon be driven against the rocks along the shore, so they threw out four anchors from the stern and prayed for daylight. ³⁰Then the sailors tried to abandon the ship; they lowered the lifeboat as though they were going to put out anchors from the prow. ³¹But Paul said to the commanding officer and the soldiers, "You will all die unless the sailors stay aboard." ³²So the soldiers cut the ropes and let the boat fall off.

³³As the darkness gave way to the early morning light, Paul begged everyone to eat. "You haven't touched food for two weeks," he said. ³⁴"Please eat something now for your own good. For not a hair of your heads will

27:27 The *Sea of Adria* is in the central Mediterranean; it is not to be confused with the Adriatic Sea. 27:28 Greek *20 fathoms . . . 15 fathoms* [37 meters . . . 27 meters].

perish." [35]Then he took some bread, gave thanks to God before them all, and broke off a piece and ate it. [36]Then everyone was encouraged, [37]and all 276 of us began eating—for that is the number we had aboard. [38]After eating, the crew lightened the ship further by throwing the cargo of wheat overboard.

[39]When morning dawned, they didn't recognize the coastline, but they saw a bay with a beach and wondered if they could get between the rocks and get the ship safely to shore. [40]So they cut off the anchors and left them in the sea. Then they lowered the rudders, raised the foresail, and headed toward shore. [41]But the ship hit a shoal and ran aground. The bow of the ship stuck fast, while the stern was repeatedly smashed by the force of the waves and began to break apart.

[42]The soldiers wanted to kill the prisoners to make sure they didn't swim ashore and escape. [43]But the commanding officer wanted to spare Paul, so he didn't let them carry out their plan. Then he ordered all who could swim to jump overboard first and make for land, [44]and he told the others to try for it on planks and debris from the broken ship. So everyone escaped safely ashore!

In a time of crisis, Paul clearly showed his trust in God by taking positive action and encouraging the sailors. When you face a time of crisis, pray to God and ask for his strength. Then encourage others with the strength God gives you.

How is God glorified when we trust in him during bad times?
Then at last the people will think of their Creator and have respect for the Holy One of Israel.
Isaiah 17:7

N O V E M B E R

While under house arrest, Paul continued to preach boldly. Why was that good?

ACTS 28:11-31
Paul in Chains
[11]It was three months after the shipwreck that we set sail on another ship that had wintered at the island—an Alexandrian ship with the twin gods* as its figurehead. [12]Our first stop was Syracuse,* where we stayed three days. [13]From there we sailed across to Rhegium.* A day later a south wind began blowing, so the following day we sailed up the coast to Puteoli. [14]There we found some believers,* who invited us to stay with them seven days. And so we came to Rome.

[15]The brothers and sisters in Rome

28:11 The *twin gods* were the Roman gods Castor and Pollux. 28:12 *Syracuse* was on the island of Sicily. 28:13 *Rhegium* was on the southern tip of Italy. 28:14 Greek *brothers.*

had heard we were coming, and they came to meet us at the Forum* on the Appian Way. Others joined us at The Three Taverns.* When Paul saw them, he thanked God and took courage.

¹⁶When we arrived in Rome, Paul was permitted to have his own private lodging, though he was guarded by a soldier.

¹⁷Three days after Paul's arrival, he called together the local Jewish leaders. He said to them, "Brothers, I was arrested in Jerusalem and handed over to the Roman government, even though I had done nothing against our people or the customs of our ancestors. ¹⁸The Romans tried me and wanted to release me, for they found no cause for the death sentence. ¹⁹But when the Jewish leaders protested the decision, I felt it necessary to appeal to Caesar, even though I had no desire to press charges against my own people. ²⁰I asked you to come here today so we could get acquainted and so I could tell you that I am bound with this chain because I believe that the hope of Israel—the Messiah—has already come."

²¹They replied, "We have heard nothing against you. We have had no letters from Judea or reports from anyone who has arrived here. ²²But we want to hear what you believe, for the only thing we know about these Christians* is that they are denounced everywhere."

²³So a time was set, and on that day a large number of people came to Paul's house. He told them about the Kingdom of God and taught them about Jesus from the Scriptures—from the five books of Moses and the books of the prophets. He began lecturing in the morning and went on into the evening. ²⁴Some believed and some didn't. ²⁵But after they had argued back and forth among themselves, they left with this final word from Paul: "The Holy Spirit was right when he said to our ancestors through Isaiah the prophet,

²⁶ 'Go and say to my people,
You will hear my words,
    but you will not understand;
you will see what I do,
    but you will not perceive its
        meaning.
²⁷ For the hearts of these people are
        hardened,
    and their ears cannot hear,
    and they have closed their eyes—
so their eyes cannot see,
    and their ears cannot hear,

Paul boldly told others about Jesus, even with guards watching and listening. He didn't let anyone keep him from preaching the Good News. If you are serious about following Jesus, don't let anyone scare you into not speaking up for him. Live boldly for Jesus, no matter who is around.

How does Paul's example encourage you to keep speaking out for Jesus?
Don't forget to pray for us, too, that God will give us many opportunities to preach about his secret plan— that Christ is also for you Gentiles. That is why I am here in chains.
Colossians 4:3

28:15a The Forum was about 43 miles (70 kilometers) from Rome. **28:15b** The Three Taverns was about 35 miles (57 kilometers) from Rome. **28:22** Greek this sect.

and their hearts cannot
understand,
and they cannot turn to me
and let me heal them.'*

²⁸So I want you to realize that this salvation from God is also available to the Gentiles, and they will accept it."*

³⁰For the next two years, Paul lived in his own rented house.* He welcomed all who visited him, ³¹proclaiming the Kingdom of God with all boldness and teaching about the Lord Jesus Christ. And no one tried to stop him.

28:26-27 Isa 6:9-10. **28:28** Some manuscripts add verse 29, *And when he had said these words, the Jews departed, greatly disagreeing with each other.* **28:30** Or *at his own expense.*

N O V E M B E R

In his letter to the Romans, Paul wrote, "Are we Jews better than others?" What answer did he give for this question?

ROMANS 3:9-26

No One Is Good

⁹Well then, are we Jews better than others?* No, not at all, for we have already shown that all people, whether Jews or Gentiles, are under the power of sin. ¹⁰As the Scriptures say,

"No one is good—
not even one.
¹¹ No one has real understanding;
no one is seeking God.
¹² All have turned away from God;
all have gone wrong.
No one does good,
not even one."*
¹³ "Their talk is foul, like the stench
from an open grave.
Their speech is filled with lies."
"The poison of a deadly snake
drips from their lips."*

¹⁴   "Their mouths are full of
cursing and bitterness."*
¹⁵ "They are quick to commit murder.
¹⁶   Wherever they go, destruction
and misery follow them.
¹⁷ They do not know what true peace
is."*
¹⁸   "They have no fear of God to
restrain them."*

¹⁹Obviously, the law applies to those to whom it was given, for its purpose is to keep people from having excuses and to bring the entire world into judgment before God. ²⁰For no one can ever be made right in God's sight by doing what his law commands. For the more we know God's law, the clearer it becomes that we aren't obeying it.

²¹But now God has shown us a different way of being right in his sight— not by obeying the law but by the way

3:9 Greek *Are we better?* **3:10-12** Pss 14:1-3; 53:1-3. **3:13** Pss 5:9; 140:3. **3:14** Ps 10:7. **3:15-17** Isa 59:7-8. **3:18** Ps 36:1.

promised in the Scriptures long ago. [22]We are made right in God's sight when we trust in Jesus Christ to take away our sins. And we all can be saved in this same way, no matter who we are or what we have done.

[23]For all have sinned; all fall short of God's glorious standard. [24]Yet now God in his gracious kindness declares us not guilty. He has done this through Christ Jesus, who has freed us by taking away our sins. [25]For God sent Jesus to take the punishment for our sins and to satisfy God's anger against us. We are made right with God when we believe that Jesus shed his blood, sacrificing his life for us. God was being entirely fair and just when he did not punish those who sinned in former times. [26]And he is entirely fair and just in this present time when he declares sinners to be right in his sight because they believe in Jesus.

Paul used Scripture to prove that no one is good. People must be perfect in order to please God. Because no one can be perfect, God sent Jesus to die for everyone's sins. Forgiveness for your sins can be received only by believing in Jesus Christ as your Savior. Have you put your trust in him?

Why do we need Jesus to save us?
There is not a single person
in all the earth who is always
good and never sins.
Ecclesiastes 7:20

N O V E M B E R

Paul wrote that it wasn't likely that someone would die for a good person. Why was Jesus' death so amazing?

ROMANS 5:1-11
God's Love
Therefore, since we have been made right in God's sight by faith, we have peace with God because of what Jesus Christ our Lord has done for us. [2]Because of our faith, Christ has brought us into this place of highest privilege where we now stand, and we confidently and joyfully look forward to sharing God's glory.

[3]We can rejoice, too, when we run into problems and trials, for we know that they are good for us—they help us learn to endure. [4]And endurance develops strength of character in us, and character strengthens our confident expectation of salvation. [5]And this expectation will not disappoint us. For we know how dearly God loves us, because he has given us the Holy Spirit to fill our hearts with his love.

[6]When we were utterly helpless, Christ came at just the right time and died for us sinners. [7]Now, no one is likely to die for a good person, though

someone might be willing to die for a person who is especially good. ⁸But God showed his great love for us by sending Christ to die for us while we were still sinners. ⁹And since we have been made right in God's sight by the blood of Christ, he will certainly save us from God's judgment. ¹⁰For since we were restored to friendship with God by the death of his Son while we were still his enemies, we will certainly be delivered from eternal punishment by his life. ¹¹So now we can rejoice in our wonderful new relationship with God—all because of what our Lord Jesus Christ has done for us in making us friends of God.

Jesus' death was amazing because he died for sinners. He died for those who loved God and for those who hated God. In his death, we see God's incredible love for us. He gave his own Son so that we might be able to live with him forever. Could you give your life for one of your enemies? That is what Jesus did for you.

Why does Jesus deserve your love and obedience?

O Lord, you are so good, so ready to forgive, so full of unfailing love for all who ask your aid.
Psalm 86:5

N O V E M B E R

Before people become Christians, they are slaves to sin. What sets a person free from sin?

ROMANS 6:5-23

Free from Sin

⁵Since we have been united with him in his death, we will also be raised as he was. ⁶Our old sinful selves were crucified with Christ so that sin might lose its power in our lives. We are no longer slaves to sin. ⁷For when we died with Christ we were set free from the power of sin. ⁸And since we died with Christ, we know we will also share his new life. ⁹We are sure of this because Christ rose from the dead, and he will never die again. Death no longer has any power over him. ¹⁰He died once to defeat sin, and now he lives for the glory of God. ¹¹So you should consider yourselves dead to sin and able to live for the glory of God through Christ Jesus.

¹²Do not let sin control the way you live;* do not give in to its lustful desires. ¹³Do not let any part of your body become a tool of wickedness, to be used for sinning. Instead, give yourselves completely to God since you have been given new life. And use your whole body as a tool to do what is

6:12 Or *Do not let sin reign in your body, which is subject to death.*

right for the glory of God. [14]Sin is no longer your master, for you are no longer subject to the law, which enslaves you to sin. Instead, you are free by God's grace.

[15]So since God's grace has set us free from the law, does this mean we can go on sinning? Of course not! [16]Don't you realize that whatever you choose to obey becomes your master? You can choose sin, which leads to death, or you can choose to obey God and receive his approval. [17]Thank God! Once you were slaves of sin, but now you have obeyed with all your heart the new teaching God has given you. [18]Now you are free from sin, your old master, and you have become slaves to your new master, righteousness.

[19]I speak this way, using the illustration of slaves and masters, because it is easy to understand. Before, you let yourselves be slaves of impurity and lawlessness. Now you must choose to be slaves of righteousness so that you will become holy.

[20]In those days, when you were slaves of sin, you weren't concerned with doing what was right. [21]And what was the result? It was not good, since now you are ashamed of the things you used to do, things that end in eternal doom. [22]But now you are free from the power of sin and have become slaves of God. Now you do those things that lead to holiness and result in eternal life. [23]For the wages of sin is death, but the free gift of God is eternal life through Christ Jesus our Lord.

God's grace sets a person free from sin. What does God's grace mean? It means that God gave his Son, Jesus, to pay the penalty for everyone's sin. Those who accept Jesus' payment for their sin by believing in him are set free from the power that sin has over their lives. If you believe that Jesus died for you, then you, too, can be set free from sin. Believe in Jesus as your Savior. He will set you free from your sin.

How can Jesus help us stop sinning?

Have mercy on me, O God, because of your unfailing love. Because of your great compassion, blot out the stain of my sins. Wash me clean from my guilt. Purify me from my sin.
Psalm 51:1-2

Paul wrote that Christians are not controlled by their sinful nature. Who or what should they be controlled by?

ROMANS 8:1-17
Life in the Spirit

So now there is no condemnation for those who belong to Christ Jesus. [2]For the power* of the life-giving Spirit has freed you* through Christ Jesus from the power of sin that leads to death. [3]The law of Moses could not save us, because of our sinful nature. But God put into effect a different plan to save us. He sent his own Son in a human body like ours, except that ours are sinful. God destroyed sin's control over us by giving his Son as a sacrifice for our sins. [4]He did this so that the requirement of the law would be fully accomplished for us* who no longer follow our sinful nature but instead follow the Spirit.

[5]Those who are dominated by the sinful nature think about sinful things, but those who are controlled by the Holy Spirit think about things that please the Spirit. [6]If your sinful nature controls your mind, there is death. But if the Holy Spirit controls your mind, there is life and peace. [7]For the sinful nature is always hostile to God. It never did obey God's laws, and it never will. [8]That's why those who are still under the control of their sinful nature can never please God.

[9]But you are not controlled by your sinful nature. You are controlled by the Spirit if you have the Spirit of God living in you. (And remember that those who do not have the Spirit of Christ living in them are not Christians at all.) [10]Since Christ lives within you, even though your body will die because of sin, your spirit is alive* because you have been made right with God. [11]The Spirit of God, who raised Jesus from the dead, lives in you. And just as he raised Christ from the dead, he will give life to your mortal body by this same Spirit living within you.

Christians should be controlled by the Holy Spirit. The Spirit helps Christians fight their natural desire to sin. Without the Holy Spirit living in a person's life, he or she cannot be a Christian and, as a result, cannot please God. Is the Holy Spirit living in you?

What can you pray when you have sinned?

Create in me a clean heart, O God. Renew a right spirit within me. Do not banish me from your presence, and don't take your Holy Spirit from me.
Psalm 51:10-11

8:2a Greek *the law;* also in 8:2b. **8:2b** Some manuscripts read *me.* **8:4** Or *accomplished by us.* **8:10** Or *the Spirit will bring you eternal life.*

¹²So, dear brothers and sisters, you have no obligation whatsoever to do what your sinful nature urges you to do. ¹³For if you keep on following it, you will perish. But if through the power of the Holy Spirit you turn from it* and its evil deeds, you will live. ¹⁴For all who are led by the Spirit of God are children of God.

¹⁵So you should not be like cowering, fearful slaves. You should behave instead like God's very own children, adopted into his family—calling him "Father, dear Father."* ¹⁶For his Holy Spirit speaks to us deep in our hearts and tells us that we are God's children. ¹⁷And since we are his children, we will share his treasures—for everything God gives to his Son, Christ, is ours, too. But if we are to share his glory, we must also share his suffering.

8:13 Greek *put it to death.*   **8:15** Greek *"Abba, Father." Abba* is an Aramaic term for "father."

N O V E M B E R

Christians will have troubles, trials, and hardships. Paul says that Christians can have victory through these hard times. How is that possible?

ROMANS 8:28-39

Victory Is Ours

²⁸And we know that God causes everything to work together* for the good of those who love God and are called according to his purpose for them. ²⁹For God knew his people in advance, and he chose them to become like his Son, so that his Son would be the firstborn, with many brothers and sisters. ³⁰And having chosen them, he called them to come to him. And he gave them right standing with himself, and he promised them his glory.

³¹What can we say about such wonderful things as these? If God is for us, who can ever be against us? ³²Since God did not spare even his own Son but gave him up for us all, won't God, who gave us Christ, also give us everything else?

³³Who dares accuse us whom God has chosen for his own? Will God? No! He is the one who has given us right standing with himself. ³⁴Who then will condemn us? Will Christ Jesus? No, for he is the one who died for us and was raised to life for us and is sitting at the place of highest honor next to God, pleading for us.

³⁵Can anything ever separate us from Christ's love? Does it mean he no longer loves us if we have trouble or calamity, or are persecuted, or are hungry or cold or in danger or threatened with death? ³⁶(Even the Scriptures say, "For your sake we are killed every day; we are being slaughtered like sheep."*) ³⁷No, despite all these things, overwhelming victory is ours through Christ, who loved us.

8:28 Some manuscripts read *And we know that everything works together.*   **8:36** Ps 44:22

399

[38]And I am convinced that nothing can ever separate us from his love. Death can't, and life can't. The angels can't, and the demons can't. Our fears for today, our worries about tomorrow, and even the powers of hell can't keep God's love away. [39]Whether we are high above the sky or in the deepest ocean, nothing in all creation will ever be able to separate us from the love of God that is revealed in Christ Jesus our Lord.

God is always with Christians, even when they suffer. There isn't any trial or trouble that can separate a Christian from God. He will never abandon his followers. If you are a Christian, you will never be separated from God's love. No trouble is so great that it can totally defeat you. You have the victory!

What encourages us when we face problems?

I cried out, "I'm slipping!" and your unfailing love, O LORD, supported me.
Psalm 94:18

N O V E M B E R

Paul wrote that Christians shouldn't seek revenge. How should they treat their enemies instead?

ROMANS 12:1-21

Overcoming Evil

And so, dear brothers and sisters, I plead with you to give your bodies to God. Let them be a living and holy sacrifice—the kind he will accept. When you think of what he has done for you, is this too much to ask? [2]Don't copy the behavior and customs of this world, but let God transform you into a new person by changing the way you think. Then you will know what God wants you to do, and you will know how good and pleasing and perfect his will really is.

[3]As God's messenger, I give each of you this warning: Be honest in your estimate of yourselves, measuring your value by how much faith God has given you. [4]Just as our bodies have many parts and each part has a special function, [5]so it is with Christ's body. We are all parts of his one body, and each of us has different work to do. And since we are all one body in Christ, we belong to each other, and each of us needs all the others.

[6]God has given each of us the ability to do certain things well. So if God has given you the ability to prophesy, speak out when you have faith that God is speaking through you. [7]If your gift is that of serving others, serve them well. If you are a teacher, do a good job

of teaching. [8]If your gift is to encourage others, do it! If you have money, share it generously. If God has given you leadership ability, take the responsibility seriously. And if you have a gift for showing kindness to others, do it gladly.

[9]Don't just pretend that you love others. Really love them. Hate what is wrong. Stand on the side of the good. [10]Love each other with genuine affection,* and take delight in honoring each other. [11]Never be lazy in your work, but serve the Lord enthusiastically.

[12]Be glad for all God is planning for you. Be patient in trouble, and always be prayerful. [13]When God's children are in need, be the one to help them out. And get into the habit of inviting guests home for dinner or, if they need lodging, for the night.

[14]If people persecute you because you are a Christian, don't curse them; pray that God will bless them. [15]When others are happy, be happy with them. If they are sad, share their sorrow. [16]Live in harmony with each other. Don't try to act important, but enjoy the company of ordinary people. And don't think you know it all!

[17]Never pay back evil for evil to anyone. Do things in such a way that everyone can see you are honorable. [18]Do your part to live in peace with everyone, as much as possible.

[19]Dear friends, never avenge yourselves. Leave that to God. For it is written,

"I will take vengeance;
  I will repay those who deserve
    it,"*
says the Lord.

[20]Instead, do what the Scriptures say:

"If your enemies are hungry, feed
    them.
If they are thirsty, give them
    something to drink,
  and they will be ashamed of
    what they have done to
    you."*

[21]Don't let evil get the best of you, but conquer evil by doing good.

Christians should show love to their enemies. For Jesus' followers, this command replaced the then-current belief that people should get revenge in the same way they were injured. The new command was a way of showing God's love for people. How can you love your enemies? Say a kind word to those who insult you, and pray for those who wrong you.

How can you show love to someone who does not like you?
And he said to David, "You are a better man than I am, for you have repaid me good for evil."
1 Samuel 24:17

12:10 Greek *with brotherly love.* **12:19** Deut 32:35. **12:20** Greek *and you will heap burning coals on their heads.* Prov 25:21-22.

In Paul's day, people in authority sometimes treated those under them poorly. Why did Paul tell Christians to obey people in authority?

ROMANS 13:1-10

Respect Authority

Obey the government, for God is the one who put it there. All governments have been placed in power by God. ²So those who refuse to obey the laws of the land are refusing to obey God, and punishment will follow. ³For the authorities do not frighten people who are doing right, but they frighten those who do wrong. So do what they say, and you will get along well. ⁴The authorities are sent by God to help you. But if you are doing something wrong, of course you should be afraid, for you will be punished. The authorities are established by God for that very purpose, to punish those who do wrong. ⁵So you must obey the government for two reasons: to keep from being punished and to keep a clear conscience.

⁶Pay your taxes, too, for these same reasons. For government workers need to be paid so they can keep on doing the work God intended them to do. ⁷Give to everyone what you owe them: Pay your taxes and import duties, and give respect and honor to all to whom it is due.

⁸Pay all your debts, except the debt of love for others. You can never finish paying that! If you love your neighbor, you will fulfill all the requirements of God's law. ⁹For the commandments against adultery and murder and stealing and coveting—and any other commandment—are all summed up in this one commandment: "Love your neighbor as yourself."* ¹⁰Love does no wrong to anyone, so love satisfies all of God's requirements.

Paul wrote that those in authority had been placed there by God. Because God put them in power, Christians should respect them by obeying the laws. Who is in authority over you? Your parents? Your teachers? The police? Show your love for God by obeying those people he has put in authority.

Why should we obey those in authority over us?
He is the Lord over every ruler and authority in the universe.
Colossians 2:10

13:9 Lev 19:18.

Paul let his readers know that just about everything they do is useless without one thing. What is that one thing?

1 CORINTHIANS 13:1-13

The Greatest Thing

If I could speak in any language in heaven or on earth* but didn't love others, I would only be making meaningless noise like a loud gong or a clanging cymbal. ²If I had the gift of prophecy, and if I knew all the mysteries of the future and knew everything about everything, but didn't love others, what good would I be? And if I had the gift of faith so that I could speak to a mountain and make it move, without love I would be no good to anybody. ³If I gave everything I have to the poor and even sacrificed my body, I could boast about it;* but if I didn't love others, I would be of no value whatsoever.

⁴Love is patient and kind. Love is not jealous or boastful or proud ⁵or rude. Love does not demand its own way. Love is not irritable, and it keeps no record of when it has been wronged. ⁶It is never glad about injustice but rejoices whenever the truth wins out. ⁷Love never gives up, never loses faith, is always hopeful, and endures through every circumstance.

⁸Love will last forever, but prophecy and speaking in unknown languages* and special knowledge will all disappear. ⁹Now we know only a little, and even the gift of prophecy reveals little!

¹⁰But when the end comes, these special gifts will all disappear.

¹¹It's like this: When I was a child, I spoke and thought and reasoned as a child does. But when I grew up, I put away childish things. ¹²Now we see things imperfectly as in a poor mirror, but then we will see everything with perfect clarity.* All that I know now is partial and incomplete, but then I will know everything completely, just as God knows me now.

¹³There are three things that will endure—faith, hope, and love—and the greatest of these is love.

Love is the one thing that gives meaning to everything we do. That is because God has commanded us to love God and to love others. Without love, all that we do is meaningless. So how can you love others? You can be patient with them when they annoy you. You can be kind to them when they don't deserve it. You can do what is best for others rather than what is best for yourself.

How can you show love to someone today?

Worry weighs a person down; an encouraging word cheers a person up.
Proverbs 12:25

13:1 Greek *in tongues of people and angels.* **13:3** Some manuscripts read *and even gave my body to be burned.* **13:8** Or *in tongues.* **13:12** Greek *see face to face.*

Some Corinthians had a few questions about the resurrection of believers. How did Paul answer their questions?

1 CORINTHIANS 15:35-58

Our Hope in Christ

³⁵But someone may ask, "How will the dead be raised? What kind of bodies will they have?" ³⁶What a foolish question! When you put a seed into the ground, it doesn't grow into a plant unless it dies first. ³⁷And what you put in the ground is not the plant that will grow, but only a dry little seed of wheat or whatever it is you are planting. ³⁸Then God gives it a new body—just the kind he wants it to have. A different kind of plant grows from each kind of seed. ³⁹And just as there are different kinds of seeds and plants, so also there are different kinds of flesh—whether of humans, animals, birds, or fish.

⁴⁰There are bodies in the heavens, and there are bodies on earth. The glory of the heavenly bodies is different from the beauty of the earthly bodies. ⁴¹The sun has one kind of glory, while the moon and stars each have another kind. And even the stars differ from each other in their beauty and brightness.

⁴²It is the same way for the resurrection of the dead. Our earthly bodies, which die and decay, will be different when they are resurrected, for they will never die. ⁴³Our bodies now disappoint us, but when they are raised, they will be full of glory. They are weak now, but when they are raised, they will be full of power. ⁴⁴They are natural human bodies now, but when they are raised, they will be spiritual bodies. For just as there are natural bodies, so also there are spiritual bodies.

⁴⁵The Scriptures tell us, "The first man, Adam, became a living person."* But the last Adam—that is, Christ—is a life-giving Spirit. ⁴⁶What came first was the natural body, then the spiritual body comes later. ⁴⁷Adam, the first man, was made from the dust of the earth, while Christ, the second man, came from heaven. ⁴⁸Every human being has an earthly body just like Adam's, but our heavenly bodies will be just like Christ's. ⁴⁹Just as we are now like Adam, the man of the earth, so we will someday be like Christ, the man from heaven.

⁵⁰What I am saying, dear brothers and sisters, is that flesh and blood cannot inherit the Kingdom of God. These perishable bodies of ours are not able to live forever.

⁵¹But let me tell you a wonderful secret God has revealed to us. Not all of us will die, but we will all be transformed. ⁵²It will happen in a moment, in the blinking of an eye, when the last trumpet is blown. For when the trumpet sounds, the Christians who have died* will be raised with transformed bodies. And then we who are living

15:45 Gen 2:7. **15:52** Greek *the dead.*

404

will be transformed so that we will never die. [53]For our perishable earthly bodies must be transformed into heavenly bodies that will never die.

[54]When this happens—when our perishable earthly bodies have been transformed into heavenly bodies that will never die—then at last the Scriptures will come true:

"Death is swallowed up in victory.*
[55] O death, where is your victory?
O death, where is your sting?"*

[56]For sin is the sting that results in death, and the law gives sin its power. [57]How we thank God, who gives us victory over sin and death through Jesus Christ our Lord!

[58]So, my dear brothers and sisters, be strong and steady, always enthusiastic about the Lord's work, for you know that nothing you do for the Lord is ever useless.

Paul said that when believers are raised from the dead, they will have new bodies. These bodies will be better than the bodies people have here on earth. If you are a follower of Jesus Christ, this is good news. Your new body will not get sick, feel pain, or get tired. In addition, your new body will never die. You will live with Jesus in heaven forever!

What can you look forward to when Jesus returns?

I heard a loud shout from the throne, saying, "Look, the home of God is now among his people! He will live with them, and they will be his people. God himself will be with them.* He will remove all of their sorrows, and there will be no more death or sorrow or crying or pain. For the old world and its evils are gone forever."
Revelation 21:3-4

15:54 Isa 25:8. **15:55** Hos 13:14. **21:3** Some manuscripts read *God himself will be with them, their God.*

N O V E M B E R

Paul knew what trouble was. He had been beaten and thrown into jail for his faith in Jesus. How did he deal with his troubles?

2 CORINTHIANS 4:7-18
Power for Pain

[7]But this precious treasure—this light and power that now shine within us— is held in perishable containers, that is, in our weak bodies.* So everyone can see that our glorious power is from God and is not our own.

[8]We are pressed on every side by troubles, but we are not crushed and broken. We are perplexed, but we don't give up and quit. [9]We are hunted down, but God never abandons us. We get knocked down, but we get up again and keep going. [10]Through suffering, these bodies of ours constantly share in

4:7 Greek *But we have this treasure in earthen vessels.*

the death of Jesus so that the life of Jesus may also be seen in our bodies.

[11]Yes, we live under constant danger of death because we serve Jesus, so that the life of Jesus will be obvious in our dying bodies. [12]So we live in the face of death, but it has resulted in eternal life for you.

[13]But we continue to preach because we have the same kind of faith the psalmist had when he said, "I believed in God, and so I speak."* [14]We know that the same God who raised our Lord Jesus will also raise us with Jesus and present us to himself along with you. [15]All of these things are for your benefit. And as God's grace brings more and more people to Christ, there will be great thanksgiving, and God will receive more and more glory.

[16]That is why we never give up. Though our bodies are dying, our spirits are* being renewed every day. [17]For our present troubles are quite small and won't last very long. Yet they produce for us an immeasurably great glory that will last forever! [18]So we don't look at the troubles we can see right now; rather, we look forward to what we have not yet seen. For the troubles we see will soon be over, but the joys to come will last forever.

Paul had the big picture. He knew that the troubles he had on earth would soon be over. Paul also knew that the joy he would have in heaven would last forever. In Paul's view, the pain he suffered would be a small price to pay for the joy he would receive in heaven. When you face problems, try to see things from Paul's point of view. Your joy in Jesus' kingdom will be much greater than your present pain. Soon your pain will be turned into joy.

Who should our refuge and strength be in times of trouble?
God is our refuge and strength, always ready to help in times of trouble.
Psalm 46:1

4:13 Ps 116:10. 4:16 Greek *our inner being is.*

N O V E M B E R

Paul was raising money for the Christians in Jerusalem. What did he teach the Christians in Corinth about giving?

2 CORINTHIANS 9:6-15
Cheerful Giver
[6]Remember this—a farmer who plants only a few seeds will get a small crop. But the one who plants generously will get a generous crop. [7]You must each make up your own mind as to how much you should give. Don't give reluctantly or in response to pressure. For God loves the person who gives

cheerfully. [8]And God will generously provide all you need. Then you will always have everything you need and plenty left over to share with others. [9]As the Scriptures say,

"Godly people give generously to
the poor.
Their good deeds will never be
forgotten."*

[10]For God is the one who gives seed to the farmer and then bread to eat. In the same way, he will give you many opportunities to do good, and he will produce a great harvest of generosity* in you.

[11]Yes, you will be enriched so that you can give even more generously. And when we take your gifts to those who need them, they will break out in thanksgiving to God. [12]So two good things will happen—the needs of the Christians in Jerusalem will be met, and they will joyfully express their thanksgiving to God. [13]You will be glorifying God through your generous gifts. For your generosity to them will prove that you are obedient to the Good News of Christ. [14]And they will

pray for you with deep affection because of the wonderful grace of God shown through you.

[15]Thank God for his Son—a gift too wonderful for words!*

The Christians in Corinth had told Paul that they would give generously to the needy Christians in Jerusalem. But they didn't keep their promise. So Paul wrote to them about generous giving. He told them that God loves it when people give cheerfully. He also told them that sometimes God provides people with more than they need so that they can share their wealth with others. God gives you everything you need. He gives you food, clothes, a place to live, and a family. Thank him for his gifts. Share what God has given you with others.

**Why should we help
those who are poor?**
It is sin to despise one's neighbors;
blessed are those who help the poor.
Proverbs 14:21

9:9 Ps 112:9. 9:10 Greek *righteousness*. 9:15 Greek *Thank God for his indescribable gift*.

N O V E M B E R

Some Christians in Galatia had a problem. They thought the freedom Jesus gave them was permission to sin. What did Paul say about that?

GALATIANS 5:13-26
Life in Christ
[13]For you have been called to live in freedom—not freedom to satisfy your

sinful nature, but freedom to serve one another in love. [14]For the whole law can be summed up in this one command: "Love your neighbor as yourself."* [15]But if instead of showing love among yourselves you are always biting and devouring one another, watch out! Beware of destroying one another.

[16]So I advise you to live according to your new life in the Holy Spirit. Then you won't be doing what your sinful nature craves. [17]The old sinful nature loves to do evil, which is just opposite from what the Holy Spirit wants. And the Spirit gives us desires that are opposite from what the sinful nature desires. These two forces are constantly fighting each other, and your choices are never free from this conflict. [18]But when you are directed by the Holy Spirit, you are no longer subject to the law.

[19]When you follow the desires of your sinful nature, your lives will produce these evil results: sexual immorality, impure thoughts, eagerness for lustful pleasure, [20]idolatry, participation in demonic activities, hostility, quarreling, jealousy, outbursts of anger, selfish ambition, divisions, the feeling that everyone is wrong except those in your own little group, [21]envy, drunkenness, wild parties, and other kinds of sin. Let me tell you again, as I have before, that anyone living that sort of life will not inherit the Kingdom of God.

[22]But when the Holy Spirit controls our lives, he will produce this kind of fruit in us: love, joy, peace, patience, kindness, goodness, faithfulness, [23]gentleness, and self-control. Here there is no conflict with the law.

[24]Those who belong to Christ Jesus have nailed the passions and desires of their sinful nature to his cross and crucified them there. [25]If we are living now by the Holy Spirit, let us follow the Holy Spirit's leading in every part of our lives. [26]Let us not become conceited, or irritate one another, or be jealous of one another.

Paul told the Galatians that the freedom Christ gave them was freedom from sin. Therefore, they were no longer slaves to sin but were free to serve God and one another. How do you use the freedom Jesus has given you? Do you serve him and others? Or do you enslave yourself to sin? Choose to serve Jesus and others. In serving Jesus, you will find real purpose and freedom in life.

Who should you enslave yourself to?

But now you are free from the power of sin and have become slaves of God. Now you do those things that lead to holiness and result in eternal life.
Romans 6:22

5:14 Lev 19:18.

Paul prayed for the Ephesians all the time. What did he pray about for them?

EPHESIANS 1:15-23

Paul's Prayers

[15]Ever since I first heard of your strong faith in the Lord Jesus and your love for Christians everywhere, [16]I have never stopped thanking God for you. I pray for you constantly, [17]asking God, the glorious Father of our Lord Jesus Christ, to give you spiritual wisdom and understanding, so that you might grow in your knowledge of God. [18]I pray that your hearts will be flooded with light so that you can understand the wonderful future he has promised to those he called. I want you to realize what a rich and glorious inheritance he has given to his people. *

[19]I pray that you will begin to understand the incredible greatness of his power for us who believe him. This is the same mighty power [20]that raised Christ from the dead and seated him in the place of honor at God's right hand in the heavenly realms. [21]Now he is far above any ruler or authority or power or leader or anything else in this world or in the world to come. [22]And God has put all things under the authority of Christ, and he gave him this authority for the benefit of the church. [23]And the church is his body; it is filled by Christ, who fills everything everywhere with his presence.

Paul prayed that the Ephesians would receive spiritual wisdom and understanding. He also prayed that they would understand God's power to work through them. What things do you pray about for your friends and family? If you don't pray for them, follow Paul's example and pray that they will receive spiritual wisdom and understanding. If you do pray for them, you can add wisdom and understanding to your prayer list.

What are some other things we can pray about for others?

I pray that from his glorious, unlimited resources he will give you mighty inner strength through his Holy Spirit.
Ephesians 3:16

1:18 Or *realize how much God has been honored by acquiring his people.*

Paul wrote about God's riches. How is God rich?

EPHESIANS 2:1-10
Alive in Jesus

Once you were dead, doomed forever because of your many sins. ²You used to live just like the rest of the world, full of sin, obeying Satan, the mighty prince of the power of the air. He is the spirit at work in the hearts of those who refuse to obey God. ³All of us used to live that way, following the passions and desires of our evil nature. We were born with an evil nature, and we were under God's anger just like everyone else.

⁴But God is so rich in mercy, and he loved us so very much, ⁵that even while we were dead because of our sins, he gave us life when he raised Christ from the dead. (It is only by God's special favor that you have been saved!) ⁶For he raised us from the dead along with Christ, and we are seated with him in the heavenly realms—all because we are one with Christ Jesus. ⁷And so God can always point to us as examples of the incredible wealth of his favor and kindness toward us, as shown in all he has done for us through Christ Jesus.

⁸God saved you by his special favor when you believed. And you can't take credit for this; it is a gift from God. ⁹Salvation is not a reward for the good things we have done, so none of us can boast about it. ¹⁰For we are God's masterpiece. He has created us anew in Christ Jesus, so that we can do the good things he planned for us long ago.

God is rich in mercy and love. He showed his mercy by not destroying everyone because of their sin. He showed his love by sending his perfect Son, Jesus, to pay the penalty for everyone's sin. Praise God for the mercy and love he has shown you.

What else can we praise God for?

So don't worry about having enough food or drink or clothing. . . . Your heavenly Father already knows all your needs, and he will give you all you need from day to day if you live for him and make the Kingdom of God your primary concern.
Matthew 6:31-33

Paul told believers how they shouldn't live.
Why shouldn't believers do the things Paul listed in this passage?

EPHESIANS 4:17–5:2
Brand-New

¹⁷With the Lord's authority let me say this: Live no longer as the ungodly* do, for they are hopelessly confused. ¹⁸Their closed minds are full of darkness; they are far away from the life of God because they have shut their minds and hardened their hearts against him. ¹⁹They don't care anymore about right and wrong, and they have given themselves over to immoral ways. Their lives are filled with all kinds of impurity and greed.

²⁰But that isn't what you were taught when you learned about Christ. ²¹Since you have heard all about him and have learned the truth that is in Jesus, ²²throw off your old evil nature and your former way of life, which is rotten through and through, full of lust and deception. ²³Instead, there must be a spiritual renewal of your thoughts and attitudes. ²⁴You must display a new nature because you are a new person, created in God's likeness—righteous, holy, and true.

²⁵So put away all falsehood and "tell your neighbor the truth"* because we belong to each other. ²⁶And "don't sin by letting anger gain control over you."* Don't let the sun go down while you are still angry, ²⁷for anger gives a mighty foothold to the Devil. ²⁸If you are a thief, stop stealing. Begin using your hands for honest work, and then give generously to others in need. ²⁹Don't use foul or abusive language. Let everything you say be good and helpful, so that your words will be an encouragement to those who hear them.

³⁰And do not bring sorrow to God's Holy Spirit by the way you live. Remember, he is the one who has identified you as his own, guaranteeing that you will be saved on the day of redemption. ³¹Get rid of all bitterness, rage, anger, harsh words, and slander, as well as all types of malicious behavior. ³²Instead,

Believers shouldn't willingly live a sinful lifestyle, because Jesus has made them new on the inside. If believers continue to live a life of sin, the new nature that Jesus gives them cannot grow. That's why Paul warned the Ephesians not to participate in any of these sinful actions and attitudes. Is there anything in this passage that you need to stop doing? If so, pray that Jesus will help you to overcome that sin.

Who gives us the strength we need to stop sinning?
God is awesome in his sanctuary. The God of Israel gives power and strength to his people. Praise be to God!
Psalm 68:35

4:17 Greek *Gentiles*. 4:25 Zech 8:16. 4:26 Ps 4:4.

be kind to each other, tenderhearted, forgiving one another, just as God through Christ has forgiven you.

5:1Follow God's example in everything you do, because you are his dear children. 2Live a life filled with love for others, following the example of Christ, who loved you and gave himself as a sacrifice to take away your sins. And God was pleased, because that sacrifice was like sweet perfume to him.

N O V E M B E R

Paul wrote part of this letter to children and slaves. What did he have to say to them?

EPHESIANS 6:1-9

Obeying Authority

Children, obey your parents because you belong to the Lord, for this is the right thing to do. 2"Honor your father and mother." This is the first of the Ten Commandments that ends with a promise. 3And this is the promise: If you honor your father and mother, "you will live a long life, full of blessing."*

4And now a word to you fathers. Don't make your children angry by the way you treat them. Rather, bring them up with the discipline and instruction approved by the Lord.

5Slaves, obey your earthly masters with deep respect and fear. Serve them sincerely as you would serve Christ. 6Work hard, but not just to please your masters when they are watching. As slaves of Christ, do the will of God with all your heart. 7Work with enthusiasm, as though you were working for the Lord rather than for people. 8Remember that the Lord will reward each one of us for the good we do, whether we are slaves or free.

9And in the same way, you masters must treat your slaves right. Don't threaten them; remember, you both have the same Master in heaven, and he has no favorites.

Paul told children to obey their parents, and he told slaves to obey their masters. He wanted Christian children and Christian slaves to respect those in authority over them. Many people find this difficult. No one likes to be told what to do. But, as Christians, we should be ready to serve others. That includes obeying people in authority over us.

Why is it important to obey your parents?

Listen, my child,* to what your father teaches you. Don't neglect your mother's teaching. What you learn from them will crown you with grace and clothe you with honor.
Proverbs 1:8-9

6:2-3 Exod 20:12; Deut 5:16. **1:8** Hebrew *my son;* also in 1:10, 15.

Christians shouldn't get into fistfights. But they should fight spiritual battles. What can Christians use to defend themselves?

EPHESIANS 6:10-20

God's Armor

[10] A final word: Be strong with the Lord's mighty power. [11] Put on all of God's armor so that you will be able to stand firm against all strategies and tricks of the Devil. [12] For we are not fighting against people made of flesh and blood, but against the evil rulers and authorities of the unseen world, against those mighty powers of darkness who rule this world, and against wicked spirits in the heavenly realms.

[13] Use every piece of God's armor to resist the enemy in the time of evil, so that after the battle you will still be standing firm. [14] Stand your ground, putting on the sturdy belt of truth and the body armor of God's righteousness. [15] For shoes, put on the peace that comes from the Good News, so that you will be fully prepared.* [16] In every battle you will need faith as your shield to stop the fiery arrows aimed at you by Satan.* [17] Put on salvation as your helmet, and take the sword of the Spirit, which is the word of God. [18] Pray at all times and on every occasion in the power of the Holy Spirit. Stay alert and be persistent in your prayers for all Christians everywhere.

[19] And pray for me, too. Ask God to give me the right words as I boldly explain God's secret plan that the Good News is for the Gentiles, too.* [20] I am in chains now for preaching this message as God's ambassador. But pray that I will keep on speaking boldly for him, as I should.

Christians can put on God's armor to defend themselves in spiritual battles. God's armor isn't made of metal. Rather, it's made of things like truth, righteousness, peace, faith, salvation, and God's Word. We can put on this armor only by staying connected with God. To do that, we need to read his Word and pray daily. Are you wearing God's armor today?

What should Christians put on?

The night is almost gone; the day of salvation will soon be here. So don't live in darkness. Get rid of your evil deeds. Shed them like dirty clothes. Clothe yourselves with the armor of right living, as those who live in the light.
Romans 13:12

6:15 Or *For shoes, put on the readiness to preach the Good News of peace with God.* **6:16** Greek *by the evil one.* **6:19** Greek *explain the mystery of the gospel.*

When Jesus came to earth, he gave up his rights as God. Why did he do this?

PHILIPPIANS 2:1-15
Jesus' Attitude

Is there any encouragement from belonging to Christ? Any comfort from his love? Any fellowship together in the Spirit? Are your hearts tender and sympathetic? [2]Then make me truly happy by agreeing wholeheartedly with each other, loving one another, and working together with one heart and purpose.

[3]Don't be selfish; don't live to make a good impression on others. Be humble, thinking of others as better than yourself. [4]Don't think only about your own affairs, but be interested in others, too, and what they are doing.

[5]Your attitude should be the same that Christ Jesus had. [6]Though he was God, he did not demand and cling to his rights as God. [7]He made himself nothing;* he took the humble position of a slave and appeared in human form.* [8]And in human form he obediently humbled himself even further by dying a criminal's death on a cross. [9]Because of this, God raised him up to the heights of heaven and gave him a name that is above every other name, [10]so that at the name of Jesus every knee will bow, in heaven and on earth and under the earth, [11]and every tongue will confess that Jesus Christ is Lord, to the glory of God the Father.

[12]Dearest friends, you were always so careful to follow my instructions when I was with you. And now that I am away you must be even more careful to put into action God's saving work in your lives, obeying God with deep reverence and fear. [13]For God is working in you, giving you the desire to obey him and the power to do what pleases him.

[14]In everything you do, stay away from complaining and arguing, [15]so

Jesus came to serve God and people, not to be served by them. Even though he is God, he humbled himself and became a servant. He even died like a criminal so people could live forever. As his followers, we need to have a humble attitude like his. We shouldn't think of ourselves too highly. Instead, we should see ourselves as God's servants and be willing to do what he asks us.

What has God promised those who humble themselves?
Then if my people who are called by my name will humble themselves and pray and seek my face and turn from their wicked ways, I will hear from heaven and will forgive their sins and heal their land.
2 Chronicles 7:14

2:7a Or *He laid aside his mighty power and glory.* **2:7b** Greek *and was born in the likeness of men and was found in appearance as a man.*

that no one can speak a word of blame against you. You are to live clean, innocent lives as children of God in a dark world full of crooked and perverse people. Let your lives shine brightly before them.

N O V E M B E R

Paul encouraged the Philippian Christians to keep growing in their faith. What would help them grow?

PHILIPPIANS 3:12–4:9

Rejoice

¹²I don't mean to say that I have already achieved these things or that I have already reached perfection! But I keep working toward that day when I will finally be all that Christ Jesus saved me for and wants me to be. ¹³No, dear brothers and sisters, I am still not all I should be,* but I am focusing all my energies on this one thing: Forgetting the past and looking forward to what lies ahead, ¹⁴I strain to reach the end of the race and receive the prize for which God, through Christ Jesus, is calling us up to heaven.*

¹⁵I hope all of you who are mature Christians will agree on these things. If you disagree on some point, I believe God will make it plain to you. ¹⁶But we must be sure to obey the truth we have learned already.

¹⁷Dear brothers and sisters, pattern your lives after mine, and learn from those who follow our example. ¹⁸For I have told you often before, and I say it again with tears in my eyes, that there are many whose conduct shows they are really enemies of the cross of Christ. ¹⁹Their future is eternal destruction. Their god is their appetite, they brag about shameful things, and all they think about is this life here on earth. ²⁰But we are citizens of heaven, where the Lord Jesus Christ lives. And we are eagerly waiting for him to return as our Savior. ²¹He will take these weak mortal bodies of ours and change them into glorious bodies like his own, using the same mighty power that he will use to conquer everything, everywhere.

⁴:¹Dear brothers and sisters, I love you and long to see you, for you are my joy and the reward for my work. So please stay true to the Lord, my dear friends.

²And now I want to plead with those two women, Euodia and Syntyche. Please, because you belong to the Lord, settle your disagreement. ³And I ask you, my true teammate,* to help these women, for they worked hard with me in telling others the Good News. And they worked with Clement and the rest of my co-workers, whose names are written in the Book of Life.

⁴Always be full of joy in the Lord. I

3:13 Some manuscripts read *I am not all I should be.* **3:14** Or *from heaven.* **4:3** Greek *true yokefellow,* or *loyal Syzygus.*

say it again—rejoice! [5]Let everyone see that you are considerate in all you do. Remember, the Lord is coming soon.

[6]Don't worry about anything; instead, pray about everything. Tell God what you need, and thank him for all he has done. [7]If you do this, you will experience God's peace, which is far more wonderful than the human mind can understand. His peace will guard your hearts and minds as you live in Christ Jesus.

[8]And now, dear brothers and sisters, let me say one more thing as I close this letter. Fix your thoughts on what is true and honorable and right. Think about things that are pure and lovely and admirable. Think about things that are excellent and worthy of praise. [9]Keep putting into practice all you learned from me and heard from me and saw me doing, and the God of peace will be with you.

Being joyful about their salvation, not worrying about their problems, and praying about everything would help these Christians grow. Doing these three things will also help us grow in our faith. Being joyful gives us the right point of view in life. When we are joyful, we can thank God for his goodness to us even when things are bad. Not worrying about our problems takes our mind off ourself and allows us to focus on Jesus. And praying about everything helps us depend on God to take care of us.

What can you do to take your mind off your problems?
Shout with joy to the LORD, O earth! Worship the LORD with gladness. Come before him, singing with joy.
Psalm 100:1-2

Spiritual growth is important for Christians. What advice did Paul have on growing?

COLOSSIANS 1:28–2:15

Roots

²⁸So everywhere we go, we tell everyone about Christ. We warn them and teach them with all the wisdom God has given us, for we want to present them to God, perfect* in their relationship to Christ. ²⁹I work very hard at this, as I depend on Christ's mighty power that works within me.

²:¹I want you to know how much I have agonized for you and for the church at Laodicea, and for many other friends who have never known me personally. ²My goal is that they will be encouraged and knit together by strong ties of love. I want them to have full confidence because they have complete understanding of God's secret plan, which is Christ himself. ³In him lie hidden all the treasures of wisdom and knowledge.

⁴I am telling you this so that no one will be able to deceive you with persuasive arguments. ⁵For though I am far away from you, my heart is with you. And I am very happy because you are living as you should and because of your strong faith in Christ.

⁶And now, just as you accepted Christ Jesus as your Lord, you must continue to live in obedience to him. ⁷Let your roots grow down into him and draw up nourishment from him, so you will grow in faith, strong and vigorous in the truth you were taught. Let your lives overflow with thanksgiving for all he has done.

⁸Don't let anyone lead you astray with empty philosophy and high-sounding nonsense that come from human thinking and from the evil powers of this world,* and not from Christ. ⁹For in Christ the fullness of God lives in a human body,* ¹⁰and

Paul told Christians to let the roots of their faith grow deep into Jesus. Roots do two things. First, they allow a plant to soak up food and water from the soil. Second, they keep the plant from falling over. The same is true of your faith in Jesus. Through your faith, you receive spiritual nourishment from Jesus. Faith also keeps you connected to Jesus, the one who can help you stand against any trial or temptation. Follow Paul's advice, and let your roots grow deep.

Why is it important to stay connected to Jesus?

Yes, I am the vine; you are the branches. Those who remain in me, and I in them, will produce much fruit. For apart from me you can do nothing.

John 15:5

1:28 Or *mature.* 2:8 Or *from the basic principles of this world;* also in 2:20. 2:9 Greek *in him dwells all the fullness of the Godhead bodily.*

you are complete through your union with Christ. He is the Lord over every ruler and authority in the universe.

¹¹When you came to Christ, you were "circumcised," but not by a physical procedure. It was a spiritual procedure—the cutting away of your sinful nature. ¹²For you were buried with Christ when you were baptized. And with him you were raised to a new life because you trusted the mighty power of God, who raised Christ from the dead.

¹³You were dead because of your sins and because your sinful nature was not yet cut away. Then God made you alive with Christ. He forgave all our sins. ¹⁴He canceled the record that contained the charges against us. He took it and destroyed it by nailing it to Christ's cross. ¹⁵In this way, God disarmed the evil rulers and authorities. He shamed them publicly by his victory over them on the cross of Christ.

D E C E M B E R

Paul talked about godly attitudes as clothing that Christians should put on. What attitudes should Christians wear?

COLOSSIANS 3:1-17
Get Dressed

Since you have been raised to new life with Christ, set your sights on the realities of heaven, where Christ sits at God's right hand in the place of honor and power. ²Let heaven fill your thoughts. Do not think only about things down here on earth. ³For you died when Christ died, and your real life is hidden with Christ in God. ⁴And when Christ, who is your* real life, is revealed to the whole world, you will share in all his glory.

⁵So put to death the sinful, earthly things lurking within you. Have nothing to do with sexual sin, impurity, lust, and shameful desires. Don't be greedy for the good things of this life, for that is idolatry. ⁶God's terrible anger will come upon those who do such things. ⁷You used to do them when your life was still part of this world. ⁸But now is the time to get rid of anger, rage, malicious behavior, slander, and dirty language. ⁹Don't lie to each other, for you have stripped off your old evil nature and all its wicked deeds. ¹⁰In its place you have clothed yourselves with a brand-new nature that is continually being renewed as you learn more and more about Christ, who created this new nature within you. ¹¹In this new life, it doesn't matter if you are a Jew or a Gentile,* circumcised or uncircumcised, barbaric, uncivilized,* slave, or free. Christ is all that matters, and he lives in all of us.

¹²Since God chose you to be the

3:4 Some manuscripts read *our*. 3:11a Greek *Greek*. 3:11b Greek *Barbarian, Scythian*.

holy people whom he loves, you must clothe yourselves with tenderhearted mercy, kindness, humility, gentleness, and patience. [13] You must make allowance for each other's faults and forgive the person who offends you. Remember, the Lord forgave you, so you must forgive others. [14] And the most important piece of clothing you must wear is love. Love is what binds us all together in perfect harmony. [15] And let the peace that comes from Christ rule in your hearts. For as members of one body you are all called to live in peace. And always be thankful.

[16] Let the words of Christ, in all their richness, live in your hearts and make you wise. Use his words to teach and counsel each other. Sing psalms and hymns and spiritual songs to God with thankful hearts. [17] And whatever you do or say, let it be as a representative of the Lord Jesus, all the while giving thanks through him to God the Father.

Christians should put on the attitudes of mercy, kindness, humility, gentleness, and patience. Putting on these attitudes helps us love others. And love is the most important attitude we should wear. Loving others, as Jesus said, is an important commandment to keep. Before you leave your house in the morning, be sure to clothe yourself with these godly attitudes for the day.

What does God do to make us better people?

"Come now, let us argue this out," says the LORD. "No matter how deep the stain of your sins, I can remove it. I can make you as clean as freshly fallen snow. Even if you are stained as red as crimson, I can make you as white as wool."
Isaiah 1:18

D E C E M B E R

The Thessalonians changed after they heard the Good News. What impact did their faith have on others?

1 THESSALONIANS 1:1-10
A Good Example
This letter is from Paul, Silas, * and Timothy.

It is written to the church in Thessalonica, you who belong to God the Father and the Lord Jesus Christ.

May his grace and peace be yours.

[2] We always thank God for all of you and pray for you constantly. [3] As we talk to our God and Father about you, we think of your faithful work, your loving deeds, and your continual anticipation of the return of our Lord Jesus Christ.

[4] We know that God loves you, dear

1:1 Greek *Silvanus.*

419

brothers and sisters, and that he chose you to be his own people. [5]For when we brought you the Good News, it was not only with words but also with power, for the Holy Spirit gave you full assurance that what we said was true. And you know that the way we lived among you was further proof of the truth of our message. [6]So you received the message with joy from the Holy Spirit in spite of the severe suffering it brought you. In this way, you imitated both us and the Lord. [7]As a result, you yourselves became an example to all the Christians in Greece.* [8]And now the word of the Lord is ringing out from you to people everywhere, even beyond Greece, for wherever we go we find people telling us about your faith in God. We don't need to tell them about it, [9]for they themselves keep talking about the wonderful welcome you gave us and how you turned away from idols to serve the true and living God. [10]And they speak of how you are looking forward to the coming of God's Son from heaven—Jesus, whom God raised from the dead. He is the one who has rescued us from the terrors of the coming judgment.

The Thessalonians were good examples of Christian living. Even in trials, they followed God and served him. Their faith changed the way they lived so much that everywhere Paul went, he heard people talking about the Thessalonians' faith. The Thessalonian believers are examples of what changed lives look like. People take notice of the changes. Do people notice a change in your life?

What changes does the Holy Spirit make in the lives of Christians?
But when the Holy Spirit controls our lives, he will produce this kind of fruit in us: love, joy, peace, patience, kindness, goodness, faithfulness, gentleness, and self-control.
Galatians 5:22-23

1:7 Greek *Macedonia and Achaia*, the northern and southern regions of Greece; also in 1:8.

D E C E M B E R

Paul warned the readers of this letter to stay alert. Why did he do that?

1 THESSALONIANS 5:1-22
Stay Awake
I really don't need to write to you about how and when all this will happen, dear brothers and sisters. [2]For you know quite well that the day of the Lord will come unexpectedly, like a thief in the night.

[3]When people are saying, "All is well; everything is peaceful and secure," then disaster will fall upon them as suddenly as a woman's birth pains begin when her child is about to be born. And there will be no escape.

[4]But you aren't in the dark about

these things, dear brothers and sisters, and you won't be surprised when the day of the Lord comes like a thief. [5]For you are all children of the light and of the day; we don't belong to darkness and night. [6]So be on your guard, not asleep like the others. Stay alert and be sober. [7]Night is the time for sleep and the time when people get drunk. [8]But let us who live in the light think clearly, protected by the body armor of faith and love, and wearing as our helmet the confidence of our salvation. [9]For God decided to save us through our Lord Jesus Christ, not to pour out his anger on us. [10]He died for us so that we can live with him forever, whether we are dead or alive at the time of his return. [11]So encourage each other and build each other up, just as you are already doing.

[12]Dear brothers and sisters, honor those who are your leaders in the Lord's work. They work hard among you and warn you against all that is wrong. [13]Think highly of them and give them your wholehearted love because of their work. And remember to live peaceably with each other.

[14]Brothers and sisters, we urge you to warn those who are lazy. Encourage those who are timid. Take tender care of those who are weak. Be patient with everyone.

[15]See that no one pays back evil for evil, but always try to do good to each other and to everyone else.

[16]Always be joyful. [17]Keep on praying. [18]No matter what happens, always be thankful, for this is God's will for you who belong to Christ Jesus.

[19]Do not stifle the Holy Spirit. [20]Do not scoff at prophecies, [21]but test everything that is said. Hold on to what is good. [22]Keep away from every kind of evil.

Paul wanted those who read his letter to know that Jesus could come back at any moment. He urged Christians to be ready for Jesus' return. Paul's message still applies to us today. Being ready means that we are living a life that pleases God. A life that pleases God is one of obedience to his commands. Are you ready for Jesus' return?

Why should we be ready and alert for Jesus' return?

And since you don't know when they will happen, stay alert and keep watch.*
Mark 13:33

13:33 Some manuscripts add *and pray.*

D E C E M B E R

*Some believers were being treated badly because of their faith in Jesus.
What could they look forward to during their trials?*

2 THESSALONIANS 1:1-12
Endurance

This letter is from Paul, Silas,* and Timothy.

It is written to the church in Thessalonica, you who belong to God our Father and the Lord Jesus Christ.

²May God our Father and the Lord Jesus Christ give you grace and peace.

³Dear brothers and sisters, we always thank God for you, as is right, for we are thankful that your faith is flourishing and you are all growing in love for each other. ⁴We proudly tell God's other churches about your endurance and faithfulness in all the persecutions and hardships you are suffering. ⁵But God will use this persecution to show his justice. For he will make you worthy of his Kingdom, for which you are suffering, ⁶and in his justice he will punish those who persecute you. ⁷And God will provide rest for you who are being persecuted and also for us when the Lord Jesus appears from heaven. He will come with his mighty angels, ⁸in flaming fire, bringing judgment on those who don't know God and on those who refuse to obey the Good News of our Lord Jesus. ⁹They will be punished with everlasting destruction, forever separated from the Lord and from his glorious power ¹⁰when he comes to receive glory and praise from his holy people.

And you will be among those praising him on that day, for you believed what we testified about him.

¹¹And so we keep on praying for you, that our God will make you worthy of the life to which he called you. And we pray that God, by his power, will fulfill all your good intentions and faithful deeds. ¹²Then everyone will give honor to the name of our Lord Jesus because of you, and you will be honored along with him. This is all made possible because of the undeserved favor of our God and Lord, Jesus Christ.*

These believers trusted God to judge those who were hurting them. They knew that God saw how badly they were treated by evil people. Like these believers, we can trust God to deal with those people who hurt us. So do not be discouraged. When Jesus comes back, he will defeat those who are evil. And he will bring you into the safety of his presence.

What can we remember when we are treated badly?
He will judge the world with justice and rule the nations with fairness.
Psalm 9:8

1:1 Greek *Silvanus*. **1:12** Or *of our God and the Lord Jesus Christ.*

D E C E M B E R

Some believers were lazy and didn't work for a living. What did Paul say to them?

2 THESSALONIANS 3:1-18
Get to Work!

Finally, dear brothers and sisters, I ask you to pray for us. Pray first that the Lord's message will spread rapidly and be honored wherever it goes, just as when it came to you. ²Pray, too, that we will be saved from wicked and evil people, for not everyone believes in the Lord. ³But the Lord is faithful; he will make you strong and guard you from the evil one.* ⁴And we are confident in the Lord that you are practicing the things we commanded you, and that you always will. ⁵May the Lord bring you into an ever deeper understanding of the love of God and the endurance that comes from Christ.

⁶And now, dear brothers and sisters, we give you this command with the authority of our Lord Jesus Christ: Stay away from any Christian* who lives in idleness and doesn't follow the tradition of hard work we gave you. ⁷For you know that you ought to follow our example. We were never lazy when we were with you. ⁸We never accepted food from anyone without paying for it. We worked hard day and night so that we would not be a burden to any of you. ⁹It wasn't that we didn't have the right to ask you to feed us, but we wanted to give you an example to follow. ¹⁰Even while we were with you, we gave you this rule: "Whoever does not work should not eat."

¹¹Yet we hear that some of you are living idle lives, refusing to work and wasting time meddling in other people's business. ¹²In the name of the Lord Jesus Christ, we appeal to such people—no, we command them: Settle down and get to work. Earn your own living. ¹³And I say to the rest of

---

The lazy Christians were not working to support themselves. Because they were not working, they had a lot of time on their hands, which they spent getting into trouble. So Paul told them to get to work. Working hard would give these Christians less free time to get into trouble. It would also improve the poor image of a Christian these lazy people presented. And they wouldn't be a burden on those people who gave them food or clothing. When it comes to work, are you lazy? Don't be like the lazy Christians in this reading. Instead, work hard in all that you do. This pleases God, and he will reward you for your work.

Why should you work?
Work brings profit, but mere
talk leads to poverty!
Proverbs 14:23

3:3 Or *from evil.* **3:6** Greek *brother;* also in 3:15.

you, dear brothers and sisters, never get tired of doing good.

¹⁴Take note of those who refuse to obey what we say in this letter. Stay away from them so they will be ashamed. ¹⁵Don't think of them as enemies, but speak to them as you would to a Christian who needs to be warned.

¹⁶May the Lord of peace himself always give you his peace no matter what happens. The Lord be with you all.

¹⁷Now here is my greeting, which I write with my own hand—PAUL. I do this at the end of all my letters to prove that they really are from me.

¹⁸May the grace of our Lord Jesus Christ be with you all.

D E C E M B E R

Paul encouraged Timothy to train himself spiritually. Why is this training important?

1 TIMOTHY 4:1-16
Spiritual Training

Now the Holy Spirit tells us clearly that in the last times some will turn away from what we believe; they will follow lying spirits and teachings that come from demons. ²These teachers are hypocrites and liars. They pretend to be religious, but their consciences are dead.*

³They will say it is wrong to be married and wrong to eat certain foods. But God created those foods to be eaten with thanksgiving by people who know and believe the truth. ⁴Since everything God created is good, we should not reject any of it. We may receive it gladly, with thankful hearts. ⁵For we know it is made holy by the word of God and prayer.

⁶If you explain this to the brothers and sisters, you will be doing your duty as a worthy servant of Christ Jesus, one who is fed by the message of faith and the true teaching you have followed. ⁷Do not waste time arguing over godless ideas and old wives' tales. Spend your time and energy in training yourself for spiritual fitness. ⁸Physical exercise has some value, but spiritual exercise is much more important, for it promises a reward in both this life and the next. ⁹This is true, and everyone should accept it. ¹⁰We work hard and suffer much* in order that people will believe the truth, for our hope is in the living God, who is the Savior of all people, and particularly of those who believe.

¹¹Teach these things and insist that everyone learn them. ¹²Don't let anyone think less of you because you are young. Be an example to all believers in what you teach, in the way you live, in your love, your faith, and your purity. ¹³Until I get there, focus on reading the Scriptures to the church,

4:2 Greek *are seared.* 4:10 Some manuscripts read *and strive.*

encouraging the believers, and teaching them.

¹⁴Do not neglect the spiritual gift you received through the prophecies spoken to you when the elders of the church laid their hands on you. ¹⁵Give your complete attention to these matters. Throw yourself into your tasks so that everyone will see your progress. ¹⁶Keep a close watch on yourself and on your teaching. Stay true to what is right, and God will save you and those who hear you.

Spiritual training is important for Christian growth. If we spend time reading the Bible and doing what it says, we will grow closer to Jesus and become more like him. That should be our goal as Christians. If this is your goal, set aside time to read the Bible and pray. Practice doing good. As Paul said, spiritual exercise "promises a reward in both this life and the next."

What does it take to stay spiritually fit?
Study this Book of the Law continually. Meditate on it day and night so you may be sure to obey all that is written in it. Only then will you succeed.
Joshua 1:8

D E C E M B E R

Paul warned Timothy about the love of money. What is wrong with loving money?

1 TIMOTHY 6:1-21
Be Content
Christians who are slaves should give their masters full respect so that the name of God and his teaching will not be shamed. ²If your master is a Christian, that is no excuse for being disrespectful. You should work all the harder because you are helping another believer* by your efforts.

Teach these truths, Timothy, and encourage everyone to obey them. ³Some false teachers may deny these things, but these are the sound, wholesome teachings of the Lord Jesus Christ, and they are the foundation for a godly life. ⁴Anyone who teaches anything different is both conceited and ignorant. Such a person has an unhealthy desire to quibble over the meaning of words. This stirs up arguments ending in jealousy, fighting, slander, and evil suspicions. ⁵These people always cause trouble. Their minds are corrupt, and they don't tell the truth. To them religion is just a way to get rich.

6:2 Greek *a brother.*

⁶Yet true religion with contentment is great wealth. ⁷After all, we didn't bring anything with us when we came into the world, and we certainly cannot carry anything with us when we die. ⁸So if we have enough food and clothing, let us be content. ⁹But people who long to be rich fall into temptation and are trapped by many foolish and harmful desires that plunge them into ruin and destruction. ¹⁰For the love of money is at the root of all kinds of evil. And some people, craving money, have wandered from the faith and pierced themselves with many sorrows.

¹¹But you, Timothy, belong to God; so run from all these evil things, and follow what is right and good. Pursue a godly life, along with faith, love, perseverance, and gentleness. ¹²Fight the good fight for what we believe. Hold tightly to the eternal life that God has given you, which you have confessed so well before many witnesses. ¹³And I command you before God, who gives life to all, and before Christ Jesus, who gave a good testimony before Pontius Pilate, ¹⁴that you obey his commands with all purity. Then no one can find fault with you from now until our Lord Jesus Christ returns. ¹⁵For at the right time Christ will be revealed from heaven by the blessed and only almighty God, the King of kings and Lord of lords. ¹⁶He alone can never die, and he lives in light so brilliant that no human can approach him. No one has ever seen him, nor ever will. To him be honor and power forever. Amen.

¹⁷Tell those who are rich in this world not to be proud and not to trust in their money, which will soon be gone. But their trust should be in the living God, who richly gives us all we need for our enjoyment. ¹⁸Tell them to use their money to do good. They should be rich in good works and should give generously to those in need, always being ready to share with others whatever God has given them. ¹⁹By doing this they will be storing up their treasure as a good foundation for the future so that they may take hold of real life.

²⁰Timothy, guard what God has entrusted to you. Avoid godless, foolish discussions with those who oppose you with their so-called knowledge. ²¹Some people have wandered from the faith by following such foolishness.

May God's grace be with you all.

Loving money leads to all kinds of problems. Paul said that some people have even stopped following Jesus in order to get more money. But getting more money and more things does not make people happy and content. Instead, real happiness and contentment come from having a healthy relationship with Jesus. Be content with what God has given you. Don't strive to obtain possessions, but strive to know Jesus and to do good.

Why shouldn't we love money?

No one can serve two masters. For you will hate one and love the other, or be devoted to one and despise the other. You cannot serve both God and money.
Matthew 6:24

DECEMBER

Paul encouraged Timothy to be a good worker for God.
What does a good worker for God do?

2 TIMOTHY 2:1-24
A Good Worker

Timothy, my dear son, be strong with the special favor God gives you in Christ Jesus. ²You have heard me teach many things that have been confirmed by many reliable witnesses. Teach these great truths to trustworthy people who are able to pass them on to others.

³Endure suffering along with me, as a good soldier of Christ Jesus. ⁴And as Christ's soldier, do not let yourself become tied up in the affairs of this life, for then you cannot satisfy the one who has enlisted you in his army. ⁵Follow the Lord's rules for doing his work, just as an athlete either follows the rules or is disqualified and wins no prize. ⁶Hardworking farmers are the first to enjoy the fruit of their labor. ⁷Think about what I am saying. The Lord will give you understanding in all these things.

⁸Never forget that Jesus Christ was a man born into King David's family and that he was raised from the dead. This is the Good News I preach. ⁹And because I preach this Good News, I am suffering and have been chained like a criminal. But the word of God cannot be chained. ¹⁰I am willing to endure anything if it will bring salvation and eternal glory in Christ Jesus to those God has chosen.

¹¹This is a true saying:

If we die with him,
    we will also live with him.
¹² If we endure hardship,
    we will reign with him.
If we deny him,
    he will deny us.
¹³ If we are unfaithful,
    he remains faithful,
    for he cannot deny himself.

¹⁴Remind everyone of these things, and command them in God's name to stop fighting over words. Such arguments are useless, and they can ruin those who hear them. ¹⁵Work hard so God can approve you. Be a good worker, one who does not need to be ashamed and who correctly explains the word of truth. ¹⁶Avoid godless, foolish discussions that lead to more and more ungodliness. ¹⁷This kind of talk spreads like cancer. Hymenaeus and Philetus are examples of this. ¹⁸They have left the path of truth, preaching the lie that the resurrection of the dead has already occurred; and they have undermined the faith of some.

¹⁹But God's truth stands firm like a foundation stone with this inscription: "The Lord knows those who are his,"* and "Those who claim they belong to the Lord must turn away from all wickedness."*

2:19a Num 16:5. 2:19b See Isa 52:11.

427

²⁰In a wealthy home some utensils are made of gold and silver, and some are made of wood and clay. The expensive utensils are used for special occasions, and the cheap ones are for everyday use. ²¹If you keep yourself pure, you will be a utensil God can use for his purpose. Your life will be clean, and you will be ready for the Master to use you for every good work.

²²Run from anything that stimulates youthful lust. Follow anything that makes you want to do right. Pursue faith and love and peace, and enjoy the companionship of those who call on the Lord with pure hearts.

²³Again I say, don't get involved in foolish, ignorant arguments that only start fights. ²⁴The Lord's servants must not quarrel but must be kind to everyone. They must be able to teach effectively and be patient with difficult people.

A good worker works hard for God. How do you work hard for God? You keep your focus on serving Jesus, and you do what Jesus has commanded you to do. What has Jesus commanded you to do? He has commanded you to believe in him and to tell others about him. He has commanded you to turn away from sin. This is how you can become a good worker for God.

What can we ask God to help us do?
Teach me, O LORD, to follow every one of your principles.
Psalm 119:33

D E C E M B E R

Paul gave Timothy a lot of good advice.
Why did he say that the Bible is so important?

2 TIMOTHY 3:10–4:5
The Bible
¹⁰But you know what I teach, Timothy, and how I live, and what my purpose in life is. You know my faith and how long I have suffered. You know my love and my patient endurance. ¹¹You know how much persecution and suffering I have endured. You know all about how I was persecuted in Antioch, Iconium, and Lystra—but the Lord delivered me from all of it. ¹²Yes, and everyone who wants to live a godly life in Christ Jesus will suffer persecution. ¹³But evil people and impostors will flourish. They will go on deceiving others, and they themselves will be deceived.

¹⁴But you must remain faithful to the things you have been taught. You know they are true, for you know you can trust those who taught you. ¹⁵You have been taught the holy Scriptures from childhood, and they have given

you the wisdom to receive the salvation that comes by trusting in Christ Jesus. [16]All Scripture is inspired by God and is useful to teach us what is true and to make us realize what is wrong in our lives. It straightens us out and teaches us to do what is right. [17]It is God's way of preparing us in every way, fully equipped for every good thing God wants us to do.

[4:1]And so I solemnly urge you before God and before Christ Jesus—who will someday judge the living and the dead when he appears to set up his Kingdom: [2]Preach the word of God. Be persistent, whether the time is favorable or not. Patiently correct, rebuke, and encourage your people with good teaching.

[3]For a time is coming when people will no longer listen to right teaching. They will follow their own desires and will look for teachers who will tell them whatever they want to hear. [4]They will reject the truth and follow strange myths.

[5]But you should keep a clear mind in every situation. Don't be afraid of suffering for the Lord. Work at bringing others to Christ. Complete the ministry God has given you.

The Bible is like a road map. It shows you what path you should take in life. Do you want to be prepared for life's good times and bad times? Read the Bible. It will prepare you for life.

Why is it important for you to read the Bible regularly?
How can a young person stay pure? By obeying your word and following its rules.
Psalm 119:9

D E C E M B E R

In his letter to Titus, Paul gave Christians a lot of good rules to live by. What did Paul say Christians should turn away from?

TITUS 2:1-15

In Control

But as for you, promote the kind of living that reflects right teaching. [2]Teach the older men to exercise self-control, to be worthy of respect, and to live wisely. They must have strong faith and be filled with love and patience.

[3]Similarly, teach the older women to live in a way that is appropriate for someone serving the Lord. They must not go around speaking evil of others and must not be heavy drinkers. Instead, they should teach others what is good. [4]These older women must train the younger women to love their husbands and their children, [5]to live

wisely and be pure, to take care of their homes, to do good, and to be submissive to their husbands. Then they will not bring shame on the word of God.

[6]In the same way, encourage the young men to live wisely in all they do. [7]And you yourself must be an example to them by doing good deeds of every kind. Let everything you do reflect the integrity and seriousness of your teaching. [8]Let your teaching be so correct that it can't be criticized. Then those who want to argue will be ashamed because they won't have anything bad to say about us.

[9]Slaves must obey their masters and do their best to please them. They must not talk back [10]or steal, but they must show themselves to be entirely trustworthy and good. Then they will make the teaching about God our Savior attractive in every way.

[11]For the grace of God has been revealed, bringing salvation to all people. [12]And we are instructed to turn from godless living and sinful pleasures. We should live in this evil world with self-control, right conduct, and devotion to God, [13]while we look forward to that wonderful event when the glory of our great God and Savior, Jesus Christ, will be revealed. [14]He gave his life to free us from every kind of sin, to cleanse us, and to make us his very own people, totally committed to doing what is right. [15]You must teach these things and encourage your people to do them, correcting them when necessary. You have the authority to do this, so don't let anyone ignore you or disregard what you say.

Paul said Christians should turn away from "godless living" and "sinful pleasures." Godless living and sinful pleasures both involve disobeying God. Jesus came to save us from godless living and sinful pleasures. He helps us learn self-control. And he promises us the power to fight sin. Trust him to help you overcome your old, sinful nature.

Who will help us escape temptation?

But remember that the temptations that come into your life are no different from what others experience. And God is faithful. He will keep the temptation from becoming so strong that you can't stand up against it. When you are tempted, he will show you a way out so that you will not give in to it.

1 Corinthians 10:13

God sent Jesus to save all people from their sin. Why did he do that?

TITUS 3:1-11
God's Love

Remind your people to submit to the government and its officers. They should be obedient, always ready to do what is good. ²They must not speak evil of anyone, and they must avoid quarreling. Instead, they should be gentle and show true humility to everyone.

³Once we, too, were foolish and disobedient. We were misled by others and became slaves to many wicked desires and evil pleasures. Our lives were full of evil and envy. We hated others, and they hated us.

⁴But then God our Savior showed us his kindness and love. ⁵He saved us, not because of the good things we did, but because of his mercy. He washed away our sins and gave us a new life through the Holy Spirit.* ⁶He generously poured out the Spirit upon us because of what Jesus Christ our Savior did. ⁷He declared us not guilty because of his great kindness. And now we know that we will inherit eternal life. ⁸These things I have told you are all true. I want you to insist on them so that everyone who trusts in God will be careful to do good deeds all the time. These things are good and beneficial for everyone.

⁹Do not get involved in foolish discussions about spiritual pedigrees* or in quarrels and fights about obedience to Jewish laws. These kinds of things are useless and a waste of time. ¹⁰If anyone is causing divisions among you, give a first and second warning. After that, have nothing more to do with that person. ¹¹For people like that have turned away from the truth. They are sinning, and they condemn themselves.

God didn't send Jesus because we had done good things and were worthy of being saved. Instead, he sent his Son because he loved us so much. We can show our thankfulness to God by doing what is good. Thank God for his mercy with an obedient life.

Why is it important to always be ready to do good?
The LORD approves of those who are good, but he condemns those who plan wickedness.
Proverbs 12:2

3:5 Greek *He saved us through the washing of regeneration and renewing of the Holy Spirit.* **3:9** Greek *discussions and genealogies.*

The writer of Hebrews urged Christians to come boldly to Jesus when they faced temptations. Why?

HEBREWS 4:12–5:9

Jesus Understands

¹²For the word of God is full of living power. It is sharper than the sharpest knife, cutting deep into our innermost thoughts and desires. It exposes us for what we really are. ¹³Nothing in all creation can hide from him. Everything is naked and exposed before his eyes. This is the God to whom we must explain all that we have done.

¹⁴That is why we have a great High Priest who has gone to heaven, Jesus the Son of God. Let us cling to him and never stop trusting him. ¹⁵This High Priest of ours understands our weaknesses, for he faced all of the same temptations we do, yet he did not sin. ¹⁶So let us come boldly to the throne of our gracious God. There we will receive his mercy, and we will find grace to help us when we need it.

⁵:¹Now a high priest is a man chosen to represent other human beings in their dealings with God. He presents their gifts to God and offers their sacrifices for sins. ²And because he is human, he is able to deal gently with the people, though they are ignorant and wayward. For he is subject to the same weaknesses they have. ³That is why he has to offer sacrifices, both for their sins and for his own sins. ⁴And no one can become a high priest simply because he wants such an honor. He has to be called by God for this work, just as Aaron was.

⁵That is why Christ did not exalt himself to become High Priest. No, he was chosen by God, who said to him,

"You are my Son.
   Today I have become your
      Father.*"

⁶And in another passage God said to him,

Jesus understands the temptations we face. When he lived on earth he faced all of the same temptations we do. But the difference between us and Jesus is that he never sinned. He overcame sin's power, and he wants to help us overcome sin, too. Therefore we can go to him for help when we are tempted. Don't be afraid to call on Jesus when you need his help.

Who can you call on to help you when you are tempted?
From the depths of despair, O LORD,
   I call for your help. Hear my cry,
O Lord. Pay attention to my prayer.
   Psalm 130:1-2

5:5 Or *Today I reveal you as my Son.* Ps 2:7.

"You are a priest forever
   in the line of Melchizedek."*

⁷While Jesus was here on earth, he offered prayers and pleadings, with a loud cry and tears, to the one who could deliver him out of death. And God heard his prayers because of his reverence for God. ⁸So even though Jesus was God's Son, he learned obedience from the things he suffered. ⁹In this way, God qualified him as a perfect High Priest, and he became the source of eternal salvation for all those who obey him.

5:6 Ps 110:4.

D E C E M B E R

Israel had many heroes. What made these people heroes?

HEBREWS 11:1-16

Real Heroes

What is faith? It is the confident assurance that what we hope for is going to happen. It is the evidence of things we cannot yet see. ²God gave his approval to people in days of old because of their faith.

³By faith we understand that the entire universe was formed at God's command, that what we now see did not come from anything that can be seen.

⁴It was by faith that Abel brought a more acceptable offering to God than Cain did. God accepted Abel's offering to show that he was a righteous man. And although Abel is long dead, he still speaks to us because of his faith.

⁵It was by faith that Enoch was taken up to heaven without dying—"suddenly he disappeared because God took him."* But before he was taken up, he was approved as pleasing to God. ⁶So, you see, it is impossible to please God without faith. Anyone who wants to come to him must believe that there is a God and that he rewards those who sincerely seek him.

⁷It was by faith that Noah built an ark to save his family from the flood. He obeyed God, who warned him about something that had never happened before. By his faith he condemned the rest of the world and was made right in God's sight.

⁸It was by faith that Abraham obeyed when God called him to leave home and go to another land that God would give him as his inheritance. He went without knowing where he was going. ⁹And even when he reached the land God promised him, he lived there by faith—for he was like a foreigner, living in a tent. And so did Isaac and Jacob, to whom God gave the same promise. ¹⁰Abraham did this because he was confidently looking

11:5 Gen 5:24.

433

forward to a city with eternal foundations, a city designed and built by God.

[11]It was by faith that Sarah together with Abraham was able to have a child, even though they were too old and Sarah was barren. Abraham believed that God would keep his promise.* [12]And so a whole nation came from this one man, Abraham, who was too old to have any children—a nation with so many people that, like the stars of the sky and the sand on the seashore, there is no way to count them.

[13]All these faithful ones died without receiving what God had promised them, but they saw it all from a distance and welcomed the promises of God. They agreed that they were no more than foreigners and nomads here on earth. [14]And obviously people who talk like that are looking forward to a country they can call their own. [15]If they had meant the country they came from, they would have found a way to go back. [16]But they were looking for a better place, a heavenly homeland. That is why God is not ashamed to be called their God, for he has prepared a heavenly city for them.

These heroes trusted God completely. What made their trust heroic was that they never saw the fulfillment of God's promise or they were asked to do things that didn't make sense. Yet each of them believed God. Out of their belief, they trusted God and obeyed him. Like these heroes of the faith, we should believe God when he says he will do something. God keeps all of his promises. You can trust him with your life.

How can you have faith like one of these heroes?
Trust in the LORD with all your heart; do not depend on your own understanding. Seek his will in all you do, and he will direct your paths.
Proverbs 3:5-6

11:11 Some manuscripts read *It was by faith that Sarah was able to have a child, even though she was too old and barren. Sarah believed that God would keep his promise.*

D E C E M B E R

The Christian life is like a race. How can you win this race?

HEBREWS 12:1-13
Run the Race
Therefore, since we are surrounded by such a huge crowd of witnesses to the life of faith, let us strip off every weight that slows us down, especially the sin that so easily hinders our progress. And let us run with endurance the race that God has set before us. [2]We do this by keeping our eyes on Jesus, on

whom our faith depends from start to finish.* He was willing to die a shameful death on the cross because of the joy he knew would be his afterward. Now he is seated in the place of highest honor beside God's throne in heaven. ³Think about all he endured when sinful people did such terrible things to him, so that you don't become weary and give up. ⁴After all, you have not yet given your lives in your struggle against sin.

⁵And have you entirely forgotten the encouraging words God spoke to you, his children? He said,

"My child, don't ignore it when
    the Lord disciplines you,
and don't be discouraged when
    he corrects you.
⁶ For the Lord disciplines those he
    loves,
and he punishes those he
    accepts as his children."*

⁷As you endure this divine discipline, remember that God is treating you as his own children. Whoever heard of a child who was never disciplined? ⁸If God doesn't discipline you as he does all of his children, it means that you are illegitimate and are not really his children after all. ⁹Since we respect our earthly fathers who disciplined us, should we not all the more cheerfully submit to the discipline of our heavenly Father and live forever*? ¹⁰For our earthly fathers disciplined

us for a few years, doing the best they knew how. But God's discipline is always right and good for us because it means we will share in his holiness. ¹¹No discipline is enjoyable while it is happening—it is painful! But afterward there will be a quiet harvest of right living for those who are trained in this way.

¹²So take a new grip with your tired hands and stand firm on your shaky legs. ¹³Mark out a straight path for your feet. Then those who follow you, though they are weak and lame, will not stumble and fall but will become strong.

You can win this race by doing two things. First, you need to get rid of any sin that is in your life. Second, you need to keep your eyes on Jesus. This means that you follow Jesus' example of living and trust him to make the needed changes in your life. And he will, because he has promised to finish the good work he started in you.

Who helps us keep running the race?
God arms me with strength; he has made my way safe. He makes me as surefooted as a deer, leading me safely along the mountain heights.
Psalm 18:32-33

12:2 Or *Jesus, the Originator and Perfecter of our faith.* 12:5-6 Prov 3:11-12. 12:9 Or *really live.*

God is perfect and powerful. How should we treat him?

HEBREWS 12:14-29

A Holy God

[14]Try to live in peace with everyone, and seek to live a clean and holy life, for those who are not holy will not see the Lord. [15]Look after each other so that none of you will miss out on the special favor of God. Watch out that no bitter root of unbelief rises up among you, for whenever it springs up, many are corrupted by its poison. [16]Make sure that no one is immoral or godless like Esau. He traded his birthright as the oldest son for a single meal. [17]And afterward, when he wanted his father's blessing, he was rejected. It was too late for repentance, even though he wept bitter tears.

[18]You have not come to a physical mountain, to a place of flaming fire, darkness, gloom, and whirlwind, as the Israelites did at Mount Sinai when God gave them his laws. [19]For they heard an awesome trumpet blast and a voice with a message so terrible that they begged God to stop speaking. [20]They staggered back under God's command: "If even an animal touches the mountain, it must be stoned to death."* [21]Moses himself was so frightened at the sight that he said, "I am terrified and trembling."*

[22]No, you have come to Mount Zion, to the city of the living God, the heavenly Jerusalem, and to thousands of angels in joyful assembly. [23]You have come to the assembly of God's firstborn children, whose names are written in heaven. You have come to God himself, who is the judge of all people. And you have come to the spirits of the redeemed in heaven who have now been made perfect. [24]You have come to Jesus, the one who mediates the new covenant between God and people, and to the sprinkled blood, which graciously forgives instead of crying out for vengeance as the blood of Abel did.

[25]See to it that you obey God, the

We should respect God and listen to him. We should also obey his commands and worship him because he is good and loving. Disobeying God is dangerous. If we reject him, we will spend eternity in hell. But if obey him, we will be with him in heaven. Choose to obey God. You won't regret it.

Why is God worthy of our respect?

How great is our Lord! His power is absolute! His understanding is beyond comprehension!
Psalm 147:5

12:20 Exod 19:13. **12:21** Deut 9:19.

one who is speaking to you. For if the people of Israel did not escape when they refused to listen to Moses, the earthly messenger, how terrible our danger if we reject the One who speaks to us from heaven! ²⁶When God spoke from Mount Sinai his voice shook the earth, but now he makes another promise: "Once again I will shake not only the earth but the heavens also."* ²⁷This means that the things on earth will be shaken, so that only eternal things will be left.

²⁸Since we are receiving a kingdom that cannot be destroyed, let us be thankful and please God by worshiping him with holy fear and awe. ²⁹For our God is a consuming fire.

12:26 Hag 2:6.

D E C E M B E R

Jesus never changes. He is always the same. Why is this important to know?

HEBREWS 13:1-21
Unchanging God

Continue to love each other with true Christian love.* ²Don't forget to show hospitality to strangers, for some who have done this have entertained angels without realizing it! ³Don't forget about those in prison. Suffer with them as though you were there yourself. Share the sorrow of those being mistreated, as though you feel their pain in your own bodies.

⁴Give honor to marriage, and remain faithful to one another in marriage. God will surely judge people who are immoral and those who commit adultery.

⁵Stay away from the love of money; be satisfied with what you have. For God has said,

"I will never fail you.
I will never forsake you."*

⁶That is why we can say with confidence,

"The Lord is my helper,
so I will not be afraid.
What can mere mortals do to me?"*

⁷Remember your leaders who first taught you the word of God. Think of all the good that has come from their lives, and trust the Lord as they do.

⁸Jesus Christ is the same yesterday, today, and forever. ⁹So do not be attracted by strange, new ideas. Your spiritual strength comes from God's special favor, not from ceremonial rules about food, which don't help those who follow them.

¹⁰We have an altar from which the priests in the Temple on earth have no right to eat. ¹¹Under the system of Jewish laws, the high priest brought the blood of animals into the Holy Place

13:1 Greek *with brotherly love.* **13:5** Deut 31:6, 8. **13:6** Ps 118:6.

as a sacrifice for sin, but the bodies of the animals were burned outside the camp. ¹²So also Jesus suffered and died outside the city gates in order to make his people holy by shedding his own blood. ¹³So let us go out to him outside the camp and bear the disgrace he bore. ¹⁴For this world is not our home; we are looking forward to our city in heaven, which is yet to come.

¹⁵With Jesus' help, let us continually offer our sacrifice of praise to God by proclaiming the glory of his name. ¹⁶Don't forget to do good and to share what you have with those in need, for such sacrifices are very pleasing to God.

¹⁷Obey your spiritual leaders and do what they say. Their work is to watch over your souls, and they know they are accountable to God. Give them reason to do this joyfully and not with sorrow. That would certainly not be for your benefit.

¹⁸Pray for us, for our conscience is clear and we want to live honorably in everything we do. ¹⁹I especially need your prayers right now so that I can come back to you soon.

²⁰⁻²¹And now, may the God of peace, who brought again from the dead our Lord Jesus, equip you with all you need for doing his will. May he produce in you, through the power of Jesus Christ, all that is pleasing to him. Jesus is the great Shepherd of the sheep by an everlasting covenant, signed with his blood. To him be glory forever and ever. Amen.

Jesus is perfect and has no need to change. This is important to know, because many people have come up with new teachings that twist the truth about who Jesus is and what he has done. But we can be sure that any teaching about Jesus that isn't grounded in the truth of the Bible is a lie. All that we need to know about Jesus is found in his Word. Get to know Jesus better. Read your Bible daily.

What can happen if you don't read your Bible regularly?

You seem to believe whatever anyone tells you, even if they preach about a different Jesus than the one we preach, or a different Spirit than the one you received, or a different kind of gospel than the one you believed.
2 Corinthians 11:4

DECEMBER

James's view of trials and troubles was different from most people's. How did he encourage Christians to view hard times?

JAMES 1:2-18

Tough Times

²Dear brothers and sisters, whenever trouble comes your way, let it be an opportunity for joy. ³For when your faith is tested, your endurance has a chance to grow. ⁴So let it grow, for when your endurance is fully developed, you will be strong in character and ready for anything.

⁵If you need wisdom—if you want to know what God wants you to do—ask him, and he will gladly tell you. He will not resent your asking. ⁶But when you ask him, be sure that you really expect him to answer, for a doubtful mind is as unsettled as a wave of the sea that is driven and tossed by the wind. ⁷People like that should not expect to receive anything from the Lord. ⁸They can't make up their minds. They waver back and forth in everything they do.

⁹Christians who are* poor should be glad, for God has honored them. ¹⁰And those who are rich should be glad, for God has humbled them. They will fade away like a flower in the field. ¹¹The hot sun rises and dries up the grass; the flower withers, and its beauty fades away. So also, wealthy people will fade away with all of their achievements.

¹²God blesses the people who pa-tiently endure testing. Afterward they will receive the crown of life that God has promised to those who love him. ¹³And remember, no one who wants to do wrong should ever say, "God is tempting me." God is never tempted to do wrong, and he never tempts anyone else either. ¹⁴Temptation comes from the lure of our own evil desires. ¹⁵These evil desires lead to evil actions, and evil

---

James told Christians to see trouble as an "opportunity for joy." He said this because he saw trouble as a test of faith and a chance to grow closer to God. We, too, can have James's view. We can see trouble as something that helps us trust God more completely. Trouble helps us learn patience and love. The next time you face trouble, don't let it get you down. Instead, see it as an opportunity to grow. You will be amazed at the peace you find when you look at trouble from God's point of view.

When we face troubles what should we do?

The godly will rejoice in the LORD and find shelter in him. And those who do what is right will praise him.

Psalm 64:10

1:9 Greek *The brother who is.*

439

actions lead to death. ¹⁶So don't be misled, my dear brothers and sisters.

¹⁷Whatever is good and perfect comes to us from God above, who created all heaven's lights.* Unlike them, he never changes or casts shifting shadows. ¹⁸In his goodness he chose to make us his own children by giving us his true word. And we, out of all creation, became his choice possession.

1:17 Greek from above, from the Father of lights.

D E C E M B E R

Some Christians were giving special treatment to rich people. What did James have to say about this?

JAMES 2:1-17

Playing Favorites

My dear brothers and sisters, how can you claim that you have faith in our glorious Lord Jesus Christ if you favor some people more than others?

²For instance, suppose someone comes into your meeting* dressed in fancy clothes and expensive jewelry, and another comes in who is poor and dressed in shabby clothes. ³If you give special attention and a good seat to the rich person, but you say to the poor one, "You can stand over there, or else sit on the floor"—well, ⁴doesn't this discrimination show that you are guided by wrong motives?

⁵Listen to me, dear brothers and sisters. Hasn't God chosen the poor in this world to be rich in faith? Aren't they the ones who will inherit the kingdom God promised to those who love him? ⁶And yet, you insult the poor man! Isn't it the rich who oppress you and drag you into court?

⁷Aren't they the ones who slander Jesus Christ, whose noble name you bear?

⁸Yes indeed, it is good when you truly obey our Lord's royal command found in the Scriptures: "Love your neighbor as yourself."* ⁹But if you pay special attention to the rich, you are committing a sin, for you are guilty of breaking that law.

¹⁰And the person who keeps all of the laws except one is as guilty as the person who has broken all of God's laws. ¹¹For the same God who said, "Do not commit adultery," also said, "Do not murder."* So if you murder someone, you have broken the entire law, even if you do not commit adultery.

¹²So whenever you speak, or whatever you do, remember that you will be judged by the law of love, the law that set you free. ¹³For there will be no mercy for you if you have not been merciful to others. But if you have been merciful, then God's mercy to-

2:2 Greek synagogue. 2:8 Lev 19:18. 2:11 Exod 20:13-14; Deut 5:17-18.

ward you will win out over his judgment against you.

¹⁴Dear brothers and sisters, what's the use of saying you have faith if you don't prove it by your actions? That kind of faith can't save anyone. ¹⁵Suppose you see a brother or sister who needs food or clothing, ¹⁶and you say, "Well, good-bye and God bless you; stay warm and eat well"— but then you don't give that person any food or clothing. What good does that do?

¹⁷So you see, it isn't enough just to have faith. Faith that doesn't show itself by good deeds is no faith at all—it is dead and useless.

James told those Christians that their motives were wrong. They shouldn't give special treatment to people just because those people were rich. One reason that is wrong is because it judges people by their appearance and not their heart. As James reminded these Christians, the poor may be rich in faith, and the rich may oppress people. Do you give special treatment to people because of their appearance or wealth? Consider James's warning and treat people equally. God doesn't decide a person's worth by his or her bank account, and neither should you.

Why is playing favorites wrong?
It is sin to despise one's neighbors; blessed are those who help the poor.
Proverbs 14:21

D E C E M B E R

Small things like a bit in a horse's mouth or a rudder on a ship have great power to guide and direct. What power does the tongue have?

JAMES 3:1-18
The Tongue
Dear brothers and sisters, not many of you should become teachers in the church, for we who teach will be judged by God with greater strictness.

²We all make many mistakes, but those who control their tongues can also control themselves in every other way. ³We can make a large horse turn around and go wherever we want by means of a small bit in its mouth.

⁴And a tiny rudder makes a huge ship turn wherever the pilot wants it to go, even though the winds are strong. ⁵So also, the tongue is a small thing, but what enormous damage it can do. A tiny spark can set a great forest on fire. ⁶And the tongue is a flame of fire. It is full of wickedness that can ruin your whole life. It can turn the entire course of your life into a blazing flame of destruction, for it is set on fire by hell itself.

[7]People can tame all kinds of animals and birds and reptiles and fish, [8]but no one can tame the tongue. It is an uncontrollable evil, full of deadly poison. [9]Sometimes it praises our Lord and Father, and sometimes it breaks out into curses against those who have been made in the image of God. [10]And so blessing and cursing come pouring out of the same mouth. Surely, my brothers and sisters, this is not right! [11]Does a spring of water bubble out with both fresh water and bitter water? [12]Can you pick olives from a fig tree or figs from a grapevine? No, and you can't draw fresh water from a salty pool.

[13]If you are wise and understand God's ways, live a life of steady goodness so that only good deeds will pour forth. And if you don't brag about the good you do, then you will be truly wise! [14]But if you are bitterly jealous and there is selfish ambition in your hearts, don't brag about being wise. That is the worst kind of lie. [15]For jealousy and selfishness are not God's kind of wisdom. Such things are earthly, unspiritual, and motivated by the Devil. [16]For wherever there is jealousy and selfish ambition, there you will find disorder and every kind of evil.

[17]But the wisdom that comes from heaven is first of all pure. It is also peace loving, gentle at all times, and willing to yield to others. It is full of mercy and good deeds. It shows no partiality and is always sincere. [18]And those who are peacemakers will plant seeds of peace and reap a harvest of goodness.

James wrote that the tongue has the power to destroy. What he meant was that people could hurt others with the things they say. He also warned people that they could get themselves into trouble by saying bad things. Have you ever said something hurtful to someone? Be careful what you say. Your tongue can not only get you into trouble but can ruin other people's lives as well.

Why should you watch what you say?

The crooked heart will not prosper;
the twisted tongue tumbles
into trouble.
Proverbs 17:20

All Christians are servants of God. Their work is to do good.
What example did Jesus leave for Christians to follow?

1 PETER 2:13-25
Free to Serve

[13]For the Lord's sake, accept all authority—the king as head of state, [14]and the officials he has appointed. For the king has sent them to punish all who do wrong and to honor those who do right.

[15]It is God's will that your good lives should silence those who make foolish accusations against you. [16]You are not slaves; you are free. But your freedom is not an excuse to do evil. You are free to live as God's slaves. [17]Show respect for everyone. Love your Christian brothers and sisters. Fear God. Show respect for the king.

[18]You who are slaves must accept the authority of your masters. Do whatever they tell you—not only if they are kind and reasonable, but even if they are harsh. [19]For God is pleased with you when, for the sake of your conscience, you patiently endure unfair treatment. [20]Of course, you get no credit for being patient if you are beaten for doing wrong. But if you suffer for doing right and are patient beneath the blows, God is pleased with you.

[21]This suffering is all part of what God has called you to. Christ, who suffered for you, is your example. Follow in his steps. [22]He never sinned, and he never deceived anyone. [23]He did not retaliate when he was insulted.

When he suffered, he did not threaten to get even. He left his case in the hands of God, who always judges fairly. [24]He personally carried away our sins in his own body on the cross so we can be dead to sin and live for what is right. You have been healed by his wounds! [25]Once you were wandering like lost sheep. But now you have turned to your Shepherd, the Guardian of your souls.

Jesus left the perfect example for Christians to follow. He served others, and he suffered at the hands of the authorities without getting even. He trusted in God the Father to deal justly with those who crucified him. Has anyone ever hurt you unfairly? How did you treat that person? Don't get even with him or her. Instead, follow Jesus' example and trust God to deal with that person. Only God can bring that person to justice.

Who will deal with those people who harm you?

Dear friends, never avenge yourselves. Leave that to God. For it is written, "I will take vengeance; I will repay those who deserve it,"* says the Lord.
Romans 12:19

12:19 Deut 32:35.

443

God gives all his followers gifts. What kinds of gifts does God give?

1 PETER 4:1-19

A Giving God

So then, since Christ suffered physical pain, you must arm yourselves with the same attitude he had, and be ready to suffer, too. For if you are willing to suffer for Christ, you have decided to stop sinning. ²And you won't spend the rest of your life chasing after evil desires, but you will be anxious to do the will of God. ³You have had enough in the past of the evil things that godless people enjoy—their immorality and lust, their feasting and drunkenness and wild parties, and their terrible worship of idols.

⁴Of course, your former friends are very surprised when you no longer join them in the wicked things they do, and they say evil things about you. ⁵But just remember that they will have to face God, who will judge everyone, both the living and the dead. ⁶That is why the Good News was preached even to those who have died—so that although their bodies were punished with death, they could still live in the spirit as God does.

⁷The end of the world is coming soon. Therefore, be earnest and disciplined in your prayers. ⁸Most important of all, continue to show deep love for each other, for love covers a multitude of sins. ⁹Cheerfully share your home with those who need a meal or a place to stay.

¹⁰God has given gifts to each of you from his great variety of spiritual gifts. Manage them well so that God's generosity can flow through you. ¹¹Are you called to be a speaker? Then speak as though God himself were speaking through you. Are you called to help others? Do it with all the strength and energy that God supplies. Then God will be given glory in everything through Jesus Christ. All glory and power belong to him forever and ever. Amen.

¹²Dear friends, don't be surprised at the fiery trials you are going through, as if something strange were happening to you. ¹³Instead, be very glad—because these trials will make you partners with Christ in his suffering, and afterward you will have the wonderful joy of sharing his glory when it is displayed to all the world.

¹⁴Be happy if you are insulted for being a Christian, for then the glorious Spirit of God will come upon you. ¹⁵If you suffer, however, it must not be for murder, stealing, making trouble, or prying into other people's affairs. ¹⁶But it is no shame to suffer for being a Christian. Praise God for the privilege of being called by his wonderful name! ¹⁷For the time has come for

judgment, and it must begin first among God's own children. And if even we Christians must be judged, what terrible fate awaits those who have never believed God's Good News? [18]And

> "If the righteous are barely saved,
> what chance will the godless
> and sinners have?" *

[19]So if you are suffering according to God's will, keep on doing what is right, and trust yourself to the God who made you, for he will never fail you.

The gifts God gives his followers are called spiritual gifts. God gives those gifts to his followers so they can serve him and others well. Peter listed two of those gifts in this passage: speaking and helping. What spiritual gift has God given you? If you know your gift, use it to serve God the best you can.

Why should we thank God for spiritual gifts?
If you sinful people know how to give good gifts to your children, how much more will your heavenly Father give good gifts to those who ask him.
Matthew 7:11

4:18 Prov 11:31.

D E C E M B E R

In his second letter, Peter told Christians that his testimony about Jesus was true. How did they know Peter wasn't lying?

2 PETER 1:2-21
Knowing God
[2]May God bless you with his special favor and wonderful peace as you come to know Jesus, our God and Lord,* better and better.

[3]As we know Jesus better, his divine power gives us everything we need for living a godly life. He has called us to receive his own glory and goodness! [4]And by that same mighty power, he has given us all of his rich and wonderful promises. He has promised that you will escape the decadence all around you caused by evil desires and that you will share in his divine nature.

[5]So make every effort to apply the benefits of these promises to your life. Then your faith will produce a life of moral excellence. A life of moral excellence leads to knowing God better. [6]Knowing God leads to self-control. Self-control leads to patient endurance, and patient endurance leads to godliness. [7]Godliness leads to love for

1:2 Or come to know God and Jesus our Lord.

other Christians,* and finally you will grow to have genuine love for everyone. [8]The more you grow like this, the more you will become productive and useful in your knowledge of our Lord Jesus Christ. [9]But those who fail to develop these virtues are blind or, at least, very shortsighted. They have already forgotten that God has cleansed them from their old life of sin.

[10]So, dear brothers and sisters, work hard to prove that you really are among those God has called and chosen. Doing this, you will never stumble or fall away. [11]And God will open wide the gates of heaven for you to enter into the eternal Kingdom of our Lord and Savior Jesus Christ.

[12]I plan to keep on reminding you of these things—even though you already know them and are standing firm in the truth. [13]Yes, I believe I should keep on reminding you of these things as long as I live. [14]But the Lord Jesus Christ has shown me that my days here on earth are numbered and I am soon to die.* [15]So I will work hard to make these things clear to you. I want you to remember them long after I am gone.

[16]For we were not making up clever stories when we told you about the power of our Lord Jesus Christ and his coming again. We have seen his majestic splendor with our own eyes. [17]And he received honor and glory from God the Father when God's glorious, majestic voice called down from heaven, "This is my beloved Son; I am fully pleased with him." [18]We ourselves heard the voice when we were there with him on the holy mountain.

[19]Because of that, we have even greater confidence in the message proclaimed by the prophets. Pay close attention to what they wrote, for their words are like a light shining in a dark place—until the day Christ appears and his brilliant light shines in your hearts.* [20]Above all, you must understand that no prophecy in Scripture ever came from the prophets themselves* [21]or because they wanted to prophesy. It was the Holy Spirit who moved the prophets to speak from God.

Peter had been a close friend of Jesus, so the Christians knew that what Peter said about Jesus was true. What Peter and Jesus' other disciples witnessed was written down and collected to form the New Testament. The New Testament contains everything we need to know about Jesus and how we can become his disciples.

What good can come from reading the Bible?

Oh, how I love your law! I think about it all day long. Your commands make me wiser than my enemies, for your commands are my constant guide.
Psalm 119:97-98

1:7 Greek *brotherly love.* **1:14** Greek *I must soon put off this earthly tent.* **1:19** Or *until the day dawns and the morning star rises in your hearts.* **1:20** Or *is a matter of one's own interpretation.*

John wrote that everyone is a sinner.
What will Jesus do if someone confesses his or her sins?

1 JOHN 1:1-10

Forgive and Forget

The one who existed from the beginning* is the one we have heard and seen. We saw him with our own eyes and touched him with our own hands. He is Jesus Christ, the Word of life. ²This one who is life from God was shown to us, and we have seen him. And now we testify and announce to you that he is the one who is eternal life. He was with the Father, and then he was shown to us. ³We are telling you about what we ourselves have actually seen and heard, so that you may have fellowship with us. And our fellowship is with the Father and with his Son, Jesus Christ.

⁴We are writing these things so that our* joy will be complete.

⁵This is the message he has given us to announce to you: God is light and there is no darkness in him at all. ⁶So we are lying if we say we have fellowship with God but go on living in spiritual darkness. We are not living in the truth. ⁷But if we are living in the light of God's presence, just as Christ is, then we have fellowship with each other, and the blood of Jesus, his Son, cleanses us from every sin.

⁸If we say we have no sin, we are only fooling ourselves and refusing to accept the truth. ⁹But if we confess our sins to him, he is faithful and just to forgive us and to cleanse us from every wrong. ¹⁰If we claim we have not sinned, we are calling God a liar and showing that his word has no place in our hearts.

Jesus will forgive anyone who confesses his or her sins to him. He will also wash that person's sins away so that he or she can live a clean life for him. Have you confessed your sins to Jesus? Don't let sin stand in the way of enjoying a clear conscience and a close relationship with God.

What can we pray to God for?
Help us, O God of our salvation!
Help us for the honor of your name.
Oh, save us and forgive our sins
for the sake of your name.
Psalm 79:9

1:1 Greek *What was from the beginning.* **1:4** Some manuscripts read *your.*

There are two signs of a real Christian. What are those signs?

1 JOHN 3:1-18

Real Christians

See how very much our heavenly Father loves us, for he allows us to be called his children, and we really are! But the people who belong to this world don't know God, so they don't understand that we are his children. ²Yes, dear friends, we are already God's children, and we can't even imagine what we will be like when Christ returns. But we do know that when he comes we will be like him, for we will see him as he really is. ³And all who believe this will keep themselves pure, just as Christ is pure.

⁴Those who sin are opposed to the law of God, for all sin opposes the law of God. ⁵And you know that Jesus came to take away our sins, for there is no sin in him. ⁶So if we continue to live in him, we won't sin either. But those who keep on sinning have never known him or understood who he is.

⁷Dear children, don't let anyone deceive you about this: When people do what is right, it is because they are righteous, even as Christ is righteous. ⁸But when people keep on sinning, it shows they belong to the Devil, who has been sinning since the beginning. But the Son of God came to destroy these works of the Devil. ⁹Those who have been born into God's family do not sin, because God's life is in them. So they can't keep on sinning, because they have been born of God. ¹⁰So now we can tell who are children of God and who are children of the Devil. Anyone who does not obey God's commands and does not love other Christians* does not belong to God.

¹¹This is the message we have heard from the beginning: We should love one another. ¹²We must not be like Cain, who belonged to the evil one and killed his brother. And why did he kill him? Because Cain had been do-

Many people claim to be Christians. But not everyone who makes this claim really is a Christian. According to John, real Christians obey God's commands and love other Christians. Do you obey God? Do you love other Christians? If you fall short of showing either of these two signs in your life and you call yourself a Christian, ask God to help you obey him and love others. It's important to be what you claim you are.

Why do you need to love others?

The second is equally important: "Love your neighbor as yourself."* No other commandment is greater than these.
Mark 12:31

3:10 Greek *his brother.* **12:31** Lev 19:18.

ing what was evil, and his brother had been doing what was right. [13]So don't be surprised, dear brothers and sisters, if the world hates you.

[14]If we love our Christian brothers and sisters, it proves that we have passed from death to eternal life. But a person who has no love is still dead. [15]Anyone who hates another Christian* is really a murderer at heart. And you know that murderers don't have eternal life within them. [16]We know what real love is because Christ gave up his life for us. And so we also ought to give up our lives for our Christian brothers and sisters. [17]But if anyone has enough money to live well and sees a brother or sister in need and refuses to help—how can God's love be in that person?

[18]Dear children, let us stop just saying we love each other; let us really show it by our actions.

3:15 Greek *his brother.*

D E C E M B E R

John wrote that God will answer his followers' prayers. How can his followers be sure of this?

1 JOHN 5:1-15
Prayer Requests

Everyone who believes that Jesus is the Christ is a child of God. And everyone who loves the Father loves his children, too. [2]We know we love God's children if we love God and obey his commandments. [3]Loving God means keeping his commandments, and really, that isn't difficult. [4]For every child of God defeats this evil world by trusting Christ to give the victory. [5]And the ones who win this battle against the world are the ones who believe that Jesus is the Son of God.

[6]And Jesus Christ was revealed as God's Son by his baptism in water and by shedding his blood on the cross*— not by water only, but by water and blood. And the Spirit also gives us the

Christians can be sure God will answer their prayers if they pray for things that are "in line with his will." That means Christians should pray for things that honor God, like the salvation of friends and family. It also means that Christians shouldn't pray for things that dishonor God, like bad things happening to their enemies. Have you seen God answer your prayers lately? If not, it may be that the things you are praying for are not "in line with his will." Think about the things you pray for. Make sure they honor God.

What can we ask God to do when we pray to him?
Listen to my cry for help, my King and my God, for I will never pray to anyone but you.
Psalm 5:2

5:6 Greek *This is he who came by water and blood.*

449

testimony that this is true. [7]So we have these three witnesses*—[8]the Spirit, the water, and the blood—and all three agree. [9]Since we believe human testimony, surely we can believe the testimony that comes from God. And God has testified about his Son. [10]All who believe in the Son of God know that this is true. Those who don't believe this are actually calling God a liar because they don't believe what God has testified about his Son.

[11]And this is what God has testified:

He has given us eternal life, and this life is in his Son. [12]So whoever has God's Son has life; whoever does not have his Son does not have life.

[13]I write this to you who believe in the Son of God, so that you may know you have eternal life. [14]And we can be confident that he will listen to us whenever we ask him for anything in line with his will. [15]And if we know he is listening when we make our requests, we can be sure that he will give us what we ask for.

5:7 Some very late manuscripts add *in heaven—the Father, the Word, and the Holy Spirit, and these three are one. And we have three witnesses on earth.*

D E C E M B E R 27

John urged Christians to love others. Why did he do this?

2 JOHN 1:1-11

Walk in Love

This letter is from John the Elder.*

It is written to the chosen lady and to her children,* whom I love in the truth, as does everyone else who knows God's truth—[2]the truth that lives in us and will be in our hearts forever.

[3]May grace, mercy, and peace, which come from God our Father and from Jesus Christ his Son, be with us who live in truth and love.

[4]How happy I was to meet some of your children and find them living in the truth, just as we have been commanded by the Father.

[5]And now I want to urge you, dear lady, that we should love one another. This is not a new commandment, but one we had from the beginning. [6]Love means doing what God has commanded us, and he has commanded us to love one another, just as you heard from the beginning.

[7]Many deceivers have gone out into the world. They do not believe that Jesus Christ came to earth in a real body. Such a person is a deceiver and an antichrist. [8]Watch out, so that you do not lose the prize for which we* have been working so hard. Be diligent so that you will receive your full reward. [9]For if you wander beyond the teaching of Christ, you will not have fellowship with God. But if you con-

1a Greek *From the elder.* **1b** Or *the church God has chosen and her members,* or *the chosen Kyria and her children.* **8** Some manuscripts read *you.*

tinue in the teaching of Christ, you will have fellowship with both the Father and the Son.

¹⁰If someone comes to your meeting and does not teach the truth about Christ, don't invite him into your house or encourage him in any way. ¹¹Anyone who encourages him becomes a partner in his evil work.

By urging Christians to love others, John was telling them to obey God. God has commanded all Christians to love others. If we follow Jesus, then we must obey his commands. He loved us, and we must love others.

How can you actively love others?
Pure and lasting religion in the sight of God our Father means that we must care for orphans and widows in their troubles, and refuse to let the world corrupt us.
James 1:27

DECEMBER

Jude warned his readers about those who were dividing the church. What advice did he give them?

JUDE 1:14-25
Hang In There
¹⁴Now Enoch, who lived seven generations after Adam, prophesied about these people. He said,

"Look, the Lord is coming
    with thousands of his holy ones.
¹⁵ He will bring the people of the world
    to judgment.
He will convict the ungodly of all
        the evil things
    they have done in rebellion
and of all the insults that godless
        sinners
    have spoken against him."*

14-15 The quotation comes from the Apocrypha: Enoch 1:9.

¹⁶These people are grumblers and complainers, doing whatever evil they feel like. They are loudmouthed braggarts, and they flatter others to get favors in return.

¹⁷But you, my dear friends, must remember what the apostles of our Lord Jesus Christ told you, ¹⁸that in the last times there would be scoffers whose purpose in life is to enjoy themselves in every evil way imaginable. ¹⁹Now they are here, and they are the ones who are creating divisions among you. They live by natural instinct because they do not have God's Spirit living in them.

²⁰But you, dear friends, must continue to build your lives on the foundation of your holy faith. And continue to pray as you are directed by the Holy Spirit.* ²¹Live in such a way that God's love can bless you as you wait for the eternal life that our Lord Jesus Christ in his mercy is going to give you. ²²Show mercy to those whose faith is wavering. ²³Rescue others by snatching them from the flames of judgment. There are still others to whom you need to show mercy, but be careful that you aren't contaminated by their sins.*

²⁴And now, all glory to God, who is able to keep you from stumbling, and who will bring you into his glorious presence innocent of sin and with great joy. ²⁵All glory to him, who alone is God our Savior, through Jesus Christ our Lord. Yes, glory, majesty, power, and authority belong to him, in the beginning, now, and forevermore. Amen.

Jude told believers to continue to live lives that please God. What does that mean to you? That means you should live obediently to God's commands found in the Bible. You should listen to the Holy Spirit's urgings about people and things to pray for. And you should show kindness to people by telling them about the hope they can have in Jesus Christ. Living a life like that pleases God.

What can you do to show that you love Jesus?

You who love the LORD, hate evil! He protects the lives of his godly people and rescues them from the power of the wicked.
Psalm 97:10

20 Greek *Pray in the Holy Spirit.* 23 Greek *mercy, hating even the clothing stained by the flesh.*

DECEMBER

29

Jesus appeared to John. What did he want John to do?

REVELATION 1:1-20
Jesus' Last Message

This is a revelation from* Jesus Christ, which God gave him concerning the events that will happen soon. An angel was sent to God's servant John so that John could share the revelation with God's other servants. ²John faithfully reported the word of God and the testimony of Jesus Christ—everything he saw.

³God blesses the one who reads this prophecy to the church, and he blesses all who listen to it and obey what it says. For the time is near when these things will happen.

⁴This letter is from John to the seven churches in the province of Asia. Grace

1:1 Or *of.*

and peace from the one who is, who always was, and who is still to come; from the sevenfold Spirit* before his throne; ⁵and from Jesus Christ, who is the faithful witness to these things, the first to rise from the dead, and the commander of all the rulers of the world.

All praise to him who loves us and has freed us from our sins by shedding his blood for us. ⁶He has made us his kingdom and his priests who serve before God his Father. Give to him everlasting glory! He rules forever and ever! Amen!

⁷Look! He comes with the clouds of heaven. And everyone will see him— even those who pierced him. And all the nations of the earth will weep because of him. Yes! Amen!

⁸"I am the Alpha and the Omega— the beginning and the end," says the Lord God. "I am the one who is, who always was, and who is still to come, the Almighty One."

⁹I am John, your brother. In Jesus we are partners in suffering and in the Kingdom and in patient endurance. I was exiled to the island of Patmos for preaching the word of God and speaking about Jesus. ¹⁰It was the Lord's Day, and I was worshiping in the Spirit.* Suddenly, I heard a loud voice behind me, a voice that sounded like a trumpet blast. ¹¹It said, "Write down what you see, and send it to the seven churches: Ephesus, Smyrna, Pergamum, Thyatira, Sardis, Philadelphia, and Laodicea."

¹²When I turned to see who was speaking to me, I saw seven gold lampstands. ¹³And standing in the middle of the lampstands was the Son of Man.* He was wearing a long robe with a gold sash across his chest. ¹⁴His head and his hair were white like wool, as white as snow. And his eyes were bright like flames of fire. ¹⁵His feet were as bright as bronze refined in a furnace, and his voice thundered like mighty ocean waves. ¹⁶He held seven stars in his right hand, and a sharp two-edged sword came from his mouth. And his face was as bright as the sun in all its brilliance.

¹⁷When I saw him, I fell at his feet as dead. But he laid his right hand on me and said, "Don't be afraid! I am the First and the Last. ¹⁸I am the living one who died. Look, I am alive forever and ever! And I hold the keys of death and the grave.* ¹⁹Write down what you have seen—both the things that are

Jesus had a message for his followers, and he wanted John to write it down. That is why he appeared to John. Part of the message Jesus gave was for certain churches. But the rest of the message was for all of his followers, past, present, and future. If you follow Jesus, the message of this book is for you, too. Read it and be encouraged that Jesus is coming back for you!

What will all Christians do when Jesus returns?

And so the LORD's fame will be celebrated in Zion, his praises in Jerusalem, when multitudes gather together and kingdoms come to worship the LORD.
Psalm 102:21-22

1:4 Greek the seven spirits. 1:10 Or in spirit. 1:13 Or one who looked like a man; Greek reads one like a son of man. 1:18 Greek and Hades.

now happening and the things that will happen later. [20]This is the meaning of the seven stars you saw in my right hand and the seven gold lampstands: The seven stars are the angels of* the seven churches, and the seven lampstands are the seven churches.

D E C E M B E R

Jesus will come again and make everything new.
Who will live with Jesus when he comes back?

REVELATION 21:1-12, 22-27
Everything Made New

Then I saw a new heaven and a new earth, for the old heaven and the old earth had disappeared. And the sea was also gone. [2]And I saw the holy city, the new Jerusalem, coming down from God out of heaven like a beautiful bride prepared for her husband.

[3]I heard a loud shout from the throne, saying, "Look, the home of God is now among his people! He will live with them, and they will be his people. God himself will be with them.* [4]He will remove all of their sorrows, and there will be no more death or sorrow or crying or pain. For the old world and its evils are gone forever."

[5]And the one sitting on the throne said, "Look, I am making all things new!" And then he said to me, "Write this down, for what I tell you is trustworthy and true." [6]And he also said, "It is finished! I am the Alpha and the Omega—the Beginning and the End. To all who are thirsty I will give the springs of the water of life without charge! [7]All who are victorious will inherit all these blessings, and I will be their God, and they will be my children. [8]But cowards who turn away from me, and unbelievers, and the corrupt, and murderers, and the immoral, and those who practice witchcraft, and idol worshipers, and all liars—their doom is in the lake that burns with fire and sulfur. This is the second death."

[9]Then one of the seven angels who held the seven bowls containing the seven last plagues came and said to me, "Come with me! I will show you the bride, the wife of the Lamb."

[10]So he took me in spirit* to a great, high mountain, and he showed me the holy city, Jerusalem, descending out of heaven from God. [11]It was filled with the glory of God and sparkled like a precious gem, crystal clear like jasper. [12]Its walls were broad and high, with twelve gates guarded by twelve angels. And the names of the twelve tribes of Israel were written on the gates.

• • •

²²No temple could be seen in the city, for the Lord God Almighty and the Lamb are its temple. ²³And the city has no need of sun or moon, for the glory of God illuminates the city, and the Lamb is its light. ²⁴The nations of the earth will walk in its light, and the rulers of the world will come and bring their glory to it. ²⁵Its gates never close at the end of day because there is no night. ²⁶And all the nations will bring their glory and honor into the city. ²⁷Nothing evil will be allowed to enter—no one who practices shameful idolatry and dishonesty—but only those whose names are written in the Lamb's Book of Life.

Those who believe in Jesus will live with him forever. Those who overcome evil will live in the beautiful new Jerusalem. Jesus will reward those who believe in him. Believe in Jesus and look forward to life in heaven with him.

Who will live with God forever?
Surely the godly are praising
your name, for they will live
in your presence.
Psalm 140:13

D E C E M B E R

John wrote down Jesus' final words to everyone. What did Jesus say?

REVELATION 22:1-21

The End

And the angel showed me a pure river with the water of life, clear as crystal, flowing from the throne of God and of the Lamb, ²coursing down the center of the main street. On each side of the river grew a tree of life, bearing twelve crops of fruit,* with a fresh crop each month. The leaves were used for medicine to heal the nations.

³No longer will anything be cursed. For the throne of God and of the Lamb will be there, and his servants will worship him. ⁴And they will see his face, and his name will be written on their foreheads. ⁵And there will be no night there—no need for lamps or sun—for the Lord God will shine on them. And they will reign forever and ever.

⁶Then the angel said to me, "These words are trustworthy and true: 'The Lord God, who tells his prophets what the future holds, has sent his angel to tell you what will happen soon.' "

⁷"Look, I am coming soon! Blessed are those who obey the prophecy written in this scroll."

⁸I, John, am the one who saw and heard all these things. And when I saw

22:2 Or *12 kinds of fruit.*

455

and heard these things, I fell down to worship the angel who showed them to me. [9]But again he said, "No, don't worship me. I am a servant of God, just like you and your brothers the prophets, as well as all who obey what is written in this scroll. Worship God!"

[10]Then he instructed me, "Do not seal up the prophetic words you have written, for the time is near. [11]Let the one who is doing wrong continue to do wrong; the one who is vile, continue to be vile; the one who is good, continue to do good; and the one who is holy, continue in holiness."

[12]"See, I am coming soon, and my reward is with me, to repay all according to their deeds. [13]I am the Alpha and the Omega, the First and the Last, the Beginning and the End."

[14]Blessed are those who wash their robes so they can enter through the gates of the city and eat the fruit from the tree of life. [15]Outside the city are the dogs—the sorcerers, the sexually immoral, the murderers, the idol worshipers, and all who love to live a lie.

[16]"I, Jesus, have sent my angel to give you this message for the churches. I am both the source of David and the heir to his throne.* I am the bright morning star."

[17]The Spirit and the bride say, "Come." Let each one who hears them say, "Come." Let the thirsty ones come—anyone who wants to. Let them come and drink the water of life without charge. [18]And I solemnly declare to everyone who hears the prophetic words of this book: If anyone adds anything to what is written here, God will add to that person the plagues described in this book. [19]And if anyone removes any of the words of this prophetic book, God will remove that person's share in the tree of life and in the holy city that are described in this book.

[20]He who is the faithful witness to all these things says, "Yes, I am coming soon!"

Amen! Come, Lord Jesus!

[21]The grace of the Lord Jesus be with you all.

Jesus urged everyone to come to him for eternal life. Those who come to Jesus will live with him forever in a place of beauty and peace. Have you come to Jesus yet? Don't delay. Time is short.

What can we look forward to as followers of Jesus Christ?
Surely your goodness and unfailing love will pursue me all the days of my life, and I will live in the house of the LORD forever.
Psalm 23:6

22:16 Greek *I am the root and offspring of David.*

WHY READ THE BIBLE?

Have you ever received a note from your best friend? Were you excited to read it? The Bible is God's note to you!

All Scripture is inspired by God and is useful to teach us what is true and to make us realize what is wrong in our lives. It straightens us out and teaches us to do what is right. It is God's way of preparing us in every way, fully equipped for every good thing God wants us to do. (2 Timothy 3:16-17)

Here are three good reasons why you should read your Bible:

You should read the Bible because it is God's main way of communicating with you.
- It tells you who God is.
- It tells you what God wants you to know.

All your words are true; all your just laws will stand forever. (Psalm 119:160)

You should read the Bible because it tells you how to have eternal life.
- It tells you to turn away from your sins.
- It tells you to believe in Jesus so that your sins will be forgiven.

For God so loved the world that he gave his only Son, so that everyone who believes in him will not perish but have eternal life. (John 3:16)

You should read the Bible because it tells you how to live.
- It records God's commands for living (Exodus 20:1-17).
- It records Jesus' life and teachings. His life is a perfect example of how you should live.

I will study your commandments and reflect on your ways. I will delight in your principles and not forget your word. (Psalm 119:15-16)

WHO IS GOD?

God Is the Creator

He created everything—even you.

Come, let us worship and bow down. Let us kneel before the LORD our maker, (Psalm 95:6)

God Is the Almighty

He is stronger than any person or machine. He controls everything.

I am the LORD, the God of all the peoples of the world. Is anything too hard for me? (Jeremiah 32:27)

God Is Our Father

All those who believe in Jesus become a part of God's family.

So you should not be like cowering, fearful slaves. You should behave instead like God's very own children, adopted into his family—calling him "Father, dear Father." For his Holy Spirit speaks to us deep in our hearts and tells us that we are God's children. (Romans 8:15-16)

God Is Love

He is a loving God. He loves you and cares for you.

We know how much God loves us, and we have put our trust in him. God is love, and all who live in love live in God, and God lives in them. (1 John 4:16)

God Is Our Savior

He saves all those who call on him for help. He saves those who believe in Jesus from sin and the coming judgment.

Praise the Lord; praise God our savior! For each day he carries us in his arms. (Psalm 68:19)

For God so loved the world that he gave his only Son, so that everyone who believes in him will not perish but have eternal life. (John 3:16)

God Is the Holy One

He is completely different from any person. He is perfect and does not sin.

He is the Rock; his work is perfect. Everything he does is just and fair. He is a faithful God who does no wrong; how just and upright he is! (Deuteronomy 32:4)

But now you must be holy in everything you do, just as God—who chose you to be his children—is holy. For he himself has said, "You must be holy because I am holy." (1 Peter 1:15-16)

God Is the Fair Judge

God is just and fair. He will correctly judge everyone.

And now the prize awaits me—the crown of righteousness that the Lord, the righteous Judge, will give me on that great day of his return. And the prize is not just for me but for all who eagerly look forward to his glorious return. (2 Timothy 4:8)

God Is Compassionate

He forgives those who repent of their sins. He patiently waits for all to come to him for salvation.

He passed in front of Moses and said, "I am the LORD, I am the LORD, the merciful and gracious God. I am slow to anger and rich in unfailing love and faithfulness. I show this unfailing love to many thousands by forgiving every kind of sin and rebellion. Even so I do not leave sin unpunished, but I punish the children for the sins of their parents to the third and fourth generations." (Exodus 34:6-7)

The Lord isn't really being slow about his promise to return, as some people think. No, he is being patient for your sake. He does not want anyone to perish, so he is giving more time for everyone to repent. (2 Peter 3:9)

YOUNG PEOPLE IN THE BIBLE

You don't have to wait until you are an adult to serve God. Find out what these young people from the Bible did.

A CHILD WITH JESUS
Jesus praised the humility of this child. (Matthew 18:2-4)

DANIEL
Daniel resolved not to disobey God's law. (Daniel 1:8)

DAVID
David trusted in God and courageously stood up to God's enemy Goliath.
(1 Samuel 17:45)

ESTHER
Esther obeyed her uncle, Mordecai. (Esther 2:10)

A JEWISH GIRL
This young girl told her Gentile mistress about the true prophet of God. (2 Kings 5:3)

JOASH
Joash became king when he was seven years old, and later in his life he repaired the Temple. (2 Kings 11:21)

JOSIAH
Josiah, as a sixteen-year-old, began to seek God, and later in his life he led the Israelites back to obeying God's law. (2 Chronicles 34:1-2)

JONATHAN
Jonathan and his young armor bearer trusted in God to help them fight the Philistines.
(1 Samuel 14:6-7)

JOSEPH
Joseph ran from temptation. (Genesis 39:12)

MIRIAM
Moses' sister, Miriam, courageously cared for Moses. (Exodus 2:3-9)

TIMOTHY
Timothy was encouraged by Paul to be an example to older Christians. (1 Timothy 4:12)

WHEN YOU ARE TEMPTED

Everyone is tempted—even Jesus was tempted. But Jesus resisted. It is not a sin to be tempted, but it is wrong to give in to temptation. When you are tempted:

1 **Pray to God like Daniel did (Daniel 6:10). Ask God to protect you from temptation.**

But remember that the temptations that come into your life are no different from what others experience. And God is faithful. He will keep the temptation from becoming so strong that you can't stand up against it. When you are tempted, he will show you a way out so that you will not give in to it. (1 Corinthians 10:13)

2 **Say no to temptation like Jesus did. He said no to Satan's plans to make him famous (Luke 4:1-13).**

So humble yourselves before God. Resist the Devil, and he will flee from you. (James 4:7)

3 **Run from temptation like Joseph did. He ran from the temptations of Potiphar's wife (Genesis 39:11-12).**

Run from anything that stimulates youthful lust. Follow anything that makes you want to do right. Pursue faith and love and peace, and enjoy the companionship of those who call on the Lord with pure hearts. (2 Timothy 2:22)

JESUS' BIRTH AND CHILDHOOD

Jesus was a kid, too! His childhood was filled with excitement. But he also had to do many of the same things other children have to do, such as obeying his parents. Here is what the Bible has to say about Jesus' childhood:

- Jesus was born in a stable in Bethlehem. (Luke 2:7)

- Jesus' birth was announced by angels. (Luke 2:8-14)

- Jesus was worshiped by shepherds and wise men. (Luke 2:16; Matthew 2:11)

- Jesus was dedicated to God at the Temple. (Luke 2:22)

- Jesus fled from evil Herod to Egypt. (Matthew 2:13-14)

- Jesus moved to the town of Nazareth. (Matthew 2:23-24)

- Jesus learned carpentry from Joseph, his earthly father. (Matthew 13:55; Mark 6:3)

- Jesus went to the Temple to worship God. (Luke 2:41-42)

- Jesus listened to religious teachers and asked questions. (Luke 2:46)

- Jesus, as a child, was wise. (Luke 2:47, 52)

- Jesus was obedient to his parents. (Luke 2:51)

- Jesus grew in wisdom. (Luke 2:52)

JESUS, OUR SAVIOR

WHO IS JESUS?

Jesus is the Son of God. He is God become human (*John 1:1-2, 14; 1 John 5:20*).

Jesus is the Messiah, the Christ. He is the one God promised to send to Israel (*Matthew 26:63-64; John 4:25-26*).

Jesus is our Savior. He died on the cross to save us from our sins. Those who believe in him will have eternal life (*John 3:16-18; Luke 2:11*).

WHAT DID JESUS DO ON EARTH?

Jesus called people to repent of their sins (*Luke 5:32*).

Jesus taught people about the Kingdom of God (*Matthew 13:24*).

Jesus healed the sick (*Mark 1:32-24; Luke 5:12-15*).

Jesus showed compassion to sinners (*Matthew 9:36; Luke 5:32*).

WHAT DOES JESUS DO FOR ME?

Jesus saves you from slavery to sin. With Jesus' power, you can resist temptation (*Romans 6:6-14; 1 John 5:18*).

Jesus forgives your sin (*Luke 24:27; 1 John 1:9*).

Jesus gives you the gift of eternal life (*John 17:2*).

Jesus sends the Holy Spirit to live in you. The Holy Spirit guides you into truth (*John 14:26*).

JESUS' PRAYER

In Matthew 6:9-13, Jesus gave all of his followers a pattern for their prayers. That pattern has four points:

1 Praise and thank God.

Praise God for who he is. He is great, perfect, and loving. Then, thank God for what he has done for you. He has given you a home, food, and clothing—he has even given you friends (*Matthew 6:9-10*).

2 Ask God for what you need.

Ask God to give you what you need, such as food, clothes, a home, and friends that will encourage you to follow him (*Matthew 6:11*).

3 Ask God to forgive you.

Ask God to forgive all your sins—both the ones you know about and the ones you do not know about (*Matthew 6:12*).

4 Ask God to protect you.

Ask God to protect you from evil. Ask him to give you the strength to resist temptation. Ask him for the wisdom to know what is right to do and the power to do it (*Matthew 6:13*).

And we can be confident that he will listen to us whenever we ask him for anything in line with his will. And if we know he is listening when we make our requests, we can be sure that he will give us what we ask for. (1 John 5:14-15)

Pray like this:
> *Our Father in heaven,*
> *may your name be honored.*
> *May your Kingdom come soon.*
> *May your will be done here on earth,*
> *just as it is in heaven.*
> *Give us our food for today,*
> *and forgive us our sins,*
> *just as we have forgiven those who have sinned against us.*
> *And don't let us yield to temptation,*
> > *but deliver us from the evil one.*

(*Matthew 6:9-13*)

GOD PROMISES . . .

Have you ever been let down by someone? Others may disappoint you, but God will never let you down. Look at what God has promised you!

God Promises Everlasting Life to All Who Believe in Jesus:
For God so loved the world that he gave his only Son, so that everyone who believes in him will not perish but have eternal life. (John 3:16)

God Promises Never to Abandon Those Who Believe in Him:
My sheep recognize my voice; I know them, and they follow me. I give them eternal life, and they will never perish. No one will snatch them away from me. (John 10:27-28)

And I am convinced that nothing can ever separate us from his love. Death can't, and life can't. The angels can't, and the demons can't. Our fears for today, our worries about tomorrow, and even the powers of hell can't keep God's love away. Whether we are high above the sky or in the deepest ocean, nothing in all creation will ever be able to separate us from the love of God that is revealed in Christ Jesus our Lord. (Romans 8:38-39)

God Promises to Hear and Answer Your Prayers:
Then if my people who are called by my name will humble themselves and pray and seek my face and turn from their wicked ways, I will hear from heaven and will forgive their sins and heal their land. (2 Chronicles 7:14)

And we can be confident that he will listen to us whenever we ask him for anything in line with his will. And if we know he is listening when we make our requests, we can be sure that he will give us what we ask for. (1 John 5:14-15)

God Promises to Forgive Your Sins:
But if we confess our sins to him, he is faithful and just to forgive us and to cleanse us from every wrong. (1 John 1:9)

God Promises to Meet All of Your Needs:
And this same God who takes care of me will supply all your needs from his glorious riches, which have been given to us in Christ Jesus. (Philippians 4:19)

God Promises to Give You Wisdom:
If you need wisdom—if you want to know what God wants you to do—ask him, and he will gladly tell you. He will not resent your asking. (James 1:5)

God Promises to Give You Strength and Courage:
Don't be afraid, for I am with you. Do not be dismayed, for I am your God. I will strengthen you. I will help you. I will uphold you with my victorious right hand. (Isaiah 41:10)

For I can do everything with the help of Christ who gives me the strength I need. (Philippians 4:13)

God Promises that He Has a Plan for You:

And we know that God causes everything to work together for the good of those who love God and are called according to his purpose for them. (Romans 8:28)

"For I know the plans I have for you," says the LORD. "They are plans for good and not for disaster, to give you a future and a hope." (Jeremiah 29:11)

All of us do something wrong at one time or another. Fortunately, God is forgiving. If we confess our wrongdoing to him, he will forgive us. But he does not stop there. He also cleans us. He washes away our sin, kind of like a person washing a dirty car. God removes our sin from his sight so that we can shine once again. And if you do something wrong in the future, you can follow these four steps to make things right with God:

 Tell God what you have done wrong. God wants you to turn to him—even when you sin.
I have come to call sinners to turn from their sins, not to spend my time with those who think they are already good enough. (Luke 5:32)

Ask God to forgive you. God will forgive. He has promised to forgive those who repent.
But if we confess our sins to him, he is faithful and just to forgive us and to cleanse us from every wrong. (1 John 1:9)

Ask God to help you not to sin again. He promises to provide a way for you to escape any temptation.
But remember that the temptations that come into your life are no different from what others experience. And God is faithful. He will keep the temptation from becoming so strong that you can't stand up against it. When you are tempted, he will show you a way out so that you will not give in to it. (1 Corinthians 10:13)

 Ask the person you wronged to forgive you. Jesus commands you not only to forgive others, but to ask others for their forgiveness.
So if you are standing before the altar in the Temple, offering a sacrifice to God, and you suddenly remember that someone has something against you, leave your sacrifice there beside the altar. Go and be reconciled to that person. Then come and offer your sacrifice to God. (Matthew 5:23-24)

A Prayer of Confession

Here is a prayer you can pray after you have sinned:

> Dear Heavenly Father,
>
> I have done something wrong. I have sinned against you.
>
> I am sorry. Please forgive me.
>
> Help me not do to it again.
>
> Thank you, Lord, for forgiving me, for accepting me as your child, and for giving me the power to resist future temptation.
>
> In Jesus' name, Amen.

WHEN EVERYTHING IS GOING WRONG

Have you ever had a bad day—and then it got worse? Your kid brother tore up your homework. Your best friend sat with someone else at lunch. The neighborhood bully stole your favorite cap. Everything went wrong! What do you do?

God is our refuge and strength, always ready to help in times of trouble. (Psalm 46:1)

Remember:
- God loves you. You are his child (1 John 3:1).
- God controls your situation and has a good plan for you (Romans 8:28).
- God wants you to learn from difficult situations (Hebrews 12:5-7).
- God wants to help you (Psalm 46:1).

And we know that God causes everything to work together for the good of those who love God and are called according to his purpose for them. (Romans 8:28)

Pray:
- Ask God to help you learn from this difficult situation.
- Ask God to give you power and wisdom.
- Trust God. He will help you overcome your problems.

But God is my helper. The Lord is the one who keeps me alive! (Psalm 54:4)

Ask:
- Ask either your parents, your teacher, or your Sunday school teacher what you should do.

Plans go wrong for lack of advice; many counselors bring success. (Proverbs 15:22)

HOW SHOULD A CHRISTIAN LIVE?

But when the Holy Spirit controls our lives, he will produce this kind of fruit in us: love, joy, peace, patience, kindness, goodness, faithfulness, gentleness, and self-control. Here there is no conflict with the law. (Galatians 5:22-23)

Fruit	Example
LOVE	Jesus loved Lazarus, Martha, and Mary. He comforted them when they were sad. (John 11:1-37)
JOY	Mary rejoiced that God had chosen her. (Luke 1:46-55)
PEACE	Abigail made peace with David by giving him gifts. (1 Samuel 25:23-28, 32-35)
PATIENCE	Simeon patiently waited for God to send the promised Savior. (Luke 2:25-35)
KINDNESS	Boaz showed kindness to Ruth. He let her collect grain from his fields. (Ruth 2:8-16)
GOODNESS	The Good Samaritan was good. He helped out someone in need. (Luke 10:25-37)
FAITHFULNESS	Daniel was faithful to God. He prayed to God, even though it was against the law. (Daniel 6:10-11)
GENTLENESS	Jesus showed gentleness by not condemning the woman who committed adultery. Instead, he saved her from being stoned to death. He also told her not to sin. (John 8:1-11)
SELF-CONTROL	David showed self-control. He did not kill his enemy Saul, even though he had the chance to do so. (1 Samuel 24:1-13)